Growth Patterns in Vascular Plants

4/25/95

4/25/95

Growth Patterns in Vascular Plants

Edited by

Muhammad Iqbal

Professor, and Head,
Department of Botany, Faculty of Science,
Hamdard University, New Delhi, India

DIOSCORIDES PRESS
Theodore R. Dudley, Ph.D., General Editor
Portland, Oregon

Copyright © 1994 by Dioscorides Press
(an imprint of Timber Press, Inc.)

ISBN 0-931146-26-7
Printed in Hong Kong

DIOSCORIDES PRESS
The Haseltine Building
133 S.W. Second Ave., Suite 450
Portland, Oregon 97204-3527, U.S.A.

Library of Congress Cataloging-in-Publication Data

Growth patterns in vascular plants / edited by Muhammad Iqbal.
        p.   cm.
   Includes bibliographical references (p.   ) and index.
   ISBN 0-931146-26-7
   1. Growth (Plants)   I. Iqbal, M. (Muhammad), 1952-
QK731.G75   1993
581.3'1--dc20   92-32755
                                                        CIP

Contents

Preface and Acknowledgments

Several books are available on the anatomy and physiology of plants, but only a few deal comprehensively with the interdependence of cellular structure and function in the development of different plant organs. The study of plant-growth processes has become multidisciplinary. No longer is it the territory of the botanist alone. Great contributions are being made by investigators trained in other disciplines, notably biochemistry, ecophysiology, and molecular biology. The many major advances made since the early 1970s in understanding ultrastructural and biochemical events in plant growth and development need to be collated and a consolidated overview created. This exercise is essential not only to disseminate information but also to determine whether new concepts are emerging from the recent data.

Coverage and synthesis of the advances in understanding of plant-growth processes has become too broad a task for any single person. The present volume, therefore, presents 16 chapters prepared by eminent scholars known for their contributions to the study of plant growth. The volume is not a compendium of reviews on divergent topics with only tenuous connection between them; rather it is an attempt to elucidate the "big picture" of plant growth from the perspectives of gametophytic growth, embryogeny, apical and radial expansion of the root and stem, development of lateral (vegetative as well as reproductive) appendages, and phylogenetic development of the vascular plants. The chapters cover the morphological, cytological, and ecophysiological aspects of plant growth and compare the growth characteristics of the major groups of vascular plants.

Because the book has been designed for a broad audience—from beginning graduate students to seasoned specialists—the discussion may sometimes overwhelm individual readers even though efforts have been made to strike a balance. Our aim has not been to provide an encyclopedic coverage of the field but to provide an overview of the trends. This approach provides the keys to a fuller understanding of plant growth at the submicroscopic, chemical, cellular, and histogenic levels, and holds interest not only for students, teachers, and researchers in plant growth and development but also for foresters, horticulturists, and botanists in general.

I am grateful to my colleagues who, despite their heavy academic and research commitments, accepted the additional burden of writing chapters. I am also indebted to Dr. P. W. Barlow of Long Ashton Research Station, Bristol, United Kingdom, Professor S. Carlquist of Rancho Santa Ana Botanic Garden, Claremont, California,

7

Professor H. L. Mogensen of the North Arizona University, Flagstaff, Dr. J. A. Romberger of the Agricultural Research Center, Beltsville, Maryland, Dr. P. S. Srivastava of Hamdard University, New Delhi, Dr. E. L. Taylor of Ohio State University, Columbus, and Professor M. T. M. Willemse of the Agricultural University, Wageningen, the Netherlands, for their help in refereeing several chapters. My several associates, especially Mahmood, Fareed, and Kamal, have been unstinting in their versatile support and deserve special appreciation and thanks.

I also thank B. A. Fineran, A. K. M. Ghouse, P. G. Mahlberg, H. L. Mogensen, Academic Press, the University of Chicago Press, Springer-Verlag, the *American Journal of Botany,* and the *Bulletin of the Torrey Botanical Club* for their generous permission to reproduce published material.

I was delighted to work with the editors at Dioscorides Press, who kept me enthusiastically engaged with this project through their expert advice and encouraging treatment throughout the preparation of the book.

I have the great pleasure of dedicating this work to commemorate the scientific contributions of Professor A. K. M. Ghouse, Chairman of the Botany Department at the Aligarh Muslim University, Aligarh, India, who initiated me into botanical research.

New Delhi   Muhammad Iqbal
January 1992

Dedication: A. K. M. Ghouse

MUHAMMAD IQBAL

Abdul Kasim Mohamed Ghouse was born on 15 June 1933 in Porto-novo (now Parangipattai) of Tamil Nadu, India. He obtained a B.S. degree at Madras University in 1955 and an M.S. (Botany) at Aligarh Muslim University in 1957, achieving First in the order of merit in the latter examination. He did research with Professor Abrar M. Khan, a leading phytopathologist of India, and was awarded the Ph.D. in Botany in 1961 on a dissertation entitled, "Studies on the Physiology of *Colletotrichum* spp. on Graminaceous Hosts."

A free-thinker while young, Professor Ghouse turned to religion in the late 1960s. He learned Arabic and Urdu so that he could read the original literature to satisfy his inquisitiveness. Islamic mysticism seems to have influenced him the most. He married Mehar Rana in 1964 and now is the father of two daughters and three sons.

Professor Ghouse joined the Aligarh Muslim University as Lecturer in Botany in 1962, became Reader in 1975 and Professor in 1984, and is now in the Chair of the Botany department. Soon after his appointment, he gained a reputation as a talented teacher by developing a new framework for teaching morphology of the vascular plants based solely on phylogenetic and systematic considerations. During the late 1970s he was instrumental in starting a special course in advanced plant anatomy for the postgraduate students of Botany.

A mycologist by training, Ghouse thrived on research in a new discipline. His independent nature did not allow him to receive dictation from the "big names" of his speciality even in academic affairs. He chose cambial studies initially. After examining about 80 tropical trees common to north India, he revealed that contrary to the earlier descriptions, fusiform initials do not necessarily constitute 90% or more of the cambial cylinder. Instead, their relative proportion in some species might be as low as only 25% of the total cambial surface. The ratio of the ray and fusiform initials occupied a greater area of the cambial cylinder in young shoots than in older stems or tree trunks. Ghouse described several taxa with multinucleate fusiform cells; their frequency was correlated to the phases of the seasonal cambial cycle in some of the species studied. Ghouse noted certain interesting correlations between cambial behavior and phenological events, the most interesting of which was related to the sequence of the formation of phloem and xylem and the tree phenology.

Ghouse also investigated the impact of variation in cambium cell-size on the component elements of cambium-derived tissues. In most species, from the top of the stem downward, the length of vessel elements on the one side and of sieve tube elements on the other varied more or less according to the variation in length of the precursor cambial initials. The proportion of the phloem that was actively conducting was noted to vary with taxa and even with the different positions within the plant axis. Ghouse therefore suggested that the use of any arbitrarily fixed values, such as Craft's 1/5 value or Münch's 2/3 value, to estimate the amount of the conducting pathway in the mass transfer studied is inappropriate and that a precise analysis of phloem is essential before undertaking any physiological investigation pertaining to photosynthate translocation.

Ghouse was the first in India to investigate the longevity of the secondary phloem in several indigenous trees. He suggested that certain macro- as well as micromorphological characters of bark, including patterns of sclerenchyma distribution and types of extension tissue, help considerably in tree identification. Through microscopy, he also elucidated diagnostic anatomical features of a large number of softwoods and hardwoods.

Ghouse directed systematic studies of the leaves of hundreds of eucalypts and conifers. He devised a computerized dichotomous key based on the foliar characteristics of the eucalypt species and reinterpreted the composition and distribution of transfusion tissue of the coniferous leaves. He investigated the structural and functional responses of a large number of plants to radiation and coal-smoke pollution. He also contributed to the disciplines of ethnobotany, pharmacognosy, and histopathology.

Ghouse has published over 200 research papers on a variety of topics and guided the research of 22 students toward the Ph.D. degree. The number of students who have obtained the Master of Philosophy degree under his guidance is still greater. In 1972, he edited *Research Trends in Plant Anatomy* (Tata McGraw Hill, New Delhi) in collaboration with Dr. M. Yunus, his first research student. He was elected Fellow of the Linnean Society of London in 1974 and Fellow of the Academy of Environmental Biology, India, in 1978. He was elected to the Academic Council of the Aligarh Muslim University in 1974 and 1976, and has long been on the executive boards of many scientific journals, including *Journal of Tree Science, Research Journal of Plant and Environment,* and *Indian Journal of Applied and Pure Biology.* He served as Professor of Botany at the Faculty of Basic Sciences of Al-Fateh University of Misurata, Libya, during 1985–1989, and was invited speaker at the 15th International Botanical Congress, Tokyo (1993). He is listed in several biographical directories of Asia's men and women of achievement. A selected 100 of his research publications are listed below.

BIBLIOGRAPHY

Plant Anatomy

Ghouse, A. K. M. 1969. Classification of woods of indigenous coniferous genera of India by microscopic structure. In *Recent Advances in the Anatomy of Tropical Seed Plants*. Ed. K. A. Chowdhury, Hindustan Publ. Corp. (India). Delhi, India: 137–149.

———. 1973. Variation in transfusion tissue in pines. *Bull. Torrey Bot. Club* 100:151–152.

———. 1973. Occurrence of transfusion tissue in the leaves of *Sequoia sempervirens* (D. Don.) Endl. *Israel J. Bot.* 22:236–238.

———. 1974. Transfusion tissue in the leaves of *Taxus baccata* L. *La Cellule* 70:159–162.

Ghouse, A. K. M., and S. Hashmi. 1976. The amount of active area of vertical conduction in the conducting phloem of some evergreen and deciduous tropical trees. *Bull. Torrey Bot. Club* 103:252–254.

———. 1977. Comparative study of cambial structure of five Indian tropical trees. *Phytomorphology* 27:35–39.

———. 1977. Cell length variation of phloem fibres within the bark of some evergreen and deciduous trees. *Bot. Jahrb. Syst. Pflanzengesch. Pflanzengeogr.* 97:503–507.

———. 1978. Seasonal cycle of vascular differentiation in *Polyalthia longifolia* (Annonaceae). *Beitr. Biol. Pflanz.* 54:375–380.

———. 1979. Cambium periodicity in *Polyalthia longifolia*. *Phytomorphology* 29:64–67.

———. 1979. Longevity of phloem in *Polyalthia longifolia* Benth. & Hook. *Bull. Torrey Bot. Club* 106:182–184.

———. 1980. Changes in the vascular cambium of *Polyalthia longifolia* Benth. et Hook. (Annonaceae) in relation to the girth of the tree. *Flora* 170:135–143.

———. 1980. Longevity of secondary phloem in *Delonix regia* Rafin. *Proc. Indian Acad. Sci. (Plant Sci.)* 89:67–72.

———. 1980. Seasonal production of secondary phloem and its longevity in *Mimusops elengi* L. *Flora* 170:175–179.

———. 1981. Developmental changes in the vascular cambium of *Delonix regia* Rafin. *Proc. Indian Acad. Sci. (Plant Sci.)* 90:143–151.

———. 1982. Impact of extension growth and flowering on the cambial activity of *Delonix regia* Rafin. *Proc. Indian Acad. Sci. (Plant Sci.)* 91:201–209.

———. 1983. Periodicity of cambium and the formation of xylem and phloem in *Mimusops elengi* L., an evergreen member of tropical India. *Flora* 173:479–487.

Ghouse, A. K. M., and M. Iqbal. 1975. A comparative study on the cambial structure of some arid zone species of *Acacia* and *Prosopis*. *Bot. Not.* 128:327–331.

———. 1977. Trends of size variation in phloem fibres and sieve tube cells within the bark of some arid zone trees. *Flora* 166:517–521.

———. 1977. Variation trends in the cambial structure of *Prosopis spicigera* L. in relation to the girth of the tree axis. *Bull. Torrey Bot. Club* 104:197–201.

———. 1978. Interspecific quantitative variation of active mass transfer medium in the main trunks of some arid zone *Acacia* and *Prosopis*. *Flora* 167:466–471.

———. 1979. Intrusive growth in the secondary phloem of *Acacia* and *Prosopis*. *New Bot.* 6:91–96.

———. 1981. Cell length variation within the bark and wood with respect to the development of trees. In *Advances in Forest Genetics*. Ed. P. K. Khosla, New Delhi, India: Ambika Publ. 192–212.

———. 1982. Comparative study of sapwood structure in *Acacia nilotica* and *Prosopis spicigera* with respect to seasonal variation. *J. Tree Sci.* 1:50–56.

Ghouse, A. K. M., M. Iqbal, F. A. Siddiqui, and A. Jamal. 1979. Taxonomic significance of sclerenchyma distribution in the secondary phloem of some Indian tropical trees. *Feddes Repert.* 90:173–178.

Ghouse, A. K. M., and A. Jamal. 1978. Studies on the bark anatomy of some *Cassia* species. *Indian J. Bot.* 1:91–97.

———. 1979. Sieve tube proportion in the secondary phloem of some *Cassia* species. *Bull. Soc. Bot. Fr.* 126:207–212.

Ghouse, A. K. M., and A. U. Khan. 1986. Growth pattern in *Dalbergia sissoo* Roxb., a timber tree of Gangetic plain. *Proc. Int. Workshop on Problems in Physiological Investigations of Tree Crops.* Kottayam, India: Rubber Res. Inst. 51–54.

Ghouse, A. K. M., and M. I. H. Khan. 1977. Seasonal variation in the nuclear number of fusiform cambial initials in *Psidium guajava* L. *Caryologia* 30:441–444.

Ghouse, A. K. M., M. I. H. Khan, and S. Khan. 1976. Amount of sieve elements in the secondary phloem of some Myrtaceae. *Flora* 165:489–492.

Ghouse, A. K. M., M. I. H. Khan, S. Khan, and A. H. Khan. 1979. Occurrence of poly-nucleate condition in the fusiform initials of some Verbenaceae. *Chromosome Inform. Serv.* 26:16–17.

Ghouse, A. K. M., M. I. H. Khan, and M. Yunus. 1972. The development of primary vascu-lar elements in the needle leaves of *Pinus roxburghii. Bull. Torrey Bot. Club* 99:190–195.

Ghouse, A. K. M., M. Salahuddin, and M. Saquib. 1985. Size variation of tracheary ele-ments across the tree trunk of *Mangifera indica. Acta Bot. Indica* 13:33–36.

Ghouse, A. K. M., and F. A. Siddiqui. 1976. Cell length variation in phloem fibres within the bark of four tropical fruit trees: *Aegle marmelos, Mangifera indica, Syzygium cumini* and *Zizyphys mauritiana. Blumea* 23:13–16.

———. 1976. Cell length variation in phloem fibres within the bark of some tropical fruit trees. I. *Anona squamosa, Emblica officinalis, Feronia limonia* and *Grewia asiatica. Phytomorphology* 26:109–111.

Ghouse, A. K. M., and M. Yunus. 1972. Leaf anatomy in the classification of Indian conifers. In *Research Trends in Plant Anatomy.* Ed. A. K. M. Ghouse and M. Yunus, New Delhi, India: Tata McGraw Hill. 123–144.

———. 1973. Some aspects of cambial development in the shoots of *Dalbergia sissoo* Roxb. *Flora* 162:549–558.

———. 1973. Some new findings on the occurrence of transfusion tissue in *Sciadopitys ver-ticillata. Phytomorphology* 23:149–151.

———. 1974. Cambial structure in *Dalbergia. Phytomorphology* 24:152–158.

———. 1974. The ratio of ray and fusiform initials in some woody species of the Ranalian complex. *Bull. Torrey Bot. Club* 101:363–366.

———. 1974. Transfusion tissue in the leaves of *Cunninghamia lanceolata* (Lambert) Hooker (Taxodiaceae). *Bot. J. Linn. Soc.* 60:147–151.

———. 1975. Intrusive growth in the phloem of *Dalbergia. Bull. Torrey Bot. Club.* 102:14–17.

———. 1975. The origin and development of phellogen in *Dalbergia sissoo* Roxb. *J. Indian Bot. Soc.* 54:183–187.

———. 1975. Transfusion tissue in the leaves of *Thuja orientalis* L. *Ann. Bot.* 39:225–227.

———. 1976. Cell length variation in the secondary phloem of *Dalbergia* spp. with increasing age of the vascular cambium. *Ann. Bot.* 40:13–16.

———. 1976. Ratio of ray and fusiform initials in the vascular cambium of certain leguminous trees. *Flora* 165:23–28.

Ghouse, A. K. M., M. Yunus, and M. Iqbal. 1976. A comparative study on the cambial structure of some *Bauhinia* species. *Bot. Jahrb. Syst. Pfanzengesch. Pflanzengeogr.* 95:411–417.

Iqbal, M. and A. K. M. Ghouse. 1977. Ontogenetic size variation in vessel elements of *Prosopis spicigera* L. *Flora* 166:187–192.

———. 1977. Ontogenetic size variation of sieve tube elements in *Prosopis spicigera* L. *Bull. Soc. Bot. Fr.* 124:445–450.

———. 1979. Anatomical changes in *Prosopis spicigera* with growing girth of stem. *Phytomorphology* 29:204–211.

_____. 1982. Comparative bark features of arid zone species of *Acacia* and *Prosopis*. *Phytomorphology* 32:373–380.

_____. 1983. An analytical study on cell size variation in some arid zone trees of India: *Acacia nilotica* and *Prosopis spicigera*. *IAWA Bull.* (n.s.) 4:46–52.

_____. 1985. Cell events of radial growth with special reference to cambium of tropical trees. In *Widening Horizons of Plant Sciences*. Ed. C. P. Malik. New Delhi, India: Cosmo Publ. 217–252.

_____. 1987. Anatomy of the vascular cambium of *Acacia nilotica* (L.) Del. var. *telia* Troup (Mimosaceae) in relation to age and season. *Bot. J. Linn. Soc.* 94:385–397.

_____. 1990. Cambial concept and organisation. In *The Vascular Cambium*. Ed. M. Iqbal. Taunton. UK: Research Studies Press. 1–36.

Jamal, A., and A. K. M. Ghouse. 1981. Interspecific variation in the cambium of *Cassia*. *New Bot.* 8:1–4.

Khan, M. I. H., and A. K. M. Ghouse 1978. Occurrence of intermittent growth waves in the shoots of *Psidium guajava* L. In *Environmental Physiology and Ecology of Plants*. Ed. D. N. Sen. Dehra Dun, India: B. Singh, M. P. Singh. 351–355.

_____. 1980. Studies on the impact of heavy flowering and fruiting on the extension growth of guava (*Psidium guajava* L.) *Flora* 169:453–455.

Siddiqui, Z. A., M. Yunus, and A. K. M. Ghouse. 1974. Studies on reaction xylem developed due to *Meloidogyne incognita* in the roots of *Lagenaria leucantha*. *Indian J. Nematol.* 4:46–52.

Yunus, M., and A. K. M. Ghouse. 1978. Transfusion tissue in the leaves of *Abies balsamia*. *New Bot.* 5:29–35.

_____. 1979. Structure and distribution of transufsion tissue in the leaves of *Cedrus* and *Picea*. *New Bot.* 6:61–66.

Microtechnique

Ghouse, A. K. M., F. Farooqui, and D. Sabir. 1974. Use of sodium hydroxide in the preparation of epidermal peels from certain coniferous leaves rich in resins and tannins. *Stain Technol.* 49:125–128.

Ghouse, A. K. M., and D. Sabir, 1973. A simple technique to demonstrate three-dimensional view of trancheary elements of *Equisetum*. *Acta Bot. Indica*. 1:73–75.

Ghouse, A. K. M., and M. Yunus. 1972. Preparation of epidermal peels from leaves of gymnosperms by treatment with hot, 60% HNO_3. *Stain Technol.* 47:322–324.

_____. 1974. Preparation of cuticle-free epidermal peels for the demonstration of primary pit fields. *Ann Bot.* 38:209–211.

Ghouse, A. K. M., M. Yunus, F. Farooqui, and D. Sabir. 1974. A simple maceration technique for the separation of sieve elements from the barks of woody plants. *Curr. Sci.* 43:424–425.

Yunus, M., and A. K. M. Ghouse. 1978. A rapid maceration technique to study reaction xylem developed due to root knot nematodes. *Micr. Acta* 80:273–275.

Environmental and Radiation Botany

Abidi, S. H., R. Kazmi, and A. K. M. Ghouse. 1979. Some acute doses of gamma irradiation and pollen fertility in *Linum usitatissimum*. L. var. T-397. In *Environmental Biology*. Ed. S. R. Verma, A. K. Tyagi, and S. K. Bansal. Muzaffar Nagar, India: Acad. Environ. Biol. (India), 165–166.

Amani, A. Z., S. H. Zaidi, A. K. M. Ghouse, and M. H. Farooqui. 1979. Studies on the trichome development and density in the different populations of *Croton* experiencing varying degrees of air pollution. *Geophytology* 9:162–164.

Ghouse, A. K. M., S. H. Abidi, P. R. Khan, and R. Pervaiz. 1981. The cambial activity of *Linum usitatissimum* var. T-397 as influenced by gamma rays. In *Contemporary Trends in Plant Sciences*. Ed. S. C. Verma. New Delhi, India: Kalyani Publ. 263–266.

Ghouse, A. K. M., Z. Ahmad, M. Saquib, and M. S. Khan. 1986. Air pollution and wood formation in *Mangifera indica* Linn. *Indian J. Appl. Pure Biol.* 1:37–39.

Ghouse, A. K. M., and F. A. Khan. 1983. Growth responses of *Melilotus indica* J. to air pollutants emerging out of coal burning. *Geobios* 10:227–228.

Ghouse, A. K. M., F. A. Khan, S. Khair, and N. R. Usmani. 1986. Micromorphological variations in *Croton bonplandianum* L. Baill. as induced by pollutants resulting from fossil fuel firing. *Res. J. Pl. Environ.* 3:93–95.

Ghouse, A. K. M., F. A. Khan, S. Khair, N. R. Usmani, and I. M. Sulaiman. 1985. Anatomical responses of *Chenopodium album* to air pollution caused by coal burning. *Acta Bot. Indica* 13:287–288.

Ghouse, A. K. M., F. A. Khan, and M. J. Pasha. 1984. Effect of air pollution on wood formation in *Dalbergia sissoo*, a timber tree of Gangetic plain. *J. Tree Sci.* 3:140–142.

Ghouse, A. K. M., F. A. Khan, M. Salahuddin, and M. A. Rasheed. 1984. Effect of air pollution on wood formation in *Tectona grandis*. *Indian J. Bot.* 7:84–86.

Ghouse, A. K. M., P. R. Khan, R. Pervaiz, S. T. Husain, and M. M. Alam. 1982. Control of IAA and GA over the adverse activity of ionizing radiation on seed germination of *Linum usitatissimum* L. var. Mukta. *J. Biol. Res.* 2:21–24.

Ghouse, A. K. M., Mahmooduzzafar, M. Iqbal, and P. Dastgiri. 1989. Effect of coal-smoke pollution on the stem anatomy of *Cajanus cajan* (L.) Mill. *Indian J. Appl. Pure Biol.* 4:147–149.

Ghouse, A. K. M., S. H. Zaidi, and A. Atique. 1984. Effect of air pollution on the foliar organs of *Solanum surattense* Burm. *J. Plant Nature* 1:20–30.

Gupta, M. C., and A. K. M. Ghouse. 1986a. Fruit quality and yield of *Abelmoschus esculentus* Moench. in relation to air pollutants. *Acta Bot. Indica* 14:191–194.

———. 1986b. The effects of coal smoke pollutants on the leaf epidermal architecture in *Solanum melongena* L. var. Pusa Purple Long. *Environ. Pollut. Ser. A* 41:315–321.

———. 1986c. Effect of coal smoke pollution on the growth performance of *Abelmoschus esculentus* Moench. *Proc. Nat. Acad. Sci. India (Plant Sci.)* 56:69–73.

———. 1987a. Cuticular geography, pigment content and anatomical traits of *Ficus benghalensis* L. under the influence of coal-smoke pollutants. *J. Tree Sci.* 6:106–110.

———. 1987b. The effect of coal smoke pollutants on the growth, yield and leaf epidermal features of *Abelmoschus esculentus* Moench. *Environ. Pollut. Ser. A* 43:263–270.

———. 1987c. Effect of coal-smoke pollutants from different sources on the growth, chlorophyll content, stem anatomy and cuticular traits of *Euphorbia hirta* L. *Environ. Pollut.* 47:221–229.

———. 1988. Leaf epidermal responses of *Tridax procumbens* L. to coal-smoke pollution. *Proc. Nat. Acad. Sci. India Sect. B* 58:93–96

Gupta, M. C., M. Salahuddin, M. Solanki, and A. K. M. Ghouse. 1988. Impact of coal smoke pollutants on flowering, fruitset and stem anatomy of *Syzygium cumini* Skeels. *Indian J. Appl. Pure Biol.* 3:27–30.

Iqbal, M., and A. K. M. Ghouse. 1982. Environmental influence on growth activites of *Prosopis spicigera*. In *Improvement of Forest Biomass*. Ed. P. K. Khosla. Solan, India: I.S.T.S. 387–393.

———. 1985. Impact of climatic variation on the structure and activity of vascular cambium in *Prosopis spicigera*. *Flora* 177:147–156.

Iqbal, M., Mahmooduzzafar, and A. K. M. Ghouse. 1987. Impact of air pollution on the anatomy of *Cassia occidentalis* L. and *Cassia tora* L. *Indian J. Appl. Pure Biol.* 2:23–26.

Khan, F. A., and A. K. M. Ghouse. 1988. Root growth responses of *Anagallis arvensis* L., Primulaceae to air pollution. *Environ. Pollut.* 52:281–288.

Mahmooduzzafar, M. Iqbal, and A. K. M. Ghouse. 1987. Anatomical responses of *Achyranthes aspera* L. to air pollution. *Indian J. Appl. Pure Biol.* 2:45–47.

Saquib, M., Z. Ahmad, and A. K. M. Ghouse. 1986. Effect of air pollution on the anatomy of *Chenopodium album* L. growing in an agroecosystem near Aligarh (India). *Indian J. Appl. Pure Biol.* 1:98–99.

Zaidi, S. H., A. Z. Amani, M. H. Farooqui, and A. K. M. Ghouse. 1979. Leaf epidermal structure of *Croton bonplandianum* Baill. in relation to air pollution. In *Environmental Biology*. Ed. S. R. Verma, A. K. Tyagi, and S. K. Bansal. Muzaffar Nagar, India: Acad. Environ. Biol. India. 239–242.

Miscellaneous

Atique, A., M. Iqbal, and A. K. M. Ghouse. 1985. Use of *Annona squamosa* and *Piper nigrum* against diabetes. *Fitoterapia* 56:190–192.

———. 1985. Ethnobotanical study of cluster fig (*Ficus racemosa*). *Fitoterapia* 56:236–240.

Ghouse, A. K. M., and M. Yunus. 1974. The effect of IAA and GA_3 on the dormant lenticels of *Melia azedarach* L. *Z. Pflanzenphysiol* 73:208–213.

Ghouse, A. K. M., and S. H. Zaidi. 1982. A preliminary study on the classification of some exotic *Eucaluptus* species on the basis of foliar morphology and stomatal characteristics. *Indian J. Forestry* 5:47–49.

Hashmi, S., A. Atique, and A. K. M. Ghouse. 1981. The botanical and histochemical characteristics of a leading bark remedy of Unani system: *Putranjiva roxburghii* Wall. syn. *Drypetes roxburghii* (Euphorbiaceae). *Indian J. Bot.* 4:201–205.

Iqbal, M., and A. K. M. Ghouse. 1980. *Acacia nilotica* (L.) Willd.—an ideal tree form of arid zone environment. *Ann. Arid Zone* 19:481–483.

Jamal, A., and A. K. M. Ghouse. 1975. Physio-biochemical differences in two varieties of *Coccinia cordifolia* Cogn. resistant and susceptible to powdery mildew *Erysiphe cichoracearum* DC. *Biochem. Physiol. Pflanzen* 167:101–104.

Section I
PRIMARY VEGETATIVE GROWTH

From Cell to System: Repetitive Units of Growth in the Development of Roots and Shoots

P. W. BARLOW

Four types of meristem are found in higher plants: apical, intercalary, cambial, and diffuse. All of them participate in either the longitudinal or latitudinal growth of organs; hence all contribute to the size and complexity of plants. Because the apical meristems are sites of morphogenetic process, they contribute most directly to the specification of plant form.

An important aspect of apical meristems is their repetitive activity. At the level of their constituent cells, mitosis repeats at approximately daily intervals to result in new cells. Where organs such as shoots or roots are concerned, there is a periodic production by their meristems of organized collections of cells such as leaf primordia and the sites of future root primordia; the time between the initiation of successive leaves (the plastochron) may typically repeat at 3–4-day intervals. At the higher level of the whole plant, there may be periods when the meristems are either active or inactive; annual phases of shoot growth and dormancy are an example of such a protracted rhythmicality. Thus, the higher the level of organization, the longer the period of the rhythm.

These rhythmic activities result in the construction of three types of structural unit that are fundamental to plant form. The first—the *cell*—is the source of other cells and ultimately of the other structural units. Their autoreproduction results in the replenishment of the meristem from which the second structural unit—the *metamer*—is constructed. Metamers compose the third, more complex, unit known as the *module*. Aspects of each of these structural units have been extensively studied in higher plants, although it should not be forgotten that lower plants—algae, fungi, and even certain lichens—are also constructed in a similarly repetitive fashion (L'Hardy-Halos 1970; Trinci 1984; Sanders 1989).

The three units, or levels, of morphological organization—cell, metamer and

From *Growth Patterns in Vascular Plants* Edited by Muhammed Iqbal

19

module—are related in a hierarchical fashion. The elements that compose any one level together construct the next, more complex, level. In the present case, the highest level of the module is ultimately constructed from cells of common ancestry by way of the intermediate level of the metamer (Figure 1.1). Combinations of modules build; in turn, an even higher level of organization: the *system* of shoots and roots. The spatial arrangement of modules determines the particular morphology of each of these systems. In the case of trees, the various geometric arrangements of modules in the shoot system fall into 23 categories, or architectural models. [These models, each named after a botanist who has contributed to their analysis, were devised using tropical trees as an extensive database. Shrubs and herbs can also be assigned to one or other of the models. However, there are cases where some trees and shrubs cannot be so definitely assigned. For example, hemlocks (*Tsuga* spp.) share features of the models of Massart, Roux, and Troll (Hibbs 1981); buffaloberries (*Shepherdia* spp.) do not fit any of the models (Hayes et al. 1990); apple (*Malus domestica*) is intermediate between the models of Rauh and Champagnat (Crabbé 1986); and so on. Further research will eventually clarify the situation, but for the present the 23 models provide a useful conceptualization of plant development.] These have been described in detail by Hallé et al. (1978). They can be simulated by applying various statistical parameters to meristem functioning (Reffye et al. 1986). Superimposed upon each model are differences in the relative rates at which leader and lateral branches grow; in trees, these relative rates determine the characteristic shape of their crown. Fisher (1984) has admirably discussed the processes by which one of these models is constructed and its possible adaptive significance.

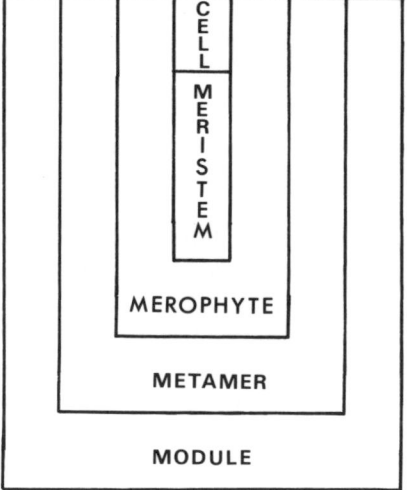

Figure 1.1.   The hierarchical composition of a module illustrating its interrelations with the lower levels of cell, merophyte and metamer. Sometimes merophyte and metamers coincide (as in shoots of mosses). The meristem is considered to reflect an increased span of the cellular level and not to be a level in its own right.

The general adaptive significance of the various architectural models is still an open question (Fournier 1979), however, particularly since an additional five theoretically possible models have not been recorded in either living or extinct species (Porter 1989). Perhaps they generate properties that are somehow incompatible with plant life. This can be demonstrated theoretically (though not in the context of the architectural models) by computer simulations that predict fitness as a result of morphological variables such as branching pattern interacting with selective forces (e.g. light): certain growth forms then become extinct (Niklas 1986). Furthermore, as far as can be established, the architecture of fossil trees corresponds to only certain of the 23 models, and Porter (1989) has suggested that other forms paid the penalty of extinction for an evolutionarily unacceptable mode of development. Only later, with further modification to the environment, could these forms be sustained. It is by no means clear, however, in what sequence the various architectural models evolved. On the other hand, Paleozoic lepidodendrales exhibit forms that correspond to three of the architectural models (Chaloner 1986), thus indicating a diversity of morphogenetic plan within this group of fossil trees.

The architectural models that pertain to root systems of tropical trees have been reviewed by Kahn (1977) and Jeník (1978). The models of root and shoot systems have so far been found to be independent of each other (Fournier 1979). Clearly, an adequate understanding of the development of the whole plant requires consideration of the architecture of both systems.

The hierarchically organized units that issue from cells in a growing apex (Figure 1.1) provide the basis for a discussion of the iterative manner in which shoot and root systems are constructed. The first part of this discussion deals with shoot and root apices and the axes that they produce, and then proceeds to the lower level of the meristematic cell and its products. A following section attempts to show how development at each level is integrated to form a complete system. The shoot systems of trees are often mentioned in this section and some details from apple (*Malus domestica*) are used to illustrate further how a shoot system is constructed. The review concludes by discussing how the activities of the elements that make up each level can be described with the aid of flow diagrams and the language of automata theory. Some consideration is given to what such approaches could contribute to future studies of plant anatomy and morphology.

MODULES AND METAMERS

Shoot Systems

The shoot apex of higher plants is often considered to consist simply of a meristematic zone that produces leaf primordia (e.g. Lyndon 1976). However, the rhythmic production of leaf primordia spaced according to a regular phyllotactic pattern, together with the associated groups of cells that become nodes and internodes with which buds (that are usually, but not always, in an axillary position) are later associated, all suggest that the apical meristem is producing more than just leaves, but rather is the originator of a coordinated and repeating set of parts that eventually comes to constitute the mature shoot. This quadripartite set of internode, node, leaf, and associated bud has been termed *metamer* and is held to represent a fundamental unit of shoot construction (White 1979, 1984). That the shoot is composed of repetitive structural units of some sort was recognized long ago, the concept having been first proposed by the French botanist C. Gaudichaud in 1841 and a little later by Asa Gray in 1849 (White 1979). These two early authors used the terms *phyton* and *phytomer,* respectively, which, by their etymology (Greek $\varphi\upsilon\tau\upsilon$ = plant), takes cognizance of the need for a botanically oriented term. Although *phytomer* is in many ways an attractive term, and is often used in contemporary morphological literature, *metamer* has the additional feature of being a term that implicates a broader biological perspective, since it can also apply to the repetitive structures that arise in animal development.

The concept of the metamer, in spite of its historical antecedents, is one that is still not well defined, particularly in dicotyledons [see White (1979) and Rutishauser and Sattler (1985) for a discussion]. For example, the anatomical constitution of the metamer of a given species varies according to the phyllotactic pattern. Decussate, whorled, and spiral phyllotaxies result in different volume-fractions of the stem being associated with the metamer: these might vary from large cylindrical segments of stem (as in distichous phyllotaxy) to small prismatic segments, as would apply, for example, in the spiral phyllotaxy of gymnosperms (Zagorska-Marek 1985, 1987). Superficially, there is in all these instances a clear repetition of similar parts along the stem that are the outcome of the activity of the apical meristem. Conceptually, it is this repetitiveness of parts *per se,* rather than the details of their construction, that is crucial for the definition of the metamer. For example, the triangular phyllotactic unit of the gymnosperm shoot, proposed by Zagorska-Marek (1987), is the externally recognizable metameric unit of that organ; but to what extent the detailed internal anatomy of such units has been considered, or indeed whether it is regarded as relevant to the metamer, requires further clarification.

The composition of the metamer can, moreover, differ during growth of the stem. In adult vines of *Parthenocissus* and *Vitis* spp., for example, a leaf and a tendril occur at two successive nodes, whereas at the third node the tendril is absent. This pattern repeats in each trio of developing nodes (Millington 1966; Critchfield 1970), each trio of nodes being the mirror image of the previous trio. The apex that gives rise to this pattern goes through a sequence of four distinct morphological states during the course of the initiation of the various primordia (Gerrath and Posluszny 1988). By contrast, during their juvenile phase, the stems bear a single leaf at each node but no tendril (Mullins et al. 1979). Thus, in this case, it is possible to speak of juvenile and adult metamers.

Additional variability in the composition of the metamer is seen in other species with a vine habit. Ray (1988), for example, has presented a detailed architectural analysis of shoots of 87 species within the Araceae. The variation in the types of appendages borne on a given metamer suggests that it may have two fundamental components, the stem unit (the internode) and the appendicular unit (which may be a leaf, prophyll, etc.). Such a double structure would accord with the leaf-skin concept of shoot organization (see Rutishauser and Sattler 1985). Each of the two subunits of the metamer undoubtedly would have its own set of genetic controls, a scheme that would easily account for the finding that mutation can alter the complement of organs associated with a metamer [for example, the heterochronic mutations that affect the morphology of the shoot of maize (Poethig 1988)]. Each set of genes would nevertheless be subordinate to factors that regulate the rhythmic production of metamers by the meristem.

As mentioned above, metamers are components of a more complex unit, the module. A module is a metamerized axis whose growth, in the case of the shoot, may be terminated by the development of an inflorescence, tendril, or spine, or by the parenchymatization of the apical meristem (White 1979); a root module may also terminate in a spine or a parenchymatous apex (Barlow 1986). From observation of the branches of trees and shrubs of temperate species, it is evident that the sequence of metamers is arranged into morphologically dissimilar groups that correspond to a pattern of growth that has been interrupted by season-related periods of dormancy of the apex. These seasonally produced units of growth will be referred to, for convenience, as *submodules,* for, although they have a definite metameric structure, they are only a part of the complete module. There are species (of tropical trees, for example), however, whose modules show continuous growth and have unbroken sequences of morphologically similar metamers (Hallé et al. 1978).

Modules branch usually as a consequence of the outgrowth of axillary buds, but sometimes they do so from adventitious buds. If the axillary bud of a submodule grows out during the season of that submodule's extension (i.e. if the bud does not exhibit a dormant period), it is termed *sylleptic*. If it grows out after the supporting submodule has finished extending, it is termed *proleptic* (Hallé et al. 1978). The branching of modules reflects a feature that helps to define further the component metamers, namely, that each metamer contains a site with the potentiality to form another module.

The shoot system is therefore a collection of metamerically constructed modules with apical meristems (terminal and axillary) of varying age and activity. Depending on both the season of the year and internal correlations within the system, these meristems are either actively growing and producing additional metamers, or they, together with a set of partially developed metamers, are contained within a dormant bud awaiting a stimulus to resume growth. When growth does resume, the major part of submodule elongation takes place in the internode portion (particularly at its distal end) of each metamer (e.g. Garrison 1973). Eventually terminal meristems become committed to floral development. In this case, some of the metamers include modified leaves that form parts of the flower.

There is some evidence that growth and development of shoot modules is a determinate process, since in some cases (in maize and tobacco, for example) it has been experimentally shown that a fixed number of metamers are produced before the formation of a terminal inflorescence. However, these pre-floral metamers develop only if some inductive event switches the shoot apex to a determinate mode of growth; prior to the occurrence of this determining event, metamer production is apparently unlimited (McDaniel 1980; Irish and Nelson 1988).

The modules of many species of trees and shrubs show a periodicity of development that is not related to the more controlled constant environmental conditions (e.g. trees of *Theobroma cacao* studied by Greathouse et al. 1971). The reasons for this endogenous developmental rhythm is unknown, but very likely involve correlative interactions between the entire system of shoot and root modules (Champagnat et al. 1986). Such rhythms can be shown theoretically to arise even when growth conditions are apparently constant (Borchert 1973).

Not all buds in a growth unit are equivalent. Axillary buds, for instance, may be of unequal sizes and potentialities (Cutter 1966) and sometimes can lie quite deep within the stem tissue: in the Araucariaceae, for example, they lie more than 1 mm below the stem surface (Burrows 1987). Their different potentialities for growth lead to the particular branching patterns of the shoot system. An axillary bud may be directed toward forming either a new leading shoot or a distinct type of short shoot; or it may form a flower, or remain dormant. In trees, the terminal bud of a leading shoot or a side branch might, when it resumes growth, continue as a long leading shoot, or it too might form a flower (see e.g. Maillette 1982). Short shoots of some species (e.g. *Malus domestica*) frequently form a flower, but those of some other species (e.g. *Pyrus* spp.) often convert to a spine; in both these cases the capacity for further apical growth is arrested and growth of the module is terminated.

Module growth therefore continues only as long as the apical meristem is active; but the cessation of this activity may be the stimulus for an axillary bud to become active and thus bring about branching of the module. New modules sometimes arise from older, epicormic buds in the stem. These can often play a vital role in regeneration, as, for example, in fire-damaged eucalyptus trees in which new modules rapidly grow out from buds concealed within the lignotuber (a structural modification of the stem base) (Chattaway 1958).

The type of module or submodule (i.e. whether it is a long shoot, short shoot, or terminates in a flower or inflorescence) that arises from a sequence of metamers depends upon its position and orientation within the shoot system as a whole. Module type and its position on a supporting axis together contribute to the characteristic form of the plant. The angles with which modules insert into their supporting axes, as well as their azimuthal angles, confer additional information (both topological and physiological) that contributes to a more complete specification of shoot form. Presumably the distribution of the various module types within the frame of a shoot system has some bearing on the capture and utilization of energy and minerals that in turn influence fitness (cf. Niklas 1986).

The question of what type of module (e.g. long or short shoot) will form at a particular location on an axis, or what type of appendage will form on a metamer, is one that could theoretically be resolved in terms of the information inherent in the shoot system as a whole. Different types of modules, and different types of metamers, are attended by different "physiological states," i.e. the net result of all the previous inflows and outflows of information specified in large measure by hormones, nutrients, and other factors such as temperature and light that affect growth. These states, therefore, create, within a multibranched system of axes, a physiological system replete with mutual interactions; hence it is rich in information that is potentially useful for specifying the future course of development (Champagnat 1954; Nozeran et al. 1971; Nozeran 1984). By means of this information, the state of any given location on an axis can be assessed and responded to by the meristems, which grow or not as the circumstances dictate. In this regard, light seems to be a particularly important environmental factor (e.g. Jones and Harper 1987; Novoplansky et al. 1989); water availability, determined by branch patterns, may be another important factor for regulating bud growth (Cottignies and Jennane 1988).

Because the shoot system grows by the addition of new axes, the position of a module is a relative, not a fixed, property. The addition and growth of new modules causes the relative positions and states of the already existing modules to change, and this in turn may influence the potentialities of the buds and the receptive meristems that they bear. It is this sort of interaction between parts of the growing system that has permitted branching patterns to be simulated by deterministic algorithms and hence analyzed in a rigorous way (Lück et al. 1990). As Hardwick (1986) has pointed out, as the number of modules (n) in the system increases, the potential number of flows of information between modules increases as n^2. Yet growth continues to maintain "harmonious relationships" (cf. "die Harmonie der Baumgestalt" (Münch 1938)) in the overall form of the shoot system.

Additional features relating to the shoot system and its modules will become evident when further details are presented below of the behavior of the various types of modules found in the shoot system of apple and other trees.

Root Systems

Another major class of apical meristems gives rise to the root system. This system also has a modular character evident from its branching pattern. Primary roots and first-, second-, and higher order lateral roots (each of decreasing diameter) are all modules from which the root system is constructed; up to six orders of branching have been described in the root system of *Malus sylvestris* (crab apple) (Kolesnikov 1930). A detailed description of the development of the root system and its component types of root has been made for *Acer rubrum* by Lyford and Wilson (1964) and the ecological significance of root system morphology in general has been discussed by Sen (1980) and Kummerow (1981).

By comparison with the shoot system, distinct types of root modules are neither so common nor so well known; however, the so-called "heterorhizis" of tree root systems (where there are both long roots of unlimited growth and determinate short roots) is familiar to students of forestry (Kubíková 1967), and in herbaceous angiosperms lateral roots with a distinctive appearance are sometimes also found. For example, dauciform roots, certain types of very fine root, and the thickened roots found in response to drought, all seem to be particular types of lateral root (Peterson and Peterson 1986) and therefore constitute distinct types of root modules. Aerial roots, storage roots, root spines, and pneumatorhizae are the types of modules that are different from the common type of terrestrial root module with which, in certain species, they regularly coexist (Barlow 1986). Likewise, in water plants, the upward-growing aerenchymatous roots and the horizontal fibrous water roots also constitute modules distinct from their respective coexistent partners, the downward-growing roots and the mud roots.

Lateral roots generally emerge from the parent root axis shortly after their initiation as primordia. The primordia rarely seem to enter a prolonged period of dormancy, although a brief period of reduced cell proliferation in the meristem may occur just prior to lateral emergence (MacLeod and McLachlan 1975). The growth pattern of lateral root primordia thus seems to be analogous to the sylleptic buds of the shoot system. Sometimes, lateral root primordia are initiated on a parent root axis out of the normal acropetal sequence with which they are initiated at the distal end of the axis. These give rise to the so-called "adventive" laterals (Barlow 1986) and are analogous to the adventitious and epicormic axes on the shoot system. Initiation and subsequent emergence of lateral roots are under separate controls. The degree to which either process occurs in a strictly acropetal sequence is for the most part unknown, but at least in maize roots there is no precise order in which laterals either initiate or emerge as the main apex grows forward. The zone of primordium initiation does not usually overlap with that of lateral emergence, however (MacLeod 1990).

The lack of a prolonged dormant phase may be evidence that lateral root primordia, unlike the dormant buds of prospective shoot modules, are not subject to multiple correlative influences from elsewhere in the root system. Instead, they are subject primarily to the influence of the apex from which they are descended, and this determines both the distance from the apex at which the primordia are initiated and the position at which they later emerge as young lateral roots. The relative "strength" of the apical dominance on axes of different orders will therefore influence the patterns of initiation and emergence of laterals of the next higher order. That is, the dominance of the apex of the primary root (an axis of zero order) specifies the pattern of first-order laterals; the apex of first-order laterals in turn specifies the pattern of second-order laterals; and so on. On the other hand, if primordia do become dormant, or if they develop adventively, their subsequent fate could become subject to correlative influences. This would be manifested in the timing of their emergence as adventive laterals and perhaps also in the type of root that emerges. For example, certain combinations of environmental and correlative influences may cause dormant primordia to emerge adventively as dauciform roots (Peterson and Peterson 1986). Furthermore, in certain circumstances the primordia may develop as shoots (e.g. Torrey 1958).

As indicated above, there are definite relationships between the growth of the various orders of laterals. For example, there is a close relationship between the diameters of the primary root of maize and that of its laterals (Yamazaki and Kaeriyama 1983). In cereals, the diameter of the roots roughly halves with each successive order of branching. Moreover, the extension rate and spacing between branch roots also decreases the higher the order of branching (May et al. 1985). These effects have important consequences for the uptake of minerals and hence the nutrition and growth of the shoot system.

Before leaving this section, the question whether root modules are developed independently of the modules of the shoot, or whether roots and shoots together form an inclusive suprasystem of modules, should be briefly discussed. Although it is generally accepted that roots and shoots are evolutionarily distinct classes of organs (e.g. Groff and Kaplan 1988), root modules (e.g. aerial roots) often grown out at quite precise sites on the shoot system (Weber 1936; Gill 1969). Moreover, the root system can also give rise to shoots (Peterson 1975). In many of these latter cases, the shoots form at sites of physiological disturbance such as wounding. These sites are functionally equivalent to locations where roots can be artificially induced at the base of stems or leaves, as, for example, when cuttings are taken. Roots or shoots induced in this way do not arise at sites especially laid aside for their formation; however, the primordia that naturally form on both root and shoot axes show a certain plasticity of behavior. They are essentially indeterminate, their fate being decided by the milieu in which they find themselves (Torrey 1958). Usually, this leads to shoot buds being borne on shoots and root buds on roots, but occasionally the parent axis can support a module of the other type. Since these sites yield only locally to the other system, and moreover do so at intercalary and not at terminal positions, roots and shoots should be regarded as two independent categories of modular systems that may nevertheless be physiologically interdependent.

METAMERS AND MERISTEMS

Shoot Apices

Externally, shoot apices differ greatly in their shape and size as well as in the arrangement and sequence of the leaf primordia that they form (Clowes 1961). Some of these features may be interrelated: for example, experimentally induced alterations to the curvature of the apex can lead to changes in the vertical spacing and phyllotaxy of the primordia (Schwabe 1971).

Internally, shoot apices (at least those of angiosperms) differ relatively little in their construction. All have a superficial mantle of cells that constitutes the tunica that in turn encloses the corpus (Schmidt 1924). The number of cellular layers that make up the tunica varies: one to three layers are quite typical, but this number can vary depending on the types of shoot examined. All cells in the tunica consistently divide anticlinally; indeed, its layered structure exists only for as long as this plane of division is maintained. In the corpus, cells divide in all planes.

Differences are also found in the cytochemical properties of the apex, but these do not necessarily coincide with the arrangement of cells into tunica and corpus. For example, sectioned apices stained for nucleic acids (DNA and RNA) reveal a group of cells at the summit of the apex with less of these substances than cells elsewhere (Lance 1957; Nougarède 1967). This weakly staining zone includes cells of both tunica and corpus; it also corresponds to a zone that other methods show to have low rates of DNA synthesis and cell division. The French workers who made many of the original histochemical observations named it "zone axiale" (axial zone). Cells immediately surrounding the axial zone are richer in RNA and often divide more frequently. They function as initials and hence are the major source of new cells that feed into the remainder of the meristem. They are not, however, the only source of new cells, because the frequency of divisions in the axial zone is not negligible; in fact, a fraction of cells in this zone regularly enters the initial zone during each plastochron. For example, Catesson (1953) plotted the distribution of mitoses in apices of *Luzula pedemontana* and concluded that the axial zone, together with the surrounding initials, tilted from side to side during successive plastochrons. Only a narrow, lens-shaped portion of the axial zone persisted for any length of time at the summit. Such a zone, even if consisting of only a few cells, is sufficient to constitute a permanent group of founder cells from which all the initials are ultimately derived. Notwithstanding observations such as those of Ball (1972) (who, having recorded the displacement of marker particles on the surface of shoot apices, was led to a view that no cell, or group of cells, has any permanence within the apex), a body of evidence, particularly from studies of chimeras, strongly indicates that the apex has a stable structure with regular and predictable divisions in the axial zone and its surrounding initials (Stewart and Dermen 1970; Rogers and Bennett 1989).

Only a few studies have related the duration of the cell division cycle in the meristematic apical dome to the duration of the plastochron. Both these pieces of information are important for integrating cellular behavior with the development of shoot metamers. In this regard, observations by Saint-Côme (1985) on the apex of *Coleus blumei* (with opposite and decussate phyllotaxy) are of interest, particularly the results relating to cell division and the plastochron (Table 1.1.A). The rate of cell production in the apex varies throughout the plastochron; the flank zone sometimes divides up to twice as fast as the axial zone. One consequence of this is that the apical dome increases in size throughout its development. Interestingly, the rate of division of the axial zone is roughly similar to the rate at which metamers (with pairs of leaf primordia) are produced. Yet this similarity of rates, which might suggest that the axial zone delivers exactly enough cells to the initial zone for it to construct each metamer, is not apparent in other species. For example, during the sixth plastochron of the shoot apex of *Chrysanthemum segetum* (an apex with spiral phyllotaxy), the doubling time of the axial zone cell population is approximately six days, while it is two to three days

Table 1.1. Rates of development at the vegative shoot apices of *Coleus blumei* and *Chrysanthemum segetum*.

Species	Plastochron number	Mean duration (± SE) (days)			
		Plastochron	Cell cycle		
			Axial zone	Flank zone	Medullary meristem
A. *C. blumei*	7	9.7±1.5	10.7±1.1	5.1±0.6	7.5±0.9
	9 (prefloral)	4.3±0.7	5.4±0.6	4.9±0.4	—
B. *Ch. segetum*	6	3.8	5.8	2.0	2.9
	28 (prefloral)	2.1	2.2	2.0	4.1

Data from Saint-Côme (1985)—*Coleus*; and Lance (1957), Rembur and Nougarède (1977), and Nougarède et al. (1987)—*Chrysanthemum*.

in the surrounding initials (Rembur & Nougarède 1977). The plastochron has a duration of 3.75 days (Lance 1957) (Table 1.1). Assuming steady conditions, this means
that the axial zone supplies new cells to the surrounding initials at about half the rate
at which the initials produce enough cells to construct a new leaf primordium. A
similar imbalance between division rate in the axial zone and the rate of leaf initiation
also holds in *Pisum sativum* (data not shown). Moreover, the independence of the rate
of apical cell division and the plastochron can be seen in plants of *C. segetum* grown in
different light regimes (A. Nougarède, personal communication). However, in *C.
segetum* a synchronization between cell production and leaf initiation is achieved
when apices reach the prefloral stage (Table 1.1.B, and compare with results for *Coleus*
at a similar, prefloral stage). Thus it appears that the rhythm of the plastochron does
not necessarily depend upon the rhythm of division in the axial zone or elsewhere in
the apex. The process of metamerization is superimposed upon the apex, the size of
which will increase, decrease, or remain steady according to the rate of cell production therein.

Leaf primordia come into being following a change in the orientation of growth
and division of cells in both the tunica and the corpus. Simultaneous with the initiation of a primordium, the groups of cells that ultimately become node and internode
are also specified; so is the potential site for bud formation, the leaf axil. The
morphological definition of node, internode, and axil is partly due to their topological
relationship to the adjacent leaf primordium. Only when the meristem region below the
apical dome has produced a sufficient number of cells, however, can node and internode begin to be differentiated. Thus, the plastochron has a greater significance than
merely defining the rate of leaf production: it also defines the rate of metamer production by the apex. Interestingly, when Askenasy (1880) first proposed the concept of the
plastochron, he had in mind the production of internode units (metamers) of the alga
Chara.

The cytological definition, as opposed to the positional definition, of prospective
node and internode has largely gone unnoticed, even though cells within the nodal
region must eventually be distinguishable from those in the internode on account of the
different amounts of growth that each will eventually undergo—at least in modules in
which the internodes do not remain compressed (as in shoots with a rosette of leaves).
A remarkable set of observations on young shoots of *Sambucus racemosa* (with
opposite and decussate phyllotaxy) by Zobel (1985a,b) has demonstrated that cells in
the two zones of node and internode differ not only biochemically but also in their relative amounts of growth. In the apex of this species, the outer pith contains tannin
cells. The first visible tannin mother cells, as recognized by light microscopy, occur
nine cell layers from the shoot surface. Once formed, a tannin mother cell ceases to
divide and becomes polyploid through the continued replication and division of its
nucleus. By making squash preparations of shoot apices, Zobel (1985b) was able to
show that tannin cells run the entire length of each internode (Figure 1.2). The internode must, therefore, originate from a transverse layer of cells one cell deep. The
nodal region, which links successive internodes, is always free of tannin cells.
Although the number of cell-layers from which the node originates was not specifically
documented, this number could also be as few as one.

The presence of tannin-containing and tannin-fee mother cells close to the apex
of *Sambucus* suggests that node and internode mother cells may be differentiated at the
same time. If so, node and internode are not simply passively defined by their position
relative to the accompanying pair of leaf primordia but are determined before the
primordia become visible. The alternation of tannin and nontannin cells in node and
internode suggests a rhythmic activity in the apex that is integrated with the initiation

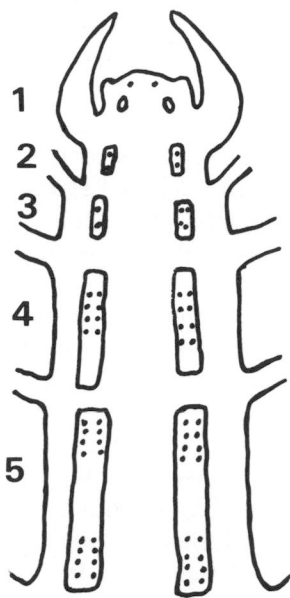

Figure 1.2. Distribution of tannin coenocytes in the internodal portions of a young stem of *Sambucus nigra*. The nodal portions lack these coenocytes. Internodes are numbered 1–5 in order of increasing age. The *dots* in each coenocyte represent the nuclei; these double in number in successively older internodes. Redrawn from a photograph in Zobel (1985b).

of each leaf. Furthermore, the tannin mother cells arise by periclinal divisions in cell layers just below the tunica (Zobel 1989b). Thus, node and internode are prefigured at a very early stage of shoot development. These observations from *Sambucus* suggest that the metamer complex of node, internode, and leaf primordium pair occupies a transverse segment of stem. This concept is seemingly at odds with that in which the stem is viewed as a collection of longitudinal sectorial units (e.g. Priestley et al. 1935; Majumdar 1942) that originate with a leaf primordium and extend along the associated orthostichy to the leaf directly below—a view that, not unexpectedly, finds correspondence in the division of the stem into physiological units (or preferential pathways) of solute transport (Watson 1986).

Lyndon (1987) arrived at a similar conclusion concerning the origin of nodes and internodes for vegetative apices of *Silene coeli-rosa* (which also has opposite and decussate phyllotaxy). Of the two cell-layers with which each pair of leaf primordia are associated, one is fated to develop as internode, the other as node. Later, in the development of the flower, the cell-layer normally contributing to the internode is absent and the remaining single cell-layer is associated with petals and stamens. More recent observations of Zobel (1989a,b) have shown that other internal markers can define node and internode in a range of species. For example, in *Reynoutria japonica* and *Polygonum reynoutria,* nodal cells are defined by their phenolic contents (the converse of the *Sambucus* example above), whereas in *Rumex salicifolius* the internodes, but not the nodes, develop intercellular spaces.

Although *Sambucus racemosa* and some of the other species mentioned may prove particularly suitable species for closer investigations of metamer development, it should be noted that the coincidence of a pattern of tannin cells (or other specialized cell types) with particular parts of the metamer is not a general phenomenon. For example, *Ricinus communis* is another species with long groups of tannin cells in the stem (Bloch 1948). These also develop from single cells in the distal region of the meristem, but later in development they are found to straddle both nodes and internodes. In the future, the techniques of molecular biology might be applied to define further the determination of node and internode. Such methods have been applied to the genetic analysis of metamer development in insects [reviewed by, among others, Akam (1987)]. This analysis in turn has also raised fundamental questions about the origin of repeating patterns, such as, for example, whether the genes involved define the boundary lines between segments or define the segmental areas themselves (Lawrence 1987). That genetic activity can be closely tied to metamer formation is evidenced by the longitudinal pattern of mutant sectors in shoots of species such as maize and sunflower. Here, marker cells affected in pigment formation almost always exist in stripes that start in the leaf and terminate at the base of the internode (McDaniel and Poethig 1988; Jegla and Sussex 1989). These mutated sectors highlight the leaf/internode complex as the basic unit of the shoot metamer.

Reaction-diffusion mechanisms underlie many of the examples of patterning of morphogenesis and have been proposed to regulate the repeating units in animals (Harrison and Tan 1988). Such mechanisms may operate within the "reaction field" of the shoot apex (Wardlaw 1955).

Important information concerning the relationship between meristematic activity and metamer production by the shoot is provided by many lower plants, including bryophytes and pteridophytes, which have an apex surmounted by a prominent apical cell (Michaux-Ferrière and Hallet 1985). Often, this cell is a tetrahedron, which, when it divides, produces daughter cells from each of its three internal faces in a regular acropetal helix (the fourth face forms part of the outer surface of the apex). A consequence of this repeating sequence of three divisions is that the shoot, when viewed in transverse section, assumes a sectored appearance. Each of the three 120° sectors is founded by one of the three daughters of the apical cell. Each daughter cell (which is equivalent to an apical initial cell of higher plant shoots) is called a *merophyte* (Douin 1923) and may be considered to be another level in the hierarchical structure of the module (Figure 1.1). Each merophyte is then further subdivided by longitudinal and transverse cell divisions. Despite these additional divisions, the outline of its original boundary wall can still be recognized (cf. Figure 1.3.a). Such apices with their particular patterns of internal divisions are useful in determining the contribution of the merophyte to the metamer: that is, whether each merophyte produces a leaf and a subtending portion of node and internode, together with an axil where a new bud may form. This is certainly the case in the bryophyte *Fontinalis antipyretica* (Clowes 1961), in which each leaf primordium arises as a bulge on a cell at the outer surface of each merophyte; but whether the axil so formed has the potentialities for bud formation is not known for this species, although in other species of mosses bud formation is quite well known and arises with the inception of a new, secondary apical cell in some of the merophytes. In the pteridophyte *Equisetum arvense,* however, the sites of leaf initiation are apparently not related to the radial boundaries of the merophyte (i.e. the 120° sector boundaries) (Golub and Wetmore 1948). This is evident from the fact that the leaves are formed in whorls that occupy a different location along the length of each sector. Although Golub and Wetmore (1948) did not seek such a particular piece of evidence, from their illustrations of *Equisetum* apices it is possible to imagine that each whorl of leaf primordia has its origin within the longitudinal limits of each gyre of three merophytes. Indeed, the coincidence of leaves and the longitudinal extent of the merophytes appears to be borne out by earlier observations on other *Equisetum* species made by Reess (1867) and Vidal (1912). Unfortunately, recent investigations of the *Equisetum* apex, which take account of the histogenetic activity of the apical cell (Gifford and Kurth 1983; Hauke 1985), stop short of elucidating the relationship between merophytes and leaf primordia. Likewise, recent investigations into the morphology of the leaf primordia (Rutishauser and Sattler 1987) do not trace their cellular origin. Thus, an unfortunate gap that has opened between morphological cellular studies of the shoot apex could be closed by paying greater attention to the merophytic nature of the apex.

The relation between merophytes and leaf initiation is a little clearer in the ferns. In some species a one-to-one correspondence between merophyte and leaf primordium has been claimed, e.g. in *Trichomanes crispiforme* and *Dicksonia squarrosa* (Hébant-Mauri 1973, 1975). *Ceratopteris thalictroides,* by contrast, deviates somewhat from this plan, for here leaf initiation occurs in only two of the three merophytes in each gyre (Hébant-Mauri 1977). This pattern resembles that found in the roots of this species in which two lateral root primordia form in each trio of successive merophytes (see below). Clearly there is some factor, perhaps endogenous, that suppresses the mitoses that would otherwise give rise to these primordia. The correspondence of merophytes and leaf primordia is especially interesting because it is not hard to imagine that a characteristic pattern of cell division in each merophyte could in some way be related to the formation of a specialized cell, or group of cells, from which a leaf is subsequently developed. Unfortunately, none of the published patterns of cell divisions in the apex are extensive enough to give evidence on this point, but the problem is obviously of great importance from a theoretical point of view (Lück and Lück 1985).

A correspondence between merophytes and metamers could be suspected if the rates of leaf primordium formation and of merophyte production by the apical cell were the same. This is the case in three species of bryophyte, *Polytrichum formosum, Leucobryum glaucum,* and *Thuidium tamariscinum,* in which the duration of the plastochron (15 hr) is the same as the duration of the mitotic cycle of the apical cell (Hallet 1977). Moreover, in certain bryophytes, the cells from which each primordium is formed always bears the same familial relationship to the apical cell. One may speculate that each merophyte somehow contains all the information necessary for its own further construction by virtue of the geometrical disposition of its cells (cf. Lück and Lück 1986). There is something harmonious and esthetically pleasing about a relationship in which the functional attributes of a structure (i.e. the siting of leaves on a stem) is precisely coincident with its geometry (i.e. the arrangement of its cells).

The examples of apical construction offered by ferns and mosses indicate both the differences and the similarities between metamers and merophytes. Metamers are portions of stem whose boundaries are set by successive leaf primordia (or whorls of primordia) and their associated nodes and internodes, whereas merophytes correspond to groups of cells common descent that, owing to their distinctive origin from a single cell, are arranged along the stem in staggered sectors. In this regard, they are similar to the longitudinal sectional units proposed by Priestley et al. (1935). Both types of structural unit contain, however, the same reiterated groups of differentiated (or differentiating) cells. The contrasting concepts of merophyte and metamer arise from two views of plant structure; one is a cellular point of view leading to the recognition of the merophyte, the other is based on external morphology and recognizes the metamer. Since the two types of unit coexist, but their boundaries may not exactly coincide (as in *Equisetum*), it seems safest to regard them as distinct but complementary structural entities (cf. Rutishauser and Sattler 1985).

Higher plants lack a prominent apical cell of the type described above, and consequently the anatomy of their apices does not reveal clearly defined cellular sectors. Instead, the summits of their apices have a multicellular organization. The descendants of these summit cells can often be recognized as multicellular groups, or packets. Many packets of cells, each originating from a different mother cell, therefore construct the apical meristem. The layered nature of the tunica, brought about by the anticlinal divisions of its cells, assures that a multicellular packet initiated in one of the tunica layers remains independent of packets initiated in contiguous layers. This is proved by the persistence of mericlinal sectors in periclinal chimeras (Rogers and Bonnett 1989).

Evidence from plants that are sectorial chimeras suggests that there may be relatively few cells at the summit of the apex from which the shoot is ultimately constructed and, moreover, demonstrates a sectorial organization of the shoot. For example, the sectorial chimeras of *Epilobium hirsutum,* described by Bartels (1961), indicate that in this species all the tissues of the shoot are derived from a minimum of four cells in each layer of the tunica. More recently, a group of four cells has been demonstrated to be the source of all cells in the superficial tunica layer of shoots of *Actinidia arguta* (Puławska 1986). Each of the four cells was the source of a multicellular complex occupying a 90° sector of the apical surface. Since the shoot of *Actinidia* has a discretely layered tunica, the four cells are initials only for the layer in which they were identified and not for any other layer. In some circumstances it may be possible to follow the cell complexes of the corpus in the axial plane, as Puławska (1982) has found in shoot apices of *Aristolochia clematitis.*

At first sight it may seem that the pattern of cell division in a given layer of the tunica has little or no connection with the development of metamers. Lück and Lück (1985) have argued, however, that the geometry of anticlinal walls in the multicellular complexes of the shoot apex might be a direct cause of the initiation of leaf primordia, and hence of phyllotactic patterning. Obviously, the influence of the wall geometry on the behavior of the tunica, with its pattern of anticlinal-radial and anticlinal-circumferential divisions, would be of great developmental significance, for it is the tunica that initiates the leaf primordia.

If, as seems possible, the geometrical arrangement of cell walls can influence cellular behavior within a layer, then interactions between layers are perhaps even more likely (e.g. Hake and Freeling 1986). Thus, it could be imagined that cell divisions are organized within apical meristems in such a way that they comprise an infallible source of information for morphogenesis and cell differentiation. If so, then the further construction of each metamer would be a direct outcome of the cellular patterning in a preceding developmental epoch. This appears to be the case in certain bryophytes. Clearly, the topic is of great interest for students of plant development and deserves close attention.

Root Apices

Many of the concepts mentioned above in the context of shoot architecture and construction are applicable in a discussion of the relationships between meristem and metamer, and between metamer and module, of root systems. For example, the same evolutionary scheme holds wherein roots with a prominent apical cell are present in pteridophytes, whereas roots with a multicellular apical zone are characteristic of angiosperms (Clowes 1961). Moreover, when a tetrahedral apical cell is present, it divides, as it does in shoots, with a regular helical sequence, producing merophytes that undergo further divisions. Such roots do not have an obvious metameric construction, since they cannot be resolved externally into segmented units. But internally, the merophyte appears to have some equivalence to the metamer—perhaps more so than in the shoot—for not only is it a reiterated structural unit, but it also has the potentiality to initiate new root modules. Construction of roots of angiosperms is examined below; these roots seem to possess neither metamers nor merophytes.

An instructive example of merophytic root construction in a lower plant is provided by the water fern, *Azolla pinnata*. The anatomy of its roots has been studied in detail by Gunning et al. (1978), who, incidentally, revived Douin's (1923) term *mérophyte,* used by that author to designate the daughter of an apical cell. The apical cell of the *Azolla* root produces a repeating sequence of three daughters, which, after further divisions, give rise to three longitudinal groups of cell-files, each occupying a 120° sector of the root. Divisions in the merophyte are at first longitudinal (periclinal and radial), and the sequence in which they occur is repeated in each merophyte. These divisions provide the root with all the files of cells from which the various cell types will later differentiate. When this class of divisions is complete, transverse divisions occur and multiply the number of cells in each file.

Each merophyte is therefore an assemblage of precisely ordered cells and, since merophytes are reiterated structures, there might be some grounds for considering them to be equivalent to metamers. Roots of *Azolla pinnata,* however, do not form lateral roots by which a metameric structure would be externally recognizable. In this instance, therefore, the merophytes are not the basis for any further development, since they are incapable of generating primordia from which new root modules arise; they might be regarded as "sterile" metamers. The only structures that they do produce and that project away from the root axis are the root hairs (these may be up to 2–3 mm long). They are formed from cells occupying a characteristic location on the outer cell layer of each merophyte. Indeed, so precise is the vertical spacing between the hairs that it is possible thereby to deduce the limits of each merophyte with a hand lens.

Some other ferns whose roots possess a tetrahedral apical cell do produce lateral roots. Species whose patterns of merophyte division have been analyzed and related to lateral primordium production are *Ceratopteris pteridoides* (Chiang 1970), *C. thalictroides* (Chiang and Gifford 1971), *Marsilea coromandelica* (Charlton 1983), and *M. quadrifolia* (Liu 1984). In *Ceratopteris,* one primordium forms in a merophytic sector (Figure 1.3.a); in *Marsilea,* two or more may do so. In all four species, lateral root

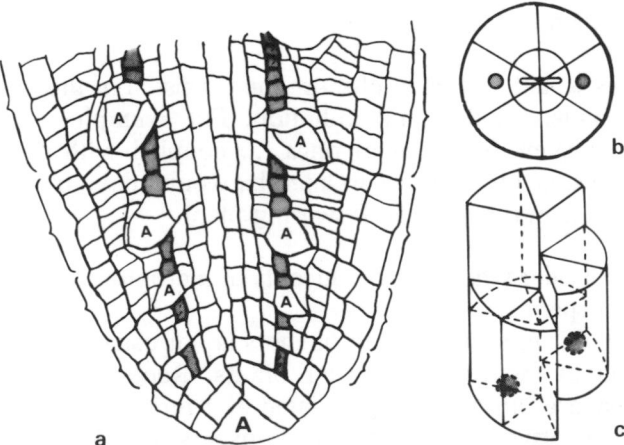

Figure 1.3. (a) Median longitudinal section through a root apex of *Ceratopteris pteridoides* showing a primary apical cell, A, in the main root axis and a secondary apical cell in each lateral root primordium. The proximal and distal limits of merophytes are indicated by *brackets*. The endodermis, which is the cell layer in which secondary apical cells develop, is *stippled*. Redrawn from Chiang (1970). (b) Diagram of a cross section of a root of *Ceratopteris* illustrating the location of two lateral primordia (*stippled*) opposite the poles of the diarch xylem system and its relation to the sextant of tissue layers. (c) Cutaway diagram of three successive merophytes of a root of *Ceratopteris* showing the location of lateral root primordia (*stippled*) at the distal end of two of the merophytes; (b) is modified, and (c) is redrawn, from Chiang & Gifford (1971).

primordia develop from a particular cell in the endodermal lineage; and they do so only after a certain sequence of divisions—both longitudinal and transverse—has been accomplished. In each case, the cell that initiates the primordium lies at the distal end of the merophyte; once formed, it begins to function like an apical cell, cutting off merophytes, which then reiterate the root-building sequence of divisions displayed by the primary apical cell of the parent axis (Chiang 1970). Additional primordia (secondary apical cells) form in other endodermal cells and do so according to a particular longitudinal pattern. In all cases, the secondary apical cells result from an unequal division (Charlton 1983; Liu 1984).

In *Ceratopteris,* the coincidence between lateral formation and merophyte development makes it possible to use the rate of lateral formation as a measure of the rate of division of the primary apical cell. In the rapidly growing roots of *C. pteridoides* [studied by Chiang (1970)], an average of 1.5 pairs (or 1.66 gyres) of laterals were produced each day. This means that the duration of the mitotic cycle in the primary apical cell was approximately 5 hr. Thus, the rate of division of the apical cell is also the rate of merophyte formation, which, in turn, bears a direct relation to the rate of formation of new root modules (cf. examples of the shoot apices of mosses, mentioned above).

Not every merophyte forms a lateral root primordium, however. In the species mentioned above, secondary apical cells arise in only two of the three merophyte sectors per gyre (Figure 1.3.b,c); presumably, a similar cell is potentially present in the appropriate position in the third sector, but does not develop or divide further. One possible reason for this irregularity is that the positioning of the vascular elements influences primordium formation: the stele is diarch, and primordia only form opposite the xylem pole (Figure 1.3.b). The result is that lateral roots tend to arise in pairs; a gap between each pair corresponds to the sector of the sterile merophyte.

From the above example it is clear that although a certain pattern of divisions is necessary for a new module to be initiated, it is not the only requirement. As Charlton (1983) has pointed out regarding the sequences of equal and unequal divisions that lead to primordium initiation in *Marsilea,*

> Minor changes would suffice to obscure the precision of the relationship between cell division pattern and lateral initiation. For example, substitution of equal longitudinal divisions for unequal ones ... coupled with delay in the enlargement of cells destined to give rise to laterals, would make the arrangement almost as obscure as it is in the average flowering plant.

Thus, we have to consider whether the concepts of merophyte and metamer also apply to the roots of angiosperms.

As mentioned above, segmentation of roots is not usually obvious; however, one exception is found in the roots of water plants. Roots of turtle grass, *Thalassia testudinum,* for instance, are visibly articulated at 1 mm intervals by the interposition among the elongated cortical cells of regular transverse diaphragms consisting of short cells (Tomlinson 1969). These segments might be regarded as metamers of a sort, though the roots that possess them never develop any lateral branches. The morphology of the diaphragms and the interdiaphragm segments is reminiscent of nodes and internodes along the shoot; like them, diaphragms and interdiaphragm segments result from a rhythmic activity in a meristem that thereby generates cells of alternating properties.

Repeated cellular units of another type are sometimes found in roots of higher plants. Some Gramineae and Cyperaceae, for example, show anticlinal sectors of cells, particularly in their epidermis-cortex complex, that resemble merophytes of ferns.

Kadej (1963) described an example in *Cyperus gracilis* and compared it with the sectored cellular pattern of roots of the fern, *Matteuccia struthiopteris*. Like the merophytes, the sectors reflect a previous history of anticlinal divisions in one or a few cells at the summit of the root. Should the apex have a single cell exactly at its summit where the cortical cell-files converge, it would be surrounded, on average, by six cells (cf. Kadej 1963). These cells could, in theory, serve as the initials for six longitudinal sectors (or sextants); however, in transverse sections it is usually not possible to observe such sextants on the basis of the arrangement of cell walls, even when they have been carefully searched for [e.g. in *Cyperus* (Kadej 1963) and in *Zea mays* and *Oryza sativa* (P. W. Barlow unpublished)]. In transverse sections of roots of *Brassica napus,* Kuras (1980) believed he was able to recognize four cellular sectors tracing to 16 initial cells encircling two tiers of central cells in the stele and cortex, one tier for each tissue. Each central group of cells originated from four progenitor cells (cf. the four progenitor cells at the summit of the *Actinidia* shoot apex mentioned above). The cap and dermatogen arose from a third tier of cells. Kuras proposed that the metaxylem vessels developed with a fixed relation to the sector boundaries within the stele and also suggested that the row of xylem cells across the diarch stele might owe its orientation to the direction of the first segmentation wall in the apical cell of the proembryo.

It is likely that in many species some sort of sectoring of the stele and cortex occurs, but the boundaries wander during the course of root growth as the pattern of cells at the summit of each cell-complex changes due to shifts in the orientation of cell division. This might apply particularly to species whose roots show a "closed" type of construction in which there are discrete boundaries at the root pole between cap and root, and between stele and cortex. In species whose roots show an "open" construction, these boundaries do not converge to the apex: there is no discontinuity between the cap initials and the root, and the stele and cortex are consequently continuous with the tissues of the cap. At the pole of the root proper, because of the relative infrequency of periclinal divisions, the number of cells from which the cell-files of the root appear to originate is nearly the same as the final number of files. Thus, no eye-catching anticlinal sectoring of the root is possible in these species.

In the above quotation from Charlton (1983), any geometrical pattern of division that is intimately, and perhaps causally, linked to primordium initiation seems to have disappeared in the angiosperm root, particularly in those with an open construction. The siting of primordia appears to have succumbed almost entirely to physiological influences that emanate from the vascular tissue. In many species, primordia form in the pericycle opposite the xylem poles, in some they form opposite the phloem, whereas in others they form between the xylem and the phloem. The reason for this variation is unknown, but it is tempting to believe that there might still be some residual influence of the cell lineage system that predisposes certain cells in the pericycle to form primordia, as has been argued elsewhere (Barlow and Adam 1988). Another line of evidence that could support this notion is that although primordia lie in definite ranks, or *orthostichies,* there is a definite distance (or multiples of that distance) between each of them (Barlow and Adam 1988). Although the rank-like arrangement of laterals might be attributable to the influence of the vasculature, the longitudinal spacing between them could be the result of a particular pattern of transverse divisions. Here it should be recalled that in *Ceratopteris* the lateral root primordia also have a fixed longitudinal spacing related to the length of the merophyte.

In the roots of angiosperms, presumptive pericycle cells divide transversely once they have left the confines of the quiescent center (a group of cells in some ways both structurally and functionally analogous to the axial zone of shoots). In the cortex of

Zea mays, the sequence of transverse divisions that a cell undergoes shows a considerable degree of ordering (Barlow 1987). It might be anticipated, therefore, that in the pericycle a similar ordered pattern of division, perhaps resulting in a particular pattern of cytoplasmic inheritance, exists and specifies which cell in the resulting packet of cells will develop as a primordium (Barlow and Adam 1988). Thus, even though merophytes occupying large anticlinal sectors may not exist in roots of higher plants, smaller groupings of cells, which trace to a set of initials lying on the proximal surface of the quiescent center, certainly do exist. The packets of cells to which each of these initial cells gives rise behave similarly to the larger merophyte cell-groupings that issue from a primary apical cell. All of the pericycle cell packets might therefore have the potentiality to give rise to new root modules, but only some have access to a signal supplied by the vascular tissue that induces the additional cell growth and division necessary for primordium formation. This would seem to be similar to the situation in the *Ceratopteris* root, except that in this species every merophyte that contains a potential primordium traces to a single primary apical cell.

As we have seen, in roots of the fern *Ceratopteris* there are grounds for considering that the terms merophyte and metamer are in some respects interchangeable. But this need not be the case in higher taxa. So, even if the applicability of the concept of metamers to roots of higher plants is rejected on the grounds that their roots do not have a regularly segmented structure, they may still contain traces of an underlying merophytic organization that is fragmented into a collection of cell packets. These packets have as their immediate origin the initials lying on the surface of the quiescent center, which, in the case of roots of closed construction, derive from a few cells at the pole of the root. This situation seems little different from that in shoots, where leaf primordia and their associated structures derive from a small group of cells in and around the axial zone. One difference, however, is that lateral root primordia arise internally from the pericycle, whereas leaf primordia arise superficially from the tunica. Another difference is that, unlike leaf primordia with their often complex forms of spiral phyllotaxis, there is often no equivalent patterning of the lateral roots on the parent root axis.

MODULES, METAMERS, AND MERISTEMS OF APPLE
AND SOME OTHER TREES

Let us integrate some of the features of shoot module development discussed in the previous sections. The shoot system of the apple tree, *Malus domestica* Borkh. (cv. Cox's Orange Pippin), is taken as a specific example, since much is known of the structure of the different types of shoots (modules) and of their relative positions within the canopy. The modules of apple trees develop with features of both Rauh's and Champagnat's architectural model (Crabbé 1986). The morphology and anatomy of the shoots and roots of these species has been recently reviewed by Pratt (1990).

Four types of module growth unit develop from the meristematic buds and apices of apple shoots in each growing season. The type of unit (submodule) that actually develops is reasonably predictable and depends on the location of the bud on the module axis (cf. Porter 1988; Crabbé 1984). With knowledge of the interactions between the population of buds and morphogenetic factors, it should be possible to formalize the particular pattern of module development by means of a suitable logical system. Various model schemes have already been proposed for apple bud development (Jankiewicz 1972; Schmidt 1973; Landsberg and Thorpe 1975), but these are based on hormonal and physiological interactions that are imperfectly understood. In one case, it has been demonstrated that the phyllotaxy of the metamers influences the development of their buds (Crabbé 1985).

The branches, twigs, and spurs of an apple tree consist of four types of growth unit, which have been described by Boyes (1922) and Bijhouwer 1924). Boyes was responsible for introducing into the English scientific literature the French terms for the various types of shoot. Although nowadays these terms have a somewhat arcane ring to them, when one considers their original French meaning it will be appreciated that they actually provide accurate and useful names for the various shoots. The first type, the *brindille,* includes all shoots longer than 10 cm: leading shoots, as well as long side-shoots, are brindilles. The second type is the *dard,* a shoot similar in construction to the first, but shorter, being 2.5–10 cm long. The third type, the *lambourde,* is <2.5 cm in length, and in the summer of its growth is surrounded by a rosette of leaves. The fourth type, the *bourse,* is a short (<1 cm), swollen shoot that bears flowers. I shall refer to these four types of shoots as growth units, or submodules, 1, 2, 3, and 4, respectively. Development by means of long and short shoots is common among trees: the structure of the crown is determined by the long shoots, while the majority of the leaves are borne by the short shoots.

In common with the growth of the other submodules, the development of the type 1 submodule is completed over a period of two growing seasons and consists of two phases. The first phase is one of morphogenesis. It begins with the formation of a bud in June–July. The distal surface of the apical meristem is flat and has an area of about 0.1 mm^2 (Figure 1.4). Beneath the surface there are 4–5 cell layers of tunica (see also Hilkenbäumer and Buchloh 1954; Hanke 1981). At this stage there are 10 metamers with spirally arranged primordia (⅝ phyllotaxy) contained within the growing apex (the apex here refers to the structure enclosed within, and including, the unexpanded leaves). The internodes cease to elongate when the bud begins to form, but the apical meristem remains active and produces 6 more metamers at a rate of about 1 per week (Luckwill and Silva 1979). The resulting set of 16 metamers is typical of a full-grown bud that will continue vegetative growth as a type 1 submodule in the following year.

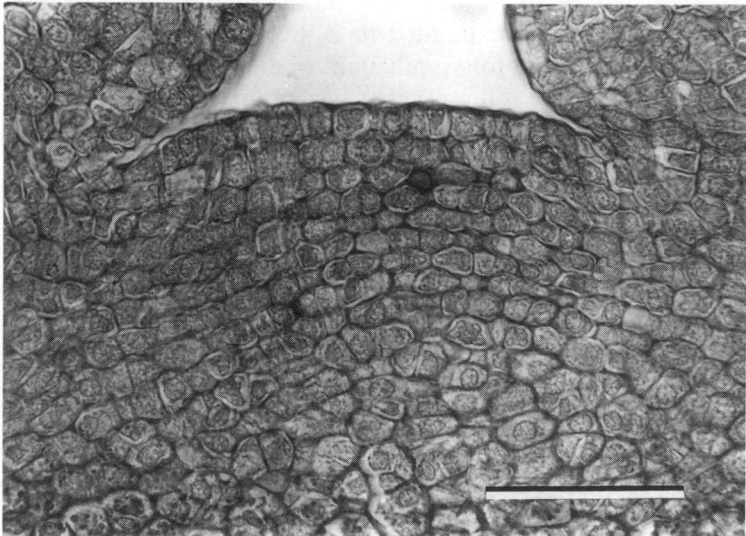

Figure 1.4. Longitudinal section through a dormant terminal bud of a leading shoot (submodule type 1) of an apple tree (*Malus domestica* cv. Cox's Orange Pippen). There are four layers of tunica. Scale bar represents 50 μm.

The bud in which these new metamers are being formed is often referred to as being in a state of "summer dormancy." This is a somewhat inappropriate term, since the apex is obviously not dormant in the sense that it is quiescent: it is, in fact, actively developing, and the apparent dormancy is only the result of the nonelongation of the internodes. Romberger (1963), who has reviewed the various types of dormancy and their controls in woody plants, refers to this pseudodormant state as one of "correlative inhibition." This state, or the period in which it occurs, is denoted as R1 (R standing for Rest). In August, this first, morphogenetic phase of submodule growth is complete and the bud then enters a state (or period) of true dormancy, or "winter dormancy," denoted as R2.

When winter dormancy has been broken by a suitable period of cool temperature, and perhaps also by the number of heat units accumulated (cf. Remphrey 1989a), the second phase of submodule development begins. Not only do the metamers enclosed within the bud resume their growth, but the apical meristem also becomes morphogenetically active and produces new metamers at a rate of 1 per 2–3 days (Abbott 1970). The plastochron is therefore about three times more rapid than it was during the first phase of growth. When growth resumes, the junction between the new submodule and the older one below can be recognized by the short internodes and the scars of fallen bud scales. In neither phase of growth is anything known about the duration of the mitotic cell cycle. Given what is known about its duration in shoots of other (mainly herbaceous) species it would not be surprising if it was about two days during the period of rapid growth.

The two phases of type 1 submodule development are more formally summarized in Figure 1.5.a. At the beginning of R1, the young submodule already possesses a set of metamers, y_b. The meristematic dome continues to produce a further set of metamers, y_a, which remain within the apex. Throughout the dormant R2 period, the bud therefore contains a total of y metamers (where $y = y_b + y_a$) surmounted by a mitotically inactive apical dome. In the second phase of growth, internode elongation commences and increases the length of most of y to Y. At the same time, the apical dome becomes active and produces a further set of metamers that adds to the remainder of y. These are *neoformed* metamers (cf. Remphrey and Powell 1984). The apex now contains a new set of metamers, z. At the time the apex re-enters R1, a fraction of the z metamers (z_a) has expanded to Z, but the remaining portion of z (z_b) is "trapped" in the bud and is therefore equivalent to metamers y_b of the previous growth period. Placing precise values on the number of metamers that make up sets Y and Z is difficult because these vary depending on environmental conditions during the growing season. Because of the biphasic nature of submodule growth, however, a certain fraction of the set of y metamers produced during the R1 period must transform into the z metamers in the second phase of growth. To illustrate this point, Figure 1.6.a shows the frequency of various numbers of metamers found within buds of type 1 submodules of apple trees sampled during the R2 period of 1986 and the number of metamers that subsequently grew out from such buds in the following year.

Publications that describe the rates of leaf initiation within the bud and their subsequent export and elongation during the following growing period are reviewed for various tree species by Hallé et al. (1978). Other thorough studies published since that review refer to *Acer saccharum* (Gregory 1980), *Arctostaphylos uva-ursi* (Remphrey and Steeves 1984), *Betula papyrifera* (Macdonald and Mothersill 1983; Macdonald et al. 1984), *Fraxinus pennsylvanica* (Rehmphrey 1989a,b), *Larix laricina* (Remphrey and Powell 1984), and *Shepherdia argentea* and *S. canadensis* (Hayes et al. 1989). An example with features similar to the one of apple is that of *Populus trichocarpa* (Critchfield 1960). Certainly one of the most thorough studies of the morphogenetic and

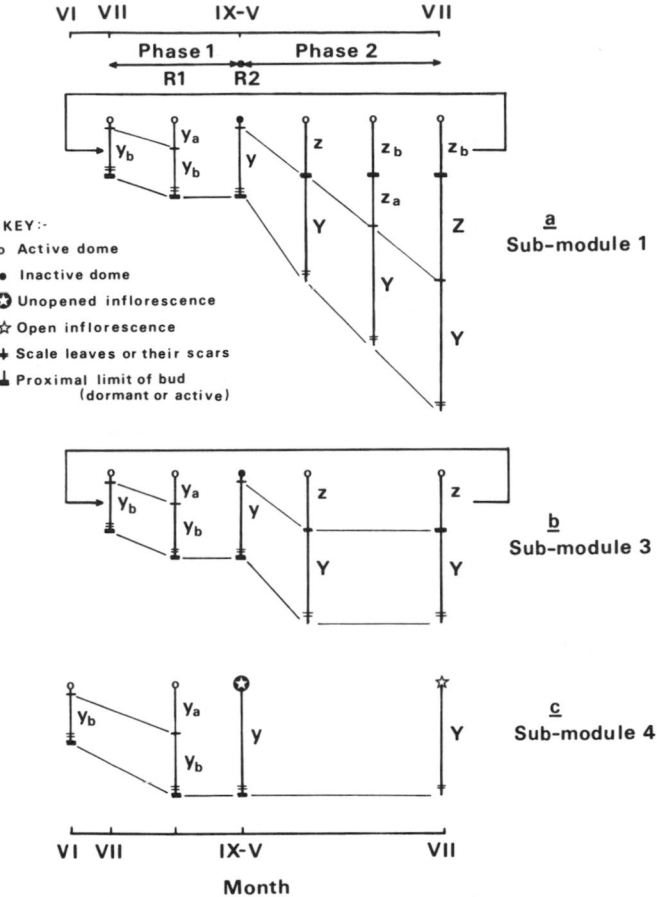

Figure 1.5. Scheme to show the development of a terminal bud through two years of growth. The month of the year is indicated by a Roman numerals (I, January; XII, December). (a), (b), and (c) refer to seasonal growth units (submodules) 1, 2, and 4, respectively. For further details, see text. Note that in submodule 4 (c), the first, morphogenetic period of growth (R1) commences in June (VI).

growth phases of a module, which also include details of mitotic activity within the apical meristem, is given by Hallé and Martin (1968) for young shoots of the rubber tree, *Hevea brasiliensis*. All the examples mentioned are of trees and shrubs. An example of bud activity in a herbaceous plant is given by Arney (1953a, b) for strawberry (*Fragaria vesca*). He showed that during the winter months the apex added to itself one new leaf primordium and exported none, whereas in summer the rate of export slightly exceeded the rate of production and the apex appeared to lose a primordium. The latter example very well illustrates that the growth of buds and submodules is essentially a problem of how the relative rates of initiation and export of primordia (metamers) are regulated.

Further details of metamer in a type 1 submodule of the apple shoot are revealed by dissecting buds at different times after their entry into the R1 state. Each plastochron sees the formation of a leaf primordium (P), an associated node (N), a proximal internode (I), and the regeneration of the meristematic dome ($\dot{D}$). The adaxial angle between P and I is the site at which the apical dome of an axillary bud will form (Figure 1.7a). When the shoot is actively growing, this axil or potential dome ($\dot{D}$)

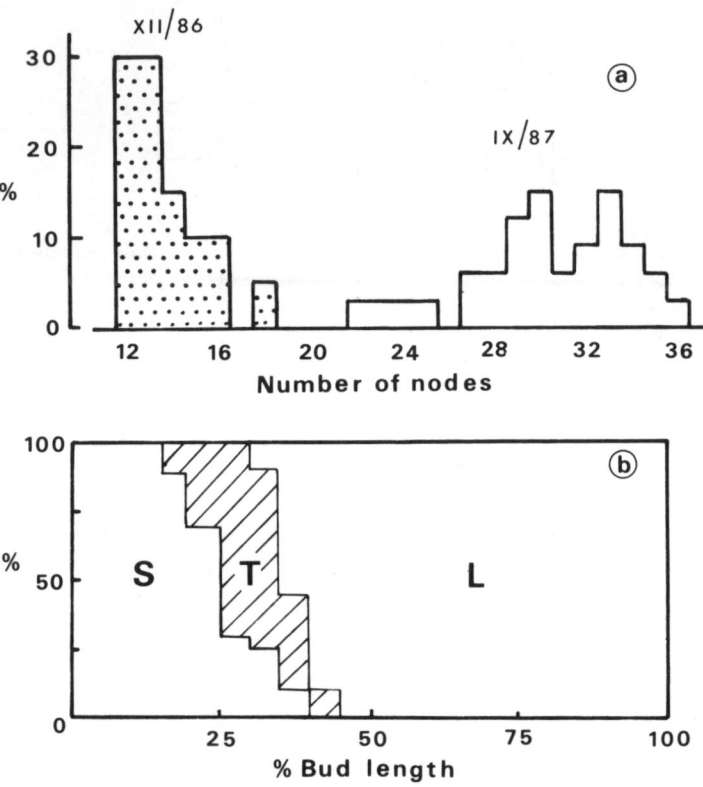

Figure 1.6. Analysis of a leading shoot (submodule type 1) of apple (*Malus domestica* cv. Cox's Orange Pippen). (a) Stippled histogram: the frequency of the different numbers of nodes (metamers) counted within dormant terminal buds collected in December 1986 (preformed metamers). Open histogram: the frequency of the different numbers of nodes that developed from a similar sample of dormant buds during the subsequent growth season (preformed plus neoformed metamers), collected at the end of their growth period in September 1987. (b) The frequency of scales (S), transition leaves (T), and true leaves (L) at various positions along the dormant buds referred to in (a). Length along the bud is given as a percentage of the total number of nodes (i.e. the total number of nodes in a bud is referred to as 100%, regardless of the actual number).

becomes an actual meristematic dome (Figure 1.7c,d) after seven further metamers have been produced. The first signs of this redirection of meristematic activity is the formation of a *shell-zone* in the axil of the third or fourth leaf primordium (Figure 1.7b) (see also Pratt 1967). The quadruplet of derivatives of D, [P N I D], produced in each plastochron, constitutes a metamer. During dormancy (R2 phase), each of the metamers is arrested at a different state of development. In particular, the dormant axillary buds show different degrees of maturity related to their age; this in turn is reflected in their subsequent behavior wherein the oldest buds grow the least.

Not all the above-mentioned metamers with their quadruplet structure that fill the portion y develop similarly in the second phase of growth. The final structures within the elongated portion Y of the submodule fall into three groups: m_1, m_2, and m_3 (Figure 1.6.b). Group m_1 consists of the four most proximal metamers, numbered 1–4, which were already present at the start of bud development. Their internodes fail to extend and m_1 thus consists of seven suppressed internodes, each of which in associated with a scale leaf. At first, scales develop (during R1) in the same way as leaves, but when the young leafy structure in nearly complete, the distal portion, which otherwise would

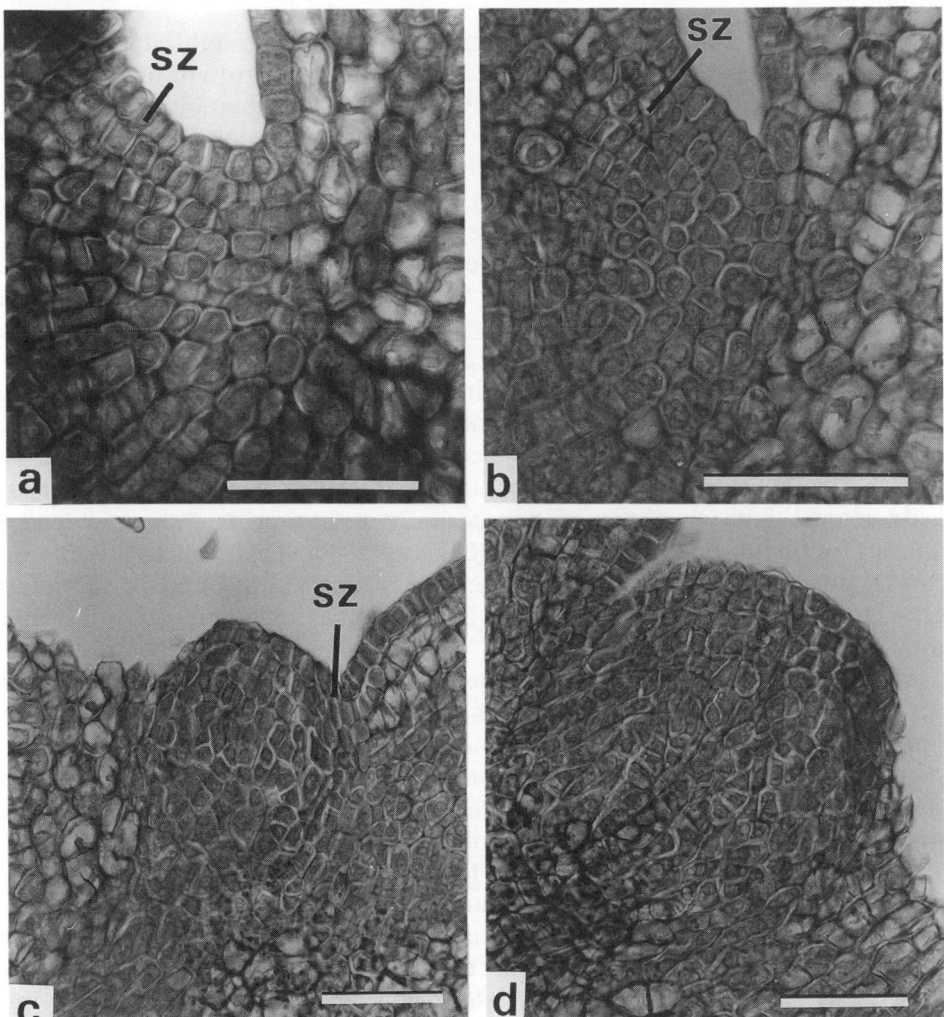

Figure 1.7. Different stages in the development of axillary buds on a dormant terminal shoot apex of a leading shoot of apple (*Malus domestica* cv. Cox's Orange Pippen). (*a*) An incipient axillary bud is indicated by the presence of a "shell zone" (sz). (*b*) The first signs of bud development within the "shell zone" (sz). (*c*), (*d*) Further growth of the bud has taken place. Each scale bar represents 50 μm.

have formed the leaf lamina, aborts and the remaining proximal portion forms a scaly, waterproof covering to the bud (Abbott 1970). Group m_2 consists of metamers 5–7. These, when they elongate, give short internodes and partial leaves. The latter are formed by abortion of the most distal portion of the pre-emergent leaf. Group m_3 contains the remaining metamers 8–16. They develop long internodes and full leaves.

The pattern of development adopted by the three groups of metamers probably reflects metabolic changes in the apex during the R1 period. For example, it may be that the onset of fruit development diverts away from the apex the flow of nutrients and carbohydrates that would otherwise have been used for the expansion of its leaves. Moreover, it is believed that there is a reduction in the amount of cytokinins reaching the apex from the roots (Abbott 1970), and at the same time there may be a net inflow of abscisic acid from the leaves to the apex. The development of the bud scales also contributes to the correlative inhibition of the apex (Abbott 1970). Similar conclusions were reached by Schneider (1968) on the role of scales in regulating the dormancy of *Rhododendron* buds. Whatever the nature of these inhibitory factors, they cause the cessation of the second phase of development of a growth unit while permitting morphogenetic processes to continue within its apex, thereby initiating the first period (R1) of development of a new growth unit. Metamers already enclosed within the apex at the time of this switch (the portion denoted y_b in Figure 1.5.a) respond in accordance with the stage of development they have reached. Metamers 1–4 (which subsequently develop as group m_1) are the most advanced at this stage and are perhaps the most vulnerable to the consequences of this developmental change. Presumably, under the conditions that prevail at the start of the R1 period, metamers of this group, even though they do not elongate, continue to mature (viz. the modified partial leaves), for when growing conditions return after the dormant period, their internodes are unable to elongate and hence they remain permanently dwarfed. Likewise, their scales abscind and their axillary buds fail to grow.

Another extensively studied shoot system (on account of its commercial importance) is that of *Acer saccharum* (sugar maple). In this species, a long shoot growth unit is developed that, when mature, consists only of those metamers developed in the bud (i.e. preformed during the R1 period) (Gregory 1980). This contrasts with the long shoot of apple where many of the metamers are neoformed as opposed to preformed. The type 2 submodule of apple (the dard), however, may be totally derived from these preformed metamers.

Growth units either with or without neoformed metamers may be the rule for certain species. For instance, *Shepherdia canadensis* is a shrub whose terminal buds produce growth units consisting of only four metamers that were preformed in the R1 bud. Growth units of the related *S. argentea,* on the other hand, consist of many more metamers, over half of which are neoformed (Hayes et al. 1989). Although *S. argentea* may produce up to nine more metamers than *S. canadensis,* the increment of shoot growth is not necessarily greater. Clearly, there are interesting relationships still to be discovered about how metamer initiation and internode elongation are controlled. For the plant, such interrelations have ecological implications. The two *Shepherdia* species have different shoot architectures and different habitats (Hayes et al. 1990). The extent to which these ecological differences relate to the behavior of the buds is a topic to which architectural analysis can begin to provide some answers.

The same general pattern of growth and development described for long type 1 shoots of apple occurs in apple buds that give rise to the shorter growth units of types 2 and 3 (Luckwill and Silva 1979). Although the meristem is somewhat smaller than that of the buds of submodule 1 (Hanke 1981), the most marked difference between growth units of types 1 and 3 is the number of metamers that form and elongate during the second phase of growth. In type 3 there is little elongation in the internodes formed earlier in the R1 period; the full leaves are thus arranged in a rosette. Neither is there any expansion of the internodes formed in the second period of growth. The latter metamers thus re-enter the bud in the succeeding R1 period (Figure 1.5.b). In a bud of a short shoot of type 3, there may be typically 18 metamers. Group m_1 contains metamers 1–7, group m_2 metamers 8–10, and group m_3 metamers 11–18; they develop seven scales, three partial leaves, and eight full leaves, respectively, in the second period of growth.

One of the earliest studies of dimorphic shoot systems was that of *Gingko biloba* (Gunkel et al. 1949). In this tree, as in apple, there are long and short shoots (consisting of submodules that are entirely of type 1 or type 3, respectively). Neither the buds nor the meristems of the two types of growth units can be distinguished by their external appearance or their internal structure (Foster 1938; Gunckel et al. 1949), but the amounts of auxin that are extractable from their apices show characteristic differences (Gunckel and Thimann 1949). The small amount of auxin produced by short shoots may account for the lack of elongation of internodes in the second phase of their growth. Similar characteristics, including those relating to auxin status, were also found for long and short shoot apices of *Cercidiphyllum japonicum,* the Katsura tree of Japan (Titman and Wetmore 1955). A recent investigation (Looney et al. 1988) of the nonbranching, highly spurred (short-shoot) mutant of apple, 'McIntosh Wijcik', has shown that its actively growing shoot tips contain significantly less polar gibberellins (mainly GA_{19}) and significantly more cytokinin than shoots from more branched apple varieties.

Apple buds of growth unit type 4, the floral submodule (often called a "fruit bud," even though the potential "fruit" occupies only a minute fraction of the bud volume), show a different pattern of development during the R1 period. The number of cell layers in the tunica of the meristem is reduced to two (Hilkenbäumer and Buchloh 1954). The plastochron has the same seven-day duration as shown by buds that remain vegetative, but the period of metamer production is extended by six weeks. Thus, a total of 21 metamers are formed [Luckwill and Silva 1979; Schmidt and Egerer 1982 (both working with cv. Golden Delicious)], resulting in buds that may have a diameter at least 10% greater than those which remain vegetative (Adam 1981)—a feature that can permit an estimate of the coming fruitfulness of a tree. The distal six metamers, i.e. those formed during this extra period of growth, each form a flower initial in the axil of either a leaf or a bract primordium. The apical portion of the meristem also converts to a flower initial (Hilkenbäumer and Buchloh 1954; Zeller 1960). Two small buds, the so-called "bourse buds," develop in the axil of each of two leaf primordia just proximal to the floral metamers. Luckwill (1974) suggests that a "critical node number" is required before flower induction can take place. According to this hypothesis (developed with the number of nodes found in cultivars Cox's Orange Pippin and Golden Delicious in mind), if more than 16 nodes are formed in the bud, flowers appear, otherwise the bud remains vegetative. This hypothesis seems to be no more than being wise after the event, however, for there is no a priori reason that additional nodes should determine flower formation; they are, perhaps, simply part of a constellation of characters associated with inflorescence formation. A similar comment may be made regarding the suggestion that the formation of bracts is one of the key features in the switch from vegetative to reproductive development (Fulford 1965, 1972).

Expressed more formally (Figure 1.5.c), a fruit bud at the end of its first phase of growth (R1) contains the unexpanded metameric set, y, which consists of a subset y_b (the metamers present in the apex at the start of bud formation) and another subset y_a, formed by the meristem during this period. In the second phase of submodule growth, all of y elongates to Y, which, in this case, is a short stem supporting an inflorescence that is an umbel-like corymb. No further addition of metamers can occur because by this time, the apical dome has been consumed by the terminal floral primordium (Figure 1.5.c). Growth of the module, of which this growth unit is the terminal member, is now complete.

The 21 metamers of the fruit bud develop in four distinct groups. Group m_1 consists of the nine most proximal metamers (metamers 1–9) with suppressed internodes and fugacious scales, which develop as described above. Groups m_2 and m_3 each contain three internodes that fail to expand (metamers 10–12 and 13–15, respectively): they are distinguished by the fact that m_2 bears partial leaves, whereas m_3 bears true leaves. The distal group, m_4 (metamers 16–22), bears the flowers: the basal trio (16–18) is subtended by true leaves, the apical trio (19–21) is subtended by bracts, and the terminal flower (metamer 22) has neither leaf nor bract. The nodes and internodes of groups m_2, m_3, and m_4 all swell latitudinally to produce the characteristic *bourse.* The bourse buds lie in the leaf axils of group m_3 and from their apical meristem, new modules can be constructed.

After the buds have over-wintered they are ready to express their potentialities in the subsequent set of fully expanded growth units or submodules. The submodules with the most complex morphogenetic behavior are those of class 1. In apple, the branching habit of this type of growth unit is acrotonic (as is characteristic of trees), and the buds supported on its axis have the greatest range of potentialities for development. The terminal apex may have developed either as a fruit bud of submodule type 4, in which case it forms an inflorescence, or it may continue (as is more usual) in a vegetative mode. Each axillary bud may expand to give a submodule of either class 1, 2, 3, or 4. It would be of great interest to be able to predict, particularly for economically important species, which type of growth unit will develop from a given axillary bud. To a certain extent this is possible because the probability with which a given bud develops as one or another of the alternative classes of submodules depends on its position along the supporting axis. An additional factor is the previous history of that axis. For example, in apple as well as birch (*Betula papyrifera*) (Macdonald and Mothersill 1983; Macdonald et al. 1984), short shoots develop from the proximal axillary buds of a long shoot, whereas long shoots develop from the distal axillary buds but usually do so only in the season following their initiation. This might parallel the situation in *Larix* spp., in which the short shoots develop from axillary buds preformed in the first, R1, period of growth, whereas long shoots develop from buds neoformed during the second period of growth (Owens and Molder 1979). The bourse buds on submodule 4 of apple also have the potential to develop as any one of the four submodule types. If there is more than one bud on a bourse, and if fruits have been set in the adjacent metamers, usually one of them develops as a submodule of type 3 in the following season and the others remain dormant.

Once the type of submodule has been established in the first season of its growth, it often continues to grow in the same way. For example, a short shoot usually produces a terminal bud that will again become a short shoot, as do the associated axillary buds, although the occasional outgrowth of long shoots is also known, particularly as the result of pruning. In some varieties of apple as well as other species of fruit tree, however, submodules of type 1 can show alternating longer and shorter growth units in successive seasons. This coincides with rhythms of flowering. Some have argued that these rhythms are a response to fruiting and seed development (Chan and Cain 1967; Luckwill 1970) and are mediated by hormones, yet recent work has failed to provide any positive evidence that this is so (Green 1987). Moreover, *Malus* 'Magdeburgensis', which rarely fruits, shows a biennial pattern of flowering (R. L. Williams and D. L. Abbott, personal communication), thus indicating that rhythms of module development probably have a more deep-seated basis in the internal correlations of the whole organism.

These examples of module development expand material presented above in the section on Modules and Metamers. As interesting as it is, the problem of module morphogenesis in relation to the higher level of shoot architecture (which would include consideration of branch angles, effects of gravimorphism, etc.) cannot be pursued here. These aspects have been studied in apple by Jankiewicz (1956), Wareing and Nasr (1961), and Mullins and Rogers (1971). With the present details of metamer and module development, there is sufficient material to point a way to the preliminary formalization of the developmental potentialities of the buds of each class of growth unit.

FORMALIZATION OF METAMER AND MODULE DEVELOPMENT

Two main concepts underlie formal methods of representing development. Implicit in the first is that development is, within limits, invariant, and its unfolding depends upon the correct set of permissive conditions. The intervention of incorrect conditions does not permit development to continue. If development simply requires "decisions" of a yes/no type—for example, seed dormancy either breaks or continues, depending on the presence or absence of water—then the final outcome of a developmental sequence would be highly predictable. Increasing the number of alternative decisions that can be taken at each responsive stage would result in a more variable outcome.

A second concept of development regards this process as essentially self-perpetuating. Again, decisions are made as to which new developmental state is to be adopted, but the information relating to the transition is inherent to the system itself; permissive environmental conditions are regarded as axiomatic. Thus, it is the combination of the current developmental states present in various parts of the organism that determine the next set of states. In the example of seed or bud dormancy mentioned above, the outcome is a vegetative shoot because this is the only state prefigured in the previous state.

The first concept is essentially physiological and regards "processes" as the fundamental driving force of development. The second is essentially structural and regards morphological "patterns" as paramount. The two concepts are not mutually exclusive: they arise from two contrasting views of development. Once again, readers are referred to Rutishauser and Sattler's thesis (1985) of complementarity in development.

The "process" view of development can be formalized with the aid of flow diagrams: development "flows" through successive stages as a result of certain physiological conditions being met at each stage (e.g. Porter 1984). The "pattern" view of development can be realized through the language of automata theory, though this is not to say that physiological conditions are considered unimportant, only that they are implicit in any given developmental stage. Both of these views can be applied to the examples of module development described in the preceding section.

A Process Description of Module Development

A chart recording the flow of module development in apple through its various stages is given in Figure 1.8. The step from one stage to the next is facilitated by some physiological process that, in this case, is reflected in the plastochron (either long or short) and in the elongation (or nonelongation) of the metamers. For example, metamer elongation accompanies development of submodule 1 (the long shoot, or brindille), whereas its absence is characteristic of submodules 3 (the short shoot, or lambourde) and 4 (the bourse) (cf. Figure 1.5). Bud dormancy and its breaking reflect other physiological accompaniments of development. The encircled numbers beside the flow lines in Figure 1.8 refer to the developmental processes described in the following two paragraphs.

The starting point of the diagram could be the apex of an already established leading shoot, such as might be present on a young apple tree. When the dormancy of its terminal bud is broken (1), the meristem becomes active and the metamers present in the bud, as well as those formed later, elongate (2). The submodule, whose development has taken place over two successive seasons, is now complete. The terminal meristem becomes again enclosed within a bud (3), and the sequence is repeated, perhaps many times, until the growth of the module concludes with the conversion of the terminal meristem to a floral growth unit (submodule type 4) or with its death.

The metamers of the terminal bud also include axillary meristems and their associated metamers, which, by the time the submodule completes its elongation, are either one or two years old. In conformity with the proleptic branching pattern of apple, these become dormant (4). In the following season, however, these pre-formed metamers may either elongate (5), and thus make a new submodule of type 1, or fail to elongate (6), and thus make a submodule of type 3. It is possible, although there is no evidence on this point, that should the only metamers to elongate be those that were formerly enclosed within the bud (i.e. there were no subsequent neoformed metamers), then a submodule of type 2 (a dard) would result. The terminal meristem of any of these growth units may, when it enters the morphogenetic (R1) period of bud development, experience an extended period of growth and form more metamers (7). This presages flower primordium development. Flowering and fertilization lead to embryogenesis (8), whereupon the sequence of shoot module development recommences in a new generation. Meanwhile, the bourse bud on the floral submodule develops (9). Eventually it may grow out as one of the three vegetative growth units, or exceptionally as another floral unit, or it may remain dormant.

A Pattern Description of Module Development

A second class of models can be formulated in the language of automata theory. Many botanical systems have been illuminated by means of the algorithmic devices proposed by Lindenmayer and his associates (Lindenmayer 1978), and no doubt the complete modular development of shoot systems could also be represented in this way (Prusinkiewicz 1987). Another type of device, however, the Petri net, has been chosen for this purpose partly because of the stimulating work of J. and H. B. Lück, who, by this means, realized different patterns of shoot and bud development on *Tradescantia* cuttings (Lück et al. 1983). Hence, it might be possible to predict the various states of an architectural system both during its growth and following experimental interventions such as removal of modules. Since Petri nets may be unfamiliar to some readers, a brief description is given of their structure.

The theory of Petri nets was developed in Germany by C. A. Petri as a means of modeling information flow within a system. The basic idea behind his work is that the operation of a system can be represented by a graph, or net (Peterson 1977; Petri 1980). A Petri net is, therefore, an abstract, formal model of the self-generating changes in the informational state of a system. The net is constructed of two essential elements: places and transitions. Places are represented by circles, transitions by rectangles; the two elements are connected by arcs (Figure 1.9). A place is an output of information to a transition, which, in turn, may be an output to another place. The sequence in which the informational states occur is indicated by an arrow on the connecting arcs.

The Petri net has a dynamic property. This dynamism can be conveniently represented with the help of a token denoted by a black dot within a place (Figure 1.9). A place containing a token is said to be "marked." Only when all the inputs to a transition are marked can that transition be enabled. If a transition has more than one output place, new tokens are generated and one token is deposited in each. These places, now newly marked with a token, can enable other transitions. The location of the tokens, therefore, marks the current state of the net system.

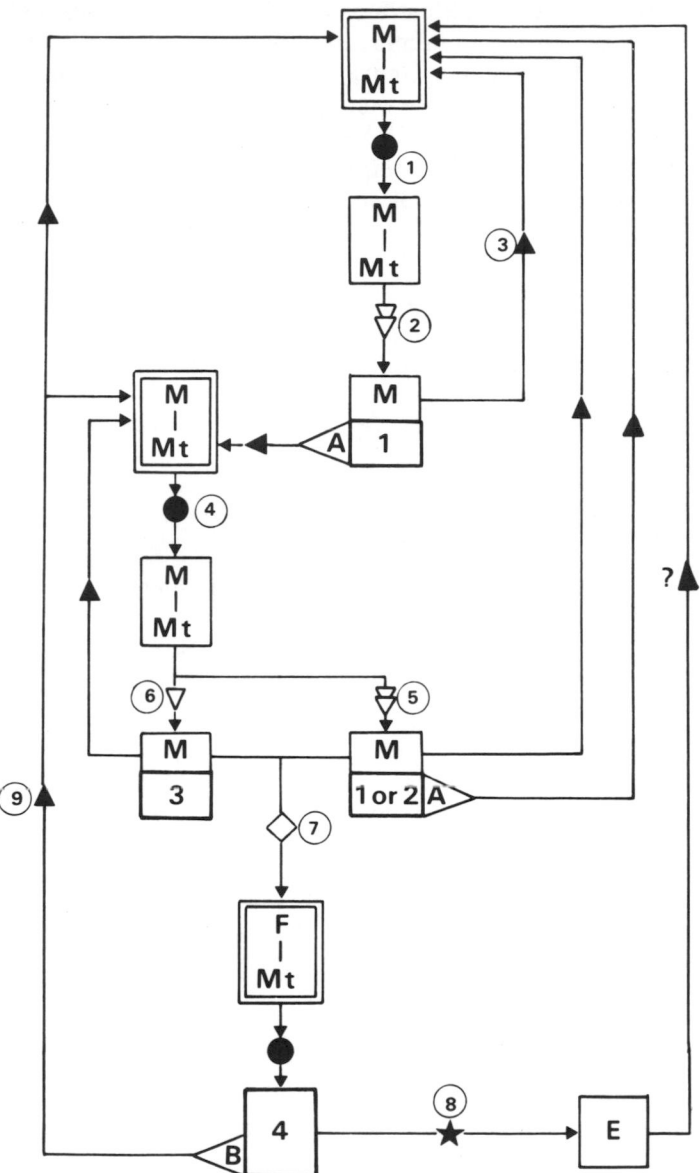

Figure 1.8. Flow chart of apple module development in terms of its apical meristems (M), axillary meristems (A), metamers (Mt), and completed seasonal growth units (or submodules) of different types represented by bold numbers **1–4** within rectangles. Submodule 4 includes a bourse bud (B) and flowers (F), whose fertilization (*) results in an embryo (E). The shoot apex is either actively growing (single-lined rectangle) or enclosed within a bud (double-lined rectangle); the completed growth of a submodule is denoted by the thickened lines of its corresponding rectangle. The plastochrons of the apex are of either long or short duration (*filled* or *open triangles,* respectively); additional plastochrons (*diamond*) accompany inflorescence development. Short plastochrons accompanied by metamer elongation are presented by *double triangles*. Dormancy (*filled circle*) is also indicated. The sequence of the present example (indicated by *numbers in circles*) depicts an apex on a leading shoot (at the *top* of the chart), initially in the morphogenetic phase of development, growing and perpetuating its apical meristem and producing axillary meristems that ultimately develop into floral submodules (type 4) during a three-year period that includes three periods of dormancy.

A simple example (Figure 1.9) illustrates the operation of a Petri net. Consider the four seasons of the year: spring, summer, autumn, and winter. Each can be represented as a place (Petri 1980). Let us mark the place "spring." The presence of the token in "spring" enables transition t_1, whereupon the token becomes deposited in the place "summer." In this new place, the token now enables transition t_2 and becomes deposited in the place "autumn." The sequence in which transitions are enabled is determined solely by the presence of a token; the start of the sequence is determined by the initial marking of the net.

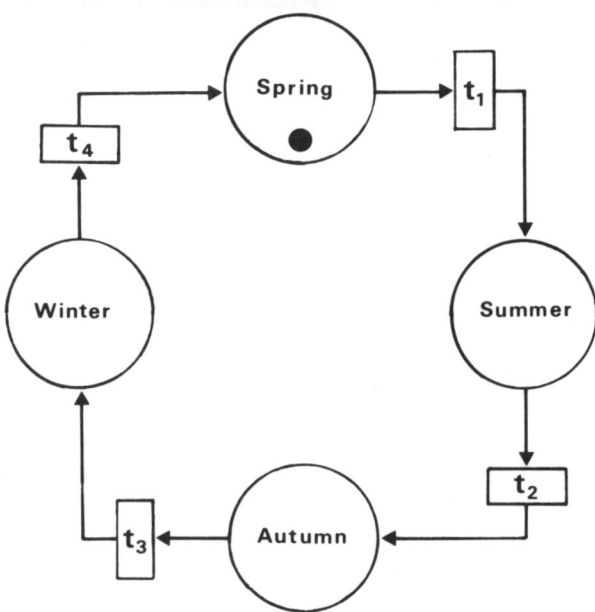

Figure 1.9. A simple Petri net representing the seasons of the year. Places are the *circles,* transitions are the *rectangles* (labeled t_1–t_4) inserted on lines that represent the arcs. The initial marking of the place "Spring" is denoted by the *solid circle.* After Petri (1980).

In the above example, no attention was paid to the calendar year in which the seasons occur; the seasons are simply states that follow each other and their sequence is known from experience. As a consequence, the net is said to be a "closed net." Nor is there any need to know the precise nature of the transition from one season to another; it is enough to know that some property of the state "winter," say, inevitably leads to the new state "spring." In reality, of course, the winter of one calendar year precedes the spring of the next; moreover, the transition of winter to spring depends upon the fulfillment of some condition contained within the motion of the Earth. In the example shown in Figure 1.9, the scope of concern has been limited to four places, or seasonal states. To include calendar years in the net would be possible, but the scope of concern would have to be enlarged to encompass perhaps an infinitude of seasonal states and the net need not then be closed.

The Petri net is not identical to a flow chart, since there is no actual "flow" of information. It is more correct to consider the Petri net as a scheme that represents potential states or conditions (the places), the means of realizing these states through enabling events (the transitions), and the relationships between places and transitions (the arcs). The Petri net is able to represent the execution of concurrent or parallel events should the net initially be marked in more than one place. Moreover, a place may itself represent an independent subnet of conditions and events that occur during this season. Thus, certain sets of conditions that hold at a given time can enable the transition to a new set of conditions. Former conditions then cease to hold, new ones arise, and the overall state of the system changes.

Nothing inherent to the Petri net specifies the passage of time. In real situations, which a net can represent, events often occur in a temporal sequence with a definite interval between each. But in the Petri net, events occur solely and immediately upon the fulfillment of the correct conditions. In the present context, time is regarded simply as an ordering of events. The Petri net can, therefore, represent time, but only by means of changes in the markings of the places. Each successive developmental state, represented by the sequence of marked places, can be regarded as a moment in the passage of "physiological time." Physical time, its counterpart, is kept by dead matter (e.g. by a clock or some other artificial device) and therefore has no place in any representation of a living, developing system.

The simple net in Figure 1.10 represents the relationships among cell, meristem, metamer, and module, and the rhythmic growth of the module. The net is marked initially at place A. The transition t_2 enables A, which may be an apical cell or a group of axial cells plus initials, to construct a meristem, D. The consequent marking of place D enables transition t_3; a series of metamers, represented by places M_1–M_4, is subsequently constructed by the enablement of transitions t_4–t_6. Enablement of transition t_7 and the consequent marking of place M_5 represents the maturation of the metamer series. When place M_5 becomes marked, transition t_8 is enabled and place A, the active meristematic apex, is regained. Rhythmic growth results from the disablement of transition t_1 when place M_1 is marked; this inhibits the autoregeneration of place A needed to make the series of metamers. Place M_5 could represent an intermediate stage in the development of a seasonal growth-unit (submodule) indicated by place M_6. If tokens are used to denote the successive marked states, it will be found that place M_6 gains a token on each occasion that the sequence of markings is completed. Table 1.2 summarizes the stages in the marking and enablement of this net.

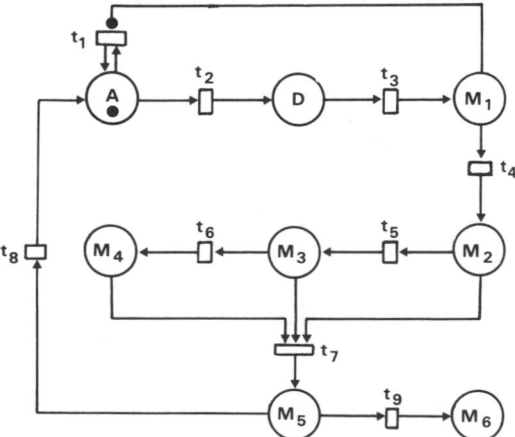

Figure 1.10. A Petri net representing rhythmic growth of a set of metamers and submodules. Symbols and notation as in Figure 1.9. Further details are described in the text and in Table 1.2.

Table 1.2. Markings of the places, and the transitions that they enable, in the Petri net shown in Figure 1.10. The number of tokens in each place is indicated at each step (μ) immediately before a transition.

	Place markings								Transitions enabled
Step	A	D	M_1	M_2	M_3	M_4	M_5	M_6	
$\mu0$	1	0	0	0	0	0	0	0	1, 2
$\mu1$	1	1	0	0	0	0	0	0	1–3
$\mu2$	1	1	1	0	0	0	0	0	2–4
$\mu3$	0	1	1	1	0	0	0	0	3–5
$\mu4$	0	0	1	1	1	0	0	0	4–6
$\mu5$	0	0	0	1	1	1	0	0	7
$\mu6$	1	0	0	0	0	0	1	0	8, 9
$\mu7$	1	0	0	0	0	0	0	1	1, 2

In the example mentioned above (Figure 1.10), rhythmic activity is endogenous to the system; it does not depend upon any outside influence, though this, of course, could be built into the structure of the net. Rhythmic activity could be abolished and growth made continuous by removal of the inhibitory arc that disables t_1. Use might be made of the presence or absence of this arc to represent differences in the physiology of a growing module. For example, during growth, the metamers may be a source, either directly or indirectly, of an inhibitor of apical activity. Likewise, formation and maturation of the metamers, represented by places M_2–M_6, may relieve this inhibition. Obviously, more detailed representations of module development, and particularly module interrelationships, could be presented with net notation; however, the main intention is to show how an algorithm for development can be presented in a concise tabular and graphic form from which a sequence of development can be reconstructed. In the future, it might be possible to formalize some of the expressions of complex correlative phenomena that accompany the development of an architectural system as a whole. Lück et al. (1983), for example, have constructed algorithms that describe the growth and development of roots and shoots of *Tradescantia* cuttings experimentally manipulated in various ways. By extending this approach, it should be possible to formalize the behavior of a system as complex as the shoot of an apple tree. Results of various shoot-pruning procedures in apple trees (Crabbé 1984, 1985; Porter 1988) show the intricacy of the correlative system operating within even a single branch—a system whose very existence depends on the mutual interactions between the meristems and the modules they produce. Nevertheless, algorithmic formulation could make explicit the "rules" that govern shoot architecture and hence open them to biological interpretation.

CONCLUDING REMARKS

This survey of the structure of shoot and root systems has ranged from the level of the cell to that of the module, and from the concrete reality of those levels to their abstract representation by graphical algorithms.

Cells are clearly the basis for module morphogenesis because they are the units within which growth and differentiation occur. The regulation of growth and differentiation results from the collective properties of the cells. Just as the individual cell receives information relevant to its plane of division and course of differentiation from its immediate surroundings, so organized groups of cells (metamers) receive information pertaining to their further development from their location within the module. Similarly, information relevant to the development of modules from buds or primordia depends on their location in the system as a whole.

The metamer is an element of module organization that stands at a level between the module and the cell. It is the smallest externally recognizable unit of morphological organization, and it usually contains a meristematic site from which a new potential module can develop. Observation of the interior of the plant reveals another category of morphological organization—the cellular complex—whose most substantial unit of organization is the merophyte. Cellular organization as exemplified by the merophyte, however, and morphological organization as exemplified by the metamer, although describing overlapping portions of the module, actually categorize two types of repeating structural unit. Both are equally valid elements that contribute to a description of module construction, but they are products of different views of plant organization—the cellular and the morphological views. Roots, particularly those of lower plants that lack an obvious metameric construction, can be usefully analyzed in terms of their merophytic organization; however, roots of higher plants do not have clearly defined merophytic cell groups, though evidence of "hidden" merophytes may be present in the siting of lateral root primordia. For the shoots of higher plants, which also lack merophytes, the metamer is so far the only useful conceptual category of multicellular organization. On the other hand, in shoots of lower plants (e.g. mosses), merophyte and metamer are one and the same unit of construction.

Abstract devices for representing development can be helpful in discovering the "rules" that govern morphogenesis at all levels of organization. With their aid it should be possible to comprehend development in an objective and rigorous way and hence make inferences about the conditions necessary for its realization. Such rules, therefore, correspond to an epigenetic code for development.

Acknowledgments

I am very grateful to Mrs. J. S. Parker, who prepared the material shown in Figures 1.4, 1.6, and 1.7, and who shared with me her extensive knowledge of apple tree development. I am also indebted to Dr. F. A. L. Clowes, Drs. J. and H. B. Lück, Professor A. Nougarède, and Mr. J. White for many interesting and helpful discussions. Mrs. Christine P. P. Cooke gave unfailingly skillful assistance in typing this chapter.

LITERATURE CITED

Abbott, D. L. 1970. The role of budscales in the morphogenesis and dormancy of the apple fruit bud. In *Physiology of Tree Crops*. Ed. L. C. Luckwill, C. V. Cutting. London: Academic Press. 65–82.

Adam, J. S. 1981. Pre-pruning assessment. *Grower* 95(5):15–16.

Akam, M. 1987. The molecular basis for metameric pattern in *Drosophila* embryo. *Development* 101:1–22.

Arney, S. E. 1953a. The initiation, growth, and emergence of leaf primordia in *Fragaria*. *Ann. Bot.* 17:477–492.

———. 1953b. Studies in growth and development in the genus *Fragaria* I. Factors affecting the rate of leaf production in Royal Sovereign strawberry. *J. Hort. Sci.* 28:73–84.

Askenasy, E. 1880. Über eine neu Methode, um die Verteilung der Wachstumsintensität in wachsenden Teilen zu bestimmen. *Verh. Naturk.-med. Ver. Heidelberg* N.F. 2:70–153.

Ball, E. A. 1972. The surface "histogen" of living shoot apices. In *The Dynamics of Meristem Cell Populations.* Ed. M. W. Miller, C. C. Kuehnert. New York: Plenum Press. 75–100.

Barlow, P. W. 1986. Adventitious roots of whole plants: Their form, functions, and evolution. In *New Root Formation in Plants and Cuttings.* Ed. M. B. Jackson. Dordrecht: M. Nijhoff. 67–110.

———. 1987. Cellular packets, cell kinetics and morphogenesis in the primary root meristem of *Zea mays* L. *New Phytol.* 105:27–56.

Barlow, P. W. and J. S. Adam. 1988. The position and growth of lateral roots on cultured root axes of tomato, *Lycopersicon esculentum* (Solanaceae). *Plant Syst. Evol.* 158:141–154.

Bartels, F. 1961. Zur Entwicklung der Keimpflanze von *Epilobium hirsutum.* IV. Der Nachweis eins Scheitelzellenwachstums. *Flora* 150:552–571.

Bijhouwer, J. 1924. De periodiciteit van de knopontwikkeling bij den appel. *Meded. Landbouwhoogschool Wageningen* 27(7):1–64.

Bloch, R. 1948. The development of the secretory cells of *Ricinus* and the problem of cellular differentiation. *Growth* 12:271–284.

Borchert, R. 1973. Simulation of rhythmic tree growth under constant conditions. *Physiol. Plant.* 29:173–180.

Boyes, D. 1922. Notes on the characters of apple tree shoots. *J. Pomol. Hort. Sci.* 3:36–46.

Burrows, G. E. 1987. Leaf axil anatomy in the Araucariaceae. *Austral. J. Bot.* 35:631–640.

Catesson, A.-M. 1953. Structure, évolution et fonctionnement du point végétatif d'une monocotylédon: *Luzula pedemontana* Boiss. et Reut. (Joncacées). *Ann. Sci. Nat. Bot. Biol. Veg.* 11ème sér. 14:253–291.

Chaloner, W. G. 1986. The lepidodendrid tree. In *Colloque International sur l'Arbre. Naturalia monspeliensia, hors series.* 475–486.

Champagnat, P. 1954. Les correlations sur le rameau d'un an des végétaux ligneux. Φyton 4:1–102.

Champagnat, P., P. Barnola, and S. Lavarenne, 1986. Quelques modalitiés de la croissance rhythmique endogène des tiges chez les végétaux ligneux. In *Colloque International sur l'Abre. Naturalia monspeliensia, hors series.* 279–302.

Chan, B. G., and J. C. Cain, 1967. The effect of seed formation on subsequent flowering in apple. *Proc. Amer. Soc. Hort. Sci.* 91:63–68.

Charlton, W. A. 1983. Patterns and control of lateral root initiation. *Br. Plant Growth Regulator Group, Monogr.* 10:1–13.

Chattaway, M. M. 1958. Bud development and lignotuber formation in eucalypts. *Austral. J. Bot.* 6:103–115.

Chiang, S.-H., and E. M. Gifford, Jr. 1971. Development of the root of *Ceratopteris thalictroides* with special reference to apical segmentation. *J. Indian Bot. Soc.* 50A:96–106.

Chiang, Y.-L. 1970. Macro- and microscopic structure of the root of *Ceratopteris pteridoides* (Hook.) Hieron. *Taiwania* 15:31–49.

Clowes, F. A. L. 1961. *Apical Meristems.* Oxford: Blackwell.

Cottignies, A. and A. Jennane. 1988. Water content, water potential, and transition from the non-cycling to the cycling state in the pea cotyledonary bud. *J. Plant Physiol.* 132:1–4.

Crabbé, J. J. 1984. Vegetative vigor control over location and fate of flower buds in fruit trees. *Acta Hort.* 149:55–63.

———. 1985. Aspects of the apical control on branching on one-year-old caulinary axes of woody plants. *Acta Univ. Agric. (Brno) Fac. Agron.* 33:555–560.

———. 1986. Hierarchie et opportunisme dans le developpement de l'appareil caulinaire des arbres. In *Colloque International sur l'Abre. Naturalia monspeliensia, hors series.* 339–350.

Critchfield, W. B. 1960. Leaf dimorphism in *Populus trichocarpa. Amer. J. Bot.* 47:699–711.

———. 1970. Shoot growth and leaf dimorphism in Boston Ivy (*Parthenocissus tricuspidata*). *Amer. J. Bot.* 57:535–542.

Cutter, E. G. 1966. Patterns of organogenesis in shoots. in *Trends in Plant Morphogenesis.* Ed. E. G. Cutter. London: Longmans. 220–234.

Douin, C. 1923. Recherches sur le gamétophyte des Marchantiées. III.—Le thalle stérile des Marchantiées développement basilaire des feuilles et autres organes latéraux chez les Muscinées. *Rév. Gen. Bot.* 23:487–508.

Fisher, J. B. 1984. Tree architecture: relationships between structure and function. In *Contemporary Problems in Plant Anatomy.* Ed. R. A. White, W. C. Dickison. Orlando. FL: Academic Press. 541–589.

Foster, A. S. 1938. Structure and growth of the shoot apex of *Gingko biloba. Bull. Torrey Bot. Club* 65:531–556.

Fournier, A. 1979. *Is Architectural Radiation Adaptive?* Diplome d'Etudes Approfondies d'Ecologie Générale et Appliquée. Université des Sciences et Techniques du Languedoc, Montpellier. 38 p.

Fulford, R. M. 1965. The morphogenesis of apple buds. III. The inception of flowers. *Ann. Bot.* 30:207–219.

———. 1972. Leaves, fruit and flower initiation. *Proc. 18th Int. Hort. Congr. Tel Aviv* 4:143–150.

Garrison, R. 1973. The growth and development of internodes in *Helianthus annuus. Bot. Gaz.* 134:246–255.

Gerrath, J. M., and U. Posluszny. 1988. Morphological and anatomical development in the Vitaceae. I. Vegetative development in *Vitis riparia. Can. J. Bot.* 66:209–224.

Gifford, E. M., E. Kurth. 1983. Quantitative studies of the vegetative shoot apex of *Equisetum scirpoides. Amer. J. Bot.* 70:74–79.

Gill, A. M. 1969. The ecology of an elfin forest in Puerto Rico, 6. Aërial roots. *J. Arnold Arbor.* 50:197–209.

Golub, S. J., and R. H. Wetmore. 1948. Studies of development in the vegetative shoot of *Equisetum arvense* L. I. The shoot apex. *Amer. J. Bot.* 35:755–767.

Greathouse, D. C., W. M. Laetsch, and B. O. Phinney. 1971. The shoot-growth rhythm of a tropical tree, *Theobroma cacao. Amer. J. Bot.* 58:281–286.

Green, J. R. 1987. *The Hormonal Control of Biennial Bearing in Cider Apples.* Ph.D. Thesis, University of Bristol. 171. p.

Gregory, R. A. 1980. Annual cycle of shoot development in sugar maple. *Can. J. For. Sci.* 10:316–326.

Groff, P. A., and D. R. Kaplan. 1988. The relation of root systems to shoot systems in vascular plants. *Bot. Rev.* 54:387–422.

Gunckel, J. E., and K. V. Thimann. 1949. Studies of development in long shoots and short shoots of *Ginkgo biloba* L. III. Auxin production in shoot growth. *Amer. J. Bot.* 36:145–151.

Gunckel, J. E., K. V. Thimann, and R. H. Wetmore. 1949. Studies of development in long shoots and short shoots of *Gingko biloba* L. IV. Growth habit, shoot expression and the mechanism of its control. *Amer. J. Bot.* 36:309–316.

Gunning, B. E. S., J. E. Hughes, and A. R. Hardham. 1978. Formative and proliferative cell divisions, cell differentiation, and developmental change in the meristem of *Azolla* roots. *Planta* 143:121–144.

Hake, S., and M. Freeling. 1986. Analysis of genetic mosaics shows that the extra epidermal cell divisions in *Knotted* mutant maize plants are induced by adjacent mesophyll cells. *Nature* 320:621–623.

Hallé, F., and R. Martin. 1968. Etude de la croissance rythmique chez l'Hevea (*Hévéa brasiliensis* Mull. Arg. Euphorbiacées-Crotonoidées). *Adansonia* (N.S.) 8:475–503.

Hallé, F., R. A. A. Oldeman, and P. B. Tomlinson. 1978. *Tropical Trees and Forests. An Architectural Analysis.* Berlin: Springer-Verlag.

Hallet, J.-N. 1977. Le cycle cellulaire de l'apicale muscinale: données nouvelles et caractères originaux. *Bryophyt. Biblio.* 13:1–20.

Hanke, V. 1981. Morphogenetische Untersuchungenen am vegetativen Apikalmeristem bei Apfelknospen. *Arch. Gartenbau* 29:315–329.

Hardwick, R. C. 1986. Physiological consequences of modular growth in plants. *Philos. Trans. R. Soc. London Ser. B* 313:161–173.

Harrison, L. G., and K. Y. Tan. 1988. Where may reaction-diffusion mechanisms be operating in metameric patterning of *Drosophila* embryos? *BioEssays* 8:119–128.

Hauke, R. L. 1985. The transition from vegetative to reproductive growth of shoot apices of holoheterophyadic species of *Equisetum*: phenology, morphology and anatomy. *Can. J. Bot.* 63:2430–2438.

Hayes, P. A., T. A. Steeves, and B. R. Neal. 1989. An architectural analysis of *Shepherdia canadensis* and *Shepherdia argentea*: patterns of shoot development. *Can. J. Bot.* 67:1870–1877.

Hayes, P. A., T. A. Steeves, and B. R. Neal. 1990. An architectural analysis of *Shepherdia canadensis* and *Shepherdia argentea* (Eleagnaceae): the architectural models. *Can. J. Bot.* 68:719–725.

Hébant-Mauri, R. 1973. Fonctionnement apical et ramification chez quelques fougères du genre *Trichomanes* L. (Hyménophyllacées). *Adansonia,* 2ème sér. 13:495–526.

———. 1975. Apical segmentation and leaf initiation in the tree fern *Dicksonia squarrosa*. *Can. J. Bot.* 53:764–772.

———. 1977. Segmentation apicle et initiation foliare chez *Ceratopteris thalictroides* (Fougère leptosporangiée). *Can. J. Bot.* 55:1820–1828.

Hibbs, D. E. 1981. Leader growth and the architecture of three North American hemlocks. *Can. J. Bot.* 59:476–480.

Hilkenbäumer, F., and G. Buchloh. 1954. Zur Histogenese der Übergangsknospen beim Apfel. *Gartenbauwissenschaft* 1(19):7–21.

Irish, E. E., and T. M. Nelson. 1988. Development of maize plants from cultured shoot apices. *Planta* 175:9–12.

Jankiewicz, L. S. 1956. The effect of auxins on crotch angles in apple trees. *Bull. Acad. Polon. Sci.* Cl.II 4:173–178.

———. 1972. A cybernetic model of growth correlation in young apple trees. *Biol. Plant.* (Prague) 14:52–61.

Jegla, D., and I. M. Sussex. 1989. Cell lineage patterns in the shoot meristem of the sunflower embryo in the dry seed. *Develop. Biol.* 131:215–225.

Jeník, J. 1978. Roots and root systems in tropical trees: morphologic and ecologic aspects. In *Tropical Trees as Living Systems*. Ed. P. B. Tomlinson, M. H. Zimmermann. Cambridge: Cambridge University Press. 323–349.

Jones, M., and J. L. Harper. 1987. The influence of neighbours on the growth of trees. II. The fate of buds on long and short shoots in *Betula pendula*. *Proc. R. Soc. London Ser. B* 232:19–33.

Kadej, F. 1963. Interpretation of the pattern of the cell arrangement in the root apical meristem of *Cyperus gracilis* L. var. *alternifolius*. *Acta Soc. Bot. Pol.* 32:296–301.

Kahn, F. 1977. Analyse structurale des systèmes racinaires des plantes ligneuses de la forét tropicale dense humide. *Candollea* 32:321–358.

Kolesnikov, V. A. 1930. The root system of fruit tree seedlings. *J. Pomol. Hort. Sci.* 8:197–203.

Kubíková, J. 1967. Contribution to the classification of root systems of woody plants. *Preslia* 39:236–243.

Kummerow, J. 1981. Structure of roots and root systems. In *Ecosystems of the World*. Ed. F. DiCastri, D. W. Goodall, R. L. Specht. Amsterdam: Elsevier Science. 11:269–288.

Kuras, M. 1980. Activation of embryo during rape (*Brassica napus* L.) seed germination. II. Transversal organization of radicle apical meristem. *Acta Soc. Bot. Pol.* 49:387–395.

Lance, A. 1957. Recherches cytologiques sur l'évolution de quelques méristèmes apicaux et sur ses variations provoquées par des traitements photopériodiques. *Ann. Sci. Nat. Bot.,* 11ème sér. 18:91–421.

Landsberg, J. J., and M. R. Thorpe. 1975. The mechanism of apple bud morphogenesis: analysis and a model. *Ann. Bot.* 39:689–699.

Lawrence, P. 1987. Pair-rule genes: Do they paint stripes or draw lines? *Cell* 51:879–890.

L'Hardy-Halos, M. T. 1970. Recherches sur les Céramiacées (Rhodophycées-Céramiales) et leur morphogénèse. I. Structure de l'appareil végétatif et des organes reproducteurs. *Rev. Gen. Bot.* 77:221–287.

Lindenmayer, A. 1978. Algorithms for plant development. *Acta Biotheoret.* 27(suppl.):37–81.

Liu, B.-L. L. 1984. *Studies of Lateral Root Initiation in* Marsilea quadrifolia L. Ph.D. Thesis. Ohio State University.

Looney, N. E., J. S. Taylor, and R. P. Pharis. 1988. Relationship of endogenous gibberellin and cytokinin levels in shoot tips to apical form in four strains of 'McIntosh' apple. *J. Amer. Soc. Hort. Sci.* 113:395–398.

Lück, H. B., and J. Lück. 1986. Unconventional leaves (an application of map 0L-systems to biology). In *The Book of L*. Ed. G. Rozenberg, A. Salomaa. Berlin: Springer-Verlag. 275–289.

Lück, J., and H. B. Lück. 1985. Comparative plant morphogenesis founded on map and stereomap generating systems. In *Dynamical Systems and Cellular Automata*. Ed. J. Demongeot, E. Golès, M. Tchuente. London: Academic Press. 111–121.

Lück, J., H. B. Lück, and M. Bakkali. 1990. A comprehensive model for acrotonic, mesotonic, and basitonic branchings in plants. *Acta Biotheoret.* 38:257–288.

Lück, J., F. Raoul, and H. B. Lück, 1983. Le determinisme de la ramification chez *Tradescantia fluminensis* a la lumière des reseaux de Petri. *Actes 3ème Seminaire de l'Ecole de Biologie Théorique du CNRS*. Bordeaux: Presse Universitaire. 27–39.

Luckwill, L. C. 1970. The control of growth and fruitfulness of apple trees. In *Physiology of Tree Crops*. Ed. L. C. Luckwill, C. V. Cutting. London: Academic Press. 237–253.

———. 1974. A new look at the process of fruit bud formation in apple. *Proc. 19th Int. Hort. Congr. Warsaw*. 3:237–245.

Luckwill, L.C. and J. M. Silva. 1979. The effects of daminozide and gibberellic acid on flower initiation, growth and fruiting of apple cv. Golden Delicious. *J. Hort. Sci.* 54:217–223.

Lyford, W. H., and B. F. Wilson. 1964. Development of the root system of *Acer rubrum* L. *Harvard Forest Paper* 10:1–17.

Lyndon, R. F. 1976. The shoot apex. In *Cell Division in Higher Plants*. Ed. M. M. Yeoman. London: Academic Press. 285–314.

———. 1987. Initiation and growth of internodes and stem and flower frusta in *Silene coeli-rosa*. In *The Manipulation of Flowering*. Ed. J. G. Atherton. London: Butterworths. 301–314.

McDaniel, C. N. 1980. Influence of leaves and roots on meristem development in *Nicotiana tabacum* L. cv. Wisconsin 38. *Planta* 148:462–467.

McDaniel, C. N, and R. S. Poethig. 1988. Cell-lineage patterns in the shoot apical meristem of the germinating maize embryo. *Planta* 175:13–22.

MacDonald, A. D., and D. H. Mothersill. 1983. Shoot development in *Betula papyrifera*. I. Short-shoot morphogenesis. *Can. J. Bot.* 61:3049–3065.

MacDonald, A. D., D. H. Mothersill, and J. C. Caesar. 1984. Shoot development in *Betula papyrifera*. III. Long shoot organogenesis. *Can J. Bot.* 62:437–445.

MacLeod, R. D. 1990. Lateral root primordium inception in *Zea mays* L. *Environ. Exp. Bot.* 30:225–234.

MacLeod, R. D., and S. M. McLachlan. 1975. The development of large primordia in *Vicia faba* L.: some cytological and anatomical changes. *Protoplasma* 85:291–304.

Maillette, L. 1982. Structural dynamics of silver birch. I. The fate of buds. *J. Appl. Ecol.* 19:203–218.

Majumdar, G. P. 1942. The organization of the shoot in *Heracleum* in the light of development. *Ann. Bot.* 6:49–81.

May, L. H., F. H. Chapman, and D. Aspinall. 1985. Quantitative studies on root development. I. Influence of nutrient concentration. *Austral. J. Biol. Sci.* 18:25–35.

Michaux-Ferrière, N., and J. N. Hallet. 1985. La cellule apicale: son rôle dans la controle de l'activité méristematique caulinaire. *Bull. Soc. Bot. Franc. Actual. Bot.* 132:49–61.

Millington, W. F. 1966. The tendril of *Parthenocissus inserta*: determination and development. *Amer. J. Bot.* 53:74–81.

Mullins, M. G., and W. S. Rogers. 1971. Growth in horizontal apple shoots: effects of stem orientation and bud position. *J. Hort. Sci.* 46:313–321.

Mullins, M. G., Y. Nair, and P. Sampet. 1979. Rejuvenation *in vitro*: induction of juvenile characters in an adult clone of *Vitis vinifera* L. *Ann. Bot.* 44:623–627.

Münch, E. 1938. Untersuchungen über die Harmonie der Baumgestalt. *Jahrb. Wiss. Bot.* 86:581–673.

Niklas, K. J. 1986. Computer-simulated plant evolution. *Sci. Amer.* 254 (3): 67–75.

Nougarède, A. 1967. Experimental cytology of the shoot apical cells during vegetative growth and flowering. *Internat. Rev. Cytol.* 21:203–351.

Nougarède, A., J. Rembur, and R. Saint-Côme. 1987. Rates of cell division in the young prefloral shoot apex of *Chrysanthemum segetum* L. *Protoplasma* 138:156–160.

Novoplansky, A., D. Cohen, and T. Sachs. 1989. Ecological implications of correlative inhibition between plant shoots. *Physiol. Plant.* 77:136–140.

Nozeran, R. 1984. Integration of organismal development. In *Positional Controls in Plant Development*. Ed. P. W. Barlow, D. J. Carr. Cambridge: Cambridge University Press. 375–401.

Nozeran, R., L. Bancilhon, and P. Neville. 1971. Intervention of internal correlations in the morphogenesis of higher plants. *Adv. Morphogen.* 9:1–66.

Owens, J. N., and M. Molder. 1979. Bud development in *Larix occidentalis*. I. Growth and development of vegetative long shoots and vegetative short shoot buds. *Can. J. Bot.* 57:687–700.

Peterson, J. L. 1977. Petri nets. *Comput. Surveys* 9:223–252.

Peterson, R. L. 1975. The initiation and development of root buds. In *The Development and Function of Roots*. Ed. J. G. Torrey, D. T. Clarkson. London: Academic Press. 125–161.

Peterson, R. L., and C. A. Peterson, 1986. Ontogeny and anatomy of lateral roots. In. *New Root Formation in Plants and Cuttings*. Ed. M. B. Jackson. Dordrecht: Nijhoff. 1–30.

Petri, C. A. 1980. Introduction to general net theory. *Lect. Notes Comp. Sci.* 84:1–19.

Poethig, R. S. 1988. Heterochronic mutations affecting shoot development in maize. *Genetics* 119:959–973.

Porter, J. R. 1984. A model of canopy development in winter wheat. *J. Agric. Sci.* 102:383–392.

_____. 1988. Pruning, canopy architecture and plant productivity. In *Manipulation of Fruiting*. Ed. C. J. Wright. London: Butterworths, 293–304.

_____. 1989. Modules, models and meristems in plant architecture. In *Plant Canopies: Their Growth, Form and Function*. Ed. G. Russell, B. Marshall, P. G. Jarvis. *SEB Seminar Ser.* 31:143–159. Cambridge: Cambridge University Press.

Pratt, C. 1967. Axillary buds in normal and irradiated apple and pear. *Rad. Bot.* 7:113–122.

_____. 1990. Apple trees: morphology and anatomy. *Hort. Rev.* 12:265–305.

Priestley, J. H., L. I. Scott, and E. C. Gillett. 1935. The development of the shoot in *Alstroemeria* and the unit of shoot growth in monocotyledons.*Ann. Bot.* 49:161–179.

Prusinkiewicz, P. 1987. Applications of L-systems to computer imagery. *Lect. Notes Comp. Sci.* 291:534–548.

Puławska, Z. 1982. Tissues development in stems of *Aristolochia clematitis* L. in the point of view of multicellular complexes formation. *Acta Soc. Bot. Pol.* 51:107–125.

_____. 1986. The sequence of cell divisions in the I tunic layer of *Actinidia arguta* Planch. in light of the development of twin cell complexes. *Acta Soc. Bot. Pol.* 55:171–179.

Ray, T. S. 1988. Survey of shoot organisation in the Araceae. *Amer. J. Bot.* 75:56–84.

Reess, M. 1867. Entwicklungsgeschichte der Stammspitze von *Equisetum. Jahrb. Wiss. Bot.* 6:209–236.

Reffye, P. de, C. Edlin, M. Jaeger, and C. Cabart. 1986. Simulation de l'architecture des arbres. In *Colloque International sur l'Abre. Naturalia monspeliensia, hors series*. 223–240.

Rembur, J., and A. Nougarède, 1977. Duration of cell cycles in the shoot apex of *Chrysan-*

themum segetum L. *Z. Pflanzenphysiol.* 81:173–179.

Remphrey, W. R. 1989a. Shoot ontogeny in *Fraxinus pennsylvanica* (green ash). I. Seasonal cycle of terminal meristem activity. *Can. J. Bot.* 67:1624–1632.

———. 1989b. Shoot ontogeny in *Fraxinus pennsylvanica* (green ash). II. Development of the inflorescence. *Can. J. Bot.* 67:1966–1978.

Remphrey, W. R., C. G. Davidson, and M. J. Blouw. 1987. A classification and analysis of crown form in green ash (*Fraxinus pennsylvanica*). *Can. J. Bot.* 65:2188–2195.

Remphrey, W. R., and G. R. Powell. 1984. Crown architecture of *Larix laricina* saplings: shoot preformation and neoformation and their relationships to shoot vigour. *Can. J. Bot.* 62:2181–2192.

Remphrey, W. R., and T. A. Steeves. 1984. Shoot ontogeny in *Arctostaphylos uva-ursi* (bearberry): the annual cycle of apical activity. *Can. J. Bot.* 62:1925–1932.

Rogers, S. O., and H. T. Bonnett. 1989. Evidence for apical initial cells in the vegetative shoot apex of *Hedera helix* cv. Goldheart. *Amer. J. Bot.* 76:539–545.

Romberger, J. A. 1963. Meristems, growth, and development in woody plants. An analytical review of anatomical, physiological, and morphogenic aspects. U. S. Dept. Agric., *Techn. Bull.* No. 1293. 214. p.

Rutishauser, R., and R. Sattler. 1985. Complementarity and heuristic value of contrasting models in structural botany I. General considerations. *Bot. Jahrb. Syst.* 107:415–455.

———. 1987. Complementarity and heuristic value of contrasting models in structural botany. II. Case study on leaf whorls: *Equisetum* and *Ceratophyllum*. *Bot. Jahrb. Syst.* 109:227–255.

Saint-Côme, R. 1985. *Cycles cellulaires dans le méristème caulinaire de* Coleus blumei Benth. *de la germination à la floriason. Aspects morphogénétiques et cytophysiologiques.* Ph.D. Thesis, Univ. Pierre et Marie Curie, Paris. 300 p.

Sanders, W. B. 1989. Growth and development of the reticulate thallus in the lichen *Ramalina menziesii*. *Amer. J. Bot.* 76:666–678.

Schmidt, A. 1924. Histologische Studien an phanerogamen Vegetatsionpunkten. *Bot. Arch.* 8:345–404.

Schmidt, S. 1973. Modelvorstellungen zum Entwicklungsrhythmus von Apfelbaumen. *Arch. Gartenbau* 21:587–601.

Schmidt, S., and J. Egerer. 1982. Wachstum und RNS-Haushalt von Apfelknospen in Beziehung zur generativen Entwicklung. *Arch. Gartenbau* 30:249–261.

Schneider, E. F. 1968. The rest period of *Rhododendron* flower buds. I. Effect of the bud scales on the onset and duration of rest. *J. Exp. Bot.* 19:817–824.

Schwabe, W. W. 1971. Chemical modification of phyllotaxis and its implications. *Symp. Soc. Exp. Biol.* 25:301–311.

Sen, D. N. 1980. Root system and root ecology. In *Environment and Root Behaviour*. Ed. D. N. Sen. Jodhpur, India: Geobios International. 1–24.

Stewart, R. N., and H. Dermen. 1970. Determination of number and mitotic activity of shoot apical initial cells by analysis of mericlinal chimeras. *Amer. J. Bot.* 57:816–826.

Titman, P. W., and R. H. Wetmore. 1955. The growth of long and short shoots in *Cercidiphyllum*. *Amer. J. Bot.* 42:364–372.

Tomlinson, P. B. 1969. On the morphology and anatomy of turtle grass, *Thalassia testudinum* (Hydrocharitaceae). II. Anatomy and development of the root in relation to function. *Bull. Marine Sci.* 19:57–71.

Torrey, J. G. 1958. Endogenous bud and root formation by isolated roots of *Convolvulus* grown *in vitro*. *Plant Physiol.* 33:258–263.

Trinci, A. P. J. 1984. Regulation of hyphal branching and hyphal orientation. In *The Ecology and Physiology of the Fungal Mycelium*. Ed. D. H. Jennings, A. D. M. Rayner. Cambridge: Cambridge University Press. 23–52.

Vidal, L. 1912. La croissance terminale de la tige et la formation des bourgeons chez l'*Equisetum palustre*. *Ann. Sci. Nat. Bot.*, 9ème sér. 15:1–38.

Wardlaw, C. W. 1955. Evidence relating to the diffusion-reaction theory of morphogenesis. *New Phytol.* 54:39–48.

Wareing, P. F., and T. A. A. Nasr. 1961. Gravimorphism in trees. 1. Effects of gravity on growth and apical dominance in fruit trees. *Ann. Bot.* 25:321–340.

Watson, M. A. 1986. Integrated physiological units in plants. *Trends Ecol. Evol.* 1:119–123.

Weber, H. 1936. Vergleichend-morphologische Studien über die Sproßbürtige Bewurzelung. *Nova Acta Leopold. N. F.* 4:229–298.

White, J. 1979. The plant as a metapopulation. *Annu. Rev. Ecol. Syst.* 10:109–145.

———. 1984. Plant metamerism. In *Perspectives on Plant Population Ecology.* Ed. R. Dirzo, J. Sarukhán. Sunderland, MA: Sinauer. 15–47.

Yamazaki, K., and N. Kaeriyama. 1983. The diameter of primary roots and the lateral root formation in corn plants. *Jpn. J. Crop Sci.* 52:59–64. (In Japanese)

Zagorska-Marek, B. 1985. Phyllotactic patterns and transitions in *Abies balsamea. Can. J. Bot.* 63:1844–1854.

———. 1987. Phyllotaxis triangular unit: phyllotactic transitions as the consequences of the apical wedge disclinations in a crystal-like pattern of the units. *Acta Soc. Bot. Pol.* 56:229–255.

Zeller, O. 1960. Entwicklungsgeschichte der Blütenknospen und Fruchtanlagen an einjahrigen langtrieben von Apfelbuschen I. Entwicklungsverlauf und Entwicklungs-morphologie der Blüten am einjahrigen Langtrieb. *Z. Pflanzenzücht.* 44:175–214.

Zobel, A. 1985a. Ontogenesis of tannin coenocytes in *Sambucus racemosa* L. II. Mother tannin cells. *Ann. Bot.* 56:91–104.

———. 1985b. The internode of *Sambucus racemosa* L. originates from a single cell layer. *Ann. Bot.* 56:105–107.

———. 1989a. Origin of nodes and internodes in plant shoots. I. Transverse zonation of apical parts of the shoot. *Ann. Bot.* 63:199–208.

———. 1989b. Origin of nodes and internodes in plant shoots. II. Models of node and inter-node origin from one layer of cells. *Ann. Bot.* 63:209–220.

Chapter 2

Root Tip Organization and the Spatial Relationships of Differentiation Events

THOMAS L. ROST

The classical view of the root tip is that it consists of three defined regions: the meristematic zone, the elongation zone, and the maturation zone. The exact origin of this model is lost in the early literature of root structure, but early workers probably never intended to imply that the boundaries for each zone are the same for every cell file. Instead, it is quite clear that each file and/or tissue is independently regulated.

Analysis of root tip organization requires visualizing some kind of multilevel mechanism whereby differentiation events can be regulated within cell files and between development zones. Ivanov (1973) analyzed root development in terms of transition points. According to his view, the important factor that differentiates between root cell-files is the position of the transition points between cell division and elongation, and between the cessation of cell growth at the end of the elongation zone and the start of final maturation. Changing the position of one transition point will necessarily affect the position of another.

Several questions relating to the regulation of key differentiation events in root development remain unanswered. For example, what regulates the differences between adjacent cell-files? Cells of two very different files may share a common cell wall and be connected to each other by plasmodesmata. According to positional control theory (Warren Wilson and Warren Wilson 1984), local morphogens induce specific differentiation events. If this is so, the mechanism must be extremely precise in order to separate target cells with common walls.

Another question concerns the mechanism regulating the spatial modulation of the transition points. For example, transition points can move within a cell-file relative to the growth rate of the root. In fast-growing roots, differentiation events occur farther from the tip than in slow-growing roots. This kind of positional modulation occurs rapidly; if it involves the DNA/RNA/protein apparatus, it will require a very fast response time. A consideration of the structure of the root tip and the nature of the relationships and characteristics of the transition points for differentiation events will be a primary goal of this review.

From *Growth Patterns in Vascular Plants* Edited by Muhammed Iqbal

THE ORGANIZATION AND BOUNDARIES
OF THE ROOT MERISTEM

Meristem Organization

An important difference among root tips of various species is the organization of cells in the apex. Popham (1966), citing older works, especially Janczewski (1874), categorized the roots of vascular plants into six types and two subtypes. All of these incorporate one of two common developmental schemes. In the first, all cell-file lineages can be directly followed to a specific tier of initial cells. These initials, or histogens (Hanstein 1868), may contribute to different tissues; for example, in the most common monocot type there are three initial layers for stele, cortex/epidermis, and root cap (Zea mays, Figure 2.1.A), whereas the most common type in dicots also has three layers, but in this case, for stele, cortex, and epidermis/root cap. This kind of organization is called *closed*.

In the second type, cell lineages do not connect to distinct initial layers, but instead can be followed to a zone of cells lacking any special organization. Both monocots (*Allium;* Figure 2.1.B) and dicots (*Pisum;* Figure 2.1.C) are examples. This type of organization is referred to as *open,* since specific cell lineages do not connect to specific initials. Popham (1955) studied the pea root tip (*Pisum sativum*) and suggested that the initial zone between the root body and cap should be called a *transverse meristem* (marked with dashed lines between stars in Figure 2.1.C), because he had concluded that cells within this region acted as initials to supply cells to both the cap and body. Apices with open organization, however, are not all alike. *Pisum* and other legumes have a broad transverse meristem, and the identity of mature tissues is not clearly apparent for some distance basipetal to the tip. In other plants with open organization, for example *Allium* (Figure 2.1.B), a transverse meristem is apparently lacking, and the identity of tissues can be determined much closer to the tip.

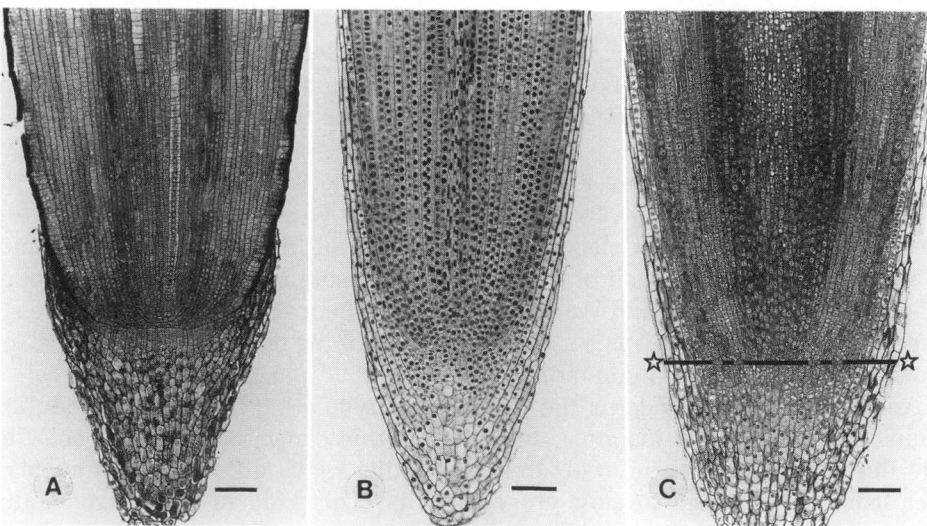

Figure 2.1. Median longitudinal sections of root tips; line scales = 100 μm. (A) Corn (Zea mays) with a closed apical organization. (B) Onion (*Allium cepa*) with an intermediate type of open apical organization. (C) Pea (*Pisum sativum*) with an open apical organization and a transverse meristem (*----*).

Clowes (1981) and Deysson (1980) considered the differences between open and closed apices in slightly different terms. A *closed apex* is one with a distinct initial layer for the root cap (Figure 2.1.A), and an *open apex* shows apparent interchange of cells between cortex and cap (Figure 2.1.C). Deysson (1980) contended that the epidermis in most plants is either derived from the innermost layer of the root cap or the outermost layer of the cortex. This notion seems valid for roots with closed apices, and it accurately describes the most common condition in monocots like corn, in which one initial layer forms the cortex and epidermis, and in dicots like *Coleus*, in which one initial layer forms the root cap and epidermis. Applying such interpretations to roots with open organization becomes a problem, however, because the differentiation of epidermis does not occur until perhaps 2 mm, and the root cap or cortical association of the tissue is impossible to determine (Rost et al. 1988).

Clowes (1958) discovered quiescent cells positioned at the boundary of root body and cap. This quiescent center is composed of cells that progress through the cell cycle very slowly. The peripheral cells comprise the distal and proximal meristems (Torrey and Feldman 1977) that cycle more rapidly.

Clowes (1981) compared the quiescent centers of *Zea* and *Helianthus*, which have closed and open organization, respectively. [Janczewski (1874, as described in Popham 1966) classified *Helianthus* as having closed organization.] Guttenberg (1960) studied stages of *Helianthus* root development and reported that the organization was closed during early growth and open during late growth. *Helianthus* and other members of the Asteraceae are marginal examples of open organization in that they are convertible from one type to the other (Armstrong and Heimsch 1976). Members of the Convolvulaceae also fall into the convertible category (Seago and Heimsch 1969).

In *Zea*, the quiescent center is a hemispherical cell mass with a flattened acroscopic surface composed of approximately 330 cells (Clowes 1981). It includes all of the histogen layers, including those for the epidermis and cortex (tier 1), but not those of the root cap. The quiescent center in *Helianthus* is very small (approximately 80 cells) with a convex acroscopic surface. Clowes reported that the quiescent center is variable in size, and that in some roots it includes tiers 1 and 2 distal to it (Figure 2.2, only tier 1 shown) and in other instances does not. Armstrong and Heimsch (1976) examined the apical organization in members of the Asteraceae. They reported that apices could change from open to closed during stages of root elongation, and presented two possible explanations for this change: (a) the cells distal to the quiescent center could become quiescent, or (b) the cortex could intrude between the stele pole (quiescent center) and the root cap initials. Clowes (1981) has shown in *Helianthus* that the former mechanism probably accounts for such occurrences. If tiers 1 and 2 were to become inactive by inclusion into the quiescent center, they would no longer form initials and cell lineages would no longer connect to them. If tiers 1 and 2 became quiescent, a closed organization would result; if not, an open organization would occur.

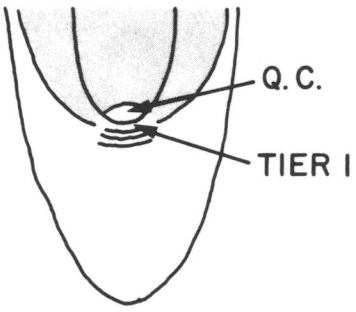

Figure 2.2. Redrawing of a sunflower (*Helianthus annuus*) root apex (from Clowes 1981) showing the quiescent center (Q.C.) and the tier of cells (tier 1) immediately acropetal to the Q.C. If tier 1 cells are quiescent, apices such as this will be closed; if they are active and form initials, the apex will be open.

This type of switching mechanism could perhaps also occur in an open organization root such as *Allium* (Figure 2.1.B), in which a more or less apparent difference can be seen between the root body and the root cap but histogen layers are lacking. It seems unlikely that such a mechanism could occur in an open apex, such as *Pisum* (Figure 2.1.C), in which the transverse meristem is very broad, histogen layers are lacking, the epidermis is not delineated for some distance, and the body/cap boundary is clearly lacking.

Meristem Boundaries

Jensen and Kavaljian (1958) plotted the distribution of cell division activity in *Allium cepa* root tips. They reported that cell division is most active in the cortical region between 600–1500 μm from the root tip, in the protoderm primarily between 1500–1800 μm, and in the stele between 500–1200 μm. Their work demonstrated that cell division activity is tissue-specific and that the boundaries of the meristem are not the same for all tissues.

Luxová and Murín (1973) and Luxová (1975) did similar studies with *Vicia faba, Hordeum vulgare,* and *Zea mays* root tips. In corn, cell division activity remained active longest in the epidermis, whereas in *Vicia* it remained active longest in the pericycle and inner cortex cells opposite the xylem.

In pea roots (Rost et al. 1988), cell division activity follows a pattern of cylindrical and vascular sector distribution (Figure 2.3). Moving basipetally from the root cap/body junction, back to approximately 250 μm, cell division occurs randomly (Figures 2.3.A, 2.4.A). At approximately 350 μm, cells in the pith and middle cortex have mostly stopped dividing and have begun to mature, and two cylinders, consisting of the inner root cap/epidermis/outer cortex (outer cortex cylinder) and the inner cortex/pericycle/vascular tissue (inner cortex cylinder), continue to divide (Figure 2.3.B). At about 600 μm, the protophloem matures, and the cells within the phloem sector of the inner cortex cylinder stop dividing. Basipetally from this level, the only cells still dividing in the inner cortex cylinder are those in the xylem sector, consisting

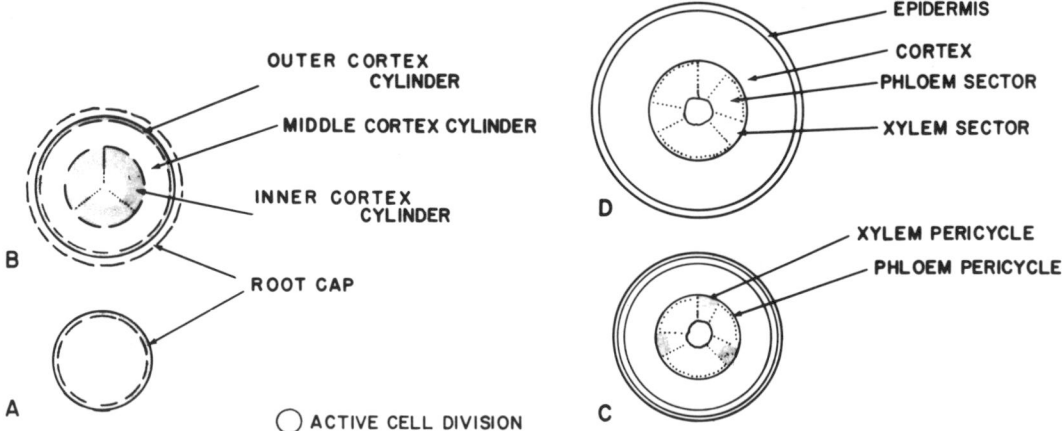

Figure 2.3. Diagrams of transverse sections of a pea root showing the distribution of cell division activity (*shading*). The approximate levels of each section are: A. 100 μm, B. 400 μm, C. 1.5 mm, D. 4.0 mm.

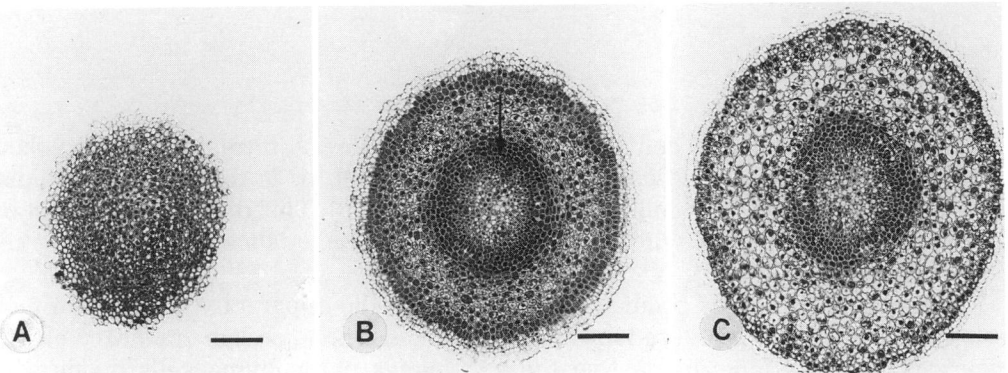

Figure 2.4. Transverse sections of pea root. (A) 40 μm. (B) 600 μm. (C) 1.5 mm. Line scales = 100 μm.

mostly of the three-layered xylem pericycle (Figure 2.4.B). Some cells are still dividing in the outer cortex cylinder at about 1800 μm, and the epidermis completes its maturation by about 2 mm (Figures 2.3.C, 2.4.C).

The protoxylem tracheary elements (PTE) form unlignified secondary cell walls and are almost mature at about 5 mm. The exact location is dependent on the total length and growth rate of the root (Rost and Baum 1988). As PTE maturation occurs, the cells in the multilayered pericycle opposite the protoxylem stop dividing and mature soon after. At the molecular level, Tanimoto et al. (1993) have shown that histone H2A mRNA is expressed in these same cycling cells in pea roots. Some pericycle and nearby cells continue infrequent cell division, but in effect they remain inactive until stimulated to divide again as lateral root primordia.

The pericycle in pea roots consists of one cell layer opposite the phloem, and three to four layers opposite the xylem (Popham 1955; Toriyama 1978; Allan & Trewavas 1986; Rost et al. 1988). Cell division in the pericycle opposite the phloem is switched off after the protophloem matures. The phloem pericycle does not contribute to the formation of either lateral roots or vascular cambium (Hinchee 1981).

Luxová and Murín (1973) observed cell division activity opposite the xylem poles in *Vicia faba* roots similar to that now also reported in pea. They interpreted the xylem cell group to be composed of inner cortex, including the endodermis, the pericycle, and a few layers of cells internal to and adjacent to the pericycle. Van't Hof et al. (1986) observed another group of cells with a similar distribution. They reported on vascular parenchyma precursor cells that replicate their DNA in a unique pattern after sucrose starvation of roots *in vitro*. These cells end up with elongated nuclei and are distributed similarly to the division activity reported by Rost et al. (1988). That is, they are at first uniformly distributed, then in the form of a "peri-stelar" ring, and finally outside the three protoxylem points. Van't Hof et al. (1986) call them *vascular parenchyma cells*.

Toriyama (1978) fixed pea roots with Lillie's neutral formalin and stained them with methyl blue. He noted that the cells opposite the phloem stained lighter than those opposite the xylem. The phloem pericycle cells were designated β-cells and were noted to contain dense granules of some kind. The xylem pericycle cells were called α-cells by Toriyama (1978) and stained very densely with methyl blue. Rost et al. (1988), Toriyama (1978), and Van't Hof et al. (1986) probably all described the same pea root cells.

TYPES OF CELL CYCLES AND THEIR ROLES IN DIFFERENTIATION

Roles of Cell Division

There are two types of cell divisions within cell-files. A formative division occurs on the periphery of the quiescent center (Barlow 1982), or is the initial longitudinal division that starts any new cell-file (Gunning et al. 1978). This division is the first in a file and its derivative cells will usually retain the characteristics of the existing cells within the same file.

Proliferative divisions occur within a file. Each file apparently maintains a more-or-less set number of proliferative divisions. For example, xylem tracheary element precursors in *Vicia faba* divide five times, whereas parenchyma cells divide seven times (Luxová and Murín 1973). The number of divisions that occur is inversely related to final cell length. Cells that are long at maturity will cease dividing close to the body/cap junction, and cells that are short at maturity will cease dividing farther back.

If cell division is inhibited in a root tip, cell maturation will occur closer to the tip (Rost and Baum 1988). Such cells usually continue to differentiate as they would normally, but they tend to be much shorter (Heimsch 1951). Proliferative cell divisions have at least two functions. They provide a continuous supply of new cells to ensure the growth of the root, and they also coordinate cell length through the regulation of the number of divisions in each file.

IS CELL DIVISION A PREREQUISITE FOR MATURATION?

An ongoing discussion in the literature concerns whether cell division is a prerequisite for a specific maturation event (Aloni 1987). In my view, maturation of specific cell types does not specifically require cell division in a programming sense. Dodds (1981) has supported this view. The cell cycle consists of four stages: G_1–S–G_2–M. Within the cycle there are two control points, at G_1 and G_2 (Van't Hof 1969). Once a cell passes a certain critical point, say in G_1, it will naturally progress to S and on to G_2. Once it progresses past a certain critical point in G_2, it will progress into M, and so on under ideal circumstances. If a critical cell cycle factor is missing at that point, the cell in question will go on to differentiate further without dividing or progressing through S again. This means that differentiation depends on the absence, at a critical time, of a certain cell cycle factor that will allow the cell to recycle. If that factor is missing, the cell in question will switch to a maturation path prescribed for the cells in the file it occupies (see also Chapter 9).

In recent years the nature of the G_1/G_2 control point has perhaps been identified. Paul Nurse and others (e.g. Moreno et al 1989) have characterized a 34,000 MW protein kinase (p34) coded for in yeast by a gene named *cdc2*. The homolog for this protein has now been identified in a number of plants, including *Pisum, Arabidopsis,* and *Daucus* (John et al. 1989; Gorst et al. 1991). John et al. (1990) examined the levels of this protein in wheat leaves and observed that it is highest in the meristem and decreased in mature cells. Peter John (personal communication) has observed this same distribution of $p34_{cdc2}$ in pea root tips. This suggests a possible developmental correlation, wherein the lack of $p34_{cdc2}$ precludes the ability of cells to cycle.

POLYPLOIDIZATION CYCLES IN ROOT TIP CELLS

A general view of a hypothetical root cortical cell-file is shown in Figure 2.5. After a certain number of rounds of proliferative cell divisions, a transition point is reached at which G_2–M is switched off. These cells will now continue to cycle several more times, but by a truncated cell cycle not including M. This endoreduplication may involve complete replication of the genome, or partial replication of only certain genes. After a certain number of replications, this cycle will also terminate. The role of endocycles in root cell-files is not fully understood, but its presence is common, if not universal, and should be discussed.

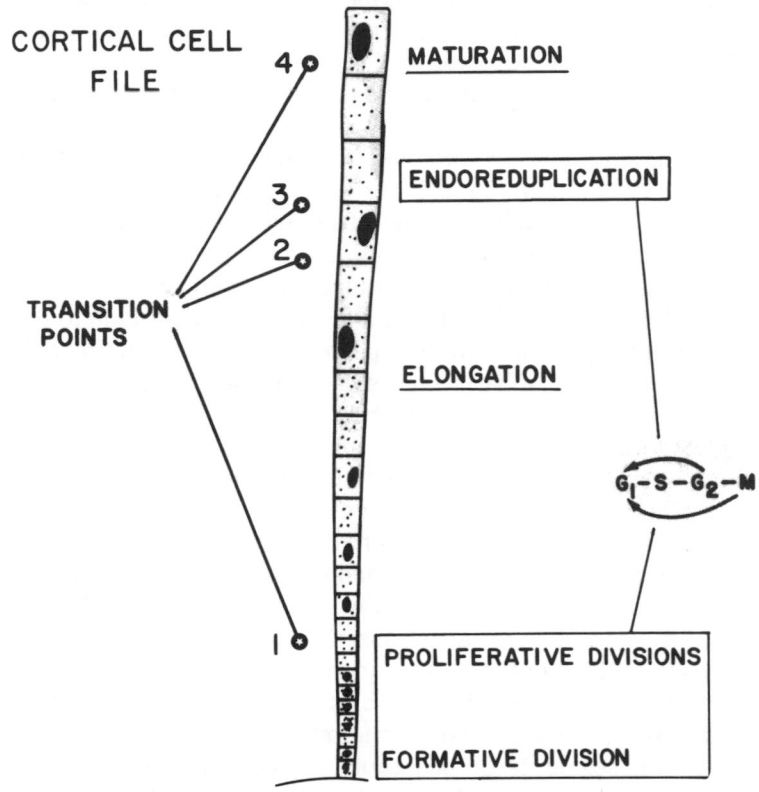

Figure 2.5. Diagram of a hypothetical cortical parenchyma cell-file showing the position of transition points (TP). TP 1 indicates the basipetal boundary for cell division activity. At this TP G_2–M is stopped, but an endoreduplicative cycle continues replicating DNA for several rounds. TP 2 marks the termination of cell elongation. At TP 3 endoreduplication is stopped. TP 4 shows the position of cell maturation.

Brodsky and Uryvaeva (1985) and Nagl (1978) have written about the occurrence and possible significance of polyploidization and other types of endoreduplication cycles in cells of various tissues in plants and animals. No specific role for polyploidization can be generally described, except that it occurs predictably in cells having secretory or storage functions, such as the tapetum, the suspensor, and cotyledon parenchyma cells (Dyer 1976; Nagl 1978). In such cases, an obvious role for polyploidization is to replicate multiple copies of genes needed for the synthesis of abundant gene products (Nagl 1982). Gene amplification, whereby only certain genes or gene sequences are replicated, may also be an important type of replication in specialized cells such as metaxylem tracheary elements (Avanzi et al. 1973).

The absolute necessity of endoreduplication of DNA as a prerequisite for cytodifferentiation in root cells is an open question. Apparently it is a required step in the differentiation of several cell types, but it is probably best considered as simply a step in a differentiation sequence and not a prerequirement (Dyer 1976). Endoreduplication cycles have not been commonly reported in ferns or in gymnosperms (Nagl 1978), although List (1963) did report multinucleate metaxylem tracheary elements in *Marsilea* roots. There is also some question as to whether polyploid cells are found in sunflower (*Helianthus annuus*) roots. Evans and Van't Hof (1974) and Cavallini and Cionini (1986) propose that there are none, whereas Nagl and Capesius (1976) report that polyploid cells are present. This apparent conflict may arise from differences in measurement technique, or from differences among taxa, since the two groups used different cultivars. Because common cell types occur in these groups and individuals, duplicating the entire genome must not be a requirement for the differentiation of cells in general.

List (1963) directly measured the cell volume, nuclear volume, and relative DNA contents of metaxylem cells in the roots from 50 angiosperm and fern genera, including *Zea mays*. In angiosperms, he observed generally that a more or less linear relationship existed between DNA amount and cell size. As metaxylem tracheary elements increased in size, their DNA content also increased, to as high as 32-ploid. Avanzi et al. (1973) used an rRNA–DNA hybridization technique to measure ribosomal cistron DNA reduplication in *Allium cepa* root metaxylem tracheary elements. They observed an 8C amount of DNA in metaxylem tracheary elements by 800 μm from the root tip, and up to almost 32C by 6000 μm.

No one seems to have directly measured ploidy changes in *Pisum sativum* root tracheary elements. The relationship between tracheary element differentiation and polyploidization in pea roots has been developed entirely from tissue culture observations of root segments. Torrey and Fosket (1970) cultured 1 mm segments of pea roots excised 10–11 mm from the root tip. In medium lacking cytokinin, only pericycle cells divided in these cultures. When cytokinin was added, the cortical parenchyma cells also divided, and some of them also passed through endoreduplication cycles. These polypoloid cells then differentiated into tracheary elements. The pericycle cells always remained as diploid cells and did not form tracheary elements. Phillips and Torrey (1973) refined this process by using microexcision to isolate only the cortex and epidermis of 1 mm segments of pea roots. Again, these cells did not divide unless cytokinin was in the medium. The nuclei of cortex cells then underwent endoreduplication and differentiated into tracheary elements.

Van Parijs and Vandendriessche (1966) observed polyploidization in elongating cortical cells at the base of germinating pea roots. Such cells have also been observed in the radicles of *Anchusa capensis* before germination, and in *Spinacia oleracea* radicles three days after germination (Nero-Buffalino and Witkus 1984). Evans and Van't Hof (1975) measured polyploid cells in pea root segments taken 6–6.5 mm from the root tip, and Evans and Van't Hof (1974) found them in the 12–14 and 20–22 mm segments as well. Wipf and Cooper (1940) found tetraploid mitotic figures in cortical cells in the root hair zone of pea roots. Presumably, the cells became tetraploid much closer to the tip in these roots. These observations are contrary to Matthysse and Torrey (1969) and Libbenga and Torrey (1973), who found no polyploid cells in the 10–11 mm segment of pea roots. From these conflicting observations, we can conclude that polyploid cells are present in pea root cortical parenchyma cells, but their exact position remains to be determined.

THE SPATIAL RELATIONSHIP AND MODULATION
OF DIFFERENTIATION EVENTS

Maturation Position and Meristem Size

In pea roots, the position of protoxylem tracheary element (PTE) maturation has been correlated to primary root length and the size of the root tip meristem (Rost and Baum 1988). This correlation is a natural three-part modulation effect (Figure 2.6). In short roots (4–40 mm), as the root elongates, the PTE maturation position becomes farther from the root body/cap junction. In midlength primary roots (40–80 mm), the position of PTE maturation remains approximately constant at 5 mm from the tip. In longer roots, the maturation position becomes increasingly close to the tip. The primary root of pea is determinate but can become as long as 500 mm in some seedlings. The final length of the root is temperature-dependent in peas. The longest final lengths occur in roots grown at 10 to 15°C (P. Lu, D. Gladish, and T. Rost, unpublished observations). Many seedlings tend to lose primary root dominance and have longer lateral roots. The position of PTE maturation in the longest possible primary roots has not been determined, but it is presumably less that 1 mm from the body/cap junction.

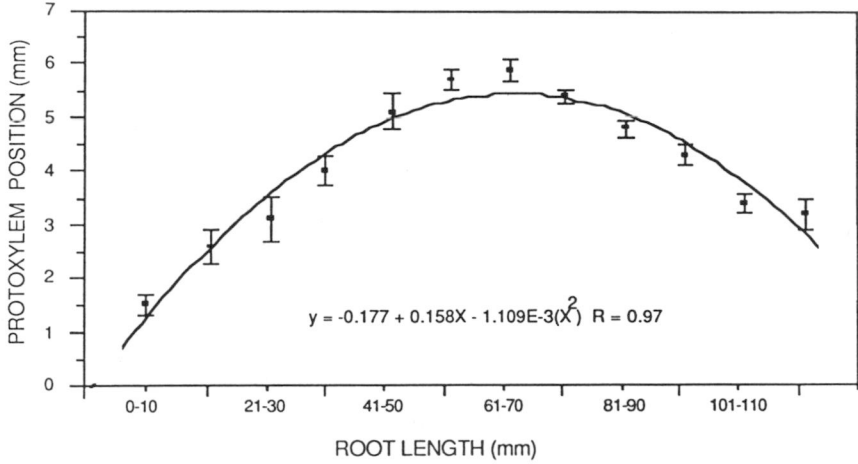

Figure 2.6. Curve showing the relationship of protoxylem tracheary element (PTE) position to root length. PTE position is closer to the tip in short roots, farthest in medium length roots, and closer again in longer roots. (With permission, Rost and Baum 1988.)

The relative size of the meristem was measured by Rost and Baum (1988), who determined the meristem height as the distance from the root body/cap junction to a position at which the distance between Feulgen-stained cortical cell nuclei exceeded approximately two nuclear diameters. This is a relative measure, because it did not take into account that cell-files for different tissues terminate at different levels. With this measure, however, the relationship of root length to meristem height also followed a three-part correlation (Figure 2.7). In short roots, the meristem height increased with increasing root length. In midlength roots, meristem height remained constant at approximately 2.5 mm, and in longer roots it became shorter. Meristem width and volume (Rost and Baum 1988) followed a linear relationship whereby short roots tended to have wide, high volume meristems and longer roots had narrower, smaller

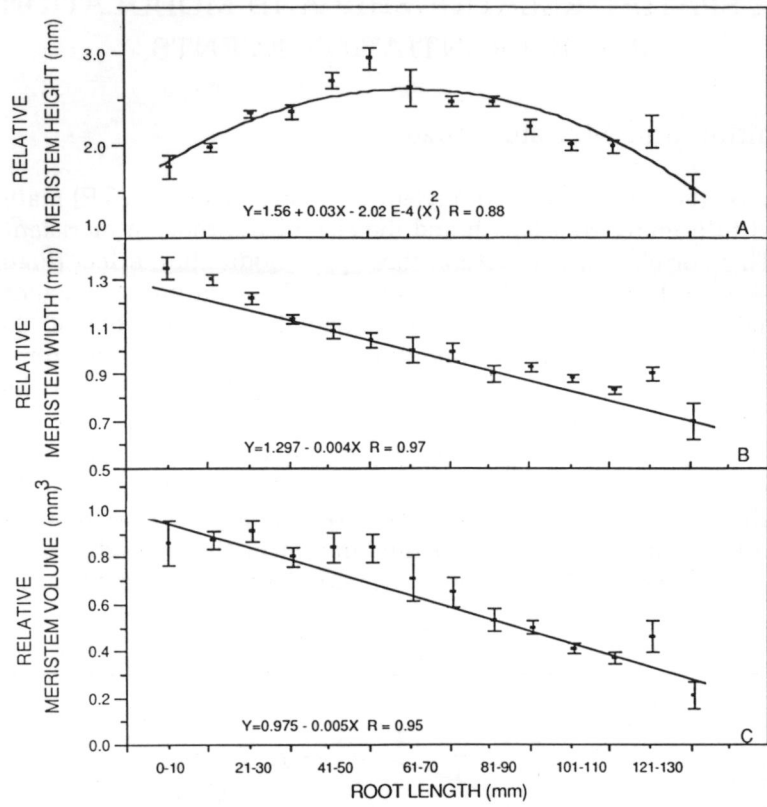

Figure 2.7. Graphs of relative meristem size plotted against root length. (A) Relative meristem height has a curve relationship to root length, while width (B) and volume (C) best fit a linear relationship. (With permission, Rost and Baum, 1988.)

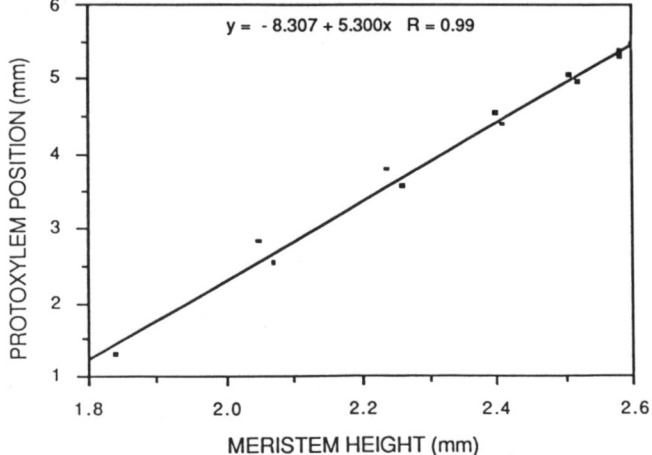

Figure 2.8. Plot of PTE position versus meristem height. Based on the slope of the line, for every 0.19 mm increase or decrease in meristem height, the PTE position changes correspondingly by 1.0 mm. (With permission, Rost and Baum, 1988.)

meristems (Figure 2.7.B,C). This means that the meristem is a dynamic structure that changes its shape in correlation with the developmental status (length in this case) of the primary root.

Rost and Baum (1988) plotted the factors of relative meristem height and PTE position against each other and reported a linear relationship (Figure 2.8). The slope of this line showed that for each 0.19 mm change in meristem height, the PTE maturation position changed by 1 mm. In roots with short meristems, PTEs mature close to the tip; in those with tall meristems, PTE maturation occurs farther back.

On the Modulation of Maturation Position

In addition to the natural modulation of PTE position relative to root length, several other factors and growth conditions have been reported to influence maturation position. Esau (1965) discussed the general course of xylem development in roots and reported, based on published studies, that xylem maturation occurs farther from the tip in fast-growing roots than in slow-growing roots. Torrey (1953) made a similar observation in cultured pea roots; as the rate of elongation of a 5 mm root increased after recovery from excision, so did the distance to the most proximal PTE. Popham (1955) observed that PTE matured closer to the tip in old pea (21 d) roots than in younger (5 d) roots. He also reported that roots grown in aerated medium grew faster than in nonaerated medium, and the position of PTE maturation was farther from the tip. Peterson (1967) made the identical observation in white mustard roots grown in aerated and non-aerated media.

Wilcox (1954) compared active and dormant fir roots. He demonstrated that the most proximal PTE was 7 mm from the tip in roots growing 6 mm/d, but that the most proximal PTE occurred at 0.5 mm in roots that had stopped elongating. In a dormant fir root, the most proximal PTE was 0.05 mm from the apical initial cells. When cell division stopped, so did elongation, but maturation continued acropetally so that the mature cells near the tip were always short. Heimsch (1951) had reported similar observations: When cell division ceased in an old barley root, vascular tissue matured near the tip without much elongation.

Barghoorn (1942) used one-proline to increase cotton root elongation rates. PTEs matured farther from the tip in fast growing roots than in slow-growing roots. Odhnoff (1963) used GA_3 to decrease bean root growth rate and induced xylem maturation closer to the tip. Treatment with phenylboric acid stimulated root elongation by 35%, and xylem maturation was farther from the tip.

Roots are very sensitive to manipulation. Simply transferring a seedling from one medium to another is enough to inhibit elongation and cause differentiation events to occur closer to the root tip (Burstrom 1956; Rost and Baum 1988). Severe treatments of various types can induce a three-part response that is common for many roots: (a) inhibition of cell division and elongation; (b) induction of lateral swelling of the sub-apical tissue; and (c) premature maturation of cells. As an example, Dunlop & Schmidt (1964) exposed Narcissus tazetta roots to a strong magnetic field. The root meristem cells stopped dividing, the tip swelled, and vascular tissues matured very near the root tip. In a general sense, any stress factor that inhibits growth, cell division, or cell elongation seems to induce, secondarily, subapical swelling and premature maturation.

Therefore, it appears that xylem maturation, and presumably other cells and tissues as well, can be modulated by influencing the levels at which the transition points for cell division and cell elongation are triggered. Modulations occur naturally according to primary root length (Rost and Baum 1988), developmental age (Heimsch 1951; Wilcox 1954; Popham 1955), growth rate (Popham 1955; Peterson 1967; Rost and Baum 1988), and by experimental induction (Barghoorn 1942; Torrey 1953; Odhnoff 1963; Rost and Baum 1988).

DEVELOPMENTAL UNITS

There are at least five levels of organization in the root—individual cells, cell packets, cell-files, tissue cylinders, and tissue sectors (Figure 2.9). Researchers have concentrated on each level to determine the basic structural unit and the causal mechanisms that regulate root structural pattern and development. Isolating each level is probably the wrong approach, since development is an integrative process involving simultaneous events at each level.

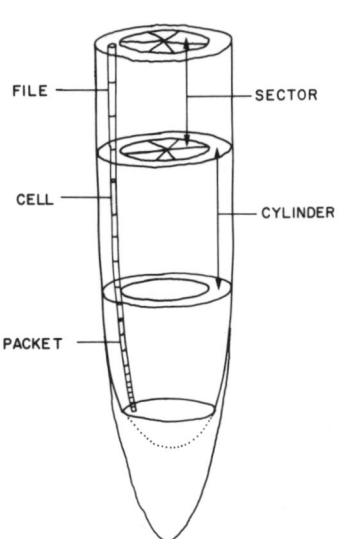

Figure 2.9. Diagram showing five different development units—cell, cell packet, cell-file, tissue sector, and tissue cylinder—present in a root tip. Each unit is an independent functional unit, yet each is dependent on the next higher level. Any model explaining root development must account for organization at each level.

Merophytes and Packets

Gunning (1981) has described the organization of the *Azolla* root tip. These roots have a large apical cell that divides sequentially from three basiscopic surfaces. The apical cell divides a preprogrammed number of times to produce derivative cells. Each of these in turn divides a determined number of times within the confines of the original derivative cell wall. This developmental unit, or *merophyte,* divides, differentiates, and enlarges in a set pattern, resulting in mature cells and tissues. A merophyte system has been reported in other ferns but not in the roots of higher vascular plants.

Barlow (1987) has described a somewhat analogous structural unit in corn roots. He traced the development of single cells in the radicle of ungerminated embyros through their subsequent divisions during and after germination. These cells and their derivatives divided a set number of times. The outer wall of the original mother cell remained thickened during these divisions, forming recognizable cell packets, each consisting of 2–16 cells. Cells in cortical cell packets divided in basipetal sequence; the apical-most cell in each packet divided first. The first division of the original mother cell in the series tended to be asymmetric. The large derivatives were all positioned acropetally and divided sequentially. This pattern was not consistent in different tissues, however, since stelar cell packets did not follow a constant division sequence. Cell packets may also be found in roots of other plants (Webster 1980). The cell packet is a developmental unit not unlike the merophyte, but is tissue-specific and lacking in the precise development pattern found in fern merophytes.

Cell-Files

Cell-files are the next order of organization. A file is of indefinite length. Depending on the forces impinging upon it, cells within it may undergo one or more formative divisions to produce a branching cell-file. Cells within cell-files are strongly connected to each other by plasmodesmatal connections mostly within their transverse walls, with fewer between files (Juniper and Barlow 1969; Gunning 1978). Apparently, the conduit for passage of cytoplasmic signals is through the plasmodesmata (Gunning and Robards 1976; Gunning and Overall 1983). Since most plasmodesmata lie within the transverse walls of the cell-files, presumably that is the best route for signal transduction.

Tissue Cylinders and Sectors

Although most plasmodesmatal connections lie in the transverse cell walls, aggregates of cell-files (tissues) often act as developmental units (sectors and cylinders) (Figure 2.9). For example, the middle cortex cylinder in pea roots (Figure 2.4.B) is composed of an aggregate of similar cells. These cells stop dividing and differentiate together as a unit. The signals inducing this behavior must affect all cells within the unit together. Presumably such a signal would readily move from cell to cell within the unit, to the exclusion of other nearby cells. This would imply that the hypothetical signal is unique to the unit (cylinder), or that the nearby cells are immune to its effect.

In peas, the vascular cylinder can be further subdivided into xylem and phloem sectors. The xylem PTEs stop dividing very near the body/cap junction, while the pericycle and adjoining cells continue to divide as a unit some distance farther back. Cells of the xylem pericycle stop dividing at a position corresponding closely to the level of protoxylem maturation, a finding that suggests a regulatory connection between xylem pericycle cells and maturing xylem tracheary elements.

For a full understanding of root development, all levels of organization must be considered. Most likely, not one or even two interacting signals, morphogens, physical factors, or cues will explain root development. Instead, since the root is a composite of individual cells, cell packets, cell-files, and tissue sectors and cylinders, a complicated network of interacting and coordinated signals must operate in root development.

CONCLUSION

In conclusion, I describe the position, transition points, and relationships of three cell-files in a hypothetical root tip (Figure 2.10). I highlight the relationships of the transition points to each other and briefly speculate as to their nature.

In the cortical parenchyma cell file, the transition point for cell division occurs about 250 μm from the body/cap junction in a pea root. At this point the G_2–M control

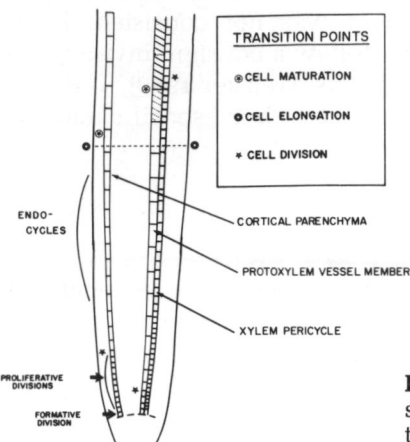

Figure 2.10. Diagram of a median longitudinal section of a root tip showing the comparative positions of the transition points for three cell-files.

point terminates cell division. The nature of this transition point is unknown, but it could logically involve the cytoskeleton or the expression of p34[cdc2] genes.

In the protoxylem vessel member file, cell division is terminated close to the tip, and again only the G_2–M control point is affected; these cells also have a high ploidy level when mature. The exact position for turning off endoreduplication is unknown, but it probably accompanies cell maturation. In both cell-files, two kinds of cell-cycle transition points occur, one for the G_2–M control point that is located very close to the tip and another, farther back in the file, for the G_1–S.

The xylem pericycle files have a different cell cycle regulation mechanism. In pea roots (Rost et al. 1988) and in *Vicia faba* roots (Luxová and Murín 1973), the xylem pericycle cells continue to cycle quite far from the body/cap junction (greater than 10 mm in pea roots). This finding means that the cells will continue to divide past the point at which cell elongation is terminated and that derivative cells formed after that time will be shorter than their parental cells (Figure 2.10). At some location, the transition point for cell cycling will occur in these cells, only in this case, both the G_2–M and G_1–S control points will be affected. Apparently these cells do not become polyploid, since they are involved in lateral root initiation (Van't Hof et al. 1986). This transition point is different from that in the cortical parenchyma and xylem PTE files, since it involves both cell-cycle control points simultaneously.

The transition point for cell elongation in a straight-growing root will be the same for all cell-files. In a root following a bent or curved path, this transition point will allow the cells on one surface to continue elongation or to elongate at a faster rate, thus resulting in a curved root. Plant growth regulators are known to be involved in cell elongation, along with specific enzymes for cell-wall synthesis. The lack of any event or process would probably inhibit elongation. The specific transition point that would terminate elongation at a specific position and at a specific cell length is unknown.

The transition points for cell maturation will be different for each cell-file. This position is modulated by several factors, however, as discussed above. In pea roots, for example, maturation of PTEs is modulated in relation to meristem height. In roots with tall meristems, PTEs mature farther from the root tip. Stress factors also modulate the position of this transition point. Generally, any factor that inhibits growth will cause maturation to occur closer to the root tip. These observations show that growth events, cell division and cell elongation, are intimately tied to maturation events, but that they may also be independent of each other. Hence, cell division, *per se,* is not a prerequisite for a specific maturation event. One role for cell division and cell elongation in the root tip is to maintain the spatial distance between the tip and the mature cells.

SUMMARY

1. There are two basic types of apical organization—open and closed. In closed apices, cell-files connect directly to tiers of initial cells. In open apices, they terminate in a zone at the root body/cap junction. In closed organization roots, the tissue identity of cell-files is apparent at the time of the first formative cell division; in open organization roots, the tissue identity of cell-files is usually not apparent for some distance basipetal to the apex.

2. The root meristem does not have a common boundary for all cell-files. Instead, each cell-file is regulated by a transition point involved in switching off the cell cycle at a cell-file and tissue-specific location. The transition point may act on only a single cell or an entire tissue cylinder or sector.

3. At least two types of cell cycle are found in most root tips. Formative cell divisions occur at the initiation site of a cell-file, and proliferative divisions occur within a cell-file. The formative division occurs once per file, and the proliferative divisions usually occur a set number of times specific to the cell-file.

    In some cells, a transition point occurs that switches off the G_2–M portion of a proliferative cell cycle. In these instances such cells may continue to cycle, but in an endoreduplicative mode. These cells increase their DNA content to a certain level, apparently to create many copies of genes essential to a specific development process. The presence of formative and proliferative cell cycles and endoreduplication cycles implies that there are different kinds of transition points regulating their behavior. The nature of the G_1 and G_2 control points is apparently different.

4. Maturation position is related to meristem height. In roots with short meristems, maturation will occur relatively closer to the root tip than in the same root with a tall meristem.

5. Maturation is also modulated by root growth rate. Slow-growing roots will show mature cells closer to the tip than fast-growing roots. Stress factors that slow or stop growth will induce maturation closer to the root tip.

6. There are at least five levels of organization in a root tip: individual cells, cell packets, cell-files, tissue sectors, and tissue cylinders. The control of differentiation depends on the presence and activity of transition points. These transition points act at each level and also involve interaction between levels.

Acknowledgments

Dr. Todd Jones (Du Pont, Inc., Wilmington, Delaware) and Mr. Stuart Baum (University of California, Davis) are acknowledged for their contributions and help with our research on pea root tips. Dr. Judy Jernstedt and Mr. Gene Tanimoto (both of the University of California, Davis) are acknowledged for their assistance in preparing this manuscript.

LITERATURE CITED

Allan, E. F., and A. Trewavas. 1986. Tissue-dependent heterogeneity of cell growth in the root apex of *Pisum sativum*. *Bot. Gaz.* 147:258–269.

Aloni, R. 1987. Differentiation of vascular tissues. *Annu. Rev. Plant Physiol.* 38:179–204.

Armstrong, J. E. and C. Heimsch. 1976. Ontogenetic reorganization of the root meristem in the Compositae. *Am. J. Bot.* 63:212–219.

Avanzi, S., F. Maggini, and A. M. Innocenti.1973. Amplification of ribosomal cistrons during the maturation of metaxylem in the roots of *Allium cepa*. *Protoplasma* 76:197–210.

Barghoorn, E. S. Jr. 1942. The effects of 1-proline on proliferation of cells and differentiation of protoxylem in roots of cotton and bean. *Growth* 6:23–31.

Barlow, P. W. 1976. Towards an understanding of the behaviour of root meristems. *J. Theor. Biol.* 57:433–451.

Barlow, P. W. 1982. Root development. In *The Molecular Biology of Plant Development*. Ed. H. Smith, D. Grierson. Berkeley: Univ. Calif Press. 185–222.

Barlow, P. W. 1984. Positional controls in root development. In *Positional Controls in Plant Development*. Ed. P. W. Barlow, D. J. Carr. Cambridge: Cambridge Univ. Press 281–318.

Barlow, P. W. 1987. Cellular packets, cell division and morphogenesis in the primary root meristem of *Zea mays* L. *New Phytol.* 105:27–56.

Brodsky, V. Y. and I. V. Uryvaeva. 1985. *Genome Multiplication in Growth and Development: Biology of Polyploidy and Polytene Cells*. Cambridge: Cambridge Univ. Press.

Burstrom, H. 1956. Temperature and root cell elongation. *Physiol. Plant* 9:682–692.

Cavallini, A., and P. G. Cionini. 1986. Nuclear DNA content in differentiated tissues of sunflower (*Helianthus annuus* L.) *Protoplasma* 130:91–97.

Clowes, F. A. L. 1958. Development of quiescent centres in root meristems. *New Phytol.* 57:85–88.

Clowes, F. A. L. 1981. The difference between open and closed meristems. *Ann. Bot.* 48:761–767.

Deysson, G. 1980. Control of cell multiplication in root meristems of higher plants. *Biol. Cell.* 38:75–80.

Dodds, J. H. 1981. Relationship of the cell cycle to xylem cell differentiation: A new model. *Plant Cell Environ.* 4:145–146.

Dunlop, D. W., and B. L. Schmidt. 1964. Biomagnetics. I. Anomalous development of the root of *Narcissus tazetta* L. *Phytomorphology* 14:333–342.

Dyer, A. F. 1976. Modifications and errors of mitotic cell division in relation to differentiation. In *Cell Division in Higher Plants*. Ed. M. M. Yeoman. New York: Academic Press. 199–249.

Esau, K. 1965. *Vascular Differentiation in Plants*. New York: Holt, Rinehart and Winston.

Evans, L. S., and J. Van't Hof. 1974. Is the nuclear DNA content of mature root cells prescribed in the root meristem? *Am. J. Bot.* 61:1104–1111.

Evans, L. S., and J. Van't Hof. 1975. Is polyploidy necessary for tissue differentiation in higher plants? *Am. J. Bot.* 62:1060–1064.

Gorst, J. R., P. C. L. John, and F. J. Sek. 1991. Levels of p34cdc2-like protein in dividing, differentiating and dedifferentiating cells of carrot. *Planta* 185:304–310.

Gunning, B. E. S. 1978. Age-related and origin-related control of the numbers of plasmodesmata in cell walls of developing *Azolla* roots. *Planta*. 143:181–190.

Gunning, B. E. S. 1981. Microtubules and cytomorphogenesis in a developing organ: The root primordium of *Azolla pinnata*. In *Cytomorphogenesis in Plants*. Ed. O. Kiermayer. Berlin: Springer-Verlag 301–325.

Gunning B. E. S., A. R. Hardham, and J. E. Hughes. 1978. Pre-prophase bands of microtubules in all categories of formative and proliferative cell division in *Azolla* roots. *Planta* 143:145–160.

Gunning, B. E. S., and R. L. Overall. 1983. Plasmodesmata and cell-to-cell transport in plants. *BioScience* 33:260–265.

Gunning, B. E. S., and A. W. Robards, Eds. 1976. *Intercellular Communication in Plants: Studies on Plasmodesmata.* Berlin: Springer-Verlag.

Guttenberg, H. von. 1960. Grundzüge der Histogenese höhere Pflanzen. I. Die Angiospermen. *Handbuch Pflanzenanat.* 8:3. Berlin: Gebrüder Borntraeger.

Hanstein, J. 1868. Die Scheitelzellgrupe im Vegetationspinkt der Phanerogamen. *Festchr. Niederrhein. Ges. Natur. Heilkunde* 1868:109–134.

Heimsch, C. 1951. Development of vascular tissues in barley roots. *Am. J. Bot.* 38:523–537.

Hinchee, M. A. W. 1981. *Factors Controlling Lateral Root Development in Seedlings of Pea* (Pisum sativum cv. *Alaska*). Ph.D Thesis. Davis: Univ. Calif.

Ivanov, V. B. 1973. Growth and reproduction of cells in roots. In *Physiology of Roots.* Ed. N. V. Obrucheva. Moscow: Uniiti. 1–40.

Janczewski, E. De. 1874. Recherches sur l'accroissement terminal des racines dans les phanerogames. *Ann. Sci. Nat. Ser. 5* 20:162–201.

Jensen, W. A., and L. G. Kavaljian. 1958. An analysis of cell morphology and the periodicity of division in the root tip of *Allium cepa. Am. J. Bot.* 45:365–372.

John, P. C. L., F. J. Sek, and M. G. Lee. 1989. A homolog for the cell cycle control protein p34[cdc2] participates in the division cycle of *Chlamydomonas,* and a similar protein is detectable in higher plants of remote taxa. *Plant Cell* 1:1185–1193.

John, P. C. L., F. J. Sek, J. P. Carmichael, and D. W. McCurdy. 1990. p34[cdc2] homologue level, cell division, phytohormone responsiveness and cell differentiation in wheat leaves. *J. Cell Sci.* 97:627–630.

Juniper, B. E., and P. W. Barlow. 1969. The distribution of plasmodesmata in the root tip of maize. *Planta* 89:352–360.

Libbenga, K. R., and T. G. Torrey. 1973. Hormone-induced endoreduplication prior to mitosis in cultured pea root cortex cells. *Am. J. Bot.* 60:293–299.

List, A. Jr. 1963. Some observations on DNA content and cell and nuclear volume growth in the developing xylem cells of certain higher plants. *Am. J. Bot.* 50:320–329.

Luxová, M. 1975. Some aspects of the differentiation of primary root tissues. In *The Development and Function of Roots.* Ed. J. G. Torrey, D. T. Clarkson. New York: Academic Press 73–90.

Luxová, M., and A. Murín. 1973. The extent and differences in mitotic activity of the root tip of *Vicia faba* L. *Biol. Plant. (Praha)* 15:37–43.

Matthysse, A. G., and J. G. Torrey. 1969. Factors limiting the stimulation of polyploid mitoses in intact pea roots and excised root segments. *Bot. Gaz.* 130:62–69.

Moreno, S., J. Hayles, and P. Nurse. 1989. Regulation of p34[cdc2] protein kinase during mitosis. *Cell* 58:361–372.

Nagl, W. 1978. *Endopolyploidy and Polyteny in Differentiation and Evolution.* Amsterdam: Elsevier North Holland.

Nagl, W. 1982. DNA endoreduplication and differential DNA replication. In *Nucleic Acids and Proteins in Plants II.* Ed. B. Parthier, D. Boulter. Berlin: Springer-Verlag. 111–123.

Nagl, W., and I. Capesius. 1976. Endopolyploidy in *Helianthus annuus* (Asteraceae), a scanning cytophotometry study. *Plant Syst. Evol.* 125:261–268.

Nero-Buffalino, L. del, and R. Witkus. 1984. The first appearance of polyploid nuclei in primary roots of two diploid angiosperms. *Ann. Bot.* 53:53–58.

Odhnoff, C. 1963. The effect of gibberellin and phenylboric acid on xylem differentiation and epidermal cell elongation in bean roots. *Physiol. Plant* 16:474–483.

Peterson, R. L. 1967. Differentiation and maturation of primary tissues in white mustard root tips. *Can. J. Bot.* 45:319–331.

Phillips, R., and J. G. Torrey. 1973. DNA synthesis, cell division and specific cytodifferentiation in cultured pea root cortical explants. *Dev. Biol.* 31:336–347.

Popham, R. A. 1955. Zonation of primary and lateral root apices of *Pisum sativum. Am. J. Bot.* 42:267–273.

Popham, R. A. 1966. *Laboratory Manual for Plant Anatomy.* St. Louis, MO: C. V. Mosby Co.

Rost, T. L., and S. Baum. 1988. On the correlation of primary root length, meristem size and protoxylem tracheary element position in pea seedlings. *Am. J. Bot.* 75:414–424.

Rost, T. L., T. J. Jones, and R. H. Falk. 1988. The distribution and relationship of cell division and maturation events in *Pisum sativum* (Fabaceae) seedling roots. *Am. J. Bot.* 75:1571–1583.

Seago, J. L., and C. Heimsch. 1969. Apical organization in roots of the Convolvulaceae. *Am. J. Bot* 56:131–138.

Tanimoto, E. Y., T. L. Rost, and L. Comai. 1993. Histone H_2A expression during S-phase: Histological co-localization of H_2A mRNA and DNA synthesis in pea root tips. In *Molecular and Cell Biology of the Plant Cell Cycle*. Ed. J. C. Ormrod and D. Francis. Dordrecht, The Netherlands: Kluwer Academic Publishers. 85–95.

Toriyama, H. 1978. Observational and experimental studies of the meristem of leguminous plants. II. Differentiation of the pericycle in the root tips of *Pisum sativum*. *Cytologia* 43:705–716.

Torrey, J. G. 1953. The effect of certain metabolic inhibitors on vascular tissue differentiation in isolated pea roots. *Am. J. Bot.* 40:525–533.

Torrey, J. G., and L. J. Feldman 1977. The organization and function of the root apex. *Am. Sci.* 65:334–344.

Torrey, J. G., and D. W. Fosket. 1970. Cell division in relation to cytodifferentiation in cultured pea root segments. *Am. J. Bot.* 57:1072–1080.

Van Parijs, R., and L. Vandendriessche. 1966. Changes in the DNA content of nuclei during the process of cell elongation in plants. I. The formation of polytene chromosomes. *Arch. Int. Physiol. Biochem.* 74:579–586.

Van't Hof, J. 1969. Two principal points of control in the mitotic cycle of pea meristem cells. In *Advances in Radiation Research*. Ed. J. F. Dunlap, A. Chapiro. Vol. 2:881–894. New York: Gordon and Breach Sci. Pub.

Van't Hof, J., C. A. Bjerknes, and S. S. Lamm. 1986. Meristematic precursors of vascular parenchyma differentiate from G_2 phase after replicating DNA discontinously. *Am. J. Bot.* 73:87–95.

Warren Wilson, P. M., and J. Warren Wilson. 1984. Control of tissue patterns in normal development and regeneration. In *Positional Controls in Plant Development*. Ed. P. W. Barlow, D. J. Carr. Cambridge: Cambridge Univ. Press 223–280.

Webster, P. L. 1980. Analysis of heterogeneity of relative division rates in root apical meristems. *Bot. Gaz.* 141:353–359.

Wilcox, H. 1954. Primary organization of active and dormant roots of noble fir, *Abies procera*. *Am. J. Bot.* 41:812–821.

Wipf, L., and D. C. Cooper. 1940. Somatic doubling of chromosomes and nodular infection in certain Leguminosae. *Am. J. Bot.* 27:821–824.

Chapter 3

The Dynamics of Root Growth and Gravitropism

RANDY MOORE

Roots respond to many environmental stimuli, including light, gravity, and physical pressure. These responses are concentrated in the terminal 2–3 cm of the roots, where stimuli are sensed and primary growth occurs (Feldman 1984). Thus, understanding root growth requires that we understand the structure of root tips.

STRUCTURE OF ROOT TIPS

Root tips are covered by a thimble-shaped root cap that protects and helps the root move through soil. Behind the root cap is a quiescent center of 500–2000 inactive cells arrested in the G_1 phase of mitosis. The quiescent center organizes patterns of primary growth. Since the root cap effectively but imperfectly protects the root, the root apical meristem is occasionally damaged as the root forces its way through the soil. When this occurs, cells of the quiescent center divide and re-form the meristem and root cap. Thus, the quiescent center also functions as a reservoir of genetically healthy cells.

Surrounding the quiescent center is a subterminal, dome-shaped apical meristem located 0.5–1.5 mm behind the root tip. This meristematic region is the so-called *zone of cellular division,* and is made of small, isodiametric cells. Cellular divisions in root tips are strongly influenced by ethylene and rarely occur past 1 cm behind the root tip.

Also comprising the root apical meristem are transitional meristems: protoderm that forms epidermis, procambium that forms vascular tissues (i.e. xylem and phloem), and ground meristem that forms ground tissue (e.g. cortex). These transitional meristems extend through the regions of cellular elongation and maturation located 3–10 mm behind the root tip. Cellular elongation shoves the root through the soil, and is responsible for roots' responses to environmental stimuli such as gravity. Primary roots

From *Growth Patterns in Vascular Plants* Edited by Muhammed Iqbal

elongate as much as 2–4 cm/d, whereas secondary roots usually grow significantly slower (e.g. 0.05–0.5 cm/d). Auxin typically inhibits cellular elongation in roots, but low concentrations of ethylene (e.g. 0.02–0.1 ppm) stimulate elongation. Two other factors are required for cellular elongation (i.e. primary growth) in roots:

1. *Loosening of the cell wall so that it can stretch:* One means by which walls are loosened is by secretion of acids into the walls. These acids loosen the cell wall by activating pH-dependent enzymes that break bonds between cellulose molecules in the wall. Wall acidification associated with cellular elongation is strongly influenced by auxin.

2. *Positive turgor:* Turgor is generated by accumulations of ions and salts in vacuoles, which causes an osmotically driven uptake of water. Thus, filling the vacuole with water is what "fills up" an expanding cell. This means of cellular enlargement is energetically more efficient than making an equal volume of cytoplasm.

The direction of cellular elongation is determined by which cell wall is most stretchable; this in turn, is determined by orientation of the wall's cellulose microfibrils. Microtubules strongly influence deposition of these microfibrils; for example, treating roots with microtubule-disrupting drugs such as colchicine produces spherical rather than elongate cells. Cells behind the elongating zone do not elongate.

Cellular elongation is completed in the zone of cellular maturation, which is located just behind the zone of cellular elongation. The maturation zone is characterized by the presence of ephemeral root hairs that increase the absorptive surface area of the root.

GRAVITROPISM

The downward growth of primary roots of most plants results from three events: (a) perception of gravity; (b) transformation of gravity into a physiological stimulus; and (c) a stimulus-directed response characterized by differential growth that produces downward curvature.

Perception of Gravity

Charles Darwin and his son Francis were among the first botanists to study root gravitropism. One of their earliest experiments demonstrated that removing the root cap rendered roots nonresponsive to gravity. This experiment, which has been repeated several times, suggests that the root cap is necessary for graviresponsiveness, and prompted Darwin (1881) to write that "there is no structure in plants more wonderful as far as its functions are concerned, than the tip of the radicle."

Figure 3.1 shows a cap of primary root of *Zea mays*. At the base of a root cap is the *calyptrogen,* or cap meristem. Cellular divisions in the calyptrogen continually push cells into the cap, where they sequentially differentiate into columella and peripheral cells. Columella cells each contain 15 to 30 amyloplasts that sediment to the lower sides of the cells (Figure 3.2). This sedimentation of amyloplasts in columella cells and their possible interactions with other cellular structures such as the

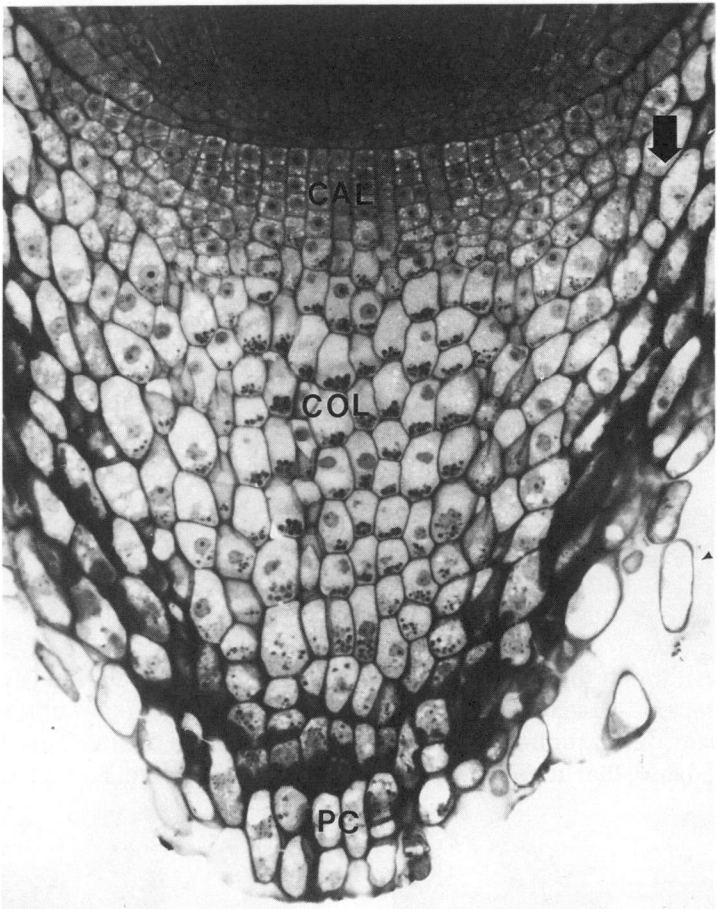

Figure 3.1. Optical micrograph of a cap of a primary root of *Zea mays*. The calyptrogen (CAL) at the base of the cap produces cells that sequentially differentiate into columella cells (COL) in the center of the cap and peripheral cells (PC) at the cap's edge. The gravity vector is indicated by an *arrow* in the upper right corner of the photo.

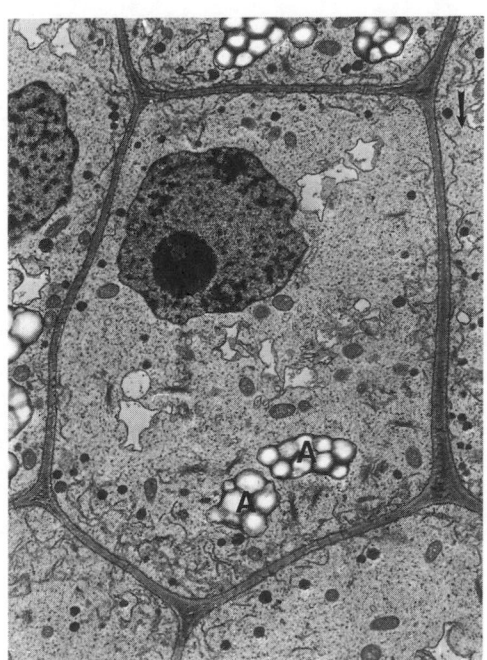

Figure 3.2. Electron micrograph of a columella cell from a primary root of *Zea mays*. Columella cells contain numerous amyloplasts (A) that sediment to the lower side of the cell. The gravity vector is indicated by an *arrow* in the upper right of the photo.

endoplasmic reticulum and/or plasmalemma are thought by many to underlie how roots perceive gravity. This conclusion is based on the following observations:

1. Amyloplasts sediment in columella cells before the onset of root gravicurvature (see review by Audus 1979).

2. Removing the root cap renders roots nonresponsive to gravity (see review by Jackson and Barlow 1981). Replacing the detached cap restores graviresponsiveness. Recovery of graviresponsiveness by decapped roots usually occurs within 24 hr after decapping and correlates positively with sedimentation of amyloplasts in cells of their tips (Barlow 1974; Hillman and Wilkins 1982). This nongraviresponsiveness of decapped roots has been interpreted as indicating that the root cap is the site of graviperception and is therefore necessary for gravitropism (see discussion in (Jackson and Barlow 1981; Moore and Evans 1986); however, decapped roots regain graviresponsiveness long before a root cap is regenerated, thus indicating that a root cap *per se* is not necessary for graviresponsiveness.

3. Treatments that dissolve starch from amyloplasts render roots nonresponsive to gravity. These destarched roots regain graviresponsiveness when they regenerate starch in their tips (Iversen 1969).

Although these correlations are convincing, correlation is not causality. Indeed, several recent observations have questioned the role of columella amyloplasts as gravity sensors in roots. For example, sedimentation of amyloplasts in columella cells does not ensure that a root responds to gravity (Ransom and Moore 1983; Olsen and Iversen

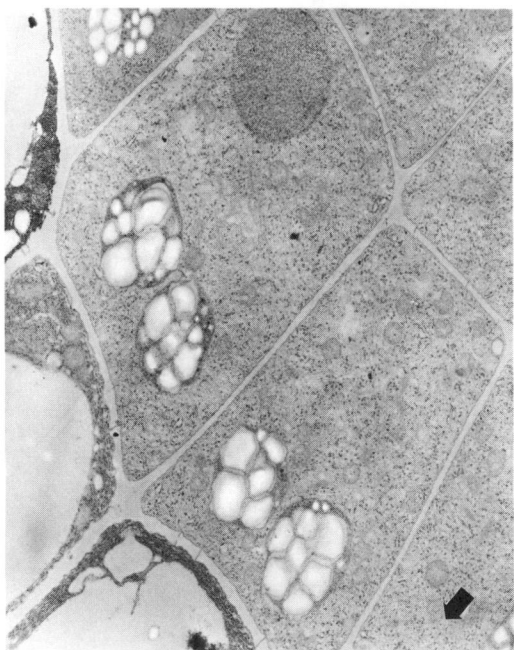

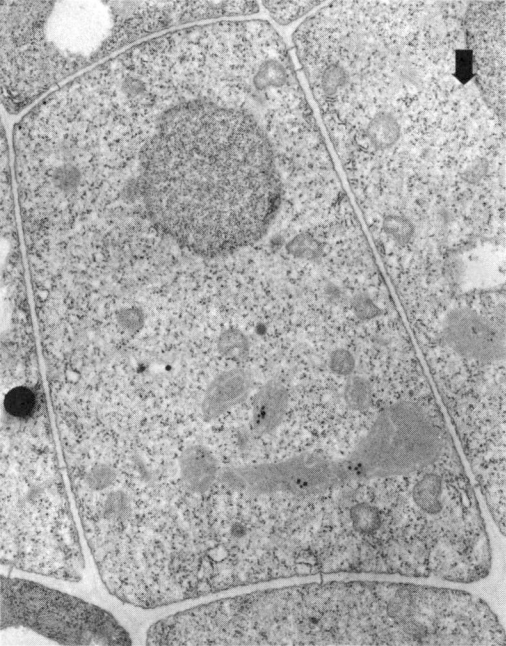

Figure 3.3. Electron micrograph of columella cells of a wild-type seedling of *Arabidopsis*. The gravity vector is indicated by an *arrow*.

Figure 3.4. Electron micrograph of columella cells of a mutant seedling of *Arabidopsis*. Mutants lack starch and amyloplasts, yet are graviresponsive. The gravity vector is indicated by an *arrow*.

1980; Moore 1985a,b). More importantly, roots of the TC7 *Arabidopsis* mutant contain no starch or amyloplasts yet respond to gravity (Figures 3.3, 3.4; Caspar and Pickard 1989). This observation indicates that amyloplasts are not necessary for root graviresponsiveness, and therefore are not necessary for perception of gravity. Saether and Iversen (1991), however, claim that plastids in roots of the TC7 mutant do contain starches and sediment in response to gravity. Recent evidence suggests that (a) integrin-like proteins in the cell/extracellular matrix junction may be required for gravisensing (Wayne 1992), and (b) roots respond to gravity by sensing gravitational pressures exerted by the protoplast and not by sedimentation of amyloplasts (Lee et al. 1992).

Response to Gravity: Differential Growth

Although the root cap may be involved in perceiving gravity, the downward curvature characteristic of root gravitropism occurs in the elongating zone, which is 2–4 mm behind the cap. Orienting roots horizontally reduces growth along the lower side of the root (Audus and Brownridge 1957; Pilet and Ney 1981; Darbelly and Perbal 1984). This causes the root to curve down, usually within 10–30 min after reorientation. Some signal that inhibits growth presumably moves from the cap to the elongating zone of the root. Several studies have suggested that this signal is an inhibitor:

1. Decapped roots elongate faster than intact roots (Pilet 1972; Wilkins and Wain 1974), and applying a second cap to an intact root decreases elongation (Pilet 1972).

2. Inserting impermeable barriers between the root cap and elongating zone causes roots to curve away from the side of the root into which the barrier was inserted (Shaw and Wilkins 1973).

3. Removing half of the root cap causes roots to curve toward the side of the root with the half-cap, irrespective of the root's orientation (Gibbons and Wilkins 1970; Shaw and Wilkins 1973).

Some studies originally suggested that this inhibitor was abscisic acid (ABA; Wilkins and Wain 1975; Pilet and Chanson 1981; Pilet and Rivier 1981); however, recent observations indicate that this conclusion was wrong. For example,

1. ABA initially *stimulates* root growth over a wide range of concentrations, whereas it inhibits growth only at high concentrations after prolonged periods (Mulkey et al. 1983).

2. Mutants and chemically treated roots having undetectable amounts of ABA are strongly graviresponsive (Moore and Smith 1984, 1985; Feldman and Sun 1986).

3. If root gravicurvature is due to a gradient of ABA, one would expect gravicurvature to be reduced or eliminated when roots are submerged in a solution of ABA. Such treatments do not significantly reduce gravitropism (unpublished data of Katekar, cited by Jackson and Barlow 1981).

Therefore, ABA is probably not the effector controlling root gravitropism. Rather, the following observations suggest that indoleacetic acid (IAA) is important for gravitropism:

1. Exogenously applied IAA inhibits growth at concentrations 100–1000× lower than those at which abscisic acid is effective (see discussion in Mulkey et al. 1983).

2. Auxin applied to the upper side of the elongating zone of horizontally oriented roots moves to the lower side of the elongating zone (Hasenstein and Evans 1988).

3. Artificially induced asymmetries of IAA across root tips induce gravitropic-like curvature (Mulkey et al. 1983; Schurzmann and Hild 1980).

4. Root gravicurvature is preceded by asymmetric acid efflux that is strongest along the upper (i.e. rapidly growing) side of the elongating zone. Inhibitors of auxin-induced proton secretion (e.g. orthovanadate) and auxin transport abolish asymmetric acid efflux and gravicurvature (Mulkey and Evans 1981, 1982; Mulkey et al. 1983).

Therefore, auxin probably controls the differential growth that causes gravitropism.

Transforming the Gravitational Signal

Perception of gravity by roots is presumably based on movement of one or more cellular components called *statoliths,* which, in turn, initiate the physiological changes that ultimately cause gravicurvature. Several models have suggested that transduction of the gravitational signal involves amyloplasts contacting the plasmalemma or *distal complex* of the endoplasmic reticulum (Volkmann and Sievers 1979; Sievers and Heyder-Caspers 1983; Hensel 1984). These interactions then somehow alter production and/or transport of growth regulators affecting gravicurvature.

Although appealing, these models are probably not generally valid for root gravitropism. For example:

1. Sedimented amyloplasts seldom, if ever, touch the plasmalemma of columella cells (Audus 1979; Volkmann and Sievers 1979; Ransom and Moore 1983; Barlow et al. 1984).

2. Columella cells of most roots examined so far do not have a "distal complex" of endoplasmic reticulum (Juniper 1976; Ransom and Moore 1983; Stoker and Moore 1984; Moore and Pasieniuk 1984b). Furthermore, sedimented amyloplasts seldom touch endoplasmic reticulum (Moore and McClelen 1983; Barlow et al. 1984).

3. Recent investigations (especially those with the starch-free *Arabidopsis* mutant) question the role of amyloplasts as statoliths in roots (Figures 3.3, 3.4; Caspar and Pickard 1989.)

Not all models for transformation of the gravitational signal are based on amyloplast movement and the resulting cellular interactions. For example, Hertel (1971) suggests that physical pressure exerted by the weight of the protoplast rather than movement or pressure exerted by amyloplasts *per se* could affect gravitropism by altering transport properties of membranes. Audus (1962), however, believes that this force would be insignificant compared to the osmotic force of the cytoplasm, and therefore that it could not be important for sensing gravity.

Wilkins (1978) has suggested that electrical charges on amyloplasts could induce an electrical polarity affecting permeability and transport across the plasmalemma. Interestingly, amyloplasts have a potential of approximately −19 mV (Sack et al. 1983). Although intriguing, this hypothesis cannot explain graviresponsiveness by starchless (and amyloplastless) mutants of *Arabidopsis* (see above). Our poor understanding of how roots perceive gravity has hindered our understanding of how roots transform gravity into a physiological response.

Transduction of the gravitational signal into differential growth probably involves some type of communication between the cap and elongating zone. Recent studies suggest that a root's perception of and response to gravity are linked by free and mobile calcium (Ca^{2+}), as shown by the following examples:

1. Applying Ca^{2+} asymmetrically to root tips induces curvature toward the side of the root to which Ca^{2+} was applied (Lee et al., 1983a,b).

2. Calcium-deficient roots are not graviresponsive, and chelating Ca^{2+} in root tips with EDTA renders roots nonresponsive to gravity. Graviresponsiveness is restored when EDTA is replaced with Ca^{2+} (Lee et al. 1983b).

3. Calcium moves downward across tips of horizontally oriented roots. Such polar transport of Ca^{2+} does not occur across decapped roots (Lee et al. 1983a). Downward transport of Ca^{2+} is not a consequence of gravicurvature because a gradient of endogenous Ca^{2+} forms before the onset of gravicurvature (Moore and Fondren, unpublished).

4. Inhibitors of Ca^{2+} translocation (e.g. 2,3,5-triiodobenzoic acid, naphthylphthalmic acid) also abolish auxin transport and gravitropism (Lee et al. 1984).

These observations suggest that Ca^{2+} moves to the lower side of tips of horizontally oriented roots, and that the resulting gradient of Ca^{2+} somehow influences gravicurvature. The nature of this influence is unknown, but probably involves activation of calmodulin, a small protein that activates many enzymes important to cellular function. This conclusion is based on the following observations:

1. Calmodulin is abundant in root tips (Stinemetz and Evans 1985), and applying inhibitors of calmodulin to root tips abolishes gravitropism (see discussion in Björkman and Leopold 1987).

2. Aluminum (Al^{3+}) binds to calmodulin and inhibits its activation by calcium (Siegel and Haug 1983). Correspondingly, unilateral application of Al^{3+} to root tips has an effect opposite that of Ca^{2+}—roots grow away from the Al^{3+} (Hasenstein and Evans 1988; Hasenstein et al. 1988).

3. In corn roots requiring red light for gravisensitivity, mRNA coding for calmodulin increase within 5 min after exposure to light (L. Feldman, unpublished, cited in Björkman and Leopold 1987).

4. Applying Al^{3+} unilaterally to a root cap stimulates movement of auxin to the concave side of the elongating zone of a curving root (Hasenstein and Evans 1988).

Calmodulin may activate Ca^{2+} or auxin "pumps" in the plasmalemma, which could then produce apoplastic gradients in the root tip that affect gravicurvature.

We do not know what controls the accumulation of Ca^{2+} and/or other effectors along the lower side of the root tip. Electrical asymmetries may be involved. For example, electric current in vertically oriented roots is symmetrical; current flows out of the elongating zone and into the root tip. Electric currents (carried by H^+) become asymmetrical within 2–6 min after roots are oriented horizontally: current along the upper side of the cap flows out of the cap, while current along the lower side of the root flows into the cap. This upward flow of H^+ may balance and indirectly reflect a downward flow of Ca^{2+} toward the lower side of the cap (Behrens et al. 1982). Furthermore, inhibitors of calmodulin abolish gravicurvature and gravity-induced electrical currents (Björkman and Leopold 1987). Gravity-induced electrical asymmetries may redistribute Ca and other ions across root tips (see discussion in Moore and Evans 1986; Björkman and Cleland 1991).

Peripheral and epidermal cells of root tips produce large amounts of mucigel, a hydrated polysaccharide containing sugars, organic acids, vitamins, enzymes, and amino acids. Mucigel has several important functions (e.g. protection, lubrication, absorbing water and nutrients), one of which may be to provide a route for movement of gravitropic effectors. This conclusion is based on and/or is consistent with the following observations:

1. Calcium is abundant in mucigel (Duke et al. 1985; Moore 1986). When roots are oriented horizontally, endogenous Ca^{2+} accumulates along the lower side of the root (Moore and Fondren 1988). Also, Ca^{2+} enhances auxin transport (Dela Fuente 1984).

2. Calcium applied to mucigel along the upper surface of roots can be collected from mucigel covering the lower surface of the roots (Lee et al. 1983a, 1984; Moore 1985b). There is no evidence for symplastic movement of Ca^{2+} across the columella tissue or elongating zone of horizontally oriented roots (Moore 1986).

3. Applying mucigel asymmetrically to root tips induces gravitropic-like curvature (Marcum and Moore unpublished). Roots naturally lacking mucigel are nonresponsive to gravity (Moore, Evans, and Fondren 1990; Miller and Moore 1990), and continually washing mucigel from roots significantly reduces gravicurvature (see discussion in Moore 1985c). Adding mucigel-like material to roots lacking mucigel induces gravicurvature (Moore, Evans, and Fondren 1990).

4. The onset of graviresponsiveness by decapped roots is preceded by production and accumulation of mucilage at their tips (Barlow and Sargent 1978; Hillman and Wilkins 1982).

5. Orienting roots horizontally produces a distinct and rapid differential in the apoplastic calcium activity between the upper and lower sides of gravistimulated tips of maize roots. This differential is necessary for gravitropism (Björkman and Cleland 1991).

Taken together, these results suggest that gravitropic effectors moving from the root cap to the elongating zone move at least partially through the apoplast. This is consistent with Clarkson's suggestion that Ca moves out of cells into the apoplast during gravitropism (Clarkson 1984).

The Role of Outer Cell Layers in Root Gravicurvature

Several reports suggest that growth and gravitropism by roots are controlled by the outer cell layers of the root (Iwami and Masuda 1974). Nelson and Evans (1986) made a similar claim when they observed that (a) primary roots of *Zea mays* are nonresponsive to gravity when their outer cell layers are removed; and (b) when the outer cell layers are removed from one side of a vertically oriented root, the root curves away from the side of the root having an intact surface. Consistent with this suggestion, the most prominent asymmetries of Ca^{2+} in the elongating zone of intact roots occur in the mucigel and cell wall (i.e. apoplast) of epidermal cells (Moore et al. 1989). Perhaps this is not surprising, since mucilage is an integral part of walls of epidermal cells (Charboud and Rougier 1986). Also, the concentration of Ca^{2+} in epidermal cells differs significantly from that of cortical cells (Moore et al. 1989), a finding consistent with observations that epidermal and cortical cells have different ionic properties (Mertz and Higinbotham 1976). These results suggest that intact outer cell layers are necessary for root gravitropism. Björkman and Cleland (1988a,b) have shown, however, that root segments of *Z. mays* lacking epidermis and most of their cortex are graviresponsive. These results prompted Björkman and Cleland to suggest that the condition of the endodermis, rather than the epidermis or cortex, is critical for root gravicurvature. Because both the epidermis and endodermis lack intercellular spaces, this feature may be important for the differential growth associated with root gravicurvature.

Calcium and Auxin: A Model for Root Gravitropism

I suggest the following model for root gravitropism:

- In vertically oriented roots, auxin moves through the stele toward the cap, where its flow branches and is redirected toward the cortical and epidermal tissues of the root. This acropetal flow of auxin through the stele accounts for the large amounts of IAA present in root caps (Jackson and Barlow 1981). In tips of vertically oriented roots, pumps and symmetric electrical currents distribute Ca^{2+} symmetrically in the apoplast.

- Orienting roots horizontally induces electrical asymmetries favoring movement of Ca^{2+} back and downward through the apoplast. As a result, Ca^{2+} accumulates along the lower side of the root tip.

- The resulting accumulation of Ca^{2+} along the lower side of the root tip activates calmodulin, which, in turn, activates pumps that redirect auxin toward the lower side of the root tip. Calcium may also sensitize epidermal, cortical, and/or endodermal cells to auxin.

- The increased amount of auxin along the lower side of the root inhibits cellular elongation, thereby causing downward curvature.

NONGRAVIRESPONSIVE ROOTS

Almost all research regarding root gravitropism has centered on the primary roots of a few cultivated species such as corn. However, most roots do not grow straight down, but grow at various angles relative to gravity, and as a result more efficiently explore the soil for water and minerals.

I have recently begun studying nongraviresponsive roots because they represent an ideal "control" for distinguishing events correlated with gravitropism from those critical to gravitropism. Secondary roots of several species (e.g. *Phaseolus vulgaris, Ricinus communis, Helianthus annuus*) do not "seek" a lateral orientation. Rather, they grow in whatever direction they are initiated (Ransom and Moore 1983) and tend to grow laterally only because they are initiated perpendicular to vertically growing (and graviresponsive) primary roots.

Columella cells of lateral (i.e. nongraviresponsive) roots contain sedimented amyloplasts like columella cells of graviresponsive primary roots (Figure 3.5; Ransom and More 1983; Moore and Pasieniuk 1984a,b; Stoker and Moore 1984). Therefore, if roots sense gravity via sedimentation of amyloplasts in columella cells, then nongraviresponsive lateral roots perceive gravity as do graviresponsive primary roots. Furthermore, tips of lateral roots placed asymmetrically on detipped primary roots induce gravitropic-like curvature (Ransom and Moore 1985). These results suggest that lateral roots produce gravitropic effectors. If lateral roots perceive gravity and produce gravitropic effectors, why then do they not respond to gravity? I suggest that lateral roots do not respond to gravity because they do not establish significant gradients of gravitropic effectors. Their inability to accomplish this may relate to the size of their columella tissue. Indeed, (a) lateral roots have significantly less columella tissue than do graviresponsive primary roots (Ransom and Moore 1983, 1985); (b) the onset of graviresponsiveness by secondary roots of plants such as *Ricinus* correlates positively with dramatic increases in the length, width, and volume of their columella tissue (Moore and Pasieniuk 1984b; Moore 1985c); and (c) differing degrees of graviresponsiveness by primary roots correlate positively with the amount of columella tissue in their caps (Pilet 1982).

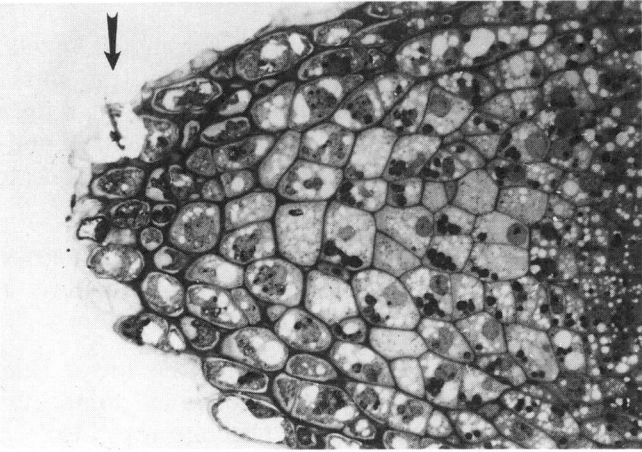

Figure 3.5. Longitudinal section of a cap of a lateral (i.e. nongraviresponsive) root of sunflower (*Helianthus annuus*). Columella cells in the center of the cap contain sedimented amyloplasts. Caps of nongraviresponsive roots are typically smaller than those of graviresponsive roots. The gravity vector is indicated by an *arrow* in the upper left corner of the photo.

Acknowledgments

Some of the work reported in this chapter was supported by Grant No. NAGW–734 from the National Aeronautics and Space Administration (NASA). I thank Eddie McClelen for his excellent help.

LITERATURE CITED

Audus, L. J. 1962. The mechanism of the perception of gravity in plants. *Symp. Soc. Exp. Biol.* 16:197–226.

_____. 1979. Plant geosensors. *J. Exp. Bot.* 30:1051–1073.

Audus, L. J. and M. E. Brownridge. 1957. Studies on geotropisms of roots. I. Growth rate distribution during response and the effects of applied auxins. *J. Exp. Bot.* 8:235–249.

Barlow, P. W. 1974. Regeneration of the cap of primary roots of Zea mays. *New Phytol.* 73:937–954.

Barlow, P. W., C. R. Hawes, and J. C. Horne. 1984. Structure of amyloplasts and endoplasmic reticulum in the root caps of *Lepidium sativum* and *Zea mays* observed after selective membrane staining and by high-voltage electron microscopy. *Planta* 160:363–371.

Barlow, P. W., and J. A. Sargent. 1978. The ultrastructure of the regenerating root cap of *Zea mays* L. *Ann. Bot.* 42:791–799.

Behrens, H. M., M. H. Weisensell, and A. Sievers. 1982. Rapid changes in the pattern of electric current around the root tip of *Lepidium sativum* L. following gravistimulation. *Plant Physiol.* 70:1079–1083.

Björkman, T., and R. E. Cleland. 1988a. The epidermis does not control gravitropism in maize roots. In *Abstr. Annu. Meet. Amer. Soc. Grav. Space Biol.*, Washington, DC, Oct. 20–23, p. 48.

_____. 1988b. The role of the epidermis and cortex in gravitropic curvature of maize roots. *Planta* 176:513–518.

_____. 1991. The role of extracellular free-calcium gradients in gravitropic signalling in maize roots. *Planta* 185:379–384.

Björkman, T., and A. C. Leopold 1987. Effect of inhibitors of auxin transport and of calmodulin on a gravisensing-dependent current in maize roots. *Plant Physiol.* 84:847–850.

Caspar, T., and B. G. Pickard. 1989. Gravitropism in a starchless mutant of *Arabidopsis*. Implication for the start-statolith theory of gravity sensing. *Planta* 177:185–197.

Charboud, A., and M. Rougier. 1986. Ultrastructural study of the maize epidermal root surface. I. Preservation and extent of the mucilage layer. *Protoplasma* 130:73–79.

Clarkson, D. T. 1984. Calcium transport between tissues and its distribution in the plant. *Plant Cell Environ.* 7:449–456.

Darbelly, N., and G. Perbal. 1984. Gravity and cell differentiation in the lentil root. *Physiologist* (Suppl.) 27:121–122.

Darwin, C. 1881. *The Power of Movement in Plants*. London: J. Murray.

Dela Fuente, R. K. 1984. The role of calcium in the polar secretion of indoleacetic acid. *Plant Physiol.* 76:342–346.

Duke, S. O., K. C. Vaughn, and R. D. Wauckope. 1985. Effects of glyphosate on uptake, translocation, and intracellular localization of metal cations in soybean (*Glycine max*) seedlings. *Pest. Biochem. Physiol.* 24:384–394.

Feldman, L. 1984. Regulation of root development. *Annu. Rev. Plant Physiol.* 35:223–242.

Feldman, L. J., and P. S. Sun. 1986. Effects of norflurazon, an inhibitor of carotenogenesis, on abscisic acid and xanthoxin in the caps of gravistimulated maize roots. *Physiol. Plant.* 67:472–476.

Gibbons, G. S. B., and M. B. Wilkins. 1970. Growth inhibitor production by root caps in relation to geotropic responses. *Nature* 226:558–559.

Hasenstein, K. H., and M. L. Evans. 1988. The influence of calcium and pH on growth of primary roots of *Zea mays*. *Physiol. Plant.* 72:466–470.

Hasenstein, K. H., M. L. Evans, C. L. Stinemetz, R. Moore, W. M. Fondren, E. C. Koon, M. A. Higby, and A. J. M. Smucker. 1988. Comparative effectiveness of metal ions in inducing curvature of primary roots of *Zea mays*. *Plant Physiol.* 86:885–889.

Hensel, W. 1984. A role of microtubules in the polarity of statocytes from roots of *Lepidium sativum* L. *Planta* 162:404–414.

Hertel, R. 1971. Aspects of the geotropic stimulus in plants. In *Gravity and the Organism*. Ed. S. A. Gordon, M. J. Cohen. Chicago, Ill.: Univ. of Chicago Press.40–50.

Hillman, S. K., and M. B. Wilkins. 1982. Gravity perception in decapped roots of *Zea mays*. *Planta* 155:267–271.

Iversen, T. H. 1969. Elimination of geotropic responsiveness in roots of cress (*Lepidium sativum*) by removal of statolith starch. *Physiol. Plant* 22:1251–1262.

Iwami, S., and Y. Masuda. 1974. Geotropic response of cucumber hypocotyls. *Plant Cell Physiol.* 15:121–129.

Jackson, M. B., and P. W. Barlow. 1981. Root geotropism and the role of growth regulators from the cap: a re-examination. *Plant Cell Environ.* 4:107–123.

Juniper, B. E. 1976. Geotropism. *Annu. Rev. Plant Physiol.* 27:385–406.

Lee, S. W., S. Y. Kim, A. Jeyabalasinkham, R. Wayne, K. Schneider, M. L. Vaughn, and T. J. Mulkey. 1992. Effect of solution density on gravitropic response of maize roots. *Plant Physiol.* 99:63.

Lee, J. S., T. J. Mulkey, and M. L. Evans. 1983a. Gravity-induced polar transport of calcium across root tips of maize. *Plant Physiol.* 73:874–876.

———. 1983b. Reversible loss of gravitropic sensitivity in maize roots after tip application of calcium chelators. *Science* 220:1375–1376.

———. 1984. Inhibition of polar calcium movement and gravitropism in roots treated with auxin-transport inhibitors. *Planta* 160:536–543.

Mertz, S. M., and N. Higinbotham. 1976. Transmembrane electropotential in barley roots as related to cell type, cell location, and cutting and aging effects. *Plant Physiol.* 57:123–128.

Miller, I., and R. Moore. 1990. Defective secretion of mucilage is the cellular basis for agravitropism in primary roots of *Zea mays* cv. Ageotropic. *Ann. Bot.* 66:169–178.

Moore, R. 1985a. A morphometric analysis of the redistribution of organelles in columella cells in primary roots of normal seedlings and a gravitropic mutants of *Hordeum vulgare*. *J. Exp. Bot.* 36:1275–1286.

———. 1985b. Calcium movement, graviresponsiveness and the structure of columella cells and columella tissues in roots of *Allium cepa* L. *Ann. Bot.* 56:173–187.

———. 1985c. Dimensions of root caps and columella tissues of primary roots of *Ricinus communis* characterized by differing degrees of graviresponsiveness. *Ann. Bot.* 55:375–380.

———. 1986. Cytochemical localization of calcium in cap cells of primary roots of *Zea mays* L. *J. Exp. Bot.* 37:73–79.

Moore, R., I. Cameron, and N. K. R. Smith. 1989. Movement of endogenous calcium in graviresponding roots of *Zea mays*. *Ann. Bot.* 64:122–126.

Moore, R., and M. L. Evans. 1986. How roots perceive and respond to gravity. *Am. J. Bot.* 73:574–587.

Moore, R., M. L. Evans, and W. M. Fonderen. 1990. Inducing gravitropic curvature of primary roots of *Zea mays* cv. Ageotropic. *Plant Physiol.* 92:310–315.

Moore, R., and W. M. Fondren. 1988. A gradient of endogenous calcium forms in mucilage of graviresponding roots of *Zea mays*. *Ann. Bot.* 61:113–116.

Moore, R., and C. E. McClelen. 1983. Ultrastructural aspects of cellular differentiation in the root cap of *Zea mays*. *Am. J. Bot.* 70:611–617.

Moore, R., and J. Pasieniuk. 1984a. Graviresponsiveness and the development of columella tissue in primary and lateral roots of *Ricinus communis*. *Plant Physiol.* 74:529–533.

———. 1984b. Structure of columella cells in primary and lateral roots of *Ricinus communis* (Euphorbiaceae). *Ann. Bot.* 53:715–726.

Moore, R., and J. D. Smith. 1984. Growth, graviresponsiveness, and abscisic-acid content of *Zea mays* seedlings treated with Fluridone. *Planta* 162:342–344.

———. 1985. Graviresponsiveness and abscisic-acid content of roots of carotenoid-deficient mutants of *Zea mays* L. *Planta* 164:126–128.

Mulkey, T. J., and M. L. Evans. 1981. Geotropism in corn roots: evidence for its mediation by differential acid efflux. *Science* 212:70–71.

_____. 1982. Suppression of asymmetric acid efflux and gravitropism in maize roots treated with auxin transport inhibitors or sodium orthovanadate. *J. Plant Growth Reg.* 1:259–265.

Mulkey, T. J., M. L. Evans, and K. M. Kuzmanoff. 1983. The kinetics of abscisic acid action on root growth and gravitropism. *Planta* 157:150–157.

Nelson, A. J., and M. L. Evans. 1986. Role of the epidermis in the gravitropic response of maize roots. *Abstr. Annu. Meet. Am. Soc. Grav. Space Biol.,* Charlottesville, VA, Oct. 1–3, 1986, p. 21.

Olsen, G. M., and T. H. Iversen. 1980. Ultrastructure and movements of cell structures in normal pea and in a geotropoic mutant. *Physiol. Plant* 50:275–284.

Pilet, P. E. 1982. Importance of the cap cells in maize root gravireaction. *Planta* 156:95–96.

_____. 1972. Root cap and root growth. *Planta* 106:169–171.

Pilet, P. E., and A. Chanson. 1981. Effect of abscisic acid on maize root growth: a critical examination. *Plant Sci. Lett.* 21:99–106.

Pilet, P. E., and D. Ney. 1981. Differential growth of georeacting maize roots. *Planta* 1512:146–150.

Pilet, P. E., and L. Rivier. 1981. Abscisic acid distribution in horizontal maize root segments. *Planta* 153:453–458.

Ransom, J. S., and R. Moore 1983. Geoperception in primary and lateral roots of *Phaseolus vulgaris* (Fabaceae). I. Structure of columella cells. *Am. J. Bot.* 70:1048–1056.

_____. 1985. Geoperception in primary and lateral roots of *Phaseolus vulgaris* (Fabaceae). III. A model to explain the differing gravibehaviors of primary and lateral roots. *Can. J. Bot.* 63:21–24.

Sack, F. D., D. A. Priestly, and A. C. Leopold. 1983. Surface charge on isolated maize-coleoptile amyloplasts. *Planta* 157:511–517.

Saether, N., and T. H. Iversen. 1991. Gravitropism and starch statoliths in an *Arabidopsis* mutant. *Planta* 184:491–497.

Schurzmann, M., and V. Hild. 1980. Effect of indoleacetic acid, abscisic acid, root tips and coleoptile tips on growth and curvature of maize roots. *Planta* 150:332–36.

Shaw, S., and M. B. Wilkins. 1973. The source and lateral transport of growth inhibitors in geotropically stimulated roots of *Zea mays* and *Pisum sativum*. *Planta* 109:11–26.

Siegel, N., and A. Haug. 1983. Aluminum interaction with calmodulin. Evidence for altered structure and function from optical and enzymatic studies. *Biochim. Biophys. Acta* 774:36–45.

Sievers, A., and C. Heyder-Caspers. 1983. The effect of centrifugal accelerations on the polarity of statocytes and on the graviperception of cress roots. *Planta* 157:61–70.

Stinemetz, C. L., and M. L. Evans. 1985. Correlated changes in calmodulin activity and gravitropic sensitivity in maize. *Physiologist* 28:S121-S122.

Stoker, R., and R. Moore. 1984. Structure of columella cells in primary and lateral roots of *Helianthus annuus* (Compositae). *New Phytol.* 97:205–213.

Volkmann, D., and A. Sievers. 1979. Graviperception in multicellular organs. In *Encyclopedia of Plant Physiology*. Ed. W. Haupt, M. Feinleib. 7:573–600. N. S. Berlin: Springer-Verlag.

Wayne, R., 1992. The contribution of the cell-extracellular matrix junction to gravisensing in chara. *Plant Physiol.* 99:30.

Wilkins, H., and R. L. Wain. 1974. The root cap and control of root elongation in *Zea mays* L. seedlings exposed to white light. *Planta* 121:1–8.

_____. 1975. Abscisic acid and the response of roots of *Zea mays* L. seedlings to gravity. *Planta* 126:19–23.

Wilkins, M. B. 1978. Gravity-sensing guidance mechanisms in roots and shoots. *Bot. Mag. Tokyo* 1:255–277. Special Issue.

_____ Chapter 4 _____

Shoot Apical Configuration in Gymnosperms

AMBUJA PILLAI

_____

This chapter evaluates significant facets of the gymnospermous shoot apex configuration and focuses on the basic knowledge of meristems and their control, concentrating largely on the work done during the past 20 years. Detailed treatment and assessment of the earlier literature are available in reviews by Johnson (1951), Gifford and Corson (1971), Pillai and Pillai (1976), Buvat (1989),and Fahn (1990).

STRUCTURAL CONFIGURATION

Johnson (1951) reviewed data by family, including Cycadaceae, Ginkgoales, Pinaceae, Araucariaceae, Sciadopitaceae, Taxodiaceae, Cupressaceae, Caphalotaxaceae, Taxaceae, Saxegothecaceae, Podocarpaceae, Ephedraceae, Gnetaceae, and Welwitschiaceae. Gifford and Corson (1971) discussed the gymnosperm shoot apex under the rubrics, vegetative shoot apex and transition to reproductive growth, and pointed out variations in terminology for the zones of the apex and differences in size, zonation, and growth patterns during different phases of shoot growth. Pillai and Pillai (1976) discussed Cycadales, Gnetales, Welwitschiales, Coniferophyta, and Ephedrales and summarized the details in tabular form regarding zonation as reported by different authors.

The terms *apical meristem, apical dome,* and *shoot apex* are used in the literature in different contexts. This lack of precision leads to confusion. Gregory and Romberger (1972a) clarified the term *apical meristem* as referring to that collection of meristematic cells from which, by repeated divisions, all primary tissues are derived. When only the dome above the youngest discernible lateral primordium is intended, it is called the *apical dome.* The term *shoot apex* refers to the tip of the shoot with its apical meristem and developing foliar primordia.

From *Growth Patterns in Vascular Plants* Edited by Muhammed Iqbal

In *Cycas circinalis*, Chacko et al. (1976) distinguished the following four zones in the shoot apex: *apical initials*, consisting of small groups of initials near the vertex in each of several superposed layers; the *peripheral zone*; the *central mother cell zone*; and the *pith rib meristem*. The zonation pattern resembles that of *Dioon* (Foster 1941) more than that of *Cycas revoluta* (Foster 1939, 1940). Pillai and Pillai (1976) envisaged the shoot apical configuration in *Cycas revoluta* as one of the most primitive among gymnosperms.

Pinus species have attracted the attention of many investigators. Most of the reports deal with the shoot apical configuration in mature trees. Ontogenetic data on embryonic, seedling, and young shoot apices are meager. The apex of the mature embryo is generally nonzonate, but in some it appears zonate because of a definite distribution of storage products. The seedling apex presents a fairly uniform appearance with no evident zonation (Tepper 1964; Riding 1974). In *P. ponderosa*, zonation similar to that in apices of mature trees is evident in seedlings only 64 d after planting. In *P. radiata*, Riding (1974) found cytohistological zonation similar to that in mature plants in the seedling apex 32 d after hydration. This zonation was more pronounced at 60 d. The development of zonation apparently varies among different species of pine, and it is correlated possibly with the branching pattern of the seedling.

Riding (1974) suggested that the attainment of a particular size and zonal pattern is essential for the development of adult habit in pines. In *P. resinosa*, the apices of younger trees stained uniformly, whereas those from mature trees showed a more lightly stained apical zone (Riding and MacLean 1974). Riding (1972) observed three zones after the initiation of the first needle primordia: the apical zone, peripheral zone, and pith rib meristem. He did not favor the division of the apical zone into apical initial and central mother cell zones (Tepper 1964, 1966) during early seedling development, because the zones do not have the same characteristics that demarcate the apical initial and central mother cell zones in mature plants of the same species.

Most of the studies on the apices of mature trees agree on the presence of a zonate pattern that becomes more pronounced in dormant as well as in larger apices. There are four zones: 1. *apical initials* that divide periclinally and anticlinally—anticlinal divisions add cells to the surface layer and periclinal divisions add cells to the subapical group (Gabilo and Mogensen 1973); 2. *central mother cells* (Riding 1972; Pillai and Pillai 1974; Pillai et al. 1980a,b), called *subapical initials* by some authors (Gabilo and Mogensen 1973), which are arranged irregularly and divide in various planes—anticlinal divisions contribute cells to the peripheral zone and periclinal divisions contribute cells to the subjacent central tissue zone; 3. the *peripheral zone* (flank meristem or peripheral meristem), which consists of a surface layer and a few underlying cell layers that are more chromophilic, and where leaf and cataphyll primorida arise; 4. the *pith rib meristem, central tissue zone,* or *central meristem,* formed of three or more vertical columns of cells below zone 2.

The proportion of periclinal to anticlinal divisions in the surface layer of long shoot bud apices was found to be higher during the period of new shoot elongation than during the remainder of the growing season in *Cephalotaxus* (Singh 1961), *Thuja* (Pillai 1963), and *Pinus banksiana* (Curtis and Popham 1972). A reduction in the volume of dwarf shoot apices occurs during needle initiation in *P. densiflora* (Hanawa 1967). Curtis and Popham (1972) assigned shoot apex zonation in *P. banksiana* to the *Abies-Cryptomeria* type described by Popham (1951), with four zones: surface meristem, subapical initials, central meristem, and peripheral meristem. The *Abies-Cryptomeria* type consists of two categories—one with periclinal divisions only in the apical initials, and one with periclinal divisions spread throughout the surface layer. The majority of *Pinus* species belong to the latter category. The cited authors reported a cup-shaped cambium-like zone in a few apices collected during late April and early May, thus placing them in the *Ginkgo* type. Owston (1969) described a transition zone (cambium-like zone) in the shoot apex of *Pinus strobus,* whereas Curtis and Popham (1972) did not consider this zone as equivalent to that of Foster (1939), because it does not contribute to the peripheral zone. This zone is, therefore, more appropriately termed a *central meristem.*

Reports on *Pinus canariensis* (Pillai and Pillai 1974) and six West Himalayan *Pinus* species (Pillai et al. 1980a) confirm four zones in the shoot apex. The cited authors do not agree with Sacher's (1954) division of hard and soft pines based on the larger, ginkgoid central mother cells in the soft pines. *Pinus massoniana,* a hard pine, and *Pinus wallichiana,* a soft pine, have a distinct ginkoid type of central mother cell zone. These authors also pointed out that the shoot apex of *Pinus* seems to be phylogenetically less advanced than that of other conifers and suggested that shoot apices of *Pinus* could be placed between those of the Cycads and *Ginkgo* on one side and the *Cupressus-Thuja* type on the other. Hu and Wang (1984) described four zones in the shoot apex of *Cathaya,* a member of Pinaceae. One of their illustrations shows periclinal divisions in the surface layer on the lower flanks (peripheral zone), and the zonation overall is similar to that of apices of *Pinus* species.

Gregory and Romberger (1972a,b, 1977) and Romberger and Gregory (1977) followed shoot apical ontogeny in the seedling of *Picea abies.* These authors noticed cytohistological zonation in the shoot apex of immature embryos prior to initiation of cotyledonary primordia. These apices attained the zonation characteristic of the species during early seedling development. On the basis of mathematical analysis, these authors concluded that the length of the plastochronic time interval declines appreciably as seedling age increases and also that there is a steady increase in the apical dome diameter and volume. Venkataratnam et al. (1975) reported cyto-histological zonation in the apex of mature embryos of *Picea smithiana* which becomes more pronounced during germination and seedling growth.

Interesting data are available on the dynamics of growth variables such as longi-tudinal profile, vertical position of the leaf primordia, growth rates of young inter-nodes, and volume growth within the apical dome (Romberger and Gregory 1977). Analysis of tissue-volume doubling time (TDT) indicated a decline in growth activity in the apical dome as a whole with increasing volume and age. This decline may be partly attributed to the development of a central zone of less active cells in the older domes with the peripheral cells retaining shorter TDTs than indicated by whole-dome computations. From measurements and mathematical computations, it was concluded that protoxylem differentiation in young internodes (10–12 days) is more closely related to the chronometric age of the internodes than to morphogenic age (in plastochrons) or to distance from the base of the shoot apical dome (Gregory and Romberger 1977). In Cupressaceae, differentiation of protoxylem progresses acropetally from the proximal end of the procambial trace within the axis and into the decurrent leaf base, and basipetally within the lamina. The ascending and descending protoxylem strands usually meet near the point of leaf attachment (Quinn and Gadek 1988).

The shoot apex of *Picea smithiana* was grouped (Pillai and Chacko 1978b) under the *Cupressus-Thuja* type of Pillai et al. (1972). Apical zonation in *P. smithiana* re-sembles that in *Cedrus deodara* (Pillai and Chacko 1978a), but the surface layer on the flanks is more stabilized, showing predominantly anticlinal divisions. The cells of the surface layer at the vertex can be correctly labeled as apical initials. A similar surface layer on the flanks has been reported in *Picea abies* (Gregory and Romberger 1972a,b), *Cupressus* species (S.K. Pillai, 1963), and *Thuja orientalis* (A. Pillai 1963). The develop-ment of vegetative buds is essentially the same in *P. engelmannii* (Harrison and Owens

1983), *P. glauca* (Owens et al. 1977; Owens and Molder 1977a), *P. sitchensis* (Tompsett 1978), and *P. smithiana* (Pillai and Chacko 1978b).

Harrison and Owens (1983) mention four phases of apical growth: rest phase: an early enlargement and developmental phase: a first growth phase, represented by shoot elongation: and a second growth phase, represented by the formation of a preformed vegetative bud. Terminal apices showed a pause in primordial initiation at the end of bud scale initiation. Following the pause, two types of apices were observed: *(a)* a sharp conical apex in which cells of the pith contained a dark-staining ergastic substance, which grew into vegetative apices: and *(b)* bullet-shaped apices with reduced ergastic accumulation in the pith, which grew into reproductive apices. Harrison and Owens (1983) noticed phenomenon of axillary bud abortion that was greater in the more proximal buds in *Picea engelmannii*. A meristematic plate of cells similar to a periderm or abscission zone separated the underlying shoot axis from the deteriorating bud. Unraveling the cause of apical abortion would be worthwhile.

There is no stabilized surface layer in *Cedrus deodara* (Pillai and Chacko 1978a). *Cedrus* manifests an advance over *Picea* in the reduction in size of the subapical group of cells. *Cedrus deodara* exhibits periods of dormancy, bud elongation, cataphyll formation, and foliage leaf initiation. With the advent of dormancy, a crown (nodal diaphragm) develops that separates the embryonic shoot from the older regions. The crown functions to prevent the movement of metabolites to the portion of the apex distal to it, because the vascular elements stop below the crown and fresh vasculature differentiates in the shoot apex above the crown at the resumption of growth during bud break. A similar growth periodicity and crown formation occur in *Picea smithiana* (Pillai and Chacko 1978b).

Pronounced zonation occurs in the active vegetative apices whereas zonation is indistinct in the dormant apices of *Abies amabilis* (Owens and Molder 1977b). The former show an apical zone, central mother cell zone, peripheral zone, and rib meristem. The apical initials divide infrequently by anti- and periclinal divisions. The central mother cell zone has larger cells that also divide infrequently. The protoderm does not show any periclinal divisions.

A tunica-corpus organization was reported in the vegetative apex of *Ephedra foliata* (Pillai et al. 1980b), as in *E. altissima* (Paolillo and Gifford 1961). Johnson (1951) also considered other 'higher' gymnosperms to have tunica-corpus organization.

HISTOCHEMISTRY

Vanden Born (1963) supported the concept of an anneau initial in the shoot apex, pointing out that the intensity of staining for DNA was consistent with greater activity on the flanks of the apex and hence the existence of a quiescent region. Nonetheless, the larger nuclei in the quiescent region would appear lightly stained in comparison to the smaller nuclei of the anneau initial cells, thus probably accounting for the apparent difference in the density of staining in the nuclei of the anneau initial cells and the cells of the quiescent region (Gifford and Corson 1971)

Higher concentrations of DNA, histones, and total proteins are found in the flanking zone as compared with the apical initials, subapical initials, and pith rib meristem of the vegetative apex in *Cedrus deodara* and *Picea smithiana* (Pillai and Chacko 1978a,b). The subapical initials show the same staining reactions as the apical initials and hence cannot be considered completely quiescent. The accumulation of polysaccharides and lignin-like substances is correlated with crown development. A uniform distribution of DNA, total proteins, and histones was observed in the vegetative apex of *Ephedra foliata,* whereas RNA showed greater concentration in cells of the flanking zone (Pillai et al. 1980b). Paolillo and Gifford (1961) correlated mitotic activity in dividing cells of the apical zone with a particular phase of the plastochron in *Ephedra altissima.*

More than one function seems to be attributed to peroxidase. Van Fleet (1959), Vanden Born (1963), Riding and Gifford (1973), and Pillai et al. (1980b) observed an abundance of this enzyme in the provascular strands (in the transition zone) of the apex. Localization of this enzyme in the peripheral and rib meristem areas of the apex has given rise to the suggestion that peroxidase is a forerunner of cell division. The data of Pillai et al. (1980b), however, fail to support this idea. These authors observed weak staining for peroxidase in the flanking zone where meristematic activity is high. They found indications of high peroxidase activity in mature phloem and developing xylem where divisions are infrequent. Accordingly, they suggested that peroxidase activity in the vascular regions may indicate its involvement in providing continuity between meristematic and mature tissues and may be concerned with the transport of specific metabolites.

The localization of acid phosphatase in the corpus of the vegetative apex and in the mantle cells upon transition to the reproductive phase appears to be associated with differentiation in the shoot apex (Pillai et al 1980b). The distribution of acid phosphatase may be indicative of its association with metabolic processes preceding cell division and accompanying differentiation (Riding and Gifford 1973). Distribution of succinic dehydrogenase shows that the apical and central zones are physiologically active during vegetative apex development (Riding and Gifford 1973).

REPRODUCTIVE APEX

Only a few studies deal with the early transitional stages that lead to the formation of reproductive structures. Studies on *Cupressus arizonica* by Owens and Pharis (1967) are significant in reporting an increase in the mitotic frequency on transition and that the transition involves the entire apex, the subapical mother cells, and cells of the peripheral zone, thus forming a continuous mantle of actively dividing cells. In *Thuja plicata,* developmental stages of cones in response to gibberellin treatment and under natural conditions are essentially similar in anatomical details (Owens and Pharis 1971). Owens and Molder (1977b) demonstrated the involvement of the peripheral zone, the apical zone, and the central mother cell zone in the formation of the mantle layers in the pollen and seed cone apices. In *Picea glauca,* the characteristic cytohistological zonation, i.e. an apical zone, a peripheral zone, and a pith rib meristem is maintained in the apices of male and female strobili (Owens and Molder 1977b). The apex of the female strobilus is larger than that of the male strobilus.

In *Ephedra foliata,* acid phosphatase localized in tunica, corpus, and flank regions in the reproductive apex indicated its involvement in mitotic activity. Peroxidase reached only up to the level of the youngest lateral primordium (Pillai et al. 1980b). The anatomical and histochemical data suggest that the process of changeover to the reproductive phase shows some similarity to that in the angiosperm apex. The enlargement, squaring (change in shape), and establishment of a mantle-core organization of the apex in *Ephedra foliata* (Pillai et al. 1980b), during transition to the reproductive phase is reminiscent of the condition reported in angiosperms. The cited authors questioned whether these changes are related to the establishment of a tunica-corpus organization.

Harrison and Owens (1983) observed indistinct zonation in the apices of male and female strobili, unlike the distinct zonation in the vegetative apex. Apices of female strobili are not totally utilized whereas apices of male strobili are completely utilized during microsporophyll initiation. Buds of male strobili developed almost exclusively from previously undifferentiated axillary apices. Female strobili usually develop from terminal buds during years of low tree productivity and also from axillary buds during high productivity years.

The limited information available seems to indicate the involvement of the entire apex in the formation of the female and male strobili, though the female strobili resemble the vegetative apex more than the male.

GENERAL DISCUSSION

The trends of specialization in the gymnospermous shoot apex leading to the attainment of a tunica-corpus configuration were discussed in previous reviews. The earlier view equating the gymnospermous shoot apex to a naked corpus faced strong criticism. Data favor considering the gymnosperms as having an incipient tunica, which has attained the angiosperm level in a few genera, including *Agathis*, *Araucaria*, *Gnetum*, and *Ephedra*.

The specialization trends have been traced with reference to the superficial zone of initiation, the subapical initials, the peripheral zone, and the pith meristem. Pillai et al. (1972) and Pillai and Pillai (1976) traced the course of establishment of a tunica in gymnosperms from cycads, *Ginkgo*, and Pinaceae members having a superficial zone of initiation: through *Callitris*, *Podocarpus*, etc., in which periclinal divisions are restricted to the upper flanks of the surface layer: and *Cupressus* and *Thuja*, in which periclines in the surface layer are eliminated except for a few cells near the vertex of the apical dome; to *Agathis*, *Araucaria*, and *Ephedra*, etc., in which a true tunica is realized. Reduction in size of the subapical initials is another trend. This trend culminates in the *Ephedra* apex, in which only a few cells represent this zone. Fluctuations occur in the size of the zone within the same species, depending upon the growth phase and the type of shoot.

Many investigations indicate fluctuations in the number of meristematic cells giving rise to the pith. On the basis of data on both gymnosperms and angiosperms, Pillai and Pillai (1976) suggested use of the term *pith meristem* in place of *pith rib meristem* and/or *pith mother cells*. This zone can present the appearance of a rib meristem or a small group of pith mother cells, depending on the type of shoot, season, and growth phase; e.g. Riding (1972) observed no evidence of a pith rib meristem in dormant embryos of *Pinus radiata*.

The adaptive significance of a tunica-corpus organization in meristems is unknown. According to Klekowski et al. (1985), mathematical modeling and computer simulation studies have shown that such stratified meristems promote the long-term retention of somatic mutations of positive, neutral, and negative value primarily as periclinal chimeras. In stratified apices, developmental selection deletes weak genotypes without loss of reproductive capacity (Klekowski 1988).

Histochemical and cytophotometric studies (Cecich et al. 1972) indicate that the subapical initials or the central mother cell zone is mitotically active, although to a lesser degree than the peripheral zone. Cells in the apical portion of the meristem are metabolically active during vegetative growth, and all regions are involved in the determination of vegetative form (Fosket and Miksche 1966; Riding and Gifford 1973; Pillai et al. 1980b). The results do not generally support the méristème d'attente theory of apical organization (Buvat 1955), which holds that the cells in the distal portion of the shoot (the *méristème d'attente* or *zone apicale*) are essentially devoid of cell divisions during the vegetative phase (Camefort 1956). There are many instances of nonzonate distribution for total proteins, and some show nonzonate patterns for distribution of DNA and histones as well. The majority show a zonate pattern for RNA, although not at all stages of growth. Succinic dehydrogenase localization indicating high respiratory activity has been reported throughout the vegetative apex, including the apical initials and portions of the central zone. Succinic dehydrogenase activity may decrease in the apical initials and central mother cell zone one day after irradiation by X-rays (Fosket and Miksche 1966). Moreover, the lack of a high concentration of any particular substance in any region of the apex cannot be taken as evidence for that region's totally passive nature. The central axially located cells, positionally equivalent to the *méristème d'attente* of the French school, are metabolically and mitotically active, and their contribution to vegetative growth is by no means negligible.

Cytohistological zonation could be correlated with biochemical differences between zones, and herein comes the role of enzymatic systems and their complementary location in the shoot apex. The immature embryonic apex of *Picea abies* shows zonation. In *Pinus,* many species have a nonzonate embryonic apex and zonation is established in different species at different stages of growth. Therefore, zonation does not seem to be necessary for the formation and growth of lateral organs.

At this point it may be pertinent to recall the suggestion of Pillai (1985), with reference to the presence of a less meristermatic central mother-cell zone in the angiosperm shoot apex, that zonation depends on the relative size and/or volume of the shoot apical meristem and the leaf primordium at a particular stage. Computation of the volume of shoot-apex dome and leaf primordium is used to suggest an additional factor influencing the development of zonation in the shoot apex of seed plants (Pillai and Pillai 1989).

In a few angiosperm species, Goyal (1984) calculated the volumes of the apical dome and the youngest leaf primordium by using serial sections. His basic assumption was that cells are contributed to the peripheral zone by the central mother cell zone. In plants with small apices, a sizeable proportion of the apical volume is used up in leaf-primordium formation and hence must be regenerated at every plastochron. In such cases all cells of the apical meristem are mitotically active; consequently, a semiquiescent central mother-cell zone is absent. On the other hand, when the ratio of shoot apex volume to leaf-primordial volume is higher, the tissues used up during leaf-primordium initiation can be easily replaced by a few infrequent divisions in the central mother-cell zone, followed by further divisions in the peripheral zone. This suggestion no doubt is a simplistic one and should be verified through mathematical analysis of data from a wide variety of species. At the same time, more precise and rigorous methods should be evolved to measure apices in various stages of development. Still, one should not forget that the shoot apex is a system of cells that slowly migrates, relative to the vertex, through integrated and interrelated zones. The collective activities of the cells in these zones account for morphogenesis. Hejnowicz and Romberger (1986) have proposed the theoretical concept of a cell division tensor. The suggested methods allow calculation of the relative rates of cell division at specific sites and within specific orientation classes, as well as division rates irrespective of orientation. Given the conflicting views regarding the relative mitotic activities in the distal and more basal regions of the shoot apical dome, this provides a theoretical rationale and method of calculating patterns of distribution rates and divisions in the apex. Such quantitative studies, though laborious, are feasible.

LITERATURE CITED

Buvat, R. 1955. La méristème apical de la tige. *Ann. Biol.* 31:596–656.

_____. 1989. *Ontolgeny, Cell Differentiation, and Structure of Vascular Plants.* Berlin: Springer-Verlag.

Camefort, H. 1956. Étude de la structure du point vegetatif et des variations phyllotaxiques chez quelques Gymnospermes. *Ann. Sci. Nat. Bot.* 17:1–185.

Cecich, R. A., N. R. Lersten, and J. P. Miksche. 1972. A cytophotometric study of nucleic acid and proteins in the shoot apex of white spruce. *Am. J. Bot.* 59:442–449.

Chacko, B., B. D. Deshpande, and S. K. Pillai. 1976. Shoot apical organization and leaf histogenesis in *Cycas circinalis*. *New Bot.* 3:1–5.

Curtis, J. D. and R. A. Popham. 1972. The developmental anatomy of long-branch terminal buds of *Pinus banksiana*. *Am. J. Bot.* 59:194–202.

Fahn, A. 1990. *Plant Anatomy.* 4th ed. Oxford: Pergamon.

Fosket, D. E., and J. P. Miksche. 1966. A histochemical study of the seedling shoot apical meristem of *Pinus banksiana*. *Am. J. Bot.* 53:694–702.

Foster, A. S. 1939. Structure and growth of the shoot apex of *Cycas revoluta*. *Am. J. Bot.* 26:372–385.

_____. 1940. Further studies on zonal structure and growth of the shoot apex of *Cycas revoluta* Thunb. *Am. J. Bot.* 27:487–501.

_____. 1941. Zonal structure of the shoot apex of *Dioon edule* Lindl. *Am. J. Bot.* 28:557–564.

Gabilo, E. M., and H. L. Mogensen. 1973. Foliar initiation and fate of dwarf shoot apex in *Pinus monophylla*. *Am. J. Bot.* 60:671–677.

Gifford, E. M. Jr., and G. E. Corson, Jr. 1971. The shoot apex in seed plants. *Bot. Rev.* 37:143–229.

Goyal, V. 1984. *Anatomical and Histochemical Studies on Apical Meristems.* Ph.D. Thesis University of Rajasthan, Jaipur.

Gregory, R. A., and J. A. Romberger. 1972a. The shoot apical ontogeny of the *Picea abies* seedling. I. Anatomy, apical dome diameter, and plastochron duration. *Am. J. Bot.* 59:587–597.

_____. 1972b. The shoot apical ontogeny of the *Picea abies* seedling. II. Growth rates. *Am. J. Bot.* 59:598–606.

_____. 1977. The shoot apical ontogeny of the *Picea abies* seedling. IV. Protoxylem initiation and age of internodes. *Am. J. Bot.* 64:631–634.

Hanawa, J. 1967. Growth and development in the shoot apex of *Pinus densiflora*. II. Ontogeny of the dwarf shoot and the lateral branch. *Bot. Mag. Tokyo* 80:248–255.

Harrison, D. L. S., and J. N. Owens. 1983. Bud development in *Picea engelmannii*. I. Vegetative bud development, differentiation and early development of reproductive buds. *Can. J. Bot.* 61:2291–2301.

Hejnowicz, Z., and J. A. Romberger. 1986. Calculation of rates of cell division in shoot meristem with reference to the growth tensor. *J. Theor. Biol.* 121:59–71.

Hu, Y. S., and F. H. Wang. 1984. Anatomical studies on *Cathaya* (Pinaceae). *Am. J. Bot.* 71:727–735.

Johnson, M. A. 1951. The shoot apex in gymnosperms. *Phytomorphology* 1:188–204.

Klekowski, E. J. Jr. 1988. *Mutation, Developmental Selection and Plant Evolution.* New York:Columbia Univ.

Klekowski, E. J. Jr., N. Kazarinova-Fukshansky, and H. Mohr. 1985. Shoot apical meristems and mutations: Stratified meristems and angiosperm evolution. *Am. J. Bot.* 72:1788–1800.

Owens, J. N., and M. Molder. 1977a. Bud development in *Picea glauca*. II. Cone differentiation and early development. *Can. J. Bot.* 55:2746–2760.

———. 1977b. Vegetative bud development and cone differentiation in *Abies amabilis*. *Can. J. Bot.* 55:992–1008.

Owens, J. N., M. Molder, and H. Langer. 1977. Bud development in *Picea glauca*. I. Annual growth cycle of vegetative buds and shoot elongation as they relate to date and temperature. *Can. J. Bot.* 55:2728–2745.

Owens, J. N., and R. P. Pharis. 1967. Initiation and ontogeny of the micro-sporangiate cone in *Cupressus arizonica* in response to gibberellin. *Am. J. Bot.* 54:1260–1272.

———. 1971. Initiation and development of western red cedar cones in response to gibberellin induction and under natural conditions. *Can. J. Bot.* 49:1165–1175.

Owston, P. W. 1969. The shoot apex in eastern white pine: Its structure, seasonal development and variation within the crown. *Can. J. Bot.* 47:1181–1188

Paolillo, D. J. Jr., and E. M. Gifford, Jr. 1961. Plastochronic changes and the concept of apical initials in *Ephedra altissima*. *Am. J. Bot.* 48:8–16.

Pillai, A. 1963. Shoot apex in some Cupressaceae. *Phyton* (Horn. Austria) 10:261–271.

Pillai, A. 1985. Zonation in the angiosperm shoot apex. In *Trends in Plant Research*. Ed. C. M. Govil. Meerut, India: Sarita Prakashan. 99–105.

Pillai, A., and S. K. Pillai. 1974. Shoot apical organization in some gymnosperms. *Phytomorphology* 24:68–74.

Pillai, S. K. 1963. Structure and seasonal study of the shoot apex of some *Cupressus* species. *New Phytol.* 62:335–341.

Pillai, S. K., and B. Chacko. 1978a. Anatomical and histochemical studies of the shoot apex of *Cedrus deodara*. *Phytomorphology* 29:275–283.

———. 1978b. Growth periodicity and structure of the shoot apex of *Picea smithiana* (Wall) Boiss.: An anatomical and histochemical study. *Flora* 167:515–524.

Pillai, S. K., B. Chacko, M. B. Bande, and R. Divakaran. 1972. The shoot apex in gymnosperms: Trends of specialization. In *Biology of the Land Plants*. Ed. V. Puri et al. Meerut, India: Sarita Prakashan. 44–56.

Pillai, S. K., and A. Pillai. 1976. Apical meristems in gymnosperms. In *Aspects of Plant Sciences* Ed. P. K. K. Nair. New Delhi, India: Today & Tomorrow. 157–200.

———. 1989. The shoot apex in seed plants. In *Plant Science Research in India*. Ed. M. L. Trivedi, B. S. Gill, & S. S. Saini. New Delhi, India: Today & Tomorrow. 691–695.

Pillai, S. K., A. Pillai, and B. Chacko. 1980a. Shoot apex organization in some *Pinus* species of Western Himalayas. *Phytomorphology* 30: 1–5.

———. 1980b. Anatomical and histochemical aspects of the transition of vegetative shoot apex to reproductive of *Ephedra foliata*. *Flora* 170:340–350.

Popham, R. A. 1951. Principal types of vegetative shoot apex organization in vascular plants. *Ohio J. Sci.* 51:249–270.

Quinn, C. J., and P. A. Gadek. 1988. Sequence of xylem differentiation in leaves of Cupressaceae. *Am. J. Bot.* 75:1344–1351.

Riding, R. T. 1972. Early ontogeny of seedlings of *Pinus radiata*. *Can. J. Bot.* 50:2381–2387.

———. 1974. Shoot apex of seedlings of *Pinus banksiana* and *Pinus resinosa*. *Am. J. Bot.* 61:61 (Meet. Abstr.)

Riding, R. T., and E. M. Gifford Jr. 1973. Histochemical changes occurring at the seedling shoot apex of *Pinus radiata*. *Can. J. Bot.* 51:501–512.

Riding, R. T., and A. MacLean. 1974. Short shoot apex of vegetative and mature trees of *Pinus resinosa*. *Am. J. Bot.* 61:61 (Meet. Abstr.)

Romberger, J. A., and R. A. Gregory. 1977. The shoot apical ontogeny of the *Picea abies* seedling. III. Some age-related aspects of morphogenesis. *Am. J. Bot.* 64:622–630.

Sacher, J. A. 1954. Structure and seasonal activity of the shoot apices of *Pinus lambertiana* and *Pinus ponderosa*. *Am. J. Bot.* 41:749–759.

Singh, H. 1961. Seasonal variations in the shoot apex of *Cephalotaxus drupacea*. *Phytomorphology* 11:146–153.

Tepper, H. B. 1964. Ontogeny of the shoot apex of seedlings of *Pinus ponderosa*. *Am. J. Bot.* 51:859–865.

_____. 1966. Comparative study of the long shoot apex in the genus *Pinus*. *Phytomorphology* 16:469–474.

Tompsett, P. B. 1978. Studies of growth and flowering in *Picea sitchensis* (Bong) Carr. II. Initiation and development of male, female and vegetative buds. *Ann. Bot.* 42:889–900.

Vanden Born, W. M. 1963. Histochemical studies on enzyme distribution in shoot tips of white spruce *(Picea glauca)*. *Can. J. Bot.* 41:1509–1527.

Van Fleet, D. S. 1959. Analysis of the histochemical localisation of peroxidase related to the differentiation of plant tissues. *Can. J. Bot.* 37:449–458.

Venkataratnam, K., B. Chacko, B. D. Deshpande, and S. K. Pillai. 1975. Anatomy of the mature embryo and seedling of *Picea smithiana* (Wall) Boiss. *Proc. Indian Acad. Sci.* 81B:101–110.

Chapter 5

The Influence of Light
on Leaf Development

N. G. DENGLER

The flowering plants are characterized by a striking diversity of leaf size and form. The genetic component of this diversity has yielded characteristics that are taxonomically useful at the level of species, and may additionally characterize taxa at genus, family, and higher levels. Such taxonomic variation in leaf morphology and anatomy is a reflection of the interaction between phylogenetic constraints and adaptation for a specific environment (Givnish 1987). Differences among species in effective leaf size (width of the leaf blade or its lobes or leaflets), leaf shape, orientation, thickness, pubescence, anatomy, and longevity have been shown to be related to habitat and to be significant for photosynthetic gas exchange (Givnish 1987). In addition, intraspecific genetic variation in these leaf characteristics typifies some species. For example, Björkman and Holmgren (1963) demonstrated that populations of *Solidago virgaurea* from shaded and exposed habitats showed heritable differences in photosynthetic rates and that these differences were related to leaf structural characters influencing resistance to CO_2 conductance.

Most studies concerned with the relationship among leaf morphology, anatomy, and photosynthetic rates have found, however, that variation in structural and biochemical characteristics between individual populations are *not* maintained under uniform environmental conditions; rather these are plastic responses of the genotype to environmental variability (Boardman 1977; Patterson 1980a). Because of the sessile nature of established plants, there is a need for individuals to accommodate continually to a varying environment. Plants do this through a modular pattern of growth in which development of semi-independent units reflects ambient conditions, and coordination among modules may occur primarily by competition for resources (Trewavas 1986). Three major "strategies" employed by plant species to cope with this environmental variation have been identified (Grime 1979, 1981); in two of these—stress-avoidance and stress-tolerance—plasticity is expressed primarily during vegetative growth. The competitive, stress-avoiding strategy is typical of many herbaceous,

From *Growth Patterns
in Vascular Plants*
Edited by Muhammed Iqbal

100

shrub, and tree species of stable productive habitats. Here, success depends on the ability to sustain high rates of photosynthesis and mineral nutrient uptake in a continually changing environment. Plant species employing this strategy show the greatest morphological plasticity and more rapid turnover of modular parts (Grime et al. 1986). Species that are stress-tolerant occupy habitats of low productivity and limited resources. Leaves and other organs of such species are long-lived and exhibit less plasticity in size and shape. The degree of plasticity shown by any plant population is regarded as under genetic control and is, in itself, an important adaptive characteristic (Bradshaw 1965; Schlichting 1986).

Plant growth is affected by environmental variation in light, temperature, water availability, minerals, and other factors. Extreme variation in any of these factors may lead to stress. Shade is one of the most common forms of stress, and thus light conditions are an important determinant of phenotypic plasticity (Grime 1981; Trewavas 1986). Differences in morphology and anatomy of "sun" and "shade" leaves from exposed and shaded portions of the canopy of the same individual are good examples of such plasticity and have been observed and documented over many years (Hanson 1917; Büsgen and Münch 1926; Haberlandt 1914; Penfound 1931; Wylie 1951). More recent experimental studies of the relationship between the light environment and developmental plasticity have focused primarily on the responses of shade-avoiding competitor species (e.g. Longstreth et al. 1985). Shade-tolerant species express less developmental plasticity, but are more likely to show post-developmental cytological and biochemical changes (Grime et al. 1986). These reversible physiological changes, termed *acclimation* (Björkman 1981a; Trewavas 1986), are an important aspect of plasticity.

This chapter first describes four processes associated with leaf development: initiation, morphogenesis, expansion, and histogenesis. It then considers variation in three aspects of the light environment that are known to affect plant growth: irradiance, spectral composition, and photoperiod. Next, it discusses the effect of these light properties on the rate of leaf production, leaf form, leaf size, and leaf anatomy. Finally, it explores the relationship between the degree of plasticity and the timing of developmental events.

PATTERNS OF LEAF DEVELOPMENT

Many investigations of the effects of the light environment on plant growth report characteristics of mature leaves after a period of growth under an experimental treatment. This section relates the processes of leaf development to the characteristics of mature leaves most frequently described in these studies: leaf number (initiation), leaf shape (morphogenesis), leaf size (expansion), and leaf anatomy (histogenesis). Although these processes are considered individually, there is extensive temporal overlap among them, and leaf development as a whole is a continuous, integrated process from initiation to senescence and abscission.

The underlying physiological mechanisms that control "normal" patterns of leaf development—and how these might be altered by the environmental stimuli—are still poorly understood (Dale 1986). Some studies have recognized that the factors controlling wall extensibility are clearly important in the regulation of leaf initiation and expansion, and differences in wall extension characteristics between a shade-avoiding species (*Betula pendula*) and a shade-tolerating species (*Acer pseudoplatanus*) have been demonstrated (Taylor and Davies 1985). Most developmental studies, however, have emphasized the patterns of cell division and cell enlargement that give rise to mature leaves of a certain size, shape, and anatomy. A review of this work should stress that the *control* of leaf size and shape operates at the level of the whole organ, not at the level of individual cells. Analysis of periclinal chimeras, for instance, demonstrates that the regulation of overall leaf size and form is independent of the specific pattern of cell growth (Dale 1986). The balance between the processes of cell division and cell enlargement, however, is important for yielding the distinctive cell numbers, sizes, and shapes of different tissue types within mature leaves.

A source of within-individual variation that affects leaf development in all flowering plants is *heteroblasty* (Allsopp 1967). In some species, changes in leaf form and size at successive levels of insertion are conspicuous; in others, heteroblastic changes are more subtle. Most species show heteroblastic variation in leaf initiation rate, rate of leaf expansion, mature leaf area, blade thickness and dry weight, cell number per layer, sizes of epidermal cells, volume of intercellular space, and stomatal and trichome density (Sasahara 1982; Dale and Milthorpe 1983; Tichá 1985). All these characteristics are subject to developmental plasticity as well, and caution should be used in interpreting changes induced by environmental factors without understanding their interaction with heteroblastic variation.

Development in Dicot Leaves

INITIATION

Leaves are formed on the flanks of the vegetative shoot apical meristem. The time interval between the initiation of successive leaves is a *plastochron*. The site of leaf initiation is determined by the phyllotactic system (Williams 1975), thus making it possible to predict the location of the next leaf primordium. Careful analysis of the pattern of cell division in the shoot apex of *Pisum sativum* showed that the rate of cell division at the site of leaf initiation is only slightly elevated over that of other parts of the apical meristem flank during the plastochron prior to the formation of a surface bump (Lyndon 1976, 1983). A significant change in the orientation of cell divisions, involving an increase in the proportion of periclinal divisions in the second tunica layer and underlying corpus layers, is the more important event for leaf initiation (Lyndon 1983, 1990). These divisions, and accompanying cell enlargement, form a surface protrusion on the shoot apex, the *leaf primordium*. Even before this stage, reorientation of cellulose microfibrils in epidermal cell walls may represent a "relaxation" of physical constraints, thus permitting the surface bulge (Green 1986).

A new leaf primordium becomes delimited from the shoot apical meristem by the presence of a zone of reduced growth that forms the leaf axil. In many dicotyledons the zone of leaf initiation does not have a broad tangential extent, and the new primordium takes the form of a peg-like projection that typically is flat on the adaxial side and convex on the abaxial side (Figures 5.1.A, 5.2). In species with an encircling leaf base such as *Magnolia grandifolia*, the zone of leaf initiation extends from the original site to form a low ridge around the apex (Postek and Tucker 1982). Therefore, the pattern of leaf initiation itself plays a role in the genesis of leaf form.

MORPHOGENESIS

Lamina formation usually occurs within the first 1–3 plastochrons of leaf development. While the enlarging ground meristem cells of a leaf primordium gradually become vacuolate, cells at the margins remain small and stain densely

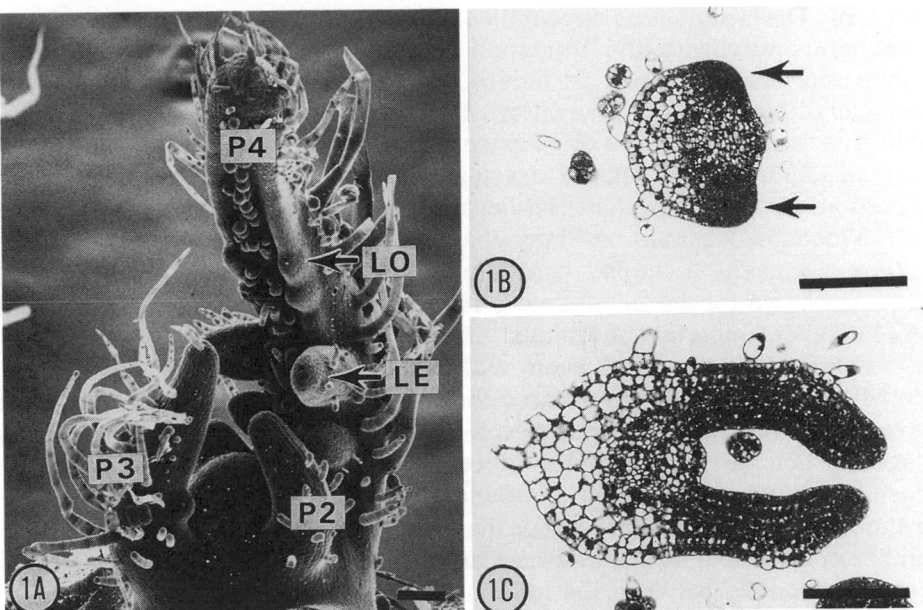

Figure 5.1. Developing leaves of *Lycopersicon esculentum*. (A) Scanning electron micrograph of the shoot apex showing leaf primordia in the second (P2), third (P3), and fourth (P4) plastochrons. Note lateral leaflet primordium (LE) and incipient lobe (LO) on margin of terminal leaflet. (B) Cross section of the terminal leaflet of a P2 leaf primordium prior to lamina formation. *Arrows,* location of marginal meristems. (C) Cross section of a terminal leaflet of a P4 leaf primordium after lamina initiation; scale = 100 μm (from Dengler 1980).

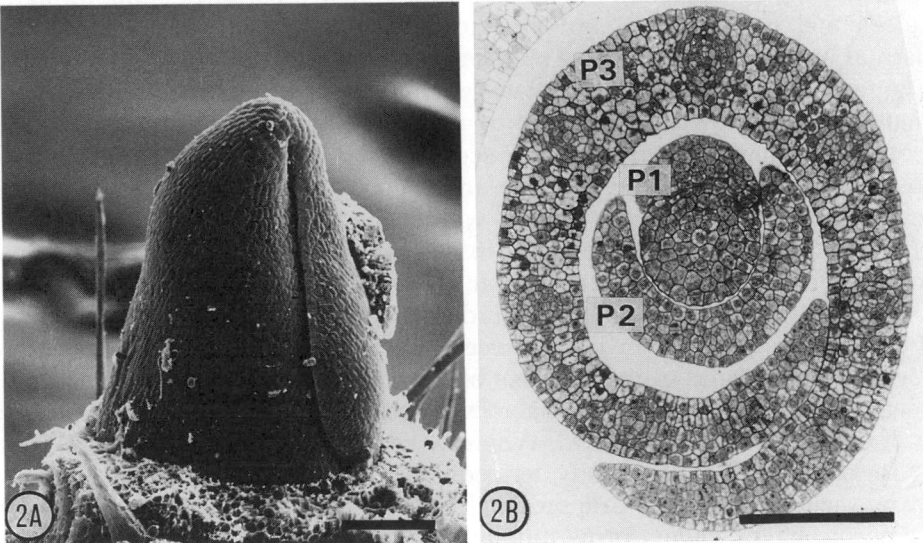

Figure 5.2. Developing leaves of *Arundinella hirsuta*. (A) Scanning electron micrograph of a leaf at a P3 stage. (B) Cross section of shoot apex with P1, P2, and P3 leaf primordia; scale = 100 μm.

(Figure 5.1.B). The histological appearance of these marginal meristematic regions is associated temporally with the formation of a rudimentary lamina (Figure 5.1.C). Although a morphogenetic role in lamina formation frequently is attributed to the marginal strip of meristematic tissue (Esau 1965), a number of investigations have indicated that this zone is not a site of elevated mitotic activity and have raised questions regarding its importance in lamina development. For instance, Poethig and Sussex (1985b) used an analysis of mutant cell lineages induced by X-irradiation in developing leaves of *Nicotiana tabacum* to show that most marginal sectors are restricted in extent, thus suggesting a limited contribution to lamina formation by the marginal meristem. As shown for the initial emergence of a leaf primordium from the flanks of an apex, however, important morphogenetic changes in shape can be achieved by a change in the *direction* of cell division, with little associated change in the rate.

Merrill (1986b) has also emphasized that the marginal strip of meristematic tissue may have a significant function during the *initiation* of the lamina and not during the later stages of lamina expansion. His investigation of *Fraxinus pennsylvanica* identified a histologically defined region of ground meristem within a 3 to 5 cell width of the margin that has a higher mitotic index than adjacent protoderm or procambial cells. The number of cells in this zone increases at the time of lamina formation. The distinction in mitotic activity between the marginal strip of cells and the proximal tissue is subsequently dampened, and the leaf primordium becomes more uniformly meristematic (Dubuc-Lebreux and Sattler 1980; Jeune 1984). A second important role for the marginal meristem is the determination of the basic number of cell layers within the extending lamina through characteristic planes of division. This aspect of marginal meristem activity was recognized by early observers of leaf development and is an important part of leaf histogenesis (Esau 1965; Maksymowych 1973).

The meristematic appearance of cells at the primordium apex also suggests a period of apical growth (Esau 1965). The plane of division in these cells is probably important in establishing the longitudinal axis of early primordium growth, and subsequent extension in primordium length is likely to be diffuse. The vacuolation of both marginal and apical cells does suggest reduced meristematic activity, although it does not indicate complete cessation of cell division. Similarly, early trichome formation on leaf apices and margins does not preclude division and expansion of intervening protodermal and underlying ground meristem cells.

Changes in leaf shape are initiated during these early morphogenetic stages. Hageman (1973) has used the concept of *meristem fractionation*, in which localized zones of meristematic activity become separated by regions of vacuolated cells, to describe the mechanism giving rise to lamina lobes and leaflets. For example, the mitotic index of incipient leaf lobes within the lamina margin of *Tropaeolum peregrinum* is significantly higher than in adjacent regions; after lobe initiation, the mitotic index becomes uniform throughout the lamina (Fuchs 1975). Jeune (1984) has emphasized, however, that leaflet primordia in some species having pinnately compound leaves are produced in close succession from "generative centers" located at distal or proximal regions of the incipient blade. In this model, the shape changes associated with leaflet formation can be recognized in a uniformly meristematic zone before "fractionation" takes place. Whereas the lobes of leaves (and leaflets) are usually formed as part of an already defined lamina margin, leaflets are usually formed directly on the axis of the leaf primordium (Figure 5.1.A). Leaflet primordia and whole-leaf primordia have similar forms initially and then undergo the same processes of lamina formation (Dengler 1984; Merrill 1986a). In compound leaves, the pattern of lamina initiation is identical to that of simple leaves, but the timing is delayed (Dengler 1984; Merrill 1986a).

This delimitation of leaf-blade shape typically occurs early in leaf development, during the first 4–5 plastochrons while the leaf is still enclosed in the bud. At this stage, the short, adaxially flattened petiole region can be distinguished by an absence of laminar growth. In some species, localized, periclinal divisions, referred to as an *adaxial meristem*, contribute to growth in thickness of the petiole and future midrib (Esau 1965). In leaves in which the leaf-base zone gives rise to stipules, the stipules develop simultaneously with blade formation (e.g. Postek and Tucker 1982). Although many aspects of leaf shape are determined within the bud, leaf shape may be significantly altered during the phase of leaf expansion. This is particularly true if expansion in different dimensions is not equivalent: for instance, initial shape differences between compound- and simple-leaved *Lycopersicon* mutants are amplified by differing allometric relationsips between growth in length and width (Dengler 1984).

EXPANSION

Exponential growth of the leaf (as measured by length, width, area, volume, and thickness) begins while the leaf is still enclosed in the bud (Williams 1975; Poethig and Sussex 1985a). Most observers have measured leaf expansion after the stage of unfolding from the bud; however, destructive sampling allows a complete time course of development from initiation to completion of expansion (Figure 5.3). Growth rates are not uniform over the surface of the leaf. Poethig and Sussex (1985a) followed expansion of the leaf blade of *Nicotiana tabacum* by marking a leaf with India ink and photographing the leaf on successive days. They showed that the relative rate of area growth in the distal region of the leaf almost ceases before peak rates are achieved near the leaf base. Similar heterogeneity of surface growth has been shown for *Xanthium strumarium* and *Vitis vinifera* (Silk 1983).

After the early establishment of leaf form by localized meristematic activity, the pattern of cell division within the immature leaf becomes more diffuse. These divisions and accompanying cell enlargement extend the area of the lamina and are referred to as *plate meristem activity* (Esau 1965). The orientation of divisions within the plate meristem is primarily anticlinal, thus maintaining the continuity of the cell

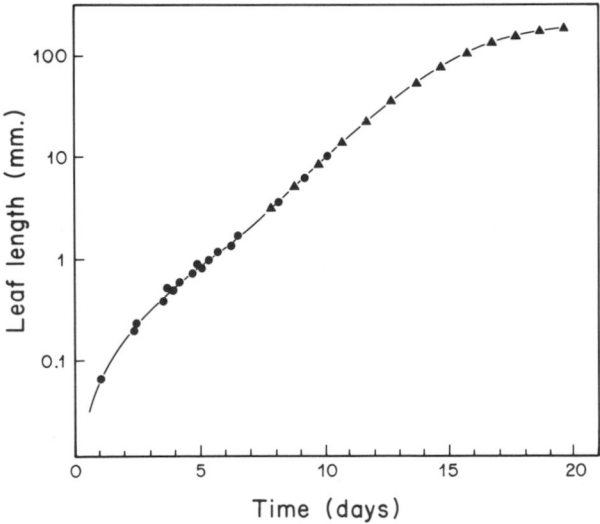

Figure 5.3. Increase in leaf length with time in *Nicotiana tabaccum. Circles,* lengths of leaf primordia dissected from bud; *triangles,* successive measurements of a single leaf (from Poethig and Sussex 1985a).

layers established by the marginal meristem within the leaf blade. Cell division within the plate meristem continues throughout much of the period of lamina extension. In *Helianthus annuus* and *Lupinus albus* (Sunderland 1960), *Trifolium repens* (Denne 1966), and *Fagus grandifolia* (Dengler et al. 1975), cell division does not cease until the leaf reaches 50% or more of its final area. Considerable spatial variation in cell division also occurs during leaf expansion. For example, in *Nicotiana tabacum*, mitotic index is highest in the distal third of the leaf when the leaf is about 10% of its final length; by the time the leaf reaches 20% of final length, cell division has ceased near the leaf apex (Poethig and Sussex 1985a). The general pattern of cessation of cell division is basipetal, although differences in the duration of cell division occur among tissues within the leaf. Cell division continues longest in the palisade layer and usually ceases first in the upper epidermis (Maksymowych 1963; Denne 1966; Dengler et al. 1975; Coleman and Greyson 1976). In all tissues, the proportion of cells dividing gradually decreases as the leaf expands (Dale 1976; Dale and Milthorpe 1983), but no one has succeeded yet in identifying the populations of dividing cells and concurrent changes in cell-cycle times.

In some species, cell divisions may occur at such a rate that a net decrease in cell size may occur, particularly in the palisade layer (Maksymowych 1963; Dengler et al. 1975). More generally, cell enlargement keeps pace with cell division, and, as the rate of cell division gradually decreases, mean cell size in all cell layers increases. There is considerable overlap during leaf extension between the periods of cell enlargement and the increase in cell number (Figure 5.4). The pattern of cell enlargement shows a basipetal trend similar to that seen for cell division (Isebrands and Larson 1973; Maksymowych 1973; Sanchez-Burgos and Dengler 1988).

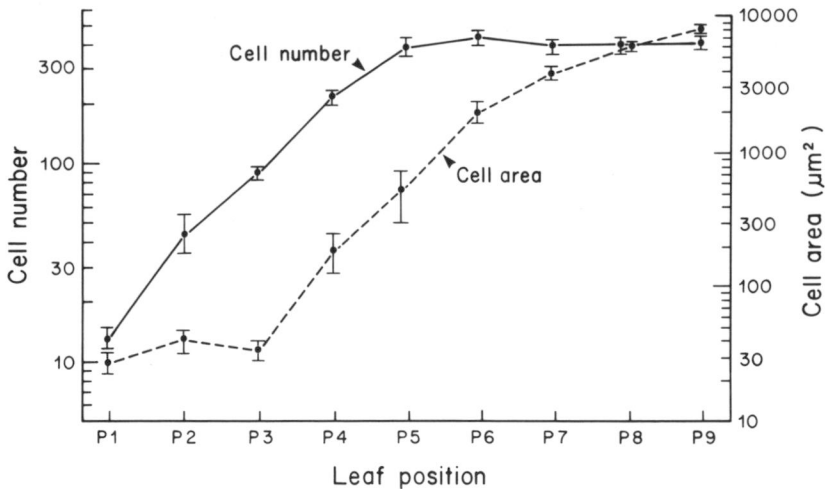

Figure 5.4. Changes in number and area of adaxial epidermis cells during development of the foliage leaves of *Pentadenia orientandina* (from Sanchez-Burgos and Dengler 1988).

HISTOGENESIS

Differences in cell size, degree of vacuolation, and plane of division between the ground meristem and protoderm are present from leaf inception (Coleman and Greyson 1976; Merrill 1986a). Leaf trace procambium, differentiating acropetally within the stem, enters the leaf primordium early, usually during the first plastochron (Coleman and Greyson 1976; Isebrands and Larson 1980). As lamina formation begins, secondary vein procambium differentiates in a continuous acropetal pattern toward the margin.

During expansion of the lamina by plate meristem activity, minor vein procambium becomes delimited within the middle layers of ground tissue by altered planes of division and cell expansion, starting near the apex and moving basipetally (Isebrands and Larson 1973; Coleman and Greyson 1976). New areoles are formed by extension of the procambium across zones of ground meristem cells. Apparently, freely ending veinlets are formed where preexisting procambium is of a substantially different developmental stage (Lersten 1965). Phloem differentiation within major veins is typically continuous and acropetal, whereas xylem differentiation is initially discontinuous, appearing first within the leaf base and differentiating basipetally and acropetally. Differentiation of minor vein xylem and phloem begins at the leaf apex and progresses basipetally (Lersten 1965; Isebrands and Larson 1973; Coleman and Greyson 1976).

Differentiation of mesophyll tissues is concurrent with that of the vascular tissues. From initially homogeneous ground meristem cells, palisade and spongy parenchyma become distinguished by differing patterns of cell expansion (Figures 5.5.A–D, 5.6.A). Palisade parenchyma cells elongate in the vertical plane, whereas spongy parenchyma expansion is usually greater in the horizontal plane (Denne 1966; Maksymowych 1973; Dengler et al. 1975). The timing of intercellular space formation is closely correlated with that of cell enlargement within both palisade and spongy parenchyma tissue (Figure 5.6.A,B) (Dengler et al. 1975; Nyman and Dengler 1978). Intercellular space formation usually begins first in the spongy mesophyll and reaches a greater final volume in this tissue (Isebrands and Larson 1973; Dengler et al. 1975; Dengler 1980).

As cells of the leaf epidermis grow in volume, the greatest axis of expansion is in the horizontal plane (Maksymowych 1973). In some species, no differences in the patterns of cell division and enlargement between the upper and lower epidermis are detected; in others, the upper epidermis shows earlier and/or greater increase in cell diameter (Dengler et al. 1975; Nyman and Dengler 1978; Dengler 1980). Stomata

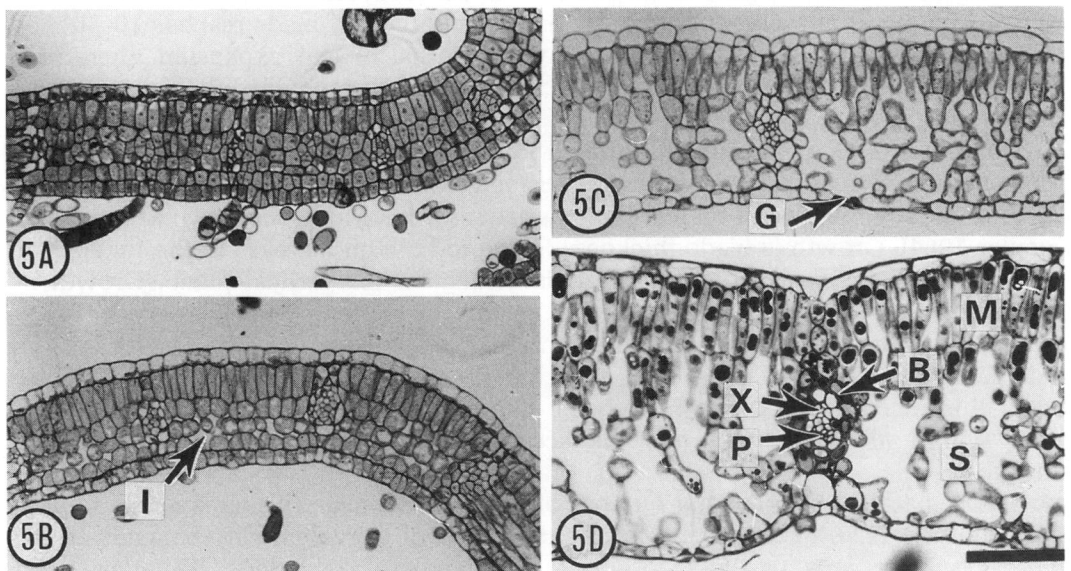

Figure 5.5. Cross sections of leaves expanding from winter buds in *Fagus grandifolia*. (A) Seven days after bud swelling; (B) 14 days; (C) 21 days; (D) 42 days (mature leaf). Note palisade (M) and spongy (S) mesophyll, formation of intercellular space (I) and stomata (G), differentiation of minor vein xylem (X), phloem (P), and sclerenchymatous bundle sheath (B); scale = 50 μm (from Dengler et al. 1975).

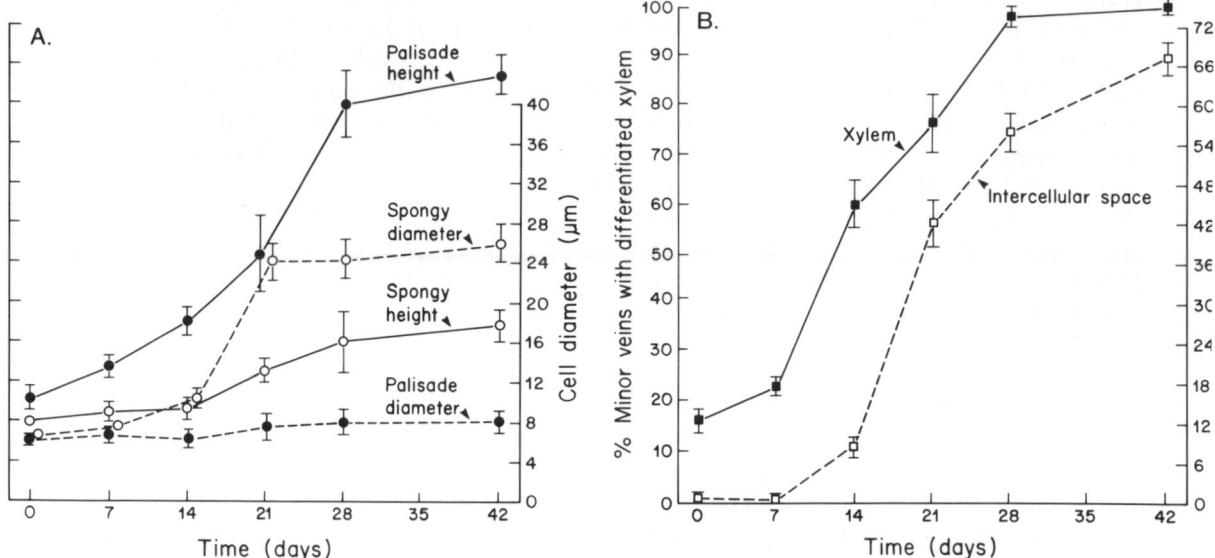

Figure 5.6. Anatomical changes in expanding leaves of *Fagus grandifolia*. (A) Changes in palisade and spongy parenchyma cell height and diameter. (B) Changes in percentage of minor vein length having differentiated xylem tracheary elements and in area of intercellular space in leaf cross sections 100 μm in width (from Dengler et al. 1975).

develop in one or both epidermal layers, first near the leaf apex and then basipetally throughout the leaf blade; usually stomatal initiation coincides with intercellular space formation (Isebrands and Larson 1973; Coleman and Greyson 1976). The formation of stomatal initials is asynchronous and continues until the leaf blade reaches 10–50% of its final area (Tichá 1985). During most of the period of leaf expansion, there is a decrease in stomatal density as other epidermal cells divide and expand (Dengler 1980; Tichá 1985).

Differentiation of mesophyll tissues is frequently associated with periclinally oriented divisions within the ground meristem, which increase the number of cell layers originally established by marginal meristems (Maksymowych 1973; Mueller and Dengler 1984). Growth in blade thickness is due to both an increase in the number of cell layers within the lamina and cell enlargement in the vertical plane. Growth in blade area and growth in thickness are usually coincident (Maksymowych 1973), although in some species leaf thickness continues to increase after area growth is complete (Dengler 1980). Leaf dry weight also changes after leaf expansion ceases (Dengler 1980); this increase results from both the deposition of primary and secondary cell walls within all leaf tissues and the accumulation of photosynthates within the mesophyll.

During leaf expansion, the number of chloroplasts per cell increases up to 4–5-fold (Whatley 1980; Fagerberg 1984). The mean size of individual chloroplasts and the internal surface area of the chloroplast membranes also increase (Whatley 1980; Fagerberg 1984; Kutik 1985). The biosynthesis of chloroplast proteins and lipids parallel these structural changes (Leech 1985, 1986). Photosynthetic rates increase during leaf expansion, usually reach a maximum *before* leaf expansion is complete, and then steadily decrease until leaf senescence (Constable and Rawson 1980; Šesták et al. 1985).

A leaf is initially heterotrophic and imports carbohydrates from older parts of the shoot system through the early differentiated major vein phloem. Gradually, with the formation of stomata, intercellular space, and differentiated mesophyll cells, the import of photosynthate ceases and the export begins (Larson et al. 1980; Dale and Milthorpe 1983; Dale 1985). As a reflection of the spatial pattern of tissue differentiation within the leaf, photosynthesis and carbohydrate export begin first in the apical portion of the leaf blade and then extend basipetally. Therefore, the expanding leaf may be a significant source of the carbon required for its own growth (Dale and Milthorpe 1983; Dale 1985). This suggests that leaf development is most strongly influenced by nutrients and other conditions within the shoot while it remains in the bud. During expansion, however, the photosynthetic rates of mature tissues at the leaf apex may influence the cellular processes associated with growth of leaf area and tissue maturation in the proximal portion of the same leaf.

Development in Grass Leaves

INITIATION

Shoot apical meristems are elongate, and leaf primordia are initiated well down on the meristem flanks (Williams 1975). Periclinal divisions, first within the subsurface layer and then within the surface layer, mark the site of initiation (Sharman 1945). The zone of initiating divisions and accompanying cell enlargement extends around the apex, resulting in the protuberance of a crescentic to incomplete ring-shaped primordium (Sharman 1945; Barnard 1964; Williams 1975; Silvy 1982a). Growth of the primordium is most rapid at the site of initiation and establishes the longitudinal axis of leaf growth.

MORPHOGENESIS

The cells at the tip and margins of the primordium soon become vacuolate, and meristematic-appearing cells are restricted to a zone near the primordium base (Barnard 1964). As a result of primarily transverse divisions in this basal zone, files of cells are produced acropetally. Longitudinal cell divisions, leading to an increase in the number of cell-files and the width of the primordial leaf, characterize most grass species examined (Sharman 1945; Silvy 1982a). Growth in width results in overlap of the leaf primordium margins above the level of insertion (Figure 5.2.A,B). Although at first there is no distinction between blade and sheath, a narrow band of small compact cells differentiates, separating the intercalary meristem of the leaf blade from that of the leaf sheath (Barnard 1964; Soper and Mitchell 1956; Silvy 1982a). The ligule arises from the adaxial epidermis at the boundary of blade and sheath.

EXPANSION

Williams (1975) has carried out a detailed quantitative analysis of leaf expansion in Triticum aestivum. Leaves undergo an early period of exponential growth in length while they are tightly enclosed within the sheath of the next oldest leaf. As the leaf blade extends beyond physical contact with the encircling sheath (but still within the encircling blade), its relative rate of extension increases to a maximum and then gradually decreases until extension growth ceases. Williams (1975) suggested that physical constraints on leaf primordia within the bud limit the early growth rate of the leaf, and that the sharp rise in relative growth rate is possible because of the release from this constraint. In Hordeum vulgare, Silvy (1982b) has shown that the maximum relative growth rate of the whole leaf corresponds to the maximum relative growth rate of the blade alone. In this species, rapid sheath extension begins after cessation of blade growth and results in blade emergence (Figure 5.7). If this pattern is characteristic of most grass species, the zone of most active cell division and enlargement within the blade is never exposed to external conditions. Cells exposed to direct light for the first time would have already reached mature size and their differentiation would be little influenced by ambient conditions (Begg and Wright 1962; Dale 1982).

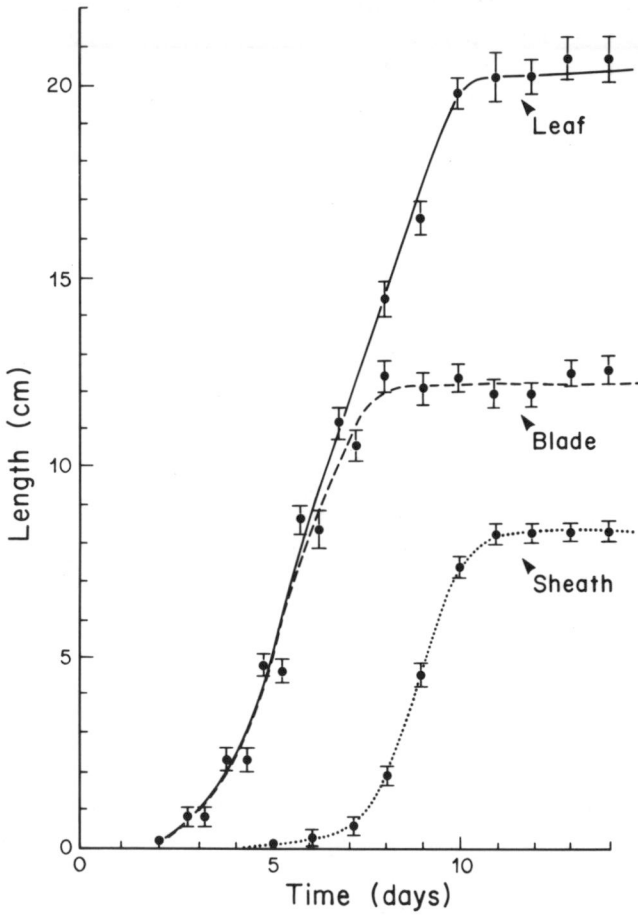

Figure 5.7. Growth in length of blade and sheath of the first leaf of *Hordeum vulgare* (from Silvy 1982b).

HISTOGENESIS

As during the early development of dicot leaves, protoderm and ground meristem can be recognized in grass leaf primordia from inception; procambium is also present during the first one or two plastochrons (Figure 5.2.B) (Barnard 1964). Unlike dicot species, the procambium of the leaf midvein and major lateral veins first appears near the level of leaf insertion in most grass species examined. The procambium then develops basipetally to join stem bundles and acropetally toward the leaf apex (Patrick 1972). As the width of the incipient leaf blade increases, new minor vein procambia are formed in the expanding panels of ground meristem between preexisting veins (Soper and Mitchell 1956; Dengler et al. 1985). In *Triticum*, Patrick (1972) found that differentiation of protophloem and protoxylem follows a discontinuous, bidirectional pattern; phloem precedes xylem differentiation by 1–2 days. The rate of basipetal sieve-tube element differentiation is generally sufficient to maintain the continuity of phloem across the intercalary meristem (Patrick 1972). The establishment of phloem continuity between a pre-emergent leaf and the youngest mature photosynthetic leaf also coincides with the rapid increase in the relative rate of leaf extension (Patrick 1972; Williams 1975).

Like vascular tissue differentiation, the development of dermal and ground tissues begins well before leaf emergence; however, the greatest changes in cell cross-sectional area, intercellular space enlargement, and plastid growth occur just before the leaf blade emerges (Figures 5.8.A–E; 5.9.A,B) (Dengler et al. 1986). The basipetal pattern of cell maturation characteristic of dicot leaves is accentuated in grass leaves by the pattern of emergence of the blade from encircling older leaves. This developmental feature has often been exploited in physiological studies, because the spatial sequence from blade tip to base should reflect the temporal sequence of cellular differentiation (Kirchanski 1975; Leech 1985, 1986). Chloroplast size and levels of chlorophyll, chloroplast RNA, cytoplasmic RNA, and photosynthetic enzymes have been shown to increase from the base to apex of the grass leaf (Leech 1986). Photosynthetic rates continue to rise throughout leaf expansion and do not decrease in mature leaves (Šesták et al. 1985); this may reflect the shorter life span of grass leaves in comparison to many dicot leaves (Langer 1979).

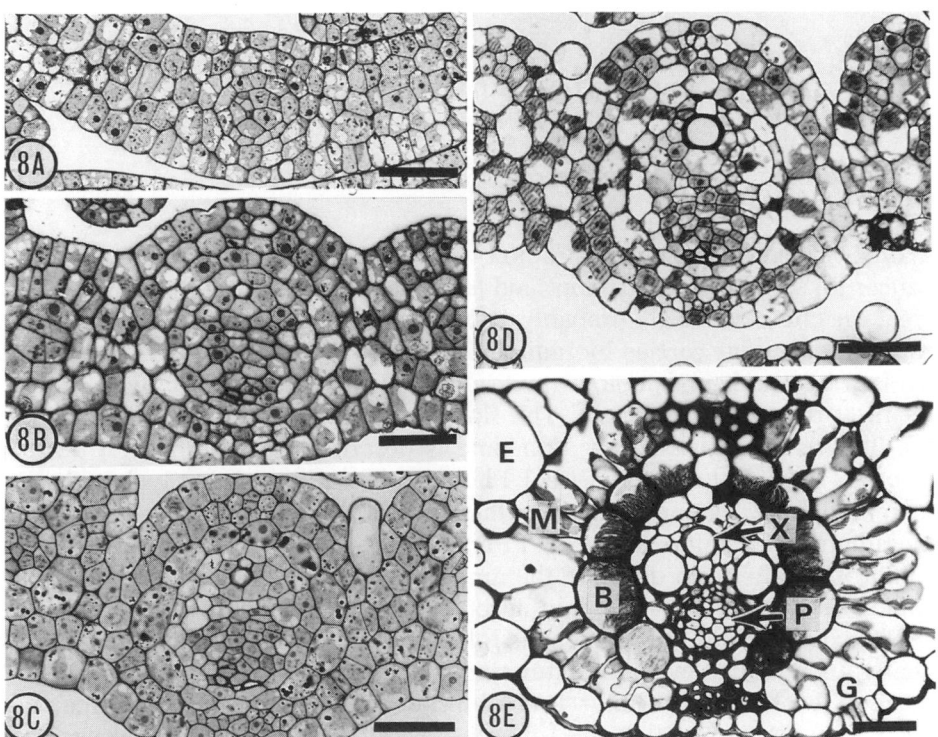

Figure 5.8. Cross sections of developing leaves of *Panicum effusum* sectioned near the midpoint of the leaf lamina. (A) P2 leaf; (B) P3 leaf; (C) P4 leaf; (D) P5 leaf; (E) mature leaf. Note changes in mesophyll cells (M), bundle sheath parenchyma (B), major vein xylem (X) and phloem (P), and bulliform (E) and guard cells (G) of the epidermis; scale = 25 μm (from Dengler et al. 1986).

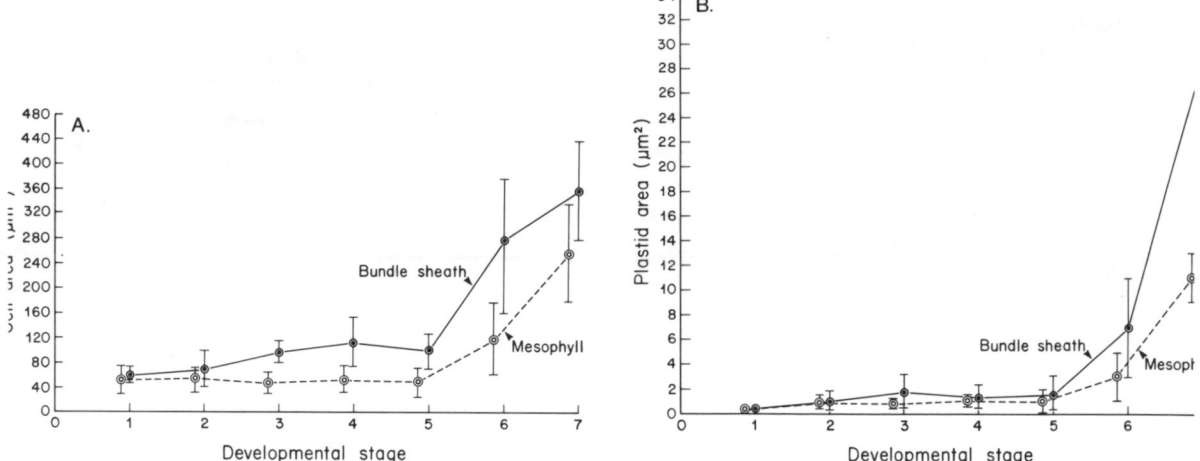

Figure 5.9. Anatomical changes in developing leaves of the C4 grass *Panicum effusum.* (A) Changes in cross-sectional area of mesophyll and bundle sheath cells. (B) Changes in chloroplast cross-sectional area in mesophyll and bundle sheath cells (from Dengler et al. 1986).

THE LIGHT ENVIRONMENT

Irradiance

Three properties of light are known to be important for plant growth: (a) irradiance; (b) spectral composition; and (c) photoperiod. Of these, irradiance, through its effect on photosynthesis, probably influences leaf development most significantly. The amount of energy carried by radiation is expressed as a quantity of radiant energy (joules, J) or by number of photons (moles, mol). The radiant energy per unit time is the energy flow rate (J/s or watt, w). The flow rate of energy falling on a flat receiving surface (in this case, a leaf) per unit time is described as the energy flux (J/m²/s or W/m²) or the photon flux (mol/m²/sec). Photosynthetically active wavelengths are those between 400 and 700 nm, and for this reason, photon flux is often limited to *photosynthetic photon flux density* (PPFD; McCree 1981). Although photon flux is the most appropriate term to describe the amount of energy falling on a flat surface per unit time, *irradiance* is also widely accepted and is used here; in general, the term "light intensity" should be avoided (Holmes 1984). Other, obsolete units that are frequently encountered in the literature include calorie (1 calorie = 4.18 joule), einstein (1 einstein = 1 mole), lux (1 lux = 4–10 W/m², depending on the light source), and foot-candle (1 foot-candle = 10.76 lux) (Larcher 1980; Holmes 1984). Discussion in this chapter retains the units used in the original investigations, even though this does not facilitate comparison among them!

Daylight consists of direct sunlight and diffuse skylight, and typical PPFD values are 1600–1900 μmol/m²/s (Smith and Morgan 1981; Smith 1982). In any plant environment, there is considerable spatial and temporal variation in irradiance, depending on surrounding vegetation, season, time of day, and cloud cover. For instance, Chazdon and Fetcher (1984) obtained peak values for a tropical rain forest site in Costa Rica of 1000 μmol/m²/s in a clearing, 100 μmol/m²/s in a 200 m² gap and 10 μmol/m²/s in the understorey. The clearing exhibited the greatest diurnal variation in PPFD and the least day-to-day variation, whereas the understorey was characterized by the least diurnal and greatest day-to-day variation (Chazdon and Fetcher, 1984). Surrounding vegetation is probably the most important source of variation in irradiance, and the growth or loss of surrounding plants are the factors most likely to alter the light environment significantly during the development of an individual leaf.

Spectral Composition

The spectral composition of light is also altered in natural shade environments. Chlorophyll within leaves absorbs wavelengths between 400 and 700 nm and transmits a proportionately greater amount of radiant energy beyond 750 nm. The spectral composition of light in full sun and under a tropical rain forest canopy are compared in Figure 5.10. This dramatic difference in spectral composition between sunlight and shade is most often expressed in terms of the absorption maxima of the pigment phytochrome: the ratio between the photon flux at 655–665 nm (red) and the photon flux at 725–735 nm (far-red) (Smith 1982). The red:far-red (R:FR) ratio in full sun is around 1.03–1.22 and in shade varies from 0.09 to 0.77 (Morgan and Smith 1981; Smith 1982; Lee 1987).

The spectral composition of daylight is also altered at twilight and in sunflecks (Morgan and Smith 1981; Smith 1982). Light reaching plants growing underwater can have changed R:FR ratios, depending on depth and season. Selective attenuation of far-red underwater is a result of reflection and refraction at the surface and absorption and scattering below the surface. R:FR ratios underwater are usually > 1.0 and may be as high as 19.6 (Morgan and Smith 1981; Spence 1981; Smith 1982). Many investigators have used artificial light sources, which further alter R:FR; for instance, ratios produced by fluorescent lights are typically around 3.0 but may be as high as 13.5 (Smith and Morgan 1983).

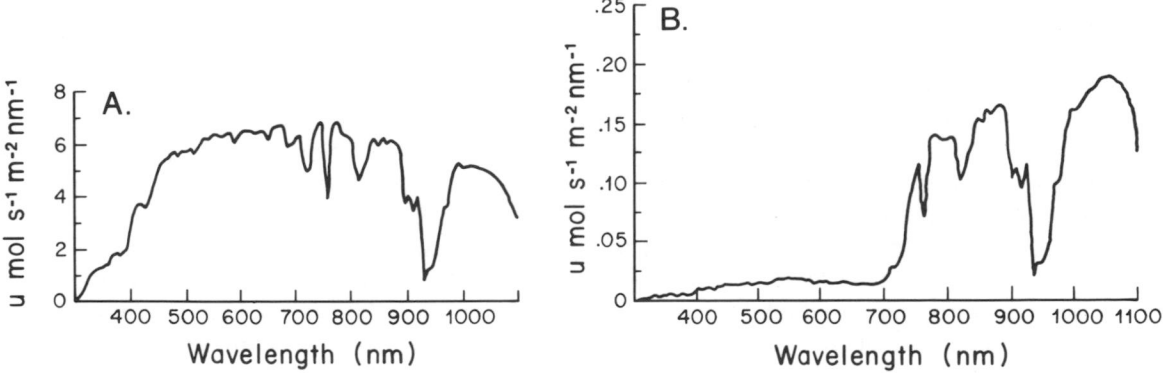

Figure 5.10. Spectral distribution of radiation at two sites at Finca La Selva, Costa Rica. (A) Full sun in a forest clearing. (B) Deep shade of the forest understorey (from Lee 1987).

Photoperiod

Plant growth may show a response to the length of the light (or dark) period. This aspect of the light environment is of less importance in the tropics than in temperate zones, where daylength varies substantially over a year, and changing daylengths give reliable information about other aspects of the environment (Larcher 1980).

EFFECT OF IRRADIANCE

Leaf Production

Both field observations (Nilsen 1986) and controlled-environment experiments (Milthorpe and Newton 1963; Newton 1963; Terry 1968; Bernáth et al. 1985; Fisher 1986; Kwesiga and Grace 1986) have shown that reduced irradiance slows leaf production in dicot species. For instance, plants of *Beta vulgaris* grown under four levels of irradiance for an 84-day period showed a close correlation between rate of leaf production and irradiance: plants grown at 110 cal./cm^2/d had a rate of 0.82 leaves/d whereas those grown under 20 cal/cm^2/d had a rate of 0.13 leaves/d (Terry 1968). Similar results have been obtained for grass species (Friend and Pomeroy 1970; Patterson 1980a; Paul and Patterson 1980). In *Imperata cylindrica*, propagules grown for 89 d in 100% available light (maximum of 2000 μE/m^2/d) produced a total of 74.1 leaves, whereas those grown under 56% and 11% shade produced 47.2 and 15.1 leaves, respectively (Patterson 1980a). Apparently, the dramatic differences reported in these studies reflect more rapid leaf production from both the main shoot apex and tiller apices.

The rate of leaf production is often assumed to be the equivalent of the rate of leaf initiation. Several developmental factors affect the relationship between initiation and visible expansion from the bud, and these may be particularly important in experiments involving plants that are transferred from one set of environmental conditions to another. Whereas the rate of leaf initiation may be constant during the ontogeny of an individual, the plastochron interval is more likely to decrease with time (Williams 1975). The time interval between the visual appearance of successive leaves has been termed a *phyllochron* (Dale and Milthorpe 1983). If the phyllochron is longer than a plastochron, the number of leaves within the apical bud will increase during ontogeny. Ambient light conditions clearly affect the rate and duration of leaf expansion, so visible changes in leaf production may not reflect changes in the rate of leaf initiation, particularly in short-term experiments.

The relationship between irradiance and leaf initiation *per se* has not been thoroughly investigated, probably because destructive sampling is required for such studies. Aspinall and Paleg (1963) showed by direct observations of shoot apices of *Hordeum vulgare* that high irradiance levels speed the rate of leaf primordium production (but not the total number of leaves produced before flowering). Barsch-Gollnau et al. (1980) also investigated the effect of light on the rate of primordium formation in seedlings of *Sinapis alba* and *Xanthium strumarium*. After initial germination in darkness, seedlings were either transferred to white light (17,000 lux) or kept in darkness for 6 d (*Sinapis*) or 12 d (*Xanthium*). Plants were then placed in continuous light to observe expansion of leaves formed during the experimental period. Based on counts of primordia made via a dissecting microscope, the white-light treatment significantly increased the number of leaf primordia formed and reduced the length of the plastochron in both species.

Leaf Shape

With few exceptions, little evidence indicates that the morphogenetic processes determining leaf shape are readily affected by irradiance level. An early study by Talbert and Holch (1957) examined 37 species growing under field conditions and compared mature leaves from the south and north peripheries of the canopies. Heteroblastic variation was avoided by sampling from the "middle" nodes of shoots. The "sun" leaves of 36 of the 37 species examined were more lobed than the "shade" leaves, and most had greater perimeters, despite having smaller areas. Since all leaves of the species examined were characterized by some lobing, it is not clear whether the changes in leaf shape reflected an early morphogenetic process or an alteration in the allometric relationship between lobe and sinus growth during leaf expansion.

In species with conspicuous shape changes of leaves in a heteroblastic series, greater irradiance may accelerate these changes. In *Ipomoea caerula*, Njoku (1956) reported that the transition from cordate to lobed leaves occurred between nodal positions 6 and 7 in shade-grown plants and between positions 2 and 3 in light grown plants (Figure 5.11.A,B). Experiments involving the transfer of seedlings between light and shade conditions at the time of unfolding of the first leaf showed that 8–14 plastochrons were required for leaf shape to respond completely to the new treatment, thus suggesting that early morphogenetic, as well as expansion, stages are essential for the genesis of appropriate leaf form (Figure 5.11.C,D). Similar results were obtained by Cameron (1970) in an investigation of the effect of irradiance on the heteroblastic development of *Eucalyptus fastigata* seedlings. Low irradiance (2–15% of full sunlight) delayed the transition from juvenile- to intermediate-form leaves and significantly reduced the number of intermediate-form leaves produced under shade conditions. These observations were interpreted as supporting the hypothesis that heteroblastic shifts in leaf form are determined by carbohydrate nutrition (Ashby 1948); however, the relationship among irradiance, nutrient level within the shoot system, and the transition from juvenile- to adult-leaf form has not yet been systematically investigated.

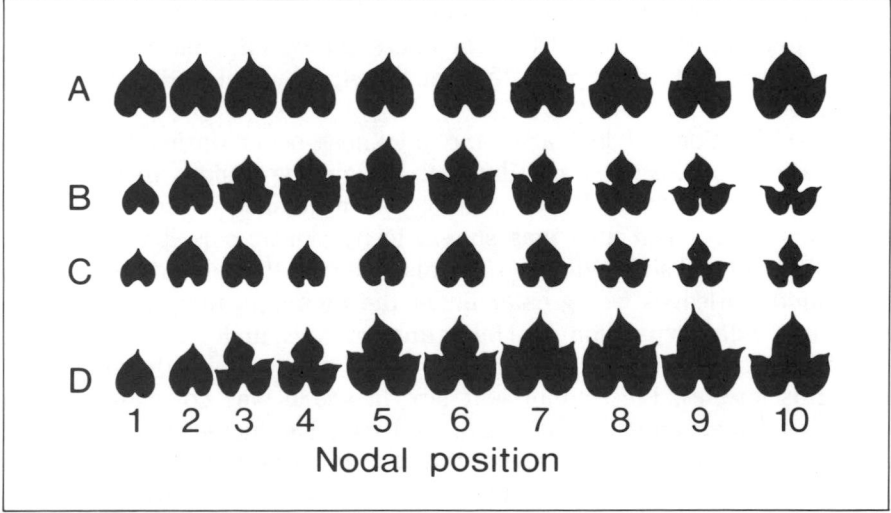

Figure 5.11. Changes in leaf shape in *Ipomoea caerula*. (A) Leaf shape at successive nodes under "shade" conditions. (B) Leaf shape at successive nodes under full daylight conditions. (C) Leaf shape in plants transferred from shade to full daylight as the second leaf unfolded. (D) Leaf shape in plants transferred from full daylight to shade as the second leaf unfolded (from Njoku 1956).

Leaf Size

Under controlled conditions of reduced irradiance, many dicot species show an increase in leaf area (Crookston et al. 1975; Rawson and Craven 1975; Pandey and Sinha 1977; Doley 1978; Clough et al. 1979; Duba and Carpenter 1980; Wild and Wolf 1980; Young and Smith 1980; Lichtenthaler et al. 1981; Longstreth et al. 1981, 1985; Fisher 1986; Kwesiga and Grace 1986). Reduced irradiance also results in decreased leaf thickness (Doley 1978; Duba and Carpenter 1980; Wild and Wolf 1980; Lichtenthaler et al. 1981; Nygren and Kellomaki 1983; Corré 1983a; Longstreth et al. 1985; Fisher 1986). Either the increase in area or the reduction in leaf thickness, but usually the combination of both, results in an increase in specific leaf area (SLA, leaf area/unit dry weight, cm^2/g) under low light levels (Doley 1978; Clough et al. 1979; Corré 1983a; Dennis and Woledge 1983; Nygren and Kellomaki 1983). This relationship is also expressed as specific leaf weight (SLW, leaf dry weight/unit area, g/cm^2), which decreases under low light intensity (Crookston et al. 1975; Fisher 1986; Hori and Oshima 1986). In grass species, reduced irradiance may also result in greater leaf area (Friend and Pomeroy 1970; Lichtenthaler et al. 1981), reduced leaf thickness (Friend and Pomeroy 1970; Lichtenthaler et al. 1981; Ward and Woolhouse 1986), increased SLA (Patterson 1980a), and decreased SLW (Ward and Woolhouse 1986). In contrast, a reduction in irradiance results in a reduction in leaf blade area in some dicot species (Butler 1963; Fitter and Ashmore 1974; Dengler 1980; Jurik et al. 1982; Oquist et al. 1982; Bernáth et al. 1985).

Species comparisons have suggested that these different responses are related to shade tolerance. *Crotalaria juncea*, a shade-intolerant species, showed a sharp decrease in mean leaf area in response to a reduction of irradiance to 80% of full sunlight, whereas *C. sericea*, a more shade-tolerant species, showed a slight *increase* in leaf area at 80% (Pandey and Sinha 1977). In experiments that varied both light level and R:FR ratio, Fitter and Ashmore (1974) found that the leaf area of *Veronica montana*, a woodland plant, was slightly affected by mild shading stress, whereas the leaf area of *V. persica*, a weed of open fields, was more dramatically reduced. A comparison of leaf structure and photosynthetic properties of the grasses *Zea mays* and *Paspalum conjugatum* showed that leaf thickness and specific leaf weight are reduced to a greater extent in the crop plant than in the shade-adapted *Paspalum* (Ward and Woolhouse 1986).

These modifications of leaf area and thickness occur during leaf development through alterations of the rates and duration of leaf expansion. In *Cucumis sativus* (Milthorpe and Newton 1963; Wilson 1966), low irradiance reduced the rate of leaf expansion, and smaller leaf area was shown to be closely correlated with epidermal cell number, but not cell size. Wilson (1966) also showed that the rate of cell division in expanding *Cucumis* leaves was greater under the high-light treatment used; duration was unaffected. Leaf expansion in *Helianthus annuus* under 25% sunlight was of longer duration and occurred at a lower rate than in full sunlight (Dengler 1980; Figure 5.13.A). In this species, the smaller leaf size in shade was correlated with smaller epidermal cell numbers and slightly smaller cell size. The increase in number occurred over the same period in both treatments, but at a greater rate under full sunlight. The rates of increase in leaf thickness and dry weight were also reduced by the shade treatment.

Experiments on the effect of irradiance and temperature on the growth of *Triticum aestivum* indicate that this grass species has a shade-intolerant type of response. Friend and Pomeroy (1970) found that leaves of *Triticum* seedlings grown under 500 ft-c had a smaller area, a narrower blade with fewer rows of epidermal cells, and were thinner than leaves of seedlings grown under 3000 ft-c. The lengths of bulli-form epidermal cells and lengths and thickness of mesophyll cells were also reduced under low light intensity. Kemp (1980) compared leaf extension rates in wheat seedlings grown in full sunlight with shade treatments of 5–20% full sun. Although he found no differences in the length of leaves expanding under the two treatments, leaves grown under low light were narrower and thinner, and the basal extension zone was 30% longer. More recently, Dale (1982) compared growth in *Triticum* under a narrower range of irradiance levels (200 and 400 μmol/m^2/s). He found no effect of light treatment on leaf area or cell number; in addition, transfer of seedlings between conditions at various times also had no effect. Friend and Pomeroy (1970), Kemp (1980), and Dale (1982) all found that reduced irradiance resulted in lower leaf dry weights and lower dry matter per cell.

Most experiments relating the light environment to leaf growth have compared different levels of irradiance, a measure of *instantaneous* flux density. Other experiments, however, designed to test the effect of *total* light energy received, have suggested that this factor is the most important determinant of leaf expansion (Hughes and Evans 1962; Chabot et al. 1979; Corré 1983a; Craker et al. 1983). Chabot et al. (1979) conducted two sets of experiments with *Fragaria virginiana*. First, peak photosynthetic photon-flux density was varied, while total PPFD over a 24-hr period was held constant. In the second set of experiments, peak PPFD was constant and total PPFD was varied. Variation in peak PPFD between 105 and 560 μE/m^2/s had no significant effect on leaf thickness, SLW, mesophyll cell volume, or maximum net photosynthesis when the total integrated daily values of PPFD were held near 5 E/m^2/d. Significant differences were found in each of these parameters when PPFD was held around 300 μE/m^2/s, and integrated daily PPFD was varied between about 6 and 20 E/m/^{2}/d. Chabot et al. (1979) argued that leaf expansion is essentially an integrative process: high photosynthetic rates under conditions of high daily PPFD result in increased investment in leaf structure in the form of thicker, heavier leaves. Despite the variation in leaf area response among species, the positive correlation between total daily PPFD and SLW appears to be general (Young 1975; Corré 1983a; Craker et al. 1983).

Because the peak relative rates of leaf expansion and cell division occur while the leaf is an importing organ, the carbohydrate balance of the whole shoot is probably the most important factor in determining final leaf area. The close correlation between leaf area and cell number suggests that control of leaf area is mediated through regulation of cell division (Dale and Milthorpe 1983; Dale 1985). This is supported by experiments on *Phaseolus vulgaris*, in which shading of the primary leaves reduced cell number and leaf area of the unshaded first trifoliate leaf (Dale 1976). The long period of developmental overlap between cell division and cell enlargement suggests that cell size will also be affected by internal shoot carbohydrate levels; however, the final stages of cell enlargement and cell differentiation occur as the leaf begins to emerge from the bud. Particularly in dicot leaves, these stages will be less influenced by the conditions under which the primordium developed, and more influenced by the light levels under which the leaf expands.

Leaf Anatomy

The reduction in leaf thickness associated with lower irradiance is closely associated with a reduction in the amount of mesophyll present (Figures 5.12.A–H, 5.13.B). The observation has been made from field-collected "shade" leaves of numerous dicot species (Haberlandt 1914; Hanson 1917; Turrell 1936; Isanogle 1944; Wylie 1951;

Cormack and Gorham 1953; Jackson 1967) as well as from leaves expanding under experimentally controlled conditions (Anderson 1955; Nobel et al. 1975; Chabot and Chabot 1977; Doley 1978; Smith and Nobel 1978; Chabot et al. 1979; Dengler 1980; Wild and Wolf 1980; Young and Smith 1980; Longstreth et al. 1981; Jurik et al. 1982; Nygren and Kellomaki 1983; Bernáth et al. 1985; Fisher 1986; Roberts-Nkrumah et al. 1986). Mesophyll thickness is strongly correlated with the development of palisade mesophyll. In some species fewer ground tissue cell layers differentiate as palisade parenchyma (Jackson 1967; Chabot and Chabot 1977; Wild and Wolf 1980; Bernáth et al. 1985; Lichtenthaler 1985; Fisher 1986). In others the number of cell layers is not

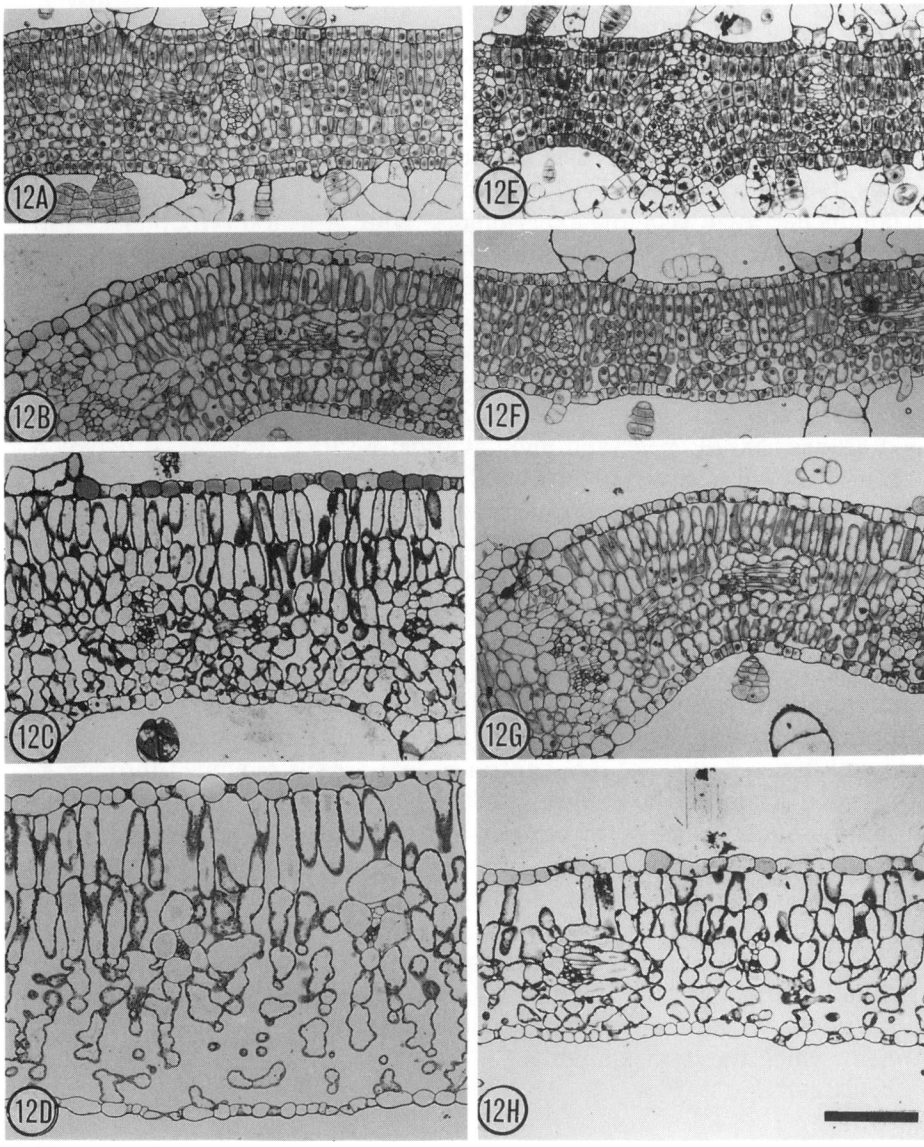

Figure 5.12.   Cross sections of the second foliage leaf of *Helianthus annuus* developing under two light treatments. (A–D) Leaves developing under full sunlight (100%). (E–H) Leaves developing under shade (25% of full sunlight). (A, E) Six days after germination. (B, F) Eight days after germination. (C, G) Ten days after germination. (D, H) Mature leaves; scale = 100 μm (from Dengler 1980).

affected, but cell "height" or total volume of palisade mesophyll shows greater reduction than that of the spongy mesophyll (Wylie 1951; Anderson 1955; Hughes 1959; Jackson 1967; Dengler 1980; Bernáth et al. 1985). In the homogeneous mesophyll of *Lolium perenne*, low irradiance results in smaller cells and fewer cells/unit leaf area (Wilson and Cooper 1969). The proportion of leaf volume occupied by intercellular space usually increases under reduced irradiance (Isanogle 1944; Wylie 1951; Chabot and Chabot 1977; Dengler 1980; Jurik et al. 1982), although the absolute volume of intercellular space may decrease (Figure 5.13.C) (Dengler 1980). Similarly, absolute thickness or volume of the epidermal layers usually decreases, but the greater reduction of mesophyll tissues may result in a greater percent thickness or volume of dermal tissue under reduced light (Dengler 1980; Jurik et al. 1982). Although they did not make a detailed analysis of anatomical characteristics, Chabot et al. (1979) showed that changes in leaf thickness and the relative volumes of mesophyll and epidermal tissues in *Fragaria virginiana* are related to total daily PPFD, not peak PPFD.

These anatomical changes observed in leaves developing under higher irradiance levels have important consequences for photosynthetic rates. The two major resis-

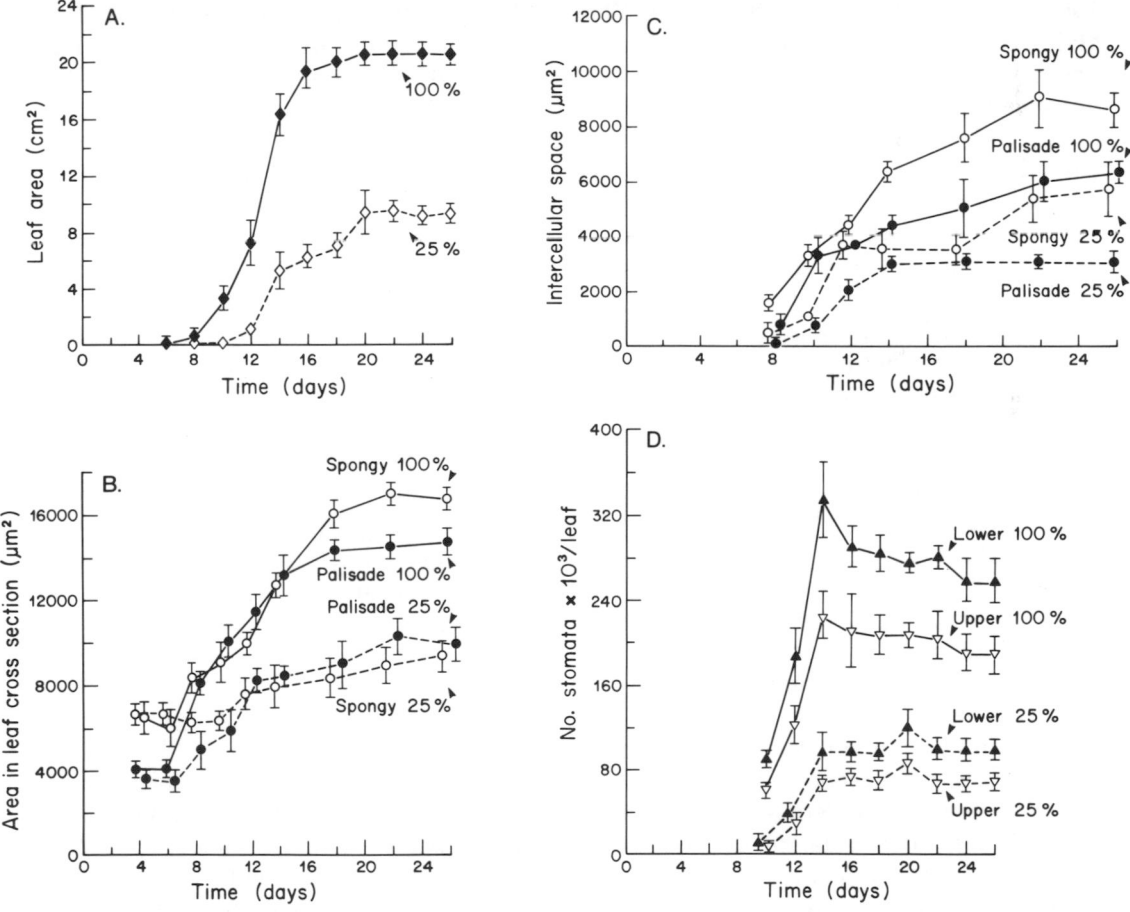

Figure 5.13. Quantitative changes in the second foliage leaf of *Helianthus annuus* developing under full sunlight (100%) and shade (25%). (A) Changes in leaf area. (B) Changes in palisade and spongy parenchyma area in leaf cross sections 100 μm in width. (C) Changes in palisade and spongy intercellular space in leaf cross sections 100 μm in width. (D) Changes in the number of stomata in upper and lower epidermal layers (from Dengler 1980).

tances to the diffusion of CO_2 into the photosynthetic cells occur at (a) the surface of photosynthetic mesophyll cells bordering the intercellular spaces and (b) the stomatal pores (Nobel and Walker 1985). An important consequence of the greater leaf thickness and mesophyll volume of "sun" leaves is the increase in surface area of mesophyll cell wall available for CO_2 uptake. Noble et al. (1975) have expressed this characteristic as A^{mes}/A, the ratio between mesophyll surface area and leaf area. A^{mes}/A is positively correlated with specific leaf weight and leaf thickness (Nobel et al. 1975; Chabot and Chabot 1977; Smith and Nobel 1978; Chabot et al. 1979; Nobel and Longstreth 1981; Oquist et al. 1982; Yun and Taylor 1986). In *Plectranthus parviflorus*, Nobel et al. (1975) found that when illumination during leaf development was raised from 900 to 42,000 lux, the mesophyll cells increased in size and number per unit leaf area, thus causing A^{mes}/A to increase 11 to 50. The net rate of photosynthesis increased four-fold, reflecting the decrease in total resistance to CO_2 uptake per unit leaf area. Variation in A^{mes}/A was large enough to account for increased CO_2 uptake under higher irradiance levels in *Encelia farinosa* (Smith and Nobel 1978) and *Hydrocotyle bonariensis* (Longstreth et al. 1981) and was shown to provide a major source of variation in photosynthetic rate with changing light levels in *Betula pendula* (Oquist et al. 1982). In *Fragaria vesca* (Chabot and Chabot 1977) *F. virginiana* (Chabot et al. 1979), and other species (Björkman 1981b), A^{mes}/A varied with differing rates of net photosynthesis associated with changing temperature, irradiance, and total PPFD; however, the relationship was not close. Björkman (1981a,b) argued that increases in photosynthetic rate under high irradiance occur only if increases in A^{mes}/A are accompanied by increases in carboxylase enzyme, electron carriers, and other chloroplast components within mesophyll cells.

The A^{mes}/A ratio also has functional implications for transpiration under sun and shade conditions. Yun and Taylor (1986) found that leaves of *Abutilon theophrasti* grown under high irradiance (600 $\mu mol/m^2/s$ were thicker and had higher values of A^{mes}/A than those grown at low irradiance (200 $\mu mol/m^2/s$). The high-light plants had higher rates of photosynthesis; however, there was little difference in transpiration rate between the two treatments, thereby yielding greater values for water use efficiency for high-light leaves.

The stomatal pores comprise a second major site of resistance to CO_2 diffusion into the leaf (Nobel and Walker 1985). Stomatal density is typically reduced in leaves developing under low light, thus increasing total resistance (Cooper and Qualls 1967; Knecht and O'Leary 1972; Crookston et al. 1975; Gay and Hurd 1975; Rawson and Craven 1975; Dengler 1980; Wild and Wolf 1980; Lichtenthaler et al. 1981; Fetcher et al 1983; Perry et al. 1986). In the amphistomatous leaves of *Lycopersicon esculentum*, stomatal density on the adaxial epidermis was reduced to $1/mm^2$ by a low-light treatment of 20 W/m^2, making the leaf essentially hypostomatous (Gay and Hurd 1975). Similarly, in *Heliocarpus appendiculatus*, shade treatments that reduced light to 1.4% of full sun also prevented stomatal differentiation in the adaxial epidermis (Fetcher et al. 1983). In some species, reduced stomatal density under shaded conditions is due entirely to greater epidermal cell expansion. In *Phaseolus vulgaris*, Knecht and O'Leary (1972) found no significant differences in *total* number of stomata/leaf, despite differences in density, among four light levels. In *Helianthus annuus*, both total number of stomata and stomatal density of both the adaxial and abaxial epidermal layers were strongly reduced by shading (Figure 5.13.D) (Dengler 1980). Resistance to CO_2 diffusion into the leaf can also be affected by the size of stomatal pores. Although stomatal pore size may not be affected by light treatment (e.g. Fetcher et al. 1983), Wild and Wolf (1980) found a small but significant reduction in pore length in *Sinapis alba* under 6 W/m^2 as compared with 60 W/m^2, and Young and Smith (1980) found a more substantial reduction (about 25%) in pore length in *Arnica cordifolia* under natural shade conditions of about 33% sunlight.

Studies of the time course of tissue differentiation show that both the rate and duration are influenced by differing light levels. In *Helianthus annuus*, reduction of light to 25% full sunlight slowed the rate of expansion of palisade and spongy mesophyll so much that even though the duration of expansion was extended by 4–5 d, tissue volumes were significantly smaller (Figure 5.13.B) (Dengler 1980). The formation of intercellular space within the mesophyll tissue paralleled cell expansion. These differences in mesophyll cell differentiation appeared early—at or shortly after leaf emergence from the bud. A similar pattern was observed in *Alternanthera philoxeroides*, in which A^{mes}/A was shown to differ between light treatments from the earliest stages of leaf expansion sampled (Longstreth et al. 1985). In *Helianthus annuus*, formation of new stomata continued until the leaf reached about 50% of its final area; formation occurred at a greater rate under high-light levels, resulting in greater stomatal densities in mature leaves, despite greater leaf expansion (Figure 5.13.D) (Dengler 1980). Wild and Wolf (1980) also found that a low-light treatment of 6 W/m^2 greatly slowed the rate and extended the duration of stomatal initiation in *Sinapis alba*.

The different photosynthetic rates among leaves expanding under various irradiance conditions can be attributed partly to the above anatomical characteristics, which affect the stomatal and mesophyll components of resistance to CO_2 diffusion (Boardman 1977; Björkman 1981a,b; Nobel and Walker 1985). The final stages of cell differentiation during leaf development under different light condition likewise result in varying cytological and biochemical mesophyll cell characteristics. In *Sinapis alba*, Wild and Wolf (1980) found that under high irradiance, palisade cells had 3.5 times as many chloroplasts and spongy parenchyma cells had 2.7 times as many chloroplasts as under low irradiance. These differences were the direct result of tissue volume differences between light treatments, since no differences were observed in chloroplast number/unit cell volume. Paul and Patterson (1980) found that chloroplasts of the bundle sheath cells in the C4 grass *Rottboellia exaltata* decreased in size under reduced light intensity. They also found a reduction in the number of mesophyll and bundle sheath plastids/unit leaf area. Low irradiance also increases the number of thylakoids/granum (Ballantine and Forde 1970; Crookston et al. 1975; Boardman 1977; Patterson 1980b; Paul and Patterson 1980; Lichtenthaler et al. 1981; Lichtenthaler 1985) and increases chlorophyll concentration/unit leaf fresh weight (Ballantine and Forde 1970; Boardman 1977; Clough et al. 1979; Wild and Wolf 1980). The reduction in the number and size of chloroplasts, however, offsets increased chlorophyll concentration, so there is less chlorophyll on a unit area basis in leaves developing under reduced irradiance (Boardman 1977; Patterson 1980a,b). Biochemical changes such as a reduction in electron carriers and carboxylation enzymes, as well as other chloroplast components, occur in leaves grown at low irradiances (Björkman 1981a,b).

Low irradiance also affects leaf longevity. After a period of maturity, leaves undergo senescence and eventually abscise. The lifespan of individual leaves varies widely with the life form of a species, and reflects a balance between the costs and benefits of making a leaf and maintaining it through unfavorable periods (Chabot and Hicks 1982). In general, conditions of high carbon gain result in more rapid leaf turnover, thereby allowing successive leaves to respond developmentally to changing light conditions. For instance, in shade-tolerant *Rhododendron maximum*, leaf survivorship was lowest (up to 3 yr) under an open canopy and highest (up to 7 yr) under the low-irradiance environment of an evergreen canopy (Nilsen 1986). In other, presumably shade-intolerant species, stress associated with low light levels and consequent low carbon gain promotes early leaf abscission (Addicott 1982).

EFFECT OF SPECTRAL COMPOSITION

The natural shade of vegetation canopies both reduces irradiance and alters the spectral composition of light, most significantly the R:FR ratio. There is strong evidence that the phytochrome within young, expanded leaves is the photoreceptor of this change in light quality (Smith 1982; Vince-Prue 1983). Light containing red wavelengths (near 660 nm) converts phytochrome to the far-red-absorbing form; upon illumination with far-red light (near 730 nm) or in darkness, the phytochrome is converted back to the red-absorbing form. Depending on the wavelengths of irradiation, an equilibrium between the two forms of phytochrome is rapidly reached. The correlation between measured phytochrome equilibria and specific plant responses, as well as the reversibility of both equilibria and plant response obtained by using red or far-red light, supports the direct involvement of phytochrome in the detection of shade (Holmes and Smith 1977; Smith 1982; Vince-Prue and Tucker 1983; Mohr 1984). To test the effects of spectral composition on plant growth, investigators have compared neutral shade (no R:FR alteration) with simulated shade (altered R:FR) (Fitter and Ashmore 1974; Frankland and Letendre 1978; Bodkin et al. 1980; Richards and Lee 1986; Inada and Nishiyama 1987), or have followed a white light photoperiod by a brief period of far-red light, a treatment that alters the phytochrome equilibrium (Sanchez 1971; Frankland and Letendre 1978).

Leaf Shape

The most frequently observed photomorphogenetic effects of shade light are increased internode extension and suppressed lateral branch growth (Morgan and Smith 1981; Smith 1982; Corré 1983b; Vince-Prue and Tucker 1983; Ballaré et al. 1987). These responses are strongest in shade-avoiding species, but are also found in shade-tolerant species (Smith 1982; Grime et al. 1986). Effects have been observed on leaf expansion and leaf shape also. In *Taraxacum officinale*, there is a heteroblastic transition from a rounded leaf shape to a deeply incised runcinate form (Sanchez 1971). Exposure of plants to far-red light at the end of a white-light photoperiod prevented this transition, and the far-red response was reversed by red light. Sanchez and Cogliatti (1975) subsequently found the effect of far-red light to be influenced by the irradiance given during the white-light photoperiod: increasing the white-light irradiance significantly decreased the effect of a given far-red exposure. They concluded that the photocontrol of leaf shape in *Taraxacum* is the result of interaction between phytochrome equilibrium and an irradiance-dependent process, presumably concentration of photosynthate within the shoot.

In contrast, changes in R:FR alone appear to control leaf-shape changes in the heterophyllous freshwater macrophyte *Hippuris vulgaris* (Bodkin et al. 1980; Spence 1981). Small scale-like leaves are produced on submerged shoots in the spring; later in the growing season, emergent shoots produce aerial-type leaves. Laboratory experiments showed that temperature, submergence, or irradiance *per se* did not determine leaf form (Bodkin et al. 1980). Even under warm temperatures and high irradiance photoperiods, shoots produced only submerged-type leaves when exposed to a high R:FR ratio during the photoperiod, or when given a brief exposure to red light after it. The same shoot produced aerial-type leaves only under a photoperiod with low R:FR or after a brief exposure to far-red light at the end of a white-light photoperiod. Similarly, Richards and Lee (1986) demonstrated that altered R:FR ratios have a signifi-

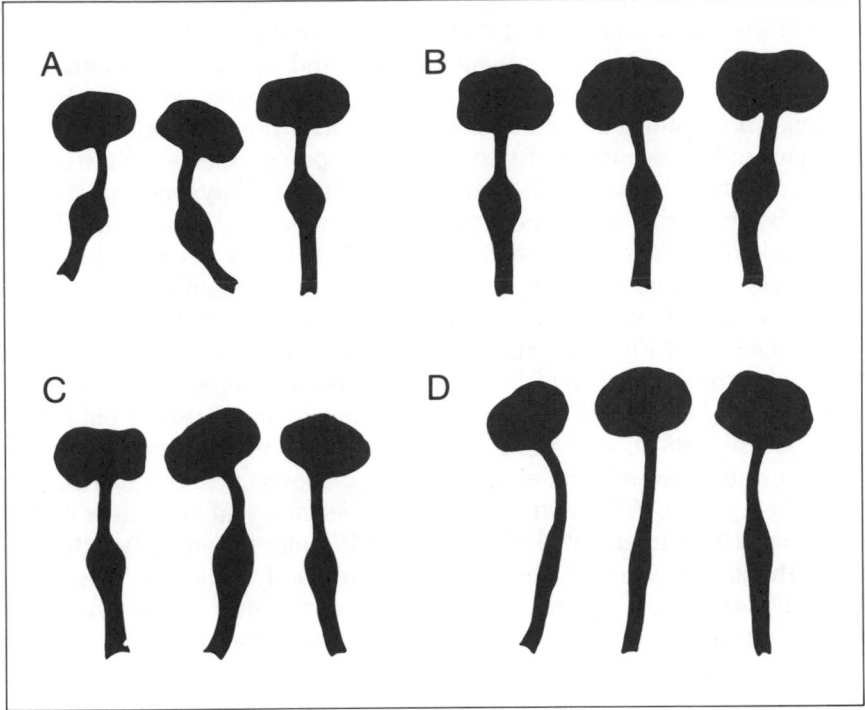

Figure 5.14. Mature leaf shape in *Eichhornia crassipes* under experimental light environments. (A) 2127 ± 142 μmol/m²/s, R:FR = 1.24 ± 0.03. (B) 1758 ± 224 μmol/m²/s, R:FR = 1.21 ± 0.00. (C) 21 ± 5 μmol/m²/s, R:FR = 1.00 ± 0.02. (D) 17 ± 9 μmol/m²/s, R:FR = 0.11 (from Richards and Lee 1986).

cant effect on leaf shape in *Eichhornia crassipes*. This aquatic macrophyte is a rosette plant that produces dense floating mats through the formation of stolons. Exposed plants at the edge of the mat have small leaves with inflated petioles, whereas shaded plants at the center of the mat have long leaves with narrow petioles. Field experiments with varied irradiance level (about 83% and 1% of full sunlight) and varied R:FR ratio (1.1 and 0.11) independently showed that shade-form leaves were produced under high-irradiance, low-R:FR conditions (Figure 5.14). The increase in petiole length under shade conditions is a response typical of rosette plants, and the net effect is comparable to the more frequently observed internode extension of nonrosette plants (Dennis and Woledge 1983; Richards and Lee 1986).

Leaf Expansion

Although spectral composition may influence the changes in leaf shape associated with heteroblastic development or with heterophylly in aquatic plants, its effect on the expansion of the leaf blade is less clear. The woodland species, *Circaea lutetiana*, responds to natural shading by decreased growth rates and increased specific leaf area (Frankland and Letendre 1978). Under controlled environmental conditions, these effects were mimicked by reducing irradiance, but not by altering the R:FR of the photoperiod or by supplying far-red light at the end of a white-light photoperiod. Neither natural nor simulated shade induced significant stem elongation in this species, a lack of response that is typical for many shade-tolerant species (Morgan and Smith 1981; Smith 1982). The differing responses of shade-tolerant and shade-avoiding

species are illustrated by the growth patterns of two species of *Veronica* under simulated shade (Fitter and Ashmore 1974). Shoot growth in the woodland perennial
species, *V. montana*, was similar in neutral shade and under far-red enhanced light of
similar intensity. In the annual weedy species, *V. persica*, specific leaf area was
increased under both reduced irradiance and enhanced far-red treatments. Similarly, in
a study comparing the responses of two tropical woody species to shade light, Kwesiga
and Grace (1986) showed the shade-tolerant seedlings of *Khaya senegalensis* were relatively insensitive to R:FR, whereas *Terminalia ivorensis*, a "light-demanding" species,
showed dramatically larger leaves with a higher SLA under decreased R:FR.

The effects of altered light quality on tissue differentiation have not been
examined specifically; however, there is some evidence that leaf thickness under shade
light is influenced by R:FR ratio. In *Rumex obtusifolius*, leaves expanding under low
R:FR (0.22) were thinner and had smaller cells and less extensive intercellular space
than leaves growing under the same irradiance but higher R:FR (3.66) (McLaren and
Smith 1978). Corré (1983b) also found that leaves of four species were thinner under
low R:FR than under neutral shade, but that this response was not related to the shade
tolerance of the species. Although they did not measure leaf thickness directly, Inada
and Nishiyama (1987) interpreted the lower SLW under spectrally altered shade as
compared with neutral shade to be a reflection of leaf thickness. Also, Child et al.
(1981) showed that far-red treatment (R:FR 0.26) at the end of the white-light period
significantly reduced stomatal density in *Chenopodium album*.

EFFECT OF PHOTOPERIOD

Plant growth responds not to absolute length of the photoperiod, but to changing
day lengths (Salisbury 1981). Such photoperiodic responses may be due to increasing
day lengths (long-day plants) or to decreasing day lengths (short-day plants). In other
species, growth is independent of day length (day-neutral plants). The mechanism of
perception of day length also involves the red:far-red reversible reaction of phytochrome (Vince-Prue and Tucker 1983; Mohr 1984). Although the best-known response
to photoperiod is floral initiation, other aspects of plant growth, including leaf development, are affected. Many experiments have shown an effect of photoperiod on leaf
expansion; however, most do not distinguish between the effects of day length and
total light energy (PPFD) received. For instance, *Arachis hypogaea* grown under short
days produced fewer and smaller leaves than plants grown under long days. Possibly,
photosynthate was limiting under short days, although the relationship was not simple
since reproductive growth was enhanced under these conditions (Ketring 1979). Dale
and Wilson (1979) also found that long days enhanced the rate of leaf primordium
initiation in three cultivars of *Hordeum vulgare*. The rate of leaf production was positively correlated with the size of the apical meristem, which in turn may be a direct
reflection of levels of photosynthate produced within the shoot under long days
(Allsopp 1967).

The effects of daylength on leaf growth are further complicated by heteroblastic
changes in leaf shape and size associated with the transition of flowering. Njoku (1956)
showed that a decrease in leaf lobing in *Ipomoea caerula* was correlated with a transition to reproductive growth. Short days induced the production of both unlobed leaves
and floral primordia at a younger nodal position than did long days.

A less equivocal effect of photoperiod on leaf shape has been shown for a few aquatic species characterized by conspicuous heterophylly. In *Proserpinaca palustris*, plants grown under short days (8 hr) produce highly divided leaves, whereas plants grown under long days (12 hr) form lanceolate-serrate leaves (Davis 1967). Production of lanceolate-serrate leaves was not dependent on flowering, since floral induction in this species requires 14-hr days. In *Ranunculus flabellaris*, continuous white-light illumination of terrestrial plants was reported to reduce leaf dissection as compared with 8 hr photoperiods, whereas in submerged plants, long days (17 hr) increased leaf dissection (Bostrack and Millington 1962).

Leaf expansion has been shown to respond to photoperiod in a number of species; generally where a response exists, leaf area is greater in long days than in short days (Cockshull 1966; Vince-Prue and Tucker 1983). In *Callistephus chinensis*, long days resulted in an acceleration of leaf-surface expansion, so that leaf area and specific leaf area were greater than under short days (Cockshull 1966). In these experiments, long days were simulated by a short (8 hr) photoperiod and a brief interruption of the dark period by low intensity white light, so it is unlikely that the response was induced by total light energy. In contrast, Young (1975) found no effect of a night-break treatment on specific leaf area in the day-neutral *Impatiens parviflora*.

DEVELOPMENTAL PLASTICITY

Most natural light environments, including those of crop plants, are characterized by spatial variation and temporal change. Leaves that were initiated on an unshaded shoot may complete expansion under shaded conditions; conversely, a leaf beginning development under shade may be exposed suddenly to direct light by loss of a neighbor. The degree of plasticity of the leaf development response to changing conditions might be expected to be correlated with the timing of environmental change. This has been supported in a general way by experiments in which plants were transferred between light treatments during the period of leaf expansion (Rumi and Carpinetti 1977).

Jurik et al. (1979) transferred plants of *Fragaria virginiana* grown under either high-light (678 μE/m^2/s) or low-light (64 μE/m^2/s) conditions to the opposite condition when a designated leaf had reached one of three stages: 1. first visible in bud; 2. expanding, but leaflets still folded together; and 3. expanded to 90% of final area. After leaf maturation under the second treatment was complete, leaf anatomy and apparent photosynthesis were compared. Leaves transferred from high to low light at stages 1 and 2 did not differ from the low-light controls in specific leaf weight, leaf thickness, mesophyll volume, or mesophyll surface area, and also had similar photosynthetic rates. Leaves transferred at stage 3 were intermediate between high-light and low-light controls. Leaves transferred from low- to high-light conditions showed a similar pattern, although the response to high light was not as complete. Jurik et al. (1979) suggested that initial development in low light simply does not allow sufficient buildup of energy reserves within the shoot to produce high light leaves. In contrast, Dennis and Woledge (1983) did not find that a low-light treatment limited growth plasticity. When *Trifolium repens* plants were transferred from a low-light (30 J/m^2/s) to a high-light (120 J/m^2/s) treatment, leaves that were "half unfolded" at the time of transfer did not differ from high-light controls in specific leaf area, petiole length, or rate of net photosynthesis. Leaves transferred "three days after becoming flat" still showed a response in specific leaf area. Gay and Hurd (1975) showed a similar plasticity in stomatal development in expanding leaves of *Lycopersicon esculentum*. Leaves beginning expansion at the time of transfer had stomatal densities intermediate between the high- and low-light controls; leaves that were younger at the time of transfer showed a greater capacity for response. Leaves show a limited capacity for structural changes even after the cessation of leaf expansion. Bunce et al. (1977) found small, but significant changes in leaf and mesophyll thickness in leaves of *Glycine max* that were transferred between high- (850 μE/m^2/s) and low- (250 μE/m^2/s) light treatments shortly after leaf expansion was complete. Other studies have shown that mature leaves retain the potential for physiological acclimation. Fagerberg (1987) demonstrated an increase in surface:volume ratio of thylakoids after 8 hr of shade in mature leaves of *Helianthus annuus*. Reciprocal transfers between high- and low-light conditions in mature leaves of *Zea mays* and *Amaranthus palmeri* resulted in significant changes in six photosynthetic enzymes within 6 d (Hatch et al. 1969).

Most transfer experiments have been carried out on leaves that are in a macroscopically visible stage of expansion. The rates and duration of the cellular processes associated with leaf expansion—cell division and cell enlargement—clearly respond to changing environmental conditions and can rapidly adjust to alter final leaf area, thickness, dry weight, and anatomy. If the experimental transfer occurs early in the expansion process, the developmental change may be of a magnitude that compensates for the original environmental conditions. This will only be true, however, if critical developmental stages do not occur before the beginning of leaf expansion from the bud. The importance of early stages is suggested by shading experiments on the expanding buds of perennial species with preformed leaves. Using five deciduous tree species, Goulet and Bellefleur (1986) artificially shaded buds from an exposed portion of the crown and exposed other buds from shaded portions of the crown by cutting away branches prior to bud break. In the three species that showed distinctive sun and shade leaf characteristics, leaf thickness, leaf area, and leaf density thickness (fresh weight/unit area) tended to be intermediate between controls for the original condition and the experimental condition. Earlier, similar experiments (Isanogle 1944; Anderson 1955) showed that preformed leaves expanding from shaded buds possessed the anatomical characteristics of "shade" leaves, whereas leaves expanding from opposite, unshaded buds were typical "sun" leaves. These experiments demonstrated the striking plasticity that can be achieved during expansion stages but did not relate the range of plasticity to conditions of the previous growing season or to control leaves, as did those of Goulet and Bellefleur (1986). The latter work suggests that developmental events during the previous growing season may indeed place constraints on leaf expansion and maturation under new conditions.

The importance of primordium initiation and early morphogenetic stages for limiting the plasticity of the final stages of leaf development has not yet been tested. Dengler and Sanchez-Burgos (1988) found some evidence supporting a key role for early morphogenetic stages in their experiments on the effect of irradiance on facultative anisophylly in *Paradrymonia ciliosa*. In this species, leaves of an opposite pair are unequal in size and may be strongly dimorphic: either leaf expansion occurs to form a simple, lanceolate blade or expansion is arrested at the time of lamina initiation so that leaves have a linear shape. The most significant effect of development under low irradiance is that a greater proportion of leaf primordia are arrested before lamina extension and mature as linear leaves. These observations suggest a threshold response to low irradiance early in leaf development, perhaps induced by low carbohydrate levels within the shoot. Some evidence indicates that low irradiance results in reduced carbohydrate levels within the shoot (Kemp 1981). Since the leaf is an importing organ until it reaches 50% of final size, reduced photosynthesis in leaves that export to a growing primordium is likely to affect developmental patterns within that leaf (Dale and Milthorpe 1983; Dale 1985).

Ashby (1948) originally suggested that one determinant of ultimate leaf size and shape is primordium size and cell number. Reduced light levels have been shown to result in smaller apical meristem size (Dale and Wilson 1979), but no one has shown whether leaf primordium size is affected, or, if affected, whether this places an irreversible constraint on the range of plasticity of later developmental stages. Experiments such as those of Jurik et al. (1979) suggest that unidentified developmental events prior to expansion from the bud may place limits on the ability of leaves to respond developmentally to increasing light levels. A series of transfer experiments, based on an adequate knowledge of the time course of important developmental conditions, is necessary to test thoroughly the hypothesis that the range of developmental plasticity becomes restricted with successive stages of leaf formation.

This hypothesis should be modified further by the recognition that not all differences in size and shape among leaves will be first expressed at early developmental stages. In *Eichhornia crassipes*, the characteristic localized petiole swelling occurs during the final stages of expansion in leaves exposed to the sun. Richards and Lee (1986) showed that transfer of shoots from full sun to growth conditions that lowered R:FR from 1.1 to 0.28 prevented the swelling, even if leaves were ½ to ¾ expanded at the time of transfer. Future experiments should employ species in which variation in irradiance, spectral composition, or photoperiod result in plasticity in leaf shape, size, and histological characteristics. Experiments in which successive transfers between growth conditions coincide with the stages of leaf initiation, morphogenesis, expansion, and tissue differentiation would provide an important contribution to the understanding of the mechanisms underlying an essential adaptive trait of all plants: phenotypic plasticity.

CONCLUSIONS

1. Alterations of mature leaf morphology and anatomy that are induced by changes in the light environment result from four aspects of leaf development: leaf initiation (which yields the number of leaves produced), morphogenesis (leaf shape), expansion (leaf size), and histogenesis (leaf anatomy). Although these aspects are considered separately, they are parts of an integrated, continuous process of leaf development.

2. In dicotyledons, a large proportion of the cell division and cell enlargement associated with leaf surface growth and tissue differentiation occur after the leaf begins to expand from the bud. Thus, these developmental processes are potentially exposed to the direct effects of environment. In contrast, blade surface growth and tissue differentiation in grasses occur before expansion from the older, ensheathing leaves.

3. Vascular connections with antecedent leaves on a shoot occur early during leaf development, and leaves are net importers of carbohydrates until maturation of photosynthetic tissues. This indicates that photosynthesis of the older leaves on a shoot will strongly influence the early developmental stages in dicot leaves and most developmental stages in grass leaves.

4. Plants grown under experimental conditions of low irradiance typically have a reduced rate of leaf production, greater leaf area, reduced leaf thickness, and lower leaf weight. Other changes such as reduced mesophyll tissue (particularly palisade parenchyma) volume, low mesophyll surface area/unit leaf surface area, reduced stomatal density, and certain biochemical and cytological changes are closely correlated with the reduced photosynthetic rates observed under low irradiance.

5. Experimental evidence indicates that total daily photon flux is more important than instantaneous photon flux for modifying leaf growth. This suggests that irradiance levels are perceived through the effect on photosynthetic rates in expanded leaves and that carbohydrate levels within the shoot will have a significant effect on the development of newly formed leaves. This may explain the acceleration of heteroblastic leaf-shape changes by high irradiance.

6. Altered spectral composition of shade light affects internode elongation and apical dominance, although at present less evidence suggests an effect on leaf expansion. Low R:FR induces larger leaf areas in some shade-intolerant terrestrial species, however, and regulates leaf shape in at least two aquatic species.

7. Photoperiod probably has the greatest influence on leaf development through its effect on total daily photon flux. Leaf-shape changes have been demonstrated to be associated with the altered phytochrome equilibria induced by daylength; these are probably the heteroblastic changes in leaf form that precede flowering.

8. Comparative studies on the effect of light on leaf development support the broad categorization of species as *stress-avoiders*, which show the greatest developmental plasticity, and *stress tolerators*, which exhibit less morphological response but are still capable of cytological and biochemical adjustments.

9. Transfer experiments between controlled light conditions indicate that the degree of plasticity of leaf development becomes limited with time and that nutritional conditions experienced by early primordium stages may constrain later ability to respond fully to changing light environment. The developmental pattern of dicot leaves suggests, however, that developmental changes such as tissue differentiation that occur during leaf expansion may respond directly to the immediate photosynthetic environment.

LITERATURE CITED

Addicott, F. T. 1982. *Abscission*. Berkeley: Univ. California Press.

Allsopp, A. 1967. Heteroblastic development in vascular plants. *Adv. Morphogenesis* 6:127–171.

Anderson, Y. O. 1955. Seasonal development in sun and shade leaves. *Ecology* 36:430–438.

Ashby, E. 1948. Studies in the morphogenesis of leaves. I. An essay on leaf shape. *New Phytol.* 47:153–176.

Aspinall, D., and L. G. Paleg. 1963. Effects of day length and light intensity on growth of barley. I. Growth and development of apex with a fluorescent light source. *Bot. Gaz.* 124:429–437.

Ballantine, J. E. M., and B. J. Forde. 1970. The effect of light intensity and temperature on plant growth and chloroplast structure in soybean. *Am. J. Bot.* 57:1150–1159.

Ballaré, C. L., R. A. Sánchez, A. L. Scopel, J. J. Casal, and C. M. Ghersa. 1987. Early detection of neighbour plants by phytochrome perception of spectral changes in reflected sunlight. *Plant, Cell Environ.* 10:551–557.

Barnard, C. 1964. Form and structure. In *Grasses and Grasslands*, Ed. C. Barnard. London: Macmillan. 47–72.

Barsch-Gollnau, S., A. Ritterbusch, and H. Mohr. 1980. Photomorphogenesis and phyllotaxis during vegetative growth in *Sinapis alba* and *Xanthium strumarium*. *Plant, Cell Environ.* 3:363–370.

Begg, J. E. and M. J. Wright. 1962. Growth and development of leaves from intercalary meristems in *Phalaris arundinacea*. *Nature* 194:1097–1098.

Bernáth, J., P. Tétényi, Z. Lassanyi, and É. Dobos. 1985. Effect of light and temperature on leaf morphology and productivity in *Digitalis lanata* Ehrh. *Acta Bot. Hung.* 31:261–268.

Björkman, O. 1981a. Ecological adaptation of the photosynthetic apparatus. In *Photosynthesis VI. Photosynthesis and Productivity, Photosynthesis and Environment*: Ed. G. Akoyunoglou. Philadelphia: Balaban Int. Sci. Serv. 191–202.

———. 1981b. Responses to different quantum flux densities. In *Encyclopedia of Plant Physiology*. 12B:57–106. Ed. O. L. Lange, P. S. Nobel, H. Ziegler. N. S. Berlin: Springer-Verlag.

Björkman, O., and P. Holmgren. 1963. Adaptability of the photosynthetic apparatus to light intensity in ecotypes from exposed and shaded habitats. *Physiol. Plant.* 16:889–914.

Boardman, N. K. 1977. Comparative photosynthesis of sun and shade plants. *Annu. Rev. Plant Physiol.* 28:355–377.

Bodkin, P. C., D. H. N. Spence, and D. C. Weeks. 1980. Photoreversible control of heterophylly in *Hippuris vulgaris*. *New Phytol.* 84:533–542.

Bostrack, J. M., and W. F. Millington. 1962. On the determination of leaf form in an aquatic heterophyllous species of *Ranunculus*. *Bull. Torrey Bot. Club* 89:1–20.

Bradshaw, A. D. 1965. Evolutionary significance of phenotypic plasticity in plants. *Adv. Genet.* 13:115–155.

Bunce, J. A., D. T. Patterson, M. M. Peel, and R. S. Alberte, 1977. Light acclimation during and after leaf expansion in soybean. *Plant Physiol.* 60:255–257.

Büsgen, M., and E. Münch. 1926. *The Structure and Life of Forest Trees*. New York: John Wiley.

Butler, R. D. 1963. The effect of light intensity on stem and leaf growth in broad bean seedlings. *J. Exp. Bot.* 14:142–152.

Cameron, R. J. 1970. Light intensity and the growth of *Eucalyptus* seedlings. I. Ontogenetic variation in *E. fastigata*. *Aust. J. Bot.* 18:29–43.

Chabot, B. F., and J. F. Chabot. 1977. Effects of light and temperature on leaf anatomy and photosynthesis in *Fragaria vesca*. *Oecologia* 26:363–377.

Chabot, B. F., and D. J. Hicks. 1982. The ecology of leaf life spans. *Annu. Rev. Ecol. Syst.* 13:229–259.

Chabot, B. F., T. Jurik, and J. F. Chabot. 1979. Influence of instantaneous and integrated light flux density on leaf anatomy and photosynthesis. *Am. J. Bot.* 66(8):940–945.

Chazdon, R. L., and N. Fetcher. 1984. Photosynthetic light environments in a lowland tropical rain forest in Costa Rica. *J. Ecol.* 72:553–564.

Child, R., D. C. Morgan, and H. Smith. 1981. Morphogenesis in simulated shadelight quality. In *Plants and the Daylight Spectrum*. Ed. H. Smith. London: Academic Press. 409–420.

Clough, J. M., R. S. Alberte, and J. A. Teeri. 1979. Photosynthetic adaptation of *Solanum dulcamera* L. to sun and shade environments. *Plant Physiol.* 64:25–30.

Cockshull, K. E. 1966. Effects of night-break treatment on leaf area and leaf dry weight in *Callistephus chinensis*. *Ann. Bot.* 30:791–806.

Coleman, W. K., and R. I. Greyson. 1976. The growth and development of the leaf in tomato (*Lycopersicon esculentum*). II. Leaf ontogeny. *Can. J. Bot.* 54:2704–2717.

Constable, G. A., and H. M. Rawson. 1980. Effect of leaf position, expansion and age on photosynthesis, transpiration and water use efficiency of cotton. *Aust. J. Plant Physiol.* 7:89–100.

Cooper, C. S., and M. Qualls. 1967. Morphology and chlorophyll content of shade and sun leaves of two legumes. *Crop Sci.* 7:672–673.

Cormack, R. G., and A. L. Gorham. 1953. Effects of exposure to direct sunlight upon the development of leaf structure of two deciduous shrub species. *Can. J. Bot.* 31:537–541.

Corré, W. J. 1983a. Growth and morphogenesis of sun and shade plants. I. The influence of light intensity. *Acta Bot. Neerl.* 32:49–62.

_____. 1983b. Growth and morphogenesis of sun and shade plants. II. Influence of light quality. *Acta Bot. Neerl.* 32:185–202.

Craker, L. E., M. Subert, and J. T. Clifford. 1983. Growth and development of radish (*Raphanus sativus* L.) under selected light environments. *Ann. Bot.* 51:59–61.

Crookston, R. K., K. J. Trehorne, P. Ludford, and J. L. Ozbun. 1975. Response of beans to shading. *Crop Science* 15:412–416.

Dale, J. E. 1976. Cell division in leaves. In *Cell Division in Higher Plants*. Ed. M. M. Yeoman. London: Academic Press 315–343.

_____. 1982. Some effects of temperature and irradiance on growth of the first four leaves of wheat, *Triticum aestivum*. *Ann. Bot.* 50:851–858.

_____. 1985. The carbon relations of the developing leaf. In *Control of Leaf Growth*. Ed. N. R. Baker, W. J. Daves, C. K. Ong. Cambridge: Cambridge University Press. 135–154.

_____. 1986. Plastic responses of leaves. In *Plasticity in Plants*. Ed. D. H. Jennings, A. J. Trewavas. Cambridge: Soc. Exp. Biol. Symp. 40. 287–305.

Dale, J. E., and F. L. Milthorpe. 1983. General features of the production and growth of leaves. In *The Growth and Functioning of Leaves*. Ed. J. E. Dale, F. L. Milthorpe. Cambridge: Cambridge University Press. 151–178.

Dale, J. E., and R. G. Wilson. 1979. The effects of photoperiod and mineral nutrient supply on growth and primordia production at the stem apex of barley seedlings. *Ann. Bot.* 44:537–546.

Davis, G. J. 1967. *Proserpinaca*: Photoperiodic and chemical differentiation of leaf development and flowering. *Plant Physiol.* 42:667–668.

Dengler, N. G. 1980. Comparative histological basis of sun and shade leaf dimorphism in *Helianthus annuus*. *Can. J. Bot.* 58:717–730.

_____. 1984. Comparison of leaf development in normal (+/+). entire (e/e), and lanceolate (La/+) plants of tomato, *Lycopersicon esculentum* 'Ailsa Craig'. *Bot. Gaz.* 145:66–77.

Dengler, N. G., R. E. Dengler and P. W. Hattersley. 1985. Differing ontogenetic origins of PCR ("Kranz") sheaths in leaf blades of C4 grasses (Poaceae). *Am. J. Bot.* 72:284–302.

_____. 1986. Comparative bundle sheath and mesophyll differentiation in the leaves of the C4 grasses *Panicum effusum* and *P. bulbosum*. *Am. J. Bot.* 73:1431–1442.

Dengler, N. G., L. B. MacKay, and L. M. Gregory. 1975. Cell enlargement and tissue differentiation during leaf expansion in beech, *Fagus grandifolia*. *Can. J. Bot.* 53:2846–2865.

Dengler, N. G., and A. A. Sanchez-Burgos. 1988. Effect of light intensity level on the expression of anisophylly in *Paradrymonia ciliosa* (Gesneriaceae). *Bot. Gaz.* 149:158–165.

Denne, M. P. 1966. Leaf development in *Trifolium repens*. *Bot. Gaz.* 127:202–210.

Dennis, W. D., and J. Woledge. 1983. The effect of shade during leaf expansion on photosynthesis by white clover leaves. *Ann. Bot.* 51:111–118.

Doley, D. 1978. Effects of shade on gas exchange and growth in seedlings of *Eucalyptus grandis* Hill ex Maiden. *Aust. J. Plant Physiol.* 5:723–738.

Duba, S. E., and S. B. Carpenter. 1980. Effect of shade on the growth, leaf morphology and photosynthetic capacity of an American sycamore clone. *Castanea* 45:219–227.

Dubuc-Lebreux, M. A., and R. Sattler. 1980 Développement des organes foliacés chez *Nicotiana tabacum* et le problème des méristèmes marginaux. *Phytomorphology* 30:17–32.

Esau, K. 1965. *Plant Anatomy*. 2nd Ed. New York: John Wiley & Sons.

Fagerberg, W. R. 1984. Cytological changes in palisade cells of developing sunflower leaves. *Protoplasma* 119:21–30.

———. 1987. Effect of short-term shading on the cytology of palisade tissue in mature leaves of the sunflower *Helianthus annuus*. *Am. J. Bot.* 74:822–828.

Fetcher, N., Strain, B. R., and S. F. Oberbauer. 1983. Effects of light regime on the growth, leaf morphology, and water relations of seedlings of two species of tropical trees. *Oecologia* 58:314–319.

Fisher, J. B. 1986. Sun and shade effects on the leaf of *Guarea* (Meliaceae): Plasticity of a branch analogue. *Bot. Gaz.* 147:84–89.

Fitter, A. H., and C. J. Ashmore. 1974. Response of two *Veronica* species to a simulated woodland light climate. *New Phytol.* 73:997–1001.

Frankland, B., and R. J. Letendre. 1978. Phytochrome and effects of shading on growth of woodland plants. *Photochem. Photobiol.* 27:223–230.

Friend, D. J. C., and M. E. Pomeroy. 1970. Changes in cell size and number associated with the effects of light intensity and temperature on the leaf morphology of wheat. *Can. J. Bot.* 48:85–90.

Fuchs, C. 1975. Ontogénèse foliare et acquisition de la forme chez le *Tropaeolum peregrinum* L. I. Les premiers stades de l'ontogénèse du lobe médian. *Ann. Sci. Nat. Bot.* 16:321–390.

Gay, A. P., and G. R. Hurd. 1975. The influence of light on stomatal density in tomato. *New Phytol.* 75:37–46.

Givnish, T. J. 1987. Comparative studies of leaf form: assessing the relative roles of selective pressures and phylogenetic constraints. *New Phytol.* 106:131–160. (Suppl.)

Goulet, F., and P. Bellefleur. 1986. Leaf morphology plasticity in response to light environment in deciduous tree species and its implication on forest succession. *Can. J. For. Res.* 16:1192–1195.

Green, P. B. 1986. Plasticity in shoot development: a biophysical view. In *Plasticity in Plants*. Ed. D. H. Jennings, A. J. Trewavas. Cambridge: Soc. Exp. Biol. Symp. 40:211–232.

Grime, J. P. 1979. *Plant Strategies and Vegetation Processes*. Chichester: John Wiley.

———. 1981. Plant strategies in shade. In *Plants and the Daylight Spectrum*: Ed. H. Smith. London: Academic Press. 159–186.

Grime, J. P., J. C. Crick, and J. E. Rincon. 1986. The ecological significance of plasticity. In *Plasticity in Plants*. Ed. D. H. Jennings, A. J. Trewavas. Cambridge: Soc. Exp. Biol. Symp. 40:5–30.

Haberlandt, G. 1914. *Physiological Plant Anatomy*. London: MacMillan.

Hageman, W. 1973. The organization of shoot development. *Rev. Biol.* 9:43–67.

Hanson, H. C. 1917. Leaf structure as related to environment. *Am. J. Bot.* 4:533–560.

Hatch, M. D., C. R. Slack, and T. A. Bull. 1969. Light-induced changes in the content of some enzymes of the C_4-dicarboxylic acid pathway of photosynthesis and its effect on other characteristics of photosynthesis. *Phytochemistry* 8:697–706.

Holmes, M. G. 1984. Radiation measurement. In *Techniques in Photomorphogenesis*. Ed. H. Smith, M. G. Holmes. London: Academic Press. 81–107.

Holmes, M. G., and H. Smith. 1977. The function of phytochrome in the natural environment. IV. Light quality and plant development. *Photochem. Photobiol.* 25:551–557.

Hori, Y, and Y. Oshima. 1986. Life history and population dynamics of the Japanese yam, *Dioscorea japonica* Thunb. I. Effects of initial plant size and light intensity on growth. *Bot. Mag.* 99: 407–418.

Hughes, A. P. 1959. Effects of the environment on leaf development in *Impatiens parviflora* DC. *J. Linn. Soc. London* 56:161–165.

Hughes, A. P., and G. C. Evans. 1962. Plant growth and the aerial environment. II. Effects of light intensity on *Impatiens parviflora*. *New Phytol.* 61:154–174.

Inada, K., and F. Nishiyama. 1987. Growth responses of sun and shade plants in simulated vegetation shade and neutral shade. *Jpn. J. Crop Sci.* 56:99–108.

Isanogle, I. T. 1944. Effects of controlled shading upon the development of leaf structure in two deciduous tree species. *Ecology* 25:404–413.

Isebrands, J. G., and P. R. Larson. 1973. Anatomical changes during leaf ontogeny in *Populus deltoides*. *Am. J. Bot.* 60:199–208.

———. 1980. Ontogeny of major veins in the lamina of *Populus deltoides*. *Am. J. Bot.* 67:23–33.

Jackson, L. W. R. 1967. Effects of shade on leaf structure of deciduous tree species. *Ecology* 48:498–499.

Jeune, B. 1984. Position et orientation des mitoses dans la zone organogène de jeunes feuilles de *Fraxinus exelsior*, *Glechoma hederacea* et *Lycopus europaeus*. *Can. J. Bot.* 62:2861–2864.

Jurik, T. W., J. F. Chabot, and B. F. Chabot. 1979. Ontogeny of photosynthetic performance in *Fragaria virginiana* under changing light regimes. *Plant Physiol.* 63:542–547.

———. 1982. Effects of light and nutrients on leaf size, CO_2 exchange, and anatomy in wild strawberry (*Fragaria virginiana*). *Plant Physiol.* 70:1044–1048.

Kemp, D. R. 1980. The location and size of the extension zone of emerging wheat leaves. *New Phytol.* 84:729–738.

———. 1981. The growth rate of wheat leaves in relation to the extension zone sugar concentration manipulated by shading. *J. Exp. Bot.* 32:141–150.

Ketring, D. L. 1979. Light effects on development of an indeterminate plant. *Plant Physiol.* 64:665–667.

Kirchanski, S. J. 1985. The ultrastructural development of the dimorphic plastids of *Zea mays* L. *Am. J. Bot.* 62:695–705.

Knecht, G. N., and J. W. O'Leary. 1972. The effect of light intensity on stomate number and density of *Phaseolus vulgaris* L. leaves. *Bot. Gaz.* 133:132–134.

Kutik, J. 1985. Chloroplast development. In *Photosynthesis During Leaf Development*. Ed. Z. Sesták. Dordrecht: Junk. 51–75.

Kwesiga, F., and J. Grace. 1986. The role of the red/far-red ratio in the response of tropical tree seedlings to shade. *Ann. Bot.* 57:283–290.

Langer, R. H. M. 1979. *How Grasses Grow*. London: Arnold.

Larcher, W. 1980. *Physiological Plant Ecology*. Berlin: Springer-Verlag.

Larson, P. R., J. G. Isebrands, and R. E. Dickson. 1980. Sink to source transition of *Populus* leaves. *Ber. Deutsch. Bot. Ges.* 93:79–90.

Lee, D. W. 1987. The spectral distribution of radiation in two neotropical rainforests. *Biotropica* 19:161–166.

Leech, R. M. 1985. The synthesis of cellular components in leaves. In *Control of Leaf Growth*. Ed. N. R. Baker, W. J. Davies, C. K. Ong. Cambridge: Cambridge University Press. 93–114.

———. 1986. Stability and plasticity during chloroplast development. In *Plasticity in Plants*. Ed. D. H. Jennings, A. J. Trewavas. Cambridge: Soc. Exp. Biol. Symp. 40. 121–154.

Lersten, N. 1965. Histogenesis of leaf venation in *Trifolium wormskioldii* (Leguminosae). *Am. J. Bot.* 52:767–774.

Lichtenthaler, H. K. 1985. Differences in morphology and chemical composition of leaves grown at different light intensities and qualities. In *Control of Leaf Growth*. Ed. N. R. Baker, W. J. Davies, C. K. Ong. Cambridge: Cambridge University Press. 201–221.

Lichtenthaler, H. K., C. Buschmann, M. Doll, H. J. Fietz, T. Bach, U. Kozel, D. Meier, and U. Rahmsdorf. 1981. Photosynthetic activity, chloroplast ultrastructure, and leaf characteristics of high-light and low-light plants and of sun and shade leaves. *Photosyn. Res.* 2:115–141.

Longstreth, D. J., J. A. Bolaños, and R. H. Goodard. 1985. Photosynthetic rate and mesophyll surface area in expanding leaves of *Alternanthera philoxeroides* grown at two light levels. *Am. J. Bot.* 72:14–19.

Longstreth, D. J., T. L. Harstock, and P. S. Nobel. 1981. Light effects on leaf development and photosynthetic capacity of *Hydrocotyle bonariensis* Lam. *Photosyn. Res.* 2:95–104.

Lyndon, R. F. 1976. The shoot apex in cell division in higher plants. In *Cell Division in Higher Plants.* Ed. M. M. Yeoman. London: Academic Press. 285–314.

_____. 1983. The mechanism of leaf initiation. In *The Growth and Functioning of Leaves.* Ed. J. E. Dale, F. L. Milthorpe. Cambridge: Cambridge University Press. 3–24.

_____. 1990. *Plant Development: The Cellular Basis.* London: Unwin Hyman.

Maksymowych, R. 1963. Cell division and cell elongation in leaf development of *Xanthium pennsylvanicum. Am. J. Bot.* 50:891–901.

_____. 1973. *Analysis of Leaf Development.* Cambridge: Cambridge University Press.

McCree, K. J. 1981. Photosynthetically active radiation. In *Physiological Plant Ecology. I. Responses to the Physical Environment:* Ed. O. L. Lange, P. S. Nobel, C. B. Osmond, H. Ziegler. Berlin: Springer-Verlag. 41–58.

McLaren, J. S., and H. Smith. 1978. Phytochrome control of the growth and development of *Rumex obtusifolius* under simulated light canopy light environments. *Plant Cell Environ.* 1:61–67.

Merrill, E. K. 1986a. Heteroblastic seedlings of green ash. II. Early development of simple and compound leaves. *Can. J. Bot.* 64:2650–2661.

_____. 1986b. Heteroblastic seedlings of green ash. III. Cell division activity and marginal meristems. *Can. J. Bot.* 64:2662–2668.

Milthorpe, F. L., and P. Newton. 1963. Studies on the expansion of the leaf surface. III. The influence of radiation on cell division and leaf expansion. *J. Exp. Bot.* 14:483–495.

Mohr, H. 1984. Criteria for photoreceptor involvement. In *Techniques in Photomorphogenesis.* Ed. H. Smith, M. G. Holmes. London: Academic Press. 13–42.

Morgan, D. C., and H. Smith. 1981. Non-photosynthetic responses to light quality. In *Physiological Plant Ecology. I. Responses to the Physical Environment.* Ed. O. L. Lange, P. S. Nobel, C. B. Osmond, H. Ziegler. *Encyclopedia of Plant Physiology* 12A:108–134. Berlin: Springer-Verlag.

Mueller, P. A., and N. G. Dengler. 1984. Leaf development in the anisophyllous shoots of *Pellionia daveauana* (Urticaceae). *Can. J. Bot.* 62:1158–1170.

Newton, P. 1963. Studies on the expansion of the leaf surface. II. The influence of light intensity and daylength. *J. Exp. Bot.* 14:458–482.

Nilsen, E. T. 1986. Quantitative phenology and leaf survivorship of *Rhododendron maximum* in contrasting irradiance environments of the southern Appalachian mountains. *Am. J. Bot.* 73:822–931.

Njoku, E. 1956. Studies on the morphogenesis of leaves. XI. The effect of light intensity on leaf shape in *Ipomoea caerulea. New Phytol.* 55:91–110.

Nobel, P. S., and D. J. Longstreth. 1981. Effects of environmental factors on leaf anatomy, mesophyll cell conductance and photosynthesis. In *Photosynthesis.* Ed. G. Akoyunoglu. Philadelphia: Balaban Int. Sci. Serv. 6:245–259.

Nobel, P. S., and D. B. Walker. 1985. Structure of leaf photosynthetic tissue. In *Topics in Photosynthesis, Vol. 6. Photosynthetic Mechanisms and the Environment.* Ed. J. Barker, N. R. Baker. Amsterdam: Elsevier. 501–536.

Nobel, P. S., L. J. Zarazoga, and W. K. Smith. 1975. Relation between mesophyll surface area, photosynthetic rate, and illumination level during development for leaves of *Plectranthus parviflorus* Henkel. *Plant Physiol.* 55:1067–1070.

Nygren, M., and S. Kellomaki. 1983. Effect of shading on leaf structure and photosynthesis in young birches, *Betula pendula* Roth. and *B. pubescens* Ehat. *Forest Ecol. Manag.* 7:119–132.

Nyman, L. P., and N. G. Dengler. 1978. Cell enlargement during leaf development in *Catharanthus roseus*. *Can. J. Bot.* 56:592–605.

Oquist, G., L. Brunes, and L. H. Ziegler. 1982. Photosynthetic efficiency of *Betula pendula* acclimated to different quantum flux densities. *Plant Cell Environ.* 5:9–15.

Pandey, B. N., and R. P. Sinha 1977. Light as a factor in growth and morphogenesis. Effect of artificial shading on *Crotalaria juncea* L. and *C. sericea* Retz. *New Phytol.* 79:431–440.

Patrick, J. W. 1972. Vascular system of the stem of the wheat plant. II. Development. *Aust. J. Bot.* 20:65–78,

Patterson, D. T. 1980a. Shading effects on growth and partitioning of plant biomass in cogongrass (*Imperata cylindrica*) from shaded and exposed habitats. *Weed. Sci.* 28:735–740.

————. 1980b. Light and temperature adaptation. In *Predicting Photosynthesis for Ecosystem Models*. Ed. J. D. Hesketh, J. W. Jones. Boca Raton: CRC Press. 205–235.

Paul, R. N., and D. T. Patterson. 1980. Effects of shading on the anatomy and ultrastructure of the leaf mesophyll and vascular bundles of itchgrass (*Rottboellia exaltata*). *Weed Sci.* 28:216–224.

Penfound, W. T. 1931. Plant anatomy as conditioned by light intensity and soil mixture. *Am. J. Bot.* 18:558–572.

Perry, M. H., D. J. C. Friend, and H. Y. Yamamoto. 1986. Photosynthetic and leaf morphological characteristics in *Leucaena leucocephala* as affected by growth under different neutral shade levels. *Photosynthesis Res.* 9:305–316.

Poethig, R. S., and I. M. Sussex. 1985a. The developmental morphology and growth dynamics of the tobacco leaf. *Planta* 165:158–169.

————. 1985b. The cellular parameters of leaf development in tobacco: a clonal analysis. *Planta* 165:170–184.

Postek, M. T., and S. C. Tucker. 1982. Foliar ontogeny and histogenesis in *Magnolia grandiflora* L. I. Apical organization and early development. *Am. J. Bot* 69:556–569.

Rawson, H. M., and C. L. Craven. 1975. Stomatal development during leaf expansion in tobacco and sunflower. *Aust. J. Bot.* 23:253–262.

Richards, J. H., and D. W. Lee. 1986. Light effects on leaf morphology in the water hyacinth, *Eichhornia crassipes* Solms. *Am. J. Bot.* 73:1741–1747.

Roberts-Nkrumah, L. B., T. U. Ferguson, and L. A. Wilson. 1986. Responses of four sweet potato cultivars to levels of shade: 1. Dry matter production, shoot morphology and leaf anatomy. *Trop. Agric.* 63:258–264.

Rumi, C. P., and R. M. Carpinetti. 1977. Effect of sunlight on the development of *Tropaeolum majus*: 1. Leaf growth. *Fyton* 35:137–143.

Salisbury, F. B. 1981. Responses to photoperiod. In *Physiological Plant Ecology I. Responses to the Physical Environment*. Ed. O. L. Lange, P. S. Nobel, C. B. Osmond, H. Ziegler. Berlin: Springer-Verlag. 135–168.

Sanchez, R. A. 1971. Phytochrome involvement in the control of leaf shape of *Taraxacum officinale* L. *Experientia* 27:1234–1237.

Sanchez, R. A., and D. Cogliatti. 1975. The interaction between phytochrome and white light irradiance in the control of leaf shape in *Taraxacum officinale*. *Bot. Gaz.* 136:281–285.

Sanchez-Burgos, A. A., and N. G. Dengler. 1988. Leaf development in isophyllous and facultatively anisphyllous species of *Pentadenia* (Gesneriaceae) *Am. J. Bot.* 75:1472–1484.

Sasahara, T. 1982. Changes in size and number of mesophyll cells, nitrogen content and photosynthesis with leaf order in Brassica spp. Ann. Bot. 50:379–383.

Schlichting, C. D. 1986. The evolution of phenotype plasticity in plants. Annu. Rev. Ecol. Syst. 17:667–693.

Sesták, Z., I. Tichá, J. Catský, J. Solárová, J. Pospíšilová, and D. Hodánová. 1985. Integration of photosynthetic characteristics during leaf development. In Photosynthesis During Leaf Development: Ed. Z. Sesták. Dordrecht: Junk. 263–286.

Sharman, B. C. 1945. Leaf and bud initiation in the Gramineae. Bot. Gaz. 106:269–289.

Silk, W. K. 1983. Kinematic analysis of leaf expansion. In The Growth and Functioning of Leaves. Ed. J. E. Dale, F. L. Milthorpe. Cambridge: Cambridge University Press. 89–108.

Silvy, A. 1982a. La première feuille des plantules d'orge. I. Morphogenese, les epidermes. Can. J. Bot. 60:2864–2876.

_____. 1982b. La première feuille des plantules d'orge. II. Croissance en longueur. Can. J. Bot. 60:2877–2881.

Smith, H. 1982. Light quality, photoreception and plant strategy. Annu. Rev. Plant Physiol. 33:481–518.

Smith, H., and D. C. Morgan. 1981. The spectral characteristics of the visible radiation incident upon the surface of the earth. In Plants and the Daylight Spectrum. Ed. H. Smith. London: Academic Press. 3–20.

_____. 1983. The function of phytochrome in nature. In Photomorphogenesis. Ed. W. Shropshire, H. Mohr. Encyclopedia of Plant Physiology 16B:491–513. Berlin: Springer-Verlag.

Smith, W. K., and P. S. Nobel. 1978. Influence of irradiation, soil water potential, and leaf temperature on leaf morphology on a desert broadleaf, Encelia farinosa Gray (Compositae) Am. J. Bot. 65:429–432.

Soper, K., and K. J. Mitchell. 1956. The developmental anatomy of perennial ryegrass (Lolium perenne L.). N. Z. J. Sci. Technol. 37:484–504.

Spence, D. H. N. 1981. Light quality and plant responses underwater. In Plants and the Daylight Spectrum: Ed. H. Smith. London: Academic Press. 245–276.

Sunderland, N. 1960. Cell division and expansion in the growth of the leaf. J. Exp. Bot. 31:68–80.

Talbert, C. M., and A. E. Holch. 1957. A study of the lobing of sun and shade leaves. Ecology 38:655–658.

Taylor, G., and W. J. Davies. 1985. The control of leaf growth of Betula and Acer by photoenvironment. New Phytol. 101:259–268.

Terry, N. 1968 Developmental physiology of the sugar beet. I. The influence of light and temperature on growth. J. Exp. Bot. 19:795–811.

Tichá, I. 1985. Ontogeny of leaf morphology and anatomy. In Photosynthesis During Leaf Development. Ed. Z. Sesták. Dordrecht: Junk. 16–50.

Trewavas, A. J. 1986. Resource allocation under poor growth conditions. A major role for growth substances in developmental plasticity. In Plasticity in Plants. Ed. D. H. Jennings, A. J. Trewavas. Cambridge: Soc. Exp. Biol. Symp. 40:31–76.

Turrell, F. M. 1936. The area of exposed internal surface of dicotyledon leaves. Am. J. Bot. 23:255–264.

Vince-Prue, D. 1983. Photomorphogenesis and flowering. In Photomorphogenesis. Ed. W. Shropshire, H. Mohr. Encylcopedia of Plant Physiology 16B:457–490. Berlin: Springer-Verlag.

Vince-Prue, D., and D. J. Tucker. 1983. Photomorphogenesis in leaves. In The Growth and Functioning of Leaves. Ed. J. E. Dale, F. L. Milthorpe. Cambridge: Cambridge University Press. 233 269.

Ward, D. A., and H. W. Woolhouse. 1986. Comparative effects of light during growth on the photosynthetic properties of NADP malic enzyme type 4-carbon pathway from open and shaded habitats. I. Gas exchange, leaf anatomy and ultrastructure. Plant Cell Environ. 9:261–270.

Whatley, J. M. 1980. Plastid growth and division in Phaseolus vulgaris. New Phytol. 86:1–16.

Wild, A., and G. Wolf. 1980. The effect of different light intensities on the frequency and size of stomata, the size of cells, the number, size and chlorophyll content of chloroplasts in the mesophyll and guard cells during the ontogeny of primary leaves of *Sinapis alba*. *Z. Pflanzenphysiol.* 97:325–342.

Williams, R. F. 1975. *The Shoot Apex and Leaf Growth*. Cambridge: Cambridge Univ. Press.

Wilson, D. and J.P Cooper. 1969. Effect of light intensity during growth on leaf anatomy and subsequent light-saturated photosynthesis among contrasting *Lolium* genotypes. *New Phytol.* 68:1125–1135.

Wilson, G. L. 1966. Studies on the expansion of the leaf surface. V. Cell division and expansion in a developing leaf as influenced by light and upper leaves. *J. Exp. Bot.* 52:440–451.

Wylie, R. B. 1951. Principles of foliar organization shown by sun-shade leaves from ten species of deciduous dicotyledonous trees. *Am. J. Bot.* 38:355–361.

Young, D. R. and W. K. Smith. 1980. Influence of sunlight on photosynthesis, water relations, and leaf structure in the understory species *Arnica cordifolia*. *Ecology* 61:1380–1390.

Young, J. E. 1975. Effects of the spectral composition of light sources on the growth of a higher plant. In *Light as an Ecological Factor II*. Ed. G. C. Evans, R. Bainbridge, O. Rackham, Oxford: Blackwell Scientific Publications.

Yun, J. I. and S. E. Taylor. 1986. Adaptive implications of leaf thickness for sun-grown and shade grown *Abutilon theophrasti*. *Ecology* 67:1314–1318.

Chapter 6

The Laticiferous System in Vascular Plants

S. K. DATTA and MUHAMMAD IQBAL

Laticifers, the specialized cells or tubes containing latex, constitute an organized storage or excretion system. Unlike gland cells, they do not discharge the inert substances that they excrete (Schnepf 1974). They occur in nearly 12,500 species belonging to 900 genera and some 22 families (Esau 1965; Metcalfe 1983), mostly of the Dicotyledonae. A few families of the Monocotyledonae and a pteridophyte genus (*Regnellidium*) of the Marsileaceae also contain laticifers (Van Die 1955; Metcalfe 1967), thus indicating the polyphyletic origin of laticifers (Rudall 1987). Most laticiferous plants belong to the dicot families Apocynaceae, Asclepiadaceae, Compositae, Euphorbiaceae, Papaveraceae, and Sapotaceae and to the monocot families Araceae, Liliaceae, and Musaceae. These may be herbs (including xeric, succulent, and water plants), shrubs, trees, or lianas. Mahlberg et al. (1987) reported fossil laticifers in Eocene brown coal deposits.

Laticiferous cells grow by intrusive as well as symplastic growth. Growing tips follow the course of middle lamella. Pectinase may be present in the latex; this may facilitate intrusive growth and also loosen wall material of the laticifer itself to simplify extension growth (Wilson et al. 1976). The basic nutritional requirements of the laticifers are obtained from adjacent cells, possibly phloem cells, to which they are often associated (Cass 1985; Fay et al. 1989).

Distribution of laticifers within the plant body varies with species. They may occur in the vascular tissues (particularly in phloem), phellem, and parenchyma. In xylem, they are often restricted to rays, running as radial tubes. Axial latex tubes enclosed in the xylem fibers are also known (*Artocarpus* spp.; Topper and Koek-Noorman 1980). Laticifers may enter leaves and develop branches, extending into the mesophyll, sometimes reaching the hypodermis or epidermis. In *Decaisnea insignis,* a Lardizabalaceae shrub, laticifers are confined to fruits, where they form a peculiar network (Metcalfe 1983). They occur in all plant parts except anther lobes, stigma nectaries, and epidermal glands of *Jatropha gossypifolia* (Castells et al. 1984), ovules

From *Growth Patterns in Vascular Plants* Edited by Muhammed Iqbal

137

and stigma of *Vallaris solanacea* (Murugan and Inamdar 1987a), and anther lobes and stigma of *Plumeria alba* (Murugan and Inamdar 1987b).

TYPES OF LATICIFERS

The laticifers are classified into (a) nonarticulated and (b) articulated types (Hartig 1862; David 1872). The nonarticulated laticifers (NAL) originate from single cells, develop with the plant, and finally become multinucleate coenocytes. In some species, they remain uninucleate. The laticifer initials grow more rapidly than the neighboring cells; their nuclei enlarge and divide without subsequent wall formation. The cells elongate mostly by apical growth, often at both ends, so that the elongating cell tips intrude between the immediately adjoining cells. The elongating apices may bifurcate repeatedly, thus forming a branched system. It is believed that nonarticulated laticifers originate in primary tissue and continue intrusive growth only in living tissues that have not lost their ability to divide (Fahn 1979). NAL are most common in the stem cortex and proliferate at the nodes, from whence they spread into leaves via the parenchymatous tissue of the petiole, and into pith through nodal leaf gaps. In some dicot taxa, they cross the vascular cambium (see Rudall 1989) and are located in wood rays (Rudall 1987, 1989; Sudo and Fujii 1987; Carlquist 1988; Fujii 1988; Fujii and Sudo 1988).

Development of multicelled articulated laticifers (AL) is analogous to that of xylem vessels. The end walls of component cells either remain entire, become porous, or disappear completely. Some laticifers anastomose laterally with the neighboring cells and are termed articulated anastomosing (branched) laticifers. The laticifers of different members in a family are often of one type: only nonarticulated laticifers are found in Apocynaceae. Euphorbiaceae, however, contain both articulated and nonarticulated laticifers; e.g. *Hevea brasiliensis* and *Manihot glaziovii* possess articulated laticifers whereas *Euphorbia* bears nonarticulated ones. Furthermore, independent systems of both types may occur in the same species, e.g. in species of *Stapelia* and *Trichocaulon*.

Several genera such as *Nerium* and *Thevetia* (Apocynaceae) (Fahn 1979), *Asclepias, Calotropis,* and *Cryptostegia* (Asclepiadaceae) (Datta and De 1986a,b), *Broussonetia, Ficus,* and *Maclura* (Moraceae) (Datta 1979; Fahn 1979), and *Euphorbia* (Euphorbiaceae) (Metcalfe 1967; Datta and Datta 1980; Figure 6.1) are known for bearing nonarticulated branched laticifers, whereas many others such as *Vinca* (Apocynaceae), *Cannabis* (Moraceae), and *Urtica* (Urticaceae) (Metcalfe 1967, 1983) are characterized by nonarticulated unbranched laticifers. Both types of laticifers have been reported in the same plant of *Jatropha,* Euphorbiaceae (Kakkar and Paliwal 1972; Dehgan and Craig 1978).

Likewise, articulated anastomosing laticifers typify *Carica* (Caricaceae), *Cichorium, Lactuca, Sonchus, Taraxacum,* and *Tragopogon* (Compositae), *Hevea* and *Manihot* (Euphorbiaceae), and all or most genera of Araceae, Campanulaceae, and Lobeliaceae (Metcalfe 1967, 1983; French 1988), whereas articulated nonanastomosing laticifers occur in *Convolvulus, Dichondra,* and *Ipomoea* (Convolvulaceae), *Allium* (Liliaceae), *Musa* (Musaceae), and *Achras* (Sapotaceae), among others (Esau 1965; Metcalfe 1983).

In the rubber plant (*Parthenium argentatum*), rubber accumulates in parenchymatous cells, instead of laticiferous cells. These cells are often confined to rays, mostly in the phloem. Rubber also accumulates in the epithelial cells of resin ducts but is not secreted into the duct lumen.

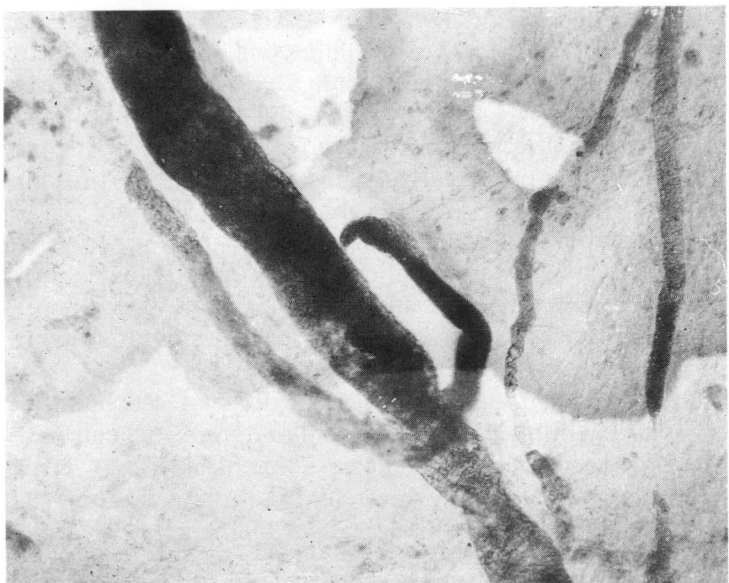

Figure 6.1. Nonarticulated branched laticifer isolated from *Euphorbia nivulia* (from Datta and Datta 1980).

LATICIFER DEVELOPMENT *IN SITU*

Origin and Progress

The unbranched nonarticulated laticifers (NALs) develop in the outer portion of the shoot apex. They continue their growth in the developing leaf until it fully matures. Branched NALs develop only in primary tissues. The laticifers entering nodes undergo complex branching. Within the leaf, they follow the vascular bundles, branching freely from vein to vein. These laticifers, commonly associated with phloem, may send out branches between palisade cells or downward between the spongy mesophyll cells. The development of branched NALs has been studied in several plants. In *Euphorbia marginata,* 12 NAL initials arise in the cotyledonary node of the embryo at its early cordate stage (Mahlberg and Sabharwal 1968). In the embryo of *Nerium oleander,* 28 laticifer initials grow and branch, penetrate into radicle and cotyledons, and grow toward the shoot apex and leaf primordia (Mahlberg 1961). The NALs in *Calotropis gigantea* originate from single cells, and develop into long tube-like structures that may branch but usually do not anastomose (Datta and De 1986b; Roy and De 1992). They exist either singly or as groups of parallel elongated cells. Later the cells undergo further elongation concomitant with free nuclear division. Subsequently the nuclei degenerate as the cell further elongates.

The entire laticiferous system in *Jatropha dioica* derives from 5–7 initials in the embryo (Cass 1985). A ring of 12 initials differentiates from the procambial cells, along the outer periphery near the cotyledonary node, during the late globular stage of embryogenesis in *Thevetia peruviana* and gives rise to nonarticulated laticifers (NAL) through bidirectional cell growth toward the radicle and cotyledon (Murugan and Inamdar 1989). In *Jatropha,* the laticifers are thought to have been derived from the innermost layer of the embryonic cortex (Cass 1985). The initials in *Glaucium flavum* first appear in the procambium of the radicle adjacent to the phloem about 48–72 hr after germination (Nessler 1982). In *Cichorium intybus,* files of laticiferous cells appear at the boundary between the phloic procambium and ground meristem. Upon seed germination, the cells develop perforations in the end walls, which later become completely resorbed (Vertrees and Mahlberg 1978).

Both primary and secondary laticiferous systems occur in *Morus nigra.* The primary laticifers arise from eight initials in the outer periphery of the future cambium near the cotyledonary node of the young heart-shaped embryo. The secondary laticiferous system comprises similar laticifers that are produced by initials of the vascular cambium. These laticifers occur in the secondary phloem of stem and root and are more numerous than the primary ones. The two systems do not fuse (Veenendaal and Outer 1990).

Anastomosing articulated laticifers (AL) are often of secondary origin, deriving from the fusiform cambial initials. In *Papaver somniferum,* AL can first be seen when roots are 2 mm in size and possess tracheary elements (Sarkany et al. 1970). These laticifers may also occur in placental traces (Fairbairn and Kapoor 1960) and in filaments extending into the anthers (Nessler and Mahlberg 1979c). In *P. bracteatum,* laticifers first differentiate in the procambium of the radicle associated with phloem. Proliferation of membrane-bound vesicles apparently of endoplasmic reticulum (ER) origin, distinguishes laticifers from adjacent cells (Nessler and Mahlberg 1978).

Protoplasm Differentiation

NAL are essentially branched coenocytes with actively growing tips continuous with the remote part of the cell, where the protoplasm is almost senescent. When the laticifer is cut, its protoplast tends to become damaged because of the sudden loss of turgor pressure (Fineran 1983). In *Nerium oleander* shoot apices, the early developmental stages of the branched NAL system are characterized by dense cytoplasm containing numerous vesicles. Mature laticifers have a thin layer of peripheral cytoplasm and a large central vacuole that encloses smaller vesicles. This vacuole apparently arises by dilation of the endoplasmic reticulum and by cellular autophagy which involves sequestering of parts of the cytoplasm in vesicles and a subsequent lysis. Limited fusion of smaller vesicles originating from the distal ER may also contribute to vacuole formation (Stockstill and Nessler 1986). The large central vacuole and the peripheral cytoplasm are typical of nonarticulated branched laticifers (cf. Giordani 1977a; Wilson and Mahlberg 1980; Rachmilevitz and Fahn 1982). Dictyosomes may be another possible source of laticifer vesicles (Wilson and Mahlberg 1980; Rachmilevitz and Fahn 1982). Cellular autophagy has been suggested to be the major mechanism for vacuole development in the nonarticulated, branched laticifers (Esau and Kosakai 1975; Buvat and Robert 1979), in which areas of the cytoplasm are enclosed by autophagic vesicles and the cellular contacts of the vesicles lysed (Marty 1968, 1970a, b; Giordani 1978; Rachmilevitz and Fahn 1982). Wilson and Mahlberg (1978) proposed that the sequestered areas of cytoplasm reported by Marty (1970a) are artifacts caused by surging of the peripheral cytoplasm due to improper fixation. Surging was not evident in the cytoplasm of *Nerium* lacticifers, however. The tonoplast was intact and patches of cytoplasm were surrounded by intact membrane (Stockstill and Nessler 1986). Vacuole formation in this species was seemingly caused by cellular autophagy, ER dilation, and fusion of small vesicles.

In *Ficus carica,* an increase in vacuolar volume appears to be followed by autophagy occurring in vacuoles. Multivesicular structures are thought to be involved in the formation of the autophagic vacuoles by supplying lytic enzymes (Rachmilevitz and Fahn 1982). Whether Golgi vesicles are the only cell components that participate in vacuole formation is not certain. Formation of vacuoles by cellular autophagy was also reported in the NAL of *Euphorbia characias* (Marty 1970a, b) and *Asclepias curassavica* (Giordani 1978). In the laticifers of *A. syriaca,* formation of vacuoles occurred by enlargement of the ER and only limited cellular autophagy (Wilson and Mahlberg 1980). In the NAL of poinsettia (*Euphorbia pulcherrima*), there is a complex system of tubular vacuoles in addition to the usual spheroidal vacuoles (Fineran 1983; Figure 6.2). Development of these vacuoles is concurrent with differentiation of the Golgi apparatus; the smooth ER associated with the dictyosomes forms both tubular and vesicular provacuoles, which later become lysosomes and eventually the central vacuoles (Marty 1978).

The progressive degeneration of cytoplasm in mature NAL has been described for several species. In *Taraxacum bicorne,* the protoplast degenerates in the following order: dictyosomes, mitochondria, ER, nucleus, and plastids (Heinrich 1967). Based on the presence of microbodies with strong peroxidase activity in laticifers of *Euphorbia characias,* Marty (1970b) suggested that peroxisomes might be involved in the initial biosynthesis of latex. Marty (1971a) also proposed that starch grains are eventually freed from the amyloplast and ejected into the vacuole, although there is evidence that they are digested or utilized by the plant. In well-fixed material of *E. pulcherrima,* however, starch grains remained within the amyloplast in both differentiating and mature parts of laticifer (Fineran 1982). Amyloplasts fail to become reduced or senescent on maturation of the laticifer cytoplasm. In *E. heterophylla* and *E. myrsinites,* the laticifers were capable of producing starch but not of consuming it; when starch reserves in other tissues were depleted, those of the laticifer remained (Biesboer and Mahlberg 1978). No starch grains were observed in the embryonal laticifers of *Thevetia peruviana* (Murugan and Inamdar 1989) or in mature laticifers of *Plumeria alba* (Murugan and Inamdar 1987b). The role of starch grains in differentiating and mature laticifers needs to be further elucidated.

Plastids have few lamellae, possess phytoferritin, and accumulate small amounts of starch in *Asclepias syriaca* (Wilson and Mahlberg 1978). It is difficult to consider laticifer phytoferritin as a storage product as suggested by Blackwell et al. (1969), because laticifer plastids do not become photosynthetically green, and presumably are not numerous enough to provide chloroplasts in the adjacent cells with a source of iron. Laticifer phytoferritin may be a byproduct accumulation (Wilson and Mahlberg 1978).

Laticifer nuclei are highly lobed and possess dilated perinuclear spaces. Milanez and Neto (1956) reported giant nuclei in embryonal laticifers of *Euphorbia pulcherrima,* which they attributed to frequent nuclear fusions. Nuclei may occur in groups in *Asclepias* (Wilson and Mahlberg 1978), without any ER bridges in embryonal laticifers, and with ER bridges in seedling laticifers. In *Jatropha* (Cass 1968), the outer nuclear membranes of adjacent nuclei are connected by segments of rough ER; this explains the linear arrangement of nuclei in the cell. The presence of a dilated perinuclear space in laticifer nuclei shortly after seed germination suggests a secretory activity or altered osmolarity for these membranes. Whether perinuclear dilation, which disappears in more mature regions of the protoplast, has a role in latex production is unknown.

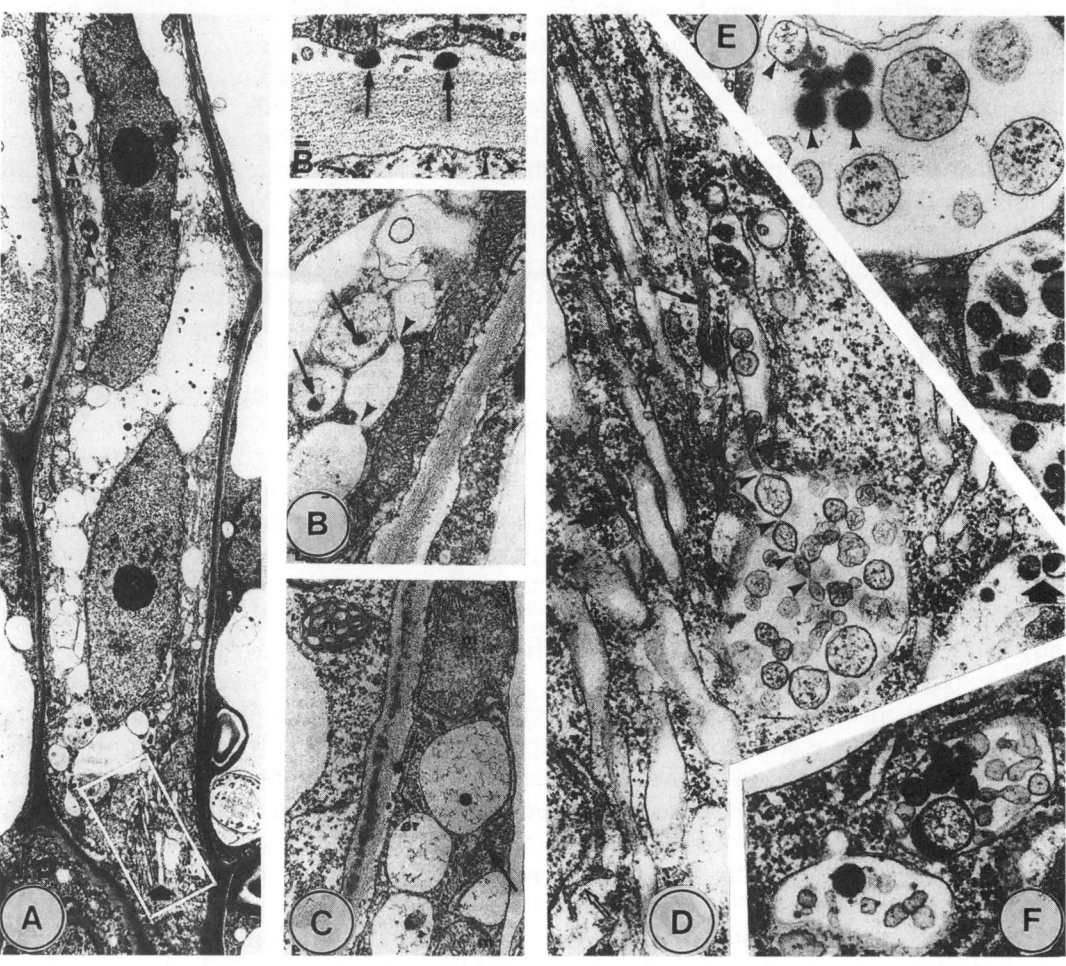

Figure 6.2. Ultrastructure of the differentiating portion of nonarticulated laticifers of *Euphorbia pulcherrima*. (A) Longitudinal section showing two large nuclei (n) and the tubular and rounded vacuoles (v) in the cytoplasm. The tubular vacuoles, mostly in the peripheral cytoplasm, are shown best toward the bottom of the micrograph (*large arrow*); × 6000. (B) Portion of two adjacent laticifers showing an elongated mitochondrion (m) and small peripheral vacuoles, some of them with latex particles (*arrows*). The expanded rounded vacuoles (*arrow heads*) are mutually connected; × 24,000. $\overline{\text{B}}$ shows the wall and adjacent cytoplasm between a laticifer (*above*) and a mesophyll cell (*below*) having microtubules associated with the plasmalemmae (*arrow heads*) and shows the electron-opaque deposits (*arrows*); the tubular vesicular materials (er) lie on the laticifer side; × 50,000. (C) Compared to the mitochondrion of a mesophyll cell (*left*), mitochondria of the differentiating laticifer (*right*) are indistinct with a few cristae and stroma of low density. A few microbodies (*arrow*) and short profiles of endoplasmic reticulum (*arrow head*) occur in the cytoplasm; × 24,000. (D) Magnified view of the parietal cytoplasm from the area indicated by the *large arrow* in Figure 6.2A showing the presence of tubular vacuoles, some with locally expanded portions. The narrower tubes (*black arrows*) possess darker contents than the wider ones. Some tubular vacuoles contain small vesicles (*curved empty arrows*) and tubelike inclusions (*straight empty arrows*). Several of the vesicles in the expanded, rounded portion of the vacuole seem to have developed by vesiculation of tubular structures (*arrow heads*). The *thick arrow* at the *right corner* indicates latex particles with cores; × 35,000. (E) Cytoplasm of a differentiating laticifer with vacuoles that contain cytoplasmic inclusions and latex particles (*arrows*). The inclusions in the top vacuole show the degenerating ribosomes and cytoplasmic matrix; × 20,000. (F) Group of small rounded vacuoles containing vesicles and some distinct latex particles at an early stage of development; × 16,000 (from Fineran 1983).

Formation of Latex

The development of a large central vacuole and formation of dense globules or particles subsequently released into the vacuole are common ultrastructural features of laticifer differentiation. Latex particles may develop in the cytoplasm (Heinrich 1967, 1970; Schulze et al 1967; Wilson and Mahlberg 1980; Rachmilevitz and Fahn 1982), in small vacuoles (Esau and Kosakai 1975), in association with rough ER (Behnke and Herrmann 1978), or in Golgi vesicles (Marty 1968). These particles originate *de novo* in the cytoplasmic matrix, where they may remain at maturity, as in *Hevea brasiliensis* (Dickenson 1969; Pujarniscle 1971; Hebant 1981), or may be shifted to the vacuole at some later stage, as in *Musa* (Trécul 1867), *Ficus elastica* (Popovici 1926; Heinrich 1970), *Euphorbia characias* (Marty 1968, 1971b), *Asclepias curassavica* (Giordani 1977a), *A. syriaca* (Wilson and Mahlberg 1980), *Ficus carica* (Rachmilevitz and Fahn 1982) and *Calotropis gigantea* (Roy and De 1992). Alternatively, latex particles may arise and remain within the vacuole, as in *Euphorbia pulcherrima* (Groeneveld 1976b).

There seem to be at least two distinct locations of particles in mature laticifers: in the cytoplasm, as naked structures (*Lactuca sativa*; Giordani 1979), and in the vacuole (*Euphorbia pulcherrima*, Fineran 1983). The naked particles may characterize articulated laticifers, whereas those located within the vacuoles may typify the nonarticulated laticifers (Giordani 1979). The latex particles in poinsettia were noted to have arisen in the tubular vacuoles at some intermediate stage during vacuolar expansion, when the vacuoles had a diameter of > 0.5 μm (Fineran 1983). Before the tubular and associated spheroidal vacuoles showed any definite latex particles, they often contained single-membrane-bound vesicles, which may represent the initials of the latex particles and may give rise to the translucent core of the mature latex particle (Fineran 1982, 1983). The limiting membrane of the vesicles seems to have been derived from the tonoplast, either by an invagination or sequestration. The vesicles, in some instances, seemingly had a more indirect origin via tubular inclusions that vesiculated (Figure 6.2; Fineran 1983).

The latex particles' electron-dense matrix may derive from the vacuolar sap and may accumulate on the vesicles that provide centers for nucleation upon initiation of latex particles (Figure 6.2). Thus, the particles in poinsettia had a composite structure, the matrix being derived from the vacuole, the core contents originally from the cytoplasm, and its limiting layer from the tonoplast. The matrix material was first deposited onto one side of the vesicle, often forming a blob, which later disappeared as the particle rounded off into a tiny sphere that enclosed the core in an asymmetrical position (Fineran 1983).

The masses of cytoplasm within the vacuole degenerate and disappear, leaving the latex particles intact. The presence of lytic enzymes in the vacuoles was demonstrated by Marty (1970a, b) and Matile et al. (1970). Sequestration of cytoplasm followed by lytic breakdown in the vacuole may represent a more efficient process for eliminating large amounts of cytoplasm than the more local invagination process by the tonoplast (Fineran 1970, 1971). The numerous latex particles contained within the smaller vacuoles of the sequestered cytoplasm can be released *en masse* into the developing central vacuoles, in contrast to the more usual process of fusion by individual vacuoles. Triterpenyl fatty acid esters in *Hoya* latices (Warnaar 1982) and cycloartenol from the latex of *E. pulcherrima* (Spilatro and Mahlberg 1986) can be used to determine the latex of tissues and thus serve as chemical markers. Measurements of cycloartenol, the laticifer-specific triterpenol, in *E. pulcherrima* showed that young leaves contain the highest latex and laticifer-starch contents on the basis of dry weight and leaf area. In older expanding leaves, laticifer growth resulted in an increased total latex volume and total laticifer starch. Laticifer growth and starch accumulation stopped upon cessation of leaf expansion (Spilatro and Mahlberg 1986). Laticifer-starch accumulation correlates with laticifer growth, but mobilization of the starch out of the laticifer is not apparent in old or senescent leaves, thus demonstrating that laticifer-starch grains function within the laticifer independently of degradation or export to other cell types. High latex content, with its toxic compontents, may provide increased protection for young leaves, which would otherwise be more susceptible than old leaves to insects and animal predation (Swain 1977). Starch concentration in laticifers differs among plant organs and appears to correlate to the proximity of primary photosynthate production sites (Spilatro and Mahlberg 1986).

Chemistry of Latex

Latex contains fuel oils, carbohydrates, organic acids, alkaloids, glycosides, etc. in solution and also various suspended particles, including terpenes, resins, and rubber (Fahn 1979; Calvin 1987). The components in the dispersed phase of the latex vary but include polyisophene, hydrocarbons, carotenes, proteins and phospholipids, in-organics, and sterols and sterol-esters (Archer et al. 1969; Groeneveld 1976a). The *Carica* latex is known to possess papain and a proteolytic enzyme (Fahn 1979), whereas *Euphorbia* latex is rich in vitamin B (Urschler 1956) and many specialized plant products such as rubber, alkanes, glycerides (Nielsen et al. 1977), C_{28}–C_{30} triterpenes and their esters (Ponsinet and Ourisson 1968), and various polyfunctional polycyclic diterpenes and cryptic irritants, the fatty acid esters of which are cocarcinogenic (Hecker 1975). Crystals of oxalates and malates are also not uncommon. Some specific materials present in the latex of certain plants include sugars (Compositae), tannins (*Musa*—Solereder and Meyer 1928), variously shaped starch grains (*Euphorbia* spp.—Mahlberg 1973, 1975), protein crystals (*Ficus callosa*—Ultee 1923; *Taraxacum bicorne*—Heinrich 1967), cardiac glycosides (certain Apocynaceae and Asclepiadaceae—Datta and De 1986a; De and Datta 1988), alkaloids (some members of Papaveraceae—Fairbairn and Wassel 1964; Matile et al. 1970; Nuemann and Muller 1972; Lalezari et al. 1974; Kamo et al. 1982), and lipids (*Plumeria alba, Vallaris solanacea*—Murugan and Inamdar 1987a,b). The cardenolides present in several plants are thought to be the latex constituents (Groeneveld and Vandermade 1982). In *Calotropis,* cardenolides in latex and osteoid starch grains are present both *in vivo* and *in vitro* (Datta and De 1986a,b). Free sterols occur in New World species of Araceae, subfamily Colocasioideae, and were localized by Fox and French (1988) in 1 μm terpenoid particles, which are abundant and account for the white-opaque appearance of the latex of these species. Starch grains in *Euphorbia* latex differ in metabolic processes and in biophysical-biochemical properties from grains of other plant cells (Spilatro and Mahlberg 1985). Although they are rare in other plants, the rod-and spindle-shaped starch grains occur widely in laticifers of the herbacious *Euphorbia* species (Biesboer and Mahlberg 1981a). Laticifer starch grains are significantly less soluble in anhydrous dimethylsulfoxide than other β-type starch grains and are rapidly hydrolyzed by amylase. The array of properties of laticifer starch grains is distinctive among β-type grains and indicates an unusually strong molecular association within the grain (Spilatro and Mahlberg 1985). Biesboer and Mahlberg (1981b) have shown that the nonutilization of laticifer starch grains during plant growth may result from a modified crystalline structure that is refractory to enzymatic hydrolysis.

Triterpenols (4,4-dimethyl-3-hydroxy-triterpenoids) and phytosterols (4-dimethyl-3-hydroxy-triterpenoids) are abundant in *Euphorbia* latex (Ponsinet and Ourisson 1968).

Triterpenoids and their esters comprise 40% of the latex dry weight in *E. pulcherrima* (Spilatro and Mahlberg 1986).

Lysosomal enzymes such as protease, RNase, and acid phosphatase have been isolated from the vacuolar fraction of the latex of articulated laticifers (Matile et al. 1970). These were reportedly involved in autophagy of the sequestered areas of cytoplasm in the laticifer vacuoles. Proteolytic enzymes were isolated from the latex of *Ficus carica* (Zuckerman-Stark and Leibowitz 1963; Zuckerman-Stark 1967). Polyphenoloxidase activity has been identified in whole plants (Ashgar and Siddiqi 1970) and in isolated latex (Roberts 1971) of *Papaver somniferum*.

In *Catharanthus roseus*, HPLC analysis of exuded latex and the fruits drained of latex confirms the presence of indole alkaloids, e.g. vindolinine and 19-epivindolinine. Strictosidine lactum was abundant in fruits but was found only in traces in latex. Ajmalicine and catharanthine occurred in traces; vindoline was absent (Eilert et al. 1985). Significantly, the biosynthesis of several secondary compunds affects development of laticifers in culture. Tissue- and organ-specific chemical differentiations have been shown in many laticiferous plants (Datta 1979; Biesboer 1983; Eilert et al 1985; Datta and De 1986a, b; Dasgupta and Datta 1989).

Articulated Laticifers

Articulated laticifers are composed of single files of cells with varying degrees of interconnection. In some taxa (*Musa*—Skutch 1927), the cells interconnect only by means of plasmodesmata; in others (*Allium*—Huang and Sterling 1970; *Cichorium intybus*—Vertrees and Mahlberg 1975; *Nelumbo nucifera*—Easu and Kosakai 1975), there are one to several perforations in the endwalls; and in still others (*Achras zapota*—Karling 1929; *Argemone maxicana*—Kapoor and Sharma 1963; *Lactuca sativa*—Olson et al. 1969), the endwalls are completely resorbed. Very few articulated laticifers form an epithelium (*Achras*—Karling 1929; Alismataceae—Stant 1964; *Mammillaria*—Mauseth 1978a). The laticifer initials often occur in young tissues and are usually larger than the surrounding parenchyma cells.

In articulated laticifers, the multinucleate condition does not involve repeated mitosis. Karyokinesis often occurs without being followed by cytokinesis (Vertrees and Mahlberg 1975). A group of 3–4 nuclei was reported in *Calystegia* (Bruni et al. 1974). During maturation of the laticifers in *Cichorium*, nucleolar material may become dispersed throughout the nucleus, thus showing a gradual degeneration. The nuclei are elongated and oriented along the longitudinal axis of the laticifers as in *Jatropha podagrica*. These nuclei often occur in densely packed groups of two or more. Cass (1968) reported some short segments of ER connecting the outer membranes of the adjacent nuclei that are perhaps ephemeral and disappear due to disruption during elongation and further maturation of the laticifers. The nuclei and plastids are the longest persisting organelles in the developing laticifers (Heinrich 1967). The protoplast may remain intact, in some cases, during maturation (Heinrich 1967; Neumann and Muller 1972). Golgi bodies degenerate very early, even before the appearance of the first rubber particle. Mitochondria and ribosomes degenerate before the dissolution of the endwall. Lutoids, i.e. the vesicles containing soluble proteins, as found in *Hevea brasiliensis*, may be involved with synthesis and disposal of the ergastic materials. The vesicles in *Chelidonium majus* are thought to be of lysosomal nature and concerned with the intracellular lytic processes during cell differentiation (Matile et al. 1970). In *Papaver somniferum*, the vesicle membrane in the initial stage appears to be either smooth or with small osmiophilic granules adhering to its exterior (Figure 6.3). It then

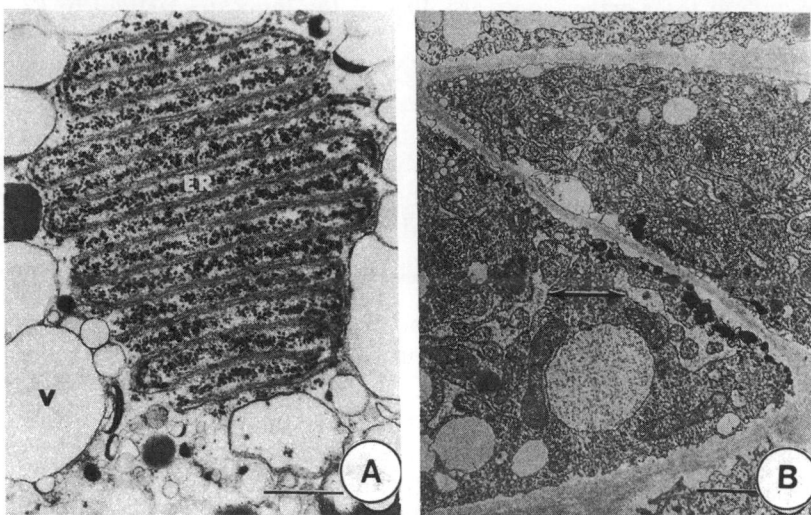

Figure 6.3. Ultrastructure of the differentiating portion of articulated laticifers of *Papaver somniferum*. (A) Laticifer cytoplasm showing stacked endoplasmic reticulum (ER) surrounded by developing vesicles (v); horizontal bar = 0.5 μm. (B) Laticifer cytoplasm showing vesicle formation by apparent dilation of rough endoplasmic reticulum (*arrow*); horizontal bar = 1 μm (from Nessler and Mahlberg 1977a).

develops 1–3 prominent cap-like osmiophilic structures (Thureson-Klein 1970; Nessler and Mahlberg 1977a). Chromoplasts (spherical bodies of high refractive index, containing β-carotene) characterize the latex of *Hevea* (Fahn 1979). They possess large osmiophilic droplets and double membranes in young laticifers.

Plastids occur as proplastids in articulated laticifers of the poppy plant (*Papaver somniferum*) and have no thylakoids or starch grains. Later, they develop electron-dense membrane-bound inclusions, which may arise from the accumulation of material within an invagination of the inner plastid membrane. The matrix of these inclusions does not consist of crystalline protein, α-amylose, amylopectin, or polysaccharides, but instead may be a lipoprotein structure comprising a lipid and diffuse enzymatic protein (Nessler and Mahlberg 1979a).

Enzymes capable of oxidizing 3, 4-dihydroxyphenylalanine (dopa), tyrosine, and diaminobenzidine (DAB) have been cytochemically localized in the membrane-bound inclusions of laticifer plastids in *P. bracteatum* (Nessler and Mahlberg 1979b). The laticifer plastids in both these *Papaver* species are similar in morphology and perhaps in physiology. In *P. bracteatum*, polyphenoloxidase activity may not induce oxidation of substrates in laticifer plastids, because the electron-opaque reaction product of this enzyme was seen in the plastids in tissues treated with the inhibitor sodium diethyldithiocarbamate (DDC) (Nessler and Mahlberg 1979b). The presence of endogenously produced hydrogen peroxide in the inclusions of laticifer plastids was also suggested.

In undifferentiated poppy laticifers, elongated profiles of the endoplasmic reticulum are abundant (Thureson-Klein 1970). The latex consists of vesicles that contain alkaloids within their vacuolar plasm (Fairbairn et al. 1974; Dickenson and Fairbairn 1975) and are derived from the ER (Nessler and Mahlberg 1977a; Figure 6.3). These vesicles have electron-dense regions, or caps, that occur early in laticifer differentiation and become less conspicuous in mature cells. Caps seem to derive from small particles that are deposited along the inner surface of the vesicle membrane and later accumulate at one or two positions along the membrane of the vesicles (Nessler and Mahlberg 1977a; Figure 6.4).

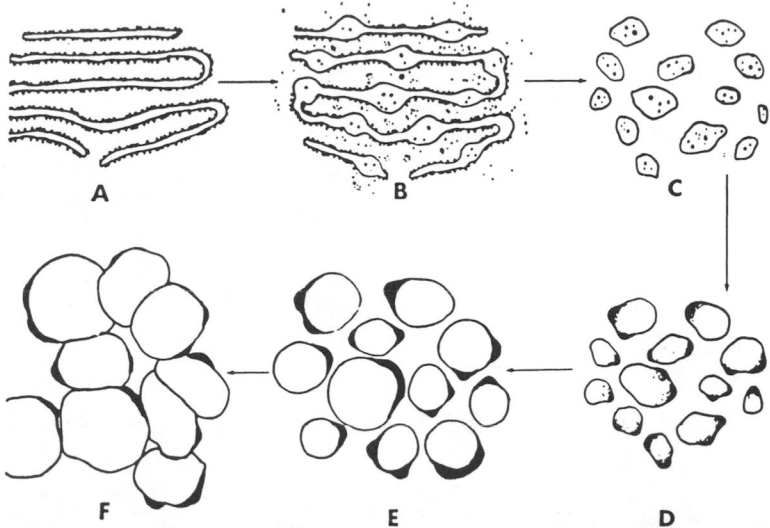

Figure 6.4. Schematic of vesicle formation through dilation of endoplasmic reticulum. (A) Stacked or unstacked endoplasmic reticulum. (B) Dilation of endoplasmic reticulum with ribosomes. (C) Small vesicles with electron-dense and electron-transparent particles. (D) Concentration of particles along the surface of enlarging vesicles. (E) Capped vesicles prior to complete vesicle expansion. (F) Large irregularly shaped vesicles in mature cells. Caps obscured by the dense packing of vesicles (from Nessler and Mahlberg 1977a).

Articulated laticifers show a range of developmental variation in members of the Papaveraceae: e.g. lack of perforations on the endwalls of the component laticifer elements (*Eschscholtzia* and *Glaucium*—Léger 1894, 1895), perforations between laticifer elements of stem but not the leaf (*Sanguinaria canadensis*—Holm 1908), and endwalls being completely resorbed (*Papaver somniferum*—Léger 1894, 1895). Likewise, articulated laticifers may remain nonanastomosing (*Chelidonium*—Schacht 1851) or form profuse anastomoses (*Papaver*—Léger 1984). Contrary to Léger's observations, Nessler (1982) found perforations on the transverse walls between the laticifer elements of *Glaucium flavum*. The perforation process seems to be incomplete, however, as evidenced by the large remnants of the transverse walls retained in mature laticifers.

The walls of laticifers are unlignified and rich in pectic substances and hemicelluloses, and hence are quite hydrated (Fahn 1979). The presence of a suberized layer within the wall of laticifers in certain members of Convolvulaceae is unique (Fineran et al. 1988). Karling (1929) described the wall-perforation process in the articulated nonanastomosing laticifers of *Achras zapota* as resulting from gradual thinning of transverse walls, usually beginning at a "pit connection" or primary pit field, either in the center of the walls or near their periphery. The transverse walls of these laticifers are thinner than their lateral walls and those of the adjacent parenchyma (Sassen 1965). Endwall perforations in laticifers of *Lactuca sativa* develop at either a unique central site or as an annular zone (Giordani 1977c). The occurrence of an annular zone of wall degradation, represented as a continuous zone of wall-thinning activity, is a curious phenomenon. Nessler and Mahlberg (1977b) studied an intermediate condition wherein wall thinning could be initiated at several random sites in the endwall. In *Papaver somniferum*, the transverse walls become thin over their entire surface, rather than at specific sites (Nessler and Mahlberg 1977b), and perforation occurs at their center or periphery before the walls are completely resorbed. Occasionally, perforated transverse walls are curved in the direction of latex flow, as indicated by the distortion of laticifer cytoplasm near a perforation site (Figure 6.5). This curved appearance of the

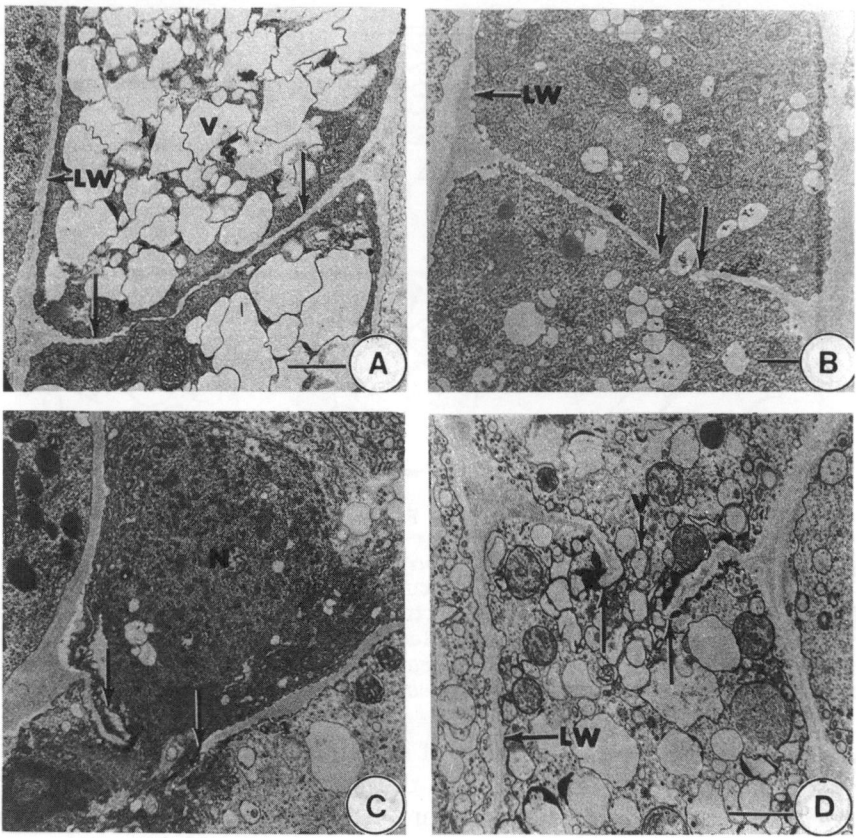

Figure 6.5. Transverse wall perforation in laticifer of *Papaver somniferum*. (A) Transverse walls (*arrows*) between two laticifer cells in the late vesiculation stage of development showing thinning over entire surface. (B) Pore (between *arrows*) in transverse walls separating two laticifer cells. (C) Perforation of the wall caused by latex surge through a thin region in walls as indicated by a nucleus flowing through the pore and the curved appearance of the walls at the pore site. (D) Group of vesicles flowing through the pore. LW, lateral wall; N, nucleus; V, vesicle; magnification lines = 1 μm (Nessler and Mahlberg 1977b).

walls may be an artifact caused by latex surging through thin regions in the walls during tissue preparation (Nessler and Mahlberg 1977b).

Lateral-wall perforations that form anastomoses also develop by thinning of common walls at specific sites between contiguous elements. Resorption of wall material occurs simultaneously on both sides of the middle lamella (Nessler and Mahlberg 1977b). Globular electron-dense deposits are occasionally associated with thinning of transverse walls and at sites of developing lateral-wall perforations (Figure 6.6) in *A. zapota* (Sassen 1965) and *P. somniferum* (Nessler and Mahlberg 1977b). Sassen found these deposits localized between the transverse walls and the plasma membrane. The black appearance of these deposits readily distinguishes them from callose, which occurs as amorphous gray masses in aged laticifers (Nessler 1976). Whether these deposits represent material from the laticifer cytoplasm accumulated at the perforation site or products derived from the thinning walls during the perforation process is unclear.

The formation of perforations by the gradual thinning of walls suggests an enzymatic basis for this process. Cellulase activity has been detected in the latex of

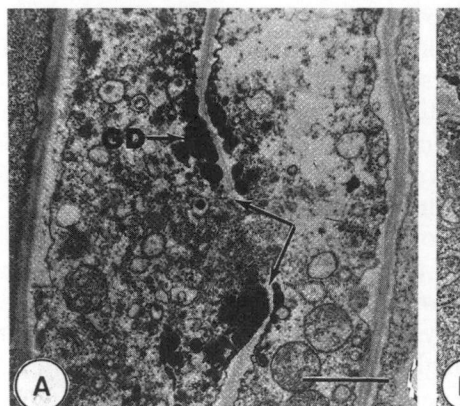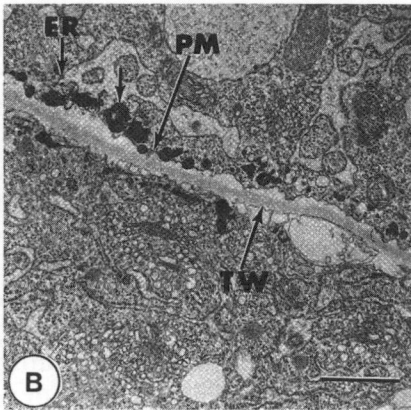

Figure 6.6. (A) Globular electron-dense deposits (GD) associated with thinning lateral walls at periphery of perforation (between *arrows*). (B) Similar deposits (*arrow*) associated with laticifer walls in initial vesiculation stage. ER, endoplasmic reticulum; PM, plasma membrane; TW, transverse laticifer wall; magnification line = 1 μm (from Nessler and Mahlberg 1977b).

several species with articulated laticifers, but not in those with nonarticulated laticifers (Sheldrake 1969; Sheldrake and Moir 1970). Therefore, cellulase may be involved in the perforation process in articulated laticifers. The involvement of cellulase in the perforation process in poppy laticifers was shown by the presence of reaction products with discrete areas of recently digested cell wall (Nessler and Mahlberg 1981).

Giordani (1977b) suggested that the concentration of peroxides in areas of laticifer wall degradation in *Lactuca sativa* might be caused by peroxidase-induced ethylene production, which in turn stimulates cellulase synthesis, or perhaps by the hydrolases responsible for wall breakdown, if they can be shown to possess peroxidase activity.

During the maturation of the anastomosing articulated laticifers of *Lacuta sativa*, the breakdown of endwalls in cells that form the laticiferous duct was accompanied by the formation of parietal vesicles from plasmalemma, which were incorporated in vacuoles (Giordani 1980). Acid phosphatase was detected on vesicles localized in the vacuoles. Cellulolytic activity occurred under plasmalemma on pectocellulosic material of the developing vesicles. Enzymatic activities were stimulated during cell wall degeneration (Giordani 1981). Acid phosphatase activity was detected on the plasmalemma, middle lamella, and primary wall of the degenerating cell wall. Incubation of the tissue with ATP at pH 5.0 showed a consistent deposition of reaction product in the hydrolyzing cell wall. Generally, the enzyme activity was highest in the pectocellulosic material. At pH 6.0, the degrading cell wall showed no cellulolytic activity; the pectic material, however, disappeared at the perforation site (Giordani 1981). The unhydrolyzed lateral walls of *Lactuca sativa* laticifers showed no hydrolase activities. The thick lateral walls remained intact, apparently unaffected by hydrolases (Giordani 1981).

Unusual Articulated Laticifers

Investigation of seven species of the cactus, *Mammillaria*, revealed a highly unusual laticifer system that can, however, be classified as articulated (Mauseth 1978a). The laticifers are derived from cells that differentiate only in older tissues, never in meristematic or young regions. The development involves a complete lysis of masses of cells, not just the perforation or resorption of the endwalls in a single file of cells. At maturity, the laticifer lumen is lined with an epithelium of one to several layers that may be quite thick. The laticifers increase in diameter with age, apparently by the lysis of the inner epithelial cells. Laticifers occur in the pith, cortex, and tubercles (the conical structures that completely cover the plant) of the vegetative body, but are not present in the roots, floral parts, vascular tissues of the vegetative shoot, or seedlings of up to eight months of age (Mauseth 1978a).

The laticifers of *Mammillaria* differ from the usual laticifers, in that they (a) have a rapid mitosis and cytokinesis that cause the laticifers to be much smaller than the surrounding parenchyma cells; (b) do not differentiate in seedlings or near the meristematic tissues; (c) involve complete lysis of cells concerned with laticifer formation; (d) bear a distinct epithelium throughout the length of the laticifers; and (e) are capable of growing in diameter with age by the continued lysis of epithelial cells (Mauseth 1978a). Of the laticifers known so far for other cacti (*Coryphantha, Leuchtenbergia, and Solisia*), those of *Solisia* (Boke 1960) resemble the laticifers of *Mammillaria* in many respects.

The laticifers in several species of the section Subhydrochylus (with semi-milky latex) of the genus *Mammillaria* are similar to those of the section Mammillaria (with milky latex) in that they are formed by the complete lysis of several rows of parenchyma cells and comprise long-branching, tubular lumens that are lined by epithelia, but their shape, lumen development, and epithelial form are comparatively irregular. They occur only as a single ring in the outermost cortex and tubercle bases, whereas those of the section Mammillaria can occur in pith, cortex, medullary rays, and throughout the tubercles (Mauseth 1978b). The laticifers of the section Subhydrochylus are postulated to be close to the ancestral type and to be the precursors for the more orderly, regular laticifers of the section Mammillaria. Two species, *M. elegans* and *M. tegelbergiana,* show an intermediate type of laticifer having traits of both the above types. The morphological variations of laticifer systems in the genus *Mammillaria* conform well to the currently accepted view of its phylogeny. It is thought (Hunt 1971) that the group without laticifers (section Hydrochylus) gave rise to the group with semi-milky laticifers (section Subhydrochylus), which in turn gave rise to the group with milky laticifers (section Mammillaria). *M. elegans* occupies an intermediate position both morphologically and phylogenetically (Mauseth 1978b).

During the early development of the latex ducts of *M. heyderi*, numerous vesicles (secondary vacuoles) develop from invaginations of the plasmalemma near the sites of wall thinning, from the ER, and from vesiculate grana of degenerate plastids. This is the only species examined in which the plastids contribute to the formation of the vesicular system (Wittler and Mauseth 1984). Plastid vesiculation is a consequence of the recruitment of mature chlorophyllous cells by the laticiferous system. New ducts can form in mature ground tissue, and the older ducts can increase in diameter by differentiation of epithelial cells from the surrounding chlorophyllous tissues (Mauseth 1978a). Thus, the parenchymatous cells of the ground tissues maintain the potential to differentiate into duct cells without apparent prior dedifferentiation. The degradative and recycling processes, which are typical of most normal laticifers and involve Golgi, endoplasmic reticulum, lysosomes (GERL), and vacuole, appear aborted in this case. Mitochondria and lipid bodies are common in young ducts, but ER is rare (Wittler and Mauseth 1984).

LATICIFER DEVELOPMENT *IN VITRO*

Attempts to grow laticifers *in vitro* have had only limited success (Fahn 1979). Snyder (1955) was unable to detect laticifers in the cultured tissue excised from *Cryptostegia grandiflora,* but Wilson and Street (1975) reported induction of laticifer fragments in the callus from *Hevea* stem explants with use of the MS medium (Murashige and Skoog 1962) containing 2,4-D and kinetin. Some cells with laticiferlike metabolism have been detected in *Asclepias syriaca* suspension culture (Biesboer 1983). The differentiation of cells to laticifers in callus and cell suspension cultures has been documented for *Calotropis procera* (Dhir et al. 1984), *Euphorbia marginata* (Bruni et al. 1981), *Hevea brasiliensis* (Wilson and Street 1975), *Papaver bracteatum* (Kutchan et al. 1983), and *P. somniferum* (Nessler and Mahlberg 1979c). Earlier workers were unable to build up any stock callus material by repeated subculturing. After several years of trials beginning in 1979 at Santiniketan, India, laticifer differentiation was established in a culture of *Calotropis gigantea* (Datta and De 1986b; Figure 6.7) and species of *Thevetia* and *Pedilanthus* (unpublished data). Callus cultures from ovary and shoot-tip explants were used for laticifer differentiation in *C. gigantea.* MS medium with auxins such as indoleacetic acid (IAA), indolebutyric acid (IBA), and naphthaleneacetic acid (NAA); cytokinins such as benzylaminopurine (BAP) and kinetin (KN); and other growth regulators, including adenine sulphate (ads) alone or in combination (at a range of concentrations), was used for callus cultures and differentiation of laticifers (Datta and De 1986b).

Laticifer formation was most frequent in the callus grown on IAA. BAP also stimulated laticifer formation after 160 d of culture. Growth and differentiation of laticifers took place only in cultures that were more that 80 d old, and usually after 120–160 d in culture. Irrespective of the hormones used, the laticifers were rarely initiated before 60 d and did not survive after 160 d of culture (Datta and De 1986b). The largest number of the NAL of *Calotropis* was obtained after 160 d of culture on media containing 1 mg/l IAA, although their initiation occurred in the same medium with 0.5 mg/l IAA after 60 d of culture. BAP and KN (of varying concentrations) in conjunction with IAA (0.5 and 1.0 mg/1) in the medium showed poor laticifer differentiation as compared to IAA alone. Observations with *Calotropis* callus show a close relationship between the phytohormone-induced initiation of laticifers and the age of the culture (Datta and De 1986b).

Young laticifers in culture grow more rapidly than neighboring parenchyma cells. Their nuclei enlarge and divide without any subsequent wall formation. Under favorable nutritional conditions, these cells elongate and differentiate into laticifers. The walls of laticifers thicken, except at the extreme tip (Fahn 1979), and become wavy at maturity *in vivo* and *in vitro. In vitro* cells are sensitive to tests for cardenolides (Table 6.1). In many cases, cultured tissues have been ineffective in producing compounds typical of intact plants. Analysis of alkaloids in cell cultures of *Catharanthus roseus* failed to show the occurrence of bisindole alkaloids and in particular, vinblastine—an antineoplastic compound. The problem associated with the nonoccurrence of vinblastine and derivatives in cell cultures might be related to the lack of specialized cells and laticifers, just as the absence of morphinan alkaloids in poppy cell cultures is related to the lack of laticifers (Nessler and Mahlberg 1979c; Kamo et al. 1982). In many plants, including *Vinca,* laticifers or laticiferlike cells are yet to be detected. The search for such cells is hampered by the deficient information on the structure and development of laticifers (Eilert et al. 1985).

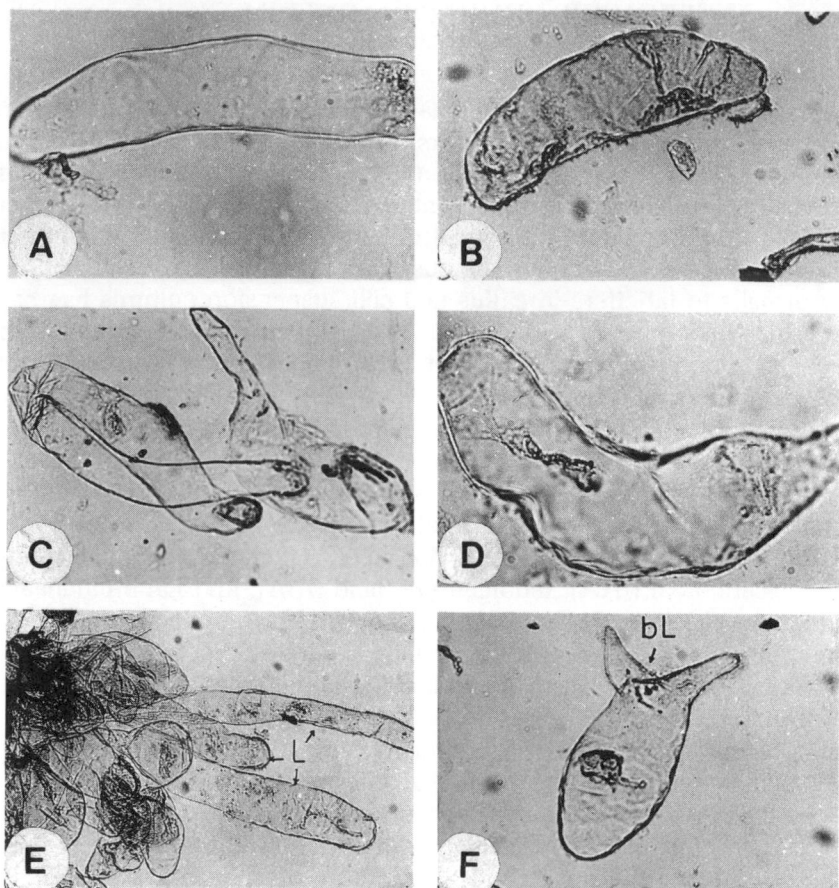

Figure 6.7. Laticifer differentiation in culture. Initiation and elongation of laticifers (A, B, D, E) and branching of a nonarticulated laticifer (C, F). L, laticifer initial; bl, branched laticifer (partly from Datta and De 1986b).

Table 6.1. Histochemical color reactions of laticifers *in vivo* and *in vitro*.[a]

Reagents	Material tested	Laticifers		Other cells		Remarks
		1[b]	2[b]	1[b]	2[b]	
Lieberman & Burchard (LB) colour reactions	Cardenolides	++++	++++	+	+	Strong
Kedde: SbC13 in 70% solution	Cardenolides	++++	+++	+	—	
Million	Protein	++++	+++	+++	++	
KOH (10%) followed by chromic acid (10%)	Latex consti-tuents	++++	++++	+	+	Strong black Violet
KI solution	Starch grains	++++	+++	+	+	Osteoid type

[a] *In situ* laticifers (from mature plant) and *in vitro* laticifers (120 days after culture) were used for this study.
[b] 1, *in vivo*; 2, *in vitro*.
Source: Modified after Datta and De (1986b).

MICROPROPAGATION OF LATICIFEROUS PLANTS

Efforts are under way to achieve mass micropropagation of laticiferous plants because many of these plants produce pharmaceutical compounds, commercial rubber, or hydrocarbons that may provide an alternative to petroleum (Nielsen et al. 1977; Calvin 1979, 1983; Hall 1980; Tideman and Hawker 1982; Eilert et al. 1985). Earlier workers (Babcock and Carew 1962; Krikorian and Steward 1969; Rao et al. 1970; Natraja et al. 1973; Langhe et al. 1974; Wilson and Street 1975; Wilson and Mahlberg 1977) had limited success with the tissue culture of latex-producing plants. Tideman and Hawker (1982) reported successful clonal propagation of a few *Euphorbia* species (*E. lathyris, E. peplus,* and *E. tannensis*), *Asclepias rotundifolia,* and *Araujia sericifera* from different explant sources such as stem node, internode, shoot-apex, leaf, and seed. Recently, Mhatre et al. (1984) have reported protoplast-derived plant regeneration in *Tylophora indica*.

Mass clonal propagation of important laticiferous plants such as *Calotropis gigantea* (Datta 1981, 1984; Datta and De 1983, 1986a), *Holarrhena antidysenterica* (Datta and Datta 1984), *Asclepias curassavica* (Pramanik and Datta 1986), and *Thevetia peruviana* (Dasgupta et al. 1987) has been performed in India. The embryogenic suspension culture of *T. peruviana* was found to contain laticifers (Dasgupta and Datta, unpublished). Mass propagation of desirable clones of plants having high economic value is a complex techinque because each species has individual requirements as to type of media, hormone balance, source of explant, and culturing methods.

EVOLUTIONARY TRENDS

There are few studies of evolutionary trends in laticifers (see Rudall 1987). Mahlberg (1973, 1975) suggested that starch grains of nonarticulated *Euphorbia* laticifers differ in morphology from grains present in other plant cells. The NAL, confined to a few families, are assumed to be of recent phylogenetic origin (Mahlberg and Sabharwal 1968). Starch grains in laticifers are elongated, whereas those in parenchymatous cells are round or oblong in many *Euphorbia* species. The elongated grains are thought to have been derived phylogenetically from the round/oblong ones of the parenchymatous cells. Deposition of additional starch at the tips of grains gave rise to the supposedly advanced osteoid grains (Mahlberg 1975), as also observed in *Calotropis* (Datta and De 1986b). In *Calotropis,* the NAL originate from single parenchymatous cells. Starch grains were round or oblong in the parenchyma, and are aggregated to form the osteoid type in laticifers. According to Fahn (1979), laticifers occur in several unrelated families and appear to have developed independently during evolution.

A study of laticifers of *Jatropha* suggests that this genus is more primitive and ancestral to other genera in the Crotonoideae (Rudall 1987). Both articulated and nonarticulated laticifers seemingly evolved either in the Acalyphoidae or in the Crotonoideae in a genus related to *Jatropha*. Laticifers are also thought to be a recently evolved cell type compared to the vascular elements, because they are so specialized and occur in so few families (Mahlberg et al. 1987).

Dehgan and Craig (1978) elucidated the importance of the study of laticifers in delimiting the sections of the subgenus *Curcas* of the genus *Jatropha* and suggested extensive re-examination of laticifers throughout the Euphorbiaceae in order to alleviate the longstanding taxonomic dilemma of this large and morphologically diverse family. French (1988) elucidated the utility of laticifers in the Araceae and evaluated the authenticity of the various Aroid subfamilies on the basis of the occurrence of anastomosing and nonanastomosing articulated laticifers. He concluded that the Colocasioideae was apparently a natural subfamily with two strongly divergent phylogenetic lines. The presence of laticifers was strongly correlated with the monoecious condition in the Araceae.

Fox and French (1988) noted that sterol profiles were qualitatively and/or quantitatively distinct for each of the New World species of Colocasioideae, Araceae that they examined. No free sterols were detected in latices of Old World genera. These are consistently clear to cloudy, lack terpenoid particles, and, typify the New World genera with white latex (Fox and French 1988). This chemical distinction conforms to other traits, including laticifer cytology, stem vasculature, pollen type and leaf type.

FUNCTIONS AND PROSPECTS

Opinions differ with regard to the function of laticifers (see Cutter 1969; Fahn 1979). Earlier workers termed laticifers "Lebenssaftgefasse" (vital sap vessels) and compared them with the blood vessels of animals. Today, laticifers are envisaged as components of secretory tissues. In some cases, they apparently produce and store mainly substances that do not re-enter plant metabolism; they may also have some role in water balance and transport of oxygen in the plant. Their main function, however, seems to be protection. Latex may play a role in wound healing and as a defense against microorganisms and herbivores. The latex of *Calotropis* and *Excoecaria agallocha* may cause injury to human eyes (Biedner et al. 1977; Datta 1979). Latex and resins are commonly thought to be by-products of metabolism; this may be disputed, however, because these substances are also metabolized (Fairbairn and Wassel 1964; Metcalfe 1983; Datta and De 1986a,b). The specific mechanism of laticifer chemodifferentiation needs further study to understand laticifer development *in vivo* and *in vitro* and biosynthesis of secondary compounds.

Copaifera multijuga (Leguminosae) is a rich source of sesquiterpene fuel materials (about 20 l/tree in 24 hr every 6 mo). The sequiterpene compounds (e.g. diesel oil) obtained from heartwood by drilling a deep hole in the trunk of the tree can be put directly into an automobile without any processing or refining. Many other laticiferous plants such as *Euphorbia lathyris, E. milli,* and *E. tirucalli* have been identified as primary sources of fuel hydrocarbons. The first species is preferred for its easy plantation and rapid production of latex: 6–10 barrels of oil/acre from planting wild seeds (Calvin 1983).

Because gene transfer technology has provided tools for genetic manipulation and improvement of crops, including petrocrops (Calvin 1987; Potrykus 1988; Weising et al. 1988), the possibility of transferring cloned genes for sesquiterpene from *Copaifera multijuga* or other related species to a suitable fast-growing plant, such as *Euphorbia lathyris,* may soon become a reality (Calvin 1983, 1987).

In *Calotropis* culture, cardenolides become evident only after laticifers are initiated; their quantity gradually increases with the age of the culture. This cycle repeats after subculturing, thus further supporting the notion that laticifers are a primary requirement for cardenolide metabolism (Datta and De 1986b). Although a basic uniformity exists in the metabolism of all photosynthetic plants, the rare occurrence of plants with unusual metabolic products such as latex suggests great scope for the study of the comparative physiology and chemotaxonomy of these plants (Metcalfe 1983). Single-cell culture and genetic engineering (gene cloning, expression, and transformation) are likely to provide an opportunity for cloning a gene or gene complex that regulates the morphology and differentiation of laticifers, and thus to produce compounds of vital interest.

Acknowledgments and Credits

Thanks are due to Dr. Sibaprasad De, Visva Bharati University, Santiniketan, India; Ms. Alexis Lansing, University of California at Davis; and Dr. Mahmooduzzafar and Mr. Mustafa K. Ansari, Aligarh Muslim University, Aligarh, India, for their help with the preparation of this chapter.

Figure 6.2 is reprinted with permission from *Annals of Botany* 52:279–293 (1983). Figures 6.3 and 6.4 are reprinted with permission from the *American Journal of Botany* 64:541–551 (1977). Figures 6.5 and 6.6 are reprinted with permission from *Botanical Gazette*, Volume 138; copyright 1977 by The University of Chicago.

LITERATURE CITED

Archer, B. L., B. G. Audley, G. P. McSweeney, and C. Hong. 1969. Studies on composition of latex, serum and 'bottom fraction' particles. J. Rubber Res. Inst. Malaya 21:560–569.

Asghar, S., and M. Siddiqi. 1970. Phenolase of *Papaver somniferum*. I. Isolation of the enzyme and its substrate specificity. *Emzymologia* 39:289–306.

Babcock, P. A., and D. P. Carew. 1962. Tissue culture of Apocynaceae. I. Culture requirements and alkaloid analysis. *Lloydia* 25:209–213

Behnke, H. D., and S. Herrmann. 1978. Fine structure and development of laticifers of *Gnetum gnemon* L. *Protoplasma* 95:371–384.

Biedner, B., L. Rothkoff, and A. Witztum. 1977. *Calotropis procera* (Sodom apple) latex keratoconjunctivities. *Israel J. Med. Sci.* 13:914–916.

Biesboer, D. D. 1983. The detection of cells with laticifer like metabolism in *Asclepias syriaca* L. suspension culture. *Plant Cell Rep.* 2:137–139.

Biesboer, D., and P. G. Mahlberg. 1978. Accumulation of non-utilizable starch in laticifers of *Euphorbia heterophylla* and *E. myrsinites. Planta* 143:5–10.

_____ . 1981a. Laticifer starch grain morphology and laticifer evolution in *Euphorbia* (Euphorbiaceae). *Nord. J. Bot.* 1:447–457.

_____ . 1981b. A comparison of alpha-amylases from the latex of three selected species of *Euphorbia* (Euphorbiaceae). *Am. J. Bot.* 68:498–506.

Blackwell, S., W. Laetsch, and B. Hyde. 1969. Development of chloroplast fine structure in aspen tissue culture. *Am. J. Bot.* 56:457–463.

Boke, N. H. 1960. Anatomy and development in *Solisia. Am. J. Bot.* 47:59–65.

Bruni, A., G. Dall'Olio, and M. P. Fasulo. 1974. Morphological aspects of the nuclei in the mature articulated laticifers of *Calystegia soldanella. Experientia* 30:1390–1393.

Bruni, A., G. L. Vannin, and G. Dall'Olio. 1981. Occurrence of laticifers in tissue cultures derived from *Euphorbia marginata*: a study by fluorescence microscopy. *Z. Pflanzenphysiol.* 103:373–377.

Buvat, R., and G. Robert. 1979. Vacuole formation in the actively growing root meristem of barley (*Hordeum sativum*). *Am. J. Bot.* 66:1219–1237.

Calvin, M. 1979. Petroleum plantations for fuel and materials. *Biosciences* 29:533–538.

———. 1983. New sources for fuel and materials. *Science* 219:24–26.

———. 1987. Fuel oils from euphorbs and other plants. *Bot. J. Linn. Soc.* 94:97–110.

Carlquist, S. 1988. *Comparative Wood Anatomy*. Berlin/Heidelberg: Springer Verlag.

Cass, D. D. 1968. Observations on the ultrastructure of the nonarticulated laticifers of *Jatropha podagrica* (Euphorbiaceae). *Experientia* 24:961–962.

———. 1985. Origin and development of non-articulated laticifers of *Jatorpha dioica*, *Phytomorphology* 35:133–140.

Castells, A. R. C., W. T. Ormond, and A. Braconi. 1984. Biology of *Jatropha gossypifolia* (Euphorbiaceae). I. Laticiferous ducts and latex glands. *Rev. Bras. Biol.* 44:149–158.

Cutter, E. G. 1969. *Plant Anatomy. Experiment and Interpretation,* London: Edward Arnold.

Dasgupta, M., and S. K. Datta. Embryogenic cell line for cardenolide biosynthesis in a tree, *Thevetia peruviana*. Unpublished.

Dasgupta, M., T. K. Pramanik, and S. K. Datta. 1987. Mass propagation and genetic variability of two cardenolide plants in vitro. *Acta Horticult.* 8:263–271.

Datta, S. K. 1979. *Pharmacognosy of Important Laticiferous Bark Drugs*. Ph.D. Thesis, Calcutta University, Calcutta.

———. 1981. In vitro study of rhizogenesis from shoot tips of *Calotropis gigantea*. *Ind. J. Exp. Biol.* 19:566–567.

———. 1984. In vitro methods applied to mass propagation of forest trees. In *Proc. Applied Biotechnology of Medicinal, Aromatic and Timber Yielding Plants*. Ed P. C. Datta. New Delhi: DST. 188–202.

Datta, S. K., and K. Datta. 1984. Auxin-induced clonal multiplication of *Holarrhena antidysenterica* by tissue culture. *J. Tree Sci.* 3:47–52.

Datta, S. K., and P. C. Datta. 1980. Laticifer in *Euphorbia nivulia*. *Cell Chromosome Res.* 3:46–47.

Datta, S. K., and S. De. 1983. In vitro study of ovary-induced callusing, rhizogenesis and presence of cardenolide in *Calotropis gigantea*. *Cell Chromosome Res.* 6:10–12.

———. 1986a. Organ specific chemodifferentiation of cardenolides of *Calotropis gigantea* in vitro. *Beitr. Biol. Pflanz.* 61:315–319.

———. 1986b. Laticifer differentiation of *Calotropis gigantea* R. Br. ex Ait. in culture. *Ann. Bot.* 57:403–406.

David, G. 1872. *Ueber die Milchzellen der Euphorbiaceen, Moreen, Apocyneen and Asclepiadeen*. Thesis, Breslau.

De, S., and S. K. Datta. 1988. Separation and HPLC identification of two cardiac glycosides from *Calotropis gigantea*. *Indian Drugs* 25:167–168.

Dehgan, B., and M. E. Craig. 1978. Types of laticifers and crystals in *Jatropha* and their taxonomic implications. *Am. J. Bot.* 65:345–352.

Dhir, S., N. Shekhawat, S. Purohit, and H. Arya. 1984. Development of laticifer cells in callus culture of *Calotropis procera* (Ait) R. Br. *Plant Cell Rep.* 3:206–209.

Dickenson, P. B. 1969. Electron microscopical studies of the latex vessel system of *Hevea brasiliensis*. *J. Rubber Res. Inst. Malaya* 21:543–559.

Dickenson, P., and J. Fairbairn. 1975. The ultrastructure of the alkaloidal vesicles of *Papaver somniferum* latex. *Ann. Bot.* 39:707–712.

Eilert, U., L. R. Nesbitt, and F. Constabel. 1985. Laticifers and latex in fruits of periwinkle, *Catharanthus roseus*. *Can. J. Bot.* 63:1540–1546.

Esau, K. 1965. *Plant Anatomy*. New York: John Wiley and Sons.

Esau, K., and H. Kosakai. 1975. Laticifers in *Nelumbo nucifera* Gaertn.: Distribution and structure. *Ann. Bot.* 39:713–719.

Fahn, A. 1979. *Secretory Tissues in Plants*. London: Academic Press.

Fay, de E., C. Sanier, and C. Hebant. 1989. The distribution of plasmodesmata in the phloem of *Hevea brasiliensis* in relation to laticifer loading. *Protoplasma* 149:155–162.

Fairbairn, J. W., and L. D. Kapoor. 1960. The laticiferous vessels of *Papaver somniferum*. *Planta Med.* 8:49–61.

Fairbairn, J., F. Hakim, and Y. Elkheir. 1974. Alkaloidal storage, metabolism and translocation in the vesicles of *Papaver somniferum* latex. *Phytochemistry* 13:1133–1139.

Fairbairn, J. W., and G. Wassel. 1964. The alkaloids of *Papaver somniferum*. III. Biosynthesis of isolated latex. *Phytocemistry* 3:583–586.

Fineran, B. A. 1970. Organization of the tonoplast in frozen-etched root tips. *J. Ultrastr. Res.* 33:574–586.

_____ . 1971. Ultrastructure of vacuolar inclusions in root tips. *Protoplasma* 72:1–18.

_____ . 1982. Distribution and organization of non-articulated laticifers in mature tissues of poinsettia (*Euphorbia pulcherrima* Willd.). *Ann. Bot.* 50:207–220.

_____ . 1983. Differentiation of non-articulated laticifers in Poinsettia (*Euphorbia pulcherrima* Willd.). *Ann. Bot.* 52:279–293.

Fineran, B. A., J. M. Condon, and M. Ingerfeld. 1988. An impregnated suberised wall layer in laticifers of Convolvulaceae, and its resemblance to that in walls of oil cells. *Protoplasma* 147:42–54.

Fox, M. G., and J. C. French. 1988. Systematic occurrence of sterols in latex of Araceae: Subfamily Colocasioideae. *Am. J. Bot.* 75:132–137.

French, J. C. 1988. Systematic occurrence of anastomosing laticifers in Araceae. *Bot. Gaz.* 149:71–81.

Fujii, T. 1988. Structure of latex and tanniniferous tubes in tropical hardwoods. *Bull. For. For. Prod. Res. Inst.* 352:113–118.

Fujii T., and S. Sudo. 1988. The cell wall structure of the latex tube in the rays of *Pimelodendron amboinicum* Hassk. (Euphorbiaceae). *Mokuzai Gakkaishi* 34:195–199.

Giordani, R. 1977a. Mise en evidence de glomerules cytoplasmiques intravacuolaries dans les cellules secretrices de latex chez *Asclepias curassavica* L. *Biol. Cell.* 30:293–296.

_____ . 1977b. Localization ultrastructurale de l' activité peroxidasique lovs du processus de perforation des parios au cours de la differenciation des laticiféres articulés de *Lactuca sativa* L. *C. R. Acad. Sci. D* 285:97–100.

_____ . 1977c. Degradation des parois terminales durant la differenciation des laticiféres articulés de *Lactuca sativa* L. *C. R. Acad. Sci. D* 284:569–572.

_____ . 1978. Autophagie cellulaire et differenciation des laticiféres non-articulés chez une Asclepiade. *Biol. Cell.* 33:253–260.

_____ . 1979. Ultrastructure des laticifers articulés de la laitue. *C. R. Acad. Sci.* 288:615–618.

_____ . 1980. Dislocation du plasmalemme et libération de vésicules pariétales lors de la dégradation des parois terminales durant la diffirenciation des laticiféres articulés. *Biol. Cell.* 38:231–236.

_____ . 1981. Activites hydrolasiques impliquées dans le processus de dégradation pariétal durant la differenciation des laticiféres articulés. *Biol. Cell.* 40:217–224.

Groeneveld, H. W. 1976a. Some morphological and chemical characteristics of the purified terpenoid particles of the latex of *Hoya australis* R. Br. ex Traill. *Acta Bot. Neerl.* 25:1–13.

_____ . 1976b. Biosynthesis of latex triterpenes in *Euphorbia*: evidence for a dual synthesis. *Acta Bot. Neerl.* 25:459–473.

Groeneveld, H. W., and L. A. Vandermade. 1982. Cardenolide and triterpene synthesis in the laticifers of *Asclepias curassavica*. *Acta Bot. Neerl.* 31:5–10.

Hall, D. O. 1980. Renewable resources (hydrocarbons). *Outlook, Agric.* 10:246–254.

Hartig, T. 1862. Über die Bewegung des Saften in den Holzpflanzen. 12 In den Milchsaftgefässen. *Bot. Z. Berlin.* 20:97–100.

Hebant, C. 1981. Ontogenie des laticiféres du systeme primaire de l'*Hevea brasiliensis*' une etude ultra structurale et cytochimique. *Can. J. Bot.* 59:974–985.

Hecker, E. 1975. Cocarcinogens and cocarcinogenesis. In *Handbook of Pathology*. Ed. E. Grundmann. Berlin: Springer-Verlag. 6:657–676.

Heinrich, G. 1967. Licht und elektronemikroskopische Untersuchungen der Milchröhren von *Taraxacum bicorne*. *Flora* 158:413–420.

_____ . 1970. Elektronenmikroskopische Untersuchungen der Milchröhren von *Ficus elastica*. *Protoplasma* 70:317–323.

Holm, T. 1908. Medicinal plants of North America. 18. *Sanguinaria canadensis* L. *Merk's Rep.* 17:209–212.

Huang, S., and C. Sterling. 1970. Laticifers in the bulb scales of *Allium*. *Am. J. Bot.* 57:1000–1003.

Hunt, D. R. 1971. Schumann and Buxbaum reconciled. *Cactus Succulent J. Gr. Br.* 33:53–72.

Kakkar, L., and G. S. Paliwal. 1972. Studies on the leaf anatomy of *Euphorbia*. IV. Terminal idioblasts. *J. Indian Bot. Soc.* 51:118–126.

Kamo, K. K., W. Kimoto, A. F. Hsu, P. G. Mahlberg, and D. D. Bill. 1982. Morphinane alkaloids in cultured tissues of redifferentiated organs of *Papaver somniferum*. *Phytochemistry* 21:219–222.

Kapoor, L. D., and B. M. Sharma. 1963. *Argemone maxicana* L. Organography and floral anatomy with reference to the laticiferous system. *Phytomorphology* 13:465–473.

Karling, J. S. 1929. The laticiferous system of *Achras zapota* L. I. A preliminary account of the origin, structure and distribution of the latex vessels in the apical meristem. *Am. J. Bot.* 16:803–824.

Krikorian, A. D., and F. C. Steward. 1969 Biosynthetic potentialities of tissues. In *Plant Physiology*. Ed. F. C. Steward. London/New York: Academic Press. 227–326.

Kutchan, T. M., S. Ayabe, R. J. Krueger, E. M. Cosica, and C. J. Cocsia. 1983. Cytodifferentiation and alkaloid accumulation in cultured cells of *Papaver bracteatum*. *Plant Cell Rep.* 2:281–284.

Lalezari, I., P. Nasseri, and R. Asgharian. 1974. *Papaver bracteatum* Lindl. population Arya II. *J. Pharm. Sci.* 63:1331–1333.

Langhe, E. D. E., P. Debergh, R. Van Rijk. 1974. In vitro culture as a vegetative propagation of *Euphorbia pulcherrima*. *Z. Pflanzenphysiol.* 71:271–274.

Léger, L. 1894. Recherches sur l'appareil vegetatif des Papaveracees. I. etude de l'anatomie generale des organes vegetatis des Papaveracees. *Soc. Linn. Normandie Caen Mem.* 18:193–516.

———. 1895. Recherches sur l'appareil vegetatif des Papaveracees. II. Etude speciale du system laticifere des papaveracees. *Soc. Linn. Normandie Caen Mem.* 18:516–624.

Mahlberg, P. G. 1959. Development of the non-articulated laticifers in proliferated embryos of *Euphorbia marginata*. *Phytomorphology* 9:156–162.

———. 1961. Embryogeny and histogenesis in *Nerium oleander*, II. Origin and development of non-articulated laticifers. *Am. J. Bot.* 48:90–99.

———. 1973. Scanning electron microscopy of starch grains from latex of *Euphorbia terracina* and *E. tirucalli*. *Planta* 110:77–80.

———. 1975. Evolution of the laticifer in *Euphorbia* as interpreted from starch grain morphology. *Am. J. Bot.* 62:577–583.

Mahlberg, P. G., D. G. Davis, D. S. Galitz, and G. D. Manners. 1987. Laticifers and the classification of *Euphorbia esula*. *Bot. J. Linn. Soc.* 94:165–180.

Mahlberg, P. G., and P. S. Sabharwal. 1968. Origin and early development of non-articulated laticifers in embryos of *Euphorbia marginata*. *Am. J. Bot.* 55:375–381.

Marty, F. 1968. Intrastructure des laticiféres differencies d'*Euphorbia characias*. *C. R. Acad. Sci.* 267:299–302.

———. 1970a. Rôle du systeme membranaire vacuolaire dans la différenciation des laticiféres d'*Euphorbia characias* L. *C. R. Acad. Sci.* 271:2301–2304.

———. 1970b. Les peroxysomes (microbodies) des laticiféres d'*Euphorbia characias* L. *J. Micros C.* 9:923–948.

———. 1971a. Differenciation des plastes dans les laticiferes d'*Euphorbia characias* L. *C. R. Acad. Sci.* 272:223–226.

———. 1971b. Vésicules autophagiques des laticiféres differencies d'*Euphorbia characias* L. *C. R. Acad. Sci.* 272:399–402.

———. 1978. Cytochemical studies on GERL, provacuoles and vacuoles in root meristematic cells of *Euphorbia*. *Proc. Nat., Acad. Sci. USA* 75:852–856.

Matile, Ph., B. Jans, and R. Rickenbacher. 1970. Vacuoles in *Chelidonium* latex: lysosomal property and accumulation of alkaloids. *Biochem. Physiol. Pflanzan* 161:447–458.

Mauseth, J. D. 1978a. The structure and development of an unusual type of articulated laticifer in *Mammillaria* (Cactaceae). *Am. J. Bot.* 65:415–420.

_____. 1978b. Further studies of the unusual type of laticiferous canals in *Mammillaria* (Cactaceae): Structure and development of the semi-milky type. *Am. J. Bot.* 65:415–420.

Metcalfe, C. R. 1967. Distribution of latex in plant kingdom. *Econ. Bot.* 21:115–126.

_____. 1983. Secretory structures. In *Anatomy of the Dicotyledons*. 2nd ed. Ed. C. R. Metcalfe, L. Chalk. London: Clarendon Press. 70–81.

Mhatre, M., V. A. Bapat, and P. S. Rao. 1984. Plant regeneration in protoplast culture of *Tylophora indica*. *J. Plant Physiol.* 115:231–235.

Milanez, F., and H. Neto. 1956. Orgem dos laticiféros do embriao de *Euphorbia pulcherrima* Willd. *Rodriguésia* 18:351–395.

Murashige, T., and F. Skoog. 1962. A revised medium for rapid growth and bioassay with tabacco tissue culture. *Physiol. Plant* 15:473–497.

Murugan, V., and J. A. Inamdar. 1987a. Studies in the laticifers of *Vallaris solanacea* (Roth) O. Ktze. *Phytomorphology* 37:209–214.

_____. 1987b. Organographic distribution, structure and ontogeny of laticifers in *Plumeria alba* Linn. *Proc. Indian Acad. Sci.* (Plant Sci.) 97:25–31

_____. 1989. Origin and development of the non-articulated laticifers of *Thevetia peruviana* Schum. *Phytomorphology* 39:189–194.

Natraja, K., M. S. Chennaveeraih, and P. Girogowda. 1973. In vitro production of shoot buds in *Euphorbia pulcherrima*. *Curr. Sci.* 42:577–578.

Nessler, C. L. 1976. *Ultrastructural and Cytochemical Investigation of Laticifer Differentiation in Intact Plants and Cultured Tissues of the Opium Poppy*, Papaver somniferum L. Ph.D. Thesis. Indiana University.

_____. 1982. Ultrastructure of laticifers in seedling of *Glaucium flavum* (Papaveraceae). *Can. J. Bot.* 60:561–567.

Nessler, C. L., and P. G. Mahlberg. 1977a. Ontogeny and cytochemistry of alkaloid vesicles in laticifers of *Papaver somniferum* (Papaveraceae). *Am. J. Bot.* 64:541–551.

_____. 1977b. Cell wall perforation in laticifers of *Papaver somniferum* L. *Bot. Gaz.* 138:402–408

_____. 1978. Laticifer ultrastructure and differentiation in seedlings of *Papaver bracteatum* Lindl. population Arya II (Papaveraceae). *Am. J. Bot.* 65:978–983.

_____. 1979a. Plastids in laticifers of *Papaver*. I. Development and cytochemistry of laticifer plastids in *P. somniferum* L. (Papaveraceae). *Am. J. Bot.* 66:266–273.

_____. 1979b. Plastids in laticifers of *Papaver* II. Enzyme cytochemistry of membrane-bound inclusions of laticifer plastids in *P. bracteatum* Lindl. (Papaveraceae). *Am. J. Bot.* 66:274–279.

_____. 1979c. Laticifers in organs redifferentiated from *Papaver somniferum* callus. *Can. J. Bot.* 57:675–685.

_____. 1981. Cytochemical localization of cellulase activity in articulated, anastomosing laticiferous system of *Papaver somniferum* L. (Papaveraceae). *Am. J. Bot.* 68:730–732.

Neumann, D., and E. Muller. 1972. Beitrage zur Physiologie der Alkaloid. III. *Chelidonium majus* und *Sanguinaria canadensis*: Ultrastruktùr der Alkaloidbehalter Alkaloidaufnahme und Verteilung. *Biochem. Phyiol. Pflanzen* 163:375–391.

Nielsen, P. E., H. Nishimura, J. M. Otvos, and M. Calvin. 1977. Plant crops as a source of fuel and hydrocarbon like materials. *Science* 198:942–944.

Olson, K. C., T. W. Tibbitts and B. E. Struckmeyer. 1969. Leaf histogenesis in *Lactuca sativa* with emphasis upon laticifer ontogeny. *Am. J. Bot.* 56:1212–1216.

Ponsinet, C., and G. Ourisson. 1968. Aspects particulieres de la Biosynthèses des triterpénes dans de latex d'*Euphorbia*. *Phytochemistry* 7:757–764.

Popovici, H. 1926. Contribution a l'etude cytologique des laticifers. *C. R. Acad. Sci.* 183:143–145.

Potrykus, I. 1988. Direct gene transfer to plants. In *Application of Plant Cell and Tissue Culture. Ciba Found, Symp.* 137:144–162. New York: Wiley.

Pramanik, T. K., and S. K. Datta. 1986. Plant regeneration and ploidy variation in culture derived plant of *Asclepias curassavica*. *Plant Cell Rep.* 3:219–222.

Pujarniscle, S. 1971. Etude biochimique des lutoides du latex d'*Hevea brasiliensis*, Mull.

Arg. Differences et analogies avec les lysosomoes. *Memoire Office de la Recherche Scientifique et Technique Outre-Mer*, 48. 100 pp.

Rachmilevitz, T., and A. Fahn. 1982. Ultrastructure and development of the laticifers of *Ficus carica* L. *Ann. Bot.* 49:13–22.

Rao, P. S., S. K. Narayanaswamy, and B. D. Benjamin. 1970. Differentiation of embryos and plantlets in stem cultures of *Tylophora indica*. *Physiol. Plant.* 23:140–144.

Roberts, M. 1971. Polyphenolases in the 1000 g fraction of *Papaver somniferum* latex. *Phytochemistry* 10:3021–3027.

Roy, A. T., and D. N. De. 1992. Studies on differentiation of laticifers through light and electron microscopy in *calotropis gigantea* (Linn.) R. Br. *Ann. Bot.* 70:443–449.

Rudall, P. J. 1987. Laticifers in Euphorbiaceae—a conspectus. *Bot. J. Linn. Soc.* 94:143–163.

Rudall, P. 1989. Laticifers in vascular cambium and wood of *Croton* spp. (Euphorbiaceae). *IAWA Bull.* (n.s.) 10:379–383.

Sarkany, S., K. Michels-Nyomarkay, and G. Venzar-Petri. 1970. Über die histologischen und feinstrukturellen Beziehungen und in die Frage der Alkaloid bildung im Samen und in die Kleinpflanzen von *Papaver somniferum* L. *Pharmazie* 10:625–629.

Sassen, M. M. A. 1965. Breakdown of the plant cell wall during the cell fusion process. *Acta Bot. Neerl.* 14:165–196.

Schacht, H. 1851. Die Songenannten Milchsaftgefasse der Euphorbiaceen. *Bot. Z.* 9:513–521.

Schnepf, E. 1974. Gland cells. In *Dynamic Aspects of Plant Ultrastructure*. Ed. A. W. Robards. 331–357. Maidenhead: McGraw Hill.

Schulze, Ch., E. Schnepf, and K. Mothes. 1967. Über die lokalisation der Kautschuk-partikel in verschiedenen Typen von Milchröhren. *Flora* 158:458–460.

Sheldrake, A. R. 1969. Cellulase in latex and its possible significance in cell differentiation. *Planta* 89:82–84.

Sheldrake, A., and G. Moir. 1970. A cellulase in *Hevea* latex *Physiol. Plant.* 23:267–277.

Skutch, A. F. 1927. Anatomy of leaf of banana. *Musa sapientum* L. var. Hort. *Gros Michel*. *Bot. Gaz.* 84:334–391.

Snyder, F. W. 1955. Growth of excised tissue from the stem of *Cryptostegia grandiflora*. *Bot. Gaz.* 177:145–155.

Solereder, H., and F. J. Meyer. 1928. *Systematische Anatomie der Monokotyledonen. Principes-synanthae-Spathiflorae*. Heft 3. Berlin: Gebrüder Brontraeger.

Spilatro, S. R., and P. G. Mahlberg. 1985. Composition and structure of nonutilizable laticifer starch grains of *Euphorbia pulcherrima* Willd. *Bot. Gaz.* 146:26–31.

———. 1986. Latex and laticifer starch content of developing leaves of *Euphorbia pulcherrima*. *Am. J. Bot.* 73:1312–1318.

Stant, M. Y. 1964. Anatomy of the Alismataceae. *Bot. J. Linn. Soc.* 59:1–42.

Stockstill, B. L., and C. L. Nessler. 1986. Ultrastructural observations on the nonarticu-lated, branched laticifers in *Nerium oleander* L. (Apocyanaceae). *Phytomorphology* 36(3,4):347–355.

Sudo, S., and T. Fujii. 1987. Latex tubes in the rays of *Pimelodendron amboinicum* Hassk. (Euphorbiaceae). IAWA Bull. (n.s.) 8:109–112.

Swain, R. 1977. Secondary compounds as protective agents. *Annu. Rev. Plant Physiol.* 28:479–501.

Thureson-Klein, A. 1970. Observations on the development and fine structure of the articu-lated laticifers of *Papaver somniferum Ann. Bot.* 34:751–759.

Tideman, J., and J. S. Hawker. 1982. In vitro propagation of latex producing plants. *Ann. Bot.* 49:273–279.

Topper, S. M. C., and J. Koek-Noorman. 1980. The occurrence of axial latex tube in the secondary xylem of some species of *Artocarpus* J. R., and G. Fosster (Moraceae). *IAWA Bull.* 1:113–119.

Trécul, M. A. 1867. Des vaisseaux propres et du tanins les Musacees. *Ann. Sci. Naturelles* (5 Ser.) 8:283–300.

Ultee, A. J. 1923. Stickstoffreiche Milchsafte. *Boll. Jar. Bot. Buitenzarg.* 5:245–246.

Urschler, I. 1956. Untersuchungen mit dem phytomyces-Test. *Protoplasma* 46:494–497.

Van Die, J. 1955. A comparative study of the particle fraction from Apocynaceae latices. *Ann. Bogor.* 2:1–124.

Veenendaal, W. L. H. van, and R. W. den Outer 1990. Distribution and development of the non-articulated branched laticifers of *Morus nigra* L. (Moraceae). *Acta Bot. Neerl.* 39:285–296.

Vertrees, G. L., and P. G. Mahlberg. 1975. Nuclei in laticifers of *Cichorium intybus*. *Phytomorphology* 25:282–288.

_____ . 1978. Structure and ontogeny of laticifers in *Cichorium intybus* (Compositae). *Am. J. Bot.* 65:764–771.

Warnaar, F. 1982. Investigation of *Hoya* species. V. Determination of the amount of latex present in *Hoya australis* R. Br. ex Fraill and *Hoya bella* Hook and its relationship with shoot development. *Z. Pflanzenphysiol.* 105:307–314.

Weising, K., G. Kahl, and J. Schell. 1988. Transfer, structure and expression of foreign genes in plants. In *Architechture of Eukaryotic Genes.* Ed. G. Kahl. Weinheim: VCH, Verlagsgesellschaft. 57–87.

Wilson, K. J., and P. G. Mahlberg. 1977. Investigations of laticifer differentiation in tissue cultures derived from *Asclepias syriaca*. *Ann. Bot.* 41:1049–1054.

_____ . 1978. Ultrastructure of non-articulated laticifers in mature embryos and seedlings of *Asclepias syriaca* L. (Asclepiadaceae). *Am. J. Bot.* 65:98–109.

_____ . 1980. Ultrastructure of developing and mature non-articulated laticifers in the milkweed *Asclepias syriaca* L. (Asclepiadaceae). *Am. J. Bot.* 67:1160–1170.

Wilson, K. J., C. L. Neesler, and P. G. Mahlberg. 1976. Pectinase in *Asclepias* latex and its possible role in laticifer growth and development. *Am. J. Bot.* 63:1140–1144.

Wilson, H. M., and H. E. Street. 1975. The growth, anatomy and morphogenetic potential of callus, and cell suspension cultures of *Hevea brasiliensis*. *Ann. Bot.* 39:671–682.

Wittler, G. H., and J. D. Mauseth. 1984. The ultrastructure of developing latex ducts in *Mammillaria heyderi* (Cactaceae). *Am. J. Bot.* 71:100–110.

Zuckerman-Stark, S. H. 1967. On proteolytic enzymes from the fig. *Enzymology.* 32:380–382.

Zuckerman-Stark, S. H., and J. Leibowitz. 1963. Researches on milk-clotting enzymes from Palestinian plant sources. II. *Enzymology* 25:252–256.

Chapter 7

Unique Tracheary Elements
in the Haustorium
of Parasitic Angiosperms

B. A. FINERAN

Graniferous tracheary elements are a unique type of xylem tracheid, or vessel element, in which the lumen of the cell contains structural inclusions (Fineran 1985). Typically, these inclusions are granules, but other configurations, such as amorphous masses or dispersed material having the same origin as the granules, may also occur. The cells are known only from parasitic flowering plants and are most frequently located in the haustorium—the organ that forms the physiological and anatomical bridge between host and parasite. Within the haustorium, these elements occur chiefly in the expanded region of xylem known as the vascular core (Fineran 1963a). Recent work based on light microscopy indicates that graniferous tracheary elements may also occur elsewhere in the parasite, especially in the stems of some mistletoes (Weber 1984; Weber and Nietfield 1984). In the root hemiparasitic representative of the order Santalales, these elements are widespread in the Santalaceae (Fineran et al. 1978) and in two species of the Loranthaceae (Fineran and Hocking 1983). They are also found in two genera of the Olacaceae (Fineran 1985; Fineran et al. 1987) and in several taxa of the Opiliaceae (Weber 1977b; Weber and Hildenbrand 1978; Kubat 1987). In addition, the cells exist in the haustorium of some aerial misletoes (Fineran 1985). Thus graniferous tracheary elements are not peculiar to the root parasitic members of the Santalales. The cells are known also from haustoria of root parasitic Scrophulariaceae (Heinricher 1895; Renaudin 1974; Fineran 1985), *Krameria* of the Krameriaceae (Fineran 1985), and *Mystropetalon* of the Balanophoraceae (Weber 1986; Fineran 1987a). These elements probably play an important role in the operation of the haustorium (Fineran and Bullock 1979), but details of the process are not yet understood.

Graniferous tracheary elements are of two distinct types in terms of the composition and origin of the granules: those with granules composed of protein, and those with granules composed of starch grains (Weber and Hildenbrand 1978; Fineran 1985).

From *Growth Patterns*
in Vascular Plants
Edited by Muhammed Iqbal

162

Graniferous tracheary elements containing starch grains are found in several unrelated families and are therefore presumed to have arisen independently, as a result of convergent evolution, among the various parasitic angiosperms. In contrast, elements with protein-type-granules have a more restricted distribution among families. But even here, the ultrastructure of the granule may provide useful new information in assessing systematic affinities among the particular groups of parasites.

RESEARCH ON GRANIFEROUS TRACHEARY ELEMENTS

Tracheary elements containing granules were first reported in parasitic plants by Heinricher (1895), in the haustorium of *Lathraea* (Scrophulariaceae). He determined histochemically that the granules were amylodextrin and suggested that the cells represented a type of storage tracheid. In 1910, Benson observed tracheary elements with granules in the haustorium of *Exocarpus cupressiformis* and in an unnamed species of *Thesium,* both of the Santalaceae, and concurred that the granules were amylodextrin. She also noted that the cells were living but did not contain a nucleus. Because the cells exhibited morphological features of both the phloem (an enucleated protoplast) and xylem (lignified secondary wall thickenings), Benson proposed that they combined the functions of phloem and xylem in transport. She therefore named them *phloeotracheides.* The only other report of granule-containing tracheary elements during the early years of the century was by Maybrook (1917), who observed them in the haustorium of *Pedicularis vulgaris* (Scrophulariaceae). Maybrook also believed that the granules were starch but, unlike Benson, found that the cells were nucleate.

Haustorial tracheary elements with structural inclusions were not described again until 1963. At first, the cells were reported as only part of a general anatomical study of the haustorium of *Exocarpus bidwillii* (Fineran 1963a,b) of the Santalaceae. Afterwards, in a similar study of *Mida salicifolia* (Simpson and Fineran 1970), also of the Santalaceae, the cells were examined more closely via the light microscope with different staining methods. At that time, Benson's name (1910) *phloeotracheide* was retained when referring to the cells. Later investigations with *E. bidwillii* and *M. salicifolia,* by means of scanning electron microscopy discovered similar cells in four other santalaceous root hemiparasites from North America (Fineran 1974). Afterwards, it was demonstrated that these distinctive tracheary elements were dead cells at maturity, like typical vessel elements or tracheids. Therefore, it was recommended that the old name be replaced by the term *graniferous tracheary element* (Fineran et al. 1978), a name descriptive of the cells without implying their function. Papers subsequently followed on the ultrastructure and differentiation of graniferous tracheary elements in *E. bidwillii* (Fineran 1979; Fineran and Bullock 1979). More recently, the scope of research has been extended to include root parasites of the Loranthaceae, namely *Atkinsonia ligustrina* and *Nuytsia floribunda* (Fineran and Ingerfeld 1982; Fineran 1983; Fineran and Hocking 1983), and *Olax phyllanthi* (Fineran et al. 1987) of the Olacacea. Preliminary observations have also been made on a variety of other parasitic angiosperms: *Lathraea squamaria* and *Euphrasia cuneata* of the Scrophulariaceae, *Krameria grayi* of the Krameriaceae, *Ximenia americana* of the Olacaceae, and *Moquiniella rubra* of the Loranthaceae (see Fineran 1985). To this must now be added *Mystropetalon thomii* (Balanophoraceae) and several species of *Arceuthobium* (Viscaceae).

During the 1970s, other groups of workers became interested in graniferous tracheary elements. Dobbins and Kuijt (1973a,b) described them briefly in *Castilleja*. Weber and his students have found the elements in five species of *Thesium* of the Santalaceae (Weber 1977a), in *Cansjera rheedii* (Weber 1977b; Weber and Hildenbrand 1978) of the Opiliaceae, in *Osyris alba* (Nietfield et al. 1983) of the Santalaceae, in several stem parasitic mistletoes (Weber 1984), among them a dwarf mistletoe (Weber and Nietfield 1984), and other taxa of the Opiliaceae (Kubat 1987). *Osyris alba* has also been studied by Benharrat (Benharrat 1986, Benharrat et al. 1987). Niranjana and Shivamurthy (1987a,b) have reported graniferous tracheary elements in *O. arborea* and *Scleropyrum wallichianum* (Santalaceae) in India.

MICROSCOPICAL METHODS INVOLVED

Graniferous tracheary elements were first observed with the light microscope (Figure 7.1), and the cells were illustrated by means of line drawings (Heinricher 1895; Benson 1910; Maybrook 1917). These early illustrations convey the essential features of the cells as we know them today.

It is generally difficult to detect graniferous tracheary elements in haustorial tissue cut by hand, except in a few taxa such as *Mida salicifolia* (Santalaceae), where granules may exceed 10 μm in diameter. Therefore, microtomed sections of paraffin

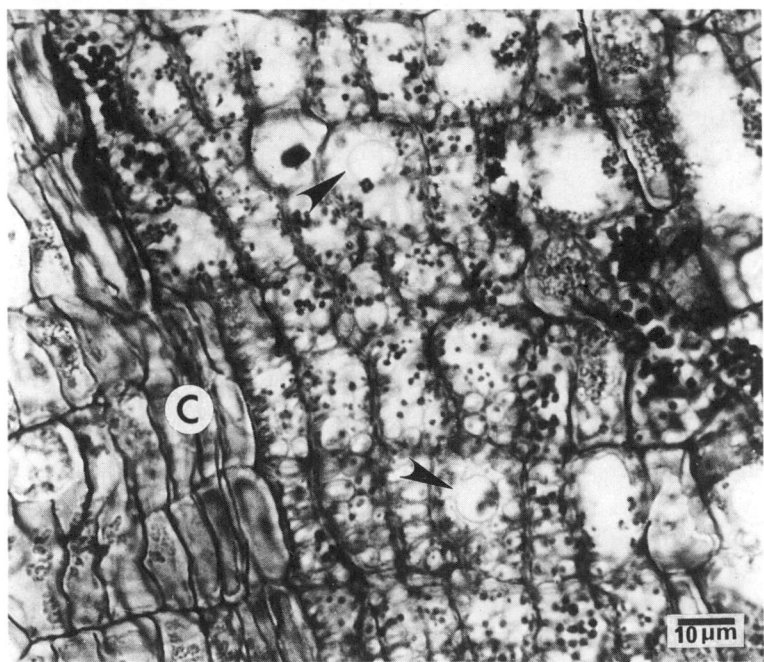

Figure 7.1. Light micrograph of graniferous tracheary element tissue in the vascular core of *Nestronia umbellulata*, a North American sandalwood. It is distinguished from other xylem of the parasite by the granules within the lumina of the tracheary elements. The tissue consists mostly of tracheids, but a few vessel elements are present showing simple perforation plates (*arrows*). The vascular cambium (C) that surrounds the vascular core is visible on the *left*. In this plant the granules are readily detected because of their size and stain reaction with safranin/fast green; × 1000.

wax-embedded material have provided the traditional means of revealing their occurrence (Fineran 1963a,b; Simpson and Fineran 1970). This approach continues to be used almost exclusively by some groups of workers today (Weber 1977a,b, 1984, 1986; Weber and Hildenbrand 1978; Weber and Nietfield 1984; Nietfield et al. 1983). Although classical methods of specimen preparation using formalin-aceto-alcohol-fixed and paraffin wax-embedded specimens provide the simplest way of assessing the presence of graniferous tracheary elements in many haustoria, and in other organs of the plant where the cells may occur, these methods have limitations. For instance, where granules are small and lie completely within the thickness of the wax ribbon, and where the tracheary elements have themselves been cut open, many granules are lost from the final preparation when sections are dewaxed, as there is no contact with the adhesive on the slide. The density of matrix within the granule also affects how much stain becomes bound to the granule and therefore, affects their visibility in the final section. If granules are smaller than about 1 μm and have a matrix of low density, they stain poorly with safranin/fast green and hence are easily overlooked in microscopic sections. The difficulty of detecting graniferous tracheary elements with small granules of low matrix density is accentuated if the granules occur in low numbers within the cell. It was probably for reasons similar to those discussed above, that Weber (1980) failed to detect graniferous tracheary elements in interspecific haustoria of *Nuytsia floribunda* (Loranthaceae), although he did find some granules in self-haustoria.

For critical work on the ultrastructure and ontogeny of graniferous tracheary elements, classical methods of specimen preparation are generally inadequate. Not so much because formalin-aceto-alcohol does not preserve the granules, but in combination with wax-embedding methods, the clarity obtainable from the slide is often inferior to that of the same material embedded in a synthetic resin. Because it is not necessary to remove the resin from the section at any stage in the procedure, small granules are not lost from the preparation. A further advantage of resin embedding is that sections can be cut thinner than in wax; this greatly improves the resolution obtainable from the sample and hence the subsequent amount of information available. For optimal light microscope work on granules composed of protein, fixation in glutaraldehyde is also preferable to formalin-aceto-alcohol. This is because the matrix of the granule is cross-linked, with minimal structural rearrangement of the protein, rather than being preserved more coarsely by coagulation. Good fixation becomes especially important if the same group of graniferous tracheary elements is to be later examined by transmission electron microscopy.

To obtain optimal preservation of the cells for light microscopy, we recommend that haustoria be fixed in glutaraldehyde (2–4% in phosphate buffer) and embedded in a synthetic resin. Resins available for this purpose include the methacrylate-based formulations, such as glycol methacrylate (O'Brien and McCully 1981), J.B.4 (Polysciences Inc.), and L. R. White's medium (London Resins Ltd), and the epoxy resins, e.g. Araldite formulations (Fineran and Bullock 1972) and Spurr's (1969) resin. With the epoxy resins, essentially the same procedure is followed in preparing the specimens for light microscopy as used for transmission electron microscope work. The main advantage with this approach is that material from the same block can be cut for light microscope survey work and later for detailed transmission electron microscope studies. In this way, a direct comparison can be made of the same structures seen with the light microscope and those observed at a greater magnification with the electron microscope. Consequently, the overall organization of graniferous tracheary elements can be interpreted better than is possible with one instrument alone, or by employing both instruments to view separate specimens processed for sectioning in different ways. Another virtue of using the same block for both light and electron microscopy is that the limited area of cells visible under the electron microscope can be related readily to the organization of the haustorium as a whole.

Sections of epoxy resin material are difficult to stain compared to those embedded in wax, but good polychrome contrast can be achieved with methylene blue/azur II (cf. Juniper et al. 1970). Almost a full range of stains may be introduced, however, if the epoxy resin is first removed by using sodium ethoxide (a saturated solution of NaOH in 100% ethanol). Following this treatment, for example, granules can be stained readily for protein, either with the mercuric chloride/bromophenol blue (Mazia et al. 1953) or the aniline blue-black schedules (Fisher 1968).

Beside bright field microscopy, other forms of light microscopy may be employed to examine graniferous tracheary elements. Nomarski interference-contrast optics have been used effectively by Weber (1977a) to show the presence of granules in some haustoria. Polarized light microscopy can be used to examine graniferous tracheary elements consisting of starch-grain granules but is of more limited application for elements with protein granules, as the granules are nonbirefringent.

Scanning electron microscopy is another technique that may be used to investigate the anatomy of haustoria and their graniferous tracheary elements (Figures 7.2; 7.4). For this purpose, haustoria may be used either as fixed specimens or as fresh tissue. By freezing living haustoria in liquid nitrogen, breaking them open under the cryogen, and then freeze-drying the material in a vacuum evaporator, it is possible to preserve granules in the near natural state. Preserved haustoria may be fixed in either formalin-aceto-alcohol or glutaraldehyde with equally acceptable results. The haustoria may be cut open with a new razor blade to produce a smooth cut surface, and then frozen in liquid nitrogen, or preferably in nitrogen "slush" produced by subjecting liquid nitrogen to a partial vacuum in a vacuum evaporator. Alternatively, the haustorium may be frozen whole and then fractured under the liquid nitrogen before freeze-drying. Fracturing produces clean surfaces of internal tissues of the haustorium, without displacement or blurring of structures that might otherwise happen during cutting. The fracturing method, however, has a disadvantage in that it is not possible to control where tissues will be fractured within the haustoria. Furthermore, snapping open a rounded organ such as an haustorium by fracturing it under liquid nitrogen is often technically difficult, other than by shattering it with a sharp blow.

Scanning electron microscopy offers the most dramatic means of visualizing graniferous tracheary elements, three-dimensionally. Furthermore, it readily provides a medium for recording their form photographically, with a greater depth of focus and magnification than is possible with the light microscope. However, for use in normal structural work, scanning electron microscopy is limited to gross topographical features of the tissue and cell, and to surface detail of individual structures. Intrinsic detail concerning the structure of granules and luminal contents derived from them and substances secondarily impregnating the granules is not revealed. Furthermore, information on the developmental origin of the granules and of their composition is not readily demonstrated. Thus, for optimal utilization of results obtained from scanning electron microscopy, these should be correlated with data from light and transmission electron microscopy. However, the application of X-ray microanalysis in scanning electron microscopy now means that the instrument can be used to provide new data on the elemental composition of granules.

The most important contribution toward our understanding of graniferous tracheary elements in modern times has come from transmission electron microscopy (Figure 7.3); it reveals the ultrastructure and development of the granules with a resolution not possible with light microscopy. The transmission electron microscope, for

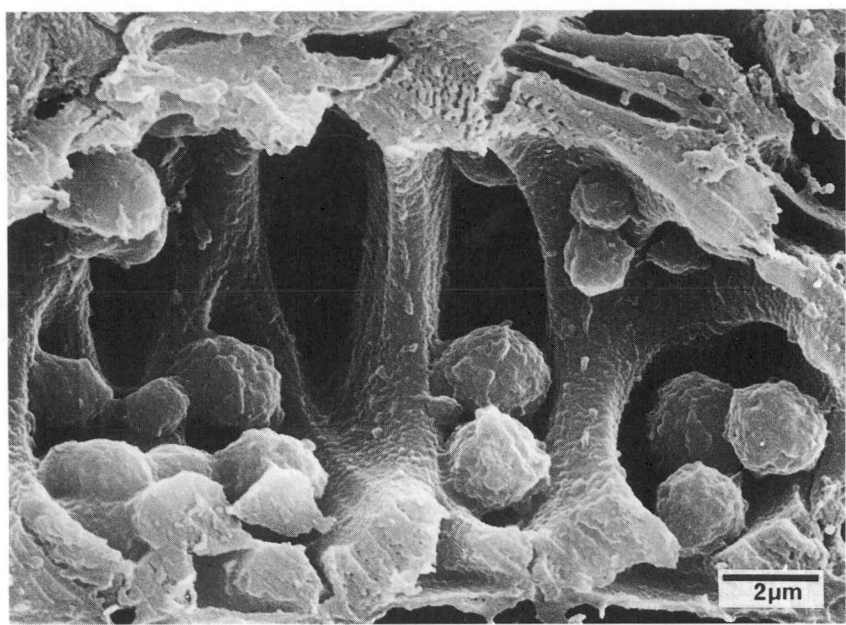

Figure 7.2. Scanning electron micrograph of a graniferous tracheid in *Thesium divaricatum*. In this European species of the Santalaceae, several spherical granules, with somewhat roughened surfaces, lie in the lumen against the wall thickenings; × 7500.

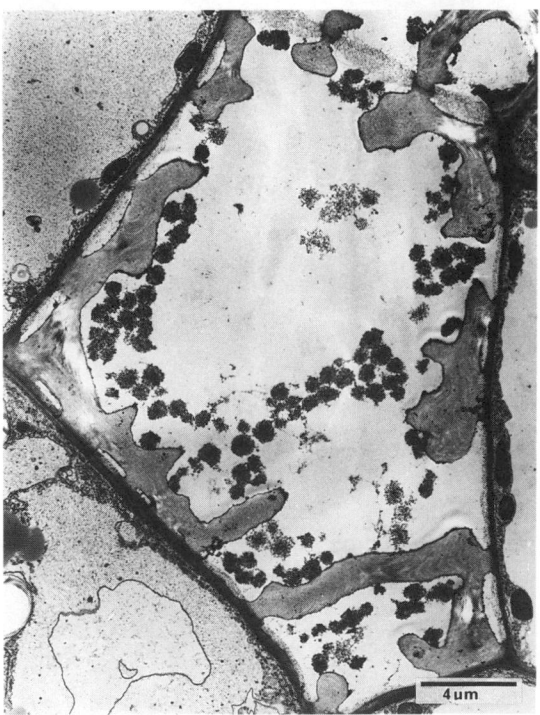

Figure 7.3. Typical appearance of a graniferous tracheid shown by conventional transmission electron microscopy in a thin section (ca. 80 nm thick). In this cell of *Colpoon compressum* (Santalaceae, southern Africa), secondary wall thickenings, primary walls, and pit membranes are visible; small naked granules also lie in the lumen. At higher magnification, such protein granules exhibit a fine fibrillar substructure; × 6000.

example, can show whether granules are naked structures within the cell lumen, or are surrounded by some kind of an envelope. Transmission electron microscopy can also determine whether the matrix of a granule is amorphous, paracrystalline, or a combination of both. The existence of a paracrystalline substructure in certain granules, for example those of *Mida salicifolia*, or the unique tubular substructure comprising the granule matrix in *Olax phyllanthi* would not have been suspected in the absence of transmission electron microscopy (Fineran et al. 1987). Moreover, the microscope has demonstrated how the matrix of some granules can become transformed as the cell ages. As a result, we can now correlate the unusual staining reactions in different parts of the haustorium, first reported by early workers in light microscope preparation, to observable ultrastructural events (Fineran and Ingerfeld 1982; Fineran 1983; Fineran et al. 1987). As a consequence, the process whereby graniferous tracheary elements become secondarily impregnated with phenolics, coinciding with the stage at which the cells appear to cease conduction, is becoming clarified (Fineran 1985).

Transmission electron microscopy is not limited to the examination of ultrathin sections, which in reality represent only a very small sample of the total structure within a cell. With the availability of high voltage electron microscopes, sections up to about 5 μm in thickness can be viewed (Figure 7.4). The use of these "semi-thick" sections, and the ability to cut them from a large block face (ca. 2 mm square), means that high voltage electron microscopy can bridge the domain between the light and conventional transmission electron microscopes for investigating tissue organization. At magnifications comparable to high power with the light microscope, because of its

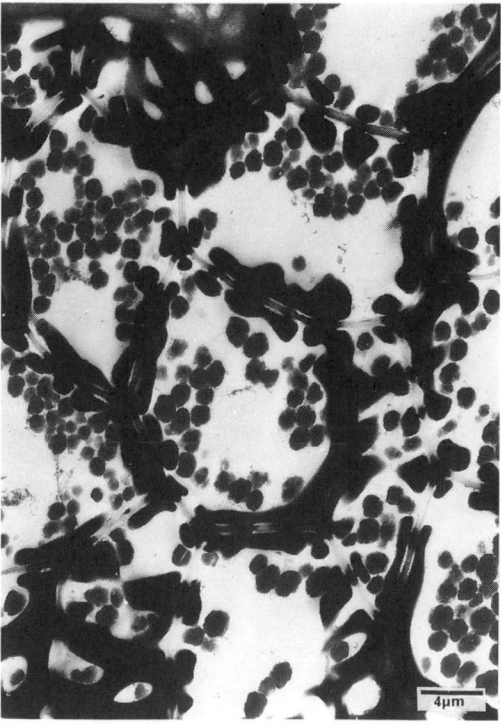

Figure 7.4. Graniferous tracheary elements in the haustorium of *Exocarpus bidwillii* (Santalaceae) visualized by high voltage (1000 kV) electron microscopy. Sample based on material fixed in glutaraldehyde, embedded in epoxy resin, and sectioned at 3 μm. Within the thickness of the section, in-depth views of cell organization are obtainable at higher magnification; × 4000.

inherently better resolution capabilities, the high voltage electron instrument produces clearer images of graniferous tracheary elements than is possible with the light microscope. The high penetration power of the electron beam also allows in-depth views of granules suspended within the cell. Furthermore, information contained in the "semi-thick" section may be enhanced with stereoscopy, whereby the specimen is examined at different angles of tilt in the microscope and photographs interpreted later as stereopairs. Modern transmission electron microscopy can also be combined with x-ray microanalysis to give qualitative and quantitative information on the elemental composition of the sample. Already this method has been applied to the graniferous tracheary elements of *Osyris alba,* where it has been shown that the granules contain calcium, potassium, and some sulfur (Benharrat et al. 1984, 1987).

No one morphological method is sufficient by itself to provide a comprehensive understanding of graniferous tracheary elements. Only by combining the advantages of each form of microscopy, and by applying different methods of specimen preparation, can we hope to obtain a balanced view of the cells in terms of their organization, origin, and function.

STRUCTURAL ORGANIZATION
OF GRANIFEROUS TRACHEARY ELEMENTS

Graniferous tracheary elements include both tracheids and vessel elements. Tracheids are often more abundant, as tracheids tend to be dominant in the xylem tissue of many haustoria. Nevertheless, graniferous vessel elements do occur in the vascular core (Figure 7.1), but the vessels here are mostly relatively short and consist of only a few elements. In haustoria of *Exocarpus bidwillii* (Fineran 1963b) and *Mida salicifolia* (Simpson and Fineran 1970), at the point where tissues of the parasite converge on the host before entering to become the sucker, the vessels are longer and contain progressively fewer granules. Within the sucker, granules often disappear from the vessels and the cells cease to be graniferous tracheary elements. In mistletoes in which graniferous tracheary elements have been found in the stem and leaf (Weber 1984; Weber and Nietfeld 1984), both tracheids and vessel elements appear to be present.

Graniferous tracheary elements are formed in both primary and secondary xylem. Haustoria typically develop their first graniferous tracheary elements during differentiation of the vascular core (Fineran 1963a), and these cells may persist throughout the life of the haustorium. In *M. salicifolia,* however, the graniferous tracheary elements of the primary xylem have fewer granules than the later-formed secondary xylem elements (Simpson and Fineran 1970). In parasites in which the haustorium functions for perhaps only one season or less, the primary xylem graniferous tracheary elements are often the only elements present. Among root hemiparasites, other examples exist, however, of the haustorium producing varying amounts of secondary thickening around the vascular core. This is the result of the initiation of a local vascular cambium around the vascular core. In species of the Santalaceae in which the secondary structure of the haustorium has been investigated (Fineran 1963b; Simpson and Fineran 1970), this cambium shows an unusual behavior in producing secondary xylem centripetally, a small quantity of secondary cortex centrifugally, but no phloem. This essentially unidirectional cambium produces secondary graniferous tracheary elements throughout the life of the haustorium, and in perennial haustoria these elements constitute the bulk of xylem tissue. With *Exocarpus bidwilli,* for example, the haustorium may live for more than six years (Fineran 1963c), and the cambium continues to form graniferous tracheary elements. Whether the elements differentiate from vascular cambia elsewhere in the plant has not been investigated. To date observations on nonhaustorial organs have been confined to primary tissues of leaves, fruits, and stems in mistletoes (Weber 1984).

Cells with Protein Granules as Luminal Inclusions

Proteinaceous granules originate as a protein body-type within dilated cisternae of the endoplasmic reticulum (Figure 7.5A), formed during ontogeny of the cell (Fineran 1979). Typically, the granules appear within the cytoplasm before the bands of secondary wall thickenings begin to differentiate. On maturation of the cell, when the cytoplasm becomes lysed (Figure 7.5.B), the granules are released from their limiting membrane sac and come to lie within the lumen, where, as naked bodies, they persist throughout the conducting life of the tracheary element (Figures 7.2–7.4). In some instances, the granules become secondarily impregnated with phenolic compounds. As indicated by the concomitant impregnation of pit membranes, this condition seems to mark the end of the cell as a conducting element.

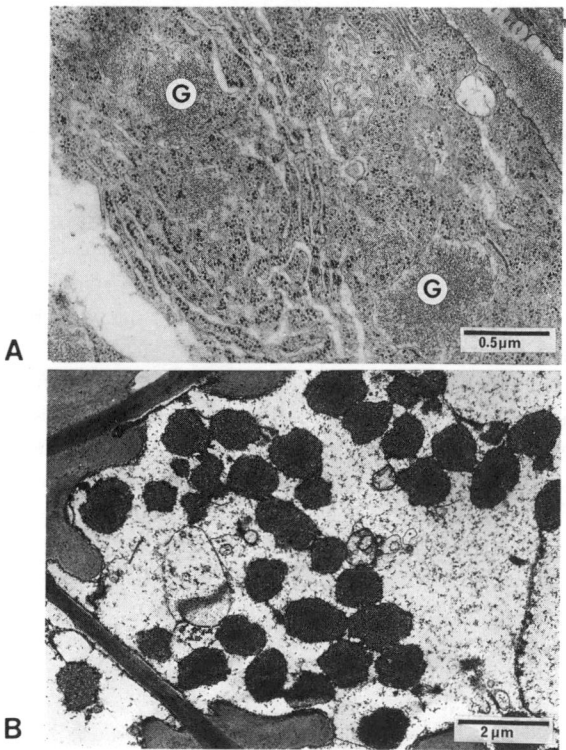

Figure 7.5. Differentiation of graniferous tracheary elements, as exemplified by *Exocarpus bidwillii* of the New Zealand Santalaceae. (A) Early stage in cell differentiation before secondary wall thickenings appear. The cytoplasm contains well-developed cisternae of endoplasmic reticulum; within its dilations the protein matrix of the granules (G) accumulates. The granules are largely fully formed by the time the secondary wall differentiates; × 44,000. (B) Late stage in which the secondary walls have developed. The cytoplasm shows advanced degeneration with only the plasmalemma, nuclear envelope, and other membrane fragments remaining. The granules are unaffected and persist in the lumen after lysis of the protoplasma is completed; × 12,000.

Graniferous tracheary elements with protein granules occur in the Santalaceae, root parasitic Loranthaceae (Fineran and Ingerfeld 1982, Fineran 1983; Fineran and Hocking 1983), and in the haustorium of the stem parasitic mistletoe *Moquiniella rubra* (Fineran 1985). So far, *Moquiniella* is the only loranthaceous stem parasite that we have examined for graniferous tracheary elements by means of transmission electron microscopy. In mistletoes of the Viscaceae, however, current work on several species of the dwarf mistletoe *Arceuthobium* has shown granules within tracheary elements of the shoot and fruit. This confirms the original observations of Weber and Nietfeld (1984), by light and scanning electron microscopy, for the existence of graniferous tracheary elements in *A. oxycedri*. The granules in *Arceuthobium* are proteinaceous, and have an ultrastructure and origin from the endoplasmic reticulum corresponding to those of the Santalaceae and Loranthaceae. In all examples from the Santalaceae, Viscaceae, and Loranthaceae, the protein of the granule is either paracrystalline or amorphous (Figure 7.6.A), and the fibrils of the amorphous granules are loosely arranged or compacted. In some species, both paracrystalline and amorphous fibrillar regions may occur in the same granule (Figure 7.6.B). The overall similarity in protein configuration, and its development within the endoplasmic reticulum (Figure 7.6A), suggests that graniferous tracheary elements in these plants might have had a common origin phylogenetically.

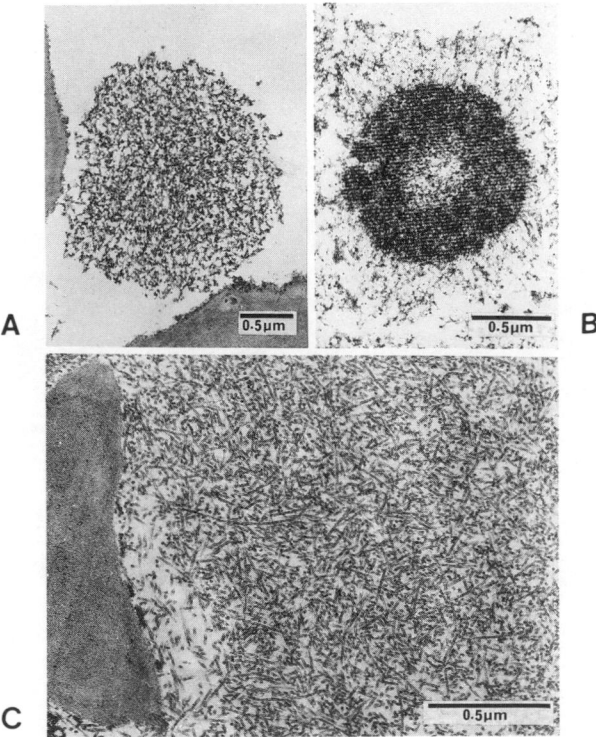

Figure 7.6. Granule ultrastructure in graniferous tracheary elements of the protein inclusion type. (A) Granule with a homogeneous protein matrix organization typical of many Santalaceae. In this example of *Rhiocarpus capensis* from southern Africa, the matrix has a somewhat coarse-textured appearance; × 28,000. (B) Granule with a paracrystalline organization surrounded by diffuse fibrillar material. *Mida salicifolia*, New Zealand Santalaceae; × 41,000. (C) Luminal contents of *Olax phyllanthi* (Olacaceae, Western Australia). Granules have disintegrated into their individual tubular substructural components. These now fill the lumen; × 64,000.

In the Olacaceae, if *Olax phyllanthi* is taken as the example, protein also forms much of the luminal material, but in contrast to the Santalaceae, the inclusions are structurally more diverse (Fineran et al. 1987). Although granules are recognizable in graniferous tracheary elements shortly after differentiation from the cambium that surrounds the vascular core, the substructure of their matrix is tubular (Figure 7.6.C). Consequently, it is completely different from any form of the protein found so far in other Santalales. The somewhat loosely constructed granules of *O. phyllanthi* mostly seem to disintegrate shortly after the cell reaches maturity, and the tubules become dispersed throughout the cell lumen (Figure 7.6.C; 7.7). The limited amount of material presently available for study has not provided sufficient stages in development of the cells for us to determine the cytoplasmic origin of the granules and their component tubules. Graniferous tracheary elements of *Olax* also contain an angular protein in the form of a crystalloid (Fineran et al. 1987). These are first seen within the vacuole during differentiation of the cell and persist in the lumen of the mature graniferous tracheary element. As a result of this vacuolar origin, the crystalloids represent a completely different class of inclusion from those differentiated within the endoplasmic reticulum, as found in the Santalaceae, Viscaceae, and Loranthaceae.

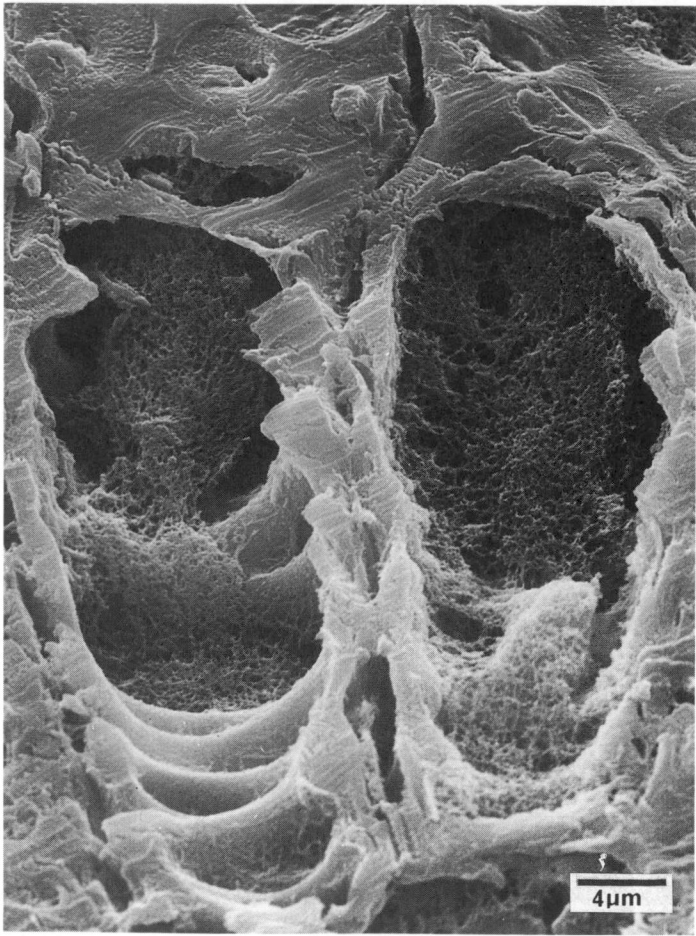

Figure 7.7. Scanning electron micrograph of graniferous tracheary elements in *Olax phyllanthi* (Olacaceae, Western Australia) in which the cells contain dispersed fibrillar material instead of granules; × 3600.

Whether these crystalloids are peculiar to *Olax,* as was at first believed (Fineran et al. 1987), is now becoming doubtful. Structures resembling them have since been seen in a graniferous tracheary element of *Thesium divaricatum* (Santalaceae) prepared for scanning electron microscopy, but information has not yet been obtained on their internal organization. More recently, in an haustorium of *Thesidium fragile* (Santalaceae), growing in association with *Mystropetalon* (Balanophoraceae), Cape province, South Africa, we have found numerous crystalloids closely resembling those of *Olax* in material examined under the transmission electron microscope. Such crystalloids are probably incidental structures to the main organization of graniferous tracheary elements, compared to the more typical granules, mainly because not all graniferous tracheary elements of the haustorium contain them.

The general protein composition of the granules in *Olax phyllanthi* agrees with that in root parasitic Santalaceae and Loranthaceae, but the distinctive tubular configuration of the *Olax* protein suggests that the relationship might not be as close as that between the various taxa of the Santalaceae and Loranthaceae. Even among related groups of parasitic plants, divergent lines of evolutionary specialization of the protein granule could have developed; the tubular condition in *Olax* may be a more divergent line than among those of the Santalaceae and Loranthaceae. Certainly, the distinctive form of the protein in *Olax* would support the notion that the Olacaceae is more distant from the other groups in the Santalales, and possibly that the family represents the more ancestral group of the Order (Kuijt, 1968).

Granules with either a tubular, paracrystalline, or an amorphous fibrillar substructure presumably represent different kinds of proteins. No work has been attempted to characterize the proteins of the granules, however, and from this to establish whether relationships can be shown to exist among the different taxa with respect to graniferous tracheary elements. Current work in our laboratory indicates that even within the same tracheary element more than one form of the protein granule may exist. For example, in *Mida salicifolia* (Santalaceae), some granules occur in paracrystalline form (Figure 7.6.B) whereas others consist of bundles of fibrils. Observations on differentiating cells reveal that both forms of granule arise within the endoplasmic reticulum but that those formed from bundles of fibrils are structurally distinct from the start. They consist of a longitudinal aggregation of fibril subunits that lack any alternate lattice plane arrangement, as shown by the other mostly paracrystalline granules. The spacing of the fibril subunits is also less than that between the lattice planes of the other larger granules.

Weber (1986) studied the haustorium of *Mystropetalon thomii,* using classical methods of histology, and reported for the first time the existence of graniferous tracheary elements in the Balanophoraceae. He noted that the cells and their granules closely resembled those of the Santalaceae, a finding that led him to discuss the possibility that the Balanophoraceae might be related to the Santalales. An affinity between these two groups had been suggested by earlier workers but argued against by others, who instead erected the separate order Balanophorales (for discussion, see Weber 1986). Using haustoria collected from the same locality in South Africa as the material examined by Weber, Fineran (1987a) confirmed the existence of graniferous tracheary elements in *Mystropetalon* (Figure 7.8) in both light and transmission electron microscope preparations. The ultrastructure of the granule matrix is compact and homogeneous when visualized at low magnification, but at high resolution the matrix reveals unusual swirling patterns consisting of what appear to be tubular components. The substructure of the granules in *Mystropetalon* is unlike anything known in the Santalales (Fineran 1985). Histochemical staining demonstrates that the granules are proteinaceous. Therefore, in terms of their general composition, the granules of

Mystropetalon thomii might support arguments for an affinity between the Balano-phoraceae and the Santalales. To support this concept fully, however, the granules would need to be shown to have the same origin in cisternae of the endoplasmic reti-culum as those of the Santalales. The origin of granules in *M. thomii* has not yet been revealed in material available for study.

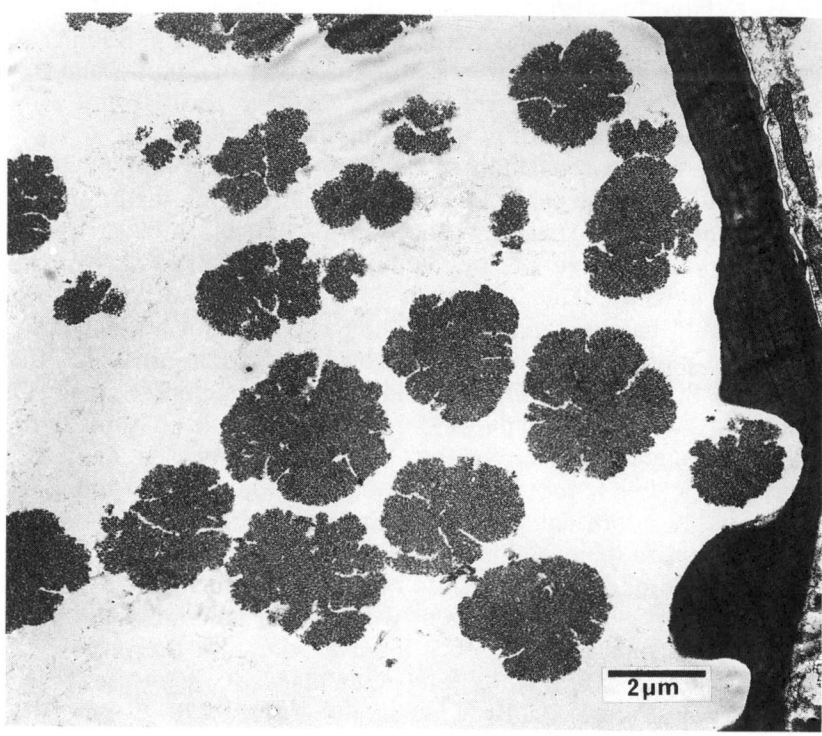

Figure 7.8. Portion of a graniferous tracheary element in the haustorium of *Mystro-petalon thomii* (Balanophoraceae). The granules measure between 1–3 μm in diameter and have a compact protein matrix consisting of an unusual swirling pattern of tubulelike components not resolvable at this magnification; × 8000.

Cells with Polysaccharide Inclusions

In the second type of graniferous tracheary element, the structural material of the lumen is a polysaccharide, usually present as starch grains. Comparatively little research has been done on the starch granule type of graniferous tracheary elements. Most of what has been done relates to root parasitic Scrophulariaceae. Heinricher (1895) illustrated two cells in the haustorium of *Lathraea* and showed the lumen filled with granules. In modern times Renaudin (1974) and Fineran (1985) have reexamined *Lathraea* by means of transmission electron microscopy and have recorded granules with an angular outline (Figure 7.9.A). Recently, we have demonstrated an amyloplast origin for the granules in *Lathraea,* based on an examination of tracheary elements at late stages of differentiation. When the graniferous tracheary element first reaches maturity, the starch grains remain as a clump within the confines of the original plastid envelope, and in light microscope preparations these usually appear as a single large body. As the tracheary elements become older, the amyloplasts disintegrate and their individual starch grains become scattered throughout the lumen (Figure 7.9A). Under the light microscope, these appear as tiny stained particles.

Musselman and Dickison (1975) made the first general survey of graniferous tracheary elements in haustoria of the Scrophulariaceae. Since then we have found starch grains in tracheary elements of *Euphrasia cuneata,* but the granules here occur in low numbers compared with the cells of *Lathraea squamaria* (Figure 7.9.A). Among the Olacaceae, starch grains have also been noted in tracheary elements in the haustorium of *Ximenia* (Fineran 1985). They were reported on briefly (Fineran and Bullock 1979) in the haustorium of *X. americana* from Florida and more recently in *X. caffra* var. *caffra* (Fineran 1985) based on field work in southern Africa. In both taxa of *Ximenia,* the granules exist within tracheary elements of the vascular core but, as in *Euphrasia cuneata,* the granules are mostly small and widely scattered among the cells. Only occasionally in *Ximenia* are graniferous tracheary elements filled with numerous granules (Fineran 1985), resembling the condition more commonly accepted for graniferous tracheary elements (Figure 7.9.A). Cytochemically, the granules in *Ximenia* react positively for polysaccharide with the Thiéry (1967) method on ultrathin sections. Preliminary studies on differentiating tracheary elements of *X. caffra* var. *caffra* also reveal that the granules originate as starch grains in amyloplasts, in the same way as they do in *Lathraea* (Scrophulariaceae). In terms of their structure and origin, the

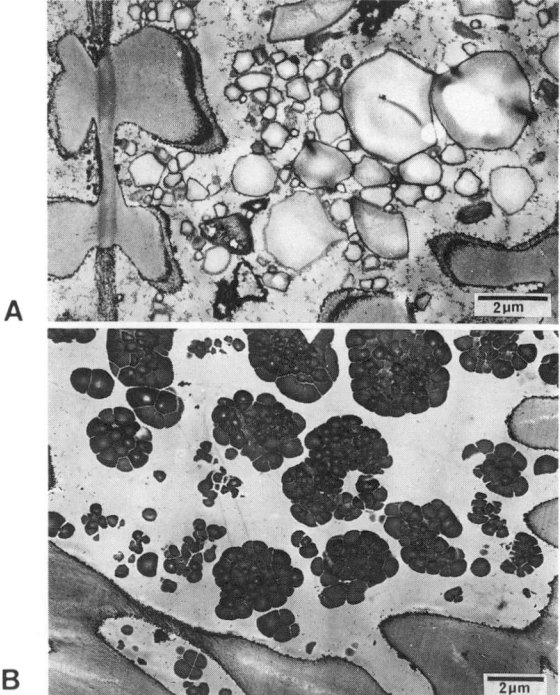

Figure 7.9.   Granule ultrastructure in graniferous tracheary elements of the starch grain inclusion type. (A) Numerous angular-shaped starch grains of various sizes fill the lumen in this cell of *Lathraea clandestina* (Scrophulariaceae, England). The granules are derived from large amyloplasts that released their starch grains on lysis of the protoplast. The granules appear mostly electron-translucent following post-staining in uranyl acetate/lead citrate; × 9000. (B) A cell in *Krameria grayi* (Krameriaceae, Arizona) containing large, mostly composite inclusions. These represent the starch grain clusters of the original amyloplasts present during the ontogeny of the cell. The starch grains are dark as a result of their positive staining for polysaccharide following the Thiéry (1967) reaction; × 7500.

granules in graniferous tracheary elements of *Ximenia*, therefore, are identical to those found in the Scrophulariaceae. As the Olacaceae and Scrophulariaceae are widely separated taxonomically, it must be concluded that the starch grain type of graniferous tracheary element has arisen independently in these families during the evolution of parasitism.

The starch grain type of graniferous tracheary element in *Ximenia* is completely different from the protein inclusion condition shown by *Olax phyllanthi*, yet both plants are placed in the Olacaceae. If graniferous tracheary elements have any taxonomic value, as they appear to have in the Loranthaceae and Santalaceaae, where their distribution and basic structure tend to strengthen existing concepts of phylogenetic relationships, then the occurrence of two types of graniferous tracheary elements in the Olacaceae is puzzling. Either the Olacaceae as currently constituted is an artificial assemblage of plants, or parasitism has arisen at least twice in the family, with the evolution of two types of graniferous tracheary elements. Regrettably, little is known about the occurrence of parasitism throughout the family as a whole, and even among taxa known to be parasitic, information on the anatomy of the haustorium is scant. Data currently available on the haustorium are insufficient to provide any framework within which a meaningful discussion could be made concerning relationships within the family. Some workers regard the Olacaceae as representing the least specialized group of Santalales, whose ancestors may have given rise to the other families of the Order (Kuijt 1968). If this is so, many clues pivotal to our understanding of affinities among graniferous tracheary elements, and of the overall structure of the haustorium in the Santalales, might exist among extant taxa of the Olacaceae. Unfortunately, most of the genera and species are tropical and widely scattered in distribution, thus making specimens difficult to obtain for comparative study.

Graniferous tracheary elements with starch grains appear to have arisen at least three times among parasitic flowering plants. Besides the Scrophulariaceae and *Ximenia* of the Olacaceae discussed above, starch grains have also been found among tracheary elements in the haustorium of *Krameria grayi* (Figure 7.9.B). The existence of granules in *Krameria* was first noted by Musselman (1975), but neither their structure nor composition was examined closely. The taxonomic status of *Krameria* has long been debated, but some recent workers favor placing the genus in its own family, the Krameriaceae (Simpson 1989). Irrespective of its systematic position, *Krameria* is so distant from other root hemiparasites that there can be little doubt that its parasitism has arisen independently. Yet, its graniferous tracheary elements are virtually identical in structure to those of *Lathraea* (Scrophulariaceae) and *Ximenia* (Olacaceae). Furthermore, the granules of *Krameria* are similarly composed of starch grains derived from amyloplasts containing numerous grains. Such parallelism is remarkable. It emphasizes the apparent similar evolutionary pressures that must have existed among unrelated groups of plants when they adopted a comparable parasitic existence. Presumably, this has been the result of similar nutritional demands and opportunities for association between organisms in adopting a parasitic mode of life.

Some graniferous tracheary elements may contain polysaccharide material other than that derived from the starch grains of amyloplasts. In *Olax phyllanthi*, for example, a reticulum made up of fine fibrils may occur that stains positively for polysaccharide with the Thiéry reaction (Fineran et al. 1987). The fibrillar meshwork can be the only structural material within the lumen, or it may coexist with other inclusions. In those graniferous tracheary elements which eventually become impregnated with phenolics, the fibrils of the meshwork provided a nucleation site for the deposition of phenolic droplets. Our current interpretation is that the polysaccharide meshwork is a secondary condition, and therefore not an integral feature of graniferous tracheary elements *per se*. The impregnation is probably a form of gummosis (Fineran et al. 1987). Similar conditions have been found in haustoria of other parasites, but the composition of the impregnating material has not been determined cytochemically. The filling of graniferous tracheary elements with polysaccharide fibrils, and the later deposition of phenolics, are phenomena requiring further study.

PROBABLE FUNCTION OF GRANIFEROUS TRACHEARY ELEMENTS

The greatest deficiency in knowledge about graniferous tracheary elements concerns their function. Partly with the aim of promoting discussion, we originally advanced the idea that graniferous tracheary elements in *Exocarpus bidwillii* (Santalaceae) might exercise some form of control over the flow of xylem sap passing through the haustorium (Fineran and Bullock 1979). This was based on the notion that the surface area created by the granules, and the presence of imperforate tracheary elements and short vessels in the vascular core, might create a mechanical drag on the flow of xylem sap passing between the host and parasite roots. It was suggested that this arrangement might be important in equalizing the pressure of xylem sap entering a parasite that simultaneously attacks a diversity of host plants having different root pressures.

While we have continued to maintain that graniferous tracheary elements in root parasitic Santalales are involved in the functioning of the haustorium, although not necessarily solely according to our original hypothesis, Weber (1984, 1986) has taken the opposite view. He contends that the granules do not have a function but are deposited in the cell as a consequence of the rapid differentiation of these xylem elements. Ultrastructural studies of differentiating graniferous tracheary elements, however, have failed to show that the cells differentiate any faster than other tracheary elements of the haustorium. That the granules follow a regular sequence of development (Fineran 1979) leads us to believe that the granules are part of the normal developmental pattern programmed for these cells. Also, it is difficult to conceive why a cell undergoing rapid differentiation would synthesize excess protein in the form of granules, which in themselves would have no function, either during differentiation or at maturity of the graniferous tracheary element. If granules have a role only during the development of the cell, one might expect them to be hydrolyzed along with the rest of the protoplast at maturity of the tracheary element; however, the granules resist hydrolysis and remain in the lumen of the dead tracheary element. In the light of such observations, we are forced to believe that the granules must have a role at the stage when the tracheary element is functioning as a conducting cell. One possibility that we have considered, from time to time but without experimental evidence, is that the granules might regulate the passage of solutes through the haustorium. With graniferous tracheary elements containing protein granules, the granules might carry a charge and in doing so could influence the movement of certain ions as the stream of xylem sap passes through the cell. The presence of parenchyma cells rich in cytoplasm associated with the graniferous tracheary elements of the vascular core, and also the interrupted zone (Fineran 1963a), presumably interacts with the conducting elements in the operation of the haustorium.

DISTRIBUTION OF GRANIFEROUS TRACHEARY ELEMENTS AMONG PARASITIC PLANTS

The full extent of graniferous tracheary elements throughout the various groups of parasitic plants is not yet known, as only a very small fraction of the total number of parasitic species have been investigated. In families such as the Rafflesiaceae, Orobancheaceae, Lennonaceae, Myzodendraceae, and Hydnoraceae, no taxa have yet been examined specifically for the occurrence of these elements. In all other families in which individual species have been studied closely, however, graniferous tracheary elements have been reported. Even in parasites whose anatomy of the haustorium had been studied by early workers and graniferous tracheary elements not seen, reinvestigation by modern methods has demonstrated the presence of the cells (Fineran 1974, 1987a; Fineran et al. 1978). In the Santalaceae, Loranthaceae, Viscaceae, Olacaceae, Opiliaceae, Krameriaceae, Scrophulariaceae, and Balanophoraceae, graniferous tracheary elements have been found in all taxa investigated (Fineran 1985). In view of these results, it seems highly probable that graniferous tracheary elements are a cell type peculiar to many groups of parasitic angiosperms. To substantiate this hypothesis, however, work is needed on a large number of different genera and species, selected from as many families as possible. Examination of a wide range of haustoria for each species is frequently necessary before the occurrence of the cells can be established with certainty. In very young haustoria, graniferous tracheary elements may not always have differentiated; consequently their apparent absence can be misleading if other stages in the growth of the haustorium are not studied. Young haustoria are typically the most visible organs in the soil because of their light color, and they also occur in larger numbers than mature haustoria. Consequently, young haustoria are the organs most likely to be sampled for anatomical study, especially by the less experienced worker.

The degree of development of graniferous tracheary elements may vary widely among haustoria, both from plant to plant and among different parasite species. In some instances, the frequency of the elements within the haustorium of a particular parasite seems to depend on the host attacked. The possible influence of the host on the expression of graniferous tracheary elements is an aspect that needs to be investigated.

CONCLUDING REMARKS

Research on graniferous tracheary elements has now reached the stage, at least in the Santalales, that an experimental approach should be made to determine the function of the cells. In particular, the hypothesis that granules might serve a mechanical function in causing a resistance to the flow of xylem sap through the haustorium (Fineran and Bullock 1979) should be tested. The concept presented in this review that the protein granules might carry a charge, and therefore influence the movement of ions through the haustorium, could also form the basis for experimentation.

The chief obstacle to experimental work to date has been the clandestine location of haustoria and the difficulty of manipulating plants under laboratory conditions while they are still attached to their hosts. Recent work by Kuo et al. (1989) on the haustorial interface relationship between *Olax phyllanthi* and its host has demonstrated the feasibility of experimenting with underground haustoria. Most root hemiparasitic Santalales are relatively slow-growing woody plants: consequently, experiments will require long-term planning if the parasites are to be grown in cultivation. For this reason, we have been establishing plants of *Colpoon compressum* (Santalaceae) and *Ximenia caffra* var. *caffra* (Olacaceae) (as well as *Buttonia superba*—Scrophulariaceae) raised from seed in containers with host plants. The original host plant selected was a species of *Chrysanthemoides,* since this was a common host at the site at which seeds of *Colpoon* were originally collected. Interestingly, when stray seedlings of *Cytisus scoparius* became established in the pots, growth of the parasite showed a marked improvement over the original host, thus indicating that *Cytisus* is a more beneficial host plant. Such plants of *Colpoon* are now well over 1m tall, after three years growth on *Cytisus* since the original *Chrysanthemoides* host was cut out. Ultimately, such parasites raised in cultivation will be used in trials to establish the pathways of conduction between host and parasite and possibly within the haustorium itself. This might involve applying tracers to the root system of the host and then following their movement into the parasite. Kuo et al. (1989) have carried out exactly this kind of experiment with *O. phyllanthi* with the inert tracers lanthanum nitrate and uranyl acetate in transmission electron microscopy. For their experiments, they were fortunate in being able to employ plants in the field growing in sandy soil. Unfortunately, with many species of root parasitic Santalales, the plants are often established in hard or rocky soil, conditions not conducive to field experiments.

An alternative approach to manipulating long-lived woody parasites, either in the field or in cultivation, might be to use herbaceous or small, semiwoody species. Although not common in the Santalales, some examples may be found among species of *Thesium.* The demonstration of graniferous tracheary elements in the haustorium of mistletoes of the Loranthaceae, as in *Moquinella rubra* (Fineran 1985), as well as in shoot tissue of *Arceuthobium oxycedri* (Weber and Nietfield 1984) of the Viscaceae, offers another type of material for experimentation. The advantage of mistletoes is that the parasite can be removed intact, along with a portion of the host branch, and placed directly in a solution containing the tracer. This approach was used successfully to demonstrate the apoplastic continuum for water transport between *Korthalsella lindsayi* and its host (Coetzee and Fineran 1987; Fineran 1987b), and also to show that lysine may follow a similar pathway into the parasite (Coetzee and Fineran 1989).

Once plant physiologists become more aware of the existence of graniferous tracheary elements among parasitic plants, there should be greater impetus for research on these unique cells. Existing ideas on the function of graniferous tracheary elements should be tested and, if rejected, replaced by new concepts. Graniferous tracheary elements may well hold the clue to some of the still unexplained phenomena related to the physiology of parasitic plants.

Acknowledgments

The author thanks Manfred Ingerfeld for technical assistance with electron microscopy. The work was supported, in part, by grants from the University of Canterbury and the University Grants Committee (No. 540894, 573097, 574430).

LITERATURE CITED

Benharrat, H. 1986. Contribution a l'etude de la biologie des phanerogames parasites: researche sur *Osyris alba* L. (Santalacees). Thèse, Universite de Nantes, France.

Benharrat, H., S. Renaudin, L. Rey, and P. Thalouarn. 1987. Sur la différenciation des trachéides dans les haustoriums d'*Osyris alba* parasitant *Hedera helix*. *Can. J. Bot.* 65:1746–1755.

Benharrat, H., L. Rey, and S. Renaudin. 1984. Étude ultrastructurale et par la microanalyse à rayons × des granules présents dans les tracheids du sucoirs d' *Osyris alba*. *Physiol. Vég.* 22:827–831.

Benson, M. 1910. Root parasitism in *Exocarpus* (with comparative notes on the haustoria of *Thesium*). *Ann. Bot. (London)* 24:667–677.

Coetzee, J., and B. A. Fineran. 1987. The apoplastic continuum, nutrient absorption and plasmatubules in the dwarf mistletoe *Korthalsella lindsayi* (Viscaceae). *Protoplasma* 136:145–153.

_____ . 1989. Translocation of lysine from the host *Melicope simplex* to the parasitic dwarf mistletoe *Korthalsella lindsayi* (Viscaceae). *New Phytol.* 112:377–381.

Dobbins, D. R. and J. Kuijt. 1973a. Studies on the haustorium of *Castilleja* (Scrophulariaceae). I. The upper haustorium. *Can. J. Bot.* 51:917–922.

_____ . 1973b. Studies on the haustorium of *Castilleja* (Scrophulariaceae). II. The endophyte. *Can. J. Bot.* 51:923–931.

Fineran, B. A. 1963a. Studies on the root parasitism of *Exocarpus bidwillii*. Hook. f. III. Primary structure of the haustorium. *Phytomorphology* 13:42–54.

_____ . 1963b. Studies on the root parasitism of *Exocarpus bidwillii* Hook. f. IV. Structure of the mature haustorium. *Phytomorphology* 13:249–267.

_____ . 1963c. Parasitism in *Exocarpus bidwillii* Hook. f. *Trans. Soc. New Zealand, Bot.* 2:109–119.

_____ . 1974. A study of 'phloeotracheids' in haustoria of santalaceous root parasites using scanning electron microscopy. *Ann Bot. (London)* 38:937–946.

_____ . 1979. Ultrastructure of differentiating graniferous tracheary elements in the haustorium of *Exocarpus bidwillii* (Santalaceae). *Protoplasma* 98:199–221.

_____ . 1983. Ultrastructure of graniferous tracheary elements in the terrestrial mistletoe *Nuytsia floribunda* (Loranthaceae). *Protoplasma* 116:57–64.

_____ . 1985. Graniferous tracheary elements in haustoria of root parasitic angiosperms. *Bot. Rev.* 51:389–441.

_____ . 1987a. Structural aspects of higher plant parasitism: graniferous tracheary elements. *XIV Int. Bot. Cong.*, Berlin (West). Abstr. p. 210.

_____ . 1987b. A structural approach towards investigating transport systems between host and parasite, as exemplified by some mistletoes and root parasites. In *Parasitic Flowering Plants*. Ed. H. C. Weber, W. Forstreuter. University of Marburg, Federal Republic of Germany. 201–220.

Fineran, B. A., and S. Bullock. 1972. A procedure for embedding plant material in Araldite for electron microscopy. *Ann. Bot.* 36:83–86.

_____ . 1979. Ultrastructure of graniferous tracheary elements in the haustorium of *Exocarpus bidwillii*, a root hemi-parasite of the Santalaceae. *Proc. R. Soc. London Ser. B.* 204:329–343.

Fineran, B. A., and P. J. Hocking. 1983. Features of parasitism, morphology and haustorial anatomy in loranthaceous root parasites. In *The Biology of Mistletoes*. Ed. D. M. Calder, P. Bernhardt. 205–277. Sydney: Academic Press.

Fineran, B. A., and M. Ingerfeld. 1982. Graniferous tracheary elements in the haustorium of *Atkinsonia ligustrina*, a root hemi-parasite of the Loranthaceae. *Protoplasma* 113:150–160.

Fineran, B. A., M. Ingerfeld, and W. D. Patterson. 1987. Inclusions of graniferous tracheary elements in the root hemi-parasite *Olax phyllanthi* (Olacaceae). *Protoplasma* 136:16–28.

Fineran, B. A., B. E. Juniper, and S. Bullock. 1978. Graniferous tracheary elements in the haustorium of the Santalaceae. *Planta* 141:29–32.

Fisher, D. B. 1968. Protein staining for ribboned epon sections for light microscopy. *Histochemie* 16:92–96.

Heinricher, E. 1895. Anatomischer Bau und Leistung der Saugorgane der Schuppen-wurz-Arten (*Lathraea clandestina* Lam. und *L. squamaria* L.). *Beitr. Biol. Pflanzen.* 7:315–406.

Juniper, B. E., G. C. Cox, A. J. Gilchrist, and P. R. Williams. 1970. *Techniques for Plant Electron Microscopy.* Oxford/Edinburgh: Blackwell Scientific Publications. 108 pp.

Kubat, R. 1987. Report of the first investigations of parasitism in Opiliaceae (Santalales). In *Parasitic Flowering Plants.* Ed. H. C. Weber, W. Forstreuter. University of Marburg, Federal Republic of Germany. 489–492.

Kuijt, J. 1968. Mutual affinities of santalalean families. *Brittonia* 20:136–147.

Kuo, J., J. S. Pate, and N. J. Davidson. 1989. Ultrastructure of the haustorial interface and apoplastic continuum between host and the root hemiparasite *Olax phyllanthi* (Labill.) R. Br. (Olacaceae). *Protoplasma* 150:27–39.

Maybrook, A. C. 1917. On the haustoria of *Pedicularis vulgaris,* Tournef. *Ann. Bot. (London)* 31:499–511.

Mazia, D., P. A. Brewer, and M. Alfert. 1953. The cytochemical staining and measurement of protein with mercuric bromophenol blue. *Biol. Bull.* 104:57–67.

Musselman, L. J. 1975. Parasitism and haustoria structure in *Krameria lanceolata* (Krameriaceae). A preliminary study. *Phytomorphology* 25:416–422.

Musselman, L. J., and W. C. Dickison. 1975. The structure and development of the haustorium in parasitic Scrophulariaceae. *Bot. J. Linn. Soc.* 70:183–212.

Nietfield, U., H. C. Weber, and F. Weberling. 1983. Zur Morphologie und Anatomie des Kontaktorgans von *Osyris alba* L. (Santalaceae). *Beitr. Biol. Pflanzen* 50:283–298.

Niranjana, R., and G. R. Shivamurthy. 1987a. Graniferous tracheary elements in the haustorium of *Osyris arborea* Wall (Santalaceae). *Ann. Bot. (London)* 59:237–243.

Niranjana, R., and G. R. Shivamurthy. 1987b. Graniferous tracheary elements in the haustorium of *Scleropyrum wallichianum* Arn. (Santalaceae). *Curr. Sci.* 56:727–730.

O'Brien, T. P. and M. E. McCully. 1981. *The Study of Plant Structure: Principles and Selected Methods.* Melbourne, Australia: Termarcarphi Pty. Ltd.

Renaudin, S. 1974. *Contribution à l'Étude de la Biologie des Phanérogames Parasites: Researches sur* Lathraea clandestina *L.* (Scrophulariacées). Ph.D. thesis. Universite de Nantes, France.

Simpson, B. B. 1989. *Krameriaceae. Flora Neoptropica.* Monograph 49. New York: Organ. Flora Neotropica, New York Botanical Garden.

Simpson, P. G., and B. A. Fineran. 1970. Structure and development of the haustorium in *Mida salicifolia. Phytomorphology* 20:236–248.

Spurr, A. R. 1969. A low-viscosity epoxy resin embedding medium for electron microscopy. *J. Ultrastruct. Res.* 26:31–43.

Thiéry, J. P. 1967. Mise en evidence des polysaccharides sur coupes fines en microscopie électronique. *J. Microscop.* 6:987–1018.

Weber, H. C. 1977a. Anatomische Studien an den Haustorien (Kontaktorganen) von *Thesium* Arten (Santalaceae). *Ber. Deutsch. Bot. Ges.* 90:439–458.

———. 1977b. Zur Anatomie des Kontaktorgans von *Cansjera rheedii* Gmel. (Opiliaceae). I. Ontogenie und Haustorialstruktur, II. Intrusives Organ. *Beitr. Biol. Pflanzen* 53:371–410.

———. 1980. Untersuchungen an australischen und neuseeländischen Loranthaceae/Viscaceae. 1. Zur Morphologie und Anatomie der unterirdischen Organe von *Nuytsia floribunda* (Labill.). R. Br. *Beitr. Biol. Pflanzen* 55:77–99.

————. 1984. Untersuchugen an australischen und neuseeländischen Lorantha-ceae/Viscaceae. 3. Granulahaltige Xylem-Leitbahnen. *Beitr. Biol. Pflanzen* 59:303–320.

————. 1986. Granulahaltige Xylem-Leitbahnen und andere den *Santalales* ähnliche anatomische Strukturen in den haustorialen Knollen von *Mystropetalon thomii* Har. (Balanophoraceae). *Flora* 178:315–328.

Weber, H. C., and M. Hildenbrand. 1978. Über die sogenannten Phloeotracheiden in den Kontaktorganen von *Cansjera rheedii* Gmel. (Opiliaceae) and einigen anderen parasitischen Angiospermen. *Ber. Deutsch. Bot. Ges.* 91:231–242.

Weber, H. C., and U. Nietfeld. 1984. Haustorialstruktur und granulahaltige Xylem-Leitbahnen bei *Arceuthobium oxycedri* (DC.) M. Bieb (Viscaceae). *Ber. Deutsch. Bot. Ges.* 97:421–431.

Section II
SECONDARY
VEGETATIVE GROWTH

_____ Chapter 8 _____

Secondary Growth in Pteridophytes

S. BHAMBIE

Radial growth is a unique phenomenon of higher vascular plants that emanates from the development and activity of vascular and cork cambia. The vascular cambium arises between primary xylem and phloem and produces secondary vascular tissues, whereas the cork cambium (phellogen) usually forms in the outermost layers of the cortex and produces the periderm layers. A number of reviews are available on various aspects of the secondary cambia in angiosperms and gymnosperms (Glock 1955; Newman 1956; Wareing 1958; Wilcox 1962; Studhalter et al. 1963; Hejnowicz 1964; Philipson and Ward 1965; Kozlowski 1971; Philipson et al. 1971; Mullik and Jenson 1973; Panikkar and Bhambie 1974; Cutler 1976; Schmidt 1976; Iqbal 1990), but this subject is relatively neglected in pteridophytes, probably because most of the living pteridophytes have shortened axes with erect, suberect, prostrate, or trailing habit and apparently need no secondary tissues for conduction and support. Extinct pterido-phytes of the Paleozoic and Mesozoic eras, however, were giant trees that often attained heights of 30 m. They possessed both vascular and cork cambia, although with marked differences in activity. This review examines the origin and function of the first cambium in the primitive land plants, its constituents, and its phylogenetic evolution. The review follows the conservative classification of pteridophytes into Psilopsida, Psilotopsida, Lycopsida, Sphenopsida, Pteropsida, and Progymnospermop-sida (Sporne 1975).

PSILOPSIDA, PSILOTOPSIDA, AND LYCOPSIDA

Lepidodendron Sternberg was an arborescent genus of the swamp forests of the Carboniferous period. The plant resembled present -day agavaceous monocots. It had a long, comparatively thin trunk (30 m × 40 cm), with a crown of successively narrow dichotomous branches at its top. The trunk was conical, not columnar (Eggert 1961a). The apical meristem had spontaneous growth for a considerable period to produce an

From *Growth Patterns*
in Vascular Plants
Edited by Muhammed Iqbal

185

undivided trunk, and it progressively increased in size, as is evident from the inverse ratio of primary and secondary tissues at different levels of the trunk (Andrews and Murdy 1958; Eggert 1961a).

In transections, the stele varied from a solid core of primary xylem (L. pettycurense) to a mixed pith (L. vasculare) or a solid pith (L. veltheimii). Most of the species had a trunk that was protostelic at the base and siphonostelic in the upper part of the main trunk and in thicker branches. The condition again became protostelic in successively smaller branches. The xylem core with exarch protoxylem groups was surrounded by a layer of parenchyma, as in the living genus Isoetes, and then by primary phloem. The extrastelar tissue comprised three distinct zones of cortex bound by a periderm.

Lepidodendron had both a vascular and a cork cambium. The vascular cambium was unifacial and gave rise on the inside to secondary xylem, which functioned in conduction, and the cork cambium gave rise to periderm, which provided mechanical support (Figure 8.1.1) (Arnold 1968; Leisman and Rivers 1974; Eggert and Kanemoto 1977; Rothwell 1984; Cichan 1985a). An irregularly bifacial cambium was reported by Lemoigne (1962, 1964, 1966) but was subsequently rejected (Lemoigne 1967). Further, the cambium was determinate in growth, unlike most present day vascular plants, as it produced a limited amount of tissue in all the specimens, whether large or small, after which it was converted into a promeristematic parenchymatous sheath (Arnold 1960; Eggert and Kanemoto 1977; Cichan 1985a). A cambium was initiated probably in the parenchymatous layer surrounding the xylem and consisted mostly of fusiform initials interrupted at places by a few ray initials (Figures 8.1.1, 8.2.A). The number of initials remained more or less constant, as proved by a recently devised method for analyzing the centrifugal enlargement of tracheids responsible for circumferential growth of the cambium. This method involves observation of serial tangential sections and reveals a complete absence of any periodic anticlinal divisions in the fusiform initials (Cichan 1985a,b). The amount of wood formed by the cambium centripetally was limited and usually depicted symmetrical arrangement, but sometimes asymmetrical. The tracheids were arranged in radial rows and were interrupted by very tall uni- or biseriate rays. The tracheids had scalariform thickenings with vertical strands of secondarily formed material, i.e. Williamson's striations (Williamson 1887). Rays were parenchymatous and were preserved only in the inner wood.

External to the wood was a lacuna caused by distortion of phloem and cortical tissue. Exterior to it lay the so-called "secretory tissue." Horizontal walls of the secretory tissue elements were absorbed in the formation of longitudinal ducts. This region of the cortex connected the parichnos of the leaf to the underground axis and helped in the aeration of the subterranean axis.

The cork cambium was indeterminate. It differentiated quite early in the ontogeny of the plant, either in peripheral or in deep-seated layers of the outer cortex. It had only one type of cell, was bifacial in activity, and produced a pronounced phellem outside and a narrow secondary cortex inside. The thick-walled phellem cells were arranged in radially aligned rows simulating the storied wood structure of certain advanced dicotyledons. They looked rectangular in cross-sections, with thickened walls and brown contents (Figures 8.1.1, 8.2.F). The cells of the secondary cortex were tightly packed and isodiametric, with walls thicker than those of the primary cortex.

The origin of the phellogen is controversial (Kirch 1913; Beck 1958; Eggert 1961a; Smith 1964). In addition to the normal activity of the phellogen, some diffuse growth around the leaf bases and a radial cortical expansion by additional tangential divisions in the cells of the middle cortex sometimes also occurred. These divisions kept pace with the increase in wood diameter through the activity of the vascular cambium and thus avoided rupture of the outer tissues. This area of growth formed the so-called "tertiary cortex" (Lemoigne 1967; Thomas 1978).

Stigmaria Brongniart, the organ-genus for the basal four-lobed underground structure, had lateral appendages or their scars. The surface of the axis was smooth due to decortication but was interrupted by scars in *S. ficoides* (Jennings 1973). A transection of a *Stigmarian* axis usually showed a central pith, rarely a solid core of xylem. The pith was surrounded by a narrow ring of endarch primary xylem bands and then by a broad zone of secondary xylem consisting of radially aligned files of tracheids interrupted by uni-, bi-, and multiseriate rays. The tracheids of both the primary and secondary xylem had spiral and scalariform thickenings. The latter also possessed Williamson's striations. Rays were quite narrow at the inner periphery of the wood but broadened toward the outer periphery. The cells of the multicellular rays gradually increased in size, became more fragile, and formed lacunae by schizogenous disruption. Concomitantly, secondary tracheids and uni- and bicellular rays also enlarged considerably, thereby increasing the size of fusiform and ray initials and eventually the circumference of the vascular cambium. The vascular cambium, unifacial and determinate, had a fixed number of initials and, after the cessation of its activity, differentiated into a "parenchymatous sheath" (Frankenberg and Eggert 1969; Cichan 1985a). In a few large specimens, however, sporadic disruptions were found in the radial files of secondary xylem. These may have been sites wherein fusiform initials divided to form a cluster of new initials (Frankenberg and Eggert 1969). The parenchymatous sheath was continuous and contained a small zone on its outer side with oval or rectangular parenchymatous cells intercepted by rays that were contiguous with the rays of the secondary xylem (see Figure 22 in Cichan 1985a). This finding suggests that the cells were derived from the cambium. This zone was followed by a cortex with a periderm a few layers beneath the outermost layers.

The phellogen began as a poorly defined single row of flattened cells in the middle cortex and produced a broad zone of phellem and a narrow zone of phelloderm. The cells of the periderm or phellem were arranged in radial files and retained the capacity for metabolic activity for a considerable duration. The cells of the phelloderm were parenchymatous or sclerenchymatous and arranged in regular rows (Figure 8.2.F). *S. stellata* was devoid of phelloderm. Further, this species had triangular wedges of thick-walled cells alternating with thin-walled cells in the outer cortex, which mostly disintegrated and formed lacunae during fossilization (Jennings 1973).

Sigillaria (Sternberg) Brongniart had a unifacial vascular cambium that produced secondary xylem around the primary xylem of a siphonostele (Cichan 1985a). The secondary xylem contained cells of varied size and mostly consisted of scalariform tracheids. The amount of primary wood was less developed in later forms, such as the Permian species *S. brardi*. Phellogen was similar in origin and activity to that of *Lepidodendron*. In *Lepidophloios* (originally spelled *Lepidofloyos*) an internal periderm layer was present adjacent to the secondary xylem (Sporne 1975; Taylor 1981; Cichan 1985a; Cichan and Beck 1986). The distinctive phellogen was bifacial as in *Lepidodendron*, but in *Lepidophloios wunenschianus* it was a three-layered zone (Smith 1964). *Bothrodendron* Lindley and Hutton lacked a vascular cambium but had a bifacial phellogen similar to that of *Lepidodendron*.

Paurodendron Fry, which existed in the Pennsylvanian and the Carboniferous periods, was a herbaceous plant with an unusual cambium somewhat similar to that of the living genus *Isoetes* (Figure 8.2.C). It had a continuous and basally expanded primary xylem, cylindrical rod from apex downwards. It had an exarch protostele (Phillips and Leisman 1966). A cambium differentiated in the lower basal region and extended laterally all around up to the middle of the axis, or *transition zone*. It produced regularly arranged files of scalariform tracheids centripetally and secondary cortex centrifugally. It was interrupted by departing root traces, which appeared V-shaped in tangential view, surrounded by ray-like parenchymatous cells and a meristematic zone, which was probably the seat of the origin of roots. There was a space between the secondary xylem and the inner cortex. The outer cortex, or *secondary cortex*, had radial files of moderately thick-walled cells filled with resinlike brown content (Phillips and Leisman 1966). The plant had bipolar activity, as in *Isoetes*, and a unique cambium surrounding the basal region of the axis (Paolillo 1982).

Lepidophloios Sternberg, *Sigillaria* (Sternberg) Brongniart, and *Paralycopodites* (Williamson) DiMichele had stigmarian type of underground axes whereas *Lepidodendropsis*, *Lepidosigillaria*, and *Protostigmaria* possessed rounded, lobed, cormlike basal axes (Jennings 1975; Pigg and Rothwell 1979). A recent study on petrified *Protostigmaria* from the Devonian period has revealed different anatomical configurations at different levels of the axis especially due to the presence of a transition region. At the proximal end of the aerial axis, the primary xylem was reduced to a point from which the surrounding secondary xylem tracheids radiated in all directions. The secondary tissue lacked any root trace and looked ellipsoidal in sectional view. Further downward in the root-producing region was a less orderly arrangement of secondary tracheids that could be branched at times and apparently arranged longitudinally and parallel to the circumference of the axis. At successively distal aerial portions of the axis was a continuous central pith containing an increased amount of exarch protoxylem and less secondary xylem, thus demonstrating an inverse ratio of primary and secondary wood like that of a *Lepidodendron*. The vascular cambium was unifacial and determinate with selective activity regarding its amount at different levels of the axis (Jennings 1975; Pigg and Rothwell 1979).

A petrified woody lycopsid stem from the Carboniferous era, tentatively thought to be related to the order Protolepidodendrales but growing in substantially drier habitat than those of the Upper Carboniferous, has been described in some detail (Cichan and Beck 1987). A transection of the axis depicted a centrally placed, relatively narrow parenchymatized protostele, surrounded by a thick cylinder of secondary xylem, then by a tripartite cortex, and ultimately by a broad periderm. Secondary xylem had narrow but too elongate tracheids, three-four times longer than those of the Upper Carboniferous lycopsids. The tracheids, interrupted by uni- and biseriate rays, attained a height of eight cells and possessed scalariform thickenings on radial and tangential walls but lacked Williamson's striations. The wide periderm formed by cork cambium had two distinct zones. The inner zone consisted of thin-walled cells that gradually gave way to thick-walled cells. The outer zone had radially arranged groups of wedge-shaped patches of cells broader than other fiber-like cells that formed fissures or "meshes". Broad and narrow tracheids are indicative of xeric habitat, thus proving that the plant hailed from drier habitat (Carlquist 1977; Metcalfe and Chalk 1983; Cutler 1984).

There were at least five genera of Mesozoic lycopsids: *Pleuromeiopsis*, *Pleuromeia*, *Nathorstiana*, *Paurodendron*, and *Isoetites*. Most of them are found in the form of impressions or casts, but associated organs prove them to be lycopods. *Pleuromeiopsis* had a once-divided stem, but its basal portion was stigmaria-like, though less extended (see Sixtel's 1962 reconstruction in Boureau 1964). *Pleuromeia* had an unbranched axis and a basally four-lobed, upturned axis (Mägdefrau 1931, 1932). *Nathorstiana*, only 20 cm high, had a very reduced axial portion and a basal portion with several longitudinal ridges. Root structure with minor anatomical variations was similar to that of stigmarian appendages (Stewart 1947, 1981, 1983; Andrews 1961; Bhambie 1962, 1970, 1972a; Taylor 1981). *Paurodendron* and *Isoetites* had bipolar growth and apparently possessed lateral meristem, i.e. a cambium and a rhizomorphic meristem (Bhambie 1962; Paolillo 1963,1982; Phillips and Leisman 1966; Schlanker and Leisman 1969; Taylor 1981). It appears that other forms might have developed a lateral meristem and subsequently secondary tissues at least in their basal portion.

These plants inform us about the changes that occurred in the environment. The swampy habitat prevalent during the Middle Devonian fostered the formation of the large stigmarian base in lepidodendroid axis, but the swamps started to recede, plants underwent gradual modification. They developed shortened lobed basal axes, as in *Pleuromeia* and *Nathorstiana,* to compete with other land plants (Taylor 1981; Thomas 1981; Thomas and Spicer 1986).

The living genus *Isoetes* Linn. usually grows in a swampy habitat. The plant body has three parts: an axis, a rosette of leaves and sporophylls above the ground, and numerous adventitious roots below the ground for anchorage. The three types of meristem found in *Isoetes* are apical, basal, and lateral. Although the apical meristem is normal in its activity and forms the stem stele, the origin and activity of the latter two are peculiar (Figure 8.1.2). The basal meristem, which can be compared with the detached meristem of *Selaginella* for the formation of rhizophore, is an embedded, self-perpetuating meristem present at the base of the rhizomorphic stele. It continues as linear strips around the horn-shaped stelar lobes up to their ends. It adds new tissue continuously to the rhizomorphic stele (Bhambie 1962, 1970). Further, it is the seat of origin of roots and is also considered a "root-producing meristem" (Bhambie 1962, 1970; Paolillo 1963, 1982; Bierhorst 1971). The peculiarity of the lateral meristem lies in its origin just outside the primary phloem of the stele [Figure 8.1.2]. It surrounds the stem stele completely just beneath the procambium, but in the rhizomorphic stelar region it is present in the form of strips bridging the gaps between two to four ridges of the stele as the basal meristem occupies the terminal face of the ridges. The vascular cambium is abnormal in its origin and is in the form of two to four strips, depending upon the number of lobes an axis has, and develops in between the ridges of the stelar lobes in the rhizomorphic region of the plant.

A transection of the axis passing through the stem (and rhizomorphic) region of ten species of *Isoetes* (*I. asiatica* Makino, *I. coromandeliana* L., *I. echinospora* Dur, *I. engelmanii* A. Br., *I. japonica* A. Br., *I. lacustris* L., *I. malinverniana* Cesat et DeNot., *I. panchananii* Pant and Sriv., *I. sahyadrii* Mahabale, and *I. sampathkumarani* Rao) shows a central bi-, tri-, and tetraradiate protostele that consists of loosely arranged tracheids and xylem parenchyma along with interspersed spaces. There is no differentiation of proto- and metaxylem. A few layers of secondarily formed tracheids have been noticed in two axes out of the 300 studied in plants with a disorganized primary xylem (Bhambie 1962). A perennial, bifacial cambium originates just adjacent to primary phloem on its outer side very early in the ontogeny of the plant (Figures 8.1.2, 8.2). It surrounds the stem stele but is in the form of 2–4 strips bridging the gaps between the radiating arms of the rhizomorphic stele. The cambium is abnormal in origin as well as in activity. It produces a small amount of secondary phloem that at times has alternate bands of secondary parenchyma centripetally and a large amount of secondary cortex centrifugally (Figure 8.2.C). The cambium consists of somewhat flattened, compactly arranged, thin-walled, densely cytoplasmic, meristematic cells. The cambium lacks typical ray initials, but in the secondary phloem, a few raylike parenchymatous cells are present that surround a leaf or root-trace when it passes through the secondary tissue. The secondary phloem consists of compactly arranged, rectangular, or tabular cells in radially arranged rows. The cells in these rows progressively enlarge peripherally in dimensions supporting the contention of Cichan (1985a)

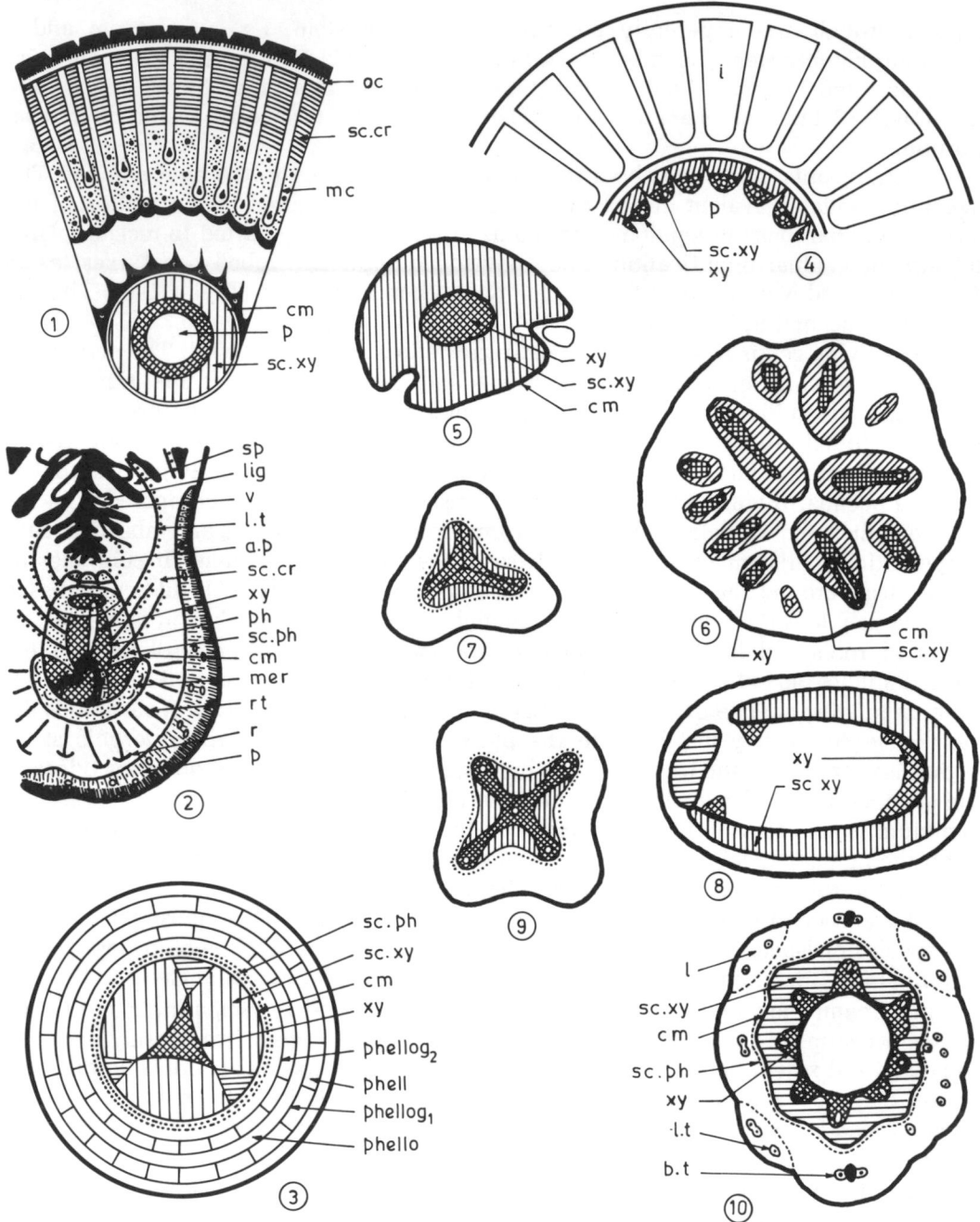

Figure 8.1. (1) Semidiagrammatic transverse section of a small stem of *Lepidodendron*. (2) Stereodiagram of a longitudinal section of *Isoetes* axis to give an integrated picture; the occurrence of bipolar growth, apical and basal meristems, and lateral cambium is noteworthy. (3–10) Semidiagrammatic transverse sections of the axis (root, stem, and phyllophore) of *Sphenophyllum* (3), *Astromyelon* (calamitean root; (4) *Schizopodium* (only xylem configuration and presumptive cambium are shown; (5) Cladoxylon (6), *Triloboxylon* (7), *Protopitys* (8), *Tetraxylopteris* (9), and *Archaeopteris* (10). a.p, apical meristem of shoot; b.t, branch trace; cm, cambium; i, cortical lacunae; l, leaf; lig, ligule; l.t, leaf trace; mc, middle cortex; mer, meristem of rhizomorph; oc, outer cortex; p, pith; ph, phloem; per, periderm; phell, phellem; phellg$_1$, phellogen I; phellog$_2$, phellogen II; phello, phelloderm; r, root; r.t, root trace; sp, developing sporangium; sc.cr, secondary cortex; sc.ph, secondary phloem; sc.xy, secondary xylem; v, velum; xy, primary xylem.

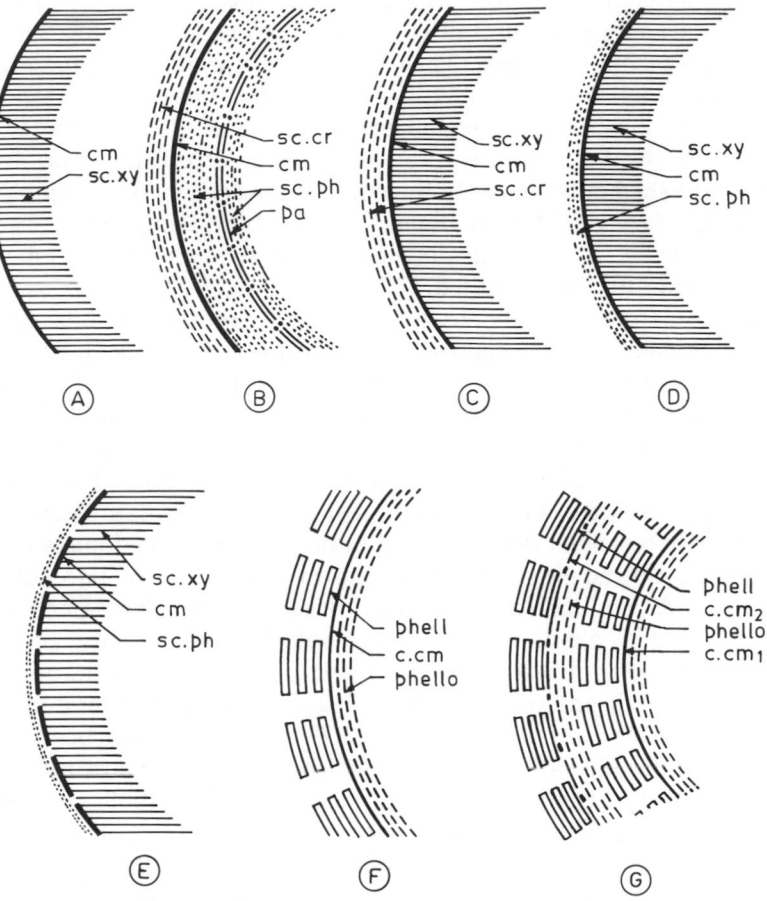

Figure 8.2. Diagrammatic representation of a part of cambium and cork cambium in extinct and extant pteridophytes. The unifacial determinate cambium (A), an anomalous cambium forming secondary phloem interrupted by layers of parenchyma or producing secondary xylem and parenchyma on the inner side and secondary cortex on the outer side (B, C, respectively), normal determinate and indeterminate bifacial cambia producing secondary xylem centripetally and secondary phloem centrifugally (D, E), normal bifacial cork cambium forming a limited amount of phelloderm and a large amount of phellem (F, G). Successive cork cambia I and II can be seen in (G). cm, cambium; c.cm, cork cambium; pa, interrupted parenchyma in secondary phloem; phell, phellem; phello, phelloderm; sc.cr, secondary cortex; sc.ph, secondary phloem; sc.xy, secondary xylem.

that the circumferential enlargement of cambium is due to progressive and gradual lengthening of individual files of secondary tissue. The sieve elements are usually enucleate cells, prismatic in appearance, without any stainable contents, and with transverse end walls. Callose occurs first around the sieve pores. Later, callose plugs are formed that block the pores; finally, callose depositions of nearby pores fuse and bands of callose occur on the walls. As the sieve pores are arranged spirally or helically, spiral and helical callose bands are observed on the walls of sieve elements. These bands have been mistaken for lignified thickenings in the past, leading to interpretations for the inner secondary tissue such as (a) secondary xylem (Smith 1900; Stokey 1909); (b) secondary parenchyma (Weber 1922); (c) "prismatic tissue" comprised of secondary xylem, phloem, and parenchyma (Scott and Hill 1900; Lang 1915; Bower 1935; Eames 1936; Bierhorst 1971; Sporne 1975); and (d) secondary phloem and secondary parenchyma (West and Takeda 1915; Bhambie 1962, 1970, 1972a). The cambium produces a large amount of secondary cortex centrifugally, which exceeds in amount the inner secondary tissue. The cambium in the rhizomorphic region occurs as strips between the radiating arms of the rhizomorphic stele, and is responsible for the formation of cortical lobes. The secondary cortical cells just adjacent to the cambium are compactly arranged in concentric rows and are interrupted by root traces. As they mature and are pushed outside due to the continuous activity of the cambium, small air spaces start appearing between them, and subsequently they become typical parenchymatous cells. A periderm develops more strongly on the lobes than in furrows, and axes are often decorticated.

Stylites Amstutz, another living genus of Isoetaceae, has two species, S. anadicola and S. gemmifera (Amstutz 1957; Rauh and Falk 1959). The axis, which is branched in one species, has unlimited growth, up to 15 cm (Bierhorst 1971). It bears sporophylls from its upper region and roots from its lower region.

The stele of the axis has two different-sized parallel cylindrical rods of primary wood lying side by side. The larger, upper one sends off traces for sporophylls on all sides, but the smaller one, which is restricted to the lower basal region, gives rise to root traces on only one side. A transection in the upper region depicts a central core of primary xylem, followed by a sheath of one or two layers of parenchyma and then primary phloem. A cambium similar to that in Isoetes, which originates quite early in the ontogeny of the plant, differentiates outside the primary phloem and acts abnormally; however, in contrast to Isoetes, it forms a limited amount of secondary tissues on either side. It produces "prismatic tissue" centripetally, and mostly secondary phloem and secondary cortex centrifugally. The cambium has been envisaged as a multiple type (Rauh and Falk 1959), but this pattern has been attributed to layers of late-maturing primary xylem and adjacent tissues (Paolillo 1963; Bierhorst 1971). The anatomy of Stylites simulates that of Isoetes triquetra, and hence Stylites is considered by some to be just a morphological variation of Isoetes (Kubitzki and Borchert 1964).

Selaginella Spring is a cosmopolitan genus with about 700 spp. having erect, creeping prostrate, or rhizomatous axes. S. selaginoides has a limited amount of secondary thickening in the hypocotyl, which is the only record of cambial activity in the whole genus (Bruchmann 1897; Schlanker and Leisman 1969; Sporne 1975). Further, it has endarch xylem in the first-formed axis whereas those developed later are exarch (Sporne 1975). It is known that it possesses a potentially active meristem for the production of unlimited numbers of roots, but generally eight roots are produced per plant. Furthermore, it has some diffuse secondary growth in the cortical zone responsible for the swelling of the basal region; however, it lacks any secondary vascular tissue or the initiation of any sort of cambium (Karrfalt 1981). A comparison with other species indicates that the centralized root system of this species can be best interpreted as a modification of the noncentralized root system prevailing in other species and probably a persistence of a juvenile phase of root production in this genus.

It would not be out of place to mention that Paurodendron has been related to Selaginella fraiponti (Schlanker and Leisman 1969) on the basis of similar reproductive anatomy, as the latter is comparable to Selaginella selaginoides, which possesses a basal hypocotylar knot due to cambium. It been suggested on the basis of anatomy, however, that Paurodendron is not Selaginella (Karrfalt 1977) and that S. selaginoides lacks any vascular cambium (Karrfalt 1981).

Psilotum Swartz has about 10 species, of which P. nudum is the most common. It has a solid, angular, or cylindrical exarch protostele. Between an endodermis and a poorly developed phloem there are a few layers of parenchyma, which in older axes are differentiated into radially arranged tracheids, which may have raylike cells adjacent to protoxylem. These cells have been designated as *secondary xylem* (Boodle 1902; Ford 1904; Stiles 1910) or part of primary xylem, as no cambial initials have ever been detected (Schoute 1938). Studies on vegetative anatomy, and especially on the transition zone, have not revealed any secondary xylem (Bierhorst 1954a,b, 1956, 1971; Roth 1963a,b; Rouffa 1967).

A feature worth mentioning is vascular differentiation in the axis. It is correlated with a reduction in the total bulk of the apical meristem (Wardlaw 1944). It has been suggested that a reduction in bulk is a direct result of apical injury (Bierhorst 1971); however, the limited growth of the aerial axes of Psilotaceae is reminiscent of the apical growth of certain fossil lycopsids and sphenopsids (Cichan 1985a, 1986).

SPHENOPSIDA

Sphenophyllum (Brongniart) Koenig was a herbaceous or shrubby fossil plant. It came into being during the Upper Devonian, flourished well in the Carboniferous and Permian, and dwindled after the Triassic. It had a subterranean, woody, rhizomatous axis bearing a few aerial axes and numerous adventitious roots (Baxter 1948; Eggert 1961b; Wilson and Eggert 1974; Batenburg 1982). the axes had nonalternating ribs. The nodes of the aerial axes had 16–18 wedge- or linear-shaped leaves, and usually lateral branches developed between the leaves. The aerial axes were of determinate growth and showed reduction in size apically.

A transection of the internode has a centrally located triarch, exarch protostele. The protoxylem appeared to be exarch as in the extant genus *Equisetum*, which might have mesarch differentiation (Bierhorst 1971). The xylem was surrounded by a layer of parenchyma and then three groups of primary phloem in the bays of the xylem arms.

A vascular cambium was initiated in the parenchymatous layer within the bays of triarch xylem (Figure 8.1.3). It subsequently enlarged on either side and surrounded the xylem. The cells of the interfascicular region were bigger than those of fascicular ones. The cambium in both regions had two types of cells: axially elongated and radially short fusiform initials, and isodiameteric ray initials (Schabilion 1969, 1975; Ma 1977; Cichan 1985b). In the interfascicular region, fusiform initials were bounded tangentially by longitudinally elongate bands of upright ray initials, 1–3 cells wide. The cambium was bifacial (Schabilion 1969; Eggert and Gaunt 1973; Ma 1977) and determinate, as it lacked any multiplicative division (Cichan and Taylor 1982, 1984; Cichan 1985a). The circumferential enlargement of the cambium was due to progressive and gradual lengthening of individual files of tracheids and rays as they moved from the inner to the outer region (Cichan and Taylor 1982; Cichan 1985a). The secondary wood formed by the cambium on its inner side was dimorphic, having wedges of large tracheids and lesser rays in the interfascicular region and smaller tracheids and more rays in the fascicular regions (Figure 8.2.E). In both of them, tracheids were arranged in files separated from all sides by ray cells, i.e. T-cell and I-cell. The radial or horizontal processes that occupied the interstices between four contiguous tracheids were cellular extensions from the tangential wall of the longitudinal upright ray cell (T-cell), which reached up to the upright cell of the ray of the other side (I-cell).

Secondary phloem consisted of sieve elements, axial parenchyma, and ray parenchyma. Sieve elements and ray parenchyma were radially arranged. Sieve elements, when seen in longisection, were axially elongated, shorter than tracheids, and had transverse end walls (Eggert and Gaunt 1973). Cichan (1985b), despite labeling it as secondary phloem, doubted that it was secondary in nature.

A deep-seated phellogen developed in the so-called "pericyclic region." It formed phellem outwards, which transformed into a periderm. The cells of the periderm were tabular in cross-section but arranged in distinct files. Cichan (1985b) tried to prove the increase in circumference mathematically by considering a triangle (primary wood) that has become a cylinder due to additional centripetal tissue that consists of linear rows of tracheids and rays. He concluded that circumferential enlargement of interfascicular cambium was due to an increase in size of the linear row of tracheids in a successive manner met within the secondary xylem whose tangential wall increased as it moved centrifugally.

The generic name *Calamites* Schlotheim, first given to the impressions and pith casts of the stems of *Arthropitys* (Binney) Hirmer et Konell, is now usually applied to the whole plant, i.e. a tree that existed during Mississippian to Permian time, but attained its peak during the Upper Carboniferous (Bierhorst 1971). The primary body of the aerial axes tapered conspicuously before joining the rhizomatous axis. However, petrified stems are still commonly designated as *Arthropitys, Arthroxylon,* and *Calamodendron,* and roots as *Astromyelon* (Taylor 1981; Cichan and Taylor 1983; Cichan 1986). A pitch cavity occupied the center of the axis in the internodal region. There was a solid pith diaphragm at the nodal region. The hollow pith cavity was followed by a ring of collateral bundles separated by parenchymatous tissue. Each bundle possessed a canal of primary xylem facing the pith. The primary xylem was considered as endarch but an ontogenetic study of its differentiation in the living genus *Equisetum* has revealed mesarchy (Bierhorst 1971). This was followed by a small amount of secondary wood lacking growth rings except in one large specimen (Andrews and Agashe 1965).

The secondary wood was formed by the vascular cambium, which also produced a limited amount of secondary tissue on its outside (Figure 8.2.D). The cambium was therefore bifacial and determinate (Wilson and Eggert 1974; Cichan 1986). The secondary wood had clear fascicular and interfascicular segments. The former consisted of linear rows of radially arranged, axially elongated, pitted tracheids interrupted rarely by parenchymatous rays, whereas the latter had sclerenchymatous or parenchymatous rays. In *Arthropitys* Goeppert, especially in *A. communis* and *A. deltoides* Cichan et Taylor, two petrified calamite axes, the circumferential enlargement was a gradual process, due partly to the significant enlargement of the fusiform initials and partly to certain changes in the interfascicular segment (Cichan 1986) (Figure 8.2.E). The cambium was followed by a limited amount of tissue on its outerside, which is presumed to be secondary phloem, although sieve elements have not been identified (Cichan 1986).

Extraxylary tissue in calamite stems consisting of cortex and periderm has been studied in detail (Agashe 1964; Andrews and Agashe 1965). The inner cortex shows a band of specialized secretory cells filled with brown contents. These cells, when observed in tangential longitudinal sections, form vertically elongated tubes. The outer cortex appears to comprise regularly arranged, thin-walled parenchymatous cells and 2–3 layers of radially elongated periderm cells.

A transection of the root, *Astromyelon* Williamson, reveals a central pith followed by 16 primary xylem strands separated by parenchyma (Wilson and Eggert 1974). A bifacial, determinate cambium differentiates outside the primary xylem and produces secondary wood consisting of radially arranged rows of tracheids interrupted at places by parenchymatous rays on its inner side and a limited amount of secondary tissue on the outer side (Figure 8.1.4). The inner cortex comprises bands of secretory cells. The middle cortex is aerenchymatous, and the outer cortex has regularly arranged, thin-walled parenchyma (Figure 8.1.4). The periderm has 2–3 layers of radially appressed cells filled with brown contents.

Equisetum has 20 extant species with a long fossil history. Its anatomy reveals xero- and hydromorphic features with a number of collateral and open vascular bundles. Cormack (1893) reported the occurrence of a possible unifacial cambium. Barratt (1920) doubted the suggested secondary nature of the bundles and considered them to be due to enlargement and displacement of protoxylem. Recent work does not support the occurrence of secondary xylem in *Equisetum* (Bierhorst 1958, 1971).

PTEROPSIDA

Cladoxylon Unger was a Middle Devonian plant. Two common species, *C. scoparium* and *C. taeniatum*, were polystelic. Each stele had a rod of primary xylem but the radiating ones were characterized by the presence of a "peripheral loop" of parenchyma surrounded by protoxylem and then by metaxylem (Taylor 1981; Stewart 1983). This was followed by radially seriated rows of tracheids. The xylem consisted of scalariform and pitted tracheids and parenchymatous rays (Figure 8.1.6).

Small axes of *Schizopodium* Moriere also grew in the Middle Devonian. It had a stellate, four-armed protostele with arms divided once or twice, usually showing exarch maturation. Some radially arranged tracheids could represent either metaxylem or secondary xylem developed by the activity of a cambium (Stewart 1983; Figure 8.1(5)). The tracheids were either cubical or vertically or radially elongated. The zone of secondary tracheids was not associated with any region of phloem or cortical tissue. Andrews (1961) suggests that this tissue is intermediate between primary and secondary xylem.

Zygopteris Corda is known from the Carboniferous and Permian (Sahni 1932; Andrews 1961; Dennis 1974). A transection of the trunk shows a very small axis, the center of which is occupied by a pentagonal or stellate protostele or circular mixed pith and primary wood in *Z. primaria* and *Z. paradoxum*, respectively. This is followed by radially aligned secondary wood consisting of tracheids and rays, reminiscent of the cambium of *Isoetes*, which produces secondary vascular tissue on its inner side and secondary cortex on its outer side (Figure 8.2.C). *Ankyropteris* Stengel was another plant of the Middle Pennsylvanian. A transection of the axis shows that there was a centrally placed penta- or heptagonal stellate protostele with exarch or mesarch primary xylem. A limited amount of secondary xylem has also been reported adjacent to the primary xylem (Bierhorst 1971).

Botrychium Linn., a present-day fern, has a short, erect, subterranean rhizomatous axis. A single frond usually develops per season along with numerous adventitious roots on the lower side. The genus is divided into three subgenera: *Sceptridium*, *Eubotrychium*, and *Osmundopteris* (Nozu 1956). Species under the subgenus *Sceptridium* have a normal cambium—a character that differs from all other living ferns. The protostele present at the base of the rhizome becomes a siphonostele and subsequently an ectophloic solenostele as it is interrupted by one or two leaf gaps.

In *Botrychium virginianum*, the cambium is normal in its activity and adds a definite amount of radially aligned rows of the secondary xylem on its inside and a few secondary phloem elements on the outside (Bierhorst 1971). The developmental anatomy of the vascular cambium and periderm in *Botrypus* (subgenus of *Botrychium*) *virginianum* (Takashi and Mansahiro 1988) shows that the cambium, originating earlier than the differentiation of the primary tissue, has fusiform and ray initials and produces enough secondary xylem, which consists of tracheids with circular bordered pits and uni- or biseriate, centripetally, and a small amount of parenchyma centrifugally. It is more active in early stages of plant development and increases in circumference with age. Phellogen is produced in the outer cortex all around the axis and forms mostly phellem or periderm. Interestingly, the Ophioglossaceae, apparently morphologically similar to Glossopteridaceae, is now being considered to be a living progymnospermous family (Takashi and Mansahiro 1988).

In addition, "presumptive cambium" has been detected in *B. multifidum* and *B. dissectum*. The cambial cells divide periclinally and add the secondary xylem, which consists of radially aligned rows of tracheids and rays only on their inside (Figure 8.2.A). The cambium is, therefore, unifacial and determinate, and simulates those of certain fossil lycopods (Stevenson 1980; Chau 1986; Takashi and Mansahiro 1988). The zone of the secondary wood is limited in *B. virginianum* but it seasonally increases in *B. dissectum* (Chau 1986). There is neither a boundary nor any structural difference between the secondary xylem and metaxylem, and the stele is considered to be eustelic as in *Ophioglossum* L. (Chau 1986). A phellogen originates in the outer cortex and produces suberized phellem and phelloderm. The cells of the phelloderm are similar to cortical parenchyma (Bierhorst 1971; Khandelwal and Goswami 1977).

In other members of Ophioglossaceae, secondary vascular tissue is of rare occurrence, but the formation of phellem or periderm is quite common (Figure 8.2.F). Of the *Ophioglossum* species, *O. costatum* and *O. vulgatum* have some secondary wood with radial seriation of tracheids in the peripheral region of the xylem (Boodle 1899; Maheshwari and Singh 1934). The species probably have a unifacial cambium as in *B. dissectum* (Chau 1986). Periderm or phellem is usually associated with secondary tissues (Fahn 1990). A phellogen, similar to that in *Botrychium*, develops in the outer cortex and produces phellem in certain rhizomes and even in roots of *Helminthostachys* Linn. and several species of *Ophioglossum* (Khandelwal and Goswami 1977).

Cyathotheca Taylor, a genus *incretae sedis*, was an unusual plant of the Upper Pennsylvanian. The primary xylem was surrounded by a well-developed zone of secondary xylem consisting of regularly arranged rows of tracheids interrupted at places by parenchymatous rays. The pattern of the secondary-tissue development indicates that fascicular cambial strips came into existence first and later extended on either side, even across a leaf gap (see Esau 1969). The secondary xylem was formed by the activity of a unifacial cambium. No secondary phloem has been noticed (Mickle and Rothwell 1986).

PROGYMNOSPERMOPSIDA

This group of plants existed from the Middle Devonian to the Mississippian and includes three orders: Aneurophytales, Archeopteridales, and Protopityales (Smith 1962; Scheckler and Banks 1971, 1972; Matten 1973; Scheckler 1976). Main and secondary axes of *Triloboxylon* Matten & Banks and *Tetraxylopteris* Beck were three- and four-lobed. In *Tetraxylopteris*, secondary xylem was responsible for the original form of the stele (Figure 8.1.7, 9). Secondary xylem had regularly arranged rows of pitted tracheids. A normal bifacial cambium gave rise to secondary xylem and secondary phloem (Bonamo and Banks 1967; Beck 1971, 1976a,b, 1979; Scheckler and Banks 1971; Wight and Beck 1984). The sieve cells had peculiar walls and lumen filled with tannin or resinlike contents. Sieve cells with excellent sieve areas have been illustrated recently (Wight and Beck 1984), however, and seem to provide evidence of the occurrence of secondary phloem during the Famennian of the Upper Devonian period. Periderm developed up to the first order of branching and subsequently split into scaly pieces, which sloughed off along with the outer cortex and epidermis.

Archaeopteris (Callixylon) Dawson was an advanced tree form during the Upper Devonian and Lower Carboniferous. The primary xylem groups of the axis, also referred to as *circummedullary strands,* were followed by a zig-zag or lobed, wide zone of secondary xylem consisting of tracheids and parenchymatous rays (Figure 8.1.10). Tracheid walls were peculiar, having alternate bands of bordered, pitted, and unpitted regions. Rays, mostly uni-, or biseriate, were four-seriate in *A. newberry.*

Protopitys (Goeppert) Walton was a single genus of the Lower Carboniferous. A cross-section of the axis, with a diameter of 45 cm in one specimen, shows abundant pycnoxylic wood (Walton 1969). The elliptical pith was enclosed by metaxylem that formed irregular groups immediately inside the secondary xylem, followed at opposite ends of the elliptical pith by protoxylem (Figure 8.1.8).

A COMPARATIVE ANALYSIS

To understand the process of radial growth in extinct and extant pteridophytes, the following points need further elucidation: (a) the origin and activity of the cambium in relation to the environment and a comparison with that in seed plants; (b) the structural variations of primary and secondary tissues and their functional aspects; (c) the cork cambium and its activity; and (d) the phylogenetic considerations of these features, if any.

Origin and Activity of Vascular Cambium

Understanding the origin and activity of the cambium requires consideration of the origin of land plants in relation to the environmental changes that occurred during that period. Vascular plants came into being in swampy habitats during the Upper Silurian and Lower Devonian. With the receding of the swamps, they had to adapt from aquatic or moisture-dependent environments to terrestrial habitat (Taylor 1981; Thomas 1981; Stewart 1983). To combat the stress of the new habitat, they developed an internal tissue system and the ability to synthesize and incorporate lignin, an organic substance consisting of a mixed polymer of phenolic derivatives of phenylpropane (Esau 1977) that is considered one of the important prerequisites of secondary growth (Barghoorn 1964). Other substances include auxin, which activates cambium, and the callose, that deposits around sieve pores in sieve elements (Esau 1950). A study of fossil plants of the Devonian period substantiates such a contention. The plant body differentiated into leaf and stem and apical dominance appeared in a number of taxa before the onset of the Middle Devonian period. Also during this period, plants started showing secondary growth (Taylor 1981; Thomas 1981).

Of psilopsids or pteropsids, *Schizopodium* of the Middle Devonian is of special interest, as it possessed an exarch protostele surrounded by radially aligned tracheids but no rays (Figure 8.1.5). This tissue has been interpreted as a product of a rudimentary cambium (Barghoorn 1964). Because it had no crushed tissues on its outer side, the cambium might have been determinate and unifacial. *Psilotum,* if it has any secondary growth in some of its older axes, is similar (Boodle 1902; Ford 1904; Stiles 1910).

Certain lycopsids such as *Lepidodendron* and *Sigillaria* possessed both vascular cambium and cork cambium. The vascular cambium was unifacial and determinate, showing comparatively little development of secondary wood centripetally. There appears to have been a compromise between primary and secondary wood, as the former decreased when the latter increased due to ontogenetic sequence of growth in these plants (Eggert 1961a; Eggert and Kanemoto 1977; Taylor 1981; Cichan 1986). The limited development of secondary wood is similar to that in present-day members of the Cactaceae. Extensive secondary cortex was responsible for a nearly 50% increase in the axis girth. In the absence of secondary phloem, its function was carried out mainly by primary phloem and probably partly by the cortex. These plants, despite their worldwide distribution, declined abruptly in the Late Paleozoic. Some semi-arborescent related forms such as *Pleuromeia* and *Pleuromeiopsis* persisted in the Early Mesozoic. *Paurodendron,* however, which existed during the Paleozoic, was unique in having bipolar axial growth as well as an unusual lateral meristem restricted to the base. It had a bifacial cambium (Phillips and Leisman 1966; Paolillo 1982). The extant genus *Isoetes,* which has a fossil history up to the Cretaceous period, also had a bifacial cambium somewhat similar to that of *Paurodendron:* It is abnormal in origin as well as in activity; develops outside the primary phloem and cuts off a limited amount of secondary xylem or phloem inside and a large amount of secondary cortex outside (Piggs and Rothwell 1979); and functionally appears to be a combination of vascular and cork cambia (Stewart 1947, 1983; Bhambie 1962, 1970; Taylor 1981).

The record of sphenopsids is more or less parallel to that of lycopsids but more diverse at the generic level. In calamite axes, the vascular cylinder was considerably thicker than those of arborescent lycopods. It had a coherent, concentric cylinder of secondary wood formed by a bifacial, determinate cambium, although whether it was indeed bifacial has been questioned (Wilson and Eggert 1974; Cichan and Taylor 1983; Cichan 1986).

The internal structure of the present-day *Equisetum,* which also has a fossil history up to the Mesozoic period, is an analog of the calamites anatomically but is devoid of cambial activity. This taxon does not appear to be a true lineal descent, however.

Sphenophyllum is another sphenopsid of Paleozoic and Mesozoic periods that deserves mention here. Its exarch protostele became surrounded by a determinate bifacial cambium. Its circumferential enlargement was caused by enhancement of individual cells (Cichan and Taylor 1982, 1984; Cichan 1985a), not by divisions in the cells of the initial layer (Schabilion 1969; Ma 1977). Secondary phloem that was formed centrifugally has been reported from *Sphenophyllum* (Eggert and Gaunt 1973) and from *Astromyelon*—the root of a calamite axis (Wilson and Eggert 1974). Whether the phloem was secondary in nature in the calamite root remains unresolved, however (Cichan 1985a; Smoot and Vande Wege 1986). After producing a limited amount of secondary xylem centripetally and secondary phloem centrifugally in *Sphenophyllum,* the vascular cambium, whether unifacial or bifacial, was usually transformed into a "parenchymatous sheath" (Taylor 1981; Cichan and Taylor 1984, 1990; Cichan 1985a,b, 1987a,b; Cichan and Beck 1986). Both unifacial and bifacial cambia apparently developed concomitantly in vascular plants after a lapse of a few years, according to the need and adaption of plants during the Early and Middle Carboniferous.

Two other modifications encountered during that age are worth mentioning: (a) a combination of vascular and cork cambia as in extinct *Paurodendron* and living *Isoetes;* and (b) the short-lived and non-multiplicative nature of cork cambium in the stem and roots of sphenopsids. In (a), the cambium produced vascular tissue centripetally and secondary cortex centrifugally (Bhambie 1972; Taylor 1981; Stewart

1983; Thomas and Spicer 1986), and in (b) the first-formed cork cambium was replaced by successive cork cambia (Figure 8.2.G), as is the vascular cambium in extinct and extant cycads, gnetopsids, and in certain present-day centrospermous seed plants. Bifacial, indeterminate and multiplicative types of cambium are of common occurrence in the present-day gymnosperms and angiosperms. Concentric rings of secondary xylem and secondary phloem are also found within extinct and extant members of cycads, gnetopsids, and the Centrospermae.

The cambium in seed plants has been categorized as unidirectional or bidirectional (Balfour 1965; Philipson and Ward 1965; Philipson et al. 1971). The unidirectional cambium has a self-perpetuating meristem. It produces secondary xylem centripetally, whereas secondary phloem patches differentiate within it, i.e. secondary xylem and phloem are formed on the same side. This characterization has been questioned, however (Esau and Cheadle 1969; Bhambie 1972a,b; Stevenson and Popham 1973; Panikkar and Bhambie 1974; Miksell and Popham 1976; Zamski 1979; Gray and Popham 1981; Metcalfe and Chalk 1983; Bhambie and Sharma 1985). The so-called unidirectional cambium of the Centrospermae has no parallel in the unifacial, non-multiplicative, and determinate cambium of extinct pteridophytes; however, a few species of the living genus *Botrychium* subgenus *Scepteridium* still possess a unifacial cambium (Stevenson 1980; Chau 1986). In certain arborescent monocots, the cambium produces secondary vascular tissue and conjunctive tissue on its inside and a limited amount of storied cortex on the outside. This cambium is reminiscent of the extinct genus *Paurodendron* and the living genus *Isoetes*.

The history of unifacial and bifacial cambia dates back 390 million years, up to Frasnian time—the lower strata of the Devonian. Pteridophytes and seed plants developed independently, however, as evolution occurred along parallel but separate lines. The secondary phloem formed centrifugally by a few extinct pteridophytes and most of the progymnospermopsids is one of the essential components of extinct and extant vascular plants. In extinct plants that possessed unifacial cambium, the function of phloem was mainly performed by primary phloem (see Cichan and Taylor 1990).

The Vascular Derivatives

Specific traits to consider in identifying sieve elements cells include: (a) an enucleate condition as nuclei degenerate and form nucleic acids; (b) the absence of any starch grains; and (c) the deposition of callose around sieve pores and the formation of callose plugs with the aging of the plant (Esau 1950, 1965; Esau et al. 1953; Zahur 1959; Shah and Fotedar 1974). The pattern of callose bands depends on the distribution of pores on the wall; bands may be annular or spiral, and can be mistaken for lignified thickenings of tracheary elements (see Bhambie 1962, 1972). Callose, a polysaccharide, can be easily detected by coralline soda (rosolic acid) and analine blue, which impart bright red and blue colors, respectively.

The phloem tissue is made up of thin-walled cells. Only rarely did it become petrified. Our earlier understanding of this tissue in fossils was based mainly on its position in the stele. A few recent publications have produced new information about the composition and structural configurations of the phloem (Satterthwaith and Schopf 1962; Esau 1969; Hebant 1969; Eggert and Gaunt 1973; Shah and Fotedar 1974; Wilson and Eggert 1974; Evert and Eichhorn 1976; Dute and Eggert 1977; Smoot and Taylor 1978, 1981; Smoot 1979, 1984, 1985; Warmbrodt and Evert 1979; Wight and Beck 1984; Smoot and Vande Wege 1986; Taylor 1987).

The primary phloem consists mainly of sieve elements and parenchyma, which function in collaboration, as in higher plants. [The use of the term *sieve element* conforms to the terminology of Esau (1979), corroborated by Dute and Evert (1977), Smoot and Vande Wege (1986), Taylor (1987, 1990), and Evert (1990), and indicates the basic cell type of phloem involved in the conduction of solutes.] The sieve element—the basic unit of conduction—is an elongate, thin-walled, tube-like cell (8.00 mm × 7.0–30.0 μm). It simulates the phloem parenchyma in its overall shape and size but possesses sieve pores either randomly distributed or aggregated in discrete oval or circular areas on all the walls. Sieve elements of two distinct sizes have been reported from a number of plants such as *Anchoropteris, Psaronius,* and *Stromatopteris,* but in length these are less than ⅓ of those of typical gymnosperms. Though they vary in size (0.6–1.0 μm or 5.0 μm), the sieve pores are present on all the walls (Bhambie 1962; Shah and Fotedar 1974); however, a tendency to be restricted to inclined or transverse end walls has been reported in a number of pteridophytes. These pores have successive depositions of callose around them, but no callose has been detected in living psilophytes, and its occurrence is doubtful in *Rhynia* (Satterthwaith and Schopf 1972; Warmbrodt 1979, 1980). Ultrastructural investigations of a sieve element reveal that it has a plasmalemma, a partial anastomosing network of smooth endoplasmic reticulum, plastids, mitochondria, and a variable number of spherules, which are mostly absent in lycopods. Callose deposition starts around each plasmodesma and results in the formation of pores. With this differentiation, there is an enlargement in the plasmodesmatal canal, unless it attains a specific size. Sieve pores are unoccluded in certain lycopods, whereas in others, tubular endoplasmic reticulum forms a cytoplasmic reticulum. Development of thick shining walls and nacreous walls due to numerous membranes or vesicles has also been noted (Warmbrodt 1979, 1980). Esau (1950) first proposed that a sieve element was differentiated from a parenchyma cell. Later his proposal was corroborated by others (Esau et al. 1953; Esau 1969; Hebant 1969; Warmbrodt 1980; Smoot and Vande Wege 1986). A parenchymatous sheath may or may not be present between xylem and phloem, but phloem parenchyma in small and large amounts, either randomly distributed, or forming vertical series (*Psaronius*) or vertical strands (*Ankyropteris*), or surrounding the secondarily developed sieve elements (*Sphenophyllum*), does exist (see Smoot and Vande Wege 1986).

Secondary phloem formed centrifugally occurred in *Sphenophyllum* and *Astromyelon* as in progymnospermopsids and seed plants, and abnormally, that is centripetally, in the living genus *Isoetes* (Bhambie 1962, 1970, 1972). In *Sphenophyllum,* secondary phloem had sieve elements and ray parenchyma, but the former varied in size around the proto- and metaxlylem poles. Around the protoxylem, these were arranged in more obvious radial files interspersed with a ray system more prominent and more specialized than around the metaxylem. Dilation in the ray cells opposite the protoxylem has also been noted (Eggert and Gaunt 1973; Cichan 1985). In *Astromyelon,* secondary phloem consists of sieve elements and ray parenchyma (Wilson and Eggert 1974). In *Isoetes,* it comprises compactly arranged sieve elements appearing tabular in transverse and longisections, at times alternating with radial bands of secondary parenchyma. It lacks any ray cells except leaf- and root traces, which are associated with a few parenchymatous cells around them. Callose deposits successively around the pores. The deposition obliterates the pore by forming plugs. The nearby callose thickenings fuse, thereby forming spiral or annular thickenings, which can be easily mistaken for the thickenings of tracheids (see Bhambie 1962).

In progymnospermopsids of the Devonian period, the members of Archaeopteridales had not only a bifacial cambium but also an extensive region of well-petrified secondary phloem. The secondary phloem in *Triloboxylon, Tetraxylopteris,* and *Proteokalon* consisted of thin-walled sieve elements, thick-walled fibers, isodiametric to elongate parenchyma, and isodiametric sclereids. The elongate tube-like sieve cell (0.3 mm × 15–25 μm) had numerous dark brown sieve areas with many sieve pores, each with a diameter of 0.6 μm (Beck 1958; Wight and Beck 1984; Taylor 1987). *Cyathotheca* had a zone of 3–30 cells of a secondary phloem consisting of sieve cells, rays, and fibers.

It appears that conducting parenchymatous cells first became sievelike cells with pores on all the walls. Later, they assumed the shape of tube-like elements that were narrower, angular, and much elongated, with more pores on transverse or inclined end walls (Esau et al. 1953). The pores in the beginning were of various shapes and sizes and were unspecialized. They became specialized and later became aggregated on transverse or inclined end walls. Concomitantly, callose development also started, which eventually plugged the pores and created the distinction between functional and nonfunctional phloem.

The secondary xylem in pteridophytes consists of radially aligned rows of tracheids interrupted by various types of rays. The xylem lacks vessels, except in 10 extant genera (*Actinopteris, Adiatum, Equisetum, Helminthostachys, Marsilea, Notholaena, Pteridium, Regnellidium, Selaginella, Woodsia*). None of them shows any secondary growth (see Madan and Bhambie 1979, 1980; Purohit and Sharma 1981). Vessel-like conducting elements have also been reported from a few extinct genera such as *Sphenophyllum* (Stewart 1983).

Secondary wood came into existence by the Middle Devonian period. Annular or helical tracheids are thought to be simpler and more primitive than reticulate, simple pitted tracheids. Circular bordered pits have developed a number of times during the course of the evolution of land plants (Bierhorst 1960, 1971; Bierhorst and Zamora 1965; White 1963a,b). In living Ophioglossales alone there are four lines of development of simple, and circular bordered pits (Madan and Bhambie 1980).

Schizopodium and *Protolepidium* were probably the first plants of the Middle Devonian period to possess secondary xylem. Tracheids of secondary wood had annular and scalariform thickenings in *Schizopodium* and scalariform and bordered pits in *Protolepidium*. In extinct arborescent lycopods, the tracheary elements were dominant, occupying 90–95% of the area of the wood in aerial axes and 80–85% of the area in subterranean axes (Cichan 1985a). These were usually narrower than primary tracheids but simulated them in possessing scalariform thickenings with Williamson's striations.

The secondary tracheids of *Calamites* were restricted to the fascicular region only. They occupied 50% of the total area of wood in the innermost region and increased gradually toward the periphery. They were elongate and extensively pitted elements that functioned mainly for conduction and provided relatively little mechanical support (Cichan 1986).

The dimorphic secondary xylem of *Sphenophyllum* had tracheids that were extensively pitted. The tracheids had maximum growth and attained a mean length of approximately 25 mm—largest among all conducting elements yet recorded in vascular plants (Cichan 1986). Among living plants, tracheids of *Araucaria cunninghamii* (a conifer) are the longest known—10.9 mm in length (Bailey and Tupper 1918; Sporne 1974).

In Progymnospermopsida, the tracheids of secondary wood show considerable variation and specialization, which may be related to their evolutionary trends (Stewart 1983). Tracheary elements of *Aneurophyton, Triloboxylon, Tetraxylopteris,* and *Protopitys* were long, arranged in radial rows, and usually had pits on all the walls. In *Aneurophyton*, the secondary tracheids had 1–5 rows of elliptical bordered pits (Sterlin and Banks 1978). In *Tetraxylopteris*, the tracheids of the inner wood had elliptical bordered pits simulating the metaxylem, whereas those of the outer wood had circular bordered pits. The pits were often multiseriate, alternately arranged, and hexagonal in outline—a condition simulating crowded araucarian-type pits (Scheckler and Banks 1971). In *Archaeopteris* and *Callixylon,* of higher strata, the secondary wood gradually diminished in amount from the proximal to distal regions. In *Protopitys,* the secondary wood simulated that of *Tetraxylopteris* in having two types of tracheids. The tracheids of the inner secondary wood had uniseriate circular bordered pits, restricted to radial walls only, whereas those of the outer wood had multiseriate circular bordered pits (Smith 1962; Walton 1969; Stewart 1983).

A mathematical model has been developed to evaluate the conducting wall area (CWA) of tracheids with various types of thickening. The space between the bars represents the conducting wall and can be calculated easily. The CWA is highest in tracheids with annular thickenings and lower in those with scalariform and alternate circular pits. Secondary-wall characteristics and cell-size data for metaxylem have exhibited moderately low CWA for psilopsids and earlier progymnospermopsids and have shown the highest CWA in arborescent lycopsids. It has been suggested that increased intercellular movement in xylem has been achieved by an increase in CWA or by structural changes that occurred in the pit membrane. These changes were a prerequisite for tracheids to acquire the mechanical properties to permit arborescent habit in plants (Cichan 1987a,b).

The Phellogen

Another secondary lateral meristem that contributes to the thickness of plant axes is phellogen. Phellogen produces phellem centrifugally and phelloderm centripetally. Tertiary thickening due to diffuse meristem has also been reported in lepidodendrids. The phellogen is bifacial and indeterminate, increases in circumference by anticlinal divisions, and increases in diameter by periclinal divisions (Bierhorst 1971; Thomas 1978; Taylor 1981; Stewart 1983; Thomas and Spicer 1986). It develops as discontinuous or continuous concentric rings that arise one after the other (Figure 8.2.G).

In *Lepidodendron, Lepidophloios,* and *Sigillaria,* the trunk had very little vascular tissue. The bulk of the stem (up to 50%) consisted of primary and a "secondary" cortex produced by phellogen centripetally. In some lepidodendrid species, the phellogen formed a continuous ring, in others a discontinuous ring, and in still others multiple concentric rings. It was 1–3 cells wide and produced a copious amount of secondary cortex which consisted of fiber cells arranged in radial files, superficially simulating cork cells, with scattered areas of thin-walled cells that might have had a secretory function. In *Sigillaria,* the thick cortex was characterized by a banded appearance caused by zones of dark secretory tissues of thin-walled cells that were radially aligned. The secondary cortex provided mechanical support to the umbrella-shaped crown. It reduced the rate of desiccation from the aerial parts of old trees where decortication had occurred. Such regions had a thicker secondary cortex (Thomas 1978; Taylor 1981; Stewart 1983; Thomas and Spicer 1986).

The disparity between tree size and the amount of mechanical tissue could be one of the reasons for the downfall of the lepidodendrid trees and their disappearance toward the end of the Carboniferous. Decortication of phellem was a common phenomenon in *Stigmaria stellata,* which had a smooth outer surface (Jennings 1973). In *Isoetes,* a few of the outermost layers became suberized to form the periderm. Decortication of entire cortical lobes as well as of periderm layers occurred due to the formation of abscission zones (Bhambie 1962; Bierhorst 1971; Taylor 1981; Stewart

1983; Thomas and Spicer 1986). The phellogen is common to the members of sphenopsids, but the nature of phellem is still an enigma in *Calamites* (Taylor 1981; Stewart 1983). In *Sphenophyllum,* a deep-seated phellogen gave rise to radially aligned cells of the phellem centrifugally and loosely arranged thin walled phelloderm centripetally, as in modern seed plants. It could be replaced by a new phellogen at times, and therefore numerous concentric rings could be seen (Taylor 1981; Stewart 1983).

There is no indication of the development of phellogen in pteropsids except in the order Ophioglossales (Bierhorst 1971; Khandelwal and Goswami 1977). A peridermlike layer, however, appears in a number of fossil and living ferns due to suberization of the epidermis or a few subepidermal layers. In Ophioglossales, a phellogen was first detected in some species of *Botrychium* (Bierhorst 1971) and subsequently in *Ophioglossum* and *Helminthostachys* rhizomes and roots (Khandelwal and Goswami 1977). In progymnospermopsids, the oldest record of phellogen comes from *Triloboxylon* of the Mid-Givetian strata of the Middle Devonian (Scheckler and Banks 1971). It has also been reported from the Frasnian strata of the Lower Devonian in plants like *Tetraxylopteris.* A phellogen initiates relatively late in contrast to vascular cambium and functions normally. Eventually the primary tissues of the axis are sloughed off in the form of fragments, thereby rendering the axis surface rough (Whitmore 1962; Bonamo and Banks 1967; Scheckler and Banks 1971, 1972; Scheckler 1976; Stewart 1981, 1983; Thomas and Spicer 1986).

In conclusion, the phellogen in pteridophytes is bifacial from the beginning. Its mode of initiation varies, as do the amounts of tissues it produces on either side. The periderm replaces the epidermis and outer primary cortex if it is deep-seated in origin. Annular increments of secondary cortex are seen in *Isoetes.* The decortication occurs in the form of ring bark or scale bark. Most of these variations can be encountered in the present-day seed plants, thus indicating that the structure and behavior of the phellogen have not changed much throughout its history. Functionally, periderm is a protective tissue, and phelloderm, in addition to increasing the axis diameter, provides mechanical support to the plant. In primitive forms, part of the periderm probably also acted as a conductive tissue.

CONCLUSION

The vascular cambium, which adds only a limited amount to radial growth in pteridophytes, is either unifacial or, rarely, bifacial. A few modifications of these two types occur, based on their origin and activity. Both of the basic types came into existence during the Middle Devonian. A unifacial, determinate type of cambium can still be seen in certain species of *Botrychium.* In extinct plants, however, in which unifacial cambium produced only secondary xylem, the function of food translocation was performed by the primary phloem. One of the important modifications of the bifacial cambium is demonstrated by the extinct *Paurodendron* and the extant *Isoetes.*

Uni- or bifacial cambia are not to be confused, however, with the unidirectional and bidirectional cambia described by Balfour (1965), Philipson and Ward (1965), and Philipson et al. (1971). The wood is manoxylic in most pteridophytes, except in progymnospermopsids, in which it was pycnoxylic. It usually lacks vessels. The phloem has sieve cells instead of sieve tubes and lacks companion cells. Rays have developed a number of times during the presumed evolution of land plants.

The phellogen is bifacial from the Paleozoic era to the present. It may be persistent or short-lived. In later cases, successive new phellogens develop. Lignification has been found to be a major step in the history of the evolution of land plants. The origin and deposition of callose and suberin are equally important and should be given due significance.

Acknowledgments

The author thanks Professors V. Puri (Meerut), K. Esau (California), M. M. McCully (Ottawa), B. S. Trivedi (Lucknow), and D. K. Jain (Meerut), Drs. J. Khurana (Michigan) and M. Rashid Ahmed (Lucknow), and Miss Minnie Mehta (Delhi) for helping in various ways.

LITERATURE CITED

Agashe, S. N. 1964. The extra-xylary tissues in certain *Calamites* from the American Carboniferous. *Phytomorphology* 14:598–611.

Amstutz, Erika. 1957. *Stylites,* a new genus of Isoetaceae. *Ann. Miss. Bot. Garden* 44:121–123.

Andrews, H. N. 1961. *Studies in Paleobotany,* New York: John Wiley & Sons, Inc.

Andrews, H. N., and S. N. Agashe. 1965. Some exceptionally large *Calamites* stems. *Phytomorphology* 15:103–108.

Andrews, H. N., and W. H. Murdy. 1958. *Lepidophloios* and ontogeny in arborescent lycopods. *Am. J. Bot.* 45:552–560.

Arnold, C. A. 1960. A lepidodendron stem from Kansas and its bearing on the problem of cambium and phloem in Paleozoic lycopods. *Contrib. Mus. Palaeontol. Univ. Mich.* 10:249–267.

―――. 1968. Current trends in palaeobotany. *Earth Sci. Rev.* 4:283–309.

Bailey, I. W., and W. W. Tupper. 1918. Size variations in tracheary cells: I. A comparison between the secondary xylems of vascular cryptogams, gymnosperms and angiosperms. *Proc. Am. Acad. Arts. Sci.* 54:149–204.

Balfour, E. 1965. Anomalous secondary thickening in Chenopodiaceae, Nyctaginaceae and Amaranthaceae. *Phytomorphology* 15:111–122.

Banks, H. P. 1970. Major evolutionary events and the geological record of plants. *Biol. Rev.* 47:451–454.

Barghoorn, E. S., Jr. 1964. Evolution of cambium in geologic time. In *The Formation of Wood in Forest Trees.* Ed. M. H. Zimmermann. New York: Academic Press. 3–17.

Barratt, K. 1920. A contribution to our knowledge of the vascular system to the genus *Equisetum. Ann. Bot.* 34:201–235.

Batenburg, L. H. 1982. Compression species and petrifaction species of *Sphenophyllum* compared. *Rev. Palaeobot. Palynol.* 36:335–359.

Baxter, W. R. 1948. A study of the vegetative anatomy of the genus *Sphenophyllum* from American coal balls. *Ann. Miss. Bot. Gard.* 35:209–231.

Beck, C. B. 1957. *Tetraxylopteris schmidtii* gen. et sp. nov., a probable pteridosperms precursor from the Devonian of New York. *Am. J. Bot.* 44:350–367.

―――. 1958. *Levicaulis arranensis* gen. et sp. nov., a lycopsid axis from the lower Carboniferous of Scotland. *Trans. Royal Soc. Edinburgh.* 58:444–457.

―――. 1971. On the anatomy and morphology of lateral branch systems of *Archaeopteris. Am. J. Bot.* 58:758–784.

―――. 1976a. Current status of the Progymnospermopsida. *Rev. Palaeobot. Palynol.* 21:5–23.

_____ . 1976b. *Origin and Early Evolution of Angiosperms.* New York: Columbia Univ. Press.

_____ . 1979. The primary vascular system of *Callixylon. Rev. Palaeobot. Palynol.* 28:103–115.

_____ . 1981. *Archaeopteris* and its role in vascular plant evolution. In *Palaeobotany, Paleoecology and Evolution, Vol. 1.* Ed. K. J. Niklas. New York: Praeger 193–230.

Beck, C. B., R. Schmid, and G. W. Rothwell. 1982. Stelar morphology and primary vascular system of seed plants. *Bot. Rev.* 48:691–815, 913–931.

Bhambie, S. 1962. Studies in Pteridophytes. II. A contribution to the anatomy of the axis of *Isoetes coromandelina* L. and some other species. *Proc. Indian. Acad. Sci.* 56:56–76.

_____ . 1970. Studies in Pteridophytes VIII. An appraisal on the nature of rhizomorph in *Isoetes. J. Indian Bot. Soc.* 50:56–62.

_____ . 1972a. Meristem in Pteridophytes. *J. Indian. Bot. Soc.* 51:72–92.

_____ . 1972b. Correlation between form, structure and habit in some lianas. *Proc. Indian. Acad. Sci.* 75:246–256.

Bhambie, S., and A. Sharma. 1985. Ontogeny of Cambium in *Amaranthus caudatus* L. and *Achyranthes aspera* L. *Proc. Indian Acad. Sci.* 95:295–301.

Bierhorst, D. W. 1954a. The gametangia and embryo of *Psilotum nudum. Am. J. Bot.* 41:274–281.

_____ . 1954b. The origin and branching in the aerial shoot of *Psilotum nudum. Virginia J. Sci.* 5:72–82.

_____ . 1956. Observations on the aerial appendages in the Psilotaceae. *Phytomorphology* 6:176–184.

_____ . 1958. Vessels in *Equisetum. Am. J. Bot.* 45:534–537.

_____ . 1960. Observations on tracheary elements. *Phytomorphology* 10:249–305.

_____ . 1971. *Morphology of Vascular Plants.* New York: MacMillan.

Bierhorst, D. W., and P. M. Zamora. 1965. Primary xylem elements and element associations of angiosperms. *Am. J. Bot.* 52:657–710.

Bonamo, P. M., and H. P. Banks. 1967. *Tetraxylopteris schmidtii:* Its fertile parts and its relationships within the Aneurophytales. *Am. J. Bot.* 54:755–768.

Boodle, L. A. 1899. Some points in the anatomy of the Ophioglossaceae. *Ann. Bot.* 13:377–394.

_____ . 1902. On the occurrence of secondary xylem in *Psilotum. Ann. Bot.* 18:505–517.

Boureau, E. 1964. *Traite' de Paléobotanique, Vol. III, Sphenophyta, Noeggerathipophyta.* Paris: Mason et Cie.

Bower, F. O. 1935. *Primitive Land Plants.* London: MacMillan.

Bruchmann, H. 1897. Unterschungen über *Selaginella.* A. B. Gotha. Cited in Schoute, J. C. 1938. Morphology. In *Manual of Pteridology.* 1:1–64. The Hague.

Carlquist, S. 1977. Ecological factors in wood evolution: A floristic approach. *Am. J. Bot.* 64:887–896.

Chau, I. R. 1986. Xylem structure in *Botrychium dissectum* Sprengel and its relevance to the taxonomic position of the Ophioglossaceae. *Am. J. Bot.* 73:1201–1206.

Cichan, M. A. 1985a. Vascular cambium and wood development in Carboniferous plants. I. Lepidodendrales. *Am. J. Bot.* 72:1163–1176.

_____ . 1985b. Vascular cambium and wood development in Carboniferous plants. II. *Sphenophyllum. Bot. Gaz.* 146:395–403.

_____ . 1986. Vascular cambium and wood development in Carboniferous plants. III. *Arthropitys* (Equisetales: Calamitaceae). *Can. J. Bot.* 64:688–695.

_____ . 1987a. Conducting wall areas in tracheids: A model. *Abstr. Am.J. Bot.* 234:678–679.

_____ . 1987b. Conducting wall area in tracheids of early land plants. *Abstr. Am. J. Bot.* 235:679.

Cichan, M. A., and C. E. Beck. 1986. An anatomically preserved lepidodendrid stem from the lower Mississippian of Kentucky. *Abs. Bot. Soc. America:* 696.

_____ . 1987. A woody lycopsid stem from the New Albany Shale (Lower Mississippian) of Kentucky. *Am. J. Bot.* 74:1750–1757.

Cichan, M. A., and T. N. Taylor. 1982a. Structurally preserved plants from Southeastern Kentucky: *Stauropteris biseriata* sp. nov. *Am. J. Bot.* 69:1491–1496.

———. 1982b. Vascular cambium development in *Sphenophyllum*: a Carboniferous arthrophyte. *IAWA Bull.* 3:155–160.

———. 1983. A systematic developmental analysis of *Arthropitys deltoides* sp. nov. *Bot. Gaz.* 144:285–294.

———. 1984. A method of determining tracheid length in petrified wood by analysis of cross section. *Ann. Bot.* 53:219–226.

———. 1990. Evolution of cambium in geologic time—A reappraisal. In *The Vascular Cambium*. Ed. M. Iqbal. Research Studies Press, Taunton, U.K.: 213–228.

Cormack, B. G. 1893. On cambial development in *Equisetum*. *Ann. Bot.* 1:63–82.

Cutler, D. F. 1976. Variation in root wood anatomy. *Leiden Bot. Ser.* 3:143–156.

———. 1984. Systematic anatomy and embryology—Recent developments: In *Current Concepts in Plant Taxonomy*, Vol. 25. Ed. V. H. Heywood, D. M. Moore. London/Orlando, FL: Academic Press.

Dennis, R. L. 1974. Studies of Paleozoic ferns: *Zygopteris* from the Middle and Late Pennsylvanian of the United States. *Palaeontographica B.* 148:95–136.

Dute, R. R., and R. F. Evert. 1977. Sieve element ontogeny in the root of *Equisetum hyemale. Am. J. Bot.* 64:421–438.

Eames, A. J. 1936. *Morphology of Vascular Plants, Lower Groups*. New York: McGraw Hill.

Eggert, D. A. 1961a. The ontogeny of Carboniferous arborescent Lycopsida. *Palaeontographica* 108B:43–92.

———. 1961b. The ontogeny of Carboniferous arborescent Sphenopsida. *Palaeontographica* 110B:99–127.

———. 1964. The question of the phylogenetic position of the Coenopteridales. *Mem. Torrey Bot. Club.* 21:38–57.

Eggert, D. A., and D. D. Gaunt. 1973. Phloem of *Sphenophyllum. Am. J. Bot.* 60:755–770.

Eggert, D. A., and N. Y. Kanemoto. 1977. Stem phloem of a middle Pennsylvanian *Lepidodendron. Bot. Gaz.* 138:102–111.

Esau, K. 1950. Development and structure of phloem tissue. *Bot. Rev.* 16:67–114.

———. 1965. *Plant Anatomy*. 2nd Ed. New York: John Wiley & Sons.

———. 1969. The Phloem. In W. Zimmermann, P. Ozenda and H. D. Wulff (Eds.) *Encyclopedia of Plant Anatomy* Vol. 5:1–505. Berlin: Gebr. Borntraeger.

———. 1977. *Anatomy of Seed Plants*. 2nd Ed. New York: John Wiley & Sons.

Esau, K., and V. I. Cheadle. 1969. Secondary growth in *Bougainvillea. Ann. Bot.* 33:807–819.

Esau, K., V. I. Cheadle, and E. M. Gifford, Jr. 1953. Comparative structure and possible trends of specialization of phloem. *Am. J. Bot.* 40:9–19.

Evert, R. F., and S. E. Eichhorn. 1976. Sieve element ultrastructure in *Platycerium bifurcatum* and some other Polypodiaceous ferns: The nacreous wall thickening and maturation of protoplast. *Am. J. Bot.* 63:30–48.

Fahn, A. 1990. *Plant Anatomy*. 4th Ed. New York: Pergamon Press.

Ford, S. O. 1904. The anatomy of *Psilotum triquetrum. Ann. Bot.* 18:589–605.

Frankenberg, J. M., and D. A. Eggert. 1969. Petrified *Stigmaria* from North America: Part 1 *Stigmaria ficoides*, the underground portions of the Lepidodendraceae. *Palaeontographica* 128B:1–47.

Glock, W. S. 1955. Growth rings and climate. *Bot. Rev.* 22:73–188.

Gray, L., and R. A. Popham. 1981. The ontogeny of the primary thickening meristem of *Atriplex hortensis* L. Chenopodiaceae. *Am. J. Bot.* 68:1042–1049.

Hébant, C. 1969. Observations sur le phloème de Filiciniées quelques tropicales. *Nat. Monpsel. Bot.* 20:135–196.

Hejnowicz, Z. 1964. Orientation of the pattern in pseudo-transverse division in cambia of some conifers. *Can. J. Bot.* 42:1685–1691.

Iqbal, M. 1990. *The Vascular Cambium*. Taunton, U.K.: Research Studies Press.

Jennings, J. R. 1973. The morphology of *Stigmaria stellata*. *Am. J. Bot.* 60:414–425.

———. 1975. *Protostigmaria*, a new plant organ from the lower Mississippian of Virginia. *Palaeontology.* 18:19–24.

Karrfalt, E. E. 1977. *Paurodendron* is not *Selaginella*. *Bot. Soc. Amer. Misc. Ser. Pub.* 154:39.

———. 1981. The comparative morphology of the root system of *Selaginella selaginoides* (L.) Link. *Am. J. Bot.* 68:244–253.

Khandelwal, S., and K. H. Goswami. 1977. Periderm in Ophioglossaceae. *Acta Soc. Bot. Pol.* 46:641–645.

Kirch, G. 1913. The physiological anatomy of the periderm of fossil lycopods. *Ann. Bot.* 27:281–320.

Kozlowski, T. T. 1971. *Growth and Development of Trees, Vol. 2. Cambial Growth, Root Growth and Reproductive Growth.* New York: Academic Press.

Kubitzki, K., and R. Borchert. 1964. Morphlogishe Studien an *Isoetes triquetra* A. Braun und Bemerkungen uber das Vertialtnis der Gattung *Stylites* E. Amstutz zur Gattung *Isoetes* L. *Ber. Deutsch. Bot. Ges.* 77:227–233.

Lang, W. H. 1915. Studies in the morphology of the stock of *Isoetes lacustris*. *Mem. Proc. Manchester Lit. Philos. Soc.* 59:1–28, 29–57.

Leisman, G. A., and R. L. Rivers. 1974. On the reproductive organs of *Lepidodendron serratum* Felix. C. R. 7 Congress Strat. Geol. Carbonifere Krefeld (1971) 3:351–365.

Lemoigne, Y. 1962. Etude de la bifurcation d'un rameau chez le *Lepidodendron selaginoides* (Sternburg). *Bull. Soc. Bot. Fr.* 109:5–13.

———. 1964. Reconnaissance du phlòeme et d'un cambium particulier dams les axes des formes Lépidodéndroides arborescentes du Paléozoique. *C. R. Acad. Sc.* 259:2265–2268.

———. 1966. Les tissus vasculairies et leur histogènese chez les Lépidophytales arborescentes du Paléozoique. *Ann. Sci. Nat. Bot. Biol. Veget.* 12:445–474.

———. 1967. Le cortex et son histogènese chez les Lépidophytales arborescentes du Paléozoique. *Ann. Sci. Nat. Bot. Biol. Veget.* 12:747–764.

Ma, P. 1977. *Anatomy of unusually large Sphenophyllum from the Carboniferous of Indiana and Illinois.* M. Sc. thesis, Western Illinois University, Macomb. 62 pp.

Madan, P., and S. Bhambie. 1979. Occurrence of vessels in *Helminthostachys zelanica* (Linn.) *Curr. Sci.* 48:689–690.

———. 1980. Tracheary elements in Ophioglossaceae. *Feddes Repert.* 91:301–307.

Mägdefrau, K. 1931. Zur Morphologie und phytogenetischen Bedeutung der fossilen Pflanzen gattung *Pleuromeia*. *Beih. Bot. Cbl.* 48:119–140.

———. 1932. Über *Nathorstiana* eine Isoetacée aus dem Neokomvon Quedlinburg a. Harz. *Beih. Bot. Cbl.* 49:706–718.

Maheshwari, P., and B. Singh. 1934. The morphology of *Ophioglossum fibrosum* Schum. *J. Indian. Bot. Soc.* 13:103–124.

Matten, L. C. 1973. The Cairoflora (Givetiana) from eastern New York. I. *Reimannia*, terete axes and lair *lamanekii* gen et. sp. n. *Am. J. Bot.* 60:619–630.

Metcalfe, C. R., and L. Chalk. 1983. *Anatomy of the Dicotyledons, Vol. 2.* 2nd Ed. Oxford:Clarendon Press.

Mickle, J. E., and G. W. Rothwell. 1986. Vegetative and fertile structure of *Cyathotheca ventilaria* from the Upper Pennsylvanian of the Appalachian. *Am. J. Bot.* 73:1474–1485.

Miksell, E., and R. A. Popham. 1976. Ontogeny and correlative relationships of the primary thickening meristem in four o'clock plants (Nyctaginaceae) maintained under long and short periods. *Am. J. Bot.* 63:427–438.

Mullik, D. B., and G. D. Jenson. 1973. New concepts of terminology of coniferous periderms. *Can. J. Bot.* 51:1459–1470.

Newman, I. V. 1956. Pattern in meristems of vascular plants. I. Cell pattern in living apices and the cambial zone in relation to the concept of initial cells and apical cells. *Phytomorphology* 6:1–19.

Nozu, Y. 1956. Anatomical and morphological studies of Japanese species of the Ophioglossaceae. II. Rhizome and root. *Jpn. J. Bot.* 15:208–288.

Panikkar, A. O. N., and S. Bhambie. 1974. Anomalous secondary growth in some vascular plants. In *Biology of the Land Plants,* Ed. V. Puri et al. Meerut, India: Sarita Prakashan Press, 100–109.

Paolillo, D. J., Jr. 1963. The developmental anatomy of *Isoetes*. III. *Biol. Monogr.* 31.

———. 1982. Meristems and evolution: Developmental correspondence among rhizomorphs of the lycopsids. *Am. J. Bot.* 69:1032–1042.

Philipson, W. R., and J. M. Ward. 1965. The ontogeny of cambium in the stem of seed plants. *Biol. Rev.* 40:534–579.

Philipson, W. R., J. M. Ward, and B. G. Butterfield. 1971. *The Vascular Cambium: Its Development and Activity*. London: Chapman & Hall.

Phillips, T. L., and A. G. Leisman. 1966. *Paurodendron,* a rhizomatous lycopod. *Am. J. Bot.* 53:1086–1100.

Pigg, K. B., and G. W. Rothwell. 1979. Stem-shoot transition of an upper Pennsylvanian woody lycopsid. *Am.J. Bot.* 66:914–924.

Purohit, S. N., and B. D. Sharma. 1980. Vessel elements in rhizome of *Adiantum incisum*. *Phytomorphology.* 30:400–402.

Rauh, W., and H. Falk. 1959. *Stylites* E. Amstutz, eine neue Isoetacee aus den Hochanden Perus. *Sitzber Heidelberg. Akad. Wiss.* V. 1–160. In *Sitzungsberichte der Heidelberger Akad. Jg.* 1959. 1. Abhandlung. Göttingen-Heidelberg: Springer.

Roth, I. 1963a. Histogenese der Luftsprosse und Bildung der "dichotomen" Verzweigungen von *Psilotum nudum. Ad. Frontier Plant Sci.* 7:157–180.

———. 1963b. Histogenese und Morphologische Deutung der Blätter von *Psilotum nudum. Flora* 153:90–111.

Rothwell, G. W. 1984. The apex of *Stigmaria* (Lycopsida) rooting organ of Lepidodendrales. *Am. J. Bot.* 71:1031–1034.

Rouffa, A. S. 1967. Induced *Psilotum* fertile-appendage aberrations. Morphogenetic and evolutionary implications. *Can. J. Bot.* 45:855–861.

Sahni, B. 1932. On the structure of *Zygopteris primaria* (Cotta) and on the relation between the genera *Zygopteris, Etapteris* and *Botrychioxylon. Philos. Trans. R. Soc. London Ser. B.* 222:29–46.

Satterwaith, D. F., and J. W. Schopf. 1972. Structurally preserved phloem zone tissue in *Rhynia. Am. J. Bot.* 59:373–376.

Schabilion, J. T. 1969. *A Study of the Anatomy and Taxonomy of the Genus Sphenophyllum*. Ph. D. thesis. University of Kansas, Lawrence. 126 pp.

———. 1975. Intercalary growth in fossil arthrophyte *Sphenophyllum. Rev. Palaeobot. Palynol.* 20:103–108.

Scheckler, S. E. 1976. Ontogeny of Progymnosperms. I. Shoots of Upper Devonian Aneurophytales. *Can. J. Bot.* 54:202–219.

———. 1978. Ontogeny of progymnosperms. II. Shoots of Upper Devonian Archaeopteridales. *Can. J. Bot.* 56:3136–3170.

Scheckler, S. E., and H. P. Banks. 1971. Anatomy of some Devonian progymnosperms from New York. *Am. J. Bot.* 58:737–751.

———. 1972. Periderm in some Devonian plants. In Y. S. Murty et al. (ed.) *Advances in Plant Morphology,* Prof. V. Puri Commemoration Vol.: 58–64, Sarita Prakashan Press, Meerut, India.

Schlanker, C. M., and G. A. Leisman. 1969. The herbaceous lycopod *Selaginella fraiponti* Comb. nov. *Bot. Gaz.* 130:35–41.

Schmidt, R. 1976. The elusive cambium—Another terminological contribution. *IAWA Bull.* 4:51–59.

Schoute, J. C. 1938. Morphology. In *Manual of Pteridology*. Ed. F. Verdoorn. The Hague: Martinus Nijhoff. 1–64.

Scott, D. H., and T. G. Hill. 1900. The structure of *Isoetes hystrix. Ann. Bot.* 14:413–454.

Shah, J. J., and R. F. Fotedar. 1974. Sieve tube members in the stem of *Cyathea gigantea*. *Am. Fern. J.* 64:27–28.

Smith, A. H. V. 1962. The palaeoecology of Carboniferous peats based on the meiospores and petrography of bituminous coals. *Proc. Yorks. Geol. Soc.* 33:423–474.

Smith, D. L. 1964. Secondary cortex in arborescent lycopods. *New Phytol.* 63:418–421.

Smith, L. P. 1962. The fructification from the Scottish Lower Carboniferous. *Palaeontology.* 5:225–237.

Smith, W. R. 1900. The structure and development of the sporophylls and sporangia of *Isoetes. Bot. Gaz.* 29:225–258, 323–346.

Smoot, E. L. 1979. The Phloem of *Etapteris leclercquii* and *Botryopteris tridentata. Am. J. Bot.* 66:511–521.

_____ . 1984. Phloem structure in the Carboniferous fern *Psaronius* (Marattiales) *Am. J. Bot.* 71:1104–1113.

_____ . 1985. Phloem anatomy of the Carboniferous coenopterid ferns *Anachoropteris* and *Ankyropteris. Am. J. Bot.* 72:191–208.

Smoot, E. L., and T. N. Taylor. 1978. Sieve areas in fossil phloem. *Science* 202:1081–1083.

_____ . 1981. Phloem histology of a lower Pennsylvanian *Psaronius. Paleobotanist* 28–29:81–85.

Smoot, E. L., and M. Vande Wege. 1986. Phloem anatomy in *Stauropteris biseriata* from the Pennsylvanian of North America. *Am. J. Bot.* 73:1043–1048.

Sporne, K. R. 1974. *The Morphology of Angiosperms.* London: Hutchinson & Co.

_____ . 1975. *The Morphology of Pteridophytes.* 4th Ed. London: Hutchinson & Co.

Sterlin, B. S., and H. P. Banks. 1978. Morphology and anatomy of *Aneurophyton* a progymnosperm from the late Devonian of New York. *Palaeontographica Americana* 8:343–353.

Stevenson, D. W. 1980. Ontogeny of the vascular system of *Botrychium multifidum* (Ophioglossaceae) and its bearing on stelar theory. *Bot. J. Linn. Soc.* 8:41–52.

Stevenson, D. W., and R. A. Popham. 1973. Ontogeny of the primary thickening meristem in the seedling of *Bougainvillea spectabilis. Am. J. Bot.* 60:1–9.

Stewart, W. N. 1947. A comparative study of stigmarian appendages and *Isoetes* roots. *Am. J. Bot.* 34:315–324.

_____ . 1981. The progymnospermopsida: The construction of a concept. *Can. J. Bot.* 59:333–340.

_____ . 1983. *Paleobotany and the Evolution of Plants.* Cambridge: Cambridge University Press.

Stiles, W. 1910. The structure of the aerial shoot of *Psilotum flaccidum. Ann. Bot.* 24:379–389.

Stokey, A. G. 1909. Anatomy of *Isoetes. Bot. Gaz.* 47:311–335.

Studhalter, R. A., W. S. Glock, and S. R. Agerter. 1963. Tree growth. *Bot. Rev.* 29:245–365.

Takashi, A., and K. Mansahiro. 1988. Developmental anatomy of the vascular cambium and periderm of *Botrypus virginianum* and its bearing on the systematic position of Ophioglossaceae. *Bot. Mag. Tokyo* 101:373–386.

Taylor, E. L. 1987. Fossil phloem tissue: Evidence for evolutionary conservatism. *Am. J. Bot.* 265:690–691 (Abstr.).

Taylor, E. L. 1990. Phloem evolution: An appraisal based on the fossil record. In *Sieve Elements: Comparative Structure, Induction, and Development.* Ed. H.-D. Behnke, R. D. Sjolund. Berlin/Heidelberg/New York: Springer-Verlag. 285–290.

Taylor, T. N. 1981. *An Introduction to Fossil Plant Biology.* New York:McGraw Hill Book Co.

Thomas, B. A. 1978. Carboniferous Lepidodendraceae and Lepidocarpaceae. *Bot. Rev.* 44:321–364.

_____ . 1981. *The Evolution of Plants and Flowers.* Spain: Europbook Ltd.

Thomas, B. A., and R. A. Spicer. 1986. *The Evolution and Paleobiology of Land Plants.* London: Chapman & Hall.

Walton, J. 1969. On the structure of a silicified stem of *Protopitys* and roots associated with it from Carboniferous (Mississippian) of Yorkshire, England. *Am. J. Bot.* 56:808–813.

Wardlaw, C. W. 1944. Experimental and analytical studies of pteridophytes. IV. Stelar morphology: The initial differentiation of vascular tissues. *Ann. Bot.* 8:173–188.

Wareing, P. F. 1958. The physiology of cambial activity. *J. Inst. Wood Sci.* 1:34–42.

Warmbrodt, R. D. 1980. Characteristics of structure and differentiation in the sieve elements of lower vascular plants. *Ber. Deutsch. Bot. Ges.*93:13–28.

Warmbrodt, R. D., and R. F. Evert. 1979. Comparative leaf structure of several species of homosporous leptosporangiate ferns. *Am. J. Bot.* 66:412–440.

Weber, U. 1922. Zur Anatomie und systematik der Gattung *Isoetes*. Hedwigia 63:219–262.

West, C., and H. Takeda. 1915. On *Isoetes japonica*. A. Br. *Bot. Trans. Linn. Soc.* (London) 8:333–376.

White, R. A. 1963a. Tracheary elements of Ferns. I. Factors which influence tracheid length: Correlation of length with evolutionary divergence. *Am. J. Bot.* 50:447–455.

―――――. 1963b. Tracheary elements in Ferns. II. Morphology of tracheary elements: conclusions. *Am. J. Bot.* 50:514–522.

Wight, D. C., and C. B. Beck. 1984. Sieve cells in phloem of a Middle Devonian progymnosperm. *Science* 225:1469–1471.

Whitmore, T. C. 1962. Why do trees have different sorts of bark? *New Scientist* 8:330–331.

Wilcox, H. 1962. Cambial growth characteristics in woody species. In *Tree Growth*. Ed. T. T. Kozlowski. New York: Ronald Press. 57–88.

Williamson, W. C. 1887. *A Monograph on the Morphology and Histology of* Stigmaria. London: Palaeontology Society.

Wilson, M. L., and D. A. Eggert. 1974. Root phloem of fossil tree sized arthrophytes. *Bot. Gaz.* 135:319–328.

Zahur, M. Z. 1959. Comparative study of secondary phloem of 423 species of woody dicotyledons belonging to 85 families. *Cornell. Univ. Agr. Exp. Sta. Mem. No.* 358:1–160.

Zamski, E. 1979. The mode of secondary growth and the three dimensional structure of phloem in *Avicennia*. *Bot. Gaz.* 140:67–76.

Chapter 9

Structural and Operational Specializations of the Vascular Cambium of Seed Plants

MUHAMMAD IQBAL

In most dicotyledons and gymnosperms, plant axes grow in girth, even after they have ceased to elongate, because of the periodic meristematic activity of cambia. Successive additions of the secondary phloem and xylem derived from the vascular cambium provide new pathways for the transportation of cell sap and assimilate to parts of the plant and additional cells for mechanical support to the branching and enlarging body of woody plants.

The cambium, when present, develops from the provascular elements between the phloem and xylem of the primary vascular system. Later it forms a continuous sheath around the wood core of the stems and roots and extends in the form of strips into leaves that experience the secondary growth. Even though the vascular cambium originates through transformation of the derivatives of the apical meristem, it may appear in residual meristem, procambium, precambium (Soh 1992), parenchyma, or callus. In some annual as well as perennial dicots, the cambium is very short-lived and becomes nonfunctional after a limited time, in contrast to the cambium in most conifers and dicots, which remains active throughout its long life. The cambium differs in cellular organization from the apical meristem in that it consists of two morphologically different types of initial and, with the activity of a single tier of initials, gives rise to specific tissues, not to organs (Berlyn 1982).

The original cambial organization into the two types of interwoven initials fulfils the requirement of a vascular thickening meristem and, in turn, implies specific cytological features. The biochemical properties and three-dimensional architecture of cambial cell walls result from polarized cell division and are prerequisites for radial growth. The conspicuous vesicular traffic and membrane exchanges in cambial cells are related to the seasonal vacuolar and cell wall cycles. The cytological and physiological properties of each cellular type ensure efficient performance of the complex dual role of the cambium as a meristematic template and bridge between the phloem and xylem (see Catesson 1990).

In most species, the cambium exhibits alternate active and dormant phases during a growth year. A few exceptions are found among the tropical species which show meristematic activity all year. Many tropical plants do not show a sharply rhythmic, cyclic growth pattern; however, close correlations between the apical growth and radial growth exist in both temperate and tropical species (see Iqbal and Ghouse 1985a; Iqbal 1990, Chapters 6 and 7). Compared to the temperate species, the tropical species are little explored regarding cambial performance. A few comprehensive reviews (Philipson et al.;1971; Catesson 1974, 1980; Berlyn 1982; Larson 1982; Iqbal and Ghouse 1985a, 1990) have elucidated the diverse, fascinating aspects of the cambial form and function.

The cambium is envisaged to be not merely a cell producer that works solely under exernal influences but also a morphogenetic organizer that could play some role in determining the fate of its derivatives (Berlyn 1982). For all this, it is thought to depend heavily on bioenergetics. Since rays are energy storage depots, the cambium ensures, by regulating the frequency of transformative cell division responsible for the development of rays from fusiform initials, that enough ray tissue is possessed by the differentiating xylem and phloem. Although the cambium of a given species is bound to produce a genetically set type of phloem and wood, it is capable of responding to extrinsic stimuli to manifest phenotypic plasticity in its products. The cambium possibly exerts a sort of epigenetic control over these phenomena by dispatching into the cytoplasm of its derivatives (the phloem mother cells and the xylem mother cells) a potential system that defines the performance of different metabolic compartments of these cells. This could be brought about by regulating organelle distribution at cell division or by including activators for the so-called chrono- or homoeotic genes (North 1983).

It is assumed that the centrifugal derivatives of the cambial initials are determined to produce phloem and the centripetal derivatives to produce xylem. This renders the *initials* the power of regulating cambial activity (cell division) as well as producing phloem and xylem (differentiation). If this is so, the cambial initials must be the cells that most influence the amounts of phloem and xylem produced each year (Savidge 1985). On the other hand, whether the initials actually exist has been controversial. Anticlinally dividing cells are thought to be initials, because these divisions initiate new radial files and add to the cell population that forms the cambial cylinder. More than a single fusiform cell of each radial file of the cambial zone may divide anticlinally, however; these cells maybe distant from one another (Savidge and Farrar 1984) and continually shift their position both radially and tangentially (Evert 1963). This suggests that any cell of the cambial zone with the essential balance of physical and chemical factors will develop and act like the hypothetical initial.

This notion agrees with the concept of a multiseriate cambial zone, in which cells are cytologically indistinguishable for initials and derivatives, as all are capable of undergoing division (details in Iqbal 1990). Meristematic shifts may occur in response to changes in cell pH and in concentrations and compositions of solutes (including hormones) that are known to differ appreciably between the inner and outer borders of the cambial zone (Savidge et al. 1982).

CAMBIAL ANATOMY AND CYTOBIOLOGY

The size and shape of the cambial cells attracted the attention of workers early in the current century. Fusiform initials were noted to be relatively short in storied cambium (e.g., 140–210 μm in *Robinia pesudoacacia*), longer in nonstoried cambium of dicotyledons (e.g., 300–350 μm in *Acer pseudoplatanus*), and still longer in conifers (e.g., 870–4000 μm in *Pinus strobus*), sometimes measuring up to 9000 μm as in *Sequoia sempervirens* (Bailey 1923). Cell size varies with species, age of the plant, climatic changes, and topography of plant habitat. Cambium cells of old plant axis generally exhibit stable features, characteristic of the species or subspecies. Berlyn (1982) postulated, possibly in reference to trees, that a fusiform initial generally needs about a 60-year span to attain its maximum (genetic) length. Dodd (1948) studied the morphology of fusiform initials of *Pinus sylvestris* and found that an initial bears 8–32 faces, with an average of 18. Each initial was in contact, on average, with 14 other cells like itself. Observations of Höhl (1960) on *Datura stramonium* (Solanaceae) revealed that the cambial cells are very similar in ultrastructure to parenchyma cells. Cambial protoplast is a complex mixture of organic compounds, including carbohydrates, lipids, proteins, amino acids, organic acids, different nitrogenous substances, certain inorganic compounds, and growth regulators (see Stewart 1966). Of the carbohydrates, which form the chief constituent, sucrose is most abundant, followed by glucose and fructose. Ultrastructural observations on cambial cytokinesis have revealed a normal cell division (Evert and Deshpande 1970; Barnett 1971; Murmanis 1971; Goosen-de Roo and Van Spronsen 1978; Timell 1979, etc.); cell plate development is obviously a prolonged process in elongate fusiform cells.

The volume of a fusiform initial is tens or hundreds of times the volume of an apical meristematic cell. The high degree of vacuolation in active cambial cells, a feature uncommon to other meristems, may be a means to minimize the amount of cytoplasmic material synthesized and thereby reduce the energy expenditures at each cell cycle. Thus, the vacuoles economically extend the reach of the cytoplasm (Wiebe 1978). The periclinal division of fusiform cambial cells, which results in the formation of a new wall in a tangential plane, violates Errera's proposal (see Dodd 1948) that new cell walls form in a plane of least surface area. Although a similar situation prevails with the elongate meristematic cells of the phellogen, the primary and secondary thickening meristems, and even the rib meristem, the condition is about 15–60 times more pronounced with the fusiform initials, among which the ratio between the largest and smallest diameters is at least 30 : 1 and may exceed 600 : 1, as is evident from the data of Bailey (1920b, 1923), Ghouse and Iqbal (1975), and Ghouse et al. (1976, 1980).

The increase of surface area ratios between newly synthesized plasma membrane after each mitosis and mother cell plasma membrane (Δ pm/pm) tends to form an asymptotic line, the value of which has been calculated to be, for example, 75% for *Acer pseudoplatanus* fusiform cells (from Catesson 1964) and 80% for *Abies concolor* cells (from Wilson 1963). In contrast, Δ pm/pm is equal to 33% when the mother cell is isodiametric and below 33% when the new cell wall is in a plane of least surface area according to Errera's law (Catesson 1990).

The cambium acts as a meristematic template for the secondary vascular tissues (xylem and phloem) and thereby bridges the gap between these tissues. This function figures as another unique feature of the cambial zone. Therefore, the cambium plays an active physiological role even when in the dormant stage (Riding and Little 1984, 1986).

Riding and Little (1984, 1986) recognized periods of activity (actively dividing cells), rest (nondividing but metabolically active cells), and quiescence during the annual cambial cycle. During the first rest period (rest 1), which follows a period of active cell division, storage of assimilates translocating through phloem and rays and probably frost- (or drought-) hardening take place. The slowing down of metabolic exchange and the cessation of cyclosis mark the beginning of quiescence.

The postquiescence phase, when a renewal of metabolic exchanges sets in, can be considered the second period of meristematic rest (rest 2). The quiescence and rest phases are sometimes reduced (*Pinus radiata*: Barnett 1973; *Acacia nilotica*: Iqbal and Ghouse, 1981) or even nil (*Ceratonia siliqua*: Liphschitz and Lev Yadun 1986). In some species, several periods of meristematic activity may occur (*Hevea brasiliensis*: Rao 1970; *Psidium quajava*: Khan 1977).

Ray initials, with well-developed cell-to-cell connections through plasmodesmata, constitute the main symplastic route for horizontal communications. The number of plasmodesmata in the tangential (T) walls between radial initials is specifically high (Murmanis 1971; Timell 1979; Barnett 1981; Rao 1985). In *Fraxinus excelsior* (Goosen-de Roo and Creyghton-Schouten 1981), the highest number of plasmodesmata per μm^2 was found in the T walls between the ray cells, and the lowest number (close to zero) was found in the T walls between the fusiform cells. The extraordinary thickening of radial (R) walls that develops during the dormant cambial phase (see Philipson et al. 1971; Iqbal and Ghouse 1985b, 1987, 1990) may be related to an increase of apoplastic translocation through cambium either when assimilates are stored in the xylem and phloem parenchyma cells or when the cambium reactivates (Sauter et al. 1973; Höhl 1975; Braun 1984; Sauter and Kloth 1986.)

Essiamah and Eschrich (1985, 1986) suggested a radial water transfer associated with cambial reactivation and sap rise. Growth substances are also transported either transversely across the cambial bridge or longitudinally along the cambium. The consequent hormonal gradient seems to bear an impact on the seasonal cambial activity and the differentiation of cambial derivatives (Savidge and Wareing 1981). Further, stress signals can be transmitted along the rays through the cambium (Shigo and Dudzik 1985). In addition to transporting assimilates from the phloem to the xylem, the rays also release sugars into vessels by means of large pits (Sauter 1982; Sauter et al. 1973). The process is too fast to accomplish by diffusion, and respiratory activity is needed for the release of sucrose into vessels.

In some plants, particularly in Pinaceae, two types of ray initial—erect cells and radially elongated cells—coexist (Wodzicki and Brown 1973) that may produce different ray parenchyma cells. The Strasburger cells, which are in close contact with the sieve cells in the phloem of Pinaceae, appear to derive from erect ray initials alone (Sauter 1980). The significance of ray initials and their derivatives in the horizontal transports necessitates maintenance of a suitable ratio between the two types of cambial initial in terms of amount and distribution. The relative proportion of the ray initials is known to vary from 0% to 75% in the cambial surface and tends to be species-specific (Catesson 1980; Iqbal and Ghouse 1990).

The maintenance of cambial integrity depends on genetically controlled species-specific rhythms (Hejnowicz 1975; Stieber 1985), growth-substance equilibrium (Savidge 1983), and external factors (Worrall 1980; Creber and Chaloner 1990). The cambial cells cultured *in vitro* do not maintain their identity (Czaninski and Catesson 1970; Catesson et al. 1971) and are no longer recognizable as "cambial cells."

Cell Wall Texture

The organization of the cambial cell wall has been studied by optical means (Kerr and Bailey 1934), X-ray (Preston and Wardrop 1949), cytochemical techniques (Northcote 1963; Roland 1978; Catesson and Roland 1981), biochemical analysis (Simson and Timell 1978a–d), and electron microscopy (Hodge and Wardrop 1950; Preston and Ripley 1954; Wardrop 1954; Mahmood 1968; Freundlich and Robards 1974; Catesson 1980, 1981; Rao 1985; etc.). A new primary wall is thought to deposit around each daughter protoplast whenever the cambial cell divides (see Mahmood, 1968, 1990). Srivastava (1966a) and Freundlich and Robards (1974) took note of the fibrillar structure of the cambial cell wall, though the chemical nature of the fibers was not clear. The fibrillar texture seems to play a significant role in regulating the direction of growth in the expanding walls (see Roland et al. 1975, 1977). The wall, composed of the usual cellulose and associated noncellulosic substances, bears numerous primary pit-fields with plasmodesmata (see Iqbal and Ghouse, 1985a). The cambial cell wall accommodates the conflicting demands of cohesion and extensibility. Maintenance of the phloem-xylem bridge requires cohesion, whereas radial expansion of the cambial cells and their derivatives necessitates extensibility. The orientation of microfibrils in the outer layer of the wall is predominantly transverse. Radial walls (R walls) are usually thicker than tangential walls (T walls), especially during the dormant phase, and their primary pit-fields are deeply depressed (see Iqbal and Ghouse 1985b, 1987). Roland (1978) found the composition of these two walls to be highly dissimilar from his mild extractions of polysaccharides in *Populus canescens* (Salicaceae), *Quercus macrocarpa* (Fagaceae), and *Sambucus nigra* (Caprifoliceae) performed with the pectin solvents pectinase and EDTA (ethylenediaminetetracetate) and the hemicellulose extractants hemicellulase and DMSO (dimethyl-sulfoxide). Observation of the remaining polysaccharides revealed that these solvents had greater impact on R walls, some areas of which were destroyed completely, with a total absence of cellulose. T walls, despite their thinness, were more homogeneous and resistant. The hemicellulose solvents revealed a very dense, criss-crossed fibrillar structure, whereas pectin solvents proved to be almost ineffective. The difference between the two types of wall may be explained as follows: T walls are produced afresh at each periclinal division and their expansion is limited, whereas R walls, forming a sort of plastic and actively extensible continuum, experience a consistent radial extension that requires a loosening of the fibrillar architecture of the wall associated with turgor pressure. Thus, the peculiar structure of the R wall agrees readily to the necessary cellular readjustments following the intrusive growth or loss of initials (see Roland and Vian 1979).

It is generally agreed that although T walls remain relatively thin throughout the year, R walls thicken markedly between pit-fields when the cambium is dormant. In *Acer pseudoplatanus,* the R walls of resting cambium are resistant to EDTA, unlike those of active cambium (Catesson 1980). DMSO treatment partly extracted both radial and tangential walls; the former appeared swollen. The wall thickening in dormant cambium was considered to be caused by the accumulation of both DMSO-extractible material (hemicellulose) and DMSO-resistant fibrillar material (probably cellulose) (Catesson 1980).

The Development and Chemistry of the Cell Wall

Vascular cambium differs from primary meristems with regard to cell-plate formation because of the length of fusiform cells and thus the extension of phragmoplast movement. At both ends of the growing cell plate, the characteristic fan-shaped tips of the phragmoplast are made up of radiating microtubules interspersed with Golgi vesicles. As the cell plate progresses toward the cell tips, microtubules disappear and vesicles fuse, leaving numerous gaps that provide ingress to rough endoplasmic reticulum tubules. The network of tubular endoplasmic reticulum present at this level might help to locate and stabilize the aggregating vesicles in a single plane (Vigil 1984). Polysaccharides can be visualized within the cell plate vesicles. As soon as the vesicles fuse, a thin fibrillar network appears as the nascent cell wall (Catesson 1990).

The nascent cambial walls in all plants examined so far exhibited (a) a high resistance to EDTA and DMSO extraction and a low resistance to hot water treatment, and (b) a strong staining with iron III hydroxylamine, which reacts specifically with methylated pectins (Catesson and Roland 1981). Thus, when the cell plate reaches the mother cell walls, the newly laid wall appears to be constituted of fibrillar polysaccharide material and methylated pectins. It does not contain any appreciable amount of EDTA-extractible acidic pectins.

All nascent cell walls, even in primary meristems, contain methylated pectins and fibrillar polysaccharides as their main components. Also, the young cell walls do not evince any segregation between pectic and fibrillar components. The addition of new polysaccharides, especially acidic pectins, during further wall maturation *within* the meristem itself (i.e. before cell elongation), causes chemical alterations that result in a complete redistribution of wall materials and the formation of a proper middle lamella (Martar et al. 1986; Martar 1987). The newly formed cambial cell walls also experience these phenomena. Tangential walls present a more typical structure of newly laid walls due to the predominance of periclinal mitoses (Catesson 1990).

The period of wall formation in sycamore cambial cell extends from the end of mitosis to the cessation of cyclosis. During this period, Golgi vesicles with polysaccharide contents are present that later fuse with plasmalemma, making it enlarged and infolded. The infoldings cross the cytoplasm and push the tonoplast into vacuoles. Paramonova (1974) proposed that such plasmalemma infoldings in the storage cells of beetroot are the sucrose pathway from the apoplast into vacuoles.

The phenomenon of the grafting of a new wall onto a preexisting cambial cell wall (Catesson and Roland 1981) involves formation of a sort of buttress at the point of contact between a thin nascent wall (T wall) and the wall of the mother cell, enlargement of the junction zone due to progressive polysaccharide apposition, rupture of the preexisting primary wall microfibrils along the buttress base that opens a gap that allows the radial middle lamella to enter the buttress and approach the tangential wall, and, ultimately, establishment of a new microfibrillar continuity between the parent and the daughter cell walls. Polysaccharide segregation then takes place in the developing wall progressing from each buttress toward the median line. Cellulose and most hemicelluloses are separated into two lateral layers that form the *primary walls* of each of the daughter cells, and acidic pectins constitute the *middle lamella*. The thickness of the new wall increases through Golgi activity and the synthesis of additional polysaccharides, and the classic tripartite organization (primary wall–middle lamella–primary wall) becomes established. The increased epimerase activity in the cambial derivatives over that in the cambial zone of sycamore (Dalessandro and Northcote 1977) may bear some correlation to the late formation of the pectic middle lamella, as the secondary walls are known for being poor in pectin content.

A delay in middle-lamella formation has also been observed in apical meristems (Martar et al. 1986; Matar 1987); cells divide in every direction, and all the walls mature from a homogeneous septum to a tripartite cell wall. When periclinal divisions dominate along the primary meristem-procambium-cambium continuum (Catesson

1964, 1984; Larson 1976a), their rhythm becomes more rapid that T wall maturation, and the apparent dissimilarity between T and R walls is progressively established (Catesson 1990). Thus, the cell walls of the cambial zone exhibit a far greater capacity of radial extension (up to 100 times) than that of tangential extension (e.g. the tangential cell diameter in *Pinus strobus* increased 2.6 times in 60 years: see Bailey 1920a). They also develop a high tangential cohesion and resistance to radial stresses.

Studies by Allsopp and Misra (1940) and Northcote (1963) showed important interspecific variations in pectin content and consequently in cellulose content. Analysis of cambial cell walls of *Acer pseudoplatanus, Betula platyphylla, Fraxinus excelsa* and *Pinus ponderosa* revealed that cell walls contain almost equal amounts of cellulose (38% to 47%) and hemicellulose (40% to 46%), whereas pectins constitute only 7% to 20% of the total weight of the component polysaccharides (Northcote 1963). These studies showed no significant difference between the pectin and cellulose of softwoods and hardwoods but revealed the fundamental difference in hemicellulose composition between the two groups. There is twice as much xylose and half as much arabinose in hardwoods as in softwoods.

Later studies (Simson and Timell 1978a) showed that wall proteins amount to 10–15% of the cell-wall dry weight and that 50% of the remaining carbohydrates are composed of pectins, 30% of hemicellulose, and 20% of cellulose. The high amount of pectins found here, compared to the earlier findings of Northcote (1963), is probably due to the inclusion of developing phloem and/or xylem in the samples used for the earlier analysis. Simson and Timell (1978b) also examined suspension-cultured cells from *Acer pseudoplatanus* and found some support for their *in vivo* observations. The main dissimilarities concern the presence of xylans and glucomannans and the lower proportion of xyloglucans in the cambial tissue than in the cultured cells.

Cambial xyloglucans isolated from *Populus tremuloides* and *Tilia americana* have an average molecular weight of 62,500 (Simson and Timell 1978b). The glucan backbone of the macromolecule contains approximately 200 sugar residues that carry about 130 xylose sidechains often bearing galactose and fucose residues. The xyloglucans also present in the cambial cell walls, are considered to be specially concerned in wall extension (Simson and Timell 1978b). The acidic glucan from aspen was identified as a methyl glucuronoxylan with an average molecular weight of 40,000 (Simson and Timell 1978d). The water-soluble arabino-galactin was probably linked to proteins and had an average molecular weight of 2,000,000. Its main chain consisted of galactose, and sidechains contained galactose, arabinose, glucuronic acid, and their methylated derivatives (Simson and Timell 1978c). The pure pectic acid extracted with EDTA gave, on hydrolysis, galacturonic acid, galactose, arabinose, and rhamnose in a molar ratio of 5 : 2 : 2 : 1 (Simson and Timell 1978d).

Cytochemical experiments and biochemical analyses have elucidated the cell-wall topochemistry and structure considerably. In radial walls, the middle lamella is almost completely extracted with EDTA, leaving a few dispersed microfibrils. It is also sensitive to DMSO but not to H_2O extraction. Thus, the matrix contains mostly acidic pectins, which is quite in accordance with the agreed characters of the middle lamella. The primary-wall skeleton, which may be observed after DMSO or methylamine (CH_3NH_2) extraction, consists of loose, mainly radially oriented microfibrils and may be interrupted in places (Roland 1978). Radial primary walls consist of a loose cellulosic skeleton embedded in xyloglucans, arabinogalactans, and a small amount of xylans, although the presence of water-soluble, highly methylated pectins cannot be excluded. The existence of xyloglucans in R walls is important in view of the crucial role attributed to these polysaccharides in cell-wall extensibility. The radial length of R walls may increase by a factor of 100 during the differentiation of a cambial cell into a vessel as in *Castanea sativa* (see Catesson 1990).

Newly formed T walls, on the contrary, exhibit no middle lamella. Extractants reveal the presence, throughout the entire wall, of a dense network of crisscrossed microfibrils. The staining of young T walls with iron III hydroxylamine indicates that the matrix probably consists of highly methylated pectins, water-soluble arabino-galactans (Simson and Timell 1978c), and some xyloglucans. The amount of acidic pectins and xylans is very low if not nil. T walls are rigid though thin. This particular characteristic may enable them to resist tensile stress known to occur in some species (Hejnowicz 1980). Whether cambial cell-wall architecture correlates with tensile and compressive stresses and ultimately with differentiation of derivative cells is a question worth investigating.

Radial walls become especially thick between the primary pit-fields, thus giving them a beaded appearance in section (Kerr and Bailey 1934; Iqbal and Ghouse 1987), whereas T wall thickening generally stops when the tripartite organization is reached (Catesson 1980, 1981). Significant Golgi activity accompanies these changes and is characteristic of the first rest period.

Strengthening of the cellulosic skeleton may cause a temporary decrease in wall plasticity (Kerr and Bailey 1934). It is suggested (see Fry 1986, Lamport 1986) that primary-wall rigidification is ensured by cross-linking of matrix polymers that include phenols. The formation of either isodityrosine bonds between extensin molecules or diferuloyl bonds between pectin molecules would require the presence of a wall peroxidase and H_2O_2, the biogenesis of which is also peroxidase dependent. An increase in wall-peroxidase activities was detected in the quiescent cambium of *Populus euramericana* by Catesson (1980). These peroxidases were strongly bound to the cell wall, unlike those in the active cambium. Cell-wall loosening, essential for the resumption of radial growth, requires the cleavage of cross linked polymers through well-bound esterases, glycanases, or proteases. Nevertheless, enzymes capable of breaking phenolic cross links are yet to be discovered in plants (see Catesson 1990). Some incidental observations suggest that a partial loosening of the wall matrix precedes the onset of mitotic activity of the cambium in spring (Rao 1985). Structural and chemical changes occurring in cambial walls during the shift from quiescence to activity deserve attention.

The Nature of Cytoplasm

Fusiform initials and ray cell initials are structurally similar in that both are vacuolate and have a parietal layer of cytoplasm with the usual complement of organelles and membranes typical of parenchyma cells. The cytoplasm is rich in mitochondria, plastids, peroxisomes, ribosomes, lipid bodies, dictyosomes, endoplasmic reticulum (ER), microtubules, amyloplasts, and lomosomes. The chloro-plast-like plastids contain thylakoid membranes that are not compiled into grana stacks. Thus, they resemble the chloroplasts of the root and hypocotyl cells of seedlings germinating under low-light conditions (Berlyn 1970).

Like other meristematic cells, active cambial cells possess a dense, polysome-studded cytoplasm, elaborate rough endoplasmic reticulum, and active dictyosomes. They differ, however, in having prominent vacuoles, larger mitochondria, and rela-tively more differentiated plastids than other meristems. Softwood and hardwood cambia exhibit minor cytoplasmic differences, if any. The cytoplasmic properties of active and dormant cambium cells vary, although in some species these variations are inconspicuous. Actively dividing initials in *Fraxinus americana,* Oleaceae, appear to be highly vacuolate and rich in endoplasmic reticulum of rough cisternal form, ribosomes, dictyosomes, coated vesicles, and microtubules (Srivastava 1966a). The coated vesicles and the rough cisternal endoplasmic reticulum are less abundant in nondividing cells. Similar features were noted for *Pinus strobus* (Srivastava and O'Brien 1966), with only a few differences in detail. The active initials possess merely one or two large vacuoles, a smooth and regular plasmalemma, and a rough cisternal form of endoplasmic reticulum. In winter cambium, vacuoles are small and numerous, the plasmalemma thrown into folds and the endoplasmic reticulum mostly in the form of smooth vesicles.

In *Salix fragilis* (Salicaceae), protein bodies, lipid droplets, and vesiculate smooth endoplasmic reticulum were abundant in the dormant cambium cells (Robards and Kidwai 1969). The dormant cambium of *Fagus sylvatica* (Fagaceae) also exhibits similar features (Kidwai and Robards 1969). Here, protein bodies occupy a larger portion of space than lipid droplets, and the vacuoles are almost completely absent. At the onset of cambial reactivation, there occurs a sequential disappearance of protein bodies, an appearance of numerous small empty vacuoles, and their gradual fusion into one or two large vacuoles. These changes undergo a reverse order at the approach of dormancy. It was suggested that the vacuoles in this species probably originate from protein bodies and that protein bodies are vacuoles filled with storage proteins (Farooqui and Robards 1979). Although the dormant initials generally possess free ribosomes, few and poorly active dictyosomes, and smooth endoplasmic reticulum (Catesson 1980) rough endoplasmic reticulum may also be present. It may be scarce as in some conifers (Tsuda 1975) or even dominant as in sycamore (Catesson 1974). Lipid droplets markedly increase in size and number. Some filamentous, possibly proteic bundles sometimes appear in the dormant cells as in ash (Srivastava 1966a), pine (Srivastava and O'Brien 1966), and sycamore (Catesson 1974). On the other hand, some similar microfilaments were observed by Tsuda (1975) in the active cambial cells of certain conifers.

The presence of a large central vacuole characterizes actively dividing cambial cells. The large vacuole divides into smaller ones during meristematic rest, and the quiescent initials, with their small, rounded vacuoles, look similar to the active apical meristematic cells. Later, during the transitional period between quiescent and active phases (rest 2), the reverse vacuolar transformation occurs. This cycle, first observed by Bailey (1930), has been confirmed by all subsequent cytological studies, especially those of temperate species. The numerous vacuoles of the dormant cells may be filled with proteins, as in beech (Farooqui and Robards 1979), or with polyphenols or sometimes with whorls of membrane-like material, as in sycamore (*Acer pseudoplatanus*: Catesson 1980). In species with a short dormant phase, the volume of individual vacuoles decreases only slightly (Barnett 1973). In ray cells, particularly in the softwood species, vacuoles are relatively little developed (Barnett 1973; Tsuda 1975; Timell 1979).

Cytoplasmic streaming is predominantly longitudinal in the thin peripheral cytoplasm of active fusiform cells; it is oblique in the anastomosing cytoplasmic strands. Small lipid globules are swept along the stream at the same velocity. Stream velocity is maximal during the active cambial phase. Values ranging from 13 to 15 μm s^{-1} were reported for white-pine cambium from mid-March to mid-July; the flow was slow during the meristematic rest (Thimann and Kaufman 1958). Ray cells exhibit a cytoplasmic streaming that is relatively slow and less precise in direction (Goosen-de Roo et al. 1983).

There may be a correlation between cytoplasmic streaming and the presence of microfilament bundles (Kamiya 1981; Parthasarathy et al. 1985). Organelle movement along the track provided by actin filaments, which form a normal component of the cytoskeleton of many plants, and/or by microtubules would be regulated by the cytoplasmic Ca^{2+} concentration (Takagi and Nagai 1986; Williamson 1986). Microfilament bundles are known to exist mostly in the active cambium of various species. In *Fraxinus excelsior,* microfilament bundles present in the peripheral cytoplasm of fusiform cells lie parallel to the long axis of the cell, the main direction of the cytoplasmic streaming. The bundles reach a length of at least 15.8 μm, contain about 16 microfilaments per bundle, and show a close association with tubules of endoplasmic reticulum running parallel to them. Shorter bundles with diverse orientation occur in the phragmoplast of fusiform cells and in the peripheral cytoplasm and cytoplasmic strands of ray initials but do not show a clear association with tubular endoplasmic reticulum (Goosen-de Roo et al. 1983). Hence, the role of microfilament bundles with respect to cytoplasmic streaming in the cambial cells remains unclear (see Catesson 1990). The presence of these bundles in quiescent cambial cells points to their probable role in protein storage.

In *Acer pseudoplatanus,* a species that grows in temperate climates with mild winters, cytoplasmic streaming is active even during the fall fragmentation of the central vacuole into a number of small elongated vacuoles (Catesson 1964, 1974). These elongated vacuoles transform into globular ones when streaming ceases. Osmotic potential also decreases, reaching a minimum value (Ca. −3.5 MPa) during quiescence. Variations of the osmotic potential during quiescence and their prominence during acute winters suggest that regulatory mechanisms are still active in quiescent cells (Catesson 1990). The water content of cambial cells in *Acer pseudoplatanus* varies from 120% of dry weight during quiescence, through 140–160% a week before bud swelling, to about 200% at the bud swelling and subsequent stage (Catesson 1964). When the temperature reaches a sufficient level, streaming is resumed, owing to an increased water content of the cells. The globular vacuoles begin to elongate and fuse. Increases in water content and vacuole enlargement induce a conspicuous swelling of the initials often observed in early spring. It has been proved experimentally that the resumption of cyclosis as well as vacuolar elongation and fusion can be achieved by increasing temperature and keeping cells under high osmotic potential.

The ray-cell cycle is similar to that of fusiform cells but the vacuoles are less developed (Barnett 1973; Tsuda 1975; Timell 1979) and the active ray cells divide less frequently. The available information suggests that the most active cells are characterized by one large vacuole, less active cells by a few smaller vacuoles, and the quiescent cells by numerous small vacuoles. Seasonal modifications of vacuoles were speculated to be closely related to variations in osmotic pressure and to sugar accumulation in sycamore (Catesson 1964; LeSaint and Catesson 1966).

Parish (1974) found the tonoplast of quiescent cells to be studded with smaller, and more numerous particles than the tonoplast of active cells. It was calculated that for the cambium cell of *Acer pseudoplatanus,* the vacuolar apparatus occupies about 75% of the cell volume in active fusiform initials and 55% in ray cells (Catesson 1990); this proportion was only 0.4% to 24% in shoot apices of a cactus (Mauseth 1982). Also, the ratio was lower in the quiescent fusiform cells (50%) than in the active ones.

The value of tonoplast surface area (including cytoplasmic strands) was estimated to be about 15,000 μm^2 for active fusiform cells and 28,000 μm^2 for quiescent ones; the increase was apparently due to the appearance of numerous tiny vacuoles. Conversely, a low amount of tonoplast in active cells should make for the resistance against any break-up of the large vacuole into a number of smaller ones (Catesson 1990). The seasonal variations in tonoplast surface area also reflect the occurrence of biosynthesis of new membranes during the shift from activity to quiescence, and of the lysis of excess tonoplast at the onset of meristematic activity. Acid phosphatase activity appears to be present in the vacuoles at least during the transitional rest periods (Catesson 1980; Rao and Catesson 1987).

Studies with both conifers (Murmanis 1971) and dicotyledons (Buvat 1956; Robards and Kidwai 1969) have shown that mitochondria occur in chains or groups in dormant cells but are widely dispersed in active cells. However, they occur singly in the cytoplasm of dormant cambial cells of *Holoptelea integrifolia* (Rao and Dave 1983a). In an active condition, mitochondria are generally ovoid or somewhat elongate, with a clear matrix and a few cristae. Seasonal variations in their shape, size, and number are not yet well documented. In *Acer pseudoplatanus* and *Robinia pseudoacacia,* mitochondria were noted to be relatively short in dormant cells, whereas they were elongated and sometimes even branched during meristematic activity (Catesson 1974, 1980; Rao 1985). In *Pinus radiata* they maintain a similar morphology all year round (Barnett 1975), but their frequency decreases during cambial activity. Dictyosomes are always active in summer, but opinions differ as to their activity in winter. They were found to be active in the winter cambium of conifers, namely *Pinus strobus* (Srivastava and O'Brien 1966), *Cryptomeria japonica* and *Pinus thunbergii* (Itoh 1971), and *Pinus radiata* (Barnett 1973) but inactive in that of certain angiosperms, namely *Fraxinus americana* (Srivastava 1966a), *Fagus sylvatica* (Kidwai and Robards 1969), *Salix fragilis* (Robards and Kidwai 1969), and *Tilia americana* (Mia 1970). However, Murmanis (1971) reported inactive dictyosomes even from *Pinus strobus*. There appears to be a distinction in this respect between hardwoods (inactive dictyosomes) and softwoods (active dictyosomes) as Barnett (1973) suggests.

Plastid forms vary with species. The stroma is somewhat dense; the thylakoid may be well developed, as in *Pinus strobus* (Murmanis 1971) or reduced to vesicles and short tubules, as in *Acer pseudoplatanus* (Catesson 1974) and *Holoptelea integrifolia* (Rao and Dave 1983a). Both conditions and even several intermediate conditions, may be present within a species (see Tsuda 1975).

The degree of differentiation of cambial cell plastids also varies with species and even within a species. All intermediates occur—from proplastids with vesicles and short tubules, as in *Acer pseudoplatanus* (Catesson 1974), to plastids with well-developed thylakoids, as in *Pinus strobus* (Murmanis 1971) and *Dianthus caryophyllus* (Y. Czaninski, unpublished observations). Prolamellar bodies were reported in quiescent cells of *Tectona grandis* (Dave and Rao 1982). In some species, plastids in ray cells are more completely differentiated or contain more starch than those in fusiform cells (Catesson 1980; Dave and Rao 1982; Rao and Dave 1983b). The most differentiated plastids, usually smaller than mesophyll chloroplasts, have few grana and generally no stroma lamellae. Owing to a probable lack of a photosystem I and the inconspicuous amount of light reaching the cambium through the bark *in situ,* photosynthesis is unlikely to occur in cambial plastids, which may serve instead as storage organelles. In addition to starch, cambial plastids often possess osmiophilic granules, which may increase in number in quiescent cells (Murmanis 1971; Barnett 1973). Paracrystalline clusters of phytoferritin are present in various species. These clusters, sometimes restricted to quiescent cells, are often thought to be a storage material (see Catesson 1990). The cambium is thought to have the highest respiration of the stem tissues apart from the apical meristem (see Berlyn and Battey 1985).

Cytoplasmic Biosynthesis and the Endomembrane System

Active cambial cells possess a dense cytoplasm with numerous polysomes and well-developed rough endoplasmic reticulum. Cisternae of rough endoplasmic reticulum are interconnected, often by smooth tubular endoplasmic reticulum, thus providing intracellular transport. The endoplasmic reticulum acts not only as the source of most of the membrane synthesis within the cell but also as the site of synthesis of many proteins and lipids.

Dictyosomes, always numerous, possess 5–7 cisternae and produce many vesicles that may differ in size (Rao 1985). The smaller vesicles (0.05 to 0.1 μm in diameter), which contain polysaccharides may contribute to cell wall formation. The purpose of the larger vesicles (0.3 to 0.5 μm in diameter), which lack polysaccharides, is unclear. Coated vesicles were observed to lie around dictyosomes (Rao and Dave 1983b; Rao 1985), though their origin from the latter was not confirmed. Lipid globules, a few peroxisomes, and microtubules (apparently axially oriented in many fusiform cells) are also present (Tsuda 1975; Farooqui and Robards 1979).

At the beginning of the meristematic rest period, cambial cells are still metabolically active: Dictyosomes keep producing many polysaccharide-containing vesicles, rough endoplasmic reticulum maintains its dominance, and plasmalemma still shows infoldings when the dormant phase starts (Catesson 1980; Riding and Little 1984; Rao 1985; Rao and Catesson 1987). Succinic dehydrogenase and peroxidase activities are maximal during this period in *Abies balsamea* (Riding and Little 1984).

Progressive changes leading to the cessation of metabolic activity mark the transitional period between rest and quiescence. Vesicular and tubular smooth endoplasmic reticulum tend to replace rough endoplasmic reticulum , and most polysomes transform into free ribosomes. In most plants, dictyosomes are rare, with only 2–4 cisternae and few vesicles. Metabolic activities become inconspicuous. However, dictyosomes surrounded by many vesicles may coexist with smooth, vesicular endoplasmic reticulum, as in *Cryptomeria japonica* and *Pinus thunbergii* (Itoh 1971). Small, rare dictyosomes, on the other hand, may accompany abundant rough endoplasmic reticulum in *Acer pseudoplatanus* (Catesson 1974, 1990). The sites of protein biosynthesis (polysomes and rough endoplasmic reticulum) and secretory structures reactivate in concurrence with the resumption of nucleolar activity when the meristematic cambial phase begins (Catesson 1980; Rao 1985).

Storage of assimilates (e.g., starch in plastids; lipids and tannins in the cytoplasm; sugar, protids, and tannins in vacuoles) forms the main feature of dormant cambial cells. Cytoplasmic tannin granules, apparently enclosed in a membrane, mostly lie near the endoplasmic reticulum or the tonoplast, and vacuolar tannins constitute globular or lens-shaped bodies closely appressed to the tonoplast inner face (Catesson 1990).

The lipid content of the cells often increases during this period (Catesson 1964, 1980; Rao and Dave 1983b; Rao 1985) especially in ray cells (Timell 1980). The phenomenon may be delayed, however, until the cells become quiescent (Riding and Little, 1984). Rao (1985) emphasized that lipids and tannin deposits look alike after conventional fixation and that they can be distinguished by the positive reaction of tannins with $FeSO_4$ and by the difference in contrast after PATAg staining.

The seasonal starch content of the cambium varies according to species. Starch may be present only in dormant cells, only in active cells, in both dormant and active cells, or in neither (for details, see Iqbal and Ghouse 1985a; Fahn and Werker 1990).

The amount of total insoluble carbohydrates in the cambium of *Abies balsamea* increases during the rest-quiescence transition and later declines. The decrease in starch content during late fall could be related to the use of food reserves during frost-hardening (Glerum and Balatinecz 1980; Riding and Little, 1984).

Osmophilic inclusions are present in certain pines, and are more abundant during the resting period (Murmanis 1971; Barnett 1973). Ferritin, presumably an iron storage product kept in readiness for differentiating tissues, was detected in Cupressaceae,

Podocarpaceae, and Taxodiaceae among conifers (Tsuda 1972) and in several hard-woods (Catesson 1974, 1980). Plastids may be identical in both fusiform and ray cells, as in beech and willow (Kidwai and Robards 1969; Robards and Kidwai 1969), or relatively well differentiated in ray cells, as in locust and sycamore (Catesson 1974). In many conifers, starch and ferritin were confined to ray-cell plastids only (Tsuda 1975). In dormant cambium of *Holoptelea integrifolia,* plastid stroma contain starch, plastoglobuli, and ribosomes; the plastid ribosomes are smaller than those of cytoplasm (Rao and Dave 1983a). Ray cells are characterized by a high starch content.

In *Gmelina arborea* and *Tectona grandis,* Verbenaceae, lipid and protein bodies are abundant in the cytoplasm of dormant cambial cells. In *Gmelina,* ray-cell initials contain a greater lipid content than fusiform initials, and the differentiating and mature vascular elements put up a larger amount of lipid globules than the cambial cells (Rao and Dave 1983). Starch grains are present only in ray initials, and only during the active cambial phase. This starch content of *Gmelina* cambium becomes depleted when the cambial activity reaches its maximum. In *Tectona* cambium, however, starch persists throughout the active period (Rao and Dave 1983c). The appearance and disappearance of starch granules seem to be correlated to the phenology. Rapid production of photosynthate and its translocation to cambial cells at leaf emergence probably enable the appearance of starch when the cambium reactivates. Active cambium consumes large amounts of carbohydrates in the production of new cambial cells and in the accretion of new phloem and xylem (Kramer and Kozlowski 1979). This is probably why the cambial cells become starch-free during peak activity. If the production of carbohydrates is in excess of cambial requirements, however, the starch remains accumulated even during the grand growth period.

Food-reserve mobilization, together with the onset of protein biosynthesis, heralds the resumption of meristematic activity. Lipase activity of cambial cells increases at this juncture in *Tilia cordata* (Höll 1975). Catesson (1990) suggests that the appearance of small electron-lucent areas in the dense matrix indicates degradation of lipids and tannins. These areas enlarge and fuse so that the matrix is reduced to a thin, dark membrane-like layer, which eventually disappears. If degradation of lipids, tannins, starch, sugars, and protids, etc. of the cambial cells does not meet the energy requirements of the dividing cambial cells, additional nutrients from the vascular storage parenchyma may be supplied through rays (Sauter 1982).

Biogenesis and Transport of Membrane

The endomembrane system represents a developmental continuum: endoplasmic reticulum-Golgi apparatus–plasma membrane and/or tonoplast. It is involved not only in synthesis but also in the intracellular transport of membranes and secretion products. The existence of endocytosis in plant cells long remained in dispute (Cram 1980; Robinson and Kristen 1982) and has been established only recently (Hübner et al. 1985). Cambial cells are ideal for the study of membrane traffic in plants because the endomembrane system of these cells undergoes seasonal changes, and an enormous amount of plasmalemma is synthesized at each division of the fusiform cells. The regulation of this traffic and its relationship to uptake and storage of nutrients and cell homeostasis, i.e. the maintenance of the dynamic equilibrium of the cytoplasm under environmental changes, constitutes an important aspect of cambial physiology.

In meristematic cells, the endomembrane complement doubles with each cell cycle. Most of this increase occurs during the interphase, whereas new plasma membrane is laid down during the late telophase phase. The amount of new plasma membrane produced at each telophase by fusiform initials seems to be far greater than the amount produced by the primary meristematic cells. The rate of Golgi-vesicle production per unit of cytoplasmic volume (number of vesicles min^{-1} μm^3 cytoplasm^{-1} is almost equivalent in the primary and secondary meristematic cells when duration of cell-plate formation is taken into account (Table 18 of Catesson 1990).

The increase in thickness of cambial cell walls that accrues during the resting period in temperate regions probably results from intense Golgi activity. In non-growing cells, obviously, such activity must result in excess production of plasma membrane; therefore, certain membrane retrieval processes must exist to maintain the necessary balance between compartments (Catesson 1990).

During wall thickening, numerous smooth or coated vesicles containing poly-saccharides appear in the cytoplasm (Rao and Catesson 1987). Concomitantly, plasmalemma invaginations (PLI), often containing vesicles or tubules become con-spicuous along the R and T walls of both ray and fusiform initials (see Catesson 1980, 1981; Timell 1980; Riding and Little 1984; Sennerby-Forsse 1986; Rao and Catesson 1987). When a plasmalemma invagination reaches a vacuole, it seemingly pushes the tonoplast inward and enters the vacuole. Eventually, the plasmalemma invagination and its ensheathing tonoplast are released into the vacuolar sap. Endoplasmic reti-culum saccules sandwiched between plasmalemma and tonoplast are also carried into the vacuoles.

Catesson (1990) concluded that plasmalemma invaginations are probably actively involved with membrane internalization in resting cambial cells and that coated vesicles may also intervene. Hübner et al. (1985) demonstrated the association of coated vesicles may also intervene. Hübner et al. (1985) demonstrated the association of coated vesicles with endocytosis in plant cells. Earlier, Traas (1984) had shown the regular presence of coated pits in plant plasma membranes. The demonstration of an for coated vesicles (Nakamura and Miki-Hirosige 1982; Pesacreta and Lucas 1985; Griffing et al. 1986).

The presence of two separate populations of coated vesicles associated with distinctly different roles, as in animal cells, has also been speculated for plant cells (Harris 1986). Evidence on the occurrence of coated vesicles and on their possible role in cambial cells is limited. The polysaccharide-containing coated vesicles and coated pits observed in fusiform cambial cells of *Aesculus* might follow an exocytotic path-way from dictyosomes to the plasma membrane, but even the reverse cannot be ruled out (Rao and Catesson 1987).

The number of plasmalemma infoldings decreases in cambial cells during the rest-quiescence transition in *Acer* (Catesson 1980), *Abies* (Riding and Little 1984), and *Aesculus* (Rao and Catesson 1987). The various membrane profiles accumulated into the vacuoles slowly disappear.

Plasmalemma invaginations obviously carry an equivalent area of tonoplast into vacuoles. Sometimes, even endoplasmic reticulum saccules find their way into vacuoles. This membrane accumulation is later lysed; however, despite this, the total surface area of tonoplast increases during this period. An entirely new set of endomembranes (especially tonoplast and plasmalemma) with different biochemical and physiological properties may form during the rest–quiescence transition (Catesson 1990). This view finds support from observations that an increase of plasmalemma invaginations, possibly due to incorporation and deletion of membrane material, often occurs during cold acclimatization (Steponkus 1984; Wisniewski and Ashworth 1985a, b, 1986). According to Riding and Little (1984), plasmalemma infoldings are related to structural alterations and consequently to functional changes of the plasma membrane. Such changes may reduce the amount of membrane-located hormone-receptor proteins

(Trewavas 1982), thus explaining why ^{14}C-labeled IAA transport declines in *Abies balsamea* (Little 1981), *Picea sitchensis* (Little and Wareing 1981) and *Fagus sylvatica* (Lachaud and Bonnemain 1982) during autumn. Conversely, the capacity for auxin transport increases during the transition from quiescence to activity (Lachaud and Bonnemain 1982). This evidently requires membrane renewal before the commencement of meristematic activity. As Cecich (1979) suggests, stored lipid bodies, which are slowly degraded during this period, may be involved as a source of phospholipid precursors in membrane biogenesis.

Dynamics of Endomembrane Traffic

During rest, i.e. the period between activity and quiescence, cambial cells accumulate sugars and other storage materials in the vacuoles. Assimilates in plant cells may accumulate in the vacuoles via an ATPase-driven H^+-sugar co-transport across the plasmalemma and/or tonoplast (Komor et al. 1984; Delrot and Bonnemain 1985). The system operative across the tonoplast is probably a sugar-proton antiport, since vacuoles have a more acidic pH than the cytoplasm (see Komor and Orlich 1986). Membrane internalization and accumulation into vacuoles has also been reported for certain sugar-storing or inulin-storing cells (Kaeser 1983; Tort et al. 1985). Study of *Stachys* tuber development showed that both pathways could intervene in succession (Auriac and Tort 1985). An active ATPase-driven transport would operate in tuber buds (Tort et al. 1985). A direct endocytotic passage from apoplast to vacuoles would occur in the growing, inulin-accumulating internodes, where the proton gradient does not favor H^+-sugar co-transport (Tort and Gendraud 1984).

Similar phenomena may occur within cambial cells. The simultaneous occurrence of plasmalemma invaginations and sugar storage in autumn suggests an endocytotic transport that allows rapid, significant sugar accumulation when H^+-sugar antiport systems are not functioning, i.e. when the vacuole pH cannot be maintained at its normal acidic value (Catesson 1990). Starch-glucose exchanges between cell compartments during quiescence and the mobilization of storage material at the onset of activity may depend on the activity of electrogenic pumps and result in vacuolar acidification. (Mellmann et al. 1986). This would explain why membrane degradation by acid phosphatase is delayed. Still to be elucidated are the rate and mechanism of vesicle formation and transport, the biochemical pathway of membrane fusion, and the factors regulating endocytosis and intracellular processing.

Endomembrane flow is believed to be influenced by the seasonal structural and functional changes in cambial cells and by the maintenance of cell polarity. Radial production of derivatives and age-dependent variations between the two tangential walls of a given initial suggest that its polar axis is either parallel (in a ray cell) or normal (in a fusiform cell) to its longitudinal axis.

We may conclude from chemical and structural differences between T and R walls of the same cell that the polysaccharide and enzyme contents of Golgi vesicles have different destinations. This outward dispatch of dissimilar vesicles is superimposed upon an inward flow toward the vacuoles. The differentiation of vesicles into extracellular and intracellular routes and the polar orientation of vesicle flow constitute the main traffic problems (Catesson 1990). Transport of the Golgi vesicles is considered a microfilament-dependent, actin-driven process (see Steer 1985; Schnepf 1986; Williamson 1986). Microfilament bundles, when present, and cytoplasmic streaming are parallel to the longitudinal axis of fusiform cells, i.e. perpendicular to the shortest route from dictyosomes to cell walls. The rates of vesicle formation and transport are related not only to traffic control but may also act as limiting factors for cell multiplication and hence for the production and growth of derivatives.

Chemical and structural dissimilarities between membranes may help in maintaining cell polarity. Vesicles with different membrane characteristics will fuse with different target membranes. Therefore, not only are the tonoplast and plasmalemma dissimilar, but each membrane contains local microdomains that show chemical and structural differences. These factors affect the process of membrane fusion, or endocytosis (Steinman et al. 1983; Steer 1985). Vesicles have been suggested to bear docking sites that may interact specifically with docking rosettes located on the plasma membrane, and to bring about fusion in the presence of Ca^{2+} (Robinson and Kristen 1982; Steer 1985). Schnepf (1986) identified close correlations among the locally restricted calcium fluxes, transcellular electrical currents, and polar cell growth. Cambial activity and cambial electrical resistance showed an inverse correlation (Wisniewski et al. 1985).

Nuclear Apparatus

Schacht (1856) may have been the first to report the presence of mulitnucleate fusiform initials, later confirmed by Russow (1882). Strasburger (1891), however, refuted these reports. On examining a variety of gymnosperms and angiosperms of tropical and temperate zones (stems, roots, and branches from trees of different size and age collected at different seasons), Bailey (1920b) concluded that fusiform initials are always uninucleate. He attributed the multinucleate appearance to a simultaneous observation of individual nuclei of several radially flattened and superimposed cells that lie close to the same focal plane. Bailey also ruled out the occurrence of polyploidy or any increase in the size of the nucleus with increasing length of fusiform initials.

The hypothesis of uninucleate cambial initials held sway in all later works until the polynucleate condition was recorded during the last two decades for certain tropical species of India, such as *Solanum melongena*, Solanaceae (Patel 1975) and several woody species of Leguminosae, Myrtaceae, and Verbenaeae (Ghouse and Khan 1977; Ghouse et al. 1979; Iqbal and Ghouse 1987). Fusiform initials of *Psidium guajava* (Myrtaceae) may have as many as five nuclei; the frequency of polynucleate cells is greater during dormancy than in the active phase of cambium (Ghouse and Khan 1977). A similar pattern is found in *Callistemon citrinus*, whereas the reverse applies to *Eugenia jambolana* (Khan 1980). No correlation was established between the polynucleate condition and seasonal variation in *Acacia nilotica* (Iqbal 1979), *Eucalyptus maculata* (Khan 1980), *Delonix regia*, *Mimusops elengi*, and *Polyalthia longifolia* (Hashmi 1977). In multinucleate cells, different nuclei may assume different shapes. In *Psidium guajava*, some degenerating nuclei elongate to become spindle-shaped and produce tail-like appendices at one or both ends. Degeneration starts from these apices, and leads to a complete disappearance of the whole nuclear body. These phenomena show no correlation with season (Ghouse and Khan 1977). In *Tectona grandis*, there may be 2–5 nuclei per fusiform cell, each nucleus with 1–2 nucleoli (Dave and Rao 1981). The number of nuclei per cell may go up to ten in *Terminalia crenulata* (Venugopal and Krishnamurthy 1989). Several other hardwood species like *Bauhinia parviflora*, *Bombax ceiba*, *Cassia fistula*, *Ficus rumphi*, and *Parkia javanica* are also reported to have polynucleate initials.

The hypothesis of multinucleate cambial cells needs further evidence, however. Reports founded solely upon ∿10–12 μm thick tangential sections are not sufficient to establish the claim, because such sections must contain several layers of "exactly superimposed" radially flattened cells (Bailey 1920b); if they do, a radial tier of 2–6 uninucleate cells may appear in tangential view as single cell with 2–6 nuclei (Catesson 1990). Conversely, with the radial width of the cambial cells in view, a 10 μm thick tangential section may contain at the most 3 cell layers and therefore, even if all over-lapping cells are in mitosis simultaneously and if all daughter nuclei are visible in the same focus, the total number of nuclei should not exceed 6. Thus, when more than 6 nuclei per cell are recorded (e.g. up to 8 nuclei in *Acacia nilotica* and *Gmelina arborea*, up to 10 nuclei in *Terminalia crenulata*), the situation deserves serious consideration. Moreover, tangential sections of the same thickness do not exhibit multinucleate fusiform initials in all species. Even all fusiform cells in a single section may not necessarily be multinucleate. In fact, only a limited portion of the cambial cell popula-tion shows polynucleation in the above-cited species. In *Psidium guajava*, for instance, at least 12–40% of fusiform initials remain uninucleate throughout the year (see Table 9.1).

Table 9.1. Percentage of fusiform initials of *Psidium guajava* L. with varying number of nuclei in the different months of a year.

Month	Percentage of fusiform cambial initials[a]				
	1-Nucleate	2-Nucleate	3-Nucleate	4-Nucleate	5-Nucleate
January	16	36	32	12	4
February	32	36	28	4	—
March	36	32	28	4	—
April	28	52	20	—	—
May	36	44	12	8	—
June	32	48	12	8	—
July	36	32	24	8	—
August	40	36	20	4	—
September	36	34	26	4	—
October	36	44	20	—	—
November	12	20	40	20	8
December	12	24	48	12	4

[a] Based on observations in 1000 initials obtained from five trees, 20 years old (from Ghouse and Khan 1977).

The origin and development of polynucleate cambial cells from precursor tissue (procambium, precambium, or parenchyma), causes of resistance to wall formation after karyokinesis, variation in the frequency of polynucleate cells with age and season, changes in the nucleocytoplasm ratio and in the shape and size of nuclei and nucleoli, and the mode of mitoses of cambial cells require special attention. Attempts to macerate cambial cells have not proved helpful because the distortion of protoplasts that occurs during maceration obscures the identity of the nuclei. With differentiation of procambial cells into fusiform cambial initials, the spherical nuclei become oval/elongated; their length can extend up to 82 μm, as in 60-year-old *Pinus strobus* (Bailey 1920b). The length of nuclei tends to increase with the length of the initial, but the ratio between nuclear size and cell size decreases. The nucleus of ray cells is almost globular and is sometimes flattened or radially elongated as in *Abies balsamea* (Timell 1979). The size and chromaticity of nuclei also vary with the season, according to periods of quiescence and activity. The nuclei are usually smaller in size and denser in chromaticity in the dormant cambium than during cambial reactivation (see Iqbal and Ghouse 1985a).

Estimation of nuclear volume (N) in relation to cellular (C) and cytoplasmic (Cp) volumes in one-year-old *Acer* and *Pinus* plants yields values for N/C of 0.6% and 1% for fusiform cells and 2.5% and 5.8% for ray initials, respectively. The value was 50 to 100 times higher for primary meristematic cells of several species (see Table 10 of Catesson 1990). Differences between ray initials and primary meristematic cells are markedly reduced in the N/Cp ratio. Earlier conclusions (Bailey 1920b) that variations in nuclear size are not related to corresponding variations in chromosomal size and number suggest the need for critically investigating the possibility of endoduplication and sequence amplification to clarify whether the nuclei of resting initials are blocked in the G1 phase of the cycle.

Generally, the nucleus of fusiform initials is elongate and has several nucleoli, whereas that of the ray cell initial is somewhat spherical and has relatively few nucleoli. Blockage of the nuclear cycle at the G1 stage has been demonstrated in shoot apices of many trees, such as *Fraxinus excelsior* (Cottignies 1979) and *Pseudotsuga menziesii* (Owens and Molder 1973). This finding was supported by experiments with the quiescent cambium of *Abies balsamea*. The blockage may be related to a change in the nuclear proteins (Riding and Little 1984). It is accompanied in dormant tissues by a reduction and sometimes a disappearance of the granular zone in the nucleolus. Moreover, RNA synthesis is reduced or ceases and DNA synthesis also ceases (see Catesson 1980; Berlyn 1982).

Several nucleoli (1 to 5) are generally present in the nucleus of a fusiform cell and one or two [rarely more, e.g. in *Abies balsamea*: Timell (1979)] in ray cells. Just before the onset of meristematic activity, nucleoli increase in volume. The nucleolus diameter decreases following the cessation of meristematic activity.

Nucleoli of the cambial nucleus are relatively large and complex and contain vacuoles filled with both amorphous and birefringent material. Contrary to Bailey's speculation, large nucleoli are not aggregates of smaller ones (Berlyn 1982). The presence of a nucleolar-like substance was detected even outside the nucleus in the egg cytoplasm of *Pinus lambertiana* (Berlyn 1982). The material was found to have come out through the nuclear membrane from the nucleolus lying within the nucleus along the nuclear membrane. In *Acer pseudoplatanus,* the large nucleoli of active cambial cells consist of an extensive granular zone interspersed in the fibrillar zone and some vacuoles, called *lacunae* by Catesson (1980). This nucleolar composition was taken by Lafontaine (1974) as typical of all meristematic, actively synthesizing cells. With the approach of dormancy, the granular zone of the nucleoli progressively decreased to a narrow peripheral band, surrounding a dense fibrillar core with a few small lacunae. At the advent of activity, the granular zone started to expand, thus rendering the nucleoli apparently less dense. This cycle conforms to one reported for other cells that showed alternate dormant and active phases (Cottignies 1977; Feldman and Torrey 1977; Satterfield et al. 1978). Whether the reduction of the granular zone is due to a complete cessation of RNA synthesis and whether the process is also accompanied by blockage of DNA synthesis are yet to be ascertained definitely.

In shoot apices, however, the cessation of DNA synthesis is also accompanied by a decrease (or cessation) of RNA synthesis and vise-versa (Cottignies 1977). Such seasonal variations are probably linked with parallel variations in the distribution and frequency of nuclear pores within nuclear envelope that are known to vary with nuclear activity (Harris 1986).

ACTIVATION AND GENERATIVE PATTERNS
OF THE CAMBIAL CELLS

Within limits set by the genome, the cambial meristem operates in the plant axis under the influence of internal physiological processes and external environmental factors. The cambium is dormant during times of stress, whether the stress is due to heat, cold, or drought. Activation of the cambial cells is a determinate process, involves several sequential events, and manifests in a variety of ways. The phenomenon of cambial generativity is periodic in most plants, and the sequence of production of the derivative tissues varies with the species.

Periodicity of Cambial Growth

Radial growth in most woody plants is, like apical growth, periodic rather than continuous. This periodicity is clearly correlated with changes in season, especially in temperate regions. In temperate species, the radial growth usually occurs in spring and summer; this is followed by a period of dormancy that extends to the following spring. Toward the Tropics, climatic periodicity becomes less acute, cambial dormancy less evident, and the number of ringless trees increases. In the Tropics, where environmental conditions are usually less limiting, the growth season tends to be longer than in temperate areas. Growth is not always continuous, however, even in ideal conditions. In the ideal and uniform growth conditions of Malaysia, only about 15% of the species exhibit a continuous radial growth (Koriba 1958). The growth rate may vary when growth is continuous. Since the climate in the Tropics is often regarded as nonseasonal, the intermittent growth in the tropical species is frequently ascribed to internal growth rhythms; however, Alvim (1964) emphasized the marked influence of environmental factors.

In Israel, woody plants exhibit three patterns of cambial periodicity (Fahn et al. 1981; Fahn and Werker 1990).

1. In Mediterranean plants, the annual rhythm is similar to that in temperate-zone plants. Cambial activity starts in the spring and ceases at the end of summer or the beginning of autumn. These plants produce more or less distinct growth rings.

2. In some desert shrubs, cambial activity starts with the rainy season (between November and December) and ceases at the beginning of the dry season (late April to early June). Some of these species possess growth rings.

3. In tropical and subtropical trees, the cambium is generally active throughout the year, but some species also form growth rings. The presence or absence of growth rings may vary even between the different specimens of the same species (Fahn et al. 1986).

These types of annual rhythm, at least in evergreens, are probably of a conservative nature; each group of plants with its specific rhythm is of a different geographic origin (Fahn 1959, 1962).

Proustia cuneifolia and *Acacia cavenia* growing under semi-arid conditions in Chile show different patterns of cambial activity. The cambium in *Proustia* remains dormant throughout the drought season and becomes active at the onset of the rainy season, as in the above Type 2 of desert plants. The behavior of *Acacia* corresponds to the above Type 3 of tropical and subtropical trees. Cambial activity decreases during the dry season, but some zones of the cambium remain active (Aljaro et al. 1972). The behavior of each tree might be related to the accessibility of underground water to the roots of each tree. Mediterranean trees can be of the following two types (Liphschitz and Lev-Yadun 1986): (a) the *temperate Mediterranean type,* in which the cambial activity takes place during spring and summer, corresponding to growing patterns in the temperate zone, where these plants probably originated; (b) the *adapted Mediterranean type,* in which cambial activity coincides with the climatic rhythm, beginning in autumn when the temperature drops and the rainy season starts, and lasting until early summer when drought stresses and high temperatures prevail.

Presumably, cambial activity in species transferred from one habitat to another is determined by the species' genetic traits developed in the original habitat and by the degree of the specimen's adaptability to conditions in the new habitat. The vigor of the individual specimen may also be a factor (Oppenheimer 1945). The cambium of *Ceratonia siliqua,* possibly of tropical origin, remains active in Israel throughout the year (Liphschitz and Lev-Yadun 1986), though with a reduced rate of activity during winter (Arzee et al. 1977), and therefore shows growth rings that vary from faint to distinct (Fahn et al. 1986). In *Eucalyptus camaldulensis,* a native to Australia, wood formation starts in Israel toward the end of the dry summer, which corresponds to the spring of Australia (Fahn 1982). In maquis trees of Israel, cambial activity begins in the branches and stems of deciduous trees 2 to 6 weeks after bud expansion. In evergreen species, the cambium reactivates in all organs simultaneously with leaf bud expansion. The different behavior of the deciduous and evergreen trees under semi-arid conditions might depend on the storage of different amounts of food reserves and growth substances. During the long dry season, the deciduous trees cannot store reserve materials sufficient for leaf development and a concurrent start of cambial activity, whereas the quantities of reserve materials stored in evergreen trees might suffice for the simultaneous start of the two processes (see Fahn and Werker 1990).

In many Indian trees, cambial activity commences sometimes in June or July and lasts until October or November (cf. Chowdhury 1968; Paliwal and Prasad 1970; Paliwal et al. 1975, 1976; Ghouse and Hashmi 1978; Iqbal and Ghouse 1982). It may be inferred from the data obtained that the growth period in the Tropics is relatively longer, if not continuous throughout the year, than in temperate regions, where it hardly exceeds 4–5 months. Chowdhury (1940, 1968, 1969) identified certain species, such as *Cedrella toona,* with a span of radial growth as long as 10 months. The cambium of tropical trees remains active for a major part of the year and, in some cases, for the whole year (see Fahn and Sarnat 1963; Lawton 1972; Rao 1970; Chou and Chiang 1973; Lu and Chiang 1975; Yunus 1976; Khan 1977; Iqbal 1979). Paliwal and Prasad (1970), Paliwal et al (1975), and Siddiqi (1991) however, showed that the growth periods of *Dalbergia sissoo, Polyalthia longifolia,* and *Ficus religiosa* are as short as in the temperate species.

In temperate regions, the annual radial growth, which usually begins in April/May and ceases around August/September, typically displays a sigmoid growth curve with a rapid increase in activity in the beginning, followed by a period of constancy, and then a gradual decline. Daubenmire and Deters (1947) suggested that the cambium shows the maximum activity in the early part of the growth period in evergreen conifers and in the later part in deciduous dicotyledons.

Cambial Reactivation vs. Phenological Events

That a relationship exists between bud break and cambial reactivation has long been suggested. Priestley (1930) was the first to suggest that cambial activity in conifers and dicots normally starts at the base of apical buds. Extension growth normally precedes radial growth by 2–12 weeks in the broad-leaved trees of India (Chowdhury 1958, 1968). A close association between cambial activity and new leaf formation was recorded in many forest trees of the tropical and subtropical belts (see Iqbal and Ghouse 1985a; Iqbal 1990; Paliwal and Paliwal 1990).

Interestingly, the cambium reactivates twice a year following two intervening periods of rest in *Psidium guajava* (Khan 1977), an Indian fruit tree that peculiarly flowers and fruits twice a year. Extension growth precedes radial growth in guava trees cultivated at Aligarh in northern India (Khan 1977). Earlier, the same species growing in China was reported to undergo a single active period, though the activity declined once during the active span; the activity began before bud burst (Chou and Chiang 1973). The discrepancy could have resulted from Chou and Chiang having obtained sections from young branches whereas Khan sampled sections from the main trunk. In some species, such as *Prosopis spicigera* (Iqbal and Ghouse 1982) and *Streblus asper* (Ajmal and Iqbal 1987a), leaf emergence and subsequent cambial reactivation are separated by a gap of several weeks, perhaps because flowering starts immediately after bud burst, and the small amounts of growth hormones produced by young leaves might be consumed, in the beginning, by the developing flowers and only become sufficiently available to the lateral meristem after a considerable lapse of time.

The connection between buds and cell division initiation is not always obligate in conifers; the cambium may become active even when buds have been removed before commencement of extension growth (Whitmore and Zahner 1966). Most workers agree, however, that auxins produced in the reactivated buds stimulate cambial division. Cambial activity was restored in certain species cultivated *in vitro* when exposed to temperatures of about 25°C (Wort 1962). Auxin reserves might be present in tissues adjacent to the cambium and be liberated by the rise of temperature, thus accounting for cambial reactivation in the absence of buds (Philipson et al. 1971).

Initiation of cambial activity in relation to bud breaks is not identical for all plant types. As reported by Ladefoged (1952), the cambium becomes active in diffuse-porous species up to a week before bud break. In ring-porous species, activity starts 1–9 days before and, in conifers, 5–15 days before bud break. In tropical trees, on the other hand, cambial growth generally commences after bud emergence (Alvim 1964; Reinders-Gouwentak 1965). Chowdhury and Tandon (1950) found that cell division in the cambium of *Michelia* (a diffuse-porous species) and *Melia* (a semi-ring-porous species), both growing in India, starts well after the cessation of the first two flushes of terminal growth. In the semi-arid Israeli maquis, the cambium of dicotyledonous trees was not active until 4–6 weeks after bud break, probably because of a shortage of stored food at the beginning of terminal growth (Fahn 1953, 1955).

The phenomenon of reactivation of the cambium is reminiscent of events that characterize the development of the seedling bud, because promordia are reactivated first, thus causing activation of the basipetal components of the associated vascular traces later. For instance, mitosis in *Fraxinus* sets in first in the leaf primordia and later in the procambial and cambial cells at the bud base (Tepper and Hollis 1967). Enzymatic activity starts in the primordia and procambial strands of *Pseudotsuga* some two weeks before bud swelling. In fact, the primordial growth causes bud swelling, and this growth activity begins some two months prior to bud burst (Owens 1968). Events of cambial growth, confluent with the stages of bud and shoot development, also seem to be correlated to the endogenous rhythms of growth-regulating substances. Growth inhibitors accumulate gradually in bud and cambial tissue with the approach of dormancy in both gymnosperms and angiosperms (Jenkins and Shepherd 1972; Michniewicz and Galoch 1972; During and Alleweldt 1973; Davison and Young 1974) and growth promoters remain at low levels (Shepherd and Rowan 1967; Alden 1971; Sládky 1972). The level of growth inhibitors declines whereas that of growth promoters rises prior to bud break (see Larson 1976b).

The ontogenetic sequence of primordial and procambial development is basically identical in both gymnosperms and angiosperms. The differences appear mainly with reference to the mode of cambial reactivation and pertain more to how the renewed cambial activity is manifested than to the underlying processes. Cambial reactivation advances rapidly down the stems of ring-porous and much more slowly down those of diffuse-porous angiosperms (Reinders-Gouwentak 1965). A single vessel may extend from the apical shoot to ground level in ring-porous species whereas vessels are markedly shorter and of determinate length in diffuse-porous species (Greenidge 1952). The differential rate of progress of cambial activity is ascribed either (a) to an auxin precursor present in the cambium of ring-porous species (Digby and Wareing 1966) or (b) to overwintering in an immature state of the first few cells nearest the ring boundary that differentiate into the first early-wood vessels in ring-porous species (Imagawa and Ishida 1972). The mode of cambial reactivation in gymnosperms is similar to that in diffuse-porous dicotyledons. The fiber matrix in hardwood and the tracheid matrix in softwood may be considered the major products of the cambial meristem that accumulate under the influence of all leaves with no one leaf predominating (Larson 1976b).

The fiber matrix is superimposed by a vessel-forming stimulus arising from the base of each leaf and progressing downward. Normally, mature leaves of angiosperms cause neither vessel formation (Elliott 1933) nor the bulk production of auxin (Eliasson 1969). Likewise, in gymnosperms, the developing needles produce a stimulus that advances basipetally and induces differentiation of the cambial derivatives below into the early-wood tracheids, which are presumably functionally analogous to the vessels in angiosperms. Mature needles, on the other hand, neither add new tracheids to their traces (see Elliott 1933) nor synthesize auxin (Egierszdorff and Tomaszewski 1973); hence, in the absence of the early-wood-forming stimulus, late-wood tracheids are usually produced when needle elongation has stopped (see Larson 1976b). This shows that, although totipotent in in vitro culture, the cambial tissue depends for its in vivo growth requirements on the other plant parts, especially the leaves. Although the cambium may use the supplementary auxin produced by cell autolysis within the zone of differentiation of the cambium derivatives, it always requires auxin from the leaves for the maintenance of its regulatory processes (Sheldrake 1973; Larson 1976b).

Larson (1976b) emphasized that although the vessel-forming stimulus in angiosperms is thought to be derived from developing leaves, mature leaves provide almost all the photosynthates required to maintain the fiber matrix of wood. Similarly, in gymnosperms, the early-wood-forming stimulus is produced by elongating needles; mature needles provide the photosynthates needed to maintain the tracheid matrix. Thus a decline in shoot and needle growth and a shift toward needle maturity tend to enhance formation of thick-walled, late-wood tracheids. Therefore, the greater the number of leaves and the faster the rate of leaf emergence, the greater the abundance of vessels in the stem wood. On the contrary, the longer mature leaves are retained on the stem in functional form, the greater the production of fibers. Similar correlations must occur between elongating needles and early wood development and between the maintenance of mature leaves on stem and the amount of late wood in conifers. Larson

(1976b) suggests that the several variables that contribute to the fiber : vessel ratio in hardwoods and the early-wood : late-wood ratio in softwoods are under genetic control and can be improved.

Onset and Advance of Cambial Activity

The initiation of periclinal division of cambial initials in the spring is usually preceded by cell swelling, i.e. conversion of the shrunken and flattened cells with dense cytoplasm into radially expanded, turgid cells containing a lighter, less dense cytoplasm. This swelling is accompanied by enlargement of nuclei and thinning of the radial walls. Cell expansion may be sizeable, as in *Dalbergia sissoo* (Yunus 1976), *Delonix regia*, and *Mimusops elengi* (Hashmi 1977), *Polyalthia longifolia* (Ghouse and Hashmi 1979) and *Prosopis spicigera* (Iqbal and Ghouse 1982), or meager as in *Pyrus communis* and *P. malus* (Evert 1960, 1963), *Robinia pseudoacacia* (Derr and Evert 1967), and *Populus tremuloides* (Davis and Evert 1968).

Swelling usually begins at the base of emerging buds (Ladefoged 1952) and spreads basipetally down the branches and trunk. Spreading is relatively slow in diffuse-porous dicots, usually taking several weeks to reach the basal part of the trunk. It is rapid, and usually too rapid to detect a time lapse, in ring-porous dicots (Wareing 1958a; Wilcox 1962). Tepper and Hollis (1967), however, found it quite slow, moving at a maximum of 6 cm a day, in two-year-old *Fraxinus* seedlings. Spread in conifers is of an intermidiate duration, and usually takes about a week (Wilcox 1962). Cessation of the activity follows approximately the same order as the initiation (Fraser 1962). Thinning of the radial walls during the cambial reactivation may render the walls weak and easily breakable so that the bark is readily separable from the wood—a phenomenon known as slipping or peeling of the bark. The slipping occurs through the cambial zone before differentiation of the cambial derivatives sets in (Priestley 1930) or, at a later stage, through the differentiating xylem in the region where cells have expanded but are still thin-walled (Bailey 1943; Evert 1960, 1963).

Swelling of the cambium is followed closely by the onset of periclinal division that leads to accumulation of the secondary tissues. Once initiated, the division continues for some months. It may take as little as only 4–6 weeks or as long as 6 months for temperate hardwoods (Philipson et al. 1971). The growth period tends to shorten in higher latitudes and lengthen toward the Equator, and is generally longer in conifers than in dicotyledons (Studhalter et al. 1963). Periclinal division begins later, reaches the highest frequency later, but stops earlier in ray cells than in fusiform cells (Evert 1963; Catesson 1964). Most anticlinal divisions in cambial initials of mature stems occur toward the end of the growth season (Bannan 1952, 1955, 1960, 1964; Evert 1961, 1963). In vigorously growing young shoots, in which the rate of periclinal division is comparatively high, anticlinal division may prevail throughout the tenure of the radial growth (Bannan 1950, 1960; Catesson 1964; Cumbie 1967; Derr and Evert 1967).

The phenomenon of cambial activiation advances basipetally down the stem but acropetally in the current-year shoot because radial growth occurs only in regions where primary tissue elements have ceased to elongate. In diffuse-porous species, the process is so slow that the tree is usually in full foliage before cell division spreads over the cambial cylinder, whereas in ring-porous species, the whole cambium is usually dividing when buds are still in expansion stage. Wareing (1951b), Digby and Wareing (1966), and several others have suggested that this quick action in ring-porous species may be ascribed to a hormone precursor in the cambium or cortical tissues before bud-break that, upon bud emergence, is converted into auxin at all levels of tree axis almost simultaneously. Nonbasipetal spread of cambial activity may occur due to such a precursor, liberated by high temperature (Wort 1962).

Small amounts of auxin are also produced in the mature leaves of some species and the stimulus for cambial activation might come from this auxin when continued activity of the cambium is not precluded by bud removal (See Wareing 1951a, 1956, 1958a; Wareing and Roberts 1956; Wareing and Black 1958; Digby and Wareing 1966). Auxin production in mature leaves, after the cessation of terminal growth, is comparatively more pronounced in ring-porous than in diffuse-porous species and hence certain ring-porous as well as coniferous species continue with cambial growth after terminal growth has stopped (Digby and Wareing 1966). Defoliation usually causes a reduction in radial growth (Glock 1955; Mott et al 1957; Studhalter et al 1963) owing to reduced carbohydrate and auxin production. Nevertheless, cambial activity after defoliation may increase, at least temporarily, due to a reduction in competition with buds and leaves for water. Auxin is also produced by the developing reproductive structures and, if other factors are not limiting, this may stimulate cambial activity. Such activity, evident in the woody species that flower before leaf emergence, is normally restricted to flowering shoots if amounts of auxin are meager.

Flower initiation stimulates the cambium of the flowering shoots to accumulate secondary tissues more rapidly than the cambium of the vegetative shoots (See Reinders-Gouwentak 1965). Once the ultimate diameter of flowering shoots has been attained, the cambium turns inactive and therefore cambial activity generally declines during flowering (See Philipson et al. 1971). Fruiting in orchard trees and heavy seeding in forest trees considerably lower cambial activity (Antevs 1925; Glock 1955; Huber and Jazewitsch 1956; Mott et al. 1957).

Cambial behavior seems to be dependent primarily on carbohydrate rather than on auxin levels. Fruit formation in apple trees requires some 35% of the total carbohydrate (Heinicke 1937), equivalent to the amount utilized in the production of structural tissues. A biennial fluctuation in cambial growth that may occur corresponds to declines in fruit production in apple, mango, and pear trees. Such variations seem to result from competition for carbohydrates. Further, ample evidence shows that translocatable carbohydrates are needed for the downward movement of growth hormones (Kozlowski 1962). Siebers and Ladage (1973) suggest that sugar rather than auxin is the most important factor for the onset of cambial growth; since the application of growth substances stimulates movement of assimilates toward the site of application (Seth and Wareing 1964; Zaerr and Mitchell 1967; Jeffcoat and Harris 1972), the phytohormones applied in decapitation experiments probably increase sugar concentration, which, in turn, accounts for the observed induction of the cambial development.

The work of Reinders-Gouwentak and colleagues revealed that a factor is needed to break the winter rest period in addition to auxin (Reinders-Gouwentak and Mass 1940; Reinder-Gouwentak 1941). Possibly, either the inhibitory substances accumulated during the previous growing season are to be removed during the rest period before auxin can exert its effect, or certain amounts of other growth substances are needed to render the auxin effective. Wareing (1958b) and Wareing et al (1964) demonstrated the interactive role of IAA with gibberellic acid (GA) in cambial reactivation and xylogenesis. The transport of signals from the developing buds downward can be understood on the basis of the polar properties of the tissues involved in auxin transport (Sachs 1969, 1981). Lachaud (1983) suggested that the resumption of the tissues' ability to polarize auxin transport in the phase of preactivation of the cambium depends on the presence of buds. Plants disbudded one month before tritiate IAA application lost their ability to activate auxin transport.

A number of intrinsic as well as extrinsic factors influence the intensity of initiation and the cessation of cambial activity. Long days and warm, humid atmosphere favor the process. In many tropical trees, the commencement of cambial activity and increased summer temperature are closely correlated (Paliwal et al. 1975; Ghouse and Hashmi 1978, 1979; Ajmal and Iqbal 1987a,b; Siddiqi 1991). The cambium could reactivate merely at a moderately high temperature; however, a high temperature and a heavy rainfall accelerate the rate of cambial cell division. Once begun, cambial activity persists even at relatively low temperatures (see Ghouse and Hashmi 1979; Iqbal and Ghouse 1982). High temperature and high humidity can induce cambial reactivation even in short-day conditions (Paliwal and Prasad 1970; Paliwal et al. 1975). A correlation between cambial activity and an external factor does not necessarily indicate a simple and direct relation between the two; however, if the factor becomes limiting, a change in the factor causes a direct response in cambium acitivy (Munting and Willemse 1987). Details of the environmental influence on cambial behavior can be gathered from Iqbal (1990), Chapters 6 and 7.

Cambial Mitosis: Planning and Discipline

The vascular cambium functions and organizes its activity so as to achieve two purposes: production of the secondary vascular tissues, and its own survival (Figure 9.1). Although, like the apical meristems, the cambium survives and operates for the entire lifetime of the plant (sometimes several thousands of years), unlike the apical meristems it is irreplaceable. It is provided with no alternative provision equivalent to the axillary buds that take up the task of the main apical meristem if the latter is damaged. Given this, cambial activity must be very efficient and precise so as to avoid the risk inherent in DNA replication. Limited cell division in the cambium is sufficient

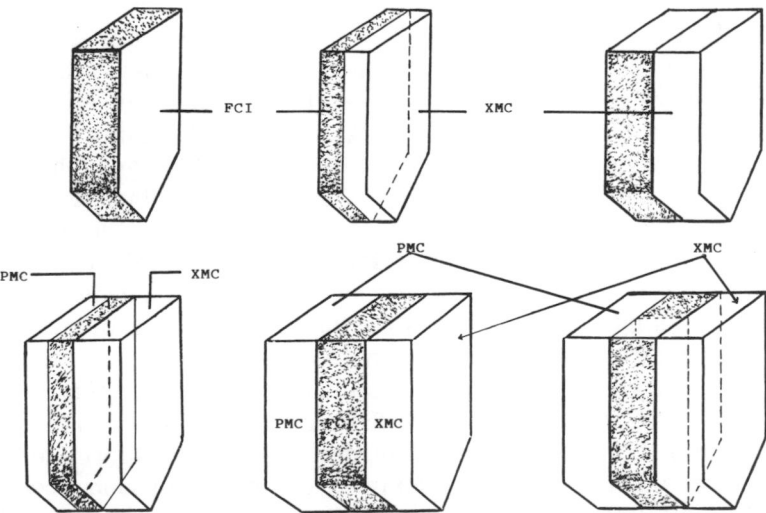

Figure 9.1. Division of fusiform cambial initial (only basal half of the cell is shown): The fusiform cambial initial (FCI) divides periclinally; of the daughter cells, the inner one acts as xylem mother cell (XMC), while the outer one continues to be a cambial initial. By further periclinal division, the same initial cuts the phloem mother cell (PMC) on the outer side. Thus, successive periclinal divisions of the initial result in several layers of xylem mother cells and phloem mother cells inside and outside the cambial initial, respectively. The initial divides anticlinally to add to its own population as the diameter of the cambial cylinder increases.

to provide new cells to the regions of the xylem mother cells and the the phloem mother cells. Further division of these newly derived cells may then result in large numbers of cells for the secondary vascular tissues. DNA copy errors and other somatic mutations in these regions of tissue mother cells are not critical, because each cell would produce a limited number of derivatives in its short lifespan. It would later differentiate and form part of the mature vascular tissue (see Mauseth 1988). Klekowski (1988) suggests that the vascular cambium must be similar to the apical meristem in that it is a step meristem with an "archival" source of genetically sound cells that slowly provides cells to regions of rapid but limited division.

In contrast, cambial initials, particularly of long-lived angiosperms, may have to divide hundreds or thousands of times in order to contribute cells to the secondary xylem and/or secondary phloem (Sachs 1981). These cells, characterized by high levels of mitotic activity, should be prone to genetic damage due to the high frequency with which external agents are available during the S and M phases of the cell cycle (Gahan 1989). An autoradiographic study of incorportaion of 3HO thymidine into nuclei of cambial initials in the stem of Lycopersicon esculentum identified subpopulations of cambial cells with varying rates of turnover (Gahan 1989). It was noted that the true initials have an exceedingly low rate of turnover and that they create a population of daughter cells that are readily identifiable, rapidly dividing cambial cells. The labeling pattern that appears substantiates the notions that (a) "cambial initials" divide at a slow rate and (b) a second group of cambial cells divide more frequently and produce cells that form phloem and xylem elements. The slowly dividing cells later cease being cambial initials and become fast-dividing cells and thus are lost from the pool of cambial initial cells. This finding may partly expain the difficulty of identifying cambial initials in many dicots and the ability of these initials to produce many daughter cells with little apparent genetic damage (Rana and Gahan 1983; Gahan 1989).

Three major functions are served by cambial cells: (a) production of derivatives on the inner and outer sides of the cambial cylinder, (b) production of new initials to keep the consistently growing cambial cylinder intact, and (c) maintenance of the specific mutual balance between the two types of cambial initial. The efficient meristem achieves these targets by additive (periclinal), multiplicative (anticlinal), and transformative (anticlinal) division, respectively (for details see Iqbal and Ghouse 1990).

The additive or periclinal division in which a new partition wall is laid down tangentially (normal to the radius of plant axis) is not confined to the "initials". Derivatives generally divide at a much greater rate than the fusiform initials. Each derivative may divide to produce up to 20 cells on the xylem side, but such divisions are fewer on the phloem side. This difference accounts for the larger amount of xylem and lower amount of phloem produced annually (Wilson 1964).

During the most active growth, the cambial initials in conifers were noted to divide only once every four to six days (Bannan 1962); The cell cycle in apical meristems was completed within 8–18 hr. The derivative of a fusiform initial may start dividing even before the mother cell has completed cytokinesis; such a cell would contain four nuclei and three phragmoplasts. Mauseth (1988) suggests that this may happen in the xylem mother cells, where division rate is greater, rather than in the cambial initials. The cell-division cycle took a total time of ten days in Pinus strobus (Wilson 1964); cell division proper took a little more than a day, including 5.3 hr for mitosis and 19.5 hr for the movement of phragmoplasts from daughter nuclei to cell tips. The average cell length is 1.1 to 1.7 mm in this species, and the rate of pharagmoplast movement is around 50 to 100 μm per hour. If a similar rate is assumed for all species in general, the time required for cell plate formation would vary from less than one hr (for the shortest fusiform cell) to about four days (for the longest cell). A total time of seven days was estimated for the cell-division cycle in *Thuja* (Bannan 1955) and two to three days for that in *Acer pseudoplatanus* (Catesson 1964, 1990).

Information about mitotic distribution across the cambial zone is scanty. Division occurs throughout the cambium but its frequency varies along the radius of the cambial zone. Further, it was suggested for *Pinus strobus* that the mitotic frequency differs among the radial files of the cambial cells and that most xylem mother cells redivide at least thrice (Wilson and Howard 1968).

In multiplicative or anticlinal division, a partition wall develops parallel to the radius of the axis, either longitudinally (in storied cambium) or pseudotransversely (in nonstoried cambium). The frequency of anticlinal division varies according to genetic as well as environmental influences. The rate of division tends to be higher in young and fast-growing shoots than in old, slow-growing stems. Also, the radial pressure exerted upon the concave arcs of the cambium in the fluted stem tends to enhance the frequency of division (Bannan 1957). A high frequency of anticlinal division yields many more fusiform initials than are actually required to keep pace with the increase in circumference of the cambial cylinder from the addition of new xylem inside the cambium. The extra initials are subsequently lost; they move out of the cambial zone and differentiate (Bannan 1950, 1951a,b, 1960; Whalley 1950; Evert 1961), although these are initials and not derivatives produced by periclinal division. In *Chamae-cyparis*, after 1100 multiplicative divisions, only 162 initials were retained in the cambial layer (Bannan 1950, 1960). The amount of circumferential growth necessary with each increase in radius is geometrically determined; less circumferential growth (low frequency of anticlinal division) is required for axes with larger radii than for those with small radii (Figure 9.2).

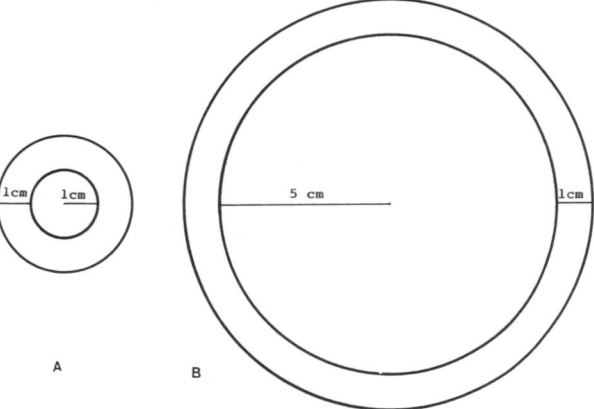

Figure 9.2.   Since circumference is $2\pi r$ (where r denotes radius), the cambium around a small twig (A) with 1 cm radius of wood core would have a circumference of 6.28 cm. For 1 cm increase in the wood radius, the cambial circumference would become $2\pi(1+1)$ = 12.57 cm. The difference being 6.29 cm, incremental circumferential growth is only 6.29/6.28 = 1, i.e. as much as was the original circumference. In a thicker axis (B) of 5 cm wood radius, the cambial circumference measures $2\pi 5$ = 31.43 cm; with 1 cm increase in the radius here, the cambial circumference would become $2\pi(5+1)$ = 37.71 cm. The difference being 6.28 cm, incremental circumferential growth here is 6.28/31.43 = 0.2, i.e. only one-fifth of the original circumference. Likewise, 1 cm radial increase to an axis of 10 cm wood radius would cause the circumference to grow by only one-tenth of the original circumference. This shows that if, for instance, A number of initials of the cambial circumference divide anticlinally to cope with the inner pressure exerted by one cm radial growth of wood in an axis of 1 cm initial wood-core radius, only 1/5th and 1/10th of A number of the cambial initials are required to divide anticlinally to withstand 1 cm radial growth in axes with 5 cm wood radius and 10 cm wood radius, respectively.

Mauseth (1988) has suggested that the excess of anticlinal division may be a mechanism that "purifies" the cambium. He further suggests:

> If a detrimental somatic mutation occurred that interfered with division, expansion, or differentiation, either in the fusiform initials or in one of the recently formed xylem mother cells, it might cause that row to expand radially less rapidly than neighboring rows; and the fusiform initials would be left behind as the rest of the cambium was pushed outward at the normal rate. If the mutation occurred in a phloem mother cell, then that row in the phloem would not expand so rapidly as the ones around it, and the whole row would be carried outward due to contact with the adjacent phloem. Being unable to expand with normal speed, the fusiform initials would again be pulled out of the cambium. Only those fusiform initials and derivatives that develop at maximum speed can remain in the cambium.

This hypothesis does not seem to explain the process of loss of extra fusiform initials, however. In fact, the initial to be lost is reduced in size through successive asymmetric periclinal divisions, thereby producing daughter cells of unequal length, the shorter one behaving as a functional initial. This cell eventually ceases to divide periclinally and is lost from the cambium; it differentiates as an anomalous phloem or xylem element and is carried into the mature vascular tissue. The gradually shortening initial is called a *declining initial*, and the row of derivatives produced by it is a *declining tier* (Srivastava 1963). The declining cells sometimes transform into ray initials after sufficient reduction and, often, segmentation (Philipson et al. 1971).

Normally, the cells that decline have poor contact with rays. Bannan and Bayly ((1956) observed that surviving cells had contact with 70% more ray initials than those that did not survive. Even shorter cells could survive if they have sufficient ray contacts, and the longer ones fail if devoid of good ray contact (Gregory and Romberger 1975). In *Pinus contorta*, however, fusiform cells without any ray contact could elongate (Savidge and Farrar 1984).

The formation of composite conduits involving a large number of component cells placed end on, such as vessels and sieve tubes in angiosperms, also deserves special attention. How the different cells in a vertical file are coordinated and are eventually adjusted to form a continuous tube requires further investigation. Derr and Evert (1967) observed that multiplicative divisions are synchronized within a vertical file of the cambial zone in *Robinia pseudoacacia*, a dicot species. Conversely, because vessel-element initials usually broaden greatly during differentiation (Zasada and Zahner 1969, among others), a precise positioning may not be needed at the initial stage and readjustments may occur during differentiation.

The transformative division, which results in the addition of new ray initials, is accomplished by transverse or anticlinal development of partition walls in the fusiform cells. New groups of ray initials derived from fusiform initials enter a cycle of development in which they increase in size and eventually are split into smaller units that may re-expand. A single ray cell may cut at the end or from the side of a fusiform initial; a declining fusiform cell may reduce to a ray cell; or a fusiform initial, partly or wholly, may become segmented by transverse partition walls and form tiers of ray initials (Barghoorn 1940a, b, Whalley 1950; Bannan 1951a; Braun 1955; Cheadle and Esau 1964). Several different methods of ray cell development can occur within a species (Ghouse and Hashmi 1980; Iqbal and Ghouse 1985a,b, 1987). When a fusiform initial next to an existing group of ray initials converts, it makes the group wider or gives it a uniseriate wing (see Iqbal and Ghouse 1985b, 1987). Because multiplicative division of a fusiform initial produces a common wall that is devoid of ray contact, and because successive division would form several such cells with no ray contacts, periodic conversion of fusiform initials into ray initials is indispensable to maintain a balanced horizontal conduction through the wood, cambium, and bark. In dicots, where multiseriate rays are quite common, ray initials may elongate and convert into fusiform initials. This conversion prevents rays from becoming too massive and creating large islands of weak parenchyma in the wood and bark (Ghouse and Iqbal 1977a, Ghouse and Hashmi 1980; Iqbal and Ghouse 1985b, 1987; Ajmal and Iqbal 1992). Ray-cell elongation mostly occurs in the central part of multiseriate rays. This process occurs in addition to splitting of rays by intrusive growth of a fusiform initial from the periphery of the ray into the mass of its component cells—a method common to both conifers and dicotyledons (detail in Philipson et al. 1971; Iqbal and Ghouse 1990).

Bünning (1956) concludes that the tangential spacing of rays is determined by the mutually inhibitory effects of the ray initials. On the contrary, Carmi et al. (1972) postulate that ray development is not necessarily dependent on the distance between them but is related to the rate of the radial growth; rays differentiate along channels of a stimulus that moves between phloem and xylem. That the cambium of fast-growing Caribbean pines have more transformative division compared to other conifers in general has been confirmed by Anoruo (1988). Since the fusiform initials with poor ray contacts have a greater chance of being lost from the cambium through differentiation, the selective loss of initials may be a regulatory mechanism to maintain distance between rays (Carmi et al. 1972).

THE FATE OF THE CAMBIAL DERIVATIVES

After the phloem and xylem mother cells are cut off by the cambium, they differentiate in sequential and overlapping phases (Kozlowski 1971; Barnett 1981; Iqbal and Ghouse 1985a). Differentiation was considered by Wilson et al. (1966) to occur in three phases: (a) the phloem and xylem mother cells may divide further, (b) the cells that have ceased dividing usually enlarge in the radial direction (in the case of vessels, even in tangential direction), and (c) subsequently, phenomena such as secondary wall formation and lignification either continue or commence. The various phases of differentiation overlap. Laying down of secondary walls in the xylem cells, for instance, frequently begins before the growth of the primary wall ends. The expansion of cells often ceases by the time lignification starts, however. Complete differentiation of a derivative cell usually takes a few to several weeks from the time of its production. The duration varies with species and cell type; for a given type of cell, it varies with the time of cell production during the growing season.

The differentiating cells enlarge in varying patterns and by varying amounts. Elongation of differentiating tracheids and fibers is normally restricted to the tips or apical portions of the cell. The growing tips penetrate between the adjoining cells where the intercellular layer is not yet lignified (Wenham and Cusick 1975). Apical intrusive growth, common to fibers and tracheids, occurs with vessel elements and sieve-tube members also (cf. Liese and Parameswaran 1972; Ghouse and Yunus 1975; Khan 1977; Ghouse and Iqbal 1979). In sieve-tube members of *Dalbergia*, not only the apical tail-like protrusions form but sometimes the whole sieve plate is pushed forward due to subapical elongation, thus forming a neck-like structure near the end wall (Figure 9.3). Ray cells and axial parenchyma undergo little change during differentiation; drastic changes occur with the component cells of vessels and sieve tubes.

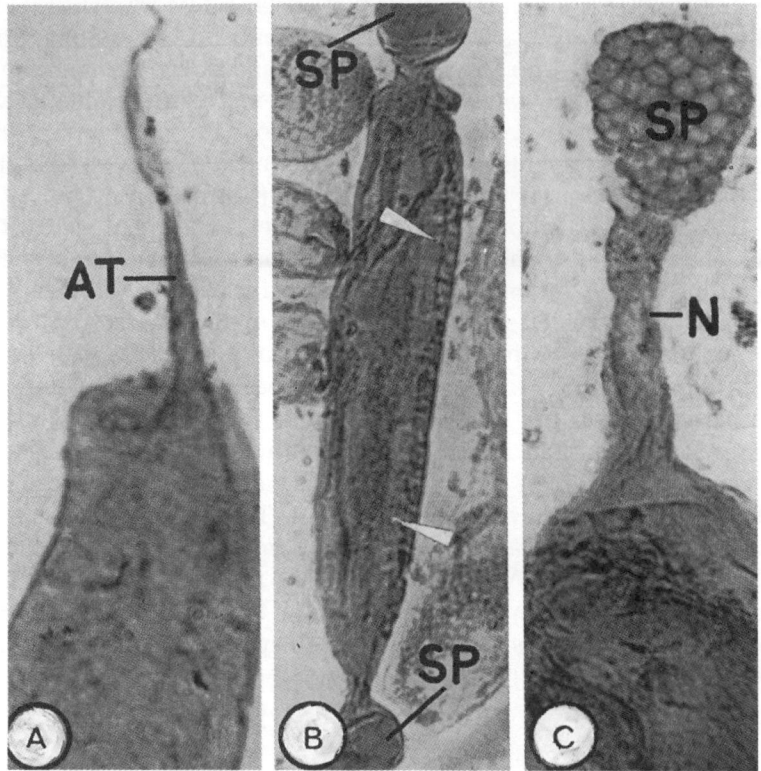

Figure 9.3. Macerated sieve-tube members of *Dalbergia* species showing apical extensions by intrusive growth on one or both cell tips. The extended tip may form apical tail (AT) or neck-like body (N) bearing the terminal sieve plate (SP); *white arrows* indicate the lateral sieve areas. A, C at × 1520, B at × 675. (from Ghouse and Yunus 1975).

Cambial Commitment for Producing Vasculature

Before examining the peculiarities of differentiation of secondary vascular tissues, let us discuss whether cambial derivatives are predetermined to be differentiated as phloem/xylem cells or whether they are forced to enter a defined course of differentiation by certain pre-existing factors. The development of multicellular eukaryotes is influenced by (a) genetic factors, which are normally set during meiosis and cause permanent changes in the genetic information available for expression; (b) epigenetic factors, which regulate the sequential and differential expression of genes during ontogeny and provide for a continuing developmental change in the eukaryote; (*epigenetics* refers to the orderly physical or chemical changes that occur to the structure of genetic information relative to the original capacity of the zygote for gene expression and that persist through replication and nuclear division); and (c) physiological factors, such as those altering enzyme activity, which are transient. These types of factors may act singly, in combination, or at cross-purposes to influence events such as cell division and cell differentiation (Savidge 1983a, 1985).

During embryogenesis, procambial and later cambial development occurs according to the genetic information that the zygote carries since its inception. The development of these meristems *per se* is not coded for in DNA, however. Rather, the genetic code contains the numerous subcellular events that comprise meristem development. Interestingly, these genes are neither randomly expressed nor expressed in total populations of apical cells (Esau 1965a; Larson 1982) but are expressed selectively in time and space. The vascular cambium may originate in the shoot apex from the layer of cells serving as pith progenitor as well as from that serving as cortex precursor (Dermen 1953). Thus, the commitment to vascular development is not ascribed to any particular cell layer in the shoot apex. Histocehmical esterase reactions were observed by Gahan (1981) in some apical cells of dicotyledons that later appeared anatomically as procambium. The procambium and cambium showed similar reactions. The procambial and cambial cells appeared to have become committed to development of the vascular tissues from the very beginning in response to auxins, cytokinins, and sucrose (Gahan 1981); however, whether these histochemical reactions provide evidence for *determination* or for *competence* of the vascular meristems remains unclear (Savidge 1985). *Determination* (or *commitment*) refers to the genome becoming restricted such that only a single differentiation pathway (for example, production of vascular tissues) can be followed (Bird et al. 1982; Wareing 1982), whereas *competence* refers to the capacity of a tissue to respond to an inductive stimulus by following a particular developmental pathway, different from one that it would follow in the absence of induction (Bird et at. 1982).

Small blocks that contained part of the cambial cylinder and the derivative tissues were surgically removed from hypocotyl of *Ricinus communis* and readjusted in their placcs with inverted polarity (keeping the xylem side outward and the phloem side toward the pith). The inverted portions of the cambium produced xylem on the bark side and phloem on the pith side (Siebers 1971a). Siebers concluded that the sites of initiation of cambium and the polarities of tissue differentiation from the cambium were determined in the embryonic shoot. In contrast, some studies with cultured callus showed that phloem formed positionally in association with an adjacent explant of mature phloem and xylem developed positionally in association with mature xylem (see Kühn 1971), thus demonstrating that the newly produced cells respond to factors that regulate the differentiation process in contiguous tissues. In other words, the cells are competent but not determined for any specific differentiation pathway.

In *Pinus contorta*, the vascular cambium disappeared in the absence of a continuing supply of the exogenons auxins (Savidge and Wareing 1981b; Savidge 1983b), thus suggesting a physiological rather than an epigenetic regulation of cambial structure (Savidge 1985). A threshold level of endogenous auxin is needed for the vascular cambium to develop in *Populus deltoides* (DeGroote and Larson 1984). Lachaud and Bonnemain (1984) proposed that cambial cells are specialized for the basipetal transport of auxin; the peculiar shapes of the fusiform initials may result from auxin-promoted polar extension and the stress-regulated planes of periclinal division (Hertel 1983; Lintilhac and Vesecky 1984).

That the *cambial derivatives* are competent but not determined for any specific differentiation pattern is also evident from the fact that they normally differentiate into a variety of elements of two different vascular tissues, asserts Savidge (1985). Because the cambial derivatives are expected to inherit, through mitosis, identical competence to their precursor *cambial initials*, the same deduction should apply to the cambial cells *per se*, and the latter must be competent to follow a variety of differentiation pathways (Savidge 1985). Similarly, the ability of the cortical or medullary cells in intact plants to be differentiated into tracheary elements also supports the assumption that differentiation occurs in response to induction by transported factors (Kučera 1978; Gahan 1981; Savidge and Wareing 1981b). By regulating the microclimate of tissue, it was possible to induce entire radial files of the cambial zone to differentiate as tracheids (Savidge and Wareing 1981a, Savidge 1983b).

Is Cell Division a Prelude to Differentiation?

In intact plants, elements of the vascular tissues differentiate from new cells that are continuously produced in the procambium or cambium by means of cell division. DNA synthesis often occurs during differentiation; this leads to endopolypoidy and to the multinucleate stages of the differentiating vascular elements. The association of vascular differentiation with DNA synthesis and cell division raises queries as to whether cell division prior to differentiation is a prelude to gene reprogramming and whether endoduplication of DNA is essential for controlling the differentiation process.

Because differentiating xylem cells are easily detectable by optical microscopy owing to their characteristic secondary wall features, and because they undergo an irreversible differentiation (the protoplast is destroyed in the final stage of maturation of the tracheary element), these cells provide a relatively good system for studying the relationship between gene action and cytodifferentiation in plants. The xylem cells derived from the vascular cambium differentiate in a particularly distinct lineage and pattern so that an entire series of developmental events can be traced along a cell line (Dodds 1981). Karyokinesis without any subsequent cytokinesis may occur during the course of fiber development, thus leading to a multinucleate condition (Kundu and Sen 1960; Pizzolato and Heimsch 1975). In some cases, cytoplasmic compartmentation occurs by formation of certain septa at the later stages of fiber development (Ghouse and Yunus 1975; Pizzolato and Heimsch 1975). Fiber initials in cultured hypocotyl segments of *Helianthus* require cytokinin at the stage of nuclear division for differentiation into fibers; more than one operating nucleus may be needed to ensure efficient control of bipolar intrusive growth of the long cell during fiber differentiation (Aloni 1982, 1987). Most evidence for and against cell division as a prelude to differentiation, however, has come from tracheary elements.

In the dividing cells, nuclei undergo certain sequential events: Mitosis (M) and DNA synthesis in preparation for the next mitosis (S) are the two main events. These events are separated by gaps in time; the gap preceding synthesis of DNA is known as G1 and the one preceding mitosis as G2. Thus a complete cell cycle comprises G1, S, G2, M (see Cooper 1979; Bryant and Francis 1985). Two types of animal cell cycles were identified by Holtzer (1970): (a) proliferative cell cycles, which result in daughter cells with the same genetic program as the original parent cell, and (b) quantal cell cycles, which yield daughter cells having different genetic programs. Dodds (1981) has suggested that in xylem cells, differentiation follows a "quantal" cell division in an appropriate inducing environment.

Whether cell division is a prerequisite for the onset of xylem cell differentiation has been examined in several experiments, usually with cultured explant systems. Induction of DNA synthesis and cell division caused by growth promoters such as cytokinin was followed by differentiation (Libbenga and Torrey 1973; Phillips and Torrey 1973; Shininger 1975; Bogers et al. 1976). Differentiation did not occur when DNA synthesis or cell division was checked by applying a DNA-synthesis inhibitor such as 5-fluorodeoxyuridine (FUdR) to explant cultures (Fosket 1968, 1970; Shininger 1975). Explants of the Jerusalem artichoke (*Helianthus tuberosus* L.) were cultured for

72 hr on a xylogenic medium in the continuous presence of tritiated (^{3}H) thymidine, a radioactive DNA precursor, so that any cell in the explant synthesizing DNA incorporated radioactive thymidine into the nucleus (Malawer and Phillips 1979). All the differentiating xylem cells analyzed by autoradiography were found to be labeled, thus showing that all cells differentiating as xylem cells had undergone at least one round of DNA synthesis. The invariably uninucleate and diploid condition in G1 of the cell cyle of these differentiating xylem cells also suggested that DNA synthesis must have been followed by mitosis and cytokinesis before the onset of differentiation (Malawer and Phillips 1979). These studies indicate that cell division must precede differentiation.

On the other hand, certain more recent studies have elucidated a direct transformation of parenchyma cells into xylem cells without intervention of a DNA-synthesis phase or cell division. The interfascicular cambium tissue of *Ricinus communis*, when isolated and cultured in the presence of high concentrations of IAA, differentiated into xylem without any preceding cell division (Siebers 1971b, 1972). Turgeon (1975) used 5-fluorodeoxyuridine (FUdR) with lettuce pith explants to confirm that no DNA synthesis is required for reprograming of the genome prior to xylem cell differentiation—albeit this conclusion was based on a small sample size. Similar inferences were derived from work on *Centaurea cyanus* (Torrey 1975) and *Zinnia elegans* (Kohlenbach and Schmidt 1975; Fukuda and Komamine 1980a, b); however this hypothesis is still poorly documented.

In plant systems where cell division must precede the onset of differentiation, research is needed to confirm whether differentiation is related to a specific point in cell cycle, as has been shown in some animal systems (Dodds 1981). Certain plant tissues often exhibit polyploidization, i.e. replication of the cell DNA without an incidence of mitosis. In a tissue in which polyploidy does not occur, use of DNA-specific Feulgen staining and scanning microdensitometry can elucidate whether xylem cells are differentiating from G1 or G2 of the cell cycle. Dodds and Phillips (1977) analyzed DNA levels by using the *Helianthus tuberosus* explant system of initial parenchyma cells prior to culture, actively dividing cultured cells, and immature differentiating tracheary elements. The DNA levels ranged between 2°C and 4°C. The immature xylem cells were exclusively diploids in G1. Later, it was shown that all differentiating xylem cells in this system synthesize DNA before differentiating, thus proving that the immature xylem cells must have experienced at least one round of cell cycle, if all these cells are in G1 (Malawer and Phillips 1979). Dodds (1981) proposed a model for xylem-cell differentiation that suggested that cells differentiating directly into xylem cells (e.g. *Zinnia* mesophyll cells) may be blocked at the G1 "early arrest" stage, go through the "critical event" section of G1, and differentiate without experiencing the S phase of the cell cycle. On the contrary, cells differentiating essentially through the cell cycle (e.g. *Helianthus tuberosus* tuber cells, pea cortical cells) must be arrested at G1 "late arrest" and therefore need to pass through S, G2, M, and "critical events" in G1 before differentiating (Figure 9.4). Tissues may contain a mixed population of cells that are arrested at both "early arrest" and "late arrest" G1 phases; thus some cells enter differentiation directly whereas others are set to divide. Later studies did not support Dodds' hypothesis, however (see Phillips and Arnott 1983).

Chromosome number has no apparent bearing on differentiation; haploid, diploid, and polyploid cells can differentiate into tracheids (Nägl 1978; Armstrong 1982). DNA synthesis or mitosis may not be indispensable, but RNA biosynthesis seems to be essential, and protein biosynthesis is a definite prerequisite for differentiation (Northcote 1982; Fukuda and Komamine 1983).

Amplification of a given area(s) of the genome that results in production of numerous specific genes, thus increasing the DNA status of a nucleus (although this is

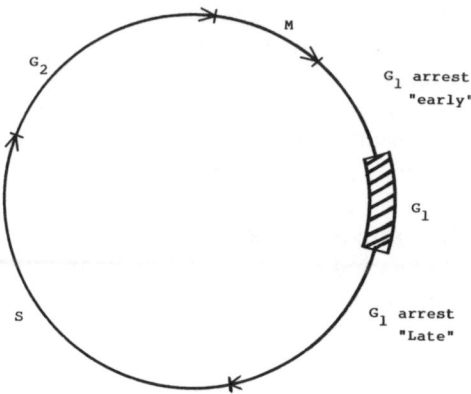

Figure 9.4. Cell cycle model for xylem–cell differentiation as suggested by Dodds (1981). G_1, Gap I; G_2, Gap II, M, Mitosis; S, Synthesis. *Hatched lines* represent critical event (S) for initiation of xylogenesis.

not in multiples of 2C, as in polyploidization), is seen in some developmental processes. This phenomenon is thought to play some role in the differentiation of xylem cells (see Innocenti and Avanzi 1971; Avanzi et al. 1973). It has also been shown that exogenously applied plant-growth hormones are capable of accelerating or retarding DNA amplification (Nägl et al. 1972); however, how the hormonal/environmental stimuli affect the cell cycle and cause a reprograming of the genome to initiate differentiation of the various cells needs further clarification.

The Phenomena of Cell Differentiation

ON THE XYLEM SIDE

The production and precise positioning of insoluble polymers outside the plasmalemma and inside most of the primary wall chiefly constitute the process of wood formation. Primary-wall dissolution and other changes may occur if needed by the differentiating cell (see Barnett 1981, 1991; Butterfield and Meylan 1982; Butterfield 1994).

The cells developing into vessel elements may elongate slightly and broaden so much that their ultimate width often exceeds their height. After the expansion is over, secondary-wall layers accumulate in characteristic patterns. Both vesicular secretion and lamellar apposition are involved in cell-wall formation in the differentiating xylem (Wardrop 1964). The vesicular secretion may relate to the incorporation of the matrix and the encrusting constituents into the wall, whereas apposition elaborates the cellulose framework. Deposition of the material for the S_1 layer of the secondary wall begins near the center of the cell and proceeds toward the apices (cf. Wardrop 1964; Barnett 1981).

The portions of the primary wall destined to give way to perforations are not covered with secondary-wall material, but thicken because of swelling of the intercellular substance (Esau and Hewitt 1940). In *Phaseolus vulgaris* L., the swelling is due to the removal of some of the matrix materials by wall-degrading enzymes and the consequent uptake of water by the remaining carbohydrates (Esau and Charvat 1978). Even though it is thicker, the perforation partition maintains complete continuity with the adjacent portions of the primary walls and the intervening middle lamella with which it is attached (Meylan and Butterfield 1981). The wall area occupied by the perforation on both sides of the plate coincides despite different patterns of wall thickening in the adjacent cells. Perforations form after the secondary walls, where they occur, are well deposited, and lignified; the mechanism involved is poorly understood. The perforation partition develops a granular surface and then numerous small holes before its final disappearance. Most noncellulosic polysaccharides are removed from the unlignified parts of the primary wall, leaving the "hydrolyzed" wall with a mat or web of cellulosic microfibrils (see Meylan and Butterfield 1981), identified by Meyer and Muhammad (1971) as reticulate (with randomly arranged microfibrils) and orthogonal (with microfibrils tranversing the scalariform openings in perpendicular direction, leaving regular rectangular spaces). These webs seemingly represent a stage in the breakdown of the perforation partition, where noncellulosic and possibly some of the cellulosic components have been digested (Benayoun et al. 1981; Meylan and Butterfield 1981). Such microfibrillar webs are absent in mature wood. Perhaps they are removed by water flow when the transpiration stream has set in (cf. Frey-Wyssling 1959; Yata et al 1970; O'Brien 1981), or perhaps they are removed by enzymatic action (cf. Roelofsen 1959, Butterfield and Meylan 1982). That these webs are commonly observed in scalariform plates and occasionally in simple plates suggests that the rate of removal of the cellulose component is much slower (Meylan and Butterfield 1981). The protoplasm dies typically after the perforation has formed. Remnants of the dead protoplasts form a lining along the walls of the tracheary elements (Scott et al. 1960).

The organelles supposedly involved in xylogenesis include microtubules, endoplasmic reticulum, dictyosome vesicles, and various boundary formations. Whether they play analogous roles in cell plate formation, primary wall development, and secondary wall synthesis is a matter of conjecture (Roberts 1969, 1976).

Hepler and Newcomb (1964) discovered the presence of microtubules and fibrillar elements within the cisternae of endoplasmic reticulum in the differentiating xylem cells of *Coleus*. They suggested that fibrils might contain either protein or carbohydrate substances for wall depostiion, whereas microtubules located in the plasmalemma adjacent to developing bands of the secondary wall might be related to the place of deposition and to the orientation of cellulose fibrils. The close correspondence of alignment between microfibrils and microtubules of the developing secondary walls was later confirmed in serveral species (Wooding and Northcote 1964; Cronshaw 1965, 1967; Cronshaw and Bouck 1965; Marchant and Hines 1979). Likewise, a possible role of plasmalemma in cell-wall synthesis was suggested (Dennis and Calvin 1965; Mühlethaler 1965, 1967). It was held that the primary-wall regions in the differentiating cells are associated with dictyosome vesicles and plasmalemma invaginations but not with microtubules, whereas the secondary-wall thickening in these cells is related to microtubules and not to dictyosome vesicles or invaginations (Cronshaw 1967). Microtubules may help maintain cell shape until the wall is sufficiently capable (Preston and Goodman 1968; Montezinos and Brown 1976, Marchant and Hines 1979). Microtubules were present in naked cells in *Oocystis apiculata*, but disappeared as wall formation started (Montezinos and Brown 1976).

Evidence is less substantial for the role of the endoplasmic reticulum than for that of dictyosome-derived vesicles and microtubules in xylem differentiation. Because it is in close association with the newly formed cell plate, the endoplasmic reticulum might have a role in cell-wall synthesis (see Porter and Machado 1960; Heslop-Harrison 1963; Hepler and Newcomb 1964; Esau et al. 1966; Pickett-Heaps and Northcote 1966; Robard 1968). On the other hand, convincing ultrastructural evidence is available for the deposition of the secondary-wall material from dictyosome-derived vesicles (see Roberts 1969, 1976), thus proving that the contents of these bodies are released directly to the developing secondary wall through plasmalemma by micropinocytosis. Biochemical changes that occur during xylem cell differentiation, particularly with reference to nucleic acids, proteins, and enzymes, have been well elucidated by Gahan (1981).

Wodzicki and Humphreys (1972, 1973) observed the formation of spherules, the breakdown of cytoplasmic strands traversing the vacuoles, and the subsequent digestion of organelles in the vacuoles during the final stages of differentiation of tracheids in *Pinus echinata*.

Lignification of the cell wall starts from primary walls adjacent to the corner deposits of the middle lamella and extends subsequently to the intercellular layer and the primary wall in general and finally to the secondary layers of the wall (see Wardrop and Bland 1959). It appears first on the tangential walls and then on the radial walls (Wardrop 1957). Concentration of lignin in the primary wall is more than double the amount in the secondary wall, and its distribution is uniform within the two layers (Frey-Wyssling 1964). Lignin-precursor substances either appear in the vascular cambium and later diffuse into the zone of the differentiating tracheary elements for conversion into lignin (Freudenberg 1964, 1965), or are synthesized within the differentiating and lignifying cells (Srivastava 1966b; Rubery and Northcote 1968). Although there is a close parallel between staining reactions of the secondary xylem and phloem fibers that would favor the concept of lignin precursors migrating from the cambium, the clear separation of lignification in the bark from cambial activity, in terms of time and space, confirms the notion that lignin precursors arise in the differentiating cells *in situ* (Srivastava 1966b). Growth regulators may influence the onset of both secondary-tissue formation and lignification (Bergmann 1964, 1965; Koblitz 1964; Parups 1964; Venketeswaran and Chen 1964; Ahuja and Doering 1967), but the nature of this relationship is still obscure (for details see Barnett 1981).

Mature tracheary elements exhibit gradients of length variation during their ontogeny. From the pith outwards, the length of vessel members may keep increasing (e.g. in *Populus tremula*) or decreasing (e.g. in *Prunus persica*) across the wood of the tree trunk (for review, see Ghouse and Iqbal 1981; Mahmooduzzafar and Iqbal 1986). The length of vessel elements, after an initial decline, increases rapidly during early secondary growth; it later slackens during the successive growth increments in most woody dicotyledons (Carlquist 1962, 1988; Sundrasivarao and Nazma 1977). The cell length may either (a) increase from the pith outward through a number of growth rings until it attains a maximum length, and stay constant during further radial growth, as in *Ulmus procera* (Sundrasivarao et al. 1973), or (b) demonstrate no regular variation except that the elements near the central core are smaller than those near the cambial cylinder, as in *Acacia nilotica* and *Prosopis spicigera* (Iqbal 1979; Iqbal and Ghouse 1983).

It has been known that the tracheary cells in the roots are generally wider than those in the stem, since the time of Nehemiah Grew (1641–1712) and has been confirmed by many subsequent studies with tracheids (Sanio 1872; Bailey 1958) and vessels (Colbert and Evert 1982; Zimmermann and Potter 1982, among others). In the roots, the diameter of tracheary cells keeps increasing with distance from the stem (Fahn 1964; Patel 1965; Sieber 1985) in both dicot and monocot species (see Tomlinson and Zimmermann 1967; Carlquist 1975, 1988; Zimmermann 1983). The increase in tracheid width from leaves to roots is positively correlated with an increase in the duration of tracheid expansion in the same direction (Denne 1972; Saks and Aloni 1985).

The basipetal increase in vessel width is accompanied by a concomitant decrease in vessel frequency per unit transverse sectional area (Fegel 1941; Carlquist 1975, 1976). The suggestion that gradients of tracheid diameter throughout the stem are positively maintained with parallel gradients of auxin fails to explain the basipetal increase in the cell diameter, although it does explain the formation of the wider tracheids in early wood and narrower tracheids in late wood (Larson 1964, 1969). In the stem the concentration of auxin decreases with increasing distance from the apical shoot, the main source of auxins. The required amount of auxin is not readily available to the differentiating cells located away from the auxin source. Consequently, the process of tracheary cell differentiation is slow in the basal parts of the stem and more so in the roots. Because cell expansion ceases after the secondary wall has been deposited, rapid differentiation yields narrow vascular elements, whereas slow differentiation allows for greater cell expansion, thus resulting in wider elements (Aloni and Zimmermann 1984; Saks and Aloni 1985; Aloni 1987). These observations are substantiated by experiments involving an external supply of auxin (Hejnowicz and Tomaszewski 1969; Aloni and Zimmermann 1983, 1984; Savidge 1983b).

Savidge (1985) proposed that cambial cells are "competent" but not "determined" for any of the several types of cellular differentiation, and that cambial derivatives are not bound to differentiate into any specific cell type in order to fulfill any subsequent physical or physiological demand of the plant. Based on these assumptions, he suggests the following:

1. The variable radial diameter and the length attained by a cambium-derived cell during differentiation are basically a function of its endogenous auxin concentration and gibberellin concentration, respectively.

2. The orientation of microfibrils during secondary-wall development is regulated by ethylene concentration.

3. A tracheid-differentiation factor (TDF), a bordered-pit factor (BPF), a lignin factor (LF), and an autolysis factor (AF) operate to regulate the mass of secondary-wall material, the number and positioning of bordered pits, the content and composition of lignin, and the occurrence of autolysis in secondary-walled elements, respectively. (The term "factor" may be more than a single entity and may lie in the realm of biophysics as well as biochemisty.)

4. High TDF concentration, in the absence of BPF, leads to the formation of libriform fibers and tracheids without bordered pits.

5. Parenchyma emanates from cambial derivatives where TDF, PBF, LF, and AF are either absent or annulled.

ON THE PHLOEM SIDE

Sieve elements are the most specialized cells of the phloem. Unlike vessel elements, sieve-elements (sieve cells/sieve-tube members) are living cells, specialized for translocation of photosynthate. During differentiation, their metabolic activity decreases, as is evident from the disorganization of the nucleus and the reduction in mitochondria and ribosomes. That the functioning of these enucleate cells is controlled by the associated nucleate companion cells has long been maintained; however, the ontogenetic connection is thought to be a secondary feature in the establishment of a specialized functional relation between the sieve-tube member and the adjacent parenchyma cell (Srivastava 1970; Esau 1973). The companion cell and other parenchymatic elements of the phloem intergrade with one another, and the two are not always unequivocally distinguishable from each other even at the ultrastructural level. Disappearance of the nucleus and tonoplast in mature sieve elements is well known; this usually occurs during the development of pores in the sieve plates (Esau 1965b, 1969) or shortly afterwards (Evert et al. 1966). The nuclear degeneration in the sieve-tube members is by chromatolysis, involving a gradual loss of stainable contents and eventual rupture of the nuclear envelope (see Thorsch and Esau 1981; Behnke and Kiritsis 1983; Behnke 1986; Evert 1990), as opposed to the pycnotic disintegration of the nucleus of the sieve cells wherein the chromatic material is aggretated into a dense mass. The nucleus disappears completely (Behnke 1969, 1973; Esau and Gill 1972; Parthasarathy 1974b; Esau 1975) but remnants of chromatin and/or nuclear membrane sometimes long persist (Esau 1972; Esau and Gill 1973; Deshpande 1975; Walsh and Evert 1975), depending largely upon the species. In many woody angiosperms, nuclear bodies have been reported in the mature elements also.

Several ultrastructural (e.g. Miyakawa et al. 1973; Deshpande 1974, 1975; Valanne and Valanne 1981; Ewers 1982; Esau and Thorsch 1984, 1985; Tippett and Hill 1984) and histochemical (e.g. Catesson 1973; Arsanto and Coulon 1974, 1975; Hebant and Fay 1980) studies have elucidated the development of sieve plates fairly well. The future sieve plate in young cells appears like any other primary wall except that it has fewer plasmodesmata (Esau 1964). Each pore site contains a single plasmodesma in the center and first becomes distinguishable from the rest of the wall by the appearance of a pair of callose platelets, one on either side of the wall. Cisternae of the endoplasmic reticulum are closely appressed to the plasmalemma bordering the callose platelets at all stages of development, and seem to be connected to the plasmodesmatal core. Rapid enlargement of the callose platelets delimits the pore sites before wall thickenings appear elsewhere on the young sieve plate. The wall thickening between pore sites soon overtakes the platelets and the pore sites then look like depressions in the plate. Perforation initiates with the removal of the cellulosic wall material that surrounds the plasmodesma and is sandwiched between the callose platelets. The opposite platelets fuse and then are broken through, giving way to the pore uniformly lined with plasmalemma and callose (Esau and Thorsch 1984, 1985). The callose platelets may prevent or inhibit deposition of cellulose microfibrils at the sites of the future pores (Evert et al. 1966; Parthasarathy 1974a), and endoplasmic reticulum at the pore site may be involved with the laying down of the platelets and later with the release of enzyme activity that leads to lysis of the callose and other wall constituents (Esau 1969). At maturity, the sieve-plate pores are unoccluded by either callose or any cytoplasmic material (see Kallarackal and Milburn 1983; Sjolund et al. 1983), but in some cases these have been reported to be occluded with P-proteins (Spanner 1978a, b). Further detail can be seen in Evert (1990) and Iqbal (1994).

The endoplasmic reticulum in mature cells is typically smooth-surfaced and breaks up into vesicles that occur either as a parietal, anastomosing system, or in stacks along the wall (see Evert 1977). Acid phosphatase and ATPase activity localized on these sites suggests that the endoplasmic reticulum may be an important source of enzymes involved in autophagic phenomena (Esau and Gill 1973; Oparka et al 1981) and possibly a specific cytoplasmic differentiation related to the conducting function of the cell (Esau and Charvat 1975). Of the various phloem-specific proteins, some are chemically distinct (usually as nuclear, plastid, and endoplasmic reticulum inclusions), whereas others (popularly known as P-proteins) are morphologically distinct at the electron-microscopy level. These P-proteins characterize all dicotyledons and several of the monocotyledons examined; the gymnosperms and lower vascular plants lack them, although some of them do contain the other phloem-specific proteins (Behnke and Sjolund 1990: Chapters 3–7, 13). P-protein, characteristic of young sieve elements, is later dispersed in the cell lumen, as the tonoplast disappears. P-protein is amorphous, granular, fibrillar, filamentous, tubular, and/or crystalline, depending on the species and the stage of differentiation of the cells. P-protein may form a network of filaments occupying the entire cell lumen, but in the majority of cases it is mostly or solely parietal in position (see Cronshaw and Sabnis 1990; Sabnis and Sabnis 1994). Normally, P-protein does not form transcellular strands or components of such strands (Evert 1977). Most abundant in the sieve elements, P-protein occurs also in the companion cells and phloem parenchyma (see Cronshaw and Sabnis 1990).

Of the cell organelles, mitochondria experience the least structural change during differentiation, sometimes having somewhat dilated cisternae (see Evert 1977). In mature sieve-tube members of *Cucurbita* and *Vitis* species, mitochondria lose their internal membranes and stroma become thin. Mitochondria may carry out at least some oxidative reactions in the mature members. Active cytochrome oxidases have been localized in mitochondria of mature sieve-tube members (Catesson 1980b), whereas nucleoside phosphatase (Gilder and Cronshaw 1973a, b), and acid phosphatase (Esau and Charvat 1975) have been localized in mitochondria of mature as well as differentiating sieve-tube members.

Two major types of plastids, i.e. S-type plastids (containing only starch), and P-type plastids (storing protein, exclusively or in addition to starch) have been recognized in dicotyledonous sieve-tube members (Behnke 1981). Unlike ordinary starch, sieve-tube starch stains brownish-red rather than blue-black with iodine.

The nacreous thickenings that are special inner-wall thickenings with a glistening or pearly appearance are observed in the sieve-tube members, often in fresh sections. The degree of the thickening may indicate the stage of cell development. In the primary phloem cells, it is maximum when the cell is approaching maturity and then disappears at the time of maturation. In the secondary phloem, the nacreous layer thickening may not essentially decrease as the cell ages (Esau and Cheadle 1958; Gilliland et al. 1984). In *Cucurbita*, these thickenings are polylamellate (Deshpande 1976a, b; Catesson 1982). Many studies (Goff 1973; Arsanto and Coulon 1974, 1975; Hoefert 1979) implicate Golgi apparatus in the development of the nacreous wall.

Sieve-tube members of the secondary phloem are generally longer near the cambium and smaller near the periderms in many tropical trees (Parameswaran and Liese 1974; Ghouse and Iqbal 1977b; Yunus et al. 1977; Iqbal and Ghouse 1983); however, the reverse was recorded for *Azadirachta indica* (Yunus et al 1977). In species with storied cambia, their length is almost constant along the radius from the cambium to periderm (Parameswaran and Liese 1974). In any case, however, the length variation is beset with many fluctuations that mar the maintenance of any steady and consistent trend of increase or decrease of the cell length (cf. Liese and Parameswaran 1972; Parameswaran and Liese 1974; Ghouse and Yunus 1976; Ghouse and Iqbal 1977b; Iqbal and Ghouse 1983, 1985a). A comprehensive account of the development, structure, and specialization of the secondary phloem has been produced by Iqbal (1993) and Iqbal and Zahur (1993).

CONCLUSIONS

From the foregoing discussion, we can draw the following generalizations:

- The vascular cambium is capable not only of producing cells but perhaps also of determining morphogenetic phenomena in response to environmental stimuli. It acts as a meristematic template and special bridge between the secondary vascular tissues, and plays an active physiological role even in the dormant stage.

- The location of the initials in the cambium is not fixed. Any cell of the cambial zone receiving the necessary balance of physical and chemical factors may act in the manner traditionally ascribed to the initials.

- The apparently thicker radial walls of cambial cells have a poorer organization of cellulose microfibrils compared to the tangential walls, and hence the thin T-walls are relatively rigid. The exceptional thickening of the R walls during the dormant cambial phase might relate to increased apoplastic translocation of assimilates through the cambium during this phase. The cambial cell walls are extendable more radially than tangentially. Any possible correlation between wall architecture, the compressive and tensile forces operative on these walls, and the course of differentiation of the derivative cells needs to be investigated.

- Cambial cells possess more prominent vacuoles, larger mitochondria, and better differentiated plastids than other meristems. Actively dividing cells are especially rich in large vacuoles, endoplasmic reticulum of rough cisternal form, dictyosomes, ribosomes, microtubules, and coated vesicles. Vacuoles are relatively little developed in ray cells, particularly of softwood species. Cytoplasmic streaming is fast in the active stage. The correlation between streaming and the microfilament bundles present in the active cambium, mostly lying parallel to the long axis of the cell (the main direction of the streaming), needs to be investigated.

- The degree of differentiation and the form of plastids in cambial cells vary with species. Plastids of ray cells are usually more completely differentiated than those of fusiform initials; the most differentiated plastids have few grana and mostly no stroma lamellae. Because of the probable deficiency of a photosystem I and the negligible amount of light reaching the cambium through the bark, the cambial plastids are unlikely to be used for photosynthesis and may serve as a storage structure.

- The seasonal starch content of cambial cells varies with species. Starch may be present during the dormant or the active phase, both phases, or neither of them. The presence/absence of starch is perhaps correlated to phenology. Rapid production of photosynthate and its supply to cambial cells might cause starch accumulation when young leaves emerge. Active cambium consumes most of the starch present in cambial cells, and consequently the cells are starch-free during peak activity. If photosynthate production is in excess of the cambial requirements, starch grains are also seen during the peak activity.

- The endomembrane system, comprising the endoplasmic reticulum, dictyosomes, plasmalemma, and/or tonoplast, discharges operations of synthesis as well as the intracellular transport of membranes and secretion products. Plasmalemma invagination seems to be involved with membrane internalization in resting cambial cells, and the coated vesicles known to occur in cambial cells of some species may relate to endocytosis. A new set of membranes is likely to develop during the rest-quiescence transition.

- The concomitant occurrence of plasmalemma invagination and sugar storage in cambium during autumn suggests an endocytotic transport, which permits rapid accumulation of sugar when H^+ sugar antiport systems are inactive and the vacuolar pH may not be maintained at its normal acidic value.

- The concept of invariably uninucleate cambial cells is no longer unequivocal. Several species are reported to possess a varying proportion of multinucleate fusiform cambial cells, which in some cases correlate to changes of season. Nucleoli are large and complex, having vacuoles filled with amorphous and birefringent substance. The nucleoli contain a granular zone intermingled with a fibrillar zone; the granular zone expands during the active phase and diminishes at the advent of dormancy. Whether this reduction occurs because of a complete blockage of RNA synthesis and whether DNA synthesis stops simultaneously still has to be confirmed.

- Reactivation of the dormant cambium begins at the base of swelling and growing buds and spreads downwards. Indole-3-acetic acid (IAA), which is produced mainly in the buds and developing shoots and is transported basipetally through the tissues, stimulates cambial reactivation.

- The emergence of new buds and young leaves precedes cambial reactivation. If leaf emergence is soon followed by flowering, most auxin produced by the young leaves is presumably consumed by the developing flowers, and cambial reactivation is delayed. Cambial reactivation occurs after growth hormones become sufficiently available. Although totipotent in *in vitro* culture and capable of utilizing the auxin produced by cell autolysis within the zone of differentiation of the derivatives, the cambium requires auxin from leaves for its *in vivo* growth and for maintaining its regulatory processes.

- The cambial zone is usually appreciably broad early in the active period when the rate of cell production by cell division is faster than the rate of differentiation of new vascular elements. The width of the cambial zone remains almost constant for the period when both cell production and cell differentiation maintain an equivalent pace. When differentiation surpasses cell production, the cambial zone becomes relatively narrow.

- IAA combined with GA_3 (gibberellic acid) is most effective in promoting cambial growth. High concentrations of IAA coupled with low concentrations of GA3 favor xylogenesis, whereas low concentrations of IAA coupled with high concentrations of GA_3 promote leptogenesis.

- Cambial activity is a periodic phenomenon in most plants, but in several tropical and subtropical species the cambium is active all year round. Cambial activity in species transferred from one habitat to another seems to be regulated by genetic factors developed in the species in the original habitat. The degree of adaptablility of the specimen to conditions prevailing in the new habitat is also significant.

- The cambium may reactivate at a moderately high temperature, but high temperature and humidity accelerate the rate of cambial cell division. Once begun, cell division may continue at relatively low temperatures.

- Because the cambium is not equipped with alternative provisions equivalent to the auxillary buds in the apical meristem that assume the job of the meristem if it is damaged, it is, unlike the apical meristems, irreplaceable and hence very calculative toward its activity to avoid the risks inherent in DNA replication. Initials divide periclinally only a few times; the derivatives undergo further divisions before differentiation. The slowly dividing initials may later act as the fast-dividing cells that form the secondary vascular tissues.

- Anticlinal division results in new initials in number far greater than required for maintaining the continuity of the expanding cambial cylinder. Hence, the extra cell population is removed from the cambial layer through successive oblique periclinal divisions to form part of the derivative tissues. The declining fusiform initials are poor in ray contacts. The loss of the initials could be a regulatory mechanism to maintain distance between rays. Several fusiform initials, normally located away from rays, convert into ray initials, thereby helping to maintain the relative distances between adjacent rays.

- Evidence gathered from various recent experiments indicates that the cambial derivatives are not *determined* for adopting any specific differentiation pathway but are *competent* to follow a variety of pathways.

- In xylem, differentiation is said to follow a *quantal* cell division that yields daughter cells with different genetic programs. Earlier studies showed that cell division must precede differentiation, whereas certain more recent works demonstrate a direct transformation of parenchyma cells into xylem elements without intervention of a DNA synthesis/mitosis phase. DNA synthesis may not be essential, but biosynthesis of RNA does appear to be essential, and that of protein is definitely a requirement for differentiation.

- Xylogenesis occurs with the active involvement of microtubules, dictyosome vesicles, endoplasmic reticulum, and various boundary formations. The primary-wall regions in differentiating cells are associated with dictyosome vesicles and plasmalemma invaginations, whereas the secondary-wall deposition in these cells involves the microtubules, which also maintain cell shape until the wall is strong enough to perform this job. The dictyosome-derived vesicles release their contents through the plasmalemma to the developing secondary wall. The endoplasmic reticulum may help in cell-wall synthesis.

- The dimensions of the cambial derivatives are determined basically by the endogenous concentrations of auxin and gibberellin, whereas the orientation of microfibrils during secondary-wall development is governed by ethylene concentration. Several other aspects of a differentiating vascular element are governed by a specific factor that may comprise one or more than one biophysical and/or biochemical component.

- Cisternae of the endoplasmic reticulum are closely associated with the deposition of callose during the development of sieve-pores in sieve-tube cells. Autophagic processes may also be involved, as is suggested from the associated phosphatase and ATPase activity. Mitochondria are least modified during differentiation of the sieve-tube members. The members exhibit certain length gradients across the width of the bark.

Credit

Figure 9.3 is reprinted with permission from the *Bulletin of the Torrey Botanical Club* 102:14–17.

LITERATURE CITED

Ahuja, M. R., and G. R. Doering. 1967. Effect of gibberellic acid on genetically controlled tumor formation and vascularization in tomato. *Nature* 216:800–801.

Ajmal, S., and M. Iqbal. 1987a. Annual rhythm of cambial activity in *Streblus asper: IAWA Bull.* (n.s.) 8:275–283.

_____ . 1987b. Seasonal rhythms of structure and behavior of vascular cambium in *Ficus rumphii. Ann. Bot.* 60:649–656.

Ajmal S., and M. Iqbal. 1992. Structure of the vascular cambium of varying age and its derivative tissues in the stem of *Ficus rumphii* Blume. *Bot. J. Linn. Soc.* 109:211–222.

Alden, T. 1971. Seasonal variations in the occurrence of indole–3-acetic acid in buds of *Pinus sylvestris. Physiol. plant.* 25:54–57.

Aljaro, M. E., E. Avila, A. Hoffman, and J. Kumerow. 1972. The annual rhythm of cambial activity in two woody species of the Chilean 'matorral'. *Am. J. Bot.* 59:879–884.

Allsopp, A., and P. Misra. 1940. The constitution of the cambium, the new wood and the mature sapwood of the common ash, the common elm and the scotch pine. *Biochem. J.* 34:1078–1084.

Aloni, R. 1982. Role of cytokinin in differentiation of secondary xylem fibers. *Plant Physiol.* 70:1631–1633.

_____ . 1987. Differentiation of vascular tissues. *Annu. Rev. Plant Physiol.* 38:179–204.

Aloni, R., and M. H. Zimmermann. 1983. The control of vessel size and density along the plant axis-a new hypothesis. *Differentiation* 24:203–208.

_____ . 1984. Length, width and pattern of regenerative vessels along strips of vascular tissue. *Bot. Gaz.* 145:50–54.

Alvim, P. De T. 1964. Tree growth and periodicity in tropical climates. In *The Formation of Wood in Forest Trees.* Ed. M. H. Zimmermann. New York/London: Academic Press. 479–495.

Anoruo, A. O. 1988. *Biotechnology, Growth Development and Wood Quality of Caribbean Pine (Pinus caribaea Mor.).* Ph.D. thesis, Yale Univ., New Haven, CT.

Antevs, E. 1925. The big tree as a climatic measure. *Carnegie Inst. Wash. Publ.* 352:115–153.

Armstrong, J. E. 1982. Polyploidy and wood anatomy of mature white ash, *Fraxinus americana. Wood Fiber* 14:331–339.

Arsanto, J. P., and J. Coulon. 1974. Détections radio-autographique et cytochimique des sites d'élaboration ou de transit des précurseurs polysaccarides pariétaux dans les cellules cirblées en cours de différenciation du métaphloème caulinaire de deux Cucurbitacées voisines (*Cucurbita pepo* L. et *Ecballuim elaterium* R.). *C. R. Acad. Sci. Paris. Ser. D* 278:2775–2778.

_____ . 1975. Application des méthodes cytochimique et radioautographique de détection ultrastructurales des polysaccarides à l'étude de la différenciation des plateaux criblées de métaphloème caulinaire de deux Cucurbitacées voisines (*Ecballium elaterium* R. et *Cucurbita pepo* L.). *C. R. Acad. Sci. Paris Ser. D* 280:601–604.

Arzee, T., E. Arbel, and L. Cohen. 1977. Ontogeny of periderm and phellogen activity in *Ceratonia siliqua* L. *Bot. Gaz.* 138:329–333.

Auriac, M. C., and M. Tort. 1985. Ultrastructural evidence for a direct transport from apoplast to vacuoles in the storage cells of japanese artichoke. *Physiol. Vég.* 23:301–307.

Avanzi, S., F. Maggini, and A. M. Innocenti. 1973. Amplification of ribosomal cistrons during the maturation of metaxylem in the root of *Allium cepa. Protoplasma* 76:197–210.

Bailey, I. W. 1920a. The formation of the cell plate in the cambium of the higher plants. *Proc. Natl. Acad. Sci. USA.* 6:197–200.

_____ . 1920b. The cambium and its derivative tissues. III. A reconnaissance of cytological phenomena in the cambium. *Am. J. Bot.* 7:417–434.

———— . 1923. The cambium and its derivative tissues. IV. The increase in girth of the cambium. *Am. J. Bot.* 10:499–509.

———— . 1930. The cambium and its derivative tissues. V. A reconnaissance of the vacuome in living cells. *Zeit. Zellforsch. Mekros. Anat.* 10:651–682.

———— . 1943. Some misleading terminologies in the literature of "plant tissue-culture". *Science* 98:539.

———— . 1958. The structure of tracheids in relation to the movement of liquids, suspensions and undissolved gases. In *The Physiology of Forest Trees.* Ed. K. V. Thimann. New York: Ronald Press. 71–82.

Bannan, M. W. 1950. Frequency of anticlinal divisions in fusiform cambial cells of *Chamaecyparis. Am. J. Bot.* 37:511–517.

———— . 1951a. The reduction of fusiform cambial cells in *Chamaecyparis* and *Thuja. Can. J. Bot.* 29:57–67.

———— . 1951b. The annual cycle of size changes in the fusiform cambial cells of *Chamaecyparis* and *Thuja. Can. J. Bot.* 29:421–437.

———— . 1955. The vascular cambium and radial growth in *Thuja occidentalis* L. *Can. J. Bot.* 33:113–138.

———— . 1957. Girth increase in white cedar stems of irregular form. *Can. J. Bot.* 35:425–434.

———— . 1960. Ontogenetic trends in conifer cambium with respect to frequency of anticlinal division and cell length. *Can. J. Bot.* 38:795–802.

———— . 1962. The vascular cambium and tree ring development. In *Tree Growth* Ed. T. T. Kozlowski. New York: Ronald Press. 3–21.

———— . 1964. Tracheid size and anticlinal divisions in the cambium of *Pseudotsuga. Can. J. Bot.* 42:603–631.

Bannan, M. W., and I. L. Bayly. 1956. Cell size and survival in conifer cambium. *Can. J. Bot.* 34:769–776.

Barghoorn, E. S. Jr. 1940a. Origin and development of the uniseriate ray in the coniferae. *Bull. Torrey Bot. Club.* 67:303–28.

———— . 1940b. The ontogenetic development and phylogenetic specialization of rays in the xylem of dicotyledons. *Am. J. Bot.* 27:918–28.

Barnett, J. R. 1971. Winter activity in the cambium of *Pinus radiata. N. Z. J. For. Sci.* 1:208–222.

———— . 1973. Seasonal variation in the ultrastructure of the cambium in New Zealand grown *Pinus radiata* D. Don. *Ann. Bot.* 37:1005–1011.

———— . 1975. Seasonal variation of organelle members in section of fusiform cambial cells of *Pinus radiata* D. Don *N. Z. J. Bot.* 13:325–332.

———— . 1981. Secondary xylem cell development. In *Xylem Cell Development.* Ed. J. R. Barnett. Tunbridge Wells, U.K.: Castle House. 47–95.

———— . 1994. Ultrastructural factors affecting xylem differentiation. In *The Cambial Derivatives.* Ed. M. Iqbal. Stuttgart: Gebrüder Borntraeger. In press.

Behnke, H. D. 1969. Aspekte der Siebröhren-Differenzierung bei Monocotylen. *Protoplasma* 68:289–314.

———— . 1972. Sieve-tube plastids in relation to angiosperm systematics. An attempt towards a classification by ultrastructural analysis. *Bot. Rev.* 38:155–197.

———— . 1981. Sieve element characters. *Nord. J. Bot.* 1:381–400.

———— . 1986. Sieve element characters and the systematic position of *Austrobaileya,* Austrobaileyaceae—with comments as to the distinction and definition of sieve cells and sieve-tube members. *Plant Syst. Evol.* 152:101–121.

Behnke, H. D., and U. Kiritsis. 1983. Ultrastructure and differentiation of sieve elements in primitive angiosperms. I. Winteraceae. *Protoplasma* 118:148–156.

Behnke, H. D., and R. D. Sjolund. 1990. *Sieve Elements: Comparative Structure, Induction and Development.* Berlin/Heidelberg: Springer Verlag.

Benayoun, J., A. M. Catesson, and Y. Czaninski. 1981. A cytochemical study of differentiation and break down of vessel-end walls. *Ann. Bot.* 47:687–698.

Bergmann, L. 1964. Der Einfluss von kinetin auf die Ligninbildung und Differenzierung in

Gewebekulturen von *Nicotiana tabacum*. *Planta* 62:221–254.

_____ . 1965. The effect of kinetin on the metabolism of plant tissue cultures. In *Proc. Int. Conf. on Plant Tissue Culture*. Eds. P. R. White and A. R. Grove. Berkeley: McCutchan Publ. Corp. 171–181.

Berlyn, G. P. 1970. Ultrastructural and molecular concepts of cell-wall formation. *Wood Fiber* 2:196–227.

_____ . 1982. Morphogenetic factors in wood formation and differentiation. In *New Perspectives in Wood Anatomy*. Ed. P. Baas. The Hague: Martinus Nijhoff. 123–150.

Berlyn, G. P., and Y. C. Battey. 1985. Metabolism and synthetic function of cambial tissue. In *Biosynthesis and Biodegradation of Wood Components*. Ed. T. Higuchi. Orlando, FL: Academic Press. 63–85.

Bird, A. P., D. E. S. Truman, and R. M. Clayton. 1982. Introductory review: The molecular basis of differentiation and competence. In *Stability and Switching in Cellular Differentiation*. Eds. R. M. Clayton, D. E. S. Truman. New York/London: Plenum. 61–64.

Bogers, R. J., H. T. M. Hooymans-Klappe, and K. R. Libbenga. 1976. The first cell cycle in explants from the mature root cortex of 7 day old *Pisum sativum*. *Plant. Sci. Lett.* 6:43–48.

Braun, H. J. 1955. Beitrage zur Entwicklungsgeschichte der Markstrahlen. *Bot Studien* 4:73–131.

_____ . 1984. The significance of the accessory tissues of the hydrosystem for osmotic water shifting as the second principle of the water ascent, with some thoughts concerning the evolution of trees. *IAWA Bull.* (n.s.) 5:275–294.

Bryant, J. A., and D. Francis. 1985. *The Cell Divison Cycle in Plants*. Cambridge/London/New York: Cambridge Univ. Press.

Bünning, E. 1965. Die Entstehung von Musterm in der Entwicklong von Pflanzen. *Handb. Pflanzenphysiol.* 15:383–408.

Butterfield, B. G. 1994. Vessel element differentiation. In *The Cambial Derivatives*. Ed. M. Iqbal. Stuttgart: Gebrüder Bortraeger. In press.

Butterfield, B. G., and B. A. Meylon. 1982. Cell wall hydrolysis in the tracheary elements of the secondary xylem. In *New Perspectives in Wood Anatomy*. Ed. P. Baas. The Hague: Martinus Nijhoff. 71–84.

Buvat, R. 1956. Variations saisonnieres du chondriome dons le cambium *Robinia pseudoacacia*. *C. R. Acad. Sci.* 243:1908–1911.

Carlquist, S. 1962. A theory of paedomorphosis in dicotyledonous woods. *Phytomorphology* 12:30–45.

_____ . 1975. *Ecological Strategies of Xylem Evolution*. Berkeley: Univ. California Press.

_____ . 1976. Wood anatomy of Roridulaceae: Ecological and phylogenetic implications. *Am. J. Bot.* 63: 1003–1008.

_____ . 1988. *Comparative Wood Anatomy: Systematic, Ecological, and Evolutionary Aspects of Dicotyledon Wood*. Berlin/Heidelberg: Springer-Verlag.

Carmi, A., T. Sachs, and A. Fahn. 1972. The relation of ray spacing to cambial growth. *New Phytol.* 71:349–353.

Catesson, A. M. 1964. Origine fonctionnement et variations cytologiques saisonnieres du cambium de l'*Acer Pseudoplatanus* L. (Aceracees). *Ann. Sci. Nat. Bot.* 12e ser. 5:229–498.

_____ . 1973. Observations cytochimiques sur les tubes cirblées de quelques angiospermes. *J. Micros. Paris.* 16:95–104.

_____ . 1974. Cambial cells. In *Dynamic Aspects of Plant Ultrastructure*. Ed. A. W. Robards. London: McGraw Hill. 358–390.

_____ . 1980a. The vascular cambium. In *Control of Shoot Growth in Trees*. Ed C. H. A. Little. Frederiction, N. B., Canada: IUFRO Workshop Proc. Maritimes Forest Research Centre.

_____ . 1980b. Localization of phloem oxidases. *Ber. Dtsch. Bot. Ges.* 93:141–152.

_____ . 1981. Le cycle saisonnier des cellules cambiales chez quelques feuillus. *Bull. Soc.*

Bot. Fr. Actualités Botaniques 128:43–51.

————. 1982. Cell wall architecture in the secondary sieve tubes of *Acer* and *Populus. Ann. Bot.* 49:131–134.

Catesson, A. M. 1984. La dynamique Cambiale. *Ann. Sci. Nat. Bot. Paris.* 13e ser. 6:23–43.

————. 1990. Cambial cytology and biochemistry. In *The Vascular Cambium.* Ed. M. Iqbal. Taunton, U.K.: Research Studies Press. 63–112.

Catesson, A. M., R. Goldberg, and M. C. Winny. 1971. Etude d'activités phosphatasiques acides dans les cellules d'*Acer Pseudoplatanus* cultivées en suspension. *C. R. Acad. Sci.* 272:2078–2081.

Catesson, A. M., and J. C. Roland. 1981. Sequential changes associated with cell-wall formation and fusion in the vascular cambium. *IAWA Bull.* (n.s.) 2:151–162.

Cecich, R. A. 1979. Development of vacuoles and lipid bodies in apical meristems of *Pinus banksiana. Am. J. Bot.* 66:895–901.

Cheadle, V. I., and K. Esau. 1964. Secondary phloem of *Liriodendron tulipifera. Univ. Calif. Publ. Bot.* 36:143–252.

Chou, T., and S. H. T. Chiang. 1973. Seasonal changes of cambial activity in the young branch of *Psidium guajava* Linn. *Taiwania* 18: 35–41.

Chowdhury, K. A. 1940. The formation of growth rings in Indian trees. II. (a) champ (b) kokko (c) sissoo (d) toon. *Indian For. Rec.* 2:41–57.

————. 1958. Extension and radial growth in tropical perennial plants. In *Modern Developments in Plant Physiology.* Ed. P. Maheshwari. Delhi: Delhi Univ.

————. 1968. *History of Botanical Researches in India, Burma and Ceylon, Part X, Wood Anatomy.* Aligarh: Aligarh Muslim University Press.

————. 1969. Cambial activities in temperate and tropical trees. *11th Internat. Bot. Congr. Seattle.* Abstr. 32.

Chowdhury, K. A., and K. N. Tandon. 1950. Extension and radial growth in trees. *Nature* 165:732–733.

Colbert, J. T., and R. F. Evert. 1982. Leaf vasculature in sugar cane (*Saccharum officinarum* L.) *Planta* 156:136–151.

Cooper, S. 1979. A unifying model for the G1 period in prokaryotes and eukaryotes. *Nature* 280:17–19.

Cottignies, A. 1977. Le nucléole dans le point végétatif dormant et non dormant du *Fraxinus excelsior* L. *Z. Phfazenphysiol.* 83:189–200.

————. 1979. The blockage in the G1 phase of the cell cycle in the dormant shoot apex of ash. *Planta* 147:15–19.

Cram, W. J. 1980. Picnocytosis in plants. *New Phytol.* 84:1–17.

Creber, G. T., and W. G. Chaloner. 1990. Environmental influences on cambial activity. In *The Vascular Cambium.* Ed. M. Iqbal. Taunton, U.K.: Research Studies Press.

Cronshaw, J. 1965. Cytoplasmic fine structure and cell wall development in differentiating xylem elements. In *Cellular Ultrastructure of Woody Plants.* Ed. W. Cote. Syracuse, NY: Syracuse Univ. Press.

————. 1967. Tracheid differentiation in tobaco pith cultures. *Planta* 72:78–90.

Cronshaw, J., and J. B. Bouck. 1965. The fine structure of differentiating xylem elements. *J. Cell Biol.* 24:415–431.

Cronshaw, J., and D. D. Sabnis. 1990. Phloem proteins. In *Sieve Elements.* Ed. H. D. Behnke, R. D. Sjolund. Berlin/Heidelberg: Springer Verlag. 257–283.

Cumbie, B. G. 1967. Developmental changes in the vascular cambium of *Leitneria floridana. Am. J. Bot.* 54:414–424.

Czaninski, Y., and A. M. Catesson. 1970. Activites peroxydasiques d'origines diverses dans les cellules D'*Acer pseudoplatanus* (tissu conducteurs et cellules en culture). *J. Microscopie* 9:1089–1102.

Dalessandro, G., and D. H. Northcote. 1977. Changes in enzymic activities of nucleoside diphosphate sugar interconversions during differentiation of cambium to xylem in sycamore and poplar. *Biochem. J.* 162:267–279.

Daubenmire, R. F., and M. E. Deters. 1947. Comparative studies of growth in deciduous and evergreen trees. *Bot. Gaz.* 109:1–12.

Dave, Y. S., and K. S. Rao. 1981. Seasonal nuclear behaviour in fusiform cambial initials of *Tectona grandis* L.f. *Flora* 171:299–305.

_____ . 1982. Plastid ultrastructure in the cambium of teak (*Tectona grandis* L.f.) *Ann. Bot.* 49:425–427.

Davis, J. D., and R. F. Evert. 1968. Seasonal development in the secondary phloem in *Populus tremuloides. Bot. Gaz.* 129:1–8.

Davison, R. M., and H. Young. 1974. Seasonal changes in the level of abscisic acid in xylem sap of peach. *Plant Sci. Lett.* 2:79–82.

De Groote, K. K., and P. R. Larson. 1984. Correlations between net auxin and secondary xylem development in young *Populus deltoides. Physiol. Plant.* 60:459–466.

Delort, S., and J. L. Bonnemain. 1985. Mechanisms and control of phloem transport. *Physiol. Vég.* 23:199–220.

Denne, M. P. 1972. A comparison of root and shoot-wood development in conifer seedlings. *Ann. Bot.* 36:579–587.

Dennis, T. L., and J. R. Calvin. 1965. The relation between cellulose biosynthesis and the structure of the cell envelope in *Acetobacler xylinum.* In *Cellular Ultrastructure of Woody Plants.* Ed. W. A. Cote, Jr. Syracuse NY: Syracuse Univ. Press. 199–212.

Dermen, H. 1953. Periclinal cytochimeras and origin of tissues in stem and leaf of peach. *Am. J. Bot.* 40:154–168.

Derr, W. F., and R. F. Evert. 1967. The cambium and seasonal development of the phloem in *Robinia pseudoacacia. Am. J. Bot.* 54:147–153.

Deshpande, B. P. 1974. Development of the sieve plate in *Saxifraga sarmentosa* L. *Ann. Bot.* 38:151–158.

_____ . 1975. Differentiation of the sieve plate of *Cucurbita*: A further view. *Ann. Bot.* 39:1015–1022.

_____ . 1976a. Observations on the fine structure of plant cell walls. II. The microfibrillar framework of the parenchymatous cell wall in *Cucurbita. Ann. Bot.* 40:439–442.

_____ . 1976b. Observations on the fine structure of plant cell walls. III. The sieve-tube wall in *Cucurbita. Ann. Bot.* 40:443–446.

Digby, J., and P. F. Wareing. 1966. The relationship between endogenous hormone levels in the plant and seasonal aspects of cambial activity. *Ann. Bot.* 30:607–622.

Dodd, J. D. 1948. On the shapes of cells in the cambial zone of *Pinus sylvestris* L. *Am. J. Bot.* 35:666–682.

Dodds, J. H. 1981. The role of the cell cycle and cell division in xylem differentiation. In *Xylem Cell Development.* Ed. J. R. Barnett. Tunbridge Wells, U.K.: Castle House Publ. 153–167.

Dodds, J. H., and R. Phillips 1977. DNA and histone content of immature tracheary elements from cultured artichoke explants. *Planta* 135: 213–216.

During, H., and G. Alleweldt. 1973. Der Jahresgang der Abscisinsaüre in vegetativen Organen von Reben. *Vitis* 12:26–32.

Egierszdorff, S., and M. Tomaszewski. 1973. Auxin dependent accumulation of photosynthates in cambium and wood formation in Scots pine. *Proc. Res. Inst. Pomol. Poland,* Ser. E. 3:181–189.

Eliasson, L. 1969. Growth regulators in *Populus tremula.* I. Distribution of auxin and growth inhibitors. *Physiol. Plant.* 22:1288–1301.

Elliott, J. H. 1933. Growth and differentiation in the vascular system during leaf development in the dicotyledon. *Proc. Leeds Philos. Lit Soc.* 2:440–450.

_____ . 1937. The development of the vascular system in evergreen leaves more than one year old. *Ann. Bot.* (n.s.) 1:107–127.

Esau. K. 1964. Aspects of ultrastructure of phloem. In *Formation of Wood in Forest Trees.* Ed. M. H. Zimmermann. New York: Academic Press. 51–63.

_____ . 1965a. *Vascular Differentiation in Plants.* New York: Holt, Rinehart and Winston.

_____ . 1965b. Anatomy and cytology of *Vitis* phloem. *Hilgardia* 37:17–72.

_____ . 1969. *The Phloem. Encyclopedia of Plant Anatomy,* Vol 5. Stuttgart: Gebrüder Borntraeger.

_____ . 1972. Changes in the nucleus and the endoplasmic reticulum during differentiation of a sieve element in *Mimosa pudica* L. *Ann. Bot.* 36:703–710.

———. 1973. Comparative structure of companion cells and phloem parenchyma cells in *Mimosa pudica* L. *Ann. Bot.* 37:625–632.

———. 1975. The phloem of *Nelumbo nucifera* Gaertn. *Ann. Bot.* 39:901–913.

Esau, K., and I. D. Charvat. 1975. An ultrastructural study of acid phosphatase localization in cells of *Phaseolus vulgaris* phloem by the use of azo dye method. *Tissue Cell* 7:619–630.

———. 1978. On vessel member differentiation in the bean (*Phaseolus vulgaris* L.). *Ann. Bot.* 42:665–677.

Esau, K., and V. I. Cheadle. 1958. Wall thickening in sieve elements. *Proc. Natl. Acad. Sci. USA.* 44:546–553.

Esau, K., V. I. Cheadle, and R. H. Gill. 1966. Cytology of differentiating tracheary elements. I. Organelles and membrane systems. *Am. J. Bot.* 53:756–764.

Esau, K., and R. H. Gill. 1972. Nucleus and endoplasmic reticulum in differentiating root protophloem of *Nicotiana tabacum*. *J. Ultrastr. Res.* 41:160–175.

———. 1973. Correlations in differentiation of protophloem sieve elements of *Allium cepa* root. *J. Ultrastr. Res.* 44:310–328.

Esau, K., and W. M. B. Hewitt. 1940. Structure of end wall in differentiating vessels. *Hilgardia* 13:229–240.

Esau, K., and J. Thorsch. 1984. The sieve plate of *Echium* (Boraginaceae): Developmental aspects and response of P-protein to protein digestion. *J. Ultrastr. Res.* 86:31–45.

———. 1985. Sieve-plate pores and plasmodesmata, the communication channels of the symplast: Ultrastructural aspects and developmental relations. *Am. J. Bot.* 72:1641–1653.

Essiamah, S., and W. Eschrich. 1985. Changes of starch content in the storage tissues of deciduous trees during winter and spring. *IAWA bull.* (n.s.) 6:97–106.

———. 1986. Water uptake in deciduous trees during winter and the role of conducting tissues in spring reactivation. *IAWA Bull.* (n.s.) 7:31–38.

Evert, R. F. 1960. Phloem structure in *Pyrus communis* L. and its seasonal changes. *Univ. Calif. Bot. Publ.* 32:127–194.

———. 1961. Some aspects of cambial development in *Pyrus communis*. *Am. J. Bot.* 48:479–488.

———. 1963. The cambium and seasonal development of the phloem in *Pyrus malus*. *Am. J. Bot.* 50:149–159.

———. 1977. Phloem structure and histochemistry. *Annu. Rev. Plant Physiol.* 28:199–222.

———. 1990. Dicotyledons. In *Sieve Elements*. Ed. H. D. Behnke, R. D. Sjolund. Berlin/Heidelberg: Springer-Verlag. 103–137.

Evert, R. F. and B. P. Deshpande. 1970. An ultrastructural study of cell division in the cambium. *Am. J. Bot.* 57:942–961.

Evert, R. F., L. Murmanis, and I. B. Sachs. 1966. Another view of the ultrastructure of *Cucurbita* phloem. *Ann. Bot.* 30:563–585.

Ewers, F. W. 1982. Developmental and cytological evidence for mode of origin of secondary phloem in needle leaves of *Pinus longaeva* (bristlecone pine) and *P. flexilis*. *Bot. Jahrb. syst.* 103:59–88.

Fahn, A. 1953. Annual wood ring development in maquis trees of Israel. *Palest. J. Bot.* 6:1–26.

———. 1955. The development of the growth ring in wood of *Quercus infectoria* and *Pistacia lentiscus* in the hill region of Israel. *Trop. Woods* 101:52–59.

———. 1959. Annual rhythm of xylem development in trees and shrubs in Israel. *Proc. 9th Int. Bot. Congr. Montreal* 110.

———. 1962. Xylem structure and annual rhythm of cambial activity in woody species of the East Mediterranean regions. *IAWA Bull.* 1962:2–6.

———. 1964. Some anatomical adaptations of desert plants. *Phytomorphology* 14:93–102.

———. 1982. *Plant Anatomy.* 3rd ed. Oxford: Pergamon Press.

Fahn, A., J. Burley, K. A. Longman, A. Mariaux, and P. B. Tomlinson. 1981. Possible contributions of wood anatomy to the determination of the age of tropical trees. In *Age and Growth of Tropical Trees.* Ed. F. H. Bormann and G. P. Berlyn. School of Forestry and Environmental Studies. Bull. 94. Yale University, New Haven: USA.

Fahn, A., and C. Sarnat. 1963. Xylem structure and annual rhythm of development in trees and shrubs of the desert. IV. shrubs. *Bull. Res. Counc. Israel* 11:198–209.

Fahn, A., and E. Werker. 1990. Seasonal cambial activity. In *The Vasuclar Cambium.* Ed. M. Iqbal. Taunton, U.K.: Research Studies Press. 139–158.

Fahn, A., E. Werker, and P. Baas. 1986. *Wood Anatomy and Identification of Trees and Shrubs from Israel and Adjacent Regions.* Jerusalem: The Israel Academy of Sciences and Humanities. 221 pp., 82 plates.

Farooqui, P., and A. W. Robards. 1979. Seasonal changes in the ultrastructure of cambium of *Fagus sylvatica* L. *Proc. Indian Acad. Sci. Sec. B.* 88:463–472.

Fegel, A. C. 1941. Comparative anatomy and varying physical properties of trunk, branch and root wood in certain north eastern trees. *Bull. NY State Coll. For. Syracuse Univ. Tech. Publ.* 55:1–20.

Feldman, L. J., and J. G. Torrey. 1977. Nuclear changes associated with cellular differentiation in pea root cortical cells cultured in vitro. *J. Cell Sci.* 28:87–106.

Fosket, D. E. 1968. Cell division and differentiation of wound vessel members in cultured stem segments of *Coleus. Proc. Natl. Acad. Sci. USA* 59:1089–1096.

_____ . 1970. The time course of differentiation and its relation to DNA synthesis in cultured *Coleus* stem segments. *Plant Physiol.* 46:64–68.

Fraser, D. A. 1962. Tree growth in relation to soil moisture. In *Tree Growth.* Ed. T. T. Kozlowski. New York: Ronald Press. 183–204.

Freudenberg, K. 1964. The formation of lignin in the tissue and in vitro. In *The Formation of Wood in Forest Trees.* Ed. M. H. Zimmermann. New York: Academic Press. 203–218.

_____ . 1965. Lignin: Its constitution and formation from p-hydroxycinnamyl alcohols. *Science* 148:595–600.

Freundlich, A., and A. W. Robards. 1974. Cytochemistry of differentiating plant vascular-cell walls with special reference to cellulose. *Cytobiologie* 8:355–370.

Frey-Wyssling, A. 1959. *Die pflanzliche Zellwand.* Berlin: Springer Verlag.

_____ . 1964. Ultraviolet and fluorescence optics of lignified cell walls. In *The Formation of Wood in Forest Trees.* Ed. M. H. Zimmermann. New York: Academic Press. 153–167.

Fry, S. C. 1986. Cross-linking of matrix polymers in the growing cell walls of angiosperms. *Annu. Rev. Plant Physiol.* 37:165–186.

Fukuda, H., and A. Komamine. 1980a. Establishment of an experimental system for the study of tracheary element differentiation from single cells isolated from the mesophyll of *Zinnia elegans. Plant Physiol.* 65:57–60.

_____ . 1980b. Direct evidence for cytodifferentiation to tracheary elements without intevening mitosis in a culture of single cells isolated from the mesophyll of *Zinnia elegans. Plant Physiol.* 65:61–64.

_____ . 1983. Changes in the synthesis of RNA and protein during tracheary element differentiation in single cells isolated from the mesophyll of *Zinnia elegans. Plant Cell Physiol.* (Tokyo) 24:603–614.

Gahan, P. B. 1981. Biochemical changes during xylem element differentiation. In *Xylem Cell Development.* Ed. J. R. Barnett. Tunbridge Wells, U.K.: Castle House. 168–191.

_____ . 1989. How stable are cambial initials? *Bot. J. Linn. Soc.* 100:319–321.

Ghouse, A. K. M., and S. Hashmi. 1978. Seasonal cycle of vascular differentiation in *Polyalthia longifolia* (Annonaceae). *Beitr. Biol. Pflanzen.* 54:375–380.

_____ . 1979. Cambium periodicity in *Polyalthia longifolia. Phytomorphology.* 29:64–67.

_____ . 1980. Changes in the vascular cambium of *Polyalthia longifolia* Benth. et Hook. (Annonaceae) in relation to the girth of the trees. *Flora* 170:135–143.

Ghouse, A. K. M., and M. Iqbal. 1975. A comparative study on the cambial structure of some arid zone species of *Acacia* and *Prosopis. Bot. Not.* 128:327–331.

_____ . 1977a. Variation trends in the cambial structure of *Prosopis spicigera* L. in relation to the girth of the tree axis. *Bull. Torrey Bot. Club* 104:197–201.

_____ . 1977b. Trends of size variation in phloem fibres and sieve-tube cells within the bark of some arid zone trees. *Flora* 166:517–521.

_____ . 1979. Intrusive growth in the secondary phloem of *Acacia* and *Prosopis*. *New Bot.* 6:91–96.

_____ . 1981. Cell length variation within the bark and wood with respect to the development of trees. In *Advances in Forest Genetics*. Ed. P. K. Khosla. New Delhi: Ambika Publ. 192–212.

Ghouse, A. K. M., and M. I. H. Khan. 1977. Seasonal variation in the nuclear number of fusiform cambial initials in *Psidium guajava* L. *Caryologia*. 30:441–444.

Ghouse, A. K. M., M. I. H. Khan, S. Khan., and A. H. Khan. 1979. Occurrence of polynucleate condition in the fusiform cambial initials of some Verbenaceae. *Chromosome Inform. Ser.* 23:16–17.

Ghouse, A. K. M., M. I. H. Khan, S. Khan, and A. H. Khan. 1980. Comparative study on the structure of vascular cambium in some Verbenaceae. *Phytomorphology* 30:32–40.

Ghouse, A. K. M., and M. Yunus. 1975. Intrusive growth in the phloem of *Dalbergia*. *Bull. Torrey Bot. Club.* 102:14–17.

_____ . 1976. Cell length variation in the secondary phloem of *Dalbergia* spp. with increasing age of the vascular cambium. *Ann. Bot.* 40:13–16.

Ghouse A. K. M., M. Yunus, and M. Iqbal. 1976. A comparative study on the cambial structure of some *Bauhinia* species. *Bot. Jahrb. Syst.* 95:411–417.

Gilder, J., and J. Cronshaw. 1973a. The distribuition of adenosine triphosphatase activity in differentiating and mature phloem cells of *Nicotiana tabacum* and its relationship to phloem transport. *J. Ultrastr. Res.* 44:388–404.

_____ . 1973b. Adenosine triophosphatase in the phloem of *Cucurbita*. *Planta* 110:189–204.

Gilliland, M. G., J. van Staden, and A. G. Bruton. 1984. Studies on the translocation system of guayule (*Parthenium argentatum* Gray). *Protoplasma* 122:169–177.

Glerum, C., and J. J. Balatinecz. 1980. Formation and distribution of food reserves during autum and their subsequent utilization in jackpine. *Can. J. Bot.* 58:40–54.

Glock, W. S. 1955. Tree growth. II. Growth rings and climate. *Bot. Rev.* 21:73–188.

Goff, C. W. 1973. Localization of nucleoside diphosphatase in the onion root tip. *Protoplasma* 78:397–416.

Goosen-de Roo, L., P. D. Burgraff, and K. R. Libbenga. 1983. Microfilament bundles associated with tubular endoplasmic reticulum in fusiform cells in the cambial zone of *Fraxinus excelsior* L. *Protoplasma* 116:204–208.

Goosen-de Roo, L. and E. A. M. Creyghton-Schouten. 1981. Plasmodesmata in cell walls in the cambial zone of *Fraxinus excelsior* L. *2nd Cell Wall Meeting, Gottingen* (Poster).

Goosen-de Roo, L. and P. Van Spronsen. 1978. Electron microscopy of the active cambial zone of *Fraxinus excelsior* L. *IAWA Bull.* 1978/4:59–64.

Greenidge, K. N. H. 1952. An approach to the study of vessel length in hardwood species. *Am J. Bot.* 39:570–574.

Gregory, R. A., and J. A. Robmerger. 1975. Cambial activity and height of uniseriate vascular rays in confiers. *Bot. Gaz.* 136:246–253.

Griffing, L. R., B. G. Mersey, and L. C. Fowke. 1986. Cell fractionation analysis of glucan synthase I and II distribution and polysaccharide secretion in soybean protoplast of coated vesicles in wall biogenesis. *Planta* 167:175–182.

Harris, N. 1986. Organization of the endomembrane system. *Annu. Rev. Plant Physiol.* 37:73–92.

Hashmi, S. 1977. *Studies on the production of secondary phloem in some tropical trees.* Ph.D. Thesis, Aligarh Muslim University, Aligarh, India.

Hebant, C., and E. de Fay. 1980. Functional organization of the bark of *Hevea brasiliensis* (rubber tree): A structural and histoenzymological study. *Z. Pflanzenphysiol.* 97:391–398.

Heinicke, A. J. 1937. Some cultural conditions influencing the manufacture of carbohydrates by apple leaves. *NY Hort. Soc. Proc.* 149–156.

Hejnowicz, Z. 1975. A model of morphogenetic map and clock. *J. Theor. Biol.* 54:345–362.

———. 1980. Tensional stress in the cambium and its developmental significance. *Am. J. Bot.* 67:1–5.

Hejnowicz, A., and M. Tomaszewski. 1969. Growth regulators and wood formation in *Pinus sylvestris*. *Physiol. Plant.* 22:984–992.

Hepler, P. K., and E. H. Newcomb. 1964. Microtubules and fibrils in the cytoplasm of *Coleus* cells undergoing secondary wall deposition. *J. Cell Biol.* 20:529–533.

Hertel, R. 1983. The mechanism of auxin transport as a model for auxin action. *Z. Pflanzenphysiol.* 112:53–68.

Heslop-Harrison, J. 1963. Ultrastructural aspects of differentiation in sporogenous tissue. In *Cell Differentiation*. Ed. G. E. Fogg. New York: Academic Press. 315–340.

Hodge, A. J., and A. B. Wardrop. 1950. An electron microscopic investigation of the cell wall organization of confier tracheids and conifer cambium. *Aust. J. Sci. Res. B* 3:265–269.

Hoefert, L. L. 1979. Ultrastructure of developing sieve elements in *Thlaspi arvense* L. I. The immuature state. *Am. J. Bot.* 66:925–932.

Hohl, H. R. 1960. Ueber die submikroskopische struktur normaler und hyper plastischer Gewebe von *Datura stramonium* L. I. Normalgewebe. *Ber. Schweiz. Bot. Ges.* 70:395–439.

Höll, W. 1975. Pattern of sugar concentration and lipase activity in trunks of *Tilia cordata* Mill. from the dormant period to the growing season. *Z. Pfanzenphysiol.* 75:158–164.

Holtzer, H. 1970. Proliferative and quantal mitosis in differentiation. In *Control Mechanisms in the Expression of Cellular Phenotypes*. Ed. H. A. Padykula. New York: Academic Press.

Huber, B., and W. V. Jazewitsch. 1956. Tree-ring studies of the Forestry-Botany Institute of Tharandt and Münich. *Tree-Ring Bull.* 21:28–30.

Hübner, R., H. Depta, and D. G. Robinson. 1985. Endocytosis in maize root cap cells. Evidence obtained using heavy metal salt solutions. *Protoplasma.* 129:214–222.

Imagawa, H., and S. Ishida. 1972. Study on the wood formation in trees. III. Occurrence of the overwintering cells in cambial zone in several ring-porous trees. *Res. Bull. Coll. Exp. For., Hokkaido Univ.* 29:207–221.

Innocenti, A. M., and S. Avanzi. 1971. Some cytological aspects of differentiation of metaxylem in the root of *Allium cepa*. *Cryptologia* 24:283–291.

Iqbal, M. 1979. *Studies on the Structure and Activity of Vascular Cambium in Acacia nilotica var. telia and Prosopis spicigera.* Ph.D. Thesis, Aligarh Muslim University, Aligarh, India.

———. 1990. *The Vascular Cambium.* Taunton, U.K.: Research Studies Press.

———. 1994. Ultrastructural differentiation of sieve elements. In *The Cambial Derivatives.* Ed. M. Iqbal. Stuttgart, Germany: Gebrüder Borntraeger. In press.

Iqbal, M., and A. K. M. Ghouse. 1980. *Acacia nilotica* (L.) Willd.—an ideal tree form of arid zone environment. *Ann. Arid Zone* 19:481–483.

———. 1982. Environmental influence on growth activities of *Prosopis spicigera*. In *Improvement of Forest Biomass.* Ed. P. K. Khosla. Dehra Dun, India: International Book House. 387–393.

———. 1983. An analytical study on cell size variation in some arid zone trees of India: *Acacia nilotica* and *Prosopis spicigera*. *IAWA Bull.* 4:46–52.

———. 1985a. Cell events of radial growth with special reference to cambium of tropical trees. In *Widening Horizons of Plant Sciences.* Ed. C. P. Malik. New Delhi: Cosmo Publications. 217–252.

———. 1985b. Impact of climatic variation on the structure and activity of vascular cambium in *Prosopis spicigera*. *Flora* 177:147–156.

———. 1987. Anatomy of the vascular cambium of *Acacia nilotica* (L.) Del. var *telia* troup (Mimosaceae) in relation to age and season. *Bot. J. Linn. Soc.* 94:385–397.

———. 1990 Cambial concept and organization. In *The Vascular Cambium.* Ed. M. Iqbal. Taunton, U.K.: Research Studies Press. 1–36.

Iqbal, M., and M. S. Zahur. 1994. Secondary phloem: Origin, structure and specialization. In *The Cambial Derivatives*. Ed. M. Iqbal. Stuttgart, Germany: Gebrüder Borntraeger. In press.

Itoh, T. 1971. On the ultrastructure of dormant and active cambium of confiers. *Wood Res.* 51:33–45.

Jeffcoat, B., and G. P. Harris. 1972. Hormonal regulation of the distribution of C-labelled assimilates in the flowering shoot of carnation. *Ann. Bot.* 36:353–361.

Jenkins, P. A., and K. R. Shepherd. 1972. Identification of abscisic acid in young stems of *Pinus radiata* D. Don. *New Phytol.* 71:501–511.

Kaeser, W. 1983. Ultrastructure of storage cells in Jerusalem artichoke tubers (*Helianthus tuberosus* L.): Vesicle formation during inulin synthesis. *Z. Pflanzenphysiol.* 111:253–260.

Kallarackal, J., and J. A. Milburn. 1983. Studies on the phloem sealing mechanism in *Ricinus* fruit stalks. *Aust. J. Plant Physiol.* 10:561–568.

Kamiya, N. 1981. Physical and chemical basis of cytoplasmic streaming. *Annu. Rev. Plant Physiol.* 32:205–236.

Kerr, T., and I. W. Bailey. 1934. The cambium and its derivative tissues X: Structure, optical properties and chemical composition of the so-called middle lamella. *J. Arnold Arbor.* 15:327–349.

Khan, M. I. H. 1977. *The Anatomical Study of the Growth Activities of Guava*. Ph.D. Thesis, Aligarh Muslim University, Aligarh, India.

Khan, S. 1980. *Studies on the Seasonal Activity of Vascular Cambium and Secondary Phloem in Some Myrtaceae*. Ph.D. Thesis, Aligarh Muslim University, Aligarh, India.

Kidwai, P., and A. W. Robards. 1969. On the ultrastructure of resting cambium in *Fagus sylvatica* L. *Planta* 89: 361–368.

Klekowski, E. K. Jr. 1988. *Mutation, Developmental Selection and Plant Evolution*. New York: Columbia University Press.

Koblitz, H. 1964. Chemisch-physiologische untersuchungen an pflanzlichen zellwaenden. *Flora Allg. Bot. Z.* 154:511–546.

Kohlenback, H. W., and B. Schmidt. 1975. Cytodifferenzierung in form einer direkten umwandlung isolierter Mesophyllen zu Tracheiden. *Z. Planzenphysiol.* 75:369–374.

Komor, E., B. H. Cho, and M. Thom. 1984. Sucrose transport and sucrose storage. *Ber. Deutsch. Bot. Ges.* 97:15–26.

Komor, E., and G. Orlich. 1986. Sugar-proton symport: From single cells to phloem loading. In *Phloem Transport*. Ed. J. Cronshaw, W. J. Lucas, and R. T. Giaquinta. New York: Alan Liss, Inc. 53–65.

Koriba, K. 1958. On the periodicity of tree-growth in the tropics, with reference to the mode of branching, the leaf fall, and the formation of the resting bud. *Gard. Bull. Singapore* 17:11–81.

Kozlowski, T. T. 1962. *Tree Growth*. New York: Ronald Press.

———. 1971. *Growth and Development of Trees*. Vol. II. New York: Academic Press.

Kramer, P. J., and T. T. Kozlowski. 1979. *Physiology of Woody Plants*. New York: Academic Press.

Kucera, L. J. 1978. Vascular nodules in the pith of yew (*Taxus baccata* L.). *IAWA Bull* 1978/4:81–85.

Kühn, A. 1971. *Lectures on Developmental Physiology*. Trans. R. Milkman. 2nd ed. Berlin/New York: Springer.

Kundu, B. C., and S. Sen. 1980. Origin and development of fibres in ramie (*Boehmeria nivea* Gaud). *Proc. Natl. Inst. Sci. India Sect. B.* (Suppl.) 26:190–198.

Lachaud, S. 1983. Xylogenese chez les Dicotyledones arborescentes. IV. Influence des bourgeons, de l'acide β-indol acetique at de l'acide gibberellique sur la reactivation cambiale et la xylogenese dans les jeunes tiges de Hetre. *Can. J. Bot.* 61:1758–1774.

Lachaud, S., and J. L. Bonnemain. 1982. Xylogenese chez les Dicotyledones arborescentes. III. Transport de l'auxine et activite cambiale dans les jeunes tiges de Hetre. *Can. J. Bot.* 60:869–876.

———. 1984. Seasonal variations in the polar-transport pathways and retention sites of

(3H) indole–3-acetic acid in young branches of *Fagus sylvatica* L. *Planta* 161:207–215.

Ladefoged, K. 1952. The periodicity of wood formation. *Klg. Danske Videnskab. Seiskab Biol. Skrifter* 7:1–98.

Lafontaine, J. G. 1974. The nucleus. In *Dynamic Aspects of Plant Ultrastructure*. Ed. A. W. Robards. London: McGraw Hill. 1–51.

Lamport, D. T. A. 1986. The primary cell wall: A new model. In *Cellulose: Structure, Modification, and Hydrolysis*. Ed. R. A. Young, R. M. Pr. Rowell. New York: John Wiley and Sons. 77–99.

Larson, P. R. 1964. Some indirect effects of environment on wood formation. In *Formation of Wood in Forest Trees*. Ed. M. H. Zimmermann. New York: Academic Press. 345–365.

_____. 1969. *Wood Formation and the Concept of Wood Quality*. Sch. For. Bull. Yale Univ. New Haven, CT. 74.

_____. 1976a. Procambium vs cambium and protoxylem vs metaxylem in *Populus deltoides* seedlings. *Am. J. Bot.* 63:1332–1348.

_____. 1976b. The leaf-cambium relation and some prospects for genetic improvement. In *Tree Physiology and Yield Improvements*. Ed. M. G. R. Cannell and F. T. Last. London: Academic Press. 261–282.

_____. 1982. The concept of cambium. In *New Perspectives in Wood Anatomy*. Ed. P. Baas. The Hague: Martinus Nijhoff. 85–122.

Lawton, J. R. 1972. Seasonal variations in the secondary phloem of some forest trees from Nigeria. II. Sturcture of the phloem. *New Phytol.* 71:335–348.

Le Saint, A. M., and A. M. Catesson. 1966. Variations simultanées des teneurs en eau, en sucres solubles, en acides amines et de la pression osmotique dans le Phloéme et le cambium de sycomore pendant les périods des repos apparent et de reprise de la croissance. *C. R. Acad. Sci.* 263:1463–1466.

Libbenga, K. R., and J. G. Torrey. 1973. Hormone induced endoreduplication prior to mitoses in cultured pea root cortical cells. *Am. J. Bot.* 60:293–299.

Liese, W., and N. Parameswaran. 1972. On the variation of cell length within the bark of some tropical hard wood species. In *Research Trends in Plant Anatomy*. Ed. A. K. M. Ghouse and M. Yunus. New Delhi: Tata McGraw Hill. 83–89.

Lintilhac, P. M., and T. B. Vesecky. 1984. Stress-induced alignment of division plane in plant tissues grown in vitro. *Nature* 307:363–364.

Liphschitz, N., and S. Lev-Yadun. 1986. Cambial activity of evergreen and seasonal dimorphics around the Mediterranean. *IAWA Bull.* 7:145–153.

Little, C. H. A. 1981. Effect of cambial dormancy state on the transport of (1–14c) Indol-3-ylacetic acid in *Abies balsamea* shoots. *Can. J. Bot.* 59:342–348.

Little, C. H. A., and P. F. Wareing. 1981. Control of cambial activity and dormancy in *Picea sitchensis* by Indol-3-ylacetic and abscisic acids. *Can. J. Bot.* 59:1480–1493.

Lu, C. Y., and S. H. T. Chiang. 1975. Seasonal activity of the cambium in the young branch of *Liquidambar formosana* Hance. *Taiwania* 20:32–47.

Mahmood, A. 1968. Cell groupings and primary wall generation in the cambial zone, xylem and phloem in *Pinus. Aust. J. Bot.* 16:177–196.

_____. 1990. The parental cell walls. In *The Vascular Cambium*. Ed. M. Iqbal. Taunton, U.K.: Research Studies Press. 113–126.

Mahmooduzzafar, and M. Iqbal. 1986. Variation in size and amount of wood elements across and within the growth ring in *Terminalia tomentosa. Flora* 178:191–196.

Malawer, C. L., and R. Phillips. 1979. The cell cycle in relation to induced xylem differentiation. Tritiated thymidine incorporation in cultured tuber explants of *Helianthus tuberosus* L. *Plant. Sci. Lett.* 15:47–55.

Marchant, H., and E. R. Hines. 1979. The role of microtubules and cell wall deposition in elongation of regenerating protoplasts of *Mougeotia. Planta* 146:41–48.

Matar, D. 1987. *Evolution Pariétale dans le Continuum Apex-Procambium-Cambium et au Cours de la Différenciation du Phloème*. 72 pp. (27 plates). These de 3eme cycle, Universite P. et M. Curie, Paris.

Matar, D., J. Chuba, and A. M. Catesson. 1986. The first steps of cell-wall maturation in the root meristem of *Phaseolus vulgaris*. *Cell Walls* 86:80–81.

Mauseth, J. D. 1982. A morphometric study of the ultrastructure of *Echinocereus engelmanii* (Cactaceae). *Am. J. Bot.* 69:551–555.

———. 1988. *Plant Anatomy*. Menlo Park, CA: Benjamin/Cummings.

Mellman, I., R. Fuchs, and A. Helenius. 1986. Acidification of the endocytic and exocytic pathways. *Annu. Rev. Biochem.* 55:553–700.

Meyer, R. W., and A. F. Muhammad. 1971. Scalariform perforation plate: fine structure. *Wood Fiber.* 3:139–145.

Meylan, B. A., and B. G. Butterfield. 1981. Perforation-plate differentiation in the vessels of hardwoods. In *Xylem Cell Development*. Ed. J. R. Barnett. Tunbridge Wells, U.K.: Castle House. 96–114.

Mia, A. J. 1970. Fine structure of active, dormant and aging cambial cells in *Tilia americana*. *Wood Sci.* 3:34–42.

Michniewicz, M., and E. Galoch. 1972. Dynamics of endogenous inhibitor of abscisic acid properties in the development of buds, newly formed shoots and adventitious roots of willow cuttings (*Salix viminalis* L.). *Bull. Acad. Pol. Sci. Cl. II Ser.* 20:333–337.

Miyakawa, M., M. Fujita, H. Saiki, and H. Harada. 1973. The cell wall structure of the secondary-phloem elements in *Cryptomeria japonica* D. Don. *Bull. Kyoto Univ. Forests* 45:181–191.

Montezinos, D., and R. M. Brown. 1976. Surface architecture of the plant cell: Biogenesis of the cell wall, with special emphasis on the role of the plasma membrane in cellulose biosynthesis. *J. Supramol. Struct.* 5:277–290.

Mott, D. G., L. D. Nairn, and J. A. Cook. 1957. Radial growth in forest trees and effects of insect defoliation. *For. Sci.* 3:286–304.

Mühlethaler, K. 1965. Growth theories and the development of the cell wall. In *Cellular Ultrastructure of Woody Plants*. Ed. W. A. Cote, Jr. New York: Syracuse Univ. Press. 51–60.

———. 1967. Ultrastructure and formation of plant cell walls. *Annu. Rev. Plant Physiol.* 18:1–24.

Munting, A. J., and M. T. M. Willemse. 1987. External influences on development of vascular cambium and its derivatives. *Phytomorphology.* 37:261–274.

Murmanis, L. 1971. Sturctural changes in the vascular cambium of *Pinus strobus* L. during an annual cycle. *Ann. Bot.* 35:133–141.

Nägl, W. 1978. *Endopolyploidy and Polyteny in Differentiation and Evolution*. Amsterdam, The Netherlands: North-Holland.

Nägl, W. J. Hendon, and W. Rucker. 1972. DNA amplification in *cymbidium* protocorms in vitro. *Cell Differen.* 1:229–237.

Nakamura, S., and H. Miki-Hirosige. 1982. Coated vesicles and cell-plate formation in the microspore mother cell. *J. Ultrastruct. Res.* 80:302–311.

North, G. 1983. Genes and development: Cloning the genes that specify fruit flies. *Nature* 303:134–136.

Northcote, D. H. 1963. Changes in the cell walls of plants during differentiation. *Symp. Soc. Exp. Biol.* 17:157–174.

———. 1982. Control of enzyme activity during plant-cell development. In *Differentiation in vitro*. Ed. M. M. Yeoman and D. E. S. Truman. London/New York: Cambridge Univ. Press. 49–64.

O'Brien, T. P. 1981. The primary xylem. In *Xylem Cell Development*. Ed. J. R. Barnett. Tunbridge Wells, U.K.: Castle House Publ. 3–37.

Oparka, K. J., R. P. C. Johnson, and J. D. Bowen. 1981. Sites of acid phsophatase in the differentiating root protophloem of *Nymphoides peltata* (S. G. Gmel) O. Kuntz. *Plant Cell Environ.* 4:27–35.

Oppenheimer, H. R. 1945. Cambial wood production in stems of *Pinus halepensis*. *Palest. J. Bot. Rehovot Ser.* 5:22–51.

Owens, J. N. 1968. Initiation and development of leaves in Douglas fir. *Can. J. Bot.* 46:271–278.

Owens, J. N., and M. Molder. 1973. A study of DNA and mitotic activity in the vegetative apex of Douglas fir during the annual growth cycle. *Can. J. Bot.* 51:1395–1409.

Paliwal, G. S., and N. V. S. R.K. Prasad. 1970. Seasonal activity of cambium in some tropical trees. I. *Dalbergia sissoo. Phytomorphology* 20:333–339.

Paliwal, G. S., N. V. S.R. K. Prasad, V. S. Sajwan, and S. K. Agarwal. 1975. Seasonal activity of cambium in some tropical trees. II. *Polyalthia longifolia. Phytomorphology* 25:478–484.

Paliwal, G. S., V. S. Sajwan, and S. K. Agarwal. 1976. Seasonal activity of cambium in some tropical trees. III. *Salvadora persica* L. *Acta Soc. Bot. Pol.* 45:303–312.

Paliwal, S. P., and G. S. Paliwal. 1990. Influence of climatic variations on the seasonal behaviour of the vascular cambium in some Himalayan trees. III. *Rhododendron arboreum* Smith. *Phytomorphology* 40:257–271.

Paramanova, N. V. 1974. Rapports structuraux fondamentaux entre le symplaste et l'apoplaste dans la racine de *Beta vulgaris* au moment de la sortie des assimilats hors de la feuille (en russe). *Physiol. Rast.* 21:578–587.

Parmeswaran, N., and W. Liese. 1974. Variation of cell length in bark and wood of tropical trees. *Wood Sci. Technol.* 8:81–90.

Parish, G. R. 1974. Seasonal variation in the membrane structure of differentiating shoot cambial-zone cells demonstrated by freeze-etching. *Cytobiologie* 9:131–143.

Parthasarathy, M. V. 1974a. Ultrastructure of phloem in palms. II. Structural changes and fate of the organelles in differentiating sieve elements. *Protoplasma* 79:93–125.

———. 1974b. Ultrastructure of phloem in palms. III. Mature phloem. *Protoplasma* 79:265–315.

Parthasarathy, M. V., T. D. Perdue, A. Witztum, and J. Alvernaz. 1985. Actin network as a normal component of cytoskeleton in many vascular plant cells. *Am. J. Bot.* 72:1318–1323.

Parups, E. V. 1964. The effect of maleic hydrazide on synthesis of lignin. *Can. J. Plant Sci.* 44:253–258.

Patel, J. D. 1975. Occurrence of multinucleate fusiform initials in *Solanum melongena. Curr. Sci.* 44:516–517.

Patel, R. N. 1965. A comparison of the anatomy of the secondary xylem in roots and stems. *Holzforschung* 19:72–79.

Pesacreta, T. C., and W. J. Lucas. 1985. Presence of a partially coated reticulum in angiosperms. *Protoplasma* 125:173–184.

Philipson, W. R., J. M. Ward, and B. G. Butterfield. 1971. *The Vascular Cambium: Its Development and Activity.* London: Chapman and Hall.

Phillips, R., and S. M. Arnott. 1983. Studies on induced tracheary element differentiation in cultured tissues of tubers of the Jerusalem artichoke, *Helianthus tuberosus. Histochem. J.* 15:427–436.

Phillips R., and J. G. Torrey. 1973. DNA synthesis, cell division and cytodifferentiation in cultured pea root cortical explants. *Dev. Biol.* 31:336–347.

Pickett—Heaps, J. D., and D. H. Northcote. 1966. The relationship of cellular organelles to the formation and development of the plant-cell wall. *J. Exp. Bot.* 17:20–26.

Pizzolato, T. D., and C. Heimsch. 1975. Ontogeny of the protophloem fibres and secondary xylem fibres within the stem of *Coleus.* I. A light microscope study. *Can. J. Bot.* 53:1658–1671.

Porter, K. R., and R. D. Machado. 1960. Studies on the endoplasmic reticulum. IV. Its form and distribution during mitosis in cells of onion root tip. *J. Biophys. Biochem. Cytol.* 7:167–180.

Preston, R. D., and G. N. Goodman. 1968. Some aspects of cellulose microfibril biosynthesis. *Proc. R. Microsc. Soc.* 88:513–527.

Preston, R. D., and G. W. Ripley. 1954. An electron microscopic investigation of the walls of conifer cambium. *J. Exp. Bot.* 5:410–413.

Preston, R. D., and A. B. Wardrop. 1949. The submicroscopic organization of the walls of confier cambium. *Biochem. Biophys. Acta* 3:549.

Priestley, J. H. 1930. Studies in the physiology of cambial activity. III. The seasonal activity of the cambium. *New Phytol.* 29:316–354.

Rana, M. A., and P. B. Gahan. 1983. Determination of fascicular, interfascicular and cork cambia in dicotyledonous plants. *Saussurea* 14:51–60.

Rao, A. N. 1970. Periodic changes in the cambial activity of *Hevea brasiliensis*. *J. Indian Bot. Soc.* 51:13–17.

Rao, K. S. 1985. Seasonal ultrastructural changes in the cambium of *Aesculus hippocastanum* L. *Ann. Sci. Nat. Bot.* (13 ème ser.) 7:213–228.

Rao, K. S., and A. M. Catesson. 1987. Changes in the membrane components of nondividing cambial cell. *Can. J. Bot.* 65:246–254.

Rao, K. S., and Y. S. Dave. 1983a. Ultrastructure of dormant cambium in *Holoptelea integrifolia* (Roxb.) Planch. *Flora* 174:165–172.

_____ . 1983b. Ultrastructure of active and dormant cambial cells in teak (*Tectona grandis* L.f.) *New Phytol.* 93:447–456.

_____ . 1983c. Seasonal histochemical changes in the cambium of *Tectona grandis* L.f. and *Gmelina arborea* Roxb. *Biol. Plant.* 25:241–245.

Reinders-Gouwentak, C. A. 1941. Cambial activity as dependent on the presence of growth hormone and the non-resting condition of stems. *Proc. Acad. Sci. Amst.* 44:654–663.

_____ . 1965. Physiology of the cambium and other secondary meristems of the shoot. In *Encyclopaedia of Plant Physiology* XV, Ed. W. Ruhland. Berlin: Springer. 1077–1105.

Reinders-Gouwentak, C. A., and A. L. Mass. 1940. Kambiumtätigkeit und Wuchsstoff: II. Meded. *Landbouwhogesch.* (*Wageningen*) 44:3–16.

Riding, R. T., and C. H. A. Little. 1984. Anatomy and histochemistry of *Abies balsamea* cambial-zone cells during the onset and breaking of dormancy. *Can. J. Bot.* 62:2570–2579.

_____ . 1986. Histochemistry of the dormant vascular cambium of *Abies balsamea*: Changes associated with tree age and crown position. *Can. J. Bot.* 64:2082–2087.

Robards, A. W. 1968. On the ultrastructure of differentiating secondary xylem in willow. *Protoplasma* 65:449–462.

Robards, A. W., and P. Kidwai. 1969. A comparative study of the ultrastructure of resting and active cambium of *Salix fragilis* L. *Planta* 84:239–249.

Roberts, L. W. 1969. The initiation of xylem differentiation. *Bot. Rev.* 35:201–250.

_____ . 1976. *Cytodifferentiation in Plants: Xylogenesis as a Model System.* London: Cambridge Univ. Press.

Robinson, D. G., and U. Kristen. 1982. Membrane flow via the Golgi apparatus of higher plant cells. *Int. Rev. Cytol.* 77:89–127.

Roelofsen, P. A. 1959. *The Plant Cell Wall.* Berlin: Gebrüder Borntraeger.

Roland, J. C. 1978. Early differences between radial walls and tangential walls of actively growing cambial zone. *IAWA Bull.* 1978. 1:7–10.

Roland, J. C., and B. Vian. 1979. The wall of growing plant cells: Its three dimensional organization. *Int. Rev. Cytol.* 61:129–166.

Roland, J. C., B. Vian, and D. Reis. 1975. Observations with cytochemistry and ultracytotomy on the fine structure of the expanding walls in actively elongating plant cells. *J. Cell Sci.* 19:239–259.

Roland, J. C., B. Vian, and D. Reis. 1977. Further observations on cell wall morphogenesis and polysaccharide arrangement during plant growth. *Protoplasma* 91:125–141.

Rubery, P. H., and D. H. Northcote. 1968. Site of phenylalanine ammonialyase activity and synthesis of lignin during xylem differentiation. *Nature* 219:1230–1234.

Russow, E. 1882. Ueber den Bau und die Entwicklung der Siebrohren und uber Bau und Entwicklung der secondaren Rinde Dicotylen und Gymnosperm. *Sitzungsher. Naturf. Gesell. Dorpat.* 6:257–327.

Sabnis D. D., and H. M. Sabnis. 1993. Phloem proteins: Structure, biochemistry and function. In *The Cambial Derivatives.* Ed. M. Iqbal. Stuttgart: Gebrüder Borntraeger. In press.

Sachs, T. 1969. Polarity and the induction of organized vascular tissues. *Ann. Bot.* 33:263–275.

_____ . 1981. The control of patterned differentiation of vascular tissues. *Adv. Bot. Res.* 9:152–261.

Saks, Y., and R. Aloni. 1985. Polar gradients of tracheid number and diameter during primary and secondary xylem development in young seedlings of Pinus pinea L. Ann. Bot. 56:771–778.

Sanio, K. 1872. Uber die Grösse der Holzellen bei der geneinen Kiefer (Pinus sylvestris). Jahrb. Wiss. Bot. 8:401–420.

Satterfield, G., J. Sparkuhl, and H. Byrne. 1978. Ribosome metabolism in excised stices of Jerusalem artichoke tuber. In Biochemistry of Wounded Plant Tissues. Ed. G. Kahl. Berlin: Walter de Gruyter. 571–594.

Sauter, J. J. 1980. The Strasburger cells equivalents of companion cells. Ber. Deutsch. Bot. Gesell. 93:29–42.

_____ . 1982. Transport in markstrahlen. Ber. Deutsch. Bot. Ges. 95:593–618.

Sauter, J. J., W. Iten, and H. Zimmermann. 1973. Studies on the release of sugar into the vessels of sugar maple (Acer saccharum). Can. J. Bot. 51:1–8.

Sauter, J. J., and S. Kloth. 1986. Plasmodesmatal frequency and radial translocation rates in ray cells of poplar (Populus × canadensis Moench 'robusta'). Planta 168:377–380.

Savidge, R. A. 1983a. The role of plant hormones in higher plant cellular differentiation. I. A critique. Histochem. J. 15:437–445.

_____ . 1983b. The role of plant hormones in higher plant cellular differentiation. II. Experiments with the vascular cambium, and sclereid and tracheid differentiation in the pine, Pinus contorta. Histochem. J. 15:447–466.

_____ . 1985. Prospects for manipulating vascular cambium productivity and xylem-cell differentiation. In Attributes of Trees as Crop Plants. Ed. M. G. R. Cannell and J. E. Jackson. Abbots Ripton, U.K.: I. T. E. 208–227.

Savidge, R. A., and J. L. Farrar. 1984. Cellular adjustment in the vascular cambium leading to spiral-grain formation in conifers. Can. J. Bot. 62:2872–2879.

Savidge, R. A., J. K. Heald, and P. F. Wareing. 1982. Non-uniform distribution and seasonal variation of endogenous indol-3-ylacetic acid in cambial region of Pinus contorta Dougl. Planta 155:89–92.

Savidge, R. A., and P. F. Wareing. 1981a. A tracheid-differentiation factor from pine needles. Planta 153:395–404.

_____ . 1981b. Plant-growth regulators and the differentiation of vascular elements. In Xylem Cell Development. Ed. J. R. Barnett. London: Castle House Publications. 196–235.

Schacht, H. 1856. Lehrbuch der Anatomie und Physiologie der Gewachse, Berlin. 1:53.

Schnepf, E. 1986. Cellular polarity. Annu. Rev. Plant. Physiol. 37:23–47.

Scott, F. M., V. Siaholm, and E. Bowler. 1960. Light and electron microscope studies on the primary xylem of Ricinus communis. Am. J. Bot. 47:162–173.

Sennerby-Forsse, L. 1986. Seasonal variation in the ultrastructure of the cambium in young stems of willow (Salix viminalis) in relation to phenology. Physiol. Plant. 67:529–537.

Seth, A., and P. F. Wareing. 1964. Interactions between auxins, gibberellins and kinins in hormone-directed transport. Life Sci. 3:1483–1486.

Sheldrake, A. R. 1973. The production of hormones in higher plants. Biol. Rev. 48:509–559.

Shepherd, K. R., and K. S. Rowan. 1967. Indoleacetic acid in cambial tissue of radiata pine. Aust. J. Biol. Sci. 20:637–646.

Shigo, A. L., and K. R. Duudzik. 1985. Response of uninjured cambium to xylem injury. Wood Sci. Technol. 19:195–200.

Shininger, T. L. 1975. Is DNA synthesis required for the induction of differentiation in quiescent root cortical parenchyma? Dev. Biol. 45:137–150.

Siddiqi, T. O. 1991. Impact of seasonal variation on the structure and activity of vascular cambium in Ficus religiosa. IAWA Bull. 12:177–185.

Sieber, M. 1985. Anatomical structure of roots of two species of Khaya in Ghana. In Xyloroma, Trends in Wood Research. Ed. L. J. Kucera. Basel: Birkhäuser. 176–183.

Siebers, A. M. 1971a. Initiation of radial polarity in the interfascicular cambium of Ricinus communis L. Acta Bot. Neerl. 20:211–220.

_____ . 1971b. Differentiation of isolated interfascicular tissue of Ricinus communis L. Acta Bot. Neerl. 20:343–355.

————. 1972. Vascular bundle differentiation and development in cultured tissue blocks excised from the embryo of *Ricinus communis* L. *Acta Bot. Neerl.* 21:327–342.

Siebers, A. M., and C. A. Ladage. 1973. Factors controlling cambial development in the hypocotyl of *Ricinus communis* L. *Acta Bot. Neerl.* 22:416–432.

Simson, B. W., and T. E. Timell. 1978a. Polysaccharides in cambial tissues of *Populus tremuloides* and *Tilia americana*. I. Isolation, fractionation, and chemical composition of the cambial tissue. *Cellulose Chem. Technol.* 12:39–50.

————. 1978b. Polysaccharides in cambial tissues of *Populus tremuloides* and *Tilia americana*. II. Isolation and structure of a xyloglucan. *Cellulose Chem. Technol.* 12:51–62.

————. 1978c. Polysaccharides in cambial tissues of *Populus tremuloides* and *Tilia americana*. III. Isolation and constitution of an arabinogalactan. *Cellulose Chem. Technol.* 12:63–77.

————. 1978d. Polysaccharides in cambial tissues of *Populus tremuloides* and *Tilia americana*. IV. 4.0 methylglucuronoxylan and pectin. *Cellulose Chem.* Technol. 12:79–84.

Sjolund, R. D., C. Y. Shih, and K. G. Jensen. 1983. Freeze-fracture analysis of phloem structure in plant tissue culture. III. P-protein, sieve area pores and wounding. *J. Ultrastr. Res.* 82:198–211.

Sladký, Z. 1972. The role of endogenous growth regulators in the differentiation process of walnut (*Juglans regia* L.) *Biol. Plant* 14:273–278.

Soh, W. Y., K. D. Kang, and W. Y. Yang. 1992. Ontogeny of the interfascicular cambium in the hypotyl of *Ricinus communis* L. In *Proc. 2nd Pacific Regional Wood Anatomy Conf.*, Oct. 1989. Ed. J. P. Rajo. Laguna, Phillipines: Forest Products Res. and Dev. Inst. 349–358.

Spanner, D. C. 1978a. Sieve plate pores, open or occluded? A critical review. *Plant Cell Environ.* 1:7–20.

————. 1978b. The Münch hypothesis, freeze substitution and the structure of Sieve-plate pores. *Ann. Bot.* 42:485–488.

Srivastava, L. M. 1963. Cambium and vascular derivatives of *Ginkgo biloba*. *J. Arnold Arbor.* 44:165–192.

————. 1966a. On the fine structure of the cambium of *Fraxinus americana* L. *J. Cell Biol.* 31:79–93.

————. 1966b. Histochemical studies on lignin. *TAPPI* 49:173–183.

————. 1970. The secondary phloem of *Austrobaileya-scandens*. *Can. J. Bot.* 48:341–359.

Srivastava, L. M., and T. P. O'Brien. 1966. On the ultrastructure of cambium and its vascular derivatives. I. Cambium of *Pinus strobus*. *Protoplasma* 61:257–276.

Steer, M. W. 1985. Vesicle dynamics. In *Botanical Microscopy*. Ed. A. W. Robards. Oxford: Science Publications. 129–155.

Steinman, R. M., I. S. Mellman, W. A. Muller, and Z. A. Cohn. 1983. Endocytosis and the recycling of plasma membrane. *J. Cell Biol.* 96:1–27.

Steponkus, P. L. 1984. Role of the plasma membrane in freezing injury and cold acclimation. *Annu. Rev. Plant Physiol.* 35:543–584.

Stewart, C. M. 1966. *The Chemistry of Secondary Growth in Trees. Div. For. Prod. Tech. Paper No.43.* Melbourne, Australia: CSIRO.

Stieber, J. 1985. Wave nature and a theory of cambial activity. *Can. J. Bot.* 63:1942–1950.

Strasburger, E. 1891. *Histologische Beitrage*. III. *Uber den Bau und die verrichtungen der Leitun-gsbahnen in den pflanzen.* (Jena).

Studhalter, R. A., W. S. Glock, and S. R. Agerter. 1963. Tree growth. *Bot Rev.* 29:245–365.

Sundrasivarao, B., and Nazma. 1977. Variation in length of vessel elements and libriform fibres within one tree. *Aesculus hippocastanum* L. *J. Jpn. Bot.* 52:179–187.

Sundrasivarao B., P. S. Prakasarao, and N. Vijayalakshmi. 1973. Variation in length of vessel elements and libriform fibers within one tree. *Ulmus procera* Salisb. *J. Jpn. Bot.* 48:304–313.

Takagi, S., and R. Nagai. 1986. Intracellular Ca^2 concentration and cytoplasmic streaming in *Vallisneria* mesophyll cells. *Plant Cell Physiol.* 27:953–960.

Tepper, H. B., and C. A. Hollis. 1967. Mitotic reactivation of the terminal bud and cambium of white ash. *Science* 156:1635–1636.

Thimann, K. V., and D. Kaufman. 1958. Cytoplasmic streaming in the cambium of white pine. In *The Physiology of Forest Trees*. Ed. K. V. Thimann. New York: Ronald Press. 479–492.

Thorsch, J., and K. Esau. 1981. Nuclear degeneration and the association of endoplasmic reticulum with the nuclear envelope and microtubules in maturing sieve elements of *Gossypium hirsutum*. *J. Ultrastr. Res.* 74:195–204.

Timell, T. E. 1979. Formation of compression wood in balsam fir *Abies balsamea*. 1. Ultrastructure of the activie cambial zone and its enlarging derivatives. *Holzforschung* 33:137–143.

_____. 1980. Organization and ultrastructure of the dormant cambial zone in compresson wood of *Picea abies*. *Wood Sci. Technol.* 14:161–179.

Tippett, J. T., and T. C. Hill. 1984. Junction complexes between sieve tubes in the secondary phloem of Myrtaceae. *Ann. Bot.* 53:421–429.

Tomlinson, P. B., and M. H. Zimmermann. 1967. The "wood" of monocotyledons. *IAWA Bull.* 2:4–24.

Torrey, J. G. 1975. Tracheary—element formation from single isolated cells in culture. *Physiol. Plant.* 35:158–165.

Tort, M., and M. Gendraud. 1984. Contribution a l'étude des pH cytoplasmique et vacuolaire en rapport avec la Crossance et l'accumulation des réserves chez le crosne du japon. *C. R. Acad. Sci.* 299 (III):431–434.

Tort, M., M. Gendraud, and J. C. Courduroux. 1985. Mechanisms of storage in dormant tubers: Correlative aspects, biochemical and ultrastructural approaches. *Physiol. Vég.* 23:289–299.

Traas, J. A. 1984. Visualization of the membrane bound cytoskeleton and coated pits of plant cells by means of dry clearing. *Protoplasma* 119:212–218.

Trewavas, A. J. 1982. Growth substance sensitivity: The limiting factor in plant development. *Physiol Plant.* 55:60–72.

Tsuda, M. 1972. Phytoferritin in plastids of the cambial zone and phloem of conifers. *Makuzai Gakkaishi* 18:367–371.

Tsuda, M. 1975. The ultrastructure of the vascular cambium and its derivatives in coniferous species. I. Cambial cells. *Bull. Tokyo Univ. For.* 67:158–226.

Turgeon, R. 1975. Differentiation of wound-vessel members without DNA synthesis, mitosis or cell division. *Nature* 257:806–808.

Valanne, N., and T. Valanne. 1981. Ultrastructure of phloem in the trunk of *Betula pubescens*. *J. Ultrastruct. Res.* 76:314.

Venketeswaran, S. and P. K. Chen. 1964. Nutritional factors affecting growth, friability, and lignification of suspension cultures of higher plant cells. *Can. J. Bot.* 42:1279–1286.

Venugopal, N., and K. V. Krishnamurthy. 1989. Organisation of vascular cambium during different seasons in some tropical timber trees. *Nord. J. Bot.* 8:631–638.

Vigil, E. L. 1984. The role of E. R. in mitosis and cytokinesis of meristematic cells in cotton apices. *J. Histochem. Cytochem.* 31:1062–1068.

Walsh, M. A., and R. F. Evert. 1975. Ultrastructure of metaphloem sieve elements in *Zea mays* L. *Protoplasma* 83:365–388.

Wardrop, A. B. 1954. The mechanism of surface growth involved in the differentiation of fibres and tracheids. *Aust. J. Bot.* 2:165–175.

_____. 1957. The phase of lignification in the differentiation of wood fibres. *TAPPI* 40:225–243.

_____. 1964. The structure and formation of the cell wall in xylem. In *The Formation of Wood in Forest Trees*. Ed. M. H. Zimmermann. London: Academic Press.

Wardrop, A. B., and D. E. Bland. 1959. The process of lignification in woody plants. In *Biochemistry of Woods*. Ed. K. Kratzl, and G. Billek. New York: Pergamon. 92–114.

Wareing, P. F. 1951a. Growth studies in woody species. III. Further photoperiodic effect in *Pinus sylvestris*. *Physiol. Plant.* 4:41–56.

_____. 1951b. Growth studies in woody species IV. Initiation of cambial activity in ring-porous species. *Physiol. Plant* 4:546–562.

———. 1956. Photoperiodism in woody plants. *Annu. Rev. Plant Physiol.* 7:191–214.

———. 1958a. The physiology of cambial activity. *J. Inst. Wood Sci.* 1:34–42.

———. 1958b. Interaction between indole-acetic acid and gibberellic acid in cambial activity. *Nature* 181:1744–1745.

———. 1982. Determination and related aspects of plant development. In *The Molecular Biology of Plant Development.* Ed. H. Smith, and D. Grierson. *Bot. Monogr.* No. 18. Oxford: Blackwell Scientific. 517–541.

Wareing, P. F., and M. Black. 1958. Photoperiodism in seeds and seedlings of woody species. In *The Physiology of Forest Trees.* Ed. K. V. Thimann. New York: Ronald Press. 529–56.

Wareing, P. F., C. E. A. Hanney, and J. Digby. 1964. The role of endogenous hormones in cambial activity and xylem differentiation. In *The Formation of Wood in Forest Trees.* Ed. M. H. Zimmermann. New York: Academic Press. 323–344.

Wareing, P. F., and L. W. Roberts. 1956. Photoperiodic control of cambial activity in *Robinia pseudoacacia* L. *New Phytol.* 55:356–366.

Wenham, M. W., and F. Cusick. 1975. The growth of secondary wood fibres. *New Phytol.* 74:247–261.

Whalley, B. E. 1950. Increase in girth of the cambium in *Thuja occidentalis* L. *Can. J. Res.* C. 28:331–340.

Whitmore, F. W., and R. Zahner. 1966. Development of the xylem ring in stems of young red pine trees. *For. Sci.* 12:198–210.

Wiebe, H. H. 1978. The significance of plant vacuoles. *Bioscience* 28:327–331.

Wilcox, H. 1962. Cambial growth characteristics. In *Tree Growth.* Ed. T. T. Kozlowski. New York: Ronald Press. 57–88.

Williamson, R. E. 1986. Organelle movements along actin filaments and microtubules. *Plant Physiol.* 82:631–634.

Wilson, B. F. 1963. Increase in cell wall surface area during enlargment of cambial derivatives in *Abies concolor.* *Am. J. Bot.* 50:95–102.

———. 1964. A model for cell poroduction by the cambium of conifers. In *The Formation of Wood in Forest Trees.* Ed. M. H. Zimmermann. New York: Academic Press. 19–36.

Wilson, B. F., and R. A. Howard. 1968. A computer model for cambial activity. *For. Sci.* 14:77–90.

Wilson, B. F., T. J. Wodzicki, and R. Zahner. 1966. Differentiation of cambial derivatives. Proposed terminology. *For. Sci.* 12:438–440.

Wisniewski, M. E., and E. N. Ashworth. 1985a. Ultrastructural changes related to cold hardiness in cortical and xylem parenchyma cells of *Prunus persica.* *Am. J. Bot.* 72:836–837.

———. 1985b. Changes in the ultrastructure of xylem parenchyma cells of peach (*Prunus persica*) and red oak (*Quercus rubra*) in response to a freezing stress. *Am. J. Bot.* 72:1364–1376.

———. 1986. A comparison of seasonal ultrastructural changes in stem tissues of peach (*Prunus persica*) that exhibit contrasting mechanisms of cold hardiness. *Bot. Gaz.* 147:407–417.

Wisniewski, M., A. L. Bogle, and C. L. Wilson. 1985. Seasonal variation in cambial electrical resistance and its relation to growth in two cultivars of peach. *Can. J. Plant Sci.* 65:345–350.

Wodzicki, T. J., and C. L. Brown. 1973. Cellular differentiation of the cambium in the Pinaceae. *Bot. Gaz.* 134:139–146.

Wodzicki, T. J., and W. J. Humphreys. 1972. Cytodifferentiation of maturing pine tracheids. The final stage. *Tissue Cell* 4:525–528.

———. 1973. Maturing pine tracheids. Organisation of intravacuolar cytoplasm. *J. Cell Biol.* 56:263–265.

Wooding, F. B. P., and D. H. Northcote. 1964. The development of the secondary wall of the xylem in *Acer pseudoplatanus.* *J. Cell Biol.* 23:327–337.

Worrall, J. G. 1980. The impact of environment on cambial growth. In *Control of Shoot Growth in Trees*. Ed. C. H. A. Little. Proc. IUFRO Workshop. Fredericton, Canada. 127–142.

Wort, D. J. 1962. Physiology of cambial activity. In *Tree Growth*. Ed. T. T. Kozlowski. New York: Ronald Press. 89–95.

Yata, S., T. Itoh, and T. Kishima. 1970. Formation of perforation plates and bordered pits in differentiating vessel elements. *Wood Res.* 50:1–11.

Yunus, M. 1976. *Anatomical Studies on the Bark of Tropical Plants of Economic Value*. Ph.D. Thesis. Aligarh Muslim Univ. Aligarh, India.

Yunus, M., M. Iqbal, and D. Yunus. 1977. Cell length variation in the secondary phloem of some medicinally important tropical trees. *La-Yaaran* 27:55–60.

Zaerr, J. B., and J. M. Mitchell. 1967. Polar transport related to mobilization of plant constituents. *Plant Physiol.* 42:863–874.

Zasada, J. C., and R. Zahner. 1969. Vessel element development in the early wood of red oak (*Quercus rubra*). *Can. J. Bot.* 47:1965–1971.

Zimmermann, M. H., and D. Potter. 1982. Vessel-length distribution in branches, stem and roots of *Acer rubrum* L. *IAWA Bull.* (n.s.) 3:103–109.

Chapter 10

Adaptive Trends
in the Wood Anatomy of Lianas

R. K. BAMBER and B. J. H. TER WELLE

Lianas are one of the most common forms of plant life in rainforests. Their presence typifies the rainforest ecosystem. Figures quoted by Richards (1952) suggest that lianas comprise 8% of the flowering plants of tropical rainforests. Although climbers are present in most plant communities, they reach their greatest development in rainforests. In Europe, for example, climbers represent only 2% of the flora (Richards 1952). The importance of lianas in tropical rainforests stands out more clearly if the contribution of liana leaves to total forest leaf area is calculated. Putz (1983) found liana leaves to comprise about 19% of a Terra Firma Forest near San Carlos de Negro in Amazonas Venezuela.

Although lianas are light-lovers, early in their life cycle they are able to tolerate deep shade. Growth in height continues until the forest canopy is reached, where full development takes place and flowering ensues. Similarly, growth is encouraged by opening of the canopy or on river banks. The seedlings of lianas usually resemble seedlings of shrubs or trees; however, after contact with the host tree or supporting structure has been made, the morphology of the liana changes rapidly and the special supporting structures, tendrils, hooks, and climbing roots develop.

This changing morphology of the developing liana is reflected in the stem. Diameter growth is restricted so that liana stems are always much smaller than forest trees. This characteristic is of interest physiologically, as lianas may have a leaf biomass equal to the biggest tree in the tropical rainforest, and implies that as lianas do not require the same amount of mechanical tissue for support as in trees, the stems are much more efficient in the conduction of water. An explanation of this phenomenon may well be found in the wood anatomy of lianas.

Anatomical studies of lianas have been, like those of barks, largely neglected. Studies of rainforest plants have concentrated on the wood anatomy of forest trees because of economic reasons, as such studies are required to provide data to enable timber identification and improve utilization. The studies reported here have aimed primarily at determining the range and pattern of anatomical variation in lianas especially in relation to tree wood.

From *Growth Patterns
in Vascular Plants*
Edited by Muhammed Iqbal

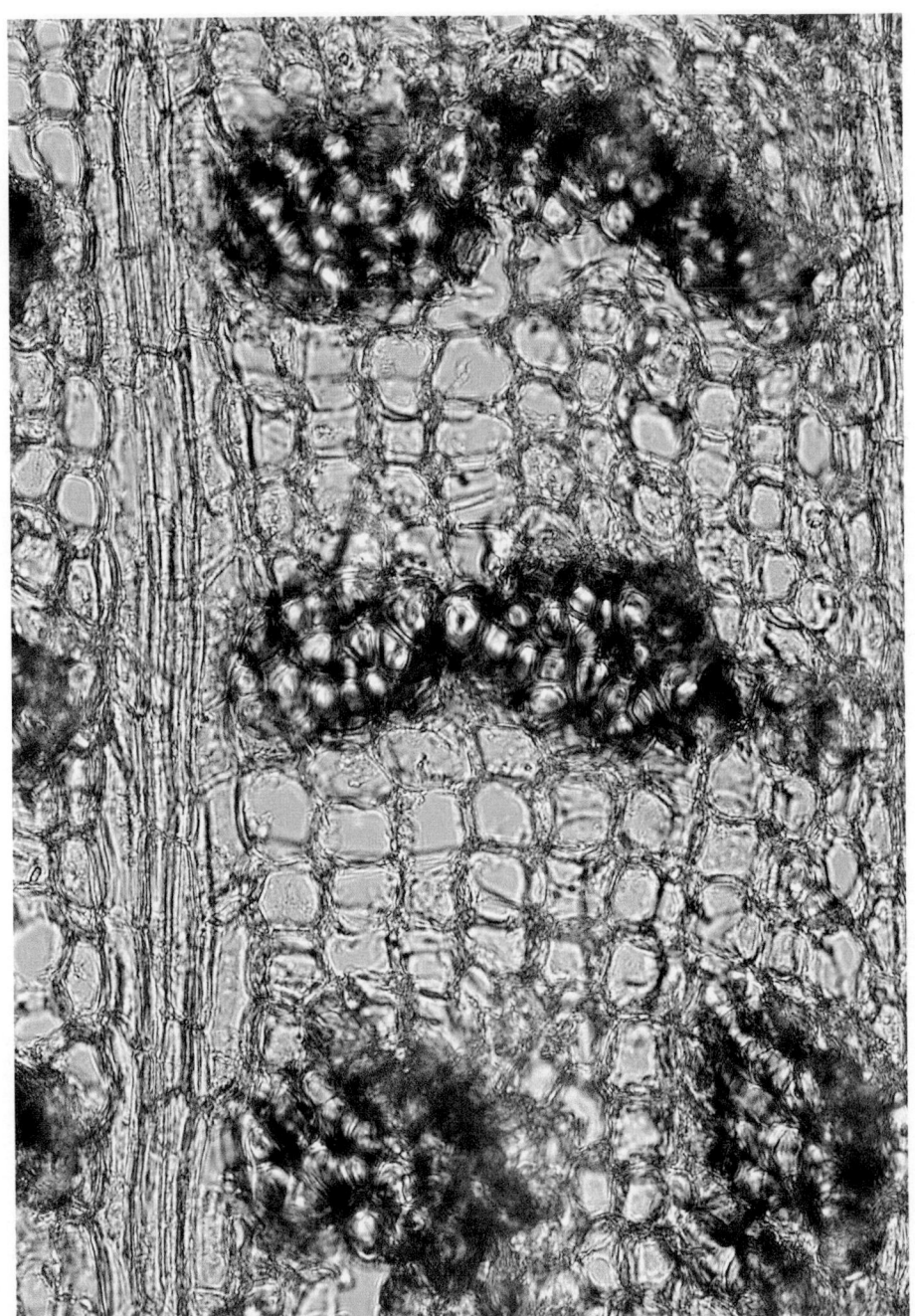

A

Figure 10.1. Transverse sections of lianas with anomalous tissue. (A) *Derris hetero-phylla*, × 60. Section stained with phloroglucinol/HCl. The undifferentiated ground mass of axial parenchyma is unstained, thus indicating the absence of lignin. The lignified fiber bundles are stained red. (B) *D. heterophylla*, × 25. Polarized light with red II filter. The undifferentiated ground mass of axial parenchyma shows a lack of birefringence typical of unthickened cells. The thickened walls of the fibers and vessels are strongly birefringent. (C) *Cardiopteris moluccana*, × 25. Phloroglucinol/HCl. The undifferentiated ground mass of axial parenchyma is unstained, thus indicating the absence of lignin. In contrast, the vessel and fiber walls are highly stained, thus indicating lignification. (D) *C. moluccana*, × 25. Polarized light. Lack of birefringence indicates the lack of secondary thickening in the walls of the undifferentiated ground mass of parenchyma.

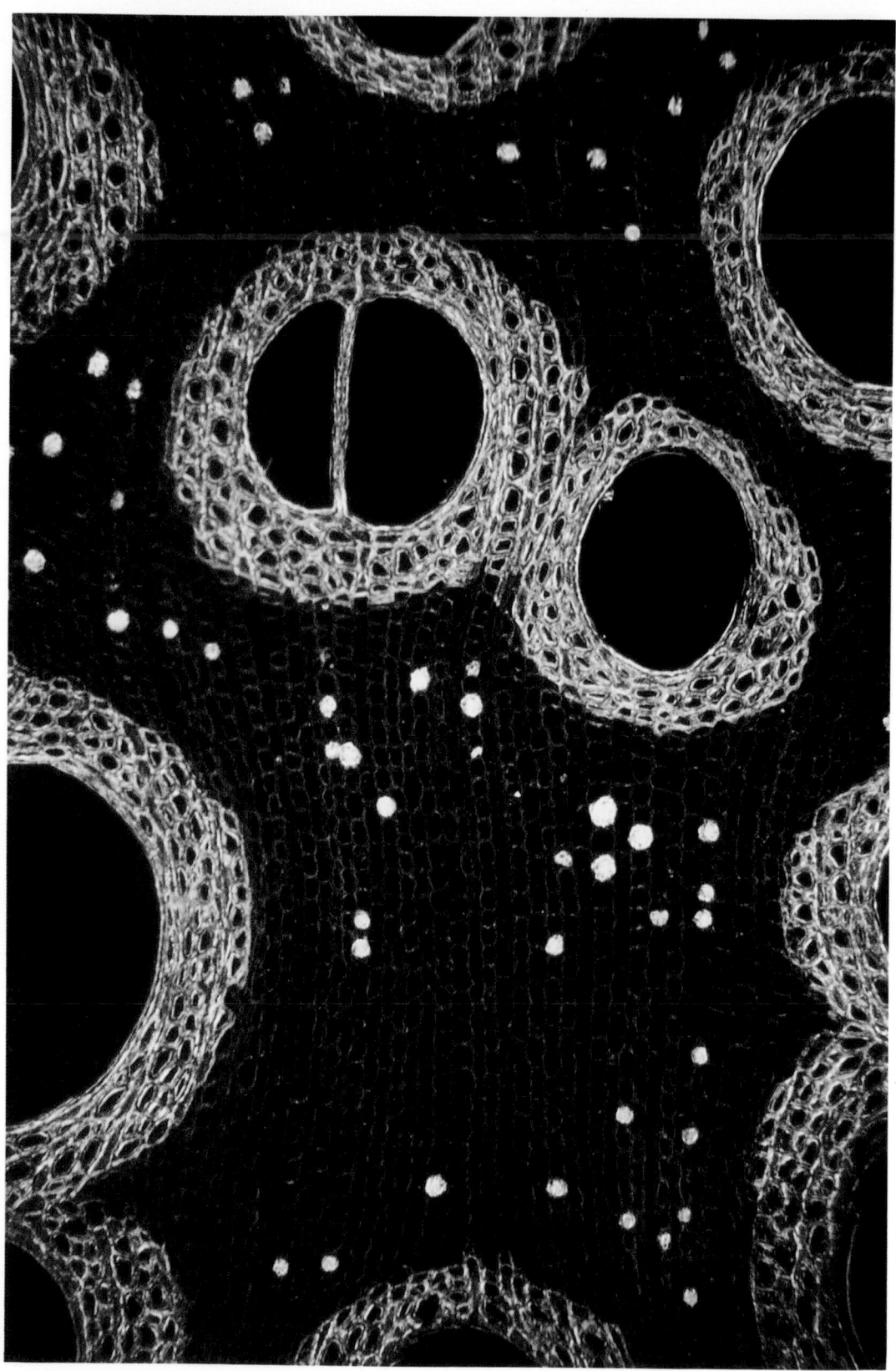

D

THE NATURE AND INCIDENCE OF ANOMALOUS GROWTH

The presence of irregular patterns of growth is apparently more common in the wood of lianas than trees and has been described by many workers (see Eames and MacDaniels 1947; Metcalfe and Chalk 1950: Esau and Cheadle 1969: Cutter 1971: Carlquist 1985, 1988). These irregular structural patterns give the impression that anomalous growth is typical of lianas. Thus Richards (1952) states, "Stems of lianas often show extraordinary anomalies in their method of secondary growth." Likewise, Obaton (1960) found anomalous secondary growth in 108 species of 21 families in material from South Africa.

The collection of 117 lianas from the rainforests of Queensland, Australia (Table 10.1) has allowed the study of the incidence and the types of the unusual secondary growth common to lianas. The two main types of anomalous growth distinguished in liana wood are (a) wood with zones of undifferentiated parenchymatous tissue in which the cell walls are without thickening or lignification (Figure 10.1.A,B [color plates]), and (b) wood characterized by the presence of included (interxylary) phloem.

Undifferentiated parenchyma occurs either as pockets in the normal ground tissue of xylem or—in reverse situation, without thickening and lignin—as the ground mass of the stem in which xylem is present in pockets. In the first case, the pockets of undifferentiated parenchyma may be small, as in Morinda salomonensis (Figure 10.2.A), or large and irregularly shaped, as in Petraeovitex multiflora (Figure 10.2.B). In the second, most specialized case, xylem ranges from pockets consisting solely of vessels surrounded by strengthening fibers, as in Cardiopteris moluccana (Figure 10.2.D), to pockets of vessels with surrounding strengthening sclerenchyma and isolated pockets of sclerenchyma arranged concentrically, as in Derris heterophylla (Figure 10.2.C).

Included phloem, likewise, shows great variation in its pattern of occurrence, ranging from irregularly distributed pockets in the axial tissue, as in Strychnos bancroftiana (Figure 10.3.B), to irregularly distributed pockets in both radial and axial tissue, as in Gouania species (Figure 10.3.C), and regular, concentrically arranged pockets in the axial tissue, as in Hypserpa decumbens (Figure 10.3.D). In a relatively few species, for example in Derris species, both undifferentiated parenchyma and included phloem are present.

On the basis of the Queensland collection, the incidence of anomalous tissue appears to be far greater in lianas than in trees. Undifferentiated parenchyma occurs in 37% of the species examined (Table 10.1) whereas 8% possess included phloem. In dicotyledonous trees, undifferentiated parenchyma, that is unthickened and unlignified tissue, mostly does not occur except for special tissue, probably of traumatic origin, such as the kino veins of Eucalyptus. The incidence of included phloem is well known, however, and is estimated to be present in some 2% of tree species. [This figure was obtained from the computerized program of the Chalk key (see Pearson and Wheeler 1981).]

Anomalous tissue arises from irregularities in cambial division. Gross irregularities can result in great irregularities in the pattern of wood development. Where masses of undifferentiated parenchyma are produced, the uneven expansion of woody and nonwoody tissue will result in the formation of ridges, as in Derris heterophylla (Figure 10.2.C) and Cardiopteris moluccana (Figure 10.2.D), where swollen vessels can be seen pushing the cambium and phloem outward. When included phloem is laid down, new successive cambia form in the inner layers of the phloem (Fahn 1985). If the included phloem forms in concentric bands, as in the mangrove Avicennia marina, the stem remains regular. Where the masses of included phloem are irregular, however, as in

Strychnos bancroftiana (Figure 10.3.B) or *Gouania* species, (Figure 10.3.C), the cambium becomes highly irregular and can produce complex patterns in the stem. The highly irregular radial pattern in *Piper nova-hollandiae* (Figure 10.3.A) arises from the long radial strips of lignified tissue that are embedded in the ground mass of undifferentiated parenchyma.

Of late, however, it has been emphasized that plants with successive cambia such as *Bougainvillea,* etc., cannot be regarded as having "included" or "interxylary" phloem since the phloem in such plants does not in fact occur in the wood but occurs where phloem typically does, outside of each cambium (Mikesell and Popham 1976: Carlquist 1988).

Reference to the presence of unlignified parenchyma in the wood of climbers was made by Solereder in 1908 (see Metcalfe and Chalk 1950). In reference to *Cissus* species, Solereder (1908) commented:

> Groundwork of wood consists of unlignified parenchyma tissue with thin walls in which are embedded groups of vessels, each group being surrounded by a sheath of lignified wood parenchyma and wood prosenchyma.

Metcalfe and Chalk (1950) also referred to the presence of compound xylem masses separated by cortical parenchyma in Sapindaceae lianas and to the presence of a soft groundwork of parenchyma in *Entada*. Earlier references to these modes of structures were cited by Solereder.

The classification of undifferentiated parenchyma as anomalous secondary growth may not accord with all opinion; for example, Carlquist (1975) places only included phloem under this heading and does not agree to the proposition that presence of large patches of axial parenchyma in otherwise "normal" wood constitutes an anomaly (see Carlquist 1988). Esau (1965), however, considers anomalous tissue to be any atypical secondary growth. According to her, the designation "anomalous" serves simply to assemble growth patterns that appear to be less common. Metcalfe and Chalk (1950) also refer to the above described unlignified and unthickened parenchyma in *Cissus* species as anomalous structures.

Table 10.1. Occurrence of anomalous secondary growth and included phloem in the wood of some rainforest lianas of Queensland, Australia.[a]

Species	Anatomical type[b]
Amaranthaceae	
Deeringia sp.	A–G
Apocynaceae	
Alyxia spicata R. Br.	N
Carissa ovata R. Br.	N
Ichnocarpus frutescens R. Br.	N
Melodinus guilfoylei F. Muell.	N
Parsonsia densvestita C. White	A–P
P. latifolia (Benth.) S. T. Blake	N
P. plaesiophylla S. T. Blake	N
P. straminea (R. Br.) F. Muell.	IP–P
P. velutina R. Br.	IP–R+P
Annonaceae	
Melodorum uhrii F. Muell.	N
Rauwenhoffia leichardtii (F. Muell.) Diels	N
Uvaria goeziana F. Muell.	N
U. membranacea Benth.	N
Araliaceae	
Motherwellia haplosciadea F. Muell.	N
Schefflera elliptica (Blume) Harms	N
Asclepiadaceae	
Gymnema sp	A–P
Secamone elliptica R. Br.	N
Austrobaileyaceae	
Austrobaileya scandens C. White	N
Bignoniaceae	
Neosepicaea jucunda (F. Muell.) Steenis	N
Neosepicaea sp.	N
Pandorea pandorana (Andr.) Steenis	N
Boraginaceae	
Tournefortia sarmentosa Lam.	N
Capparidaceae	
Capparis sepiaria L.	N
Capparis sp.	N

[a] Material was collected by B. P. M. Hyland, Division of Forest Research, CSIRO, Atherton, Australia from rainforests of Queensland.
[b] Anomalous tissue consisting of undifferentiated parenchyma is designated as A–G when this tissue forms the ground mass of the wood; A–B, when it occurs in concentric bands; A–P, when it forms isolated pockets in the axial tissue; and A–R, when it occurs in rays. Included phloem is designated as IP–B, when it occurs in concentric bands; IP–P, when it forms isolated pockets in the axial tissue: and IP–R, when it occurs in rays. Normal wood tissue is designated as N.

Table 10.1. Continued

Species	Anatomical type[b]
Celastraceae	
Celastrus subspicatus Hook.	N
Celastrus sp.	N
Hippocratea sp.	A–P
Salacia chinensis L.	IP–B
S. disepala (C. White) Ding Hou	IP–B
Salacia sp.	IP–B
Combretaceae	
Combretum trifoliatum Vent.	N
Connaraceae	
Connarus conchocarpus F. Muell.	N
Convolvulaceae	
Erycibe coccinea (Bailey) Hoogl.	IP–R
Ipomoea sp.	A–P
Merremia peltata (L.) Mer.	A–G
Operculina riedeliana (Oliv.) Ooststr.	A–R
Cucurbitaceae	
Trichosanthes pentaphylla F. Muell. ex. Benth.	A–R
Dichapetalaceae	
Dichapetalum sp.	N
Dilleniaceae	
Hibbertia scandens F. Muell.	N
Tetracera daemeliana F. Muell.	N
T. nordtiana F. Muell.	N
Elaeagnaceae	
Elaegnus triflora Roxb.	N
Escalloniaceae	
Quintinia fawkneri F. Muell.	N
Euphorbiaceae	
Croton sp.	N
Mallotus repandus (Willd.) Muell. Arg.	N
Omphalea queenslandica Bailey	N
Icacinaceae	
Cardiopteris moluccana Blume	A–G
Leguminosae	
Acacia albizioides Pedley	N
Acacia sp.	N
Austrosteenisia blackii (F. Muell.) Geesink	N
Caesalpinea bonduc (L.) Roxb.	N
C. major (Medik.) Dandy & Excell.	N
C. scortechinii (F. Muell.) Hattink	A–P
Cassia retusa Vogel	N

Table 10.1. Continued

Species	Anatomical type[b]
Dalbergia densa Benth.	N
Derris heterophylla (L.) Merr.	A–G
Derris sp.	A–G, IP–B
Kunstleria sp.	A–P
Milletia sp.	A–R
Mucuna gigantea DC.	A–G, IP–P
Timonius sp.	N
Linaceae	
Hugonia jenkinsii F. Muell.	N
Melastomaceae	
Medinilla balls-headleyi F. Muell.	N
Menispermaceae	
Carronia protensa (F. Muell.) Diels	A–P+B
Hypserpa decumbens (Benth.) Diels	IP–P+B
H. laurina (F. Muell.) Diels	N
H. reticulata Forman	A–R
Hypserpa sp.	IP–P
Legnephora moorei (F. Muell.) Miers	N
Pachygone ovata (Poir) Hook. & Thoms.	IP–B
Pycnarrhena tumefacta Miers	A–P
Monimiaceae	
Palmeria coriacea C. White	N
P. scandens F. Muell.	N
Moraceae	
Ficus pantoniana King	N
Maclura cochinchinensis (Lour.) Corner	N
Myrsinaceae	
Embelia australiana (F. Muell.) Mez.	N
Maesa dependens F. Muell.	N
M. muelleri Mez.	N
Oleaceae	
Jasminum didymum Forst.	N
Passifloraceae	
Passiflora sp.	A–P+R
Piperaceae	
Piper nova-hollandiae Miq.	A–G
Piper sp. aff. *caninum* Blume	A–G
Ranunculaceae	
Clematis sp.	A–R
Rhamnaceae	
Colubrina asiatica (L.) Brongn.	N
Gouania sp.	IP–P+R

Table 10.1. Continued

Species	Anatomical type[b]
[Rhamnaceae, continued]	
Rhamnella vitiensis (Benth.) A. C. Smith	N
Rhamnella sp.	N
Sageretia hamosa Brongn.	N
Ventilago ecorollata F. Muell.	N
Rubiaceae	
Morinda salomonensis Engl.	N
Morinda sp.	A–G
Uncaria lanosa Wallich	N
Rutaceae	
Zanthoxylum nitidum (Roxb.)DC.	N
Strychnaceae	
Strychnos minor Dennst.	IP–P
Verbenaceae	
Faradaya splendida F. Muell.	A–G
Glossocarya hemiderma Benth. & Hook.	N
Glossocarya sp.	N
Petraeovitex multiflora (Smith) Merr.	A–P
Premna limbata Benth.	N
Vitaceae	
Cayratia saponaria (Seem: ex. Benth.) Domin	A–R
Cayratia sp.	A–R
Cissus adnata Roxb.	A–R
C. hastata (Miq.) Planch.	A–R
C. hypoglauca A. Gray	A–R
C. oblonga (Benth.) Planch.	A–R
C. penninervis F. Muell.	A–R
C. sterculifolia (F. Muell. ex. Benth.) Planch.	A–R
Cissus sp. "adnata" "indica"	A–R
Cissus sp. "geranium"	A–R
Cissus sp. aff. repens	A–R
Tetrastigma nitens (F. Muell.) Planch.	A–R
Tetrastigma sp.	A–R
Vitis hypoglauca F. Muell.	A–B

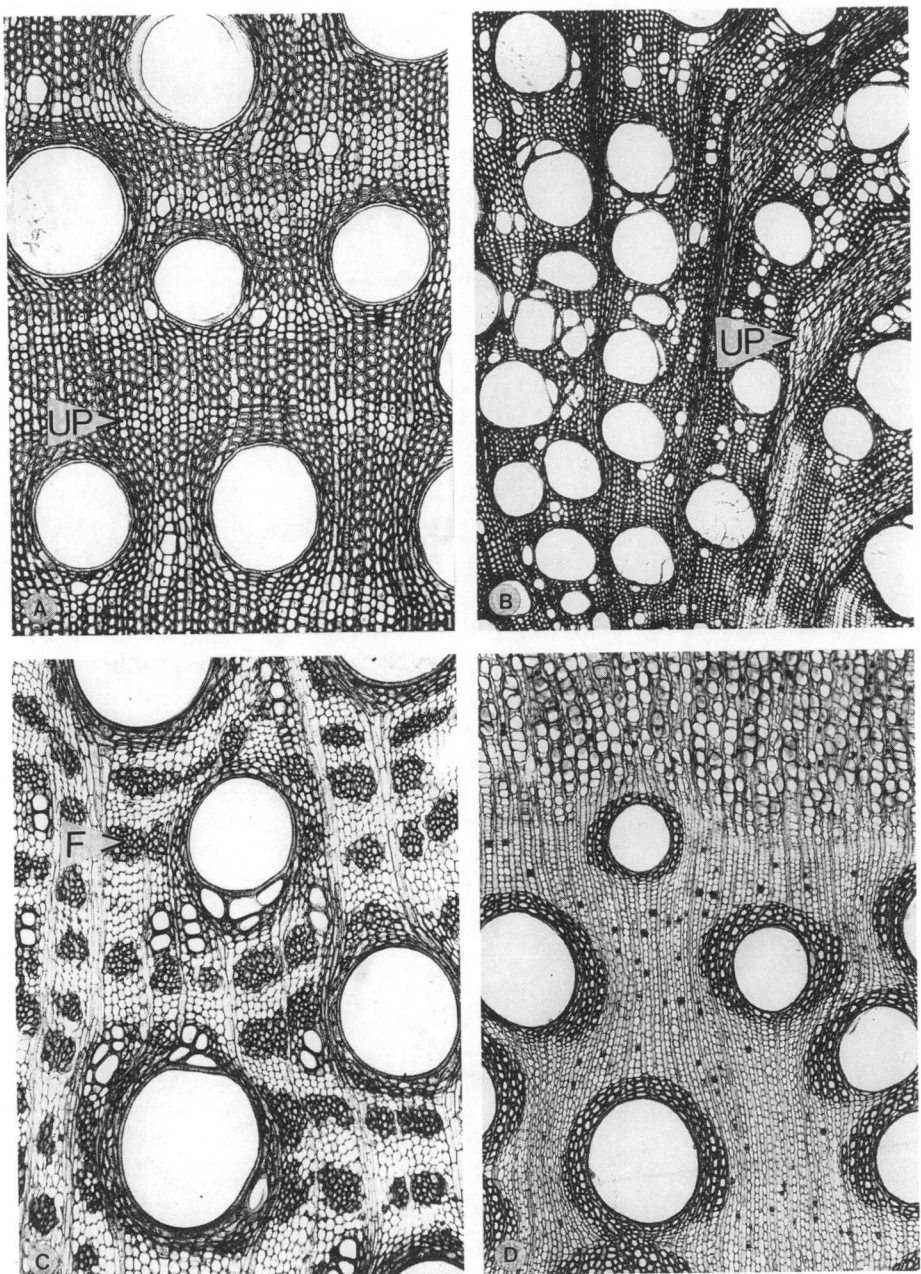

Figure 10.2.   Transverse sections of lianas showing examples of anomalous growth and included phloem. (A) *Morinda salomonensis*, × 120. Anomalous growth represented by small, isolated zones of undifferentiated parenchyma (UP), which is unlignified and unthickened. (B) *Petraeovitex multiflora*, × 120. Irregular growth pattern as a result of large pockets of undifferentiated parenchyma (UP). (C) *Derris heterophylla*, × 100. Stem formed principally of a ground tissue of undifferentiated axial parenchyma. Woody tissue is confined to vessels and surrounding cells and isolated fiber strands. (D) *Cardiopteris moluccana*, × 100. Ground tissue of undifferentiated parenchyma. Woody tissue confined to islands of vessels and surrounding fiber ("islands of xylem").

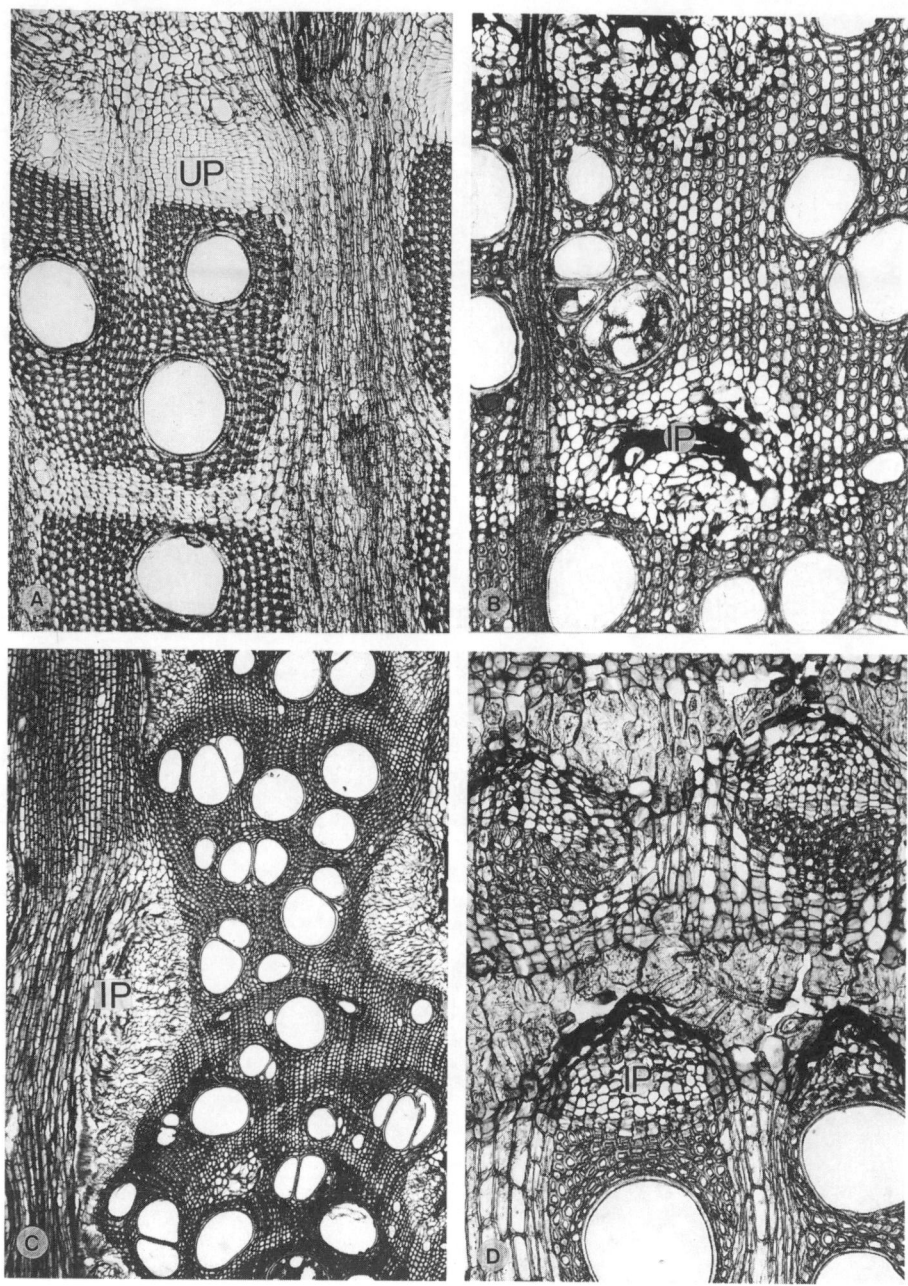

Figure 10.3.   Transverse section of lianas showing anomalous growth. (A) *Piper nova-hollandiae*, × 100. Ground mass of undifferentiated parenchyma (UP). Woody tissue occurs characteristically as long radial strips. (B) *Strychnos bancroftiana*, × 140. Included phloem (IP) occurs abundantly as pockets in the axial tissue. (C) *Gouania* sp. × 120. Included phloem occurs as large pockets in both radial and axial tissues. (D) *Hypserpa decumbens*, × 110. Included phloem occurs as pockets in the axial tissue that are arranged in distinct concentric bands.

CELL DIMENSIONS OF LIANA WOOD
IN COMPARISON WITH TREE WOOD

Cell dimensions of lianas and trees can be compared in two ways: with members of the same genera to indicate the degree of adaptation of species to the climbing habit; and by a random selection of species from the same habitat to indicate the relative conductive abilities of the two plant forms.

In Table 10.2, the cell parameters of the wood of lianas and trees from the same genus are compared (see also Figure 10.4.A–D). As Table 10.2 shows, liana vessels are some 1.9 times wider and some 2.8 times greater in proportion. Similar observations were reported by ter Welle (1985) for intrageneric comparisons; for example, with *Machaerium* he found the liana *M. macrophyllum* to have vessels about 3 times larger and about 3.7 times greater in proportion than in tree species. He found these trends to be repeated in the genera *Bauhinia* and *Aristolochia*. In the genus *Baphia*, however, although no difference was found in vessel diameter, the increase in the vessel proportion was about four-fold in the liana.

Table 10.3 compares vessel dimensions of randomly selected lianas and trees from Queensland rain forests. Vessel diameter is again larger in the lianas, some 1.8 times, and the proportion of vessels is about twice as great. The largest vessel in the Queensland rainforest lianas was 610 μm, in *Palmeria coriacea*. This shows extreme adaptation from tree species of Australian Monimiaceae, the vessels of which are

Table 10.2. A within-genus comparison of cell dimensions in the wood of some lianas and trees.[a]

Species	Tree (T) or liana (L)	Vessels			Ray parenchyma		Total parenchyma %	Fiber %
		Diameter μ			Width	Max. height		
		Mean	Max.	%	(cell no.)	(mm)		
Acacia homalophylla A. Cunn. ex Benth.	T	97	150	14	1–2	0.3	29	57
A. albizioides Pedley	L	265	450	39	2–3	1.0	36	25
Caesalpinea sappan L.	T	90	120	12	1–2	0.7	16	72
C. scortechinii (F. Muel.) Hattink	L	179	280	30	1	4.5	47	23
Celastrus cunninghamii F. Muel.	T	40	50	18	1–4	0.5	29	53
C. subspicatus Hook.	L	81	140	25	1–4	1.0	14	61
Ficus hispida Linn.	T	123	205	16	2–9	1.2	48	36
F. pantoniana King	L	238	320	57	2–6	2.5	33	10
Maclura pomifera (Ras.) C. K. Schneid.	T	116	250	11	4–5	1.8	32	57
M. cochinchinensis (Lour.) Corner	L	133	320	22	3–4	1.7	43	35
Quintinia verdonii F. Muel.	T	47	60	10	1–3	1.8	19	71
Q. fawkneri F. Muel.	L	60	180	47	1–7	8.0	16	27
Zanthoxylum suberosum C. T. White	T	56	70	14	1–2	0.3	18	63
Z. nitidum (Roxb.) DC	L	134	220	30	1–2	1.2	27	43

[a] Lianas are from the Hyland collection (see Table 10.1) and tree specimens are from the slide collection of the Forestry Commission of New South Wales.

generally quite small. For example, *Atherospermum moschatum* Labill. has a mean vessel diameter of 38 μm, *Daphnandra micrantha* (Tul.) Benth. 57 μm, and *Doryphora sassafras* Endl. 61 μm (Bamber and Erskine 1965).

These results support references to the presence of larger vessels in lianas than in trees (Metcalfe and Chalk 1950; Carlquist 1975, 1984) and also to the larger proportion of vessels (Carlquist 1975, 1984), although the proportion of liana vessels found in the Queensland material is significantly less (27%) than the figure (36%) given by Carlquist (1975).

Although liana vessels are considered to be the longest and widest in the plant kingdom (Zimmermann 1983; Ewers and Fisher 1989a,b), there is no experimental evidence to demonstrate a developmental link between these parameters. Anatomical examination of certain tropical and subtropical lianas has shown that larger-diameter stems tend to have longer as well as wider vessels (*Pithecoctenium crucigerum*: Ewers and Fisher 1989b). Narrow vessels are of smaller lengths than wider vessels; the vessel dimensions increase with stem age. In *Bauhinia fassoglensis* and *Stigmaphyllon ellipticum* that have distinct systems of inner and outer secondary xylem, the vessels of the inner system tend to be shorter and narrower than those of the outer system. Within the outer system, the longer vessels are wider, and the shorter ones are narrower (Ewers and Fisher 1989b). An individual vessel, however, can vary in diameter along its length; the widest portion in *Quercus rubra* is nearly 14% wider than the narrow portions (Akachuku 1987).

Nonetheless, large vessels are not obligatory in lianas and quite a significant number possess small vessels; for example, *Carissa ovata* and *Quintinia fawkneri* (Tables 10.1 and 10.2) have mean vessel diameters of 44 μm and 60 μm, respectively. The presence of small vessels in climbers was also recorded by Carlquist (1984) for the family Lardizabalaceae in which he found mean vessel diameters of 46 μm in *Akebia quinata*, 47 μm in *Holboellia latifolia*, 52 μm in *Stauntonia hexaphylla*, 67 μm in *Boquila trifoliata*, and 87 μm in *Lardizabala biternata*. Although these vessels average less in diameter than those of large tropical lianas, vessels of lianoid Lardizabalaceae are larger in diameter than those of shrubby Lardizabalaceae and thus they follow a pattern (Carlquist 1988).

Such a reduction in vessel diameter in lianas is compensated by an increase in vessel frequency so that, relatively speaking, the proportion of vessels remains higher on average than in trees. This relationship between lianas and trees is demonstrated in Figure 10.5.

The functional and evolutionary reasons, if any, for the correlation of vessel length and width are not yet clear. Perhaps the selective pressure to minimize the extent of damage from embolism causes a reduction of vessel dimensions for plants of a certain specific environment, or perhaps selective pressure to enhance hydraulic conductance favors an increase in vessel length and diameter. Flow through tracheary elements could be limited both by lumen resistance and pit resistance (Zimmermann 1983; Gibson et al. 1985).

Carlquist (1975) refers to the greater proportion of ray tissue in lianas exhibiting normal secondary growth than in other plant forms. While this is certainly evident in some species the most significant difference in liana and tree rays would appear to be with ray height. This is demonstrated in the intrageneric comparisons in Table 10.2 in which only one of the lianas showed no difference with the tree while the others were from two to six times higher. This intrageneric trend was also found by ter Welle (1985) who records liana rays to be about four times higher in the genus *Machaerium* and about five times higher in *Baphia* with similar trends in *Bauhinia*, *Euonymus*, and *Lonicera*.

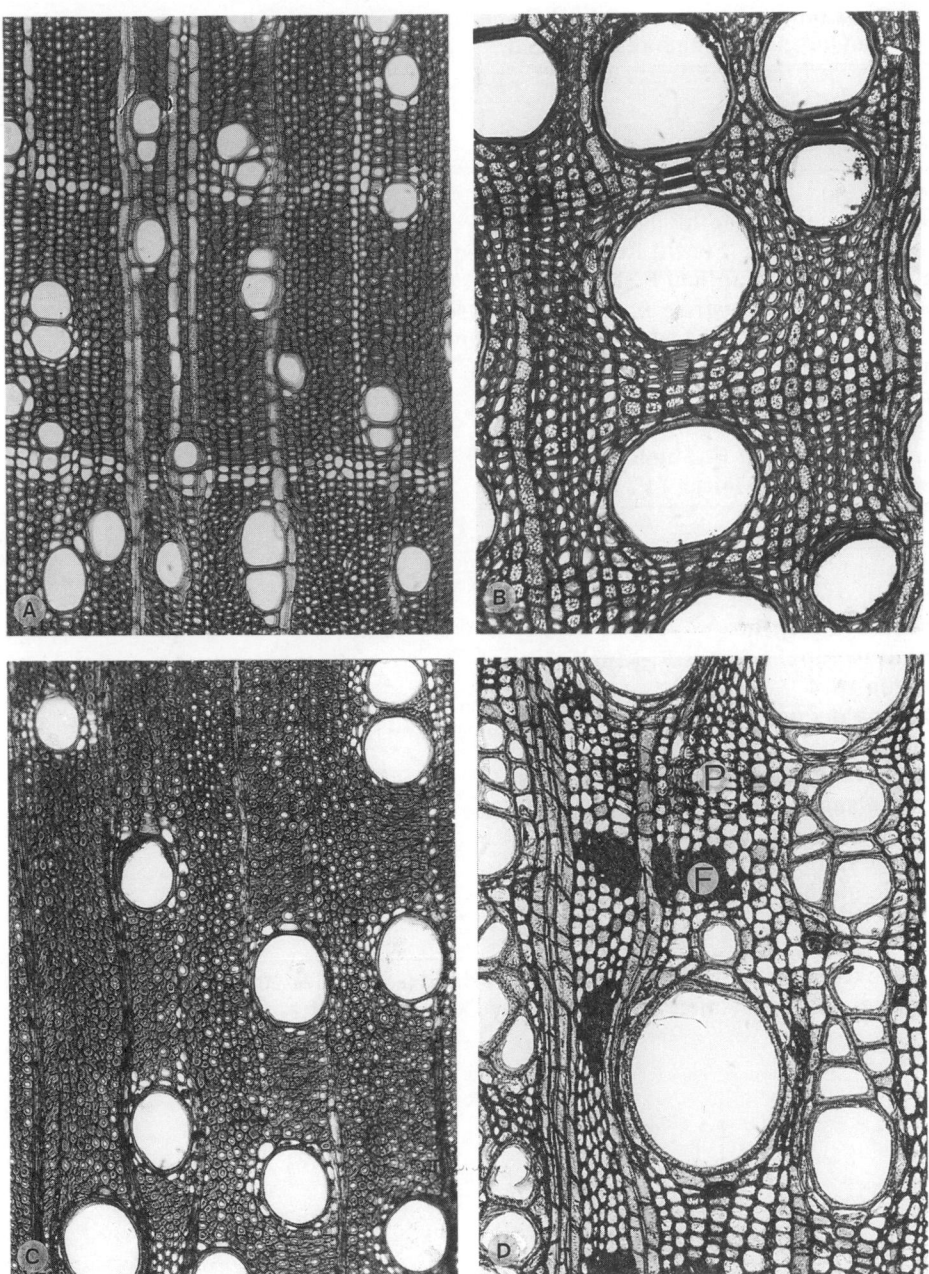

Figure 10.4. Comparison of the wood of liana and tree stems. Adaptive trends within a genus in vessel dimensions and amount of parenchyma are illustrated. Transverse sections (× 170). (A) *Zanthoxylum suberosum*, a tree. (B) *Z. nitidum*, a liana (note larger vessels). (C) *Caesalpinea sappan*, a tree. (D) *C. scortechinii*, a liana. Note larger vessels, increased amount of parenchyma (P), and the reduction in fiber (F) to small isolated strands.

Table 10.3. Comparison of mean vessel diameter and percentage of vessels in tree wood with liana wood in the Queensland rainforest material.[a]

Species	Mean vessel diameter (μ)	Vessel proportion (%)
Tree wood		
Ackama muelleri Benth.	67	21
Alphitonia excelsa (Fenzl.) Reisseck ex Benth.	80	12
Brachychiton acerifolium F. Muell.	140	11
Castanospermum australe A. Cunn. et Fraser ex Hook	119	10
Citronella moorei (F. Muell. ex Benth.) Howard	71	13
Daphnandra micrantha (Tul.) Benth.	52	26
Flindersia australis R.Br.	115	12
F. pubescens F. M. Bail.	131	16
Gmelina leichardtii F. Muell. ex. Benth.	118	16
Litsea reticulata (Meissn.) F. Muell.	120	21
Mean	101	15.9
Liana wood		
Alyxia spicata R. Br.	137	29
Carissa ovata R.Br.	44	23
Connarus conchocarpus F. Muell.	113	23
Gouania sp.	79	11
Hypserpa decumbens (Benth.) Diels	215	26
Ipomoea sp.	292	40
Menispermaceae Indeterminate species	169	23
Morinda salomonensis Engl.	218	21
Omphalea queenslandica Bailey	246	32
Palmeria coriacea C. White	175	31
Schefflera elliptica (Blume) Harms	120	40
Mean	164	27.2

[a] Lianas are from the collection of B. P. M. Hyland (see Tables 10.2, 10.2) and tree specimens are from the slide collection of the Forestry Commission of New South Wales.

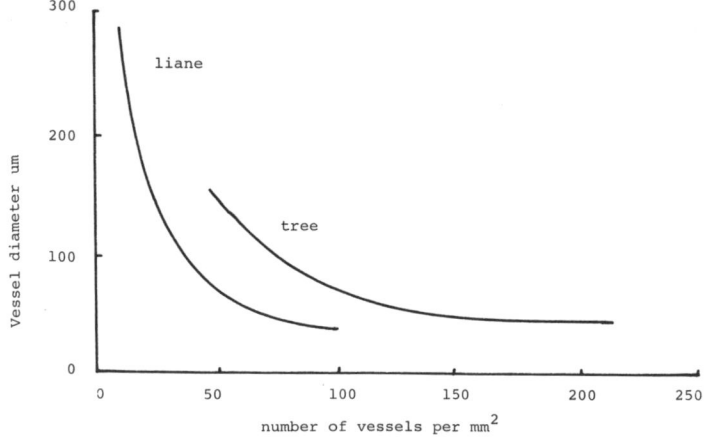

Figure 10.5. Relationship of mean vessel diameter and frequency in lianas and trees. Data taken from Tables 10.2 and 10.3.

ADAPTIVE TRENDS IN LIANA WOOD

Lianas, as a consequence of their unique pattern of growth, show significant differences in their anatomy in comparison with trees. As lianas require trees for support during growth, they represent a later stage of plant evolution: thus any differences could be considered as evolutionary adaptations.

Differences, and thus adaptations, in the anatomy of liana and tree wood are (a) marked increase in the incidence of anomalous secondary growth, (b) an increase in both vessel diameter and proportion, (c) an increase in both ray size (especially height) and proportion, and (d) a decrease in the proportion of fiber. The most spectacular of these adaptations is the increase in the incidence of anomalous secondary growth. In many of these lianas, the anomalous tissue, in the form of unthickened and unlignified parenchyma, makes up the ground mass of the "woody" stem. Such stems are clearly weak in compression in contrast to woody stems in which the ground mass is sclerenchyma, as the isolated fiber bundles provide only tensile strength for the whole stem and protection for the vessels, thus representing the ultimate adaptation to the mechanical requirements of the climbing habit.

Also significant is the increased conductive capacity of liana stems as a consequence of the increased diameter and proportion of vessels. The water flow rate in capillaries, as pointed out by Zimmermann (1983), is related to the fourth-power of the radius. Based on the data in Table 10.2, it would appear that within genera, flow rates in lianas could be some 34 times the rate in trees (per unit cross-sectional area). Compared with forest trees in general (Table 10.3), the rate could be 20 times greater. Within the genus *Zanthoxylum* (Table 10.2), the liana *Z. nitidum* has the potential to conduct sap at the flow rate some 99 times greater than *Z. suberosum*, a rain forest tree.

The adaptive significance of increased ray size is not immediately clear. As the walls between rays and vessels are invariably profusely pitted, the most obvious functional adaptation of high rays would appear to be to facilitate axial conduction by providing additional intervessel pathways. Because ray cells overlap axial cells, increased ray size could provide extra strength in the radial direction, no doubt of advantage to a liana stem in view of the considerable bending to which such flexible structures are subject.

Although the number of species considered here is small in relation to the floral composition of rainforests, the trends in respect to conductive capacity of the wood are clear and suggest an important role of lianas in water movements in the rainforest ecosystem. Their increased capacity to conduct water into the forest canopy compared to trees and their abundance in rainforests may indicate that lianas play an important role in maintaining the moisture balance in rainforests. Given this, no studies of water relations in rainforests could be complete without consideration of the role of lianas.

The flexible nature of liana stems has been attributed to the presence of anomalous tissue that separates mechanical tissue into discrete zones within the ground mass of soft tissue. Richards (1952) states:

> In the main stem, the xylem commonly consists of a number of partly or completely separated strands embedded in softer tissue. The liana stem thus often resembles a rope or cable internally as well as externally and combines flexibility with great tensile strength.

Although this may be the case for those species with abundant anomalous tissue, as can be seen from Table 10.1, the majority of lianas do not possess such structures. The flexibility of most lianas must therefore be attributed to other factors such as their relatively small diameters, smaller proportion of fiber (Table 10.2), or perhaps to altered or reduced amounts of lignin in the fiber cell walls.

CONCLUDING REMARKS

The wood of lianas shows distinct adaptive trends when compared with the wood of trees. Within a genus lianas generally have larger vessel diameter, increased proportion of vessel tissue, increased ray size, and concomitant decrease in the proportion of fiber. In comparison with rainforest species in general, lianas show both increased vessel diameter and proportion.

The frequency of anomalous secondary growth is much greater in lianas than in trees. It could be concluded that anomalous tissues is an adaptive trend in lianas of advantage for the climbing habit. Anomalous growth in liana wood basically manifests as included phloem or masses of undifferentiated parenchyma with unthickened and unlignified walls. This latter tissue is very rare in the wood of dicotyledonous trees. The presence of highly irregular stems in some lianas is due to irregular cambial development associated with the formation of anomalous tissue. Apart from these adaptive trends it must be stressed that there is no typical lianoid structure; lianas exhibit a diversity in tissue organization similar to that shown by trees.

The increased diameter and proportion of vessels in lianas indicate an increased potential for the conduction of water. Per unit area compared with tree wood, lianas appear to have the potential to conduct water at a rate 34 times greater than non-lianoid congeners and 20 times greater than rainforest trees in general.

Acknowledgments

The assistance of A. Wilkins, S. Goodwin, and R. Colley of the Forestry Commission of New South Wales with the microscopy is acknowledged with thanks. The data in Table 10.2 are published with the permission of the Forestry Commission of New South Wales.

LITERATAURE CITED

Akuchuka, A. E. 1987. A study of lumen diameter variation along the longitudinal axis of wood vessels in *Quercus rubra* using cinematography. *IAWA Bull.* (n.s.) 8:41–45.

Bamber, R. K., and R. B. Erskine. 1965. Relationship of vessel diameter to lyctus susceptibility in some New South Wales hardwoods. Forestry Commission of New South Wales, Research Note, No. 15.

Carlquist, S. 1975. *Ecological Strategies of Xylem Evolution*. Berkeley: Univ. of Calif. Press.

———. 1984. Wood and stem anatomy of Lardizabalaceae, with comments on the vining habit, ecology and systematics. *Bot. J. Linn. Soc.* 88:257–277.

_____ . Observations on functional wood histology of vines and lianas: Vessel dimorphism, tracheids, vasicentric tracheids, narrow vessels, and parenchyma. *Aliso* 11:139–157.

_____ . 1988. *Comparative Wood Anatomy*. Berlin/Heidelberg: Springer-Verlag.

Cutter, E. G. 1971. *Plant Anatomy: Experiment and Interpretation. Part 2. Organs.* London: Edward Arnold.

Eames, A. J., and L. H. MacDaniels. 1947. *An Introduction to Plant Anatomy.* New York: McGraw Hill.

Esau, K. 1965. *Plant Anatomy.* New York: John Wiley & Sons.

Esau, K. and V. I. Cheadle. 1969. Secondary growth in *Bougainvillea* Ann. Bot. 33:807-819.

Ewers, F. W., and J. B. Fisher. 1989a. Techniques for measuring vessel lengths and diameters in stems of woody plants. *Am. J. Bot.* 76:645–656.

Ewers, F. W., and J. B. Fisher. 1989b. Variation in vessel length and diameter in stems of six tropical and subtropical lianas. *Am. J. Bot.* 76:1452–1459.

Fahn, A. 1985. The development of the secondary body in plants with interxylary phloem. In *Xylorama: Trends in Wood Research.* Ed. L. J. Kucera. Basel: Birkhauser. 58–67.

Gibson, A. C., H. W. Calkin, and P. S. Nobel. 1985. Hydraulic conductance and xylem structure in tracheid-bearing plants. *IAWA Bull.* (n.s.) 6:293–302.

Metcalfe, C. R., and L. Chalk. 1950. *Anatomy of the Dicotyledons.* Vols. I, II. Oxford: Clarendon Press.

Mikesell, J. E., and R. H. Popham. 1976. Ontogeny and correlative relationship of the primary thickening meristem in four o'clock plants (Nyctaginaceae) maintained under long and short photoperiods. *Am. J. Bot.* 63:427–437.

Obaton, M. 1960. Les lianes ligneuses a structure anomale des forêsts denses d'Afrique occidentale. *Ann. Sci. Nat. Bot. Ser.* 12 1:1–220.

Pearson, R. G., and E. A. Wheeler. 1981. Computer identification of hardwood species. *IAWA Bull.* (n.s.) 2:37–40.

Putz, F. E. 1983. Liana biomass and leaf area of a "Terra Firme" forest in the Rio Negro Basin, Venezuela. *Biotropica* 15:185–189.

Richards, P. W. 1952. *The Tropical Rain Forest: An Ecological Study.* Cambridge: Cambridge Univ. Press.

Solereder, H. 1908. *Systematic Anatomy of the Dicotyledons.* Trans: L. A. Boodle, F. E. Fritsch. 2 Vols. Oxford: Clarendon Press.

ter Welle, B. J. H. 1985. Differences in wood anatomy of trees and lianas. Pan-American Regional Wood Anatomy Conference, Curitiba, Brazil.

Zimmermann, M. H. 1983. *Xylem Structure and the Ascent of Sap.* Berlin: Springer-Verlag.

Chapter 11

Stem Thickening in Monocotyledons

DARLEEN A. DEMASON

Monocotyledons have very distinctive morphological features that distinguish them from dicotyledons and affect the way they occupy space in three dimensions (Holttum 1955). These features include the continual production of shoot-borne roots (homorhizic condition), typically sympodial rather than monopodial branching patterns, and ensheathing leaf bases. It may be argued that these distinctive vegetative features are modifications directly related to monocotyledons' lack of a vascular cambium as found in dicotyledons and gymnosperms. The vascular cambium is a bidirectional meristem that produces secondary xylem centripetally and secondary phloem centrifugally. Secondary xylem has the dual function of providing structural support and increased water-carrying capacity to the shoot system. The continual production of shoot-borne roots allows increased water-carrying capacity, and the ensheathing leaves, with their numerous vascular bundles, provide structural support to the shoot.

The lack of a vascular cambium does not inhibit monocotyledons from becoming large organisms. No one would deny that date palms (*Phoenix dactylifera* L.) (Figure 11.1A) are large and have wide stem axes. The thick stem in this species is produced solely by primary growth due to a lateral meristem in the shoot tip called the *primary thickening meristem*. There are two lateral meristems, the primary thickening meristem (PTM) and the *secondary thickening meristem* (STM). The PTM is commonly present in monocotyledons, but the STM occurs in only a few families, notably the Agavaceae (DeMason 1983).

This chapter is based mainly on the recent literature and dicusses (a) the structural characteristics associated with extensive activity of the PTM in monoctyledons; (b) the mechanism of stem thickening due to activity of the PTM; (c) the relationship of the STM to the PTM, and (d) the relationship between the structure of the vascular system in monocotyledons and stem development (also see DeMason 1983).

Esau (1977) defines secondary tissues as those "produced by a vascular cambium or phellogen." It is easy, then, to identify secondary tissues in a dicotyledon. In plants without a vascular cambium, however, defining secondary tissues and secondary growth becomes more difficult. As a working definition, secondary growth may be defined as the increase in thickness of a stem or root as the result of cell division activity that occurs after maturation of primary tissues at that position. Similarly, primary growth is the result of cell division and cell enlargement in cells that are produced by the apical meristem and subsequent meristems. As the names imply, the PTM is a primary meristem, since it occurs immediately beneath the apical meristem in the shoot tip, and the STM is a secondary meristem because it occurs lower in the stem in a region of mature primary tissues.

This chapter discusses *Allium cepa* (the common onion), *Yucca whipplei,* and *Cordyline terminalis* to demonstrate the principles of stem thickening in monocotyledons. *Allium cepa* has a rosette shoot system, i.e. it has very little internodal elongation in the vegetative shoot, and the stem is compressed (Figure 11.1.B). *Yucca whipplei* also has a rosette shoot, unlike its arborescent relative, *Yucca brevifolia* (Figure 11.1.C). Finally, *Cordyline terminalis* differs from the other two species in that it has significant internodal elongation (Figure 11.1.D). All these species possess primary thickening via a PTM. In addition, the latter two species are members of the Agavaceae and possess true secondary growth via a STM.

Figure 11.1. Whole plant views. (A) *Phoenix dactylifera* L. in a commercial grove, Coachella Valley, California. (B) *Allium* bulb; stem portion is stained with neutral red. (C) *Yucca whipplei* in native habitat near Santa Barbara, California. (D) *Cordyline terminalis* growing in greenhouse.

ANATOMICAL CHARACTERISTICS ASSOCIATED
WITH PRIMARY THICKENING

A median longitudinal section of the adult onion stem reveals the lack of inter-nodal elongation (Figure 11.2.A–D). The stem is approximately as wide as it is tall. The top of the stem or crown is concave, and the apical meristem and youngest leaf primordia are sunken below surrounding stem tissues. The central cylinder is wide and the cortex is narrow. There is a small pith in the center of the central cylinder that is devoid of vascular tissue. A higher magnification of this region shows that the cortex and all of the central cylinder is composed of radial or anticlinal files of cells (Figure 11.2.B–D). These cell-files are nearly vertically oriented in the distal portion of the stem but are more horizontally oriented in the lower stem. Also, there is a narrow region of tangentially flattened cells that has traditionally been identified as the PTM (Figure 11.2.$\overline{\text{B}}$.). The PTM is associated with shoot-borne root production (Figure 11.2.C).

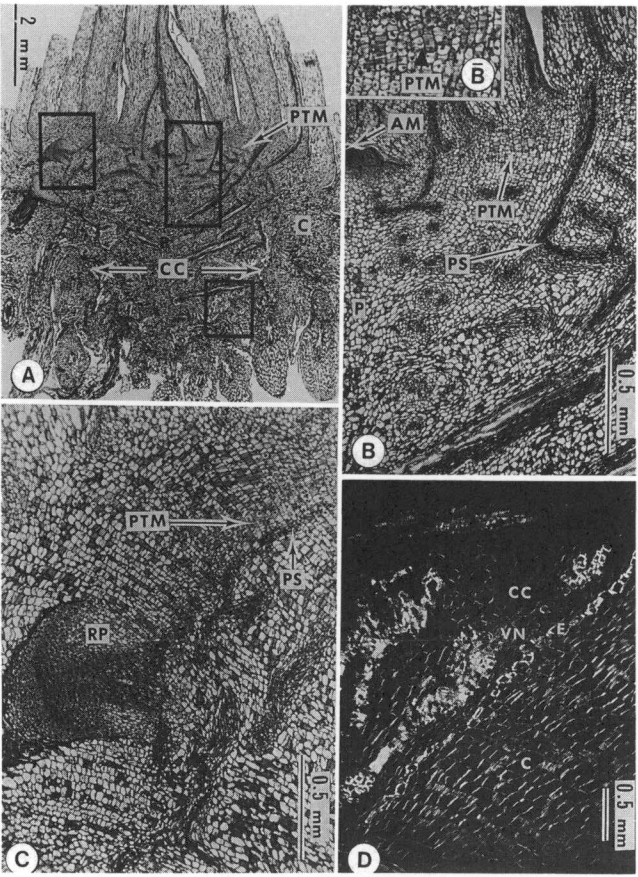

Figure 11.2. Median longitudinal sections through a 7 month old *Allium* stem. (A) Entire stem; outlined areas are enlarged as (B–D). (B) Apical meristem and pith with sub-jacent stem tissue. ($\overline{\text{B}}$) Enlargement of PTM from (B). (C) Shoot-borne root primordium. (D) Polarization micrograph of endodermoid layer, parenchyma, and vascular network between central cylinder and cortex in lower region of stem. AM, apical meristem; C, cortex; CC, central cylinder; E, endodermoid layer; P, pith; PS, procambial strand; PTM, primary thickening meristem; RP, root primordium; VN, vasculature network.

A median longitudinal section through the stem of *Yucca whipplei* shows many similarities to that of *Allium* (Figure 11.3.A,B). The stem outline is rather heart-shaped like the onion but is taller. The crown is concave with a sunken apical meristem. A small pith exists in the center of the central cylinder, and the whole stem except for the pith consists of cells arranged in distinctive radial cell-files that, again, are vertically oriented at the top of the stem and horizontally oriented in the base (Figure 11.3.C–E). A PTM is evident as a region of tangentially flattened cells in the crown. This species also possesses a STM that is continuous with the PTM in longitudinal section.

Cordyline differs from the above two species in having a significant amount of internodal elongation but has secondary growth, as does *Yucca*. A median longitudinal section through the stem reveals that the crown is only very slightly concave at the tip and that a distinct pith does not exist in the center of the central cylinder (Figure 11.4.A,B). A lightly staining region denotes a continuous lateral thickening meristem along the entire length of the stem (Figure 11.4.A) The cortex and the outer region of the central cylinder are composed of anticlinal cell-files. The majority of the central cylinder is composed of randomly oriented cells.

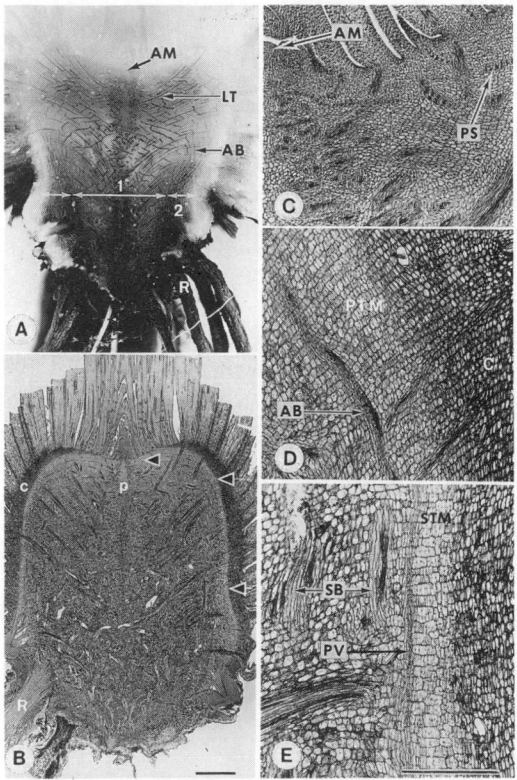

Figure 11.3. Longitudinal sections through the stem of *Yucca whipplei*. (A) Fresh hand section of a three-year-old stem showing distribution of primary and secondary tissues. (B) Median longitudinal section of one-year-old stem. *Arrows* indicate meristem; scale is 2 mm. Enlargements of the meristem in the areas indicated by *arrows* in (B). (C) Apical meristem and subadjacent stem tissue. PTM at this level is the region of dividing cells between the leaf bases and procamial strands. (D) Meristematic activity confined to a recognizable layer of tangentially flattened cells. (E) Meristem in the region of secondary growth. AB, primary axial bundle; AM, apical meristem; C, cortex; LT, leaf trace; P, pith; PS, procambial strand; PV, secondary provascular strand; R, root; SB, secondary axial bundle; PTM, primary thickening meristem; STM, secondary thickening meristem.

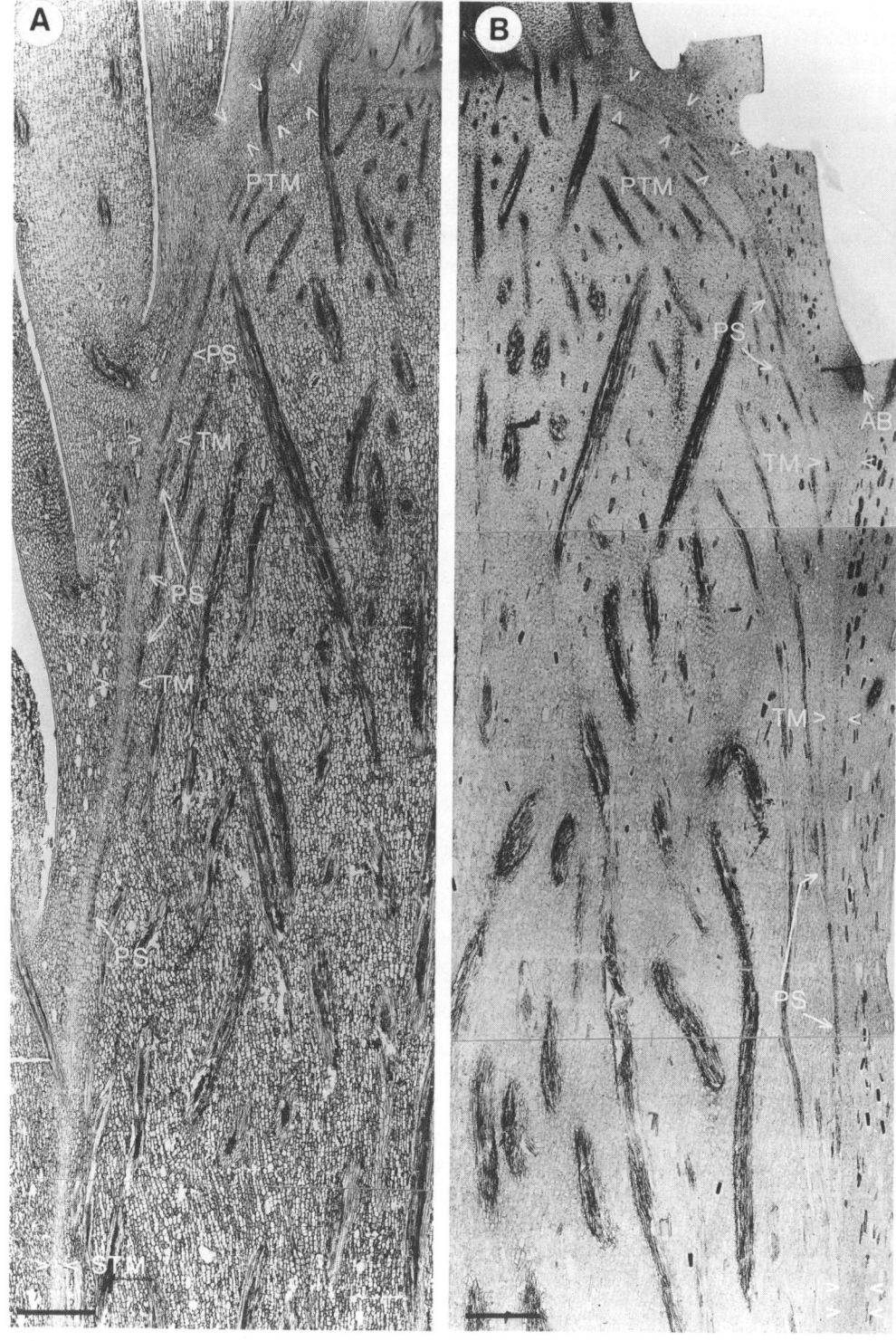

Figure 11.4.   Median longitudinal sections of *Cordyline terminalis* stem. (A) Section stained with safranin and fast green. (B) Same specimen stained with aniline blue black; scale bar is 0.5 mm. LF6, sixth leaf from apical meristem; PS, procambial strand; PTM, primary thickening meristem; STM, secondary thickening meristem; TM, thickening meristem.

A median longitudinal section of *Zea mays* illustrates further contrast to onion and *Yucca* (Figure 11.5.A,B). The shoot tip is conical and not concave as in the previous species. There is very little evidence of a lateral meristem or a pith in the center of the central cylinder. At higher magnification, there are anticlinal cell-files in the cortex, but they become obscure basipetally in the corn stem. The majority of cells in the corn stem are elongated in the longitudinal direction.

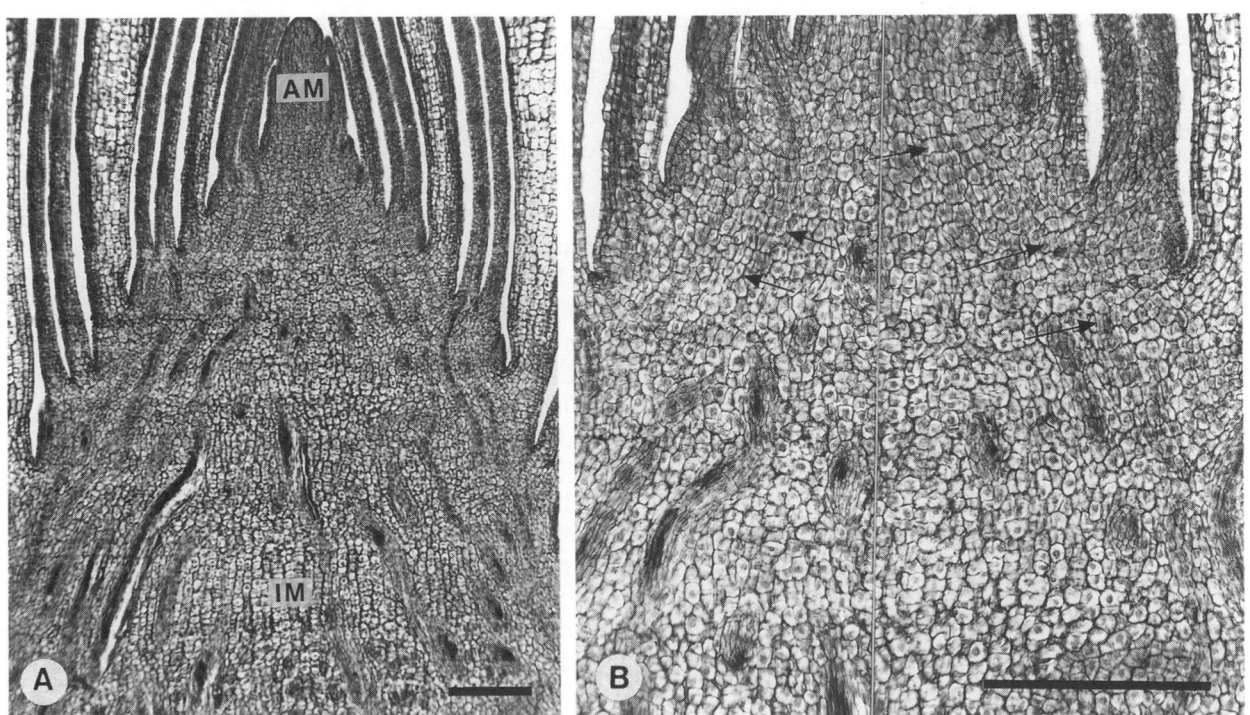

Figure 11.5. Median longitudinal sections through shoot tip of a *Zea mays* seedling; scale bar is 0.25 mm. *Arrows* indicate cell-files. AM, apical meristem; IM, intercalary meristem.

The amount of stem thickening that occurs in the four species discussed can be correlated to anatomical features to determine the mechanism of stem thickening in monocots. In rank order, from greatest amount of thickening to least, are *Yucca, Allium, Cordyline,* and finally *Zea.* The characteristics that are present extensively in *Yucca* and in *Allium* and less extensively in *Cordyline* must be important in stem thickening in monocotyledons. These morphological and anatomical characteristics include (a) an apical meristem sunken below surrounding stem tissues; (b) extensive anticlinal files of cells that run from the outer cortex into the central cylinder; and (c) a more or less distinct lateral meristem, the PTM, which is located between the cortex and the central cylinder. The first and second characteristics are less distinctive in *Cordyline,* in which the apical meristem is only slightly sunken in the shoot tip and the anticlinal files of cells do not extend as deeply into the central cylinder, but a PTM is present in the stem in this species. In *Zea,* these characteristics are essentially lacking. There are a few, short anticlinal files of cells in the shoot tip, but they are a small proportion of the total stem volume.

MECHANISM OF STEM THICKENING

The mechanism of stem thickening in monocotyledons was studied with *Allium cepa* (DeMason 1979a). Onions were planted from seed and sampled over a whole season. Morphological and anatomical changes in the stem were observed and a number of stem paramaters were measured. The first two parameters were stem height (from the base of the vasculature to the center of the apical meristem) and maximum stem width. *Allium* stems grow more rapidly in width than in height in a season (Figure 11.6). This is evidence that stem thickening is a significant process in the development of this organism. A standard height (2.5 mm) was then ascertained and the following additional parameters were measured: (a) number of cells per file in the cortex; (b) width of the central cylinder; and (c) angle of the cell-files in both the cortex and the central cylinder. The cell-files in *Allium* may be considered permanent developmental markers that allow observation of the process of development. Making these measurements at the same height on plants from different age groups is equivalent to watching a single cell-file over time. The results showed that the number of cells per file in the cortex increased through time until primary tissues were mature at that level (Figure 11.7), but the width of the central cylinder increased beyond maturation of primary tissues (Figure 11.8). The first result is evidence that *Allium* indeed has only primary growth. The angle of the cell-files in both the cortex and the central cylinder increased rapidly for the first two months and then increased more slowly before finally leveling off (Figures 11.9, 11.10). The continual increase in angle of the cell-files in the central cylinder explains why the central cylinder increases in width after cell division and cell enlargement due to primary growth has ceased. This distinct reorientation of cells is a unique phenomenon in plant development and plays an important role in the mechanism of primary thickening in monocotyledons.

Cell division activity also contributes to primary thickening, however. Identification of the PTM from the zone of tangentially flattened cells is difficult at best. Meristematic cells are usually smaller and have few small vacuoles, so these cells stain

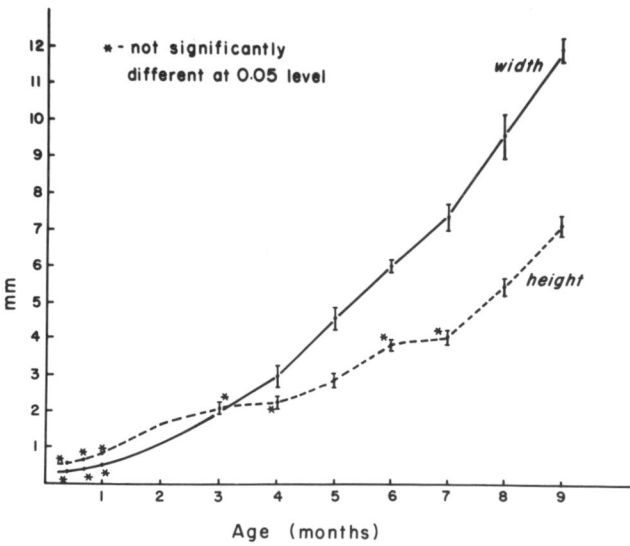

Figure 11.6. Mean heights and widths of each age group plotted as a function of time for *Allium* seedlings. *Brackets* indicate standard error.

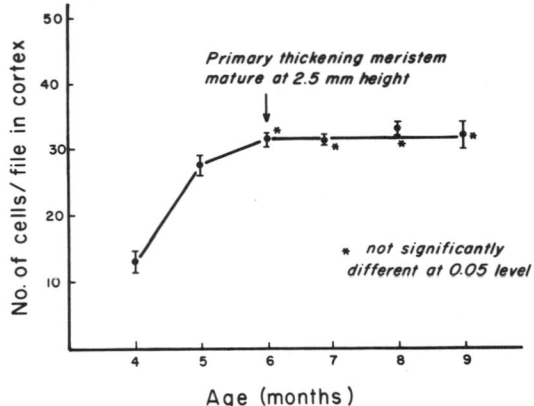

Figure 11.7. Mean number of cells per file in the cortex of each age group plotted as a function of time for *Allium* seedlings. *Brackets* indicate standard error.

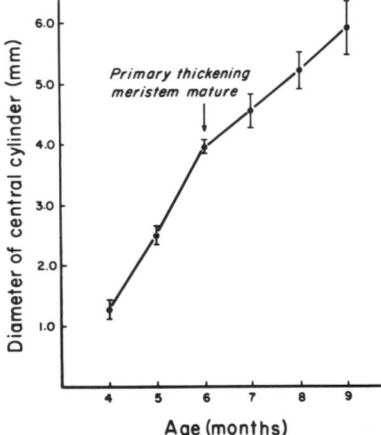

Figure 11.8. Mean diameters of central cylinder of each age group plotted as a function of time for *Allium* seedlings. *Brackets* indicate standard error.

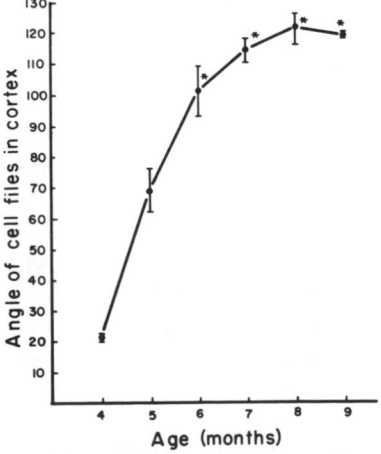

Figure 11.9. Mean angle of cell-files in the cortex of each age group plotted as a function of time for *Allium* seedlings. *Brackets* indicate standard error.

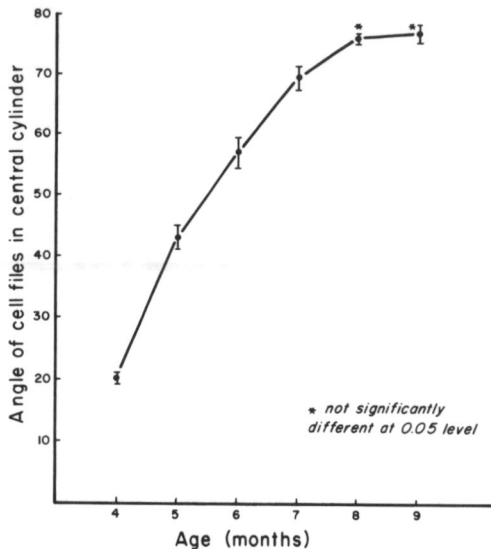

Figure 11.10.   Mean angle of cell-files in the central cylinder of each age group plotted as a function of time for *Allium* seedlings. *Brackets* indicate standard error.

darker with most cytological stains, especially those for RNA and protein, than surrounding tissue. When azure B (an RNA stain) or aniline blue black (a protein stain) are used on sections of *Allium* stems, a wide meristematic region can be recognized in the top of the stem that narrows basipetally and finally disappears below the root initiation zone (DeMason 1979a). In transverse section, it is a continuous cylinder. It is also continuous with dark staining in the apical meristem.

These staining procedures are not necessarily definitive indications of meristematic activity. The most expedient method to localize active cell division is to label plants with a radioactive DNA precursor, such as tritiated thymidine, and analyze serial autoradiograms. This was done with *Allium* stems of three ages (1–3 months), and the data were analyzed in three dimensions from serial sections (DeMason 1980). The stems were divided into three regions according to the distance below the apical meristem (A–D); the number of nuclei possessing label, the mean distance from the stem center, and the standard deviation of this mean were determined. Figure 11.11 illustrates the results for 3-month old plants. Each dot is a labeled nucleus at levels A–D. The PTM is a wide and diffuse meristem just under the apical meristem and narrows basipetally. This is confirmed by the graph of the measurements. At level A there is a smaller mean distance from the stem center and a large standard deviation for this mean. The lower levels B–D show a larger mean distance to the labeled nuclei and small standard deviations. In *Allium,* then, the zone that stains darker with cytological stains is indeed identical to the zone in which active cell division is occurring. This experiment also allows us to determine the pattern of maturation of the stem during radial growth. It is centrifugal in the central cylinder and centripetal in the cortex but occurs earlier in the central cylinder than in the cortex.

A model for the mechanism of stem thickening in monocotyledons is presented in Figure 11.12. The sequence of events has been divided into three stages that occur simultaneously but for convenience are discussed separately. The first event is the initiation of cell-files in the crown, which happens immediately adjacent to the base of the apical meristem and must occur by anticlinal cell division in the youngest cell-files.

The second event is elongation of the cell-files by both periclinal cell division activity in the PTM and by subsequent cell enlargement along the length of the files. The final event is reorientation of the cell-files to a horizontal plane. This further increases the width of the stem.

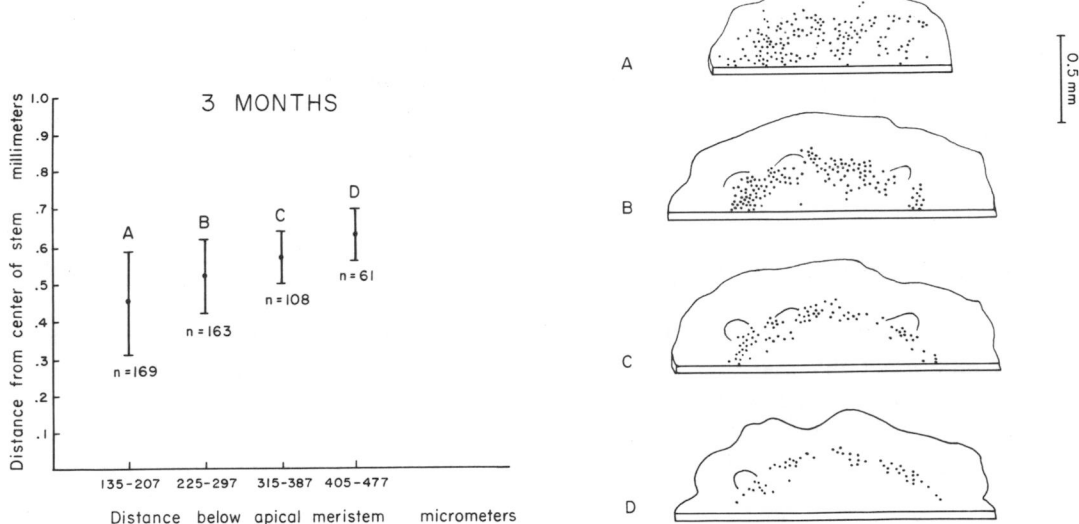

Figure 11.11. Results of three-dimensional analysis of labeled three-month-old *Allium* plants; n, number of nuclei measured; *brackets* indicate standard deviations.

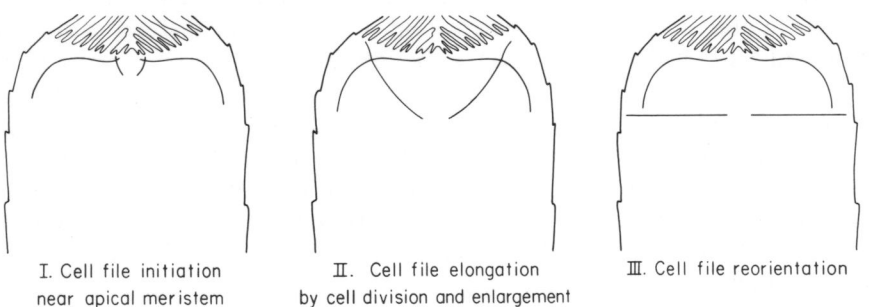

Figure 11.12. Diagrammatic representation of the mechanism of radial stem growth in monocotyledons.

RELATIONSHIP BETWEEN THE PTM AND THE STM

In considering the functional and developmental relationships of the STM to the PTM we can address the following questions: (1) How does the function of the STM relate to the function of the PTM in monocotyledons? (2) Are the two meristems longitudinally continuous in an actively growing stem? (3) At a given level in the stem, does the STM replace the PTM? (4) How does the STM arise for the first time in the stem in relation to the origin of the PTM? If the two lateral meristems are developmentally related, all criteria should be satisfied. The two meristems should be longitudinally continuous in a growing shoot, the PTM should become the STM at a given level in the stem over time, and the STM should arise after and in continuity with the PTM in a seedling.

Developmental Relationship

Longitudinal continuity in the growing shoot is simple to demonstrate. It has been shown histologically that the STM and PTM are longitudinally continuous in *Yucca* (Figure 11.3.B; Diggle and DeMason 1983a) and in *Cordyline* (Figure 11.4.A,B; DeMason and Wilson 1985). The same histochemical staining reactions have also been used for protein and for RNA to demonstrate continuity between the two lateral meristems in both species. To answer the other two questions, Diggle & DeMason (1983b) used *Yucca whipplei* and followed the anatomical changes in the stem at a standard level (2 mm above the base of the vasculature) and the initiation of the STM in seedlings. Figures 11.13.B–F illustrate the anatomical characteristics of the lateral meristem and adjacent tissues in plants 2–6 months old. At 2 months (Figure 11.13.B), the PTM is evident in the crown of the stem between the cortex and central cylinder. Mature vascular bundles are collateral in xylem and phloem arrangement and are therefore primary bundles. At 3 months, the lateral meristem is evident below the crown and radial files of cells are starting to become evident in the plane of a transverse section (Figure 11.13.C). All mature bundles are still collateral and primary. At 4 months, the lateral meristem is narrow in extent, and distinct radial files of parenchyma cells are evident in transverse section (Figure 11.13.D). Procambial strands immediately inside the meristem are in an amphivasal arrangement and therefore will mature into secondary bundles. This is the transition to secondary growth. At 5 months, the characteristic histology of the STM is evident and mature secondary, amphivasal bundles are present in the central cylinder (Figure 11.13.E). Finally, at 6 months, the STM is wide and is forming root primordia (Figure 11.13.F). Obviously, then, the PTM becomes the STM at a given level in the stem without cessation of activity of any kind.

To answer the last question, initiation of the PTM and the STM was followed in *Yucca* seedlings (Diggle and DeMason 1983b). The PTM arises in *Yucca* seedlings at germination (Figure 11.13A) and runs from the shoot apex to the base of the stem between the cortex and central cylinder. All vascular bundles initiated in the first 3 months of stem development are collateral and therefore primary. Subsequently, amphivasal bundles are initiated in the stem base while collateral bundles continue to be initiated in the crown. This is the initiation of the STM, and it is initiated in concert with the PTM in the seedling stem. All criteria proposed above to demonstrate developmental relatedness have been fulfilled.

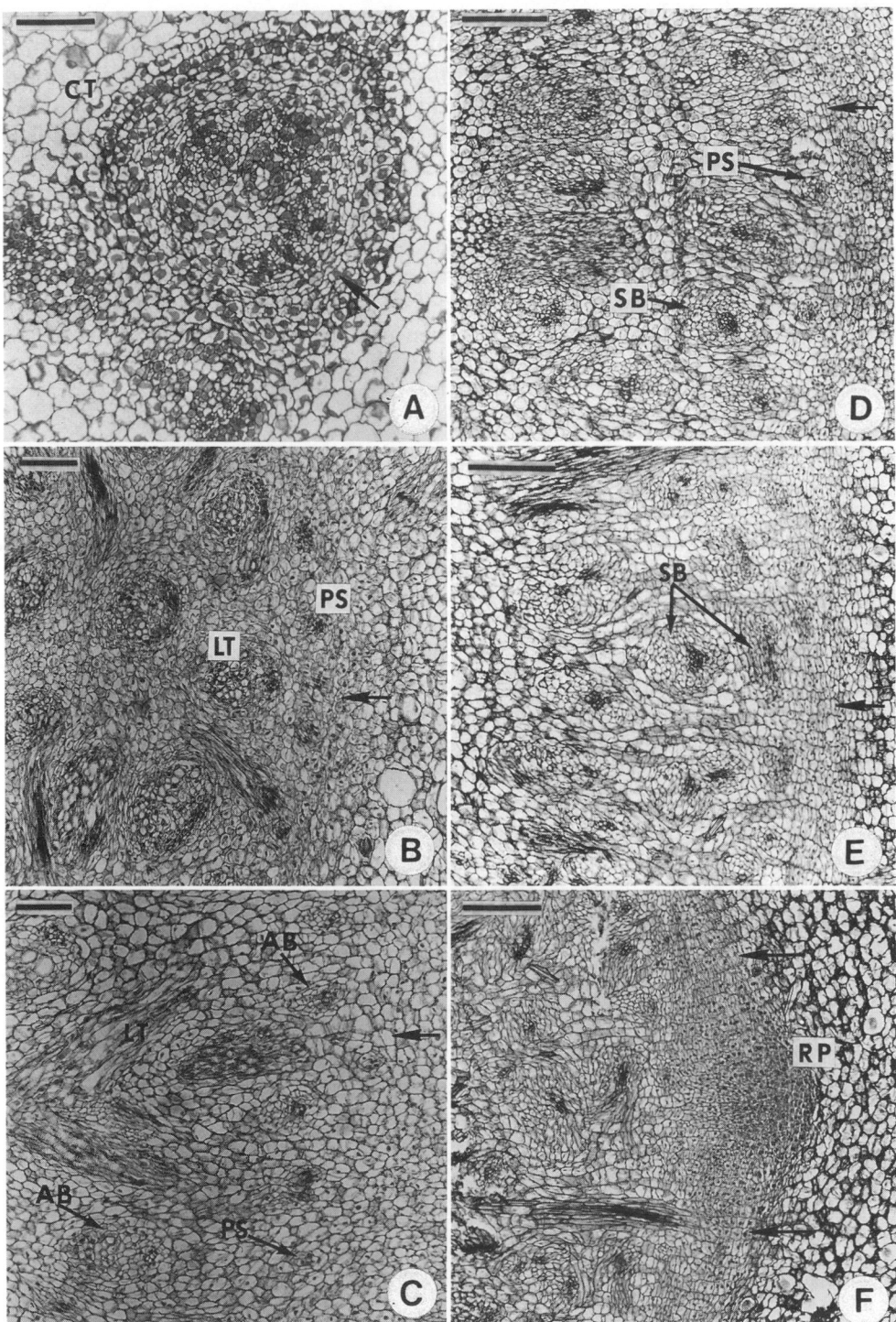

Figure 11.13. *Yucca whipplei* stem sections. (A) Transverse section of one-week-old seedling. (B–F) Transverse stem sections 2.0 mm above the stem base. (B) Two-month-old plant. (C) Three-month-old plant. (D) Four-month-old plant. (E) Five-month-old plant. (F) Six-month-old plant. *Unlabeled arrows* indicate lateral meristem; AB, primary axial bundles; CT, cotyledon; LT, leaf trace; PS, procambial strand; RP, root primordium; SB, secondary vascular bundle; scale bar, 0.1 mm in (A–C) and 0.2 mm in (D–F).

The developmental events in the transition from primary to secondary growth in a monocotyledon with true secondary growth is analogous to the development of a woody dicotyldonous axis. Following germination in a dicotyledon, development is initially primary; secondary activity is subsequently initiated in the base of the seedling. Successively formed layers of secondary tissue extend further acropetally. Continuity of meristematic activity during the transition between tissues in the plant body of dicotyledons is generally accepted (see Larson 1976), and most recent texts on plant anatomy (Esau 1965a,b, Cutter 1971; Philipson et al. 1971; Steeves and Sussex 1972; Mauseth 1988; Fahn 1990; Iqbal 1990) accept the concept that the procamium and cambium (in dicotyledons) represent sequential developmental stages of the same vascular meristem. Similarly, the PTM and STM of species in the Agavaceae probably form a continuum, and the transition between primary and secondary growth is best understood by observations of the transition in stem histology and anatomy.

Functional Relationship

To monitor the function of the PTM and the STM over time, measurements identical to those on *Allium* were made with *Yucca* plants over a season. The standard height chosen was 4 mm above the shoot base. The pattern of thymidine incorporation was also determined in seedling plants. The observations of height and width over time demonstrate that the rates of growth in the two dimensions are approximately the same (Figure 11.14). The number of cells per file in the cortex increases rapidly until primary tissues are mature and then continues to increase but less rapidly (Figure 11.15). This result is unlike the result in *Allium* and demonstrates that secondary growth does occur in *Yucca*. Like *Allium*, the width of the central cylinder continues to increase after maturation of primary tissues (Figure 11.16), and the angle of the cell-files in the cortex increases until primary tissues are mature, and then levels off (Figure 11.17). Finally, again as in *Allium*, the angle of the cell-files in the central cylinder increases rapidly until primary tissues are mature, and then increases slightly (Figure 11.18). The mechanism of stem thickening in *Yucca*, which has secondary growth, is very similar to that in *Allium*, which has no secondary growth.

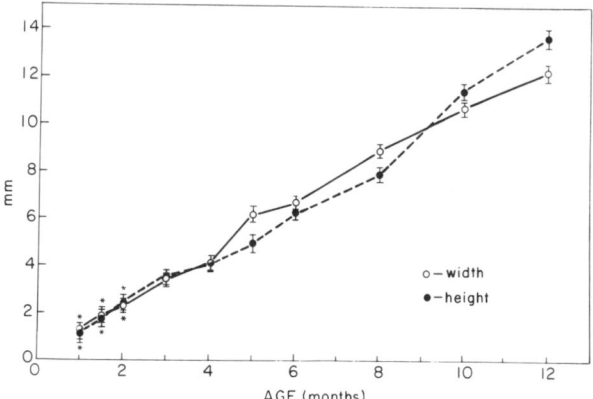

Figure 11.14.   Mean heights and widths of each age group plotted as a function of time for *Yucca* seedlings. *Brackets* indicate standard error. Adjacent *unstarred points* are significantly different ($P < 0.05$).

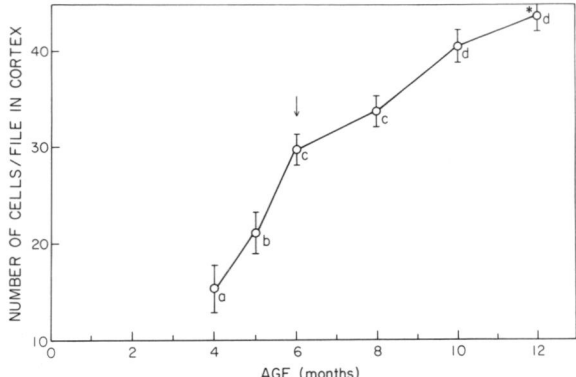

Figure 11.15. Mean number of cells per file in the cortex measured at 4 mm from stem base plotted as a function of time in *Yucca* seedlings. *Arrow* indicates transition to secondary growth at that level. *Asterisk* indicates root initiation at that level. *Brackets* indicate standard error. *Points* followed by a common letter are not significantly different ($P < 0.05$).

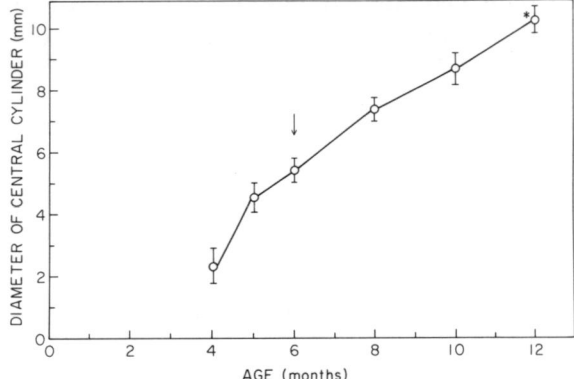

Figure 11.16. Mean diameter of central cylinder, measured at 4 mm from stem base plotted as a function of time in *Yucca* seedlings. *Arrow* indicates transition to secondary growth at that level. *Asterisk* indicates root initiation at that level. *Brackets* indicate standard error.

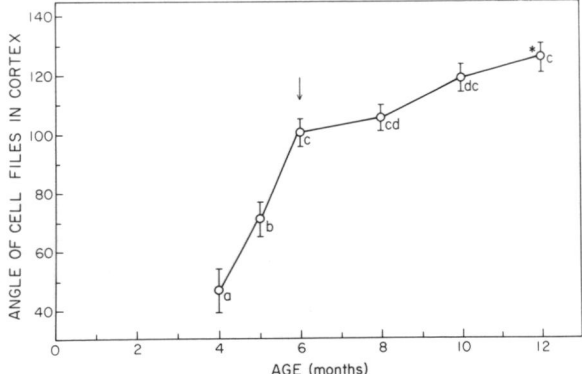

Figure 11.17. Mean angle of cell-files in cortex, measured at 4 mm above stem base, and plotted as a function of time in *Yucca* seedlings. *Arrow* indicates transition to secondary growth at that level. *Asterisk* indicates root initiation at that level. *Brackets* indicate standard error. *Points* followed by a common letter are not significantly different ($P < 0.05$).

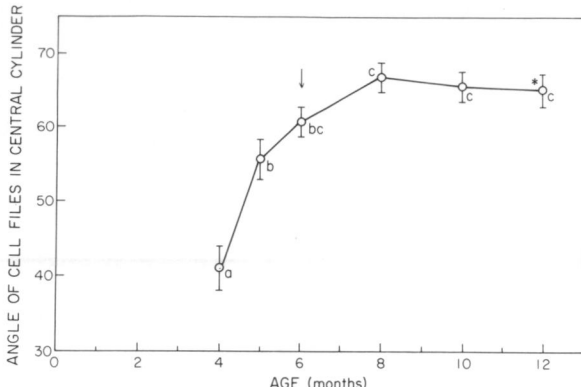

Figure 11.18. Mean angle of cell-files in central cylinder, measured at 4 mm above stem base, and plotted as a function of time. *Arrow* indicates transition to secondary growth at that level. *Asterisk* indicates root initiation at that level. *Brackets* indicate standard error. Points followed by a common letter are not significantly different ($P < 0.05$).

The results of thymidine incorporation into the lateral meristems were also similar to the results in *Allium* (Figure 11.19). The limits of the meristem as demonstrated by histochemical staining were divided into six levels; A–C were within the PTM and D–F were within the STM. Labeled nuclei appeared at all levels. In the top of the stem, the labeled nuclei were spread over a small area such that the mean distance from the stem center was small and the standard deviation was large. At successively lower levels, the position of the labeled nuclei became more distinct, as indicated by the smaller standard deviations of the mean distance from the stem center. This is exactly what we saw in *Allium*, except that the longitudinal extent of lateral meristem activity was much greater in *Yucca* (DeMason and Diggle 1984).

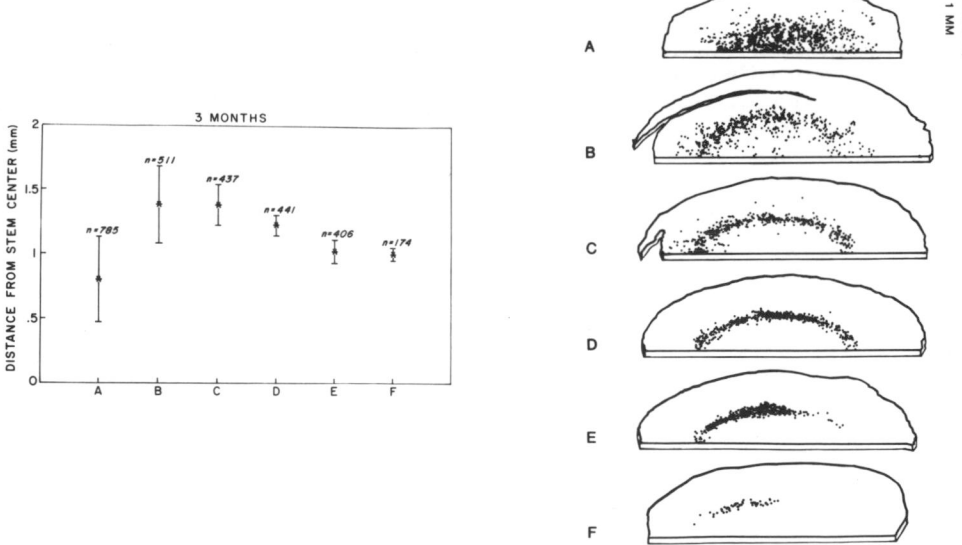

Figure 11.19. Results of three-dimensional analysis of labeled three-month-old *Yucca* plant; *n*, number of nuclei measured. *Brackets* show standard deviation. Level A is 456–504 μm below apical meristem; B is 696–744 μm below apical meristem; C is 996–1044 μm below apical meristem; D is 1164–1212 μm below apical meristem; E is 1392–1440 μm below apical meristem; F is 1512–1560 μm below apical meristem.

The stem thickens by the formation, lengthening, and reorientation of cell-files, regardless of whether there is secondary growth or solely primary growth. Another feature that supports the notion that the STM behaves similarly to the PTM is that shoot-borne roots are formed by the PTM in *Allium* but by the STM in *Yucca*. A third functional similarity between the two meristems is in the method of vascular tissue development.

DEVELOPMENT OF THE VASCULAR SYSTEM

The structure and development of the vascular system in monocotyledons have been major areas of research for the past two decades (See Tomlinson 1984). The present discussion concentrates on two specific areas: (a) the relationship of the three-dimensional structure and the transectional anatomy of the monocot vascular system to the mode of the stem development via the PTM; and (b) the relationship of the secondary vascular system to the primary vascular system in monocots with secondary growth, and how this relates to the mode of stem development via the PTM and STM. The mechanism of stem thickening in monocots places developmental constraints on the structure of the vascular system and explains some of its idiosyncrasies with respect to dicots that have not been emphasized previously.

Unique Anatomical Features

A transverse section of a monocot stem shows numerous vascular bundles widely distributed across the central cylinder. The density of these bundles increases at the periphery of the central cylinder, and the size, cell type, and cell type distribution may also differ somewhat. This arrangement is quite different from that of a dicot, which typically has a small number of bundles in a distinct cylinder that separates the cortex from the pith. In three dimensions, one can conceptually isolate individual bundles and follow their paths acropetally in the stem. Bundles can be divided by size into three classes: major, intermediate, and minor bundles, according to (a) how deeply they approach the stem center, and (b) the distance between successively formed leaf traces. The trajectory of the bundles is similar. Examining a mature bundle acropetally reveals that the bundles move in toward the stem center and then diverge out again toward the stem periphery. As a bundle diverges out, it will branch one to many times to form a leaf trace, a continuing axial bundle, and possibly bridges and satellite bundles, etc. (Figure 11.20). The continuing axial bundle then diverges in toward the stem center, and the pattern repeats over and over until it ends in a procambial strand in the PTM near the shoot apex, where it travels, destined to enter a leaf primordium (see Tomlinson 1984). The important aspects are (a) the S-shaped curving in and out of the stem center, which is not characteristic of dicots; (b) the stele consists of individual sympodia consisting of axial bundles and leaf traces; and (c) the procambial strands are open-ended and develop in the stem periphery. The latter features are similar to characteristics of other seed plants with a eustele, including dicots.

The transectional anatomy of an individual bundle depends on the type of bundle and the position of the transverse section in the three-dimensional path of the bundle. This is true of species whether they have only primary thickening or have secondary thickening as well. An example of a species with only primary thickening is the palm

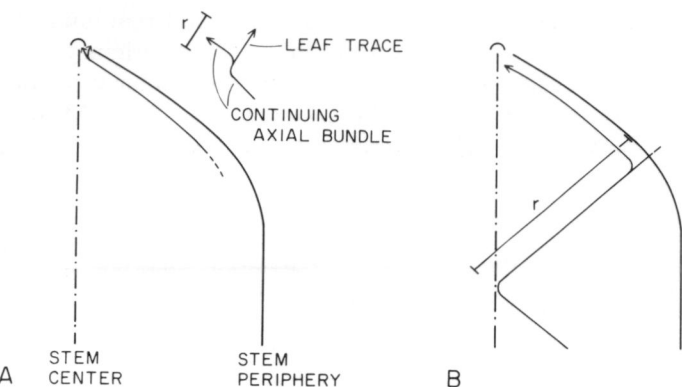

Figure 11.20. Diagrammatic representation of vascular bundle extension (r) during stem thickening in a monocotyledon. (A) illustrates before extension and (B) after extension. In this drawing, the extension occurs in the axial bundle (Bundle path type C or D from Zimmermann and Tomlinson 1974), but it could also occur in the leaf trace (type A) or in both the leaf trace and axial bundle (type B), depending where the branching occurs with respect to the radial extension during stem thickening.

Rhapis excelsa. The bundles are collateral along their entire length but the relative amounts of metaxylem and protoxylem change, depending on the position of the section in the path of the bundle and the type of bundle. The region of a major bundle that moves up toward the stem center has only metaxylem in the xylem portion of the bundle. As it turns out again, the xylem consists of both metaxylem and protoxylem, and in the stem periphery it consists only of protoxylem (Zimmermann and Sperry 1983). The minor bundles contain less protoxylem in their course and also possess a larger fiber cap on the phloem (Zimmermann and Tomlinson 1965; Tomlinson and Vincent 1984). Understanding the three-dimensional picture helps to understand the transverse section. The bundles in the center of the transectional view of a monocot stem are major bundles, and the congested bundles in the outer stem periphery are minor bundles, leaf traces, etc.

Developmental Parameters

The procambial strands are open-ended and travel in the crown in the PTM (Figure 11.20). When an axial bundle branches to form a leaf trace, the bundle bends around into the leaf primordium and then runs parallel to the anticlinal cell-files produced by the PTM. Major bundles travel closest to the apical meristem and form leaf traces that enter the young primordium early in its development. Minor bundles travel furthest from the apical meristem and form leaf traces late in the development of the leaf primordium in the base of the crown (Zimmermann and Tomlinson 1965). This explains the positions of major and minor bundles in the mature stem. The major bundles travel closer to the apical meristem; therefore, a portion of the bundles remain in the stem center after maturity. At this point, the procambial strand of a major bundle has two components: the continuing component, which grows as a procambial strand in the PTM; and the radial (r) component which runs parallel to the anticlinal cell-files. The radial component must undergo an extraordinary elongation phase, because this is the direction of cell division and elongation that causes stem thickening. The radial component also changes its angle with respect to the vertical, as the adjacent cell-files have been shown to do. This extension in the radial component is illustrated in Figure 11.20. The process of axis thickening causes the radial extension and hence the unusual (with respect to dicots) S-shape of the axial bundles of monocots. The bundles are in reality peripheral but are displaced by the process of thickening in the crown. Some elongation occurs in the other component of the strand, also due to the elongation of the shoot axis in that direction, but it is far less than the elongation that occurs parallel to the cell-files.

Because the radial component of the major axial bundle undergoes so much elongation, it is not surprising that the radial component of the bundle consists of tracheids with extensible cell thickenings, or protoxylem. From this, the radial component of the minor bundles might be predicted to have less protoxylem, since most of the axis thickening would have occurred by the time the bundles branch to form a leaf trace. (Stem maturation occurs centrifugally in the central cylinder, so the inner central cylinder matures before the outer central cylinder, where the only metaxylem found is in the radial component of the axial bundle.) This is exactly what Tomlinson and Vincent (1984) saw in their study of bundle differentiation in *Rhapis excelsa*. The process of stem thickening explains why bundle anatomy varies with respect to meta- and protoxylem in the different bundle types and in the same bundle in different positions in the mature stem. The morphology of the primary vascular system and the anatomy of the vascular bundles are directly related to the activities of the PTM in the monocotyledon shoot.

A definition of the leaf trace in monocotyledons has been a controversial issue. Beck et al. (1982) have proposed that the similarities between the vascular system in monocots and all other seed plants warrant the classical definition: A leaf trace is "a vascular bundle that extends from its connection with another vascular bundle in the stem outward to the base of the leaf." Tomlinson (1984) has defined a leaf trace in functional terms with respect to water movement in the shoot as "the extent to which protoxylem is differentiated within each leaf contact cycle." From this definition, however, follow internal inconsistencies in the same stem between major and minor bundles, and it leads to the illogical conclusion that the monocot stele is not a eustele. Laliberte and Veith (1987a,b) agree with Tomlinson and propose that the upper portion of each repeating unit (essentially, that portion with protoxylem) develops under the influence of the leaf primordium and is therefore the leaf trace. As the preceding paragraphs have shown, however, monocot vascular bundles develop similarly to those of dicots. The unusual (with respect to dicots) radial displacement is a consequence of the activities of the PTM and stem thickening in the crown. The presence of protoxylem is also expected in this region of bundle elongation. Therefore, Beck et al. (1982) appear to be justified in considering the monocot stele as a highly modified eustele and in applying the classical definition of a leaf trace.

How is the secondary vascular system related to the primary vascular system? How do the PTM and STM contribute to the development of the whole vascular system in a plant like *Cordyline* that has secondary growth? How do the roles of the PTM and STM compare in *Rhapis*, which has only primary growth? The secondary plant body in species with true secondary growth consists of discrete vascular bundles embedded in parenchymatous ground tissue that is arranged in radially aligned cell-files. In some species, the secondary bundles have a different arrangement of xylem and phloem than do the primary bundles. The relationship of the primary body to the secondary body was studied in *Yucca whipplei* and *Cordyline terminalis*, both with collateral primary bundles and amphivasal secondary bundles. Secondary bundles were identified in transverse section mainly on the basis of anatomical features such as paucity of phloem and lack of helical or annular elements in the secondary bundles

(Cheadle 1937). This feature is reminiscent of the difference in anatomy of different regions of a primary bundle in *Rhapis*.

A number of workers have used serial sections to reconstruct the vascular arrangement in a few species with true secondary growth. It now seems clear that primary bundles are continuous with secondary bundles (DeMason and Wilson 1985; Laliberte and Veith 1987a,b). The evidence for this is illustrated for *Cordyline terminalis* (Figures 11.21, 11.22; DeMason and Wilson 1985). Groups of anastomosing secondary bundles were followed acropetally in the stem. One such reconstruction is illustrated in Figure 11.21. All these bundles start as a very small group of bundles just inside the STM 17 mm below the shoot apex in the stem. They divide into a number of different bundles, some of which come very close to the stem center (VII, VIII, XII), pass out of the stem as leaf traces (II), or end as procambial strands differentiating in the PTM (IX,XI). To follow the cross-sectional anatomy of each bundle, bundle I, for example, starts as a branch from a group of secondary bundles adjacent to the STM (Figure 11.21,E,F), moves up and toward the stem center (Figures 11.21,C–F, and then travels back out as a leaf trace Figure 11.21.B,F). The bundle's anatomy changes at the different levels. At its upper extent, just before it leaves the stele as a leaf trace, the bundle has a typical collateral arrangement of xylem and phloem (Figures 11.21.F, 11.22.A). At the level closest to the stem center, it has an intermediate arrangement with protoxylem to the inside and metaxylem to the outside (Figures 11.21.F, 11.22.B). At its basal region, it is amphivasal and consists entirely of metaxylem elements (Figure 11.22.C). Further down it becomes a true secondary bundle and fuses with other secondary bundles. The beginnings of this transition can be seen in a longitudinal section in Figure 11.22.D. The cortex is at the right. At the top of the bundle is a collateral arrangement; the xylem consists of elements with extensible wall thickenings (i.e. protoxylem). At the bottom, the bundle has an intermediate arrangement with xylem on both sides of the phloem—protoxylem to the inside and metaxylem (with pitted walls) to the outside. Further down in the stem it transforms into an amphivasal bundle with metaxylem surrounding phloem. All bundles apparently do this, and therefore a direct continuity exists between the primary and secondary vascular bundles in these species. This is, of course, structurally necessary if water is to travel from the roots to the leaves and the shoot tip, and is thought to be generally true of all species with secondary growth (Tomlinson 1984).

These two lateral meristems, PTM and STM, are clearly continuous longitudinally and developmentally, and the primary and secondary vascular systems are also continuous. How do these meristems function in the production of these bundle systems? As discussed above, the vascular system consists of sympodia like those of monocots with only primary growth, but these sympodia are primary in their upper regions (in association with leaf trace formation), secondary in their basal regions (right after leaf trace formation), and intermediate in between in each repeating unit. In their upper extent, they develop in the PTM and differentiate during the process of stem thickening in the crown. In their basal region, they differentiate below this zone in immediate derivatives of the STM, simultaneously. The only developmental difference between monocots with secondary growth and those without is that the former have a much longer region in which procambial strands form. In the lower region of procambial strand development, many strands fuse with continuing axial bundles at the point of leaf trace formation (Figure 11.22.E.). This difference is minor compared to the many similarities between species. Thus, the PTM and the STM are possibly two developmental extremes of a single, continuous, thickening meristem associated with the production of a single, continuous vascular system of both primary and secondary tissues in species with true secondary growth.

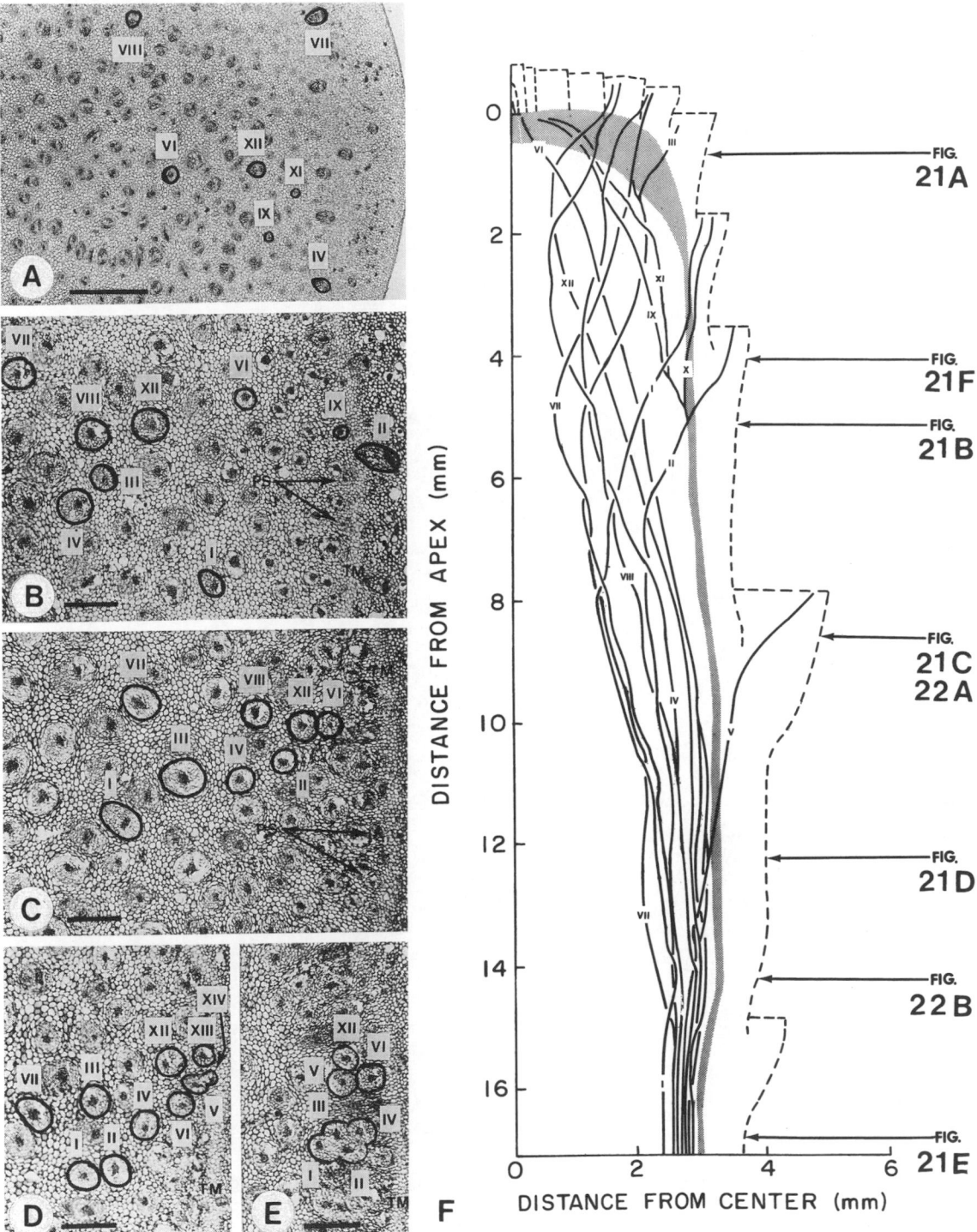

Figure 11.21. Serial sections and subsequent vascular reconstruction in *Cordyline terminalis*: (A) in region of PTM, showing only collateral bundles or procambial strands within central cylinder; (B) approximately 5 mm below apical meristem; (C) approximately 9 mm below apical meristem; (D) approximately 12 mm below apical meristem; (E) approximately 17 mm below apical meristem; scale bars, 0.5 mm; (F) reconstruction. Lateral meristem indicated by *shading*. TM, thickening meristem.

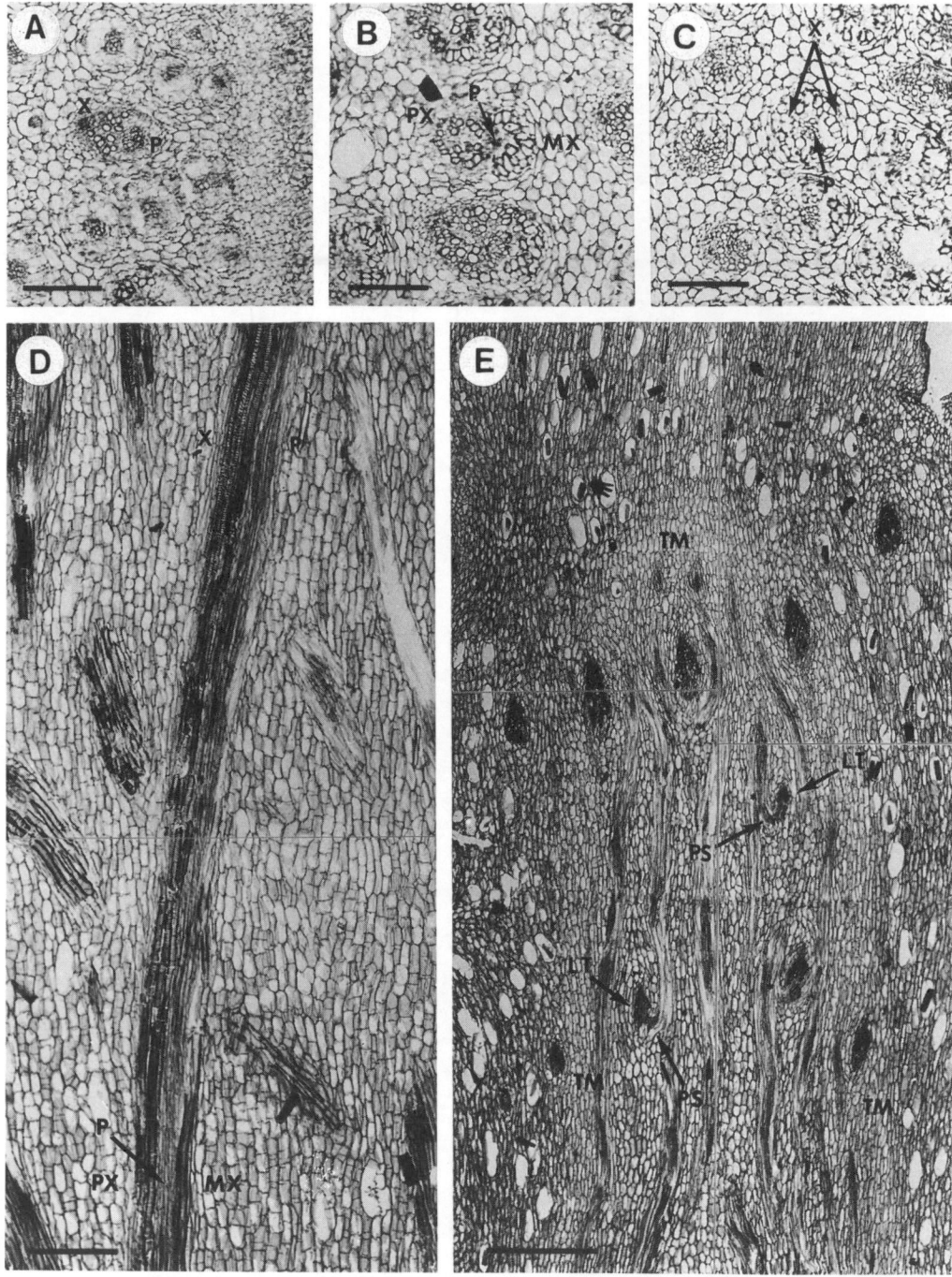

Figure 11.22. Stem anatomy of *Cordyline terminalis.* (A–C) Successive transverse sections of bundle I from previous figures showing bundle anatomy from collateral to amphivasal. (A) Collateral structure, approximately 4 mm below apical meristem. (B) Intermediate structure, adaxial protoxylem, abaxial metaxylem. (C) Amphivasal arrangement, metaxylem surrounding phloem. (D) Longitudinal section of a bundle collateral in its distal region and intermediate below. (E) Tangential section through lateral meristem with procambial axial bundles diverging from phloem side of emerging leaf traces. Scale bars, 0.5 mm; LT, leaf trace; MX, metaxylem; P, phloem; PS, procambial strand; PX, protoxylem; TM, thickening meristem; X, xylem; *, junctions of procambial strands at branching points of axial bundles and leaf traces.

CONCLUDING REMARKS

In a relatively recent paper, Kaplan (1984) explored the developmental basis of diversity in plant form. He asked:

How much of this morphological diversity is merely the result of quantitative variations in growth distribution on a common developmental theme and how much is the result of qualitatively unique developmental programs which are distinctive for individual plant groups?

Stem thickening in monocotyledons via the activities of the PTM is an example of a qualitatively unique developmental program. The lack of a vascular cambium and the presence instead of the PTM affects all structural aspects of the monocotyledonous plant. In this chapter I have shown how this program affects the morphology and anatomy of the stem and the morphology and anatomy of the vascular system. Some researchers have focused on differences rather than similarities and have consequently hypothesized unwarranted fundamental differences in vascular construction.

This unique developmental program also affects how monocotyledons occupy three-dimensional space, in that it affects rooting, morphology of the leaf, and types of branching (Holttum 1955). Stem thickening in monocotyledons via the functions of the PTM may well be the fundamental unifying feature of this unique plant group.

LITERATURE CITED

Beck, C. B., R. Schmid, and G. W. Rothwell, 1982. Stelar morphology and the primary vascular system of seed plants. *Bot. Rev.* 48:691–815.

Cheadle, V. I. 1937. Secondary growth by means of a thickening ring in certain monocotyledons. *Bot. Gaz.* 98:535–555.

Cutter, E. G. 1971. *Plant Anatomy: Experiment and Interpretation*. Part 2. *Organs*. Reading, Massachusets: Addison-Wesley.

DeMason, D. A. 1979a. Function and development of the primary thickening meristem in the monocotyledon, *Allium cepa* L. *Bot. Gaz.* 140:51–66.

_____ . 1979b. Histochemistry of the primary thickening meristem in the vegetative stem of *Allium cepa* L. *Am. J. Bot.* 66:347–350.

_____ . 1980. Localization of cell division activity in the primary thickening meristem in *Allium cepa* L. *Am. J. Bot.* 67:393–399.

_____ . 1983. The primary thickening meristem: Definition and function in monocotyledons. *Am. J. Bot.* 70:955–962.

DeMason, D. A. and P. K. Diggle. 1984. The relationship between the primary thickening meristem and the secondary thickening meristem in *Yucca whipplei* Torr. III. Observations from histochemistry and autoradiography. *Am. J. Bot.* 71:1260–1267.

DeMason, D. A. and M. A. Wilson. 1985. The continuity of primary and secondary growth in *Cordyline terminalis* (Agavaceae). *Can. J. Bot.* 63:1907–1913.

Diggle, P. K., and D. A. DeMason. 1983a. The relationship between the primary thickening meristem and the secondary thickening meristem in *Yucca whipplei* Torr. I. Histology of the mature vegetative stem. *Am. J. Bot.* 70:1195–1204.

Diggle, P. K., and D. A. DeMason. 1983b. The relationship between the primary thickening meristem and the secondary thickening meristem in *Yucca whipplei* Torr. II. Ontogenetic relationship within the vegetative stem. *Am. J. Bot.* 70:1205–1216.

Esau, K. 1965a. *Vascular Differentiation in Plants*. New York: Holt, Rinehart and Winston.
———. 1965b. *Plant Anatomy*. New York: John Wiley and Sons, Inc.
———. 1977. *Anatomy of Seed Plants*. 2nd Ed. New York: John Wiley.
Fahn, A. 1990. *Plant Anatomy*. 4th ed. Oxford, U.K.: Pergamon Press.
Iqbal, M. 1990. *The Vascular Cambium*. Taunton, U.K.: Research Studies Press.
Holttum, R. E. 1955. Growth-habits of monocotyledons—variations on a theme. *Phyto-morphology* 5:399–413.
Kaplan, D. R. 1984. Alternative modes of organogenesis in higher plants. In *Contemporary Problems in Plant Anatomy*. Ed. R. A. White, W. C. Dickison. New York: Academic Press, Inc. 261–300.
Laliberte, S. and J. Veith. 1987a. Modifications structurales des faisceaux vasculaires primaires de la tige de *Cordyline indivisa* (Agavaceae). 1. Analyse du patron de conversion. *Can. J. Bot.* 65:299–323.
———. 1987b. Modifications structurales des faisceaux vasculaires primaires de la tige de *Cordyline indivisa* (Agavaceae). 2. Repartition de differents stades structuraux dans le cylindre primaire, en fonction de la distance sous l'apex. *Can. J. Bot.* 65:324–329.
Larson, P. R. 1976. Procambium vs. cambium and protoxylem vs. metaxylem in *Populus deltoides* seedlings. *Am. J. Bot.* 63:1332–1348.
Mauseth, J. D. 1988. *Plant Anatomy*. Redwood City, CA: Benjamin Cummings.
Philipson, W. R., J. M. Ward, and B. G. Butterfield. 1971. *The Vascular Cambium: Its development and Activity.* London, U.K.: Chapman & Hall.
Steeves, T. A., and I. M. Sussex. 1972. *Patterns in Plant Development*. Englewood Cliffs, New Jersey: Prentice-Hall, Inc.
Tomlinson, P. B. 1984. Development of the stem conducting tissues in monocotyledons. In *Contemporary Problems in Plant Anatomy*. Ed. R. A. White, W. C. Dickison. New York: Academic Press, Inc. 1–51.
Tomlinson, P. B., and J. R. Vincent. 1984. Anatomy of the palm *Rhapis excelsa*, X. Differentiation of stem conducting tissue. *J. Arnold Arbor.* 65:191–214.
Zimmermann, M. H., and J. S. Sperry. 1983. Anatomy of the palm *Rhapis excelsa*. IX. Xylem structure of the leaf meristem. *J. Arnold Arbor.* 64:599–609.
Zimmermann, M. H., and P. B. Tomlinson. 1965. Anatomy of the palm *Rhapis excelsa*. I. Mature vegetative axis *J. Arnold Arbor.* 46:160–178.
———. 1974. Vascular patterns in palm stems: variations of the *Rhapis* principle. *J. Arnold Arbor.* 55:402–424.

Section III
REPRODUCTIVE GROWTH

Chapter 12

Correlative Mechanisms and Controls of Flower Development

P. S. SRIVASTAVA and MUHAMMAD IQBAL

INTRODUCTION

During post-embryonic development in higher plants, the shoot apex undergoes three discernible phases: juvenile vegetative, adult, and reproductive. The transition from the juvenile to adult phase is usually gradual and involves subtle changes in shoot morphology and physiology (see Poethig 1990). Leaf shape is one of the most conspicuous characteristics that differentiates the juvenile and adult shoots. The juvenile shoot usually has smaller and simpler leaves (e.g. *Acacia, Hedera, Morus,* etc.), although in some plants the opposite is true. The two phases can also be distinguished on the basis of phyllotaxis (*Hedera*) and leaf retention (*Fagus*). Growth habit of lateral branches, chemical composition, photosynthetic efficiency, disease resistance, and other metabolic traits vary considerably. Rooting ability of cuttings also differs; cuttings from young trees root more readily than those from adult trees. The transition from adult to reproductive state is abrupt and involves gross changes in the characters of the shoot (see McDaniel 1989).

The development of the shoot is controlled by an independently regulated, overlapping control mechanism that modifies the expression of a process necessary for growth. Evidence indicates that in maize and ivy, leaves formed during the change from juvenile to adult growth possess a combination of juvenile and adult cell types and express a variety of traits in a quantitatively intermediate fashion. Similarly, the axillary buds emerging during transition have both juvenile and adult traits. The intermediate developmental patterns are common during the transition from vegetative to reproductive state. In *Arabidopsis thaliana,* for example, the shoot produces rudimentary leaves and elongated lateral branches similar to those produced by rosette nodes. Subsequently, when inflorescence develops, leaf development is suppressed and solitary flowers originate in place of branches. In fact, differentiation of the reproductive organs is preceded by the formation of sepals and petals that have a combination of vegetative and nonvegetative characters.

For flowering, the size of the shoot is more important than its age. In several species, shoots undergo flowering on reaching a certain stage of development (Robinson and Wareing 1969). The regulatory mechanism ensures that the plant does not flower until it has attained the requisite size. This holds even in plants requiring a specific day length or chilling. In woody plants also, the transition to flowering occurs after a delay that varies with species and ranges from 1 year to 30–40 years. Once initiated, flowering recurs every year, albeit depending upon weather conditions. In tobacco (McDaniel 1980) and black currant (Schwabe and Al-Doori 1973), etc., the factor seems to originate in roots, because flowering is suppressed if shoots are rerooted before reaching the size critical for flower induction. In such cases, removal of leaves does not affect production of nodes. Inevitably, the root system appears to play a significant role in regulating the transition from vegetative to reproductive state.

That the flower is an autonomous organ and that the concept of homology of petals, stamens, and carpels with the foliage leaf is not tenable was pleaded in the late 1930s and early 1940s (see Gregoire 1938; Brooks 1940). Later, the stamens and carpels were envisaged to be basically different from sepals and petals in having a deeper initiation in the ape (Blakeslee et al. 1940; Satina and Blakeslee 1941, 1943; Barnard 1957a,b, 1958, 1960, 1961). However, sometimes even fundamentally similar appendages may differ in initiation (Merxmuller and Leins 1967); the differences do not invalidate conclusions of homology when ontogeny is similar.

MORPHOGENESIS AND THE RESULTANT STRUCTURES

Flower formation in angiosperms is a complex mechanism under the control of genes and environmental factors. It involves floral evocation (the transition of the vegetative apical meristem to a floral meristem) and development (the sequential appearance of primordia of floral organs leading to a fully differentiated flower).

The sequence of primordial inception is centripetal in the majority of flowers (Sattler 1974) and vegetative shoots. This finding has led to the interpretation of flowers as a compressed shoot with modified appendages (Eames 1931, 1961; Takhtajan 1959, 1969; Zimmermann 1959). Interestingly, in several cases the floral appendages do not originate strictly centripetally (Sattler 1974), though the sequence of primordial inception on the floral apex remains essentially centripetal even in this "special situation" (see Cheung and Sattler 1967).

Singh and Sattler (1972), in their work on *Alisma* flower, suggest that some primordia develop directly on the floral apex; these are the primary primordia (usually the primordia of sepals). Other primordia do not form on the original floral apex (circular in outline) but on the primary primordia or growth centers on the floral apex; these are the secondary primordia. The spiral direction in which the floral organs arise may reverse in the alternate whorls (e.g. *Lilium tigrinum*: Greller and Matzke 1970) or may not (e.g. *Alisma triviale*: Singh and Sattler 1972).

In most cases, the floral apex retains a two-layered tunica in all stages of development. The primordia of all floral appendages are initiated by periclinal divisions in the second tunica layer; this demonstrates a mutual homology in initiation and development (see Pande and Singh 1981). Even leaves are initiated in the second tunica layer in many cases (Pande 1978) and thus exhibit homology with floral appendages in the mode of their origin and early development. Some workers (Blakeslee et al. 1940; Satina and Blakeslee 1941, 1943; Barnard 1955, 1958, 1960; Sharman 1960), however, hold that stamens and pistils are fundamentally different from other floral appendages in having deeper initiation in the apex. Pande and Singh (1981) suggest that the adjacent tepal primordia in *Iris decora* become interconnected by the extension of growth, thus forming a complete ring of meristematic tissue in the common bases. This meristematic ring grows up by the intercalary or zonal growth and forms the perianth tube.

The French School of Anatomy gave the idea of a "waiting meristem" that becomes active only when the shoot apex enters the reproductive phase. According to Plantefol (1947), the "Anneau intial" that produces foliage leaves during vegetative growth, forms the sepals and petals also. The stamens and carpels derive from the "mersiteme de attente" (Buvat 1952a,b; Bersillon 1951; Lance 1957).

Floral Tube Formation

The calyx and corolla tube originate, in different groups of angiosperms, by (a) ontogenetic fusion of originally free parts, (b) intercalary or zonal growth beneath the originally free parts (petals and stamens), and (c) a combination of both ontogenetic fusion and zonal growth (Boke 1948). If the interprimordial growth is initially an extended growth, the mode of tube formation is a fusion of adjacent marginal meristems (Cusick 1966; Nishino 1976). This comprises the fourth mode of the origin of the floral tube.

Nishino (1978) observed that the lower part of the corolla tube in several Solanaceae is initiated by the extension of petal bases toward the lower portion of stamen primordia, while the upper part forms by the connection of the bases of petal primordia and the upward growth of this region. Sattler (1977) and Daniel and Sattler (1978) also hold that the corolla tube forms through the combined interprimordial and marginal growth of petal primordia. In general, due to the activity of the marginal meristem, the bases of the adjacent petal primordia extend and connect with the lower portion of the abaxial side of stamen primordia. Intercalary growth in the common bases of the petal and stamen primordia gives rise to the lower part of the corolla tube. Further activity of the marginal meristems in the bases of petal primordia connects these primordia in the middle of the lower abaxial base of stamen primordia. The upper part of corolla tube develops from the upward growth of the connected region. More recently, the phenomenon has been investigated for Brunoniaceae, Compositae, and Goodeniaceae (Leins and Erbar 1987, 1989; Erbar and Leins 1988). The short calyx tube forms by ontogenetic fusion of the bases of sepal primordia as observed in *Pyrostegia venusta*, Bignoniaceae (Jain and Singh 1982).

Status of the Carpel

That the carpel is the basic unit of the gynoecial apparatus and comprises the ovule and placentae has long been advocated (see Brown 1840; Van Tieghem 1871; Eames 1931; Troll 1939; Wilson and Just 1939; Douglas 1944, 1957; Joshi 1947; Guedes 1973; Puri 1951, 1961, 1964, 1978). The concept of carpel works, however, only if the gynoecial appendages (carpels) and ovules form a structural unit; it does not apply when placentae or ovules are not formed on the gynoecial primordia but on the floral apex, receptacle, or some other parts of the flower such as intercalation, e.g.

Balanophora, Fagopyrum, Illicium, Juglans, Myrica, Ochna, Scyphostegia, Stipa, Stylidium, and several Cyperaceae and Juncaceae (Sattler 1974). In Labiatae, the gynoecial primordia, which are directly formed on the floral apex, develop the gynoecial appendage, which bears placenta and ovules, but the septum is a direct extension of the floral apex (Sharma and Singh 1982).

Interpretations vary regarding the formation of syncarpus gynoecia. They are reported to form by congenital fusion, which is not, however, observed during ontogeny (Leinfellner 1950, 1951). In some taxa, such as *Tupa ignescens* (Payer 1857) and *Downingia bacigalupii* (Kaplan 1968), carpel primordia arise as C-shaped structures and then unite by way of fusion of growth centers. This fusion is also a kind of ontogenetic fusion but differs from post-genital fusion (Cusick 1966). Hageman (1970) proposes that all kinds of cups and cylindrical structures that have been described as the products of congenital fusion are formed by the process of meristematic fusion (a special type of fusion growth). The formation of the syncarpus gynoecium in Labiatae was also attributed to the process of post-genital fusion rather than to congenital fusion (cf. Sattler 1974; Sharma and Singh 1982).

In many taxa such as Acanthaceae (Singh and Jain 1975), Bignoniaceae (Jain 1977), and Labiatae (Sharma and Singh 1982), the ovary is normally mounted on a sufficiently developed gynobase (disk), which is generally four lobed and non-nectariferous (G. H. M. Lawrence 1951). This disk develops by periclinal division in the hypodermal layer of the basal region of the ovary wall. The divisions are more frequent in the four regions alternating with the four lobes of the ovary, consequently a four-lobed disk is formed. In *Lycium* (Solanaceae), also, the disk was considered to be composed of ovary tissue (Hitchcock 1932). According to J. R. Lawrence (1937), because the dorsal trace is well differentiated below the disk in Boraginaceae, the disk is a part of the ovary formed by an increased proliferation of the swollen bases of the ovary.

The disk surrounding the base of the ovary occurs in several families of Bicarpellatae, e.g. Acanthaceae, Apocynaceae, Bignoniaceae, Boraginaceae, Convolvulaceae, and Oleaceae. It is vascular in some families and nonvascular in others (Puri and Agarwal 1976). Rao (1971) maintains that the disk is an "organ sui generis" in the majority of cases and receives its vascular supply from whichever traces are conveniently located.

Parashar and Singh (1986) opine that the placentae and ovules in Solanaceae are initiated on the septum, which is an extension of the residual floral apex; therefore, the carpels have lost their significance as ovule-bearing appendages. Further, the carpellary primordia, as such, produce only stigma and style. It is therefore tempting to envisage the "gynoecium" in Solanaceae as "acarpellate" and the carpel in the traditional sense as "pseudocarpel" (cf. Lam 1947; Fagerlind 1958; Moeliono 1959, 1970); however, the ovary that has arisen by zonal growth is at least partially homologous to a gynoecial appendage.

Inferior Ovary

The morphological nature of the inferior ovary has long been a subject of interest. Inferior ovaries have been considered to be appendicular, as the ovary wall develops by the fusion of the bases of the floral appendages. This finds support from observations on several dicotyledonous families such as Ericaceae and Rosaceae (Eames 1931, 1961; MacDaniels 1940; Eames and MacDaniels 1947) as well as monocotyledonous families such as Agavaceae (Wunderlich 1950; Mogensen 1969),

Amaryllidaceae (Joshi and Pantulu 1939; Chaturvedi 1945; Rangaswami and Ramarethinum 1965; Singh 1972), and Orchidaceae (Swamy 1948).

On the basis of ontogenetic studies, formation of the floral cup in epigynous flowers has been interpreted variously. The recent research supports two hypotheses: (1) The apical meristem grows as a ring-shaped meristem and the first series of appendages emerges from the rim of the cup. (2) The so-called receptacular cup is indeed appendicular in nature and represents the connate floral whorls arising as a unit (see Pande and Singh 1981). Pande and Singh (1981) explained that there is no hollowing or sinking of the floral apex in Iridaceae. The intercalary growth in the fused bases of the floral appendages elevates the peripheral zone; the floral apex thus appears as a shallow depression that by further intercalary growth eventually develops into an inferior ovary. The receptacular cup is not fused with the ovary wall. The apparently axile-appearing placentation in the mature trilocular ovary is in fact parietal (Pande and Singh 1981).

Morphology of the Placenta

The morphology of the placenta in angiosperms has long been debated. It has been variously described as a carpellary structure and as an axial structure (see Jain and Singh 1982 for a review). In taxa with a typical axile placentation, the septum grows from what morphologically represents the summit of the floral apex and ultimately becomes fused with the carpel walls that divide the ovarian cavity into locules. The placentae that bear ovules are formed by divisions in the cells of the hypodermal layer of the septum. The placental ridges, however, develop from the lateral walls of the ovary in taxa with typically parietal placentation. An intermediate condition wherein the septum develops as in typical axile placentation and the placentae arise from the lateral walls of the ovary (fused margins of the two carpels) has been described for Labiatae; the septum is axial and the placentae appendicular in nature (Sharma and Singh 1982).

In Solanaceae, the placentae and ovules were considered axial by several earlier workers. Murray (1945) observed that the placentae are axile in position but the carpel wall, the septa, and the ovule-bearing portions of the placentae are foliar or carpellary in origin. Raud (1963) and Guedes (1964) also interpreted the solanaceous placentae as carpellary in nature. Parashar and Singh (1986) found that the placentae arise due to division and enlargement of the hypodermal and subadjacent cells of the central axis or septum. The ovules are initiated, by the active division in groups of cells in the subprotodermal layers, either before the septum fuses with the summit of the ovary, as in *Capsicum annuum*, *Lycopersicon lycopersicum*, and *Solanum nigrum*, or after the fusion, as in *Cestrum nocturnum*, *Nicotiana tabacum*, and *Withania somnifera* (Parashar and Singh 1986).

BIOPHYSICAL PRINCIPLES OF FLOWER DEVELOPMENT

In a typical angiosperm, the vegetative-growth period is followed by the floral stage. This change is cyclic and repetitive, and the resultant flower is a modified homologue of the vegetative branch. The geometry of the shoot and flower development is quite distinct and characteristic of the type of flower. The trimerous flowers originate on a stem having a distichous (zig-zag plane) leaf pattern, e.g. iris. Likewise, the flowers of *Crassula argentea*, which are star-shaped with five petals, arise on shoots with decussate phyllotaxis. Thus, the pattern of geometrical changes are species-specific.

These changes are explained on the basis of assumptions: The first links the change with differential gene expression. According to this assumption, the genome first produces the components of a reaction-diffusion system. A couple of substances, the morphogens, generate distinctive chemical profiles (Harrison and Kolar 1988; Meinhardt 1982) leading to unique reactions at specific places. Consequently, genes responsible for a specific morphogenic response are activated to produce definite structures such as leaves. The reaction-diffusion system can further create localized regions, ultimately reaching the cellular level. Thus, single cells of an organ become different from each other. This assumption does not, however, explain the formation of chemical gradient or the nature of the as yet undetected morphogens. The second assumption posits the existence of a group of organ-specific consistent genes. The organ-specific syntheses generally follow the construction rather than precede it. Thus, the two dual functions, patterning and construction, are coupled with each other (see Green 1989).

The biophysical explanation of shoot organization and development is based on the fact that plant organ can be approximated as an elongating cylinder. The transverse reinforcement on side walls of the meristem with "hoops" of cellulosic microfibrils ensures elongation at right angles to the reinforcement (Kutchera 1987). Similarly, the primordium is a hoop-reinforced, low mound representing a system of concentric circles or rings. The components of the reinforcement pattern have been deduced from polarized light images of isolated surface layers (see Green 1989). According to Gunning and Hardham (1982), the dome itself is so hoop-reinforced that the new ring patterns for appendages arise partly from the pre-existing pattern of the main axis. The cellulose alignment indeed is so, and is based on microtubule orientation. Growth during vegetative to floral development in *Vinca* has been studied by Jesuthasan and Green (1989). The bulges that occur with high curvature in the surface plane away from the dome center become primordium. The cyclic occurrence of primordia thus explains the decussate pattern (e.g. *Kalanchoe*). It has been proposed that the deformed dome parallel to the leaf base that provides a new major axis is a consequence of the expansion in girth of leaf primordium. Also, dome cells nearer the leaf base become stretched, thereby facilitating reinforcement on the dome.

Since the lateral buds appear later, the vegetative apex represents three meristematic humps along a leaf, dome, and leaf line. When floral initiation takes place, the above pattern of development is modified. The leaves become smaller and the reinforcement fields of appendages no longer extend close to the center of the dome. As the decussate pattern continues, the reinforcement in the central area shows random arrangement. As the actual transition to flowering approaches, a large central area, random in the center but reinforced at the periphery, appears. The central portion swells as a dome and a circumferential reinforcement develops. The areas between the reduced leafy bracts and the swollen central dome swell as transverse ridges and show an axial shift along the crest. This provides the hoop reinforcement. These represent the young inflorescence meristems, I-min. The consequence is that five hoop-reinforced domes (bract, I-min, flower prim, I-min, bract) in a row are visible with the meristem. The possible sequential events have been illustrated in Figure 12.1.A–D. Each I-min then becomes I-max. Subsequently, as the transition follows, the I-min gives rise to a stalk, a pair of bracts, and a central flower. Understandably, the most noticeable biophysical difference during transition is the randomly reinforced central portion of the original area that swells and forms the reinforced hoop. Other biophysical characteristics during the transition to flowering are a shift in the prominent expansion from the periphery to the central area, random reinforcement near the center, and, finally, the formation of a pre-flower mound in the center. The changes are accompanied by a mobilization and shift of growth-promoting substances toward the center of the meristem (see Green 1989).

The above findings suggest that the sequential biophysical aspects of flower development are subject to biochemical control. Gibberellic acid, through its influence on microtubules, controls the biophysical and, therefore, the morphogenic events. The progressive rounds of biophysical-biochemical interactions may thus account for organ indentity.

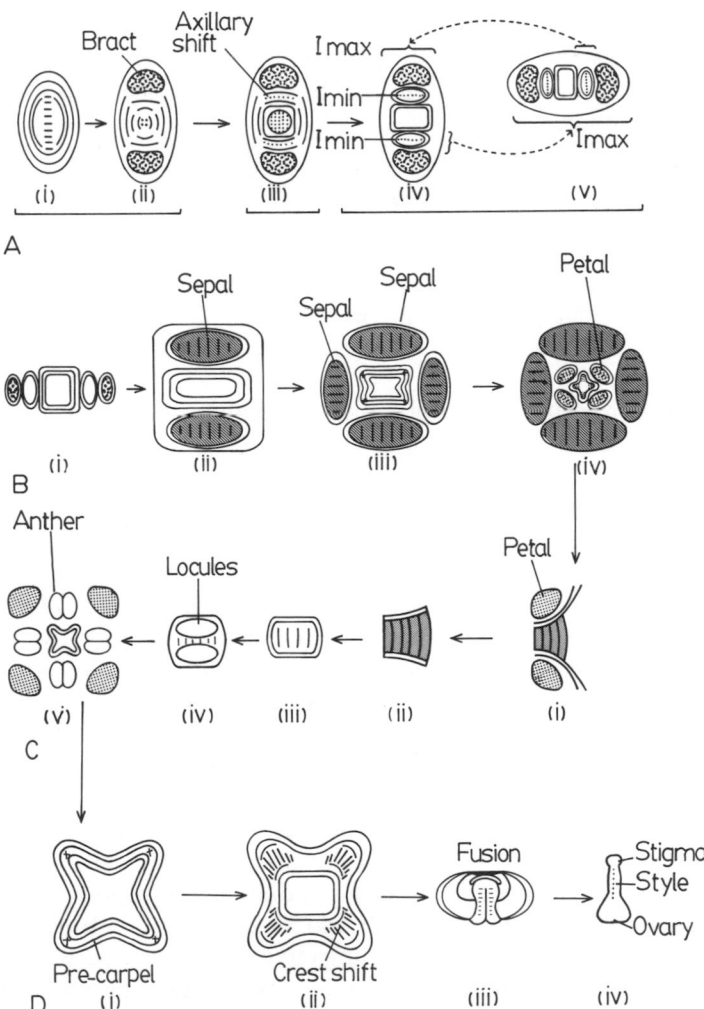

Figure 12.1. Development of floral organs—the transition process. (A) Less ordered reinforcement (*i,ii*) in the center of the dome; (*iii*) swelling of the dome and the appearance of reinforcement. The axillary shift causes formation of I-min, flower primordium, I-min (*iv,v*) see text for details. (B) Formation of sepals and petals (*i–iv*). (C) Reinforcement tangential to the petal combined with the old central field from the sepals help to form a primitive hoop reinforcement for a stamen. A four-fold symmetry is established. (D) Merging of reinforcement fields from two sets of stamens promotes a four-leaf clover-shaped precarpel structure. Arching of crests and ultimate fusion results in the hollow carpel [shown in (*iii*) and (*iv*)] (after Green 1989).

PHASE CHANGE CHARACTERISTICS

During the transition from vegetative to reproductive shoot, mitotic activity initially increases on the boundary between the central mother cell zone and the rib meristem zone and later spreads into the zone of the central mother cells. The activity almost stops in the cells of the rib meristem and the pith below it. Thus, a parenchymatous pith surrounded by meristematic cells develops in the apex; the floral apparatus arises from the meristematic cells. In all zones of the apex, the total protein and RNA and the concentration of histone in the cytoplasm increase during the transition to flowering (see Murty and Kumar 1972; Fahn 1990). Bernier et al. (1967) noted the following sequential changes leading to flower induction in Sinapis alba transferred from short to long days: (a) a rise in the mitotic index, (b) stimulation of DNA synthesis, (c) expansion of the nucleolus, (d) increase in cell volume, and (e) another rise in mitotic index. The two peaks in mitotic activity indicate floral induction and the initiation of flower buds.

Cytological Changes

The ultrastructural changes during floral induction involve an increase in the cytoplasmic volume, cytoplasmic matrix, ribosome density, number of mitochondria and dictyosomes, and size of nucleoli (see Healy 1964; Gifford and Stewart 1965; Havelange 1980; Orr 1981).

That the morphogenic transitions involve changes in specific gene expression is well established. Lyndon et al. (1983) have shown that the polypeptide complement of meristems of Sinapis changes before the transition to floral initiation. In fact, several quantitative and few qualitative differences in the recently synthesized polypeptide complement are noticeable in the meristems, thus implicating these changes in evocation. Qualitative differences in the number and location of polypeptides are also visible in Silene coeli-rosa at the start of the induction phase (Francis et al. 1988).

In Sinapis, the meristem represents a mosaic of rapidly cycling (cycling) and slowly cycling (noncycling) cells. After floral induction, as a consequence of shortening of the G_2 phase of the cycling cells and a change to cycling of noncycling G_2 cells, the first visible change is a mitotic peak at 26–30 hr after the beginning of long days (LD) (Gonthier et al. 1987). At 38 hr, because of shortening of the G_2 and S phases in cycling cells, DNA duplicates rapidly (Jacqmard and Houssa 1988). Another mitotic wave occurs at about 60 hr that coincides with the initiation of the first flower. This suggests that there is a synchrony in cell division during floral transition. The change has been partially attributed by Lejeune et al. (1988) to the supply of cytokinin from the leaves. The decrease in cell-cycle length and synchrony in cell division in the transitional meristems are corroborated by findings in other species as well, e.g. the long-day plants, Silene coelirosa (Francis and Lyndon 1985) and Lolium temulentum (Evans 1969). Mitotic inhibitors such as 5-fluorodeoxyuridine also suppress flowering in Silene, thus indicating that cell multiplication is essential to evocation (see Pharis et al. 1989).

Lolium shows 100% flowering after 90 short days (SD) at 4°C, and 30 SD at 10°C, followed by 8 LD. Gonthier and Francis (1989) observed appreciable enhancement in the mitotic index and size of the meristem in the shoot apex of long-day plants following low-temperature treatment. In fact, a cluster of mitotic cells in the apical dome of shoot apex is quite distinct in the vernalized plants exposed to 5–8 LD. An increase in the G_2 percentage is also noticed in the shoot apex following 2, 5, or 8 LD. Logically, changes in cell cycle are correlative to flowering.

Chromatin Structure

In *Pharbitis* and *Xanthium,* the first detectable change is the increase in DNA synthesis and nucleolus diameter, and the division of cells lying between the central zone and the rib meristem. Mounding of the meristem and an increase in size also ensue, accompanied by vacuolation and elongation of cells. Subsequently, small densely staining and actively dividing cells overlie a central core.

At the floral transition in *Sinapis,* Havelange and Jeanny (1984) observed a change in distribution of nuclear DNA between dispersed and condensed chromatin. An increase in the amount of DNA of the dispersed fraction occurs first in G_1 nuclei and later in G_2 nuclei. A correlation, therefore, can be made between the changes in chromatin structure and the selective expression or repression of selected genes during the transition phase.

Concomitant with the changes in cell division pattern, DNA synthesis, and chromatin structure, the apical growth pattern is also altered during the floral transition. There is a significant increase in the emergence of leaves or flowers at 72 and 120 hr after the start of LD. The uppermost embryonic internodes show an increase in length at 48 hr, and doming occurs at 54 hr. Such changes in apical growth occur in several plants (see Bernier 1988; Bernier et al. 1981a,b; Lyndon and Battey 1985).

Experiments with the radioactive precursors in *Lolium* species (long-day plants, LDP) show incorporation into RNA at the point that the flowering stimulus reaches the apex. These changes include the accompanying protein synthesis and are most pronounced in cells on the flanks of the meristem destined to form spikelets (see McDaniel 1989; Bernier 1989). In *Sinapis* also, RNA synthesis in the apical meristem cells is markedly enhanced. These events are followed by rapid DNA synthesis and later by cell division. Immunodiffusion studies show a quantitative change in proteins of the meristem of *Sinapis.* Two new proteins appear and one disappears during evocation (see Bernier 1989).

Thus, evocation is a progressive process that reaches completion only after a critical number of cells have been evoked. The accompanying increase in the number of cells involves higher use and turnover of energy-providing substances. Thus, evocation depends upon an increase in energy metabolism.

Energy Metabolism

A flower meristem shows us a relay system wherein the determination of one set of organs depends on the metabolic state of the meristem, which changes as the successive sets of organs are formed. Surgical tampering of the developing flower at different stages indicates that only the organ types not yet formed differentiate on the cut meristem. A cut made at the sepal stage in *Primula* (also reported in *Aquilegia, Nicotiana,* and *Portulaca*) resulted in the subsequent formation of the remaining organs only, i.e. petals, stamens, and carpels, but no sepals. Hence, the apex progresses through a series of metabolic states that follow each other and are specific for a certain organ at a given time.

Meristematic tissues are nonphotosynthetic and derive their energy from the more mature tissues of the plant. Energy transduction is through glycolysis and respiration.

Changes in energy metabolism occur during the transition from the vegetative to floral phase. In the apex of induced *Sinapis alba* plants, (Bernier et al. 1981a,b; Bodson 1985), the amount of sugar, ATP, starch, acid invertase, and succinic dehydrogenase and the number of mitochondria per cell increase during the early floral transition. The elevated level of sucrose is visible 10 hr after the start of the inductive long day. It appears that an early remobilization of reserve carbohydrates is an essential component of floral evocation. Such accompanying changes in energy metabolism also occur in other plants such as the LD *Brassica* (Petersen and Orr 1983) and the SD tobacco (Lu and Thomas 1988).

Genetic Considerations

That the flowering and reproductive phases in plants are gene-dependent is well recognized. Genes have very specific functions, and any change in their activity leads to various inter-related abnormalities. Flowering loci mutants of pea have yielded valuable information on the control of flowering. Six major genes, *Veg, Lf, Sn, Dne, Hr*, and *E*, that control reproductive behavior have been identified (see Jolly et al. 1987; Murfet 1989). Alleles of these genes also influence a variety of reproductive phenotypes. The genes may operate through the production of a flower-promoter and inhibitor in leaves, cotyledons, and stem, or by influencing the meristem. Perhaps flowering occurs when the balance between the promoter and inhibitor exceeds a certain threshold level (Murfet 1985; Murfet and Reid 1985; Reid 1986).

The genes, *Lf* and *Veg* are said to be involved in controlling the perception of flower stimulus by the shoot apex. Locus *Veg* is defined by a recessive mutation that is responsible for inhibiting flowering in all genotypic conditions. Alleles of *Lf* determine the length of the juvenile phase and presence of the minimum number of nodes necessary to initiate flowering. Reid and Murfet (1984) believe that the mutant genes of *Lf* and *Veg* block the preceding step prior to floral differentiation. In fact, *veg* plants do not respond to a flowering signal at all.

Sn and *Dne* control the formation of a graft-transmittable inhibitor in cotyledons and leaves, and the recessive alleles cause conditioning for early flowering. Thus, inductive photoperiods act by inhibiting the effect of genes *Sn* and *Dne*. Consequently, the ratio of promoter to inhibitor increases. The dominant alleles *Sn* and *Dne* are non-functional under light conditions (Murfet and Reid 1974). The presence of *Sn* gene in *Pisum* delays flower initiation; affects the development of vegetative traits, flower bud, fruit, and seed; and prolongs the reproductive cycle, thus increasing the yield (Murfet 1982, 1985; Murfet and Reid 1985; Reid 1979; see also Murfet 1989). The two mutant alleles *sn* and *dne* seem to be localized in leaves (Murfet 1971, 1985; Murfet and Reid 1973) and affect the biosynthetic steps involved in flower inhibition. Therefore, *sn* and *dne* genes may represent induction mutants.

Hr and *E* also seem to regulate and control the ontogenic expression of *Sn* and *Dne*; *E* suppresses the effect of *Sn* and *Dne*; and thus ensures early flowering. The effect of *Sn* and *Dne* is enhanced by *Hr* (Murfet 1971, 1973; Reid and Murfet 1977), which makes the plants photoperiodic-sensitive. It is believed that *E* acts on cotyledons and *Hr* on leaves. In addition to inhibiting flower formation, genes *Sn* and *Dne* show pleiotropic effects, prolong shoot senescence and juvenile leaf morphology, and increase the lifespan of the flower, thereby delaying fruit development (see Murfet 1989).

The *Dne*- and *Sn*-dependent response is also controlled by another gene, *Lf*, alleles of which govern a specific vegetative growth period. The duration of the vegetative period is in turn modified by *Dne* and *Sn* loci.

Genetic-combination studies by Murfet (1985) on *SDP* (requiring 8–12 hr light) with genes *Sn-sn* and *Hr-hr* produce a 9 *Sn Hr* (high node): 3 *Sn hr* (intermediate node): 4 *snHr* and *sn hr* (low node) segregation ratio. The *Sn Hr* plants bear numerous reproductive nodes with open flowers well below the apical buds. Fewer reproductive nodes with open flowers nearest the apical bud are present in plants with *sn Hr* and *sn hr* genotypes. The *Sn hr* plants have an intermediate position. It is thus obvious that *Sn Hr* loci can be used for measuring the levels of activity of *Sn Dne* genes.

Changes in gene expression related to floral induction have been studied (Arzee et al. 1970; Collins et al. 1963; Evans 1969; Ross 1970; Stiles and Davies 1976; Yoshida et al. 1967; Zeevaart 1969a) via transcription and translation inhibitors. The outcome remains inconclusive, however. Profiles of proteins of the cotyledons of *Pharbitis* subjected to LD, SD, or night-break treatments show several changes in polypeptides associated with floral-inductive treatments. Lay-Yee et al. (1987) noticed a decrease in four polypeptides (see also O'Neill 1989). Studies by Yoshida et al. (1967) on cotyledons revealed a decrease in the G+C content of mRNA after induction treatment. They proposed therefore that consequent to SD treatment, a specific floral stimulus mRNA (FS-RNA) is produced as a result of derepression of a specific gene. This mRNA encodes a protein needed for the biosynthesis of the necessary translocatable factor required for floral induction (see Yoshida et al. 1967).

Two-dimensional gel analysis of poly (A) RNA isolated from induced and noninduced cotyledons of SDP *Pharbitis* indicates a quantitative increase of a 28 kD polypeptide encoded by a single mRNA. The results corroborate the evidence that photoperiod-induced altered gene expressions, though subtle, are indeed responsible for flowering (Lay-Yee et al. 1987).

Cloning of these genes has been attempted to unravel the functional specificity and regulation mechanism. It has been possible to construct cDNA libraries in a modified vector, pCGN 1703, which facilitates identification of rare transcripts. The cDNA cloning is directional with the bacteriophage T7 RNA polymerase promoter adjacent to the 5′ end of the cDNA. Screening of cDNA libraries reveals at least one cDNA with quantitatively down-regulated expression under SD exposure. Two quantitatively up-regulated cDNA have also been identified (O'Neill 1989). Indeed, the changes in gene expression associated with floral induction are gradual and subtle.

Investigators have succeeded in constructing a cDNA library in the phage gt 10(4) from Poly (A)+ RNA isolated from floral bud (FB) explants of tobacco (see Meeks-Wagner et al. 1989; see also Huynh et al. 1985). Expression screening performed with cDNA probes from FB 7 explants helped in the identification of 52 cDNA clones. The 52 clones represent 6 gene families, FB 7-1, 2,3,4,5, and FB 7–6. It has been shown that the induction of FB 7 genes is correlative with the initiation of flowering rather than simply the presence of kinetin in the nutrient medium (see Meeks-Wagner et al. 1989).

FB 7-1, 2, and 5 genes are represented in a single copy number and each encodes for a single unique RNA. FB 7-1 and 2 are transcriptionally expressed at significant levels in the subapical pith cells of plants showing immature inflorescence. FB 7-1 transcript is detectable in the floral branch and in Poly(A)+ RNA populations of unopened flowers. FB 7–5 is absent in both. The transcripts of these genes and FB 7–5 are most abundantly present in the roots of older plants. Lower levels of these transcripts are detectable in older leaves and internode tissue (see Meeks-Wagner et al. 1989). DNA-DNA homology and DNA sequencing have revealed that FB 7-1, 2, and 5 genes are homologous to some of the pathogenesis-related (PR) genes in *Nicotiana*. Southern analysis demonstrates that 1 is homologous to chitinase and 5 to β-glucanase.

These genes are thus probably not directly involved in the transition to flowering. Nevertheless, their expression has been shown by Lotan et al. (1988) and Memelink et al. (1987) to be directed by developmental changes in healthy plants, nonpathogenic stress conditions (Brogloe et al. 1986), and also by changes in the endogenous levels of cytokinins.

Because of the availability of various morphogenic mutants, *Antirrhinum*, which has been the subject of classical genetic studies, may also prove helpful in understanding the regulation and underlying molecular processes of the development of flowers. Flowers are borne in the axils of lateral bracts on the inflorescence. The complex phenotype of class I mutants, *sterilis* and *steriloides*, indicate the interaction between gene products and hormonal effects. Both the mutants bear inflorescence only with bracts without any flowers in axil, but *steriloides* occasionally produces flowers. The other class I mutants, *squamata* and *squamosa*, interfere with the emergence of floral primordia after evocation. The phenotype of these mutants reveals that the wild-type gene establishes only the identity of the floral primordia. Therefore, primordium initiation is normal, but a shift leads to the appearance of shoots that resemble inflorescence. Also, the leaves of *squamata* show altered morphology, thus indicating the influence of the gene on vegetative as well as reproductive development (see Schwarz-Sommer et al. 1990).

The molecular basis of genetic control in plant development somewhat resembles that in animals. Cloning of the *deficiens* gene (DEF), a mutant in *Antirrhinum*, shows that DEF-A protein has a high degree of homology with the conserved DNA binding and dimerization segment of at least two transcription factors in yeast (the minichromosome maintenance gene *MCM1* produces MCM1 protein) and animals. The DEF-A protein is supposed to be a DNA-binding phosphorylated nuclear protein (see Schwarz-Sommer 1990). Surprisingly, in *Arabidopsis*, the agamus gene is also homologous to the same transcriptional unit (Yanofsky et al. 1990). The promoter sites of the *Antirrhinum* mutant, *deficiens*, and that of the *Arabidopsis* mutant share the same sequence, which resembles the serum response element (SRE) in animals. It is likely that the two plant genes have an autoregulatory system or are controlled by other factors having homology with the conserved segment of the mutant proteins.

Hybridization experiments have helped identify eight genes in the conserved segment (see Schwarz-Sommer 1990). The protein products of these genes have a 65–90% homology with the conserved DNA-binding segment of DEF-A. Four of these genes are expressed in vegetative and reproductive organs, whereas expression of the remaining four is restricted only to floral organs. Thus, the *Antirrhinum* genes coding for specific proteins have homology with transcription factors SRF and MCM1. In addition, such genes have also been reported from *Arabidopsis*, flies, frogs, and humans (see Schwarz-Sommer 1990). The genes are thus akin to the homeobox genes responsible for controlling the various mechanisms associated with differentiation.

KINEMATICS OF FLOWER GROWTH

Plant organs need to be studied in time and space for an adequate understanding of how surface growth features and intrinsic differentiation patterns contribute to the 3-D morphology of the organ as a whole. Surface-making experiments provide a picture of material (cellular) and spatial aspects of organ growth. The growing organs are marked at different places and the marks are displaced during organ ontogeny (Silk 1984). Displacement velocities from a fixed point in the organ are calculated to ascertain the relative elemental growth rate. The growth is taken to be "steady" if it is centered in the same region over time, as in an indeterminate shoot and root, whereas it is "nonsteady" if growth centers shift during ontogeny, as in determinate organs such as leaf (Silk 1984). There have been few kinematic analyses for floral development (Ritterbusch 1980; Gould and Lord 1988, 1989; Lord and Gould 1989).

In *Lilium longiflorum,* Lord and Gould (1989) describe three phases in the growth of tepals. Growth during phase I is not diffuse, but rather shows peaks and troughs that occur randomly along the tepal. Mitotic activity occurs evenly throughout the tepal. Phase II growth is steady and predominantly basal. Phase III exhibits a shift from basal to apical growth, culminating in anthesis. Of the approximately 45 days from tepal initiation to maturity, 26% of the time is spent in phase I, 53% in phase II, and 21% in phase III (Lord and Gould 1989). Growth is not continuous along the stamen but occurs in discrete areas that shift constantly in time; smaller anthers show a single growth peak, the larger ones show 2–3 peaks (possibly regions of predominantly cell division). During anther ontogeny, mitosis is followed by meiosis in pollen mother cells (PMC), and all growth subsequent to this is by cell expansion alone (Lord and Gould 1989). Factors appear to control the growth patterns, which can then modify the spatial distribution of mitosis. In the anther, the waveform persists during the phase of cell division and long after the last cell has divided; a possible mechanism for the waveform could be pulses of a growth regulator propagating at one time and being restricted at another. Alternatively, mechanical forces generated by local peaks of cell division might perpetuate the wave pattern in lily anthers (Lord and Gould 1989).

ENVIRONMENTAL CONTROL

Light is one of the major environmental factors that regulate flower development; both duration and intensity exert a marked influence. The rate of growth of reproductive organs declines in unfavorable light conditions (low intensity light for a relatively short period of time). Development never proceeds to anthesis, and failure of the whole inflorescence is inevitable. In tomato, all floral appendages are present in the first flower of the aborting inflorescence but mitotic activity and nuclear DNA synthesis are completely stopped (Kinet 1989). The cells of the sporogenous tissue in the anthers are checked at a premeiotic stage, and development in the ovules does not go beyond the early differentiation of the archesporial cell (Kinet et al. 1985). To cause flower failure in tomato light conditions need not be 100% unfavorable. The critical stage is between 5–6 and 10–12 days after the macroscopic appearance of the inflorescence, when sporogenesis occurs in the anthers of the first flower of the inflorescence (Kinet and Hachimi 1988). Unfavorable light conditions at that time cause partial abortion (Kinet 1989).

On the other hand, many species have an obvious photoperiodic requirement for reproductive growth: either facultative flowers develop in all photoperiods but faster under a favorable daylength; or absolute flower buds abort prematurely under nonsuitable photoperiodic conditions (Kinet et al. 1985).

Photoperiodic Response

Experimental evidence indicates a major role of leaves in floral regulation. Although floral induction has been proposed to result from the stimulatory action of a hormone, the florigen has not yet been identified. The transition from vegetative to photoperiodic floral phase generates a major shift, especially of assimilates from the vegetative biomass to the reproductive organs. Senescence of the parent plants in annuals follows this transition.

In *Leucospermum,* an obligatory long-short-day plant, the SD requirement can be met by a low-temperature exposure under LD conditions. Floral differentiation occurs under SD or low-temperature regime. The inflorescence is inhibited morphologically under LD but promoted in SD. The inhibitory effect can be overcome by cytokinin treatment so that all inflorescences develop simultaneously (Wallerstein 1989). Hence, physiological changes during the growth and development of plants may activate the coordinated expression of some genes.

In studies with day neutral (DN) and SD varieties of *Nicotiana tabacum* and LD species of *N. sylvestris,* Seltman (1974) and Thomas et al. (1975) showed that under certain environmental conditions, a DN or a photoperiodically sensitive plant (Gebhardt and McDaniel 1987; McDaniel et al. 1985) bears a flower after generating a specific number of nodes (see also Lang et al. 1977). Only a single or a few leaves are important for flowering (Lang 1987). In DN plants, only four apical or basal leaves of 10 cm are needed for the terminal meristem to produce the same number of nodes as meristems of plants having all their leaves (Gebhardt and McDaniel 1987; McDaniel 1980). In contrast, as few as two 10-cm apical leaves induce flowering in SD plants after the meristem has produced the same number of nodes as the untreated plants.

An interesting experiment by Hamner (see Wareing and Phillips 1985) showed that the floral stimulus is leaf-dependent. In *Xanthium,* flowering fails under SD if no leaves are present; however, the presence of only one-eighth of one leaf is sufficient to induce flowering (Figure 12.2.A). Grafting of stems between plants and exposure to SD of only one of them also causes flowering in *Xanthium* (Figure 12.2.B). Hamner's experiments thus provide additional evidence about the flowering stimulus in the leaves of both SD and LD plants.

Further grafting experiments suggested a similar nature of the stimulus. Short-day-grown vegetative shoots of *Sedum spectabile* when grafted on *Kalanchoe blossfeldiana,* also grown under SD, produced flowers along with the stock. The outcome once again implicates the existence of a flowering stimulus that caused the flowering of *Sedum,* which normally is a LD plant (Figure 12.3).

Rooting assays show that the terminal apical bud becomes florally determined before the initiation of the terminal flower. One to three leaf primordia originate afterward (McDaniel 1989; see also Poethig 1990).

In tobacco, the leaves probably transmit an inductive message that acts on organized meristems and other cells to induce the floral state. The effectiveness of the signal is genotype-environment-dependent (see Figure 12.4). The extent of the inductive signal can be modified by an input from the roots, e.g. in *N. tabacum* 'Wisconsin 38', the terminal meristem does not flower unless separated from the roots by some minimal number of nodes (McDaniel 1989). This indicates a kind of interplay between root and leaf input that involves the number of nodes.

Metabolic inhibitors have allowed measurement of the time of commitment of the apex to flower in photoperiodically sensitive plants, such as *Lolium, Sinapis,* and *Xanthium.* Use of inhibitors at different stages of induction shows that flowering in *Sinapis* can be inhibited up to 44 hr from the beginning of the inductive long day.

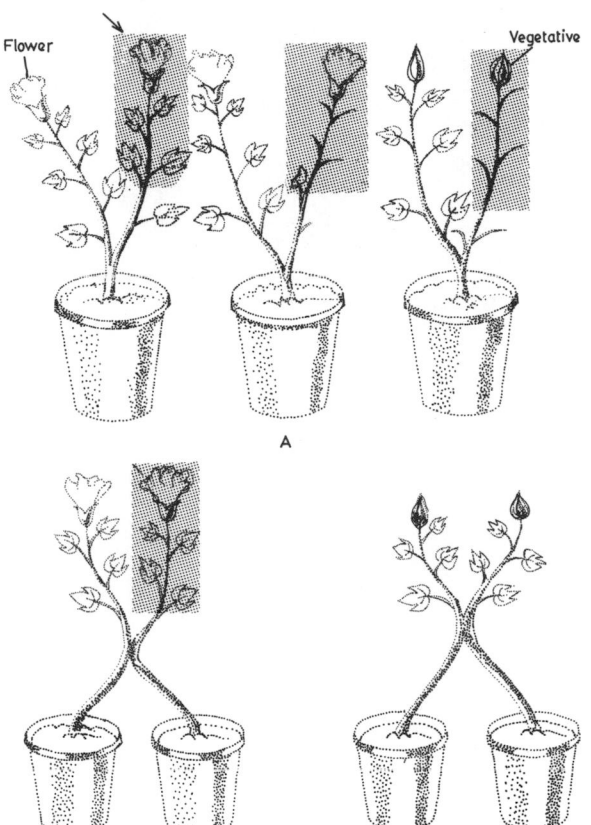

Figure 12.2. *Xanthium strumarium.* (A) Effect of leaf on flowering. (*i*) One branch exposed to short days (*arrow*) and the rest of the plant to long days. Both show flowering. (*ii*) Same as (*i*) except that only ⅛ of a leaf is present. (*iii*) Both remain vegetative if short-day exposed branch has been defoliated completely. (B) Approach grafting experiment. (*i*) Branch of one plant exposed to short days (*arrow*), while the other was maintained under long days. (*ii*) Both plants exposed to long days.

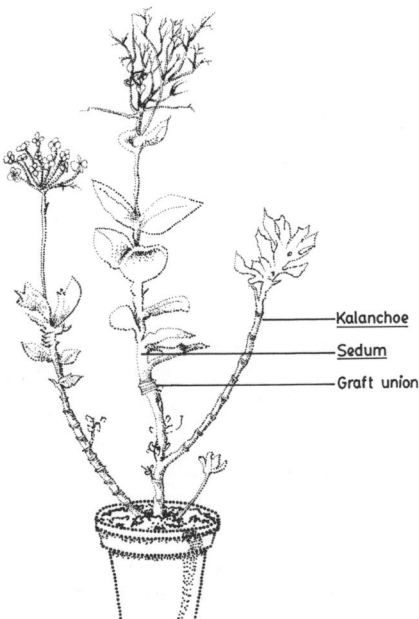

Figure 12.3. Grafting experiment to show translocation of flowering factor from short-day to long-day plant. Scion from long-day *Sedum spectabile* growing under short days grafted onto short-day flowering plant of *Kalanchoe blossfeldiana*.

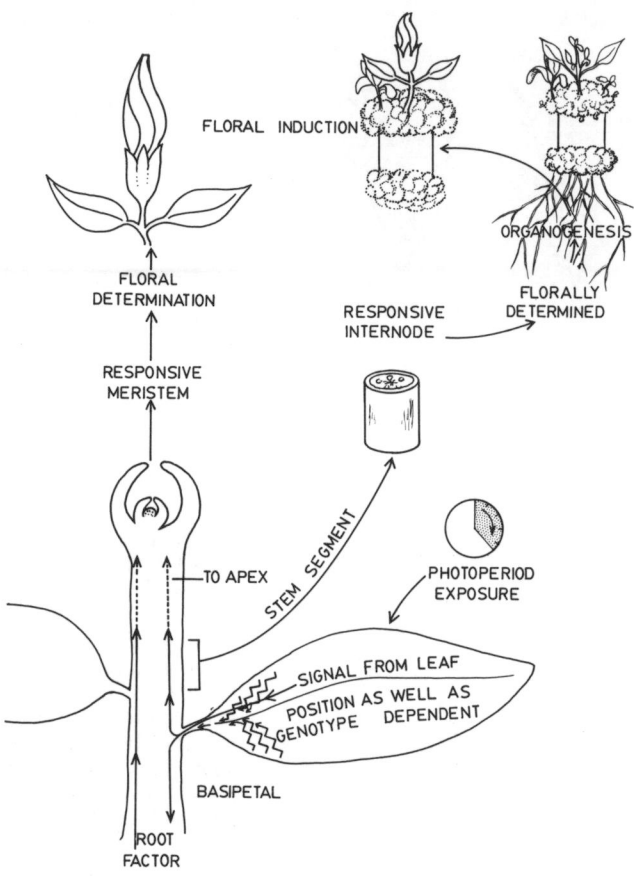

Figure 12.4. Regulation of flowering in *Nicotiana*. One or more leaves are sufficient to cause the flowering of the terminal meristem. Internode cells from the inflorescence have a high potential to differentiate floral shoots upon culture. The signal to flower is received by the leaf (modified from McDaniel 1989).

Flowering ensues afterward, however, thereby suggesting that commitment to flowering occurs within a few hours (see Wareing and Phillips 1985). Thus, several developmental events that occur prior to and during floral initiation are involved in establishing, maintaining, and expressing morphogenic states. The leaf inductive signal has a major role in floral initiation.

Role of Phytochrome

Generally, leaves or cotyledons act as photosensitive tissues, and phytochrome is the photoreceptor. A movement of the translocatable factor has been proposed (Bernier 1988; Lang 1965) from the photosensitive tissue to the apex that induces floral evocation following photoperiodic treatment. The biochemical processes triggered by the floral stimulus may be modulated by phototreatment, which coordinates or modifies the mobilization of factors reaching the shoot apex. Admittedly, the regulation of these processes occurs at the genic level. The associated changes in gene expression would initially involve a transduction of the primary floral stimulus followed by the production of an endogenous factor that causes floral evocation at the shoot apex (see Figure 12.5).

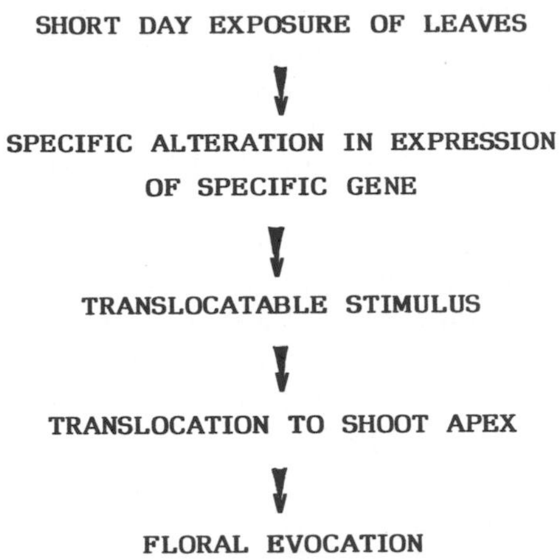

SHORT DAY EXPOSURE OF LEAVES

▼

SPECIFIC ALTERATION IN EXPRESSION
OF SPECIFIC GENE

▼

TRANSLOCATABLE STIMULUS

▼

TRANSLOCATION TO SHOOT APEX

▼

FLORAL EVOCATION

Figure 12.5. Control of flower formation in a short-day plant. The signal may be provided by specific regulation of specific genes, thus leading to translocation of the flowering stimulus at the apex.

Pharbitis nil 'Violet', a SD plant, is sensitive to photoperiodic treatment (Marushige and Marushige 1963) as early as 4 d after germination. A single 12–14 hr dark period is enough to induce flowering. The induction can be blocked by a single 10-min light exposure. Excision treatments by Imamura and Takimoto (1955) have demonstrated that cotyledons are the photoreceptive tissues at this stage, and are the source of movement of the factor that brings about floral evocation at the apex (see also Vince-Prue and Lumsden 1987). Experiments with different cultivars and related species of *Pharbitis* reveal genotypic variation in response to photoperiodic floral induction that can ultimately help in identifying the stage-specific gene expression.

Although day-length-controlled flowering in plants is well accepted (summarized in Figure 12.6), the factors involved in cellular and biochemical regulation are little understood. Enlargement of the apex or changes in the carbohydrate pool and mitotic activity have been posited to establish the transition from vegetative to reproductive phase, but these events do not reflect the metabolic regulations controlled in leaves.

Phytochrome, the gene of which has already been identified, cloned, and sequenced, seems to be the key factor in the photoperiodic induction of flowering; however, the mechanism through which it mediates various metabolic processes has not been elucidated. Phytochrome exists in at least two kinetically, spectrally, and

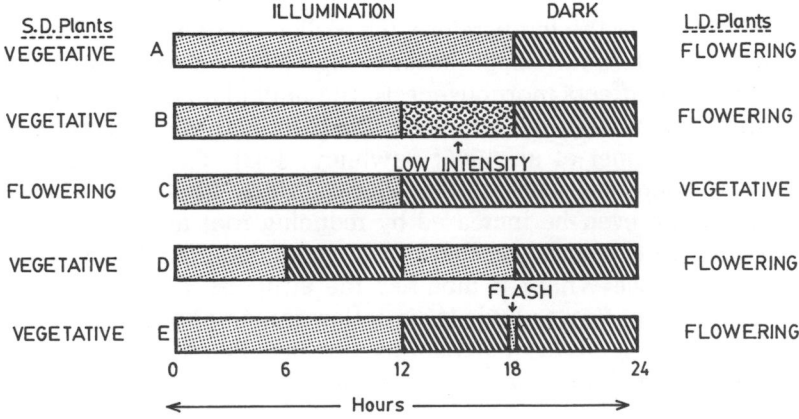

Figure 12.6. The response of short- and long-day plants to various photoperiodic exposures.

antigenically different forms; one is predominantly present in etiolated tissues (see Deitzer et al. 1979; Deitzer 1989). Different phytochrome molecules may control different physiological responses in green tissues thus implying a variable mode of action of different pools of phytochromes in photoperiodic induction. Possibly, one mode of action governs the light/dark transition, while the other controls the synthesis of the translocatable substance that initiates flowering.

The endogenous circadian rhythm-dependent response to photoperiodic induction in SD (Arzee et al. 1970) and LD (Lincoln et al. 1987) plants is well documented (see also Cumming et al. 1965; Hsu and Hamner 1967). Work by Bernier et al. (1981a,b) in *Hordeum vulgare* has linked phytochrome to rhythm-related sensitivity to far red (FR) light while plants are exposed to continuous white light. In *Hordeum*, flowering is enhanced when FR is supplied in addition to 3 d of white light. The degree of promotion is dependent upon the time when FR is provided. Sensitivity to flowering by a single 6-hr exposure to FR correlates with the circadian rhythm. The addition of FR light simultaneously promotes phytochrome-mediated flowering and changes the phase of sensitivity to further enhancement by FR light. FR light also influences the phase of the timing mechanism that regulates stomatal opening but does not inhibit net CO_2 exchange (see Deitzer 1989; see also Vince-Prue 1965).

In the SD plant *Pharbitis nil*, phytochrome-dependent time-keeping is more pronounced. Flowering can be inhibited by a single, brief pulse of red light (RL) given during the course of an inductive dark period. Surprisingly, a single 5-min pulse of RL in the presence of benzyladenine is sufficient to initiate dark-timing (Ogawa and King 1979). A second RL pulse given at different times during an extended dark period results in the circadian rhythm of floral inhibition. Experimental results have suggested that the rhythm of sensitivity to RL diminishes in continuous light longer than 6 hr. Removal of continuous light causes restart of the rhythm at a time set by the light/dark transition. The rhythm is apparently mediated by a different pool of phytochrome that inhibits flowering by a RL pulse (Lumsden et al. 1986).

The influence of FR light on flowering and stomatal rhythm in *Hordeum* resembles the effects of RL in *Pharbitis*. The effect of phytochrome in these cases seems to be mediated by a rapid shift from a low to high phytochrome photoequilibrium.

Effect of Temperature

As a rule, the higher the temperature, the earlier the opening of flowers, provided that premature failure does not occur, because high temperature may also trigger abortion. Temperature also affects morphogenesis. In many plants, such as carnation, rose, tomato, and tulip, the number of floral parts tends to increase in response to exposure to low temperatures (Kinet et al. 1985; Sawhney 1983). The number of flowers per inflorescence also increases after chilling (Lewis 1953; Phatak et al. 1966). Flower number in tomato can even be increased by reducing root temperature; this effect is graft transmissible, thus suggesting that a root-generated signal moves up to the differentiating inflorescence where it modifies the structure (Phatak et al. 1966). The development of different flower buds in an inflorescence appears to be at least partly influenced by the destiny of the neighboring flowers. Positional influences modulate the response of individual buds to the environment (see Kinet et al. 1985).

HORMONAL CONTROL

Application of growth hormones affects the growth and size of the floral organs. Gibberellins and auxins especially promote flower development. Petals and stamens are claimed sources of auxins, and stamens and ovaries of gibberellins (see Davies et al. 1982). Therefore, flower formation by photoperiodic induction may be mediated by plant growth regulators. Well-recognized alterations in gene expression associated with the transition of shoot meristem to flowering do exist and have been discussed. Once committed to floral development, the meristem transition proceeds sequentially. See Lyndon (1990) for a detailed account.

An *in vitro* organogenic system (thin cell layer, TCL) from the floral branches of flowering plants of day-neutral (DN) *Nicotiana tabacum* permits regulated studies on differentiation of floral meristems (Tran Thanh Van 1973). Depending upon the formulations of nutrient medium and culture conditions, Tran Thanh Van et al. (1985) were able to manipulate the organogenic response of TCL. After implanting the TCL in liquid medium for 20 days, they were able to induce vegetative shoots or floral buds. They concluded that the type of cytokinin used in the medium controls the morphogenic response. Whereas zeatin stimulates vegetative shoot formation, kinetin stimulates floral bud differentiation. After 45 days of culture, about 20% of the differentiated vegetative shoots having 3–4 leaves produced floral buds.

Generally, gibberellic acids (GAs) are reported to have either no effect or an inhibitory effect on flowering. In fruit trees, such as apple, pear, mango, apricot, and citrus, a severe bienniality exists in flowering and fruiting. The reason for such behavior seems to be the translocation of GAs from the developing fruits to the adjacent spur apex during floral initiation (see Pharis et al. 1989).

Application of GA_4 promotes return bloom in spur varieties of apple. GA_3 and GA_7, however, are inhibitory when applied under similar conditions. No precocious flowering is promoted by GA_4 in the woody angiosperms. In *Citrus,* flowering is thought to be negatively regulated by GAs, as development subsequent to floral induction occurs when the concentration of GAs is below a certain threshold level. The promotive effect of GA_4 is probably due to early floral initiation in induced apices, followed by a rapid mobilization that prevents the inhibitory activity.

As in woody angiosperms, GAs generally inhibit or do not promote flowering in SD plants under inductive or noninductive conditions. In some plants, such as *Pharbitis nil,* however, GAs promote flowering under noninductive conditions and only marginally under inductive conditions (Figure 12.7A,B). GA_3 is effective in low doses and so is GA_4, but over a wide range of concentrations. GA_1, the effector for vegetative growth, nevertheless promotes flowering only at high doses. Doses of GA that are inhibitory to flowering promote stem elongation. Understandably, therefore, gibberellins at low levels play a positive role in the floral induction in SD plants but play an even more positive role in GA-deficient dwarf mutants (see also Murfet and Reid 1987; O'Neill 1989). The endogenous level of GA may play a significant role in determining the concentration and extent of application of the exogenous GAs; in most cases, it is a very critical balance.

Circumstantial evidence implicates GAs in long-day plant (LDP) flowering. Pharis and King (1985) and Zeevaart (1983) estimated increased concentration of endogenous GAs in leaves of LDP. Plants transferred from SD to LD conditions also have increased concentrations of endogenous GAs. In the LDP *Lolium temulentum,* a single 24-hr inductive exposure supports the enhanced amount of bioactive GAs (Pharis et al. 1987). GA (50 µg/plant) promotes a 3–4 fold increase in stem length but little increase to

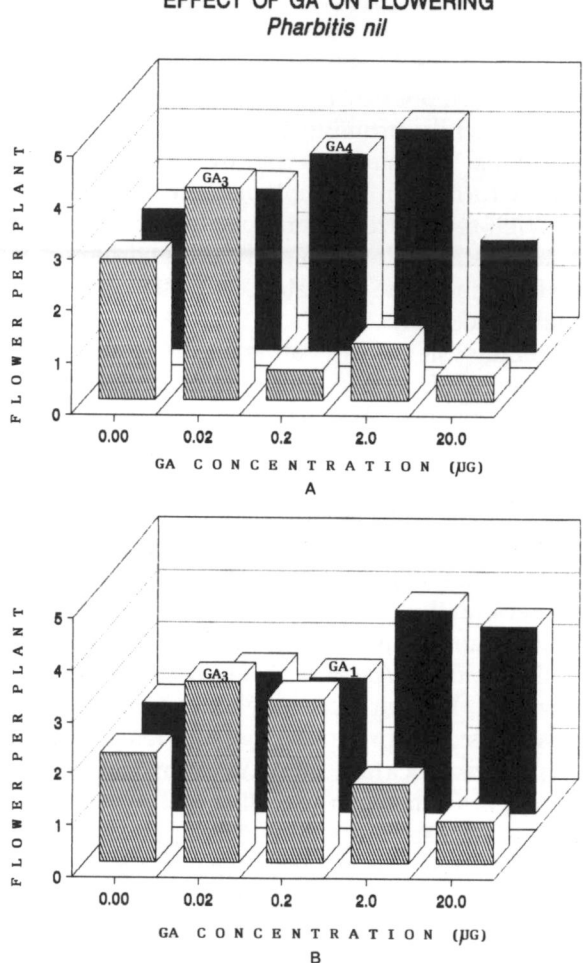

Figure 12.7. Effect of GA on flowering. (A) The hormone was supplied to the petiole 5 hr before the start of inductive cycle. (B) Hormone applied after 16 hr. Note the response with 0.02 μg in both cases (based on data of Pharis et al. 1989).

apex length. In comparison, GA_{32} stimulated flowering at 0.5 μg/plant with a negligible increase in stem length. In fact, in *Lolium temulentum,* the GA-related response to floral induction and shoot/stem elongation correlates to GA structure. For example, GA_1 with hydroxyls at C-3 and C-13 but with no double bonds in ring A, causes good vegetative growth and poor flowering. Simply adding a double bond (C-1,2) in ring A (GA_3) promotes flowering as well as stem elongation; a third hydroxyl group at C-15 further increases flowering with little effect on stem length (see Pharis et al. 1989).

A number of LDPs flower under short days when treated with GA_3. In fact, most LDPs that respond to GA by a marked elongation of internodes have a distinct rosette under short days. In *Bryophyllum* species, GA_3 substitutes for the LD requirement. Even the vernalization effect can be substituted by application of GA_3 in certain species (see Zeevaart 1969b; Wareing and Phillips 1985). Perhaps in LDPs grown under SD conditions, the endogenous level of GA_3 is too low to promote flowering, and perhaps the LD condition enhances it to the threshold level needed for flowering.

GA_3 is unable to stimulate flowering in some genotypes of *Trifolium;* however, the nonflowering genotypes do flower when both GA_3 and LD are provided. According to Henry (1989), autotetraploid *Dieffenbachia* flowers poorly in comparison to its diploid counterparts. A GA_3-treated plant, however, produces bracts, albeit without flowers.

A reduction in the amount of GA in the shoots induces flowering (Proebsting et al. 1978). Mutants that inhibit GA biosynthesis show little influence on flowering behavior, thus indicating that although GA is involved in flower initiation, it cannot promote it alone.

Factors that promote vigorous growth also bring about a quick transition to the adult phase, whereas various forms of GA induce adult-phase shoots to revert to the juvenile phase (Rogler and Hackett 1975; Zimmermann et al. 1985; see also Wallerstein and Hackett 1989; Poethig 1990).

In *Ribes,* rooted cuttings of shoots from mature plants exposed to SD for 6 wk failed to flower, but pieces of stem provided with SD before rooting produced flowers. These results implicate roots in the prevention of flower induction. Application of gibberellic acid suppresses flowering completely under SD conditions. Assays show the presence of GA in roots and juvenile stem of *Ribes.* Apparently, GA from the roots prevents the appearance of flowers in response to SD, e.g. in *Helianthus, Nicotiana,* and *Ribes* (see Wareing and Phillips 1985; Pharis et al. 1989).

The level of gibberellin in xylem sap decreases to a minimum at the beginning of floral initiation in Japanese apricot (*Prunus mume*), this in turn leads to a sharp increase in the ratio of cytokinin (CK)/GA. The concentration of zeatin in the sap increases during the formation of floral primordia (Sun and Chu 1988).

Application of CK to vegetative parts of *Sinapis* increases cell division in the central zone. Flower formation, however, fails. Sugars and cytokinins may be the substances that stimulate flowering, but they act independently and sequentially at the meristem (see Bernier 1989).

Inflorescences that abort in permanent unfavorable light conditions are markedly deficient in CK compared to inflorescences that grow normally in favorable light conditions (Leonard and Kinet 1982). On the contrary, the GA level is high in inflorescences in which early abortion occurs. High GA activity inhibits inflorescence growth at early stages. Application of the growth inhibitor 2-chloroethyltrimethyl-ammonium-chloride (CCC) during early developmental stages invariably reduces the incidence of abortion induced by a high temperature and low light. CCC also retards the yield of diffusible GAs from plant shoot tips (Abdul et al. 1978).

In tomato plant, application of GAs alone in constant unfavorable light conditions causes rapid abscission of the young flower buds after a limited elongation of the inflorescence peduncle. Cytokinins alone stimulate the growth of the inflorescence but barely to anthesis. In constant favorable light conditions, on the other hand, GAs cause abortion of many flowers at the initial stages of the growth of inflorescence. Inflorescences that avoided abortion, however, grow fast, leading to advanced anthesis (Kinet et al. 1985) and mostly increased flower numbers as a consequence of inflorescence branching. During the later stage of inflorescence development, GAs have no effect upon rate of growth but reduce the proportion of flowers that naturally abort, thus indicating a promotive effect (Kinet 1987). Treating the inflorescence first with N_6-benzylaminopurine (BA) and then with GA_{4+7} prevents abortion and triggers development up to flower opening in constant unfavorable light conditions (Kinet et al. 1978). In many other species, but perhaps not in cereals (Pharis and King 1985; Rood et al. 1988), late stages of flower development are seemingly dependent on GAs (Pharis and King 1985). The inhibition by low irradiance during sporogenesis in tomato may be mediated by the antagonist action of GAs and ethylene (Kinet 1987; Kinet and Hachimi 1988).

Application of BA + GA on inflorescences targeted for abortion in unfavorable light conditions stimulates cellular activity in the ovules of the first flower in tomato inflorescence (Kinet et al. 1985). This precedes the activity of acid invertase, a key enzyme in the control of sugar transfer from the phloem to the sink, and precedes distribution of assimilates within the plant (Ho and Baker 1982; Morris 1983). Thus, plant growth regulators act primarily as cell-division-mediating factors, and their action precedes the increased import of assimilates needed for growth. When vegetative shoot growth is limited by growth retardants or other means, metabolites are diverted for the benefit of reproductive structures (Nourai and Harris 1983), and vice versa (Iqbal and Ghouse 1982).

The axillary buds in *Pharbitis* and *Scrophularia* react to floral stimulus and form flowers at a specific developmental stage. In *Scrophularia*, the inhibitory effect of roots can be overcome by a CK, kinetin (Miginiac 1972). Sometimes, even young leaves act as inhibitors of flowering, e.g. the succulent *Kleinia* (see Lyndon 1990). These and several other examples point toward an inhibitory role of growth substances produced by leaves as well as roots.

The decisive role of growth substances in controlling meristem formation has been demonstrated in *Vitis* (Mullins 1980). Under natural conditions, the shoot apex produces lateral meristems that can form lateral shoots, tendrils, or inflorescence. Application of GA_3 to the shoot apex promotes lateral meristems, and a continued supply supports their transformation into tendrils. Application of CK to the lateral meristem, however, promotes inflorescence meristem. Thus, a lateral meristem is able to develop an inflorescence that can be inhibited by GA_3 but promoted by CK. Clearly, growth substances can control changes in perception and determination for flowering in *Vitis*.

In addition to the endogenous levels of gibberellins, some other growth factors also promote flowering in some species under certain conditions. In pineapple, for example, flowering can be induced by auxins or ethylene. Similarly, adenine and kinetin are capable of promoting flowering in *Perilla*, and zeatin in *Wolffia* (Wareing and Phillips 1985).

Nevertheless, in most SDPs and LDPs, flowering is not easy to induce by any combination of known, naturally occurring hormones. Indeed, flowering is not controlled by a single, specific hormone.

CONCLUSIONS

Leaves may produce substances capable of promoting or inhibiting flowering. The flowering response is also dependent upon the shoot apex, as the process involves several changes, including those in the apex. The stimulus generated by the leaves as a consequence of induction and reaching the apex is thought to be a single substance. Although the stimulus is graft-transmittable between different species, the notion of a single substance common for floral stimulus in related species has been unacceptable. For example, gibberellins act as floral promoters in many LD rosette plants, and auxin or ethylene elicit flowering in the bromeliads. Therefore, flowering cannot be considered as a single event requiring a single, unique promoting signal, but as a consequence of changes in the receptive leaves capable of producing substances that modify the perception and determination of the apex. The floral stimulus thus represents a sequence of substances or changes in the concentration of one or more substances that causes relevant changes in the shoot apex.

Finally, more than 200,000 species of flowering plants growing under different habitats have evolved over the centuries and have developed specific control mechanisms for floral induction that generate variation through sexual reproduction. The studies of this complex and important mechanism have provided an array of data that defies generalization.

Acknowledgments

We thank Mr. Sabah Ashraf for managing the computer print-out of the manuscript. The illustrations have been drawn by Mrs. Indu Mehra.

LITERATURE CITED

Abdul, K. S., A. E. Canham, and G. P. Harris. 1978. Effect of CCC on the formation and abortion of flowers in the first inflorescence of tomato (*Lycopersicon esculentum* Mill). *Ann. Bot.* 42:617–625.

Arzee, T., J. Gresel, and E. Galun. 1970. Flowering in *Pharbitis*: The influence of actinomycin D on growth, incorporation of nucleic acid precursors, and autoradiographic patterns. In *Cellular and Molecular Aspects of Floral Induction*. Ed. G. Bernier. London: Longmans Green & Co. Ltd. 93–107.

Barnard, C. 1955. Histogenesis of the inflorescence and flower of *Triticum aestivum*. *Aust. J. Bot.* 3:1–20.

_____. 1957a. Floral histogenesis in the monocotyledons. I. The Graminae. *Aust. J. Bot.* 5:1–20.

_____. 1957b. Floral histogenesis in the monocotyledons. II. The Cyperaceae. *Aust. J. Bot.* 5:115–128.

_____. 1958. Floral histogenesis in the monocotyledons. III. The Juncaceae. *Aust. J. Bot.* 6:285–298.

_____. 1960. Floral histogenesis in the monocotyledons. IV. The Liliaceae. *Aust. J. Bot.* 8:213–225.

_____. 1961. The interpretation of the angiosperm flower. *Aust. J. Sci.* 24:64–72.

Bernier, G. 1988. The control of floral evocation and morphogenesis. *Annu. Rev. Plant Physiol. Plant Mol. Biol.* 39:175–219.

_____. 1989. Events of the floral transition of meristems. In *Plant Reproduction: From Floral Induction to Pollination*. Ed. E. Lord, G. Bernier. Am. Soc. Plant Physiol. Symp. Ser. I. 43–50.

Bernier, G., J-M. Kinet, and R. Bronchart. 1967. Cellular events at the meristem during floral induction in *Sinapis alba* L. *Physiol. Veg.* 5:311–324.

Bernier, G., J-M Kinet, and R. M. Sachs. 1981a. *The Physiology of Flowering. Vol. I. The Initiation of Flowers*. Boca Raton, FL: CRC Press.

_____. 1981b. *The Physiology of Flowering. Vol II. The Transition to Reproductive Growth*. Boca Raton, FL: CRC Press.

Bersillon, G. 1951. Sur le point vegetatif de *Papaver somniferum* L.: Structure et fonctionnement. *C. R. Acad. Sci. Paris* 232:2470–2472.

Blakeslee, A. F., S. Satina and A. G. Avery. 1940. Utilisation of induced periclinal chimeras in determining the constitution of organs and their origin from the three germ layers in *Datura*. *Science* 91:423.

Bodson, M. 1985. *Sinapis alba*. In *Handbook of Flowering* 4:336–354. Ed. A. H. Halevy Boca Raton, FL: CRC Press.

Boke, N. H. 1948. Development of the perianth of *Vinca rosea* L. *Am. J. Bot.* 35:413–423.

Brogloe, K. E., J. J. Gaynor, and R. M. Brogloe. 1986. Ethylene-regulated gene expression: Molecular cloning of the genes encoding an endochitinase from *Phaseolus vulgaris*. *Proc. Natl. Acad. Sci. USA* 83:6820–6824.

Brooks, R. M. 1940. Comparative histogenesis of vegetative and floral apices in *Amygdalus communis* with special reference to the carpel. *Hilgardia* 13:249–299.

Brown, R. 1840. On the relative position of the divisions of stigma and parietal placentae in the compound ovarium of plants. Misc. Bot. Works of Robert Brown. *R. Soc. London* 1:555–563.

Buvat, R. 1952a. Structure, evolution et fonctionnement du meristeme apical de quelques dicotyledones. *Ann. Sci. Nat. Bot. Ser. 11* 13:199–300.

———. 1952b. L' organisation des meristeme apicaux chez les vegetaux vasculaires. *Bull. Univ. Nat.* 40:54–66.

Chaturvedi, S. B. 1945. The nature of the inferior ovary in the Amaryllidaceae. *Curr. Sci.* 14:207.

Cheung, M., and R. Sattler. 1967. Early floral development of *Lythrum salicaria*. *Can. J. Bot.* 45:1609–1618.

Collins, W. T., F. B. Salisbury, and C. W. Ross. 1963. Growth regulators and flowering. III. Antimetabolites. *Planta* 60:131–141.

Cumming, B. G., S. B. Hendricks, and H. A. Borthnick. 1965. Rhythmic flowering responses and phytochrome changes in selection of *Chenopodium rubrum*. *Can. J. Bot.* 43:825–853.

Cusick, F. 1966. On phylogenetic and ontogenetic fusions. In *Trends in Plant Morphogenesis*. Ed. E. G. Cutter. London: Longmans Green & Co., Ltd, 170–183.

Daniel F., and R. Sattler. 1978. Development of perianth tubes in *Solanum dulcamara*: Implications for comparative morphology. *Phytomorphology* 28:151–171.

Davies, P. J., E. Emshwiller, T. J. Gainfagna, W. M. Proebsting, M. Noman, and R. P. Pharis. 1982. The endogenous gibberellins of vegetative and reproductive tissues of G_2 peas. *Planta* 154:266–272.

Deitzer, G. F. 1989. Interaction between phytochrome and the circadian clock mechanism to control the photoperiodic induction of flowering. In *Plant Reproduction: From Floral Induction to Pollination*. Ed. E. Lord, G. Bernier. *Am. Soc. Plant Physiol. Symp. Ser. I.* 1–9.

Deitzer, G. F., R. Hayes, and M. Jabben. 1979. Kinetics and time dependence of the effect of far-red light on the photoperiodic induction of flowering in winter barley. *Plant Physiol.* 64:1015–1021.

Douglas, G. E. 1944. The inferior ovary I. *Bot. Rev.* 10:125–186.

———. 1957. The inferior ovary II. *Bot. Rev.* 23:1–46.

Eames, A. J. 1931. The vascular anatomy of the flower with refutation of the theory of carpel polymorphism. *Am. J. Bot.* 18:147–188.

———. 1961. *Morphology of the Angiosperms*. New York: McGraw Hill.

Eames, A. J., and L. H. MacDaniels. 1947. *An Introduction to Plant Anatomy*. New York: McGraw Hill.

Erbar, C., and P. Leins. 1988. Studies on the floral development and pollen presentation in *Brunonia australis* Smith (Brunoniaceae) *Bot. Jahrb. Syst.* 110:263–282.

Evans, L. T. 1969. *Lolium temulentum* L. In *The Induction of Flowering, Some Case Histories*. Ed. L. T. Evans. Melbourne: MacMillan. 328–349.

Fagerlind, F. 1958. Is the gynoecium of the angiosperms built up in accordance with the phyllosporous or the stachyosporous scheme? *Sven. Bot. Tidskr.* 52:421–425.

Fahn, A. 1990. *Plant Anatomy*. 4th ed. Oxford: Pergamon Press.

Francis, D., and R. F. Lyndon. 1985. The control of the cell cycle in relation to floral induction. In *The Cell Division Cycle in Plants*. Ed. J. A. Bryant, D. Francis. Cambridge: Cambridge Univ. Press. 199–215.

Francis, D., J. Rembur, and A. Nougarede. 1988. Changes in polypeptide composition in the shoot apex of *Silene coeli-rosa* during floral induction. *C. R. Acad. Sci. Paris* 307:763–770.

Gebhardt, J. S., and C. N. McDaniel. 1987. Induction and floral determination in the terminal bud of *Nicotiana tabacum* L. cv. Maryland Mammoth, a short-day plant. *Planta* 172:526–530.

Gifford, E. M. Jr., and K. D. Stewart. 1965. Ultrastructure of vegetative and reproductive apices of *Chenopodium* album. *Science* 149:75–77.

Gonthier, R., and D. Francis. 1989. Changes in the pattern of cell division in the shoot and root meristems of *Lolium perenne* during the transition from vegetative to floral growth. *J. Exp. Bot.* 20:285–292.

Gonthier, R., A. Jacqmard, and G. Bernier. 1987. Changes in cell cycle duration and growth fraction in the shoot meristem of *Sinapis* during floral transition. *Planta* 170:55–59.

Gould, K. S., and E. M. Lord. 1988. Growth of anthers in *Lilium longiflorum*: a kinematic analysis. *Planta* 173:161–171.

_____. 1989. A kinematic analysis of tepal growth in *Lilium longiflorum*. *Planta* 177:66–73.

Green, P. B. 1989. Shoot morphogenesis, vegetative through floral, from a biophysical perspective. In Plant Reproduction: From Floral Induction to Pollination. Ed. E. Lord, G. Bernier. *Am. Soc. Plant Physiol. Symp. Ser. I.* 58–75.

Gregoire, V. 1938. La morphogenise et l'autonomie morphologique de l'appareil floral I. Le carpelle. *La Cellule* 47:287–452.

Greller, A. M., and E. B. Matzke. 1970. Organogenesis, aestivation and anthesis in the flower of *Lilium tigrinum*. *Bot. Gaz.* 131:304–311.

Guedes, M. 1964. Sur l'interpretation morphologique du placenta des Solanaćees. *Bull. Soc. Bot. Fr.* 111:135–139.

_____. 1973. Carpel morphology and axis sharing in syncarpy in some Rutaceae with further comments on 'New Morphology.' *Bot. J. Linn. Soc.* 66:55–74.

Gunning, B. E. S., and A. H. Hardham. 1982. Microtubules. *Annu. Rev. Plant Physiol.* 33:651–698.

Hageman, W. 1970. Studien zur Entwicklungsgeschichte der Angiosprmenblatter. *Bot. Jahrb.* 90:297–413.

Harrison, L. G., and M. Kolar. 1988. Coupling between reaction-diffusion prepattern and expressed morphogenesis, applied to desmids and dasyclads. *J. Theor. Biol.* 130:493–515.

Havelange, A. 1980. The quantitative ultrastructure of the meristematic cells of *Xanthium strumarium* during the transition to flowering. *Am. J. Bot.* 67:1171–1178.

Havelange, A., and J. C. Jeanny. 1984. Changes in density of chromatin in the meristematic cells of *Sinapis alba* during transition to flowering. *Protoplasma* 122:222–232.

Healy, P. L. 1964. *Histochemistry and Ultrastructure in the Shoot of* Pharbitis *Before and After Induction*. Ph.D. Thesis, Univ. Calif., Berkeley.

Henry, R. J. 1989. Floral induction in 2n and 4n *Dieffenbachia maculata*, perfection after treatment with gibberellic acid. *Hort. Science* 24:307–308.

Hitchcock, C. L. 1932. A monographic study of the genus *Lycium* of the Western hemisphere. *Ann. Missouri Bot. Garden* 19:179–348.

Ho, L. C., and D. A. Baker. 1982. Regulation of loading in transport systems. *Physiol. Plant.* 56:225–230.

Hsu, J. C. S., and K. C. Hamner. 1967. Studies on the involvement of an endogenous rhythm in the photoperiodic response of *Hyoscyamus niger*. *Plant Physiol.* 42:725–730.

Huynh, T. V., R. A. Young, and R. W. Davis. 1985. Constructing and screening cDNA libraries in lambda gt 10 and lambda gt 11. In *DNA Cloning: A Practical Approach*, Vol. 1. Ed. D. M. Glover. Oxford: IRL Press. 49–78.

Imamura, S.,and A. Takimoto. 1955. Photoperiodic responses in Japanese morning glory, *Pharbitis nil* Choic., a sensitive short-day plant. *Bot. Mag.* 68:235–241.

Iqbal, M., and A. K. M. Ghouse. 1982. Environmental influence on growth activities of *Prosopis spicigera*. In *Improvement of Forest Biomass*. Ed. P. K. Khosla. Dehra Dun: Int. Book House. 387–393.

Jacqmard, A., and C. Houssa. 1988. DNA fiber replication during a morphogenetic switch in the shoot meristematic cells of a higher plant. *Exp. Cell Res.* 179:454–461.

Jain, D. K. 1977. *Morphological, Anatomical and Ontogenetic Studies in Bignoniaceae*. Ph.D. Thesis, Meerut University, Meerut, India.

Jain, D. K., and V. Singh. 1982. Development of the flower of *Pyrostegia venusta* (KER. GAWL.) Miers (Bignoniaceae). *J. Univ. Kuwait (Sci.)* 9:129:140.

Jesuthasan, S., and P. B. Green. 1989. On the mechanism of decussate phyllotaxis: Biophysical studies on the tunica of *Vinca major*. *Am. J. Bot.* 76:1152–1166.

Jolly, C. J., J. B. Reid, and J. J. Ross. 1987. Internode length in *Pisum*. Action of gene *lw*. *Physiol. Plant.* 69:489–498.

Joshi, A. C. 1947. Floral histogenesis and carpel morphology. *J. Indian Bot. Soc.* 26:62–74.

Joshi, A. C., and J. V. Pantulu. 1939. Origin of the inferior ovary in the Amaryllidaceae. *Curr. Sci.* 8:212–213.

Kaplan, D. R. 1968. Histogenesis of the androecium and gynoecium in *Downingia bacigalupi*. *Am. J. Bot.* 55:933–950.

Kinet, J. M. 1987. Inflorescence development in tomato: Control by light, growth regulators, and apical dominance. *Plant Physiol. (Life Sci. Adv.)* 6:121–127.

———. 1989. Environmental and chemical controls of flower development. In *Plant Reproduction: From Floral Induction to Pollination*. Ed. G. Bernier, E. Lord. *Am. Soc. Physiol. Symp. Ser.* I. 95–105.

Kinet, J. M., and H. E. A. Hachimi. 1988. Effects of ethephon, 1-aminocyclopropane-1-carboxylic acid, and ethylene inhibitors on flower and inflorescence development in tomato. *J. Plant Physiol.* 133:550–554.

Kinet, J. M., D. Jurdebise, A. Parmentier, and R. Stainer. 1978. Promotion of inflorescence development by growth substance treatments to tomato plants grown in insufficient light conditions. *J. Am. Soc. Hort. Sci.* 103:724–729.

Kinet, J. M., V. Zune, C. Linotte, A. Jacqmard, and G. Bernier. 1985. Resumption of cellular activity induced by cytokinin and gibberellin treatments in tomato flowers targeted for abortion in unfavourable light conditions. *Physiol. Plant.* 64:67–73.

Kutchera, U. 1987. Cooperation between outer and inner tissues in auxin-mediated plant organ growth. In *Physiology of Cell Expansion During Plant Growth*. Ed. D. J. Cosgrove, D. P. Knieval. Rockville, MD.: *Am. Soc. Plant Physiol.* 215–226.

Lam, H. J. 1947. A new system of the cormophyta. *Blumea* 6:282–289.

Lance, A. 1957. Recherches cytologiques sur l' evolution de quelques meristemes apicaux et sur ses variations provoquees par des traitements photoperiodiques. *Ann. Sci. Nat. Bot. Ser. 11* 18:91–42.

Lang, A. 1965. Physiology of flower initiation. In *Encycloped. Plant Physiol.* 15:1380–1536.

———. 1987. Perspective in flowering research. In *Plant Gene Systems and Their Biology*. Ed. J. L. Key, L. McLintosh. UCLA Symp. New York: Alan R. Liss. 3–24.

Lang, A., M. K. H. Chailakhyan, and I. A. Frolova. 1977. Promotion and inhibition of flower formation in day-neutral plant in grafts with a short-day plant and long-day plant. *Proc. Natl. Acad. Sci. USA* 74:2412–2416.

Lawrence, G. H. M. 1951. *Taxonomy of Vascular Plants*. New York: Mac Millan Co.

Lawrence, J. R. 1937. A correlation of the taxonomy and the floral anatomy of certain Boraginaceae. *Am. J. Bot.* 24:433–444.

Lay-Yee, M., R. M. Sachs, and M. S. Reid. 1987. Changes in cotyledon mRNA during floral induction of *Pharbitis nil* strain violet. *Planta* 171:104–109.

Leinfellner, W. 1950. Der Bauplan des synkarpen Gynozeums. *Oster. Bot. Z.* 97:403–436.

———. 1951. Die Nachamung der durch kongenitale vawachsung entstandenan

Formen des Gynozeums durch postgenitale Verschmelzungsvorgange. *Oster. Bot. Z.* 98:403–411.

Leins, P., and C. Erbar. 1987. Studies on the flower development in Compositae. *Bot. Jahrb. Syst.* 108:381–401.

_____. 1989. On the floral development and secondary pollen presentation in *Selliera radicans* Car. (Goodeniaceae). *Flora* 182:43–56.

Lejeune, P., J. M. Kinet, and G. Bernier. 1988. Cytokinin fluxes during floral induction in the long-day plant *Sinapis alba* L. *Plant Physiol.* 86:1095–1098.

Leonard, M., and J. M. Kinet. 1982. Endogenous cytokinin and gibberellin levels in relation to inflorescence development in tomato. *Ann. Bot.* 50:127–130.

Lewis, D. 1953. Some factors affecting flower production in the tomato. *J. Hort. Sci.* 28:207–220.

Lincoln, J. E., S. Cordes, E. Read, and R. L. Rischer. 1987. Regulation of gene expression by ethylene during tomato fruit development. *Proc. Natl. Acad. Sci. USA* 84:2793–2797.

Lord, E. M., and K. S. Gould. 1989. Kinematic analysis of lily flower organs. In *Plant Reproduction: from Floral Induction to Pollination.* Ed. E. Lord, G. Bernier. *Am. Soc. Plant Physiol. Symp. Ser. I.* 92–94.

Lotan, T., N. Ori, and R. Fluhr. 1988. Pathogenesis related proteins are developmentally regulated in tobacco flowers. 2nd Int. Congr. Plant Mol. Biol. Nov. 13–18. Paper No. 235 Israel.

Lu, C. C., and J. F. Thomas. 1988. Succinate dehydrogenase activity in the shoot apex of tobacco during floral initiation. *Plant Physiol.* 86:148.

Lumsden, P. J., D. Vince-Prue, and M. Furuya. 1986. Phase shifting of the photoperiodic flowering response rhythm in *Pharbitis nil* by red light pulses. *Physiol. Plant.* 67:604–607.

Lyndon, R. F. 1990. *Plant Development.* London: Unwin Hyman.

Lyndon, R. F., and N. H. Battey. 1985. Growth of the shoot apical meristem during flower initiation. *Biol. Plant.* 27:339–349.

Lyndon, R. F., A. Jacqmard, and G. Bernier. 1983. Changes in protein composition of the shoot meristem during floral evocation in *Sinapis alba. Physiol. Plant.* 59:476–480.

MacDaniels, L. H. 1940. The morphology of the apple and other pome fruits. Mem. Cornell University Agric. Exp. Stat. 230.

Marushige, K., and Y. Marushige. 1963. Photoperiodic sensitivity of *Pharbitis nil* seedlings of different ages in special reference to growth patterns. *Bot. Mag.* 76:92–99.

McDaniel, C. N. 1980. Influence of leaves and roots on meristem development in *Nicotiana tabacum* L. cv. Wisconsin 38. *Planta* 148:462–467.

_____. 1989. Floral initiation as a developmental process. In *Plant Reproduction: From Floral Induction to Pollination.* Ed. E. Lord, G. Bernier. *Am. Soc. Plant Physiol. Symp. Ser. I.* 51–57.

McDaniel, C. N., S. R. Singer, K. A. Dennin, and J. S. Gebhardt. 1985. Floral determination: Timing, stability and root influence. In *Plant Genetics.* Ed. M. Freeling. New York: Alan R. Liss. 73–87.

Meeks-Wagner, D. R., E. S. Dennis, A. Kelly, S. Shannon, R. White, J. Wahleithner, A. Neal, M. Lund, and W. J. Peacock. 1989. Gene expression during floral initiation. In *Plant Reproduction: From Floral Induction to Pollination.* Ed. E. Lord, G. Bernier. *Am. Soc. Plant Physiol. Symp. Ser. I.* 76–81.

Meinhardt, H. 1982. *Models of Biological Pattern Formation.* London: Academic Press.

Memelink, J., J. H. C. Hoge, and R. A. Schilperoort. 1987. Cytokinin stress changes the developmental regulation of several defence-related genes in tobacco. *EMBO J.* 6:3579–3583.

Merxmuller, H., and P. Leins. 1967. Die verwandtschaftsbeziehungen der kreuzblutler und mohngewachae. *Bot. Jahrb.* 86:113–129.

Miginiac, E. 1972. Cinetique d' action comparee des racines et de la kinetine sur le developpment floral de bourgeons cotyledonaires chez le *Scrofularia arguta* Sol. *Physiol. Veg.* 10:627–636.

Moeliono, B. M. 1959. A preliminary note on the placenta of *Stellaria media* (L.) Vill. and *Stellaria graminea* L. A possible axial origin of ovule. *Acta Bot. Neerl.* 8:292–303.

——— . 1970. Caulinay or carpellary placentation among dicotyledons. (Axis-borne versus leaf-borne ovules). The *Cauline Ovules of Centrosperms.* 2 Volumes. Assen, Netherlands: Van Gorcum & Co.

Mogensen, H. L. 1969. Floral ontogeny and an interpretation of the inferior ovary in *Agave parryi. Can. J. Bot.* 47:23–26.

Morris, A. A. 1983. Hormonal regulation of assimilate partition: Possible mediation by invertase. *News Bull. Br. Plant Growth Regulator Gr.* 6:23–25.

Mullins, M. G. 1980. Regulation of flowering in the grapevine. In *Plant Growth Substances.* Ed. F. Skoog, Berlin: Springer-Verlag. 323–330.

Murfet, I. C. 1971. Flowering in *Pisum:* Reciprocal grafts between known genotypes. *Aust. J. Biol. Sci.* 24:1089–1101.

——— . 1973. Flowering in *Pisum: Hr,* a gene for high response to photoperiod. *Heredity* 31:157–164.

——— . 1982. Flowering in the garden pea: Expression of gene *Sn* in the field and use of multiple characters to detect segregation. *Crop Sci.* 22:923–926.

——— . 1985. *Pisum sativum.* In *Handbook of Flowering.* Ed. A. H. Halevy. 4:97–126. FL: Boca Raton, CRC Press.

——— . 1989. Flowering genes in *Pisum.* In *Plant Reproduction: From Floral Induction to Pollination.* Ed. E. Lord, G. Bernier. *Am. Soc. Plant Physiol. Symp. Ser.* I:10–17.

Murfet, I. C., and J. B. Reid, 1973. Flowering in *Pisum:* Evidence that gene *Sn* controls a graft transmissible inhibitor. *Aust. J. Biol. Sci.* 26:675–677.

——— . 1974. Flowering in *Pisum:* The influence of photoperiod and vernalizing temperatures on expression of genes *Lf* and *Sn. Z. Pflanzenphysiol.* 71:323–331.

——— . 1985. The control of flowering and internode length in *Pisum.* In *The Pea Crop: A Basis for Improvement* Ed. P. D. Hebblethwaite, M. C. Heath, T. C. K. Dawkins. London: Butterworths. 67–80.

——— . 1987. Flowering in *Pisum:* Gibberellins and the flowering genes. *J. Plant Physiol.* 127:23–29.

Murray, M. A. 1945. Carpellary and placental structures in the Solanaceae. *Bot. Gaz.* 107:243–260.

Murty, Y. S., and V. Kumar. 1972. Vegetative to reproductive state of apex in monocotyledons. In *Advances in Plant Morphology.* Ed. Y. S. Murty, B. M. Johri, H. Y. Mohan Ram, T. M. Varghese. Meerut, India: Sarita Prakashan. 291–303.

Nishino, E. 1976. Developmental anatomy of foliage leaves, bracts, calyx and corolla in *Pharbitis nil. Bot. Mag.* 69:191–209.

——— . 1978. Corolla tube formation in four species of solanaceae. *Bot. Mag.* 91:263–277.

Nourai, A. H. A., and G. P. Harris, 1983. Effects of growth retardants on inflorescence development in tomato. *Sci. Hort.* 20:341–348.

Ogawa, Y., and R. W. King, 1979. Establishment of photoperiodic sensitivity by benzyladenine and a brief red irradiation in dark-grown seedlings of *Pharbitis nil* Chois. *Plant Cell Physiol.* 20:115–122.

O'Neill, S. D. 1989. Molecular analysis of floral induction in *Pharbitis nil.* In *Plant Reproduction: From Floral Induction to Pollination.* Ed. E. Lord, G. Bernier. *Am. Soc. Plant Physiol. Symp. Ser. I.* 19–28.

Orr, A. R. 1981. A quantitative study of cellular events in shoot apical meristem of *Brassica campestris* (Cruciferae) during transition from vegetative to reproductive conditions. *Am. J. Bot.* 68:17–23.

Pande, P. C. 1978. *Morphological, Anatomical and Ontogenetic Studies in Iridaceae.*

Ph.D. Thesis, Meerut University, Meerut, India.

Pande, P. C., and V. Singh. 1981. Floral development of *Iris decora* wall. (Iridaceae). *Bot. J. Linn. Soc.* 83:41–56.

Parashar, G., and V. Singh. 1986. Development of the gynoecium in Solanaceae. *Phytomorphology* 36:219–227.

Payer, J. B. 1857. *Traité d'Organogénie comparée de la Fleur*. Paris: Masson et Cie.

Petersen, K., and A. R. Orr. 1983. Histochemical study of enzyme activity in the shoot apical meristem of *Brassica campestris* L. during transition to flowering. I. Succinic dehydrogenase. *Bot. Gaz.* 144:338–341.

Pharis, R. P., and R. W. King. 1985. Gibberellins and reproductive development in seed plants. *Annu. Rev. Plant Physiol.* 36:517–568.

Pharis, R. P., L. T. Evans, R. W. King, and L. N. Mander. 1989. Gibberellins and flowering in higher plants: Differing structures yield highly specific effects. In *Plant Reproduction: From Floral Induction to Pollination*. Ed. E. Lord, G. Bernier. *Am. Soc. Plant Physiol. Symp. Ser. I.* 29–41.

Pharis, R. P., J. E. Webber, and S. D. Ross. 1987. The promotion of flowering in forest trees by gibberellin $A_{4/7}$ and cultural treatments: A review of the possible mechanisms. *Forest Ecol. Manag.* 19:65–84.

Phatak, S. C., S. H. Wittwer, and F. G. Teubner. 1966. Top and root temperature effects on tomato flowering. *Proc. Am. Soc. Hort. Sci.* 88:527–531.

Plantefol, L. 1947. Helices foliaires, point vegetatif et stele chez les dicotyledones. La notion d'anneau initial. *Rev. Gen. Bot.* 54:49–80.

Poethig, R. S. 1990. Phase change and the regulation of shoot morphogenesis in plants. *Science* 250:923–930.

Proebsting, W. M., P. J. Davies, G. A. Marx. 1978. Photoperiod induced changes in gibberellin metabolism in relation to apical growth and senescence in genetic lines of peas (*Pisum sativum* L.) *Planta* 141:231–238.

Puri, V. 1951. The role of floral anatomy in solution of morphological problems. *Bot. Rev.* 17:471–553.

———. 1961. The classical concept of angiosperm carpel: A reassessment. *J. Indian Bot. Soc.* 40:511–524.

———. 1964. On the relation between ovule and carpel. *J. Indian Bot. Soc.* 42:189–198.

———. 1978. On some peculiarities of angiosperm carpel. *Acta Bot. Indica* 6 (suppl.):1–14.

Puri, V., and R. M. Agarwal. 1976. On accessory floral organs. *J. Indian Bot. Soc.* 55:95–114.

Rangaswami, K., and S. Ramarethinam. 1965. Floral anatomy of *Zephyranthes carinata* Herb. with special reference to the gynoecium. *Bot. Notiser* 118:166–170.

Rao, V. S. 1971. The disc and its vasculature in the flowers of some dicotyledons. *Bot. Notiser* 124:442–450.

Raud, P. G. 1963. Organographie de la capsule du *Datura stramonium* L. *Bull. Soc. Bot. Fr.* 110:216–237.

Reid, J. B. 1979. Red-far-red reversibility of flower development and apical senescence in *Pisum*. *Z. Pflanzenphysiol.* 93:297–301.

———. 1986. Gibberellin mutants. In *Plant Gene Research: A Genetic Approach to Plant Biochemistry*. Ed. A. D. Blonstein, P. J. King. Wien: Springer-Verlag. 3:1–34.

Reid, J. B., and I. C. Murfet. 1977. Flowering in *Pisum*: the effect of genotype, plant age, photoperiod and number of inductive cycles. *J. Exp. Bot.* 28:811–819.

———. 1984. Flowering in *Pisum*: A fifth locus, *Veg. Ann. Bot.* 53:369–382.

Ritterbusch, A. 1980. The spaciotemporal patterns of growth and development in floral ontogenesis as visualised by Bildscharen and trajectories. *Flora* 169:405–423.

Robinson, S. W., and P. F. Wareing. 1969. Experiments on the juvenile adult phase change in some woody species. *New Phytol.* 68:67–78.

Rogler, C. E., and W. P. Hackett, 1975. Phase change in *Hedera helix*: Induction of the mature to juvenile phase by gibberellin A_3. *Physiol. Plant.* 34:141–147.

Rood, S. B., D. M. Bruns, and S. J. Smienk. 1988. Gibberellins in sorghum development. *Can. J. Bot.* 66:405–423.

Ross, C. 1970. Antimetabolite studies and the possible importance of leaf protein synthesis during induction of flowering in the cocklebur. In *Cellular and Molecular Aspects of Floral Induction.* Ed. G. Bernier. London: Longmans Green & Co., Ltd. 139–151.

Satina, S., and A. F. Blakeslee. 1941. Periclinal chimeras in *Datura stramonium* in relation to development of leaf and flower. *Am. J. Bot.* 28:862–871.

———. 1943. Periclinal chimeras in *Datura* in relation to the development of carpel. *Am. J. Bot.* 30:453–462.

Sattler, R. 1974. A new approach to gynoecial morphology. *Phytomorphology* 24:22–34.

———. 1977. Kronorohrenent stehung bei *Solanum dulcamara* L. and kongenitale Verwachsung. *Ber. Deutsch. Bot. Ges.* 90:529–538.

Sawhney, V. K. 1983. The role of temperature and its relationship with gibberellic acid in the development of floral organs of tomato (*Lycopersicon esculentum*). *Can. J. Bot.* 61:1258–1265.

Schwabe, W. W., and A. H. Al-Doori. 1973. Analysis of a juvenile-like condition affecting flowering in the black currant (*Ribes nigrum*). *J. Exp. Bot.* 24:669–681.

Schwarz-Sommer, Z., P. Huijser, W. Nacken, H. Seadler, and H. Sommer, 1990. Genetic control of flower development by homeotic genes in *Antirrhinum majus. Science* 250:931–936.

Seltman, H. 1974. Effect of light periods and temperatures on plant form of *Nicotiana tabacum* L. cv Hicks. *Bot. Gaz.* 135:196–200.

Sharma, M., and V. Singh. 1982. Morphology of the gynoecium in Labiatae. *Blumea* 28:61–75.

Sharman, B. C. 1960. Developmental anatomy of the stamen and carpel primordia in *Anthoxanthum odoratum. Bot. Gaz.* 121:192–198.

Silk, W. K. 1984. Quantitative descriptions of development. *Annu. Rev. Plant Physiol.* 35:479–518.

Singh, V. 1972. Floral morphology of the Amaryllidaceae. I. Subfamily Amaryllidioideae. *Can. J. Bot.* 50:1555–1565.

Singh, V., and D. K. Jain. 1975. Floral development of *Justicia gendarussa* (Acanthaceae). *Bot. J. Linn. Soc.* 70:243–253.

Singh, V., and R. Sattler. 1972. Floral development of *Alisma triviale. Can. J. Bot.* 50:619–627.

Stiles, J. I., and P. J. Davies. 1976. Qualitative analysis by isoelectric focussing of the protein content of *Pharbitis nil* apices and cotyledons during floral induction. *Plant Cell Physiol.* 17:855–857.

Sun, W., and M. Chu. 1988. The influence of cytokinin and gibberellin in the xylem sap on floral initiation of Japanese apricot, *Prunus mume* Sieb. et Zuce. *Acta Hort. Sin.* 15:73–76.

Swamy, B. G. L. 1948. The vascular anatomy of the orchid flowers. *Bot. Museum Leaflet, Harvard Univ.* 13:61–95.

Takhtajan, A. D. 1959. *Die Evolution der Angiospermen.* Jena, Germany: Gustav Fischer Verlag.

Takhtajan, A. D. 1969. *Flowering Plants: Origin and Dispersal.* Trans. C. Jeffrey. Edinburgh: Oliver & Boyd.

Thomas, T. F., C. E. Anderson, C. D. Raper Jr., and R. J. Downs. 1975. Time of floral initiation in tobacco as a function of temperature and photoperiod. *Can. J. Bot.* 53:1400–1410.

Tran Thanh Van, M. 1973. Direct flower neoformation from superficial tissue of small explants of *Nicotiana tabacum* L. *Planta* 115:87–92.

Tran Thanh Van M., P. Toubart, A. Cousson, A. G. Darvill, D. J. Gollin, P. Celf, and

P. Albersheim. 1985. Manipulation of the morphogenetic pathways of tobacco explants by oligosaccharins. *Nature* 314:615–617.

Troll, W. 1939. Die morpholigische Natur der Karpelle. *Chron. Bot.* 5:38–41.

Van Tieghem, P. H. 1871. Recherches sur la structure du pistil et sur l'anatomie comparee de la fleur. *Mem. Savants Etrangers Inst. des Sci.* 21:1–261.

Vince-Prue, D. 1965. The promoting effect of far-red light on flowering in the long-day plant *Lolium temulentum*. *Physiol. Plant.* 18:474–482.

Vince-Prue, D., and P. J. Lumsden. 1987. Inductive events in the leaves: Time measurement and photoperception in the short-day plant, *Pharbitis nil*. In *Manipulation of Flowering* Ed. J. G. Atherton. London: Butterworths. 255–268.

Wallerstein, I. 1989. Sequential photoperiodic requirement for flower initiation and development of *Leucospermum patersonii* (Proteaceae). *Israel J. Bot.* 38:25–34.

Wallerstein, I., and W. P. Hackett. 1989. The effects of pulse and continuous treatments with gibberellic and triiodobenzoic acid on the growth and rejuvenation of mature-phase *Hedera helix* plants. *Israel J. Bot.* 38:217–227.

Wareing, P. F., and I. D. J. Phillips. 1985. *Growth and Differentiation in Plants.* London: Pergamon.

Wilson, C. L., and T. Just. 1939. The morphology of the flower. *Bot. Rev.* 5:97–131.

Wunderlich, R. 1950. Die Agavaceae Hutchinsons in lichte ihrer Embryologie, ihres Gynozeum—Staubblatt—und Blattbaues. *Oster. Bot. Z.* 97:437–502.

Yanofsky, M. F., H. Ma, J. L. Bowman, G. N. Drews, K. A. Feldman, E. M. Meyerowity, 1990. The protein encoded by the *Arabidopsis* homeotic gene agamous resembles transcription factors. *Nature* 346:35–39.

Yoshida, K., K. Umemura, K. Yoshinage, and K. Oota. 1967. Specific RNA from photoperiodically induced cotyledons of *Pharbitis nil*. *Plant Cell Physiol.* 8:97–108.

Zeevaart, J. A. D. 1969a. *Perilla.* In *The Induction of Flowering: Some Case Histories.* L. T. Evans, Ed. Melbourne: Mac Millan. 116–155.

_____. 1969b. *Bryophyllum.* In *The Induction of Flowering: Some Case Histories.* Ed. L. T. Evans. Melbourne: MacMillan. 435–456.

_____. 1983. Gibberellins and flowering. In *The Biochemistry and Physiology of Gibberellins.* Ed. A. Crogier. New York: Praeger. 2:333–374.

Zimmermann, R. H., W. P. Hackett, and R. P. Pharis. 1985. Hormonal aspects of phase change and precocious flowering. *Encycloped. Plant Physiol.* (new series) 11:79–115.

Zimmermann, W. 1959. *Die Phylogenie der Pflanzen.* 2nd Ed. Stuttgart: Gustav Fisher Verlag.

Chapter 13

Gametophyte Ontogeny:
An Overview Based on *Oenothera*

INES NOHER DE HALAC and INES ADRIANA CISMONDI

Oenothera has been used as observational and experimental material since the beginning of this century. It remains of vital importance to modern work at the molecular level (Brennicke and Schwemmle 1984; Brennicke et al. 1985; Schuster and Brennicke 1985), because of characteristics such as its chromosomic rings under meiosis, balanced lethal factors (Cleland 1982), incompatibility, methods of gametophyte selection (Harte 1984) and male sterility (Harte and Bissinger 1952). The genetic work in *Oenothera* has been followed by developmental studies to correlate genetic and morphological events and address male sterility (Harte and Bissinger 1952; Noher de Halac 1982, 1985a, 1986), incompatibility (Dickinson & Lawson 1975; Cresti et al. 1983), and female gametophytic competition (Noher de Halac and Harte 1975, 1977, 1985; Noher de Halac 1980a–c; Sniezko and Harte 1984a,b, 1986).

Gametophyte ontogeny involves conversion from the diploid to haploid generation. Meiosis is not indispensable, however, because experimental work with anthers has made obtaining haploid plants through tissue culture possible. Work to develop haploid plants through *in vitro* culture of anthers, microspores, pollen, ovules, and even isolated gametes has gained immense significance for its application in plant breeding (Johri and Rao 1984; Linskens 1988). Despite the practical utility of haploid plants, their mechanisms of regeneration are still unclear and need to be elucidated through a thorough knowledge of pollen and megagametophyte ontogeny.

ANTHER DEVELOPMENT AND MALE STERILITY

Several reviews on angiosperm pollen provide an overview of pollen ontogeny (Heslop-Harrison 1971a, b; Knox 1984, 1987; Stanley and Linskens 1985), and tapetal cells (Echlin 1971; Pacini et al. 1985). One significant early work on the developmental problems presented by pollen walls in Onagraceae is that of Beer (1905). Most

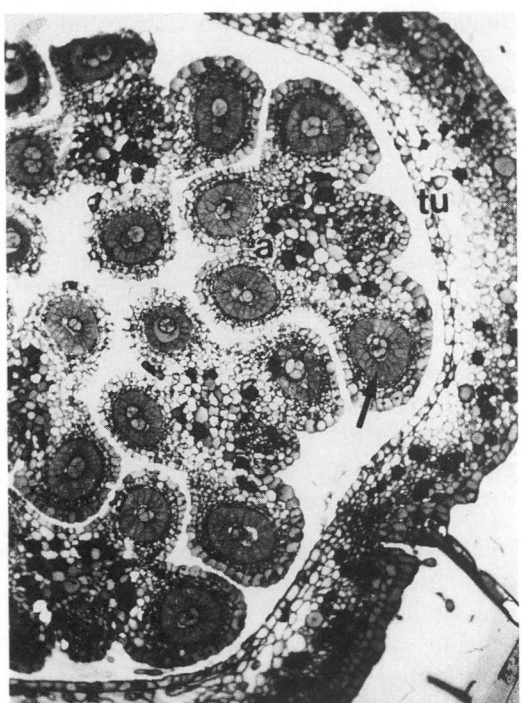

Figure 13.1. Transverse section of a flower bud of *Oenothera elata* with anthers (a) containing microspore tetrads at the middle tetrad stage (*arrow*). Complete buds were cut to detect developmental differences between anthers of the same flower; × 83; tu, tube.

electron microscopic studies on the pollen of Onagraceae ignore developmental aspects (Afzelius 1956; Diers 1963; Lepouse and Romain 1967; Rowley 1971; Skvarla et al. 1975, 1976, 1978; Cruden and Jensen 1979; Hesse 1981; Rowley et al. 1982; Cresti et al. 1983; Noher de Halac 1985a,b, 1986).

The sequential events that take place during anther growth in *Oenothera elata* HBK and in the hybrid *Oenothera elata* HBK × *O. glazioviana* Micheli were studied as part of a work on male sterility (mst) caused by recessive alleles of two loci, *fr.* and *ster.* This study compared normal pollen ontogeny with mst anther development (Noher de Halac 1982, 1985a,b, 1986; Noher de Halac et al. 1990). Inflorescences were collected at night and in the morning so as to cover the whole developmental sequence. To reveal minor developmental differences among anthers of the same flower, sections of complete buds were observed (Figure 13.1). Histochemical techniques were used to observe lipids and starch during developmental stages of normal and mst pollen (Noher de Halac and Cismondi 1992). Callose was identified with the aniline blue test and fluorescence microscopy (Eschrich and Currier 1964). Twelve developmental stages were determined from archesporium to bicellular pollen with starch (Table 13.1; Noher de Halac et al. 1990).

The development of pollen can be considered to be unique among the patterns of plant cell growth for several events (review in Knox 1984) recognized in *Oenothera*:

1. The pollen mother cells (PMCs) and newly formed microspores in the tetrad are covered by a special callose wall (Figure 13.5–13.7) whose function is assumed to be isolation of cells during meiosis (Heslop-Harrison and Mackenzie 1968; Knox and Heslop-Harrison 1970; review in Bhandari 1984).

2. Cytoplasmic changes, typical of the flow from the diploid to haploid nuclear phase, involve a sequence of organelle dedifferentiation and redifferentiation (Heslop-Harrison 1971a) and a decrease/increase of ribosome population (Dickinson and Heslop-Harrison 1977; Dickinson and Potter 1978) and formation of multimembranous bodies (Knox 1984) (Figures 13.3B, 13.4).

3. The sporophytic diploid pollen-mother cells contain the "pattern" genes that are transcribed before meiosis. The gene activity products are transferred to the cytoplasm and plasma membrane (Knox 1984).

4. Microspores develop a special wall called the *sporoderm* (Figures 13.7B, 13.8A,B, 13.9). In *Oenothera* an inner sporopolleninous layer (endexine) and a microfibrillar-cellulosic ektexine precursor layer form during early microsporogenesis prior to release of microspores from the tetrad (Noher de Halac 1986; Noher de Halac et al. 1990). This layer can be interpreted to be or to support a glycocalix with receptors for the exine wall polymer protosporopollenin or sporopollenin (Rowley and Skvarla 1974).

5. The mature pollen wall of *Oenothera* consists of the sporopolleninous exine (endexine and ektexine) and the cellulosic intine (Figure 13.11). Both layers are completed during pollen ontogeny after the release of microspores from the tetrad. The ektexine paracrystalline-beaded pattern (Skvarla et al. 1976) is thought to be contributed by the tapetal cells. The materials produced from the secretory activity of the cytoplasm of the diploid tapetal cells pass to the thecal fluid, and the ektexine is completed (Buchen and Sievers 1981) during the transfer phase of these cells.

6. The three apertures are initiated at the PMC stage (Figure 13.2). Each aperture becomes a complex structure with an apertural chamber after cytokinesis. These chambers develop through the apposition of cytoplasmic vesicles in each microspore of a tetrad and are extruded from the cytoplasm just after the microspore-release stage (Figures 13.8, 13.9). In the mature pollen grains (Figure 13.11), each apertural chamber or *oncus* has a ring of sporopolleninous material at its base (Lepouse and Romain 1967).

7. The secretory tapetum experiences sequential morphological changes that are functionally related to events affecting pollen maturation. It is thought to produce (a) callase, which helps in callose wall dissolution, (b) sporopollenin precursors for ektexine accretion, (c) lipid materials for pollen coats, and (d) hydrolytic enzymes, which characterize the last stages of tapetal-cell degradation (Noher de Halac et al. 1990).

8. Starch and lipids are produced by the diploid PMC cytoplasm. Both kinds of materials are consumed before the pollen stage and synthetized *de novo* at the pollen stage by the haploid vegetative cell. Starch grains produced by the haploid cytoplasmic activity (Figure 13.10A) differs morphologically from those of the diploid PMC (Figure 13.10B; Noher de Halac et al. 1992). The generative cell has plastids but no starch (Figure 13.10B; Diers 1963).

Table 13.1. Normal ontogenesis of pollen in *Oenothera*.

	Characteristics								
	Reproductive cells				Tapetum				
Ontogenesis	Callose	Lipids	Starch	Vacuoles	No. of nuclei	Cell wall	Laby-rinth	Lipids	Vacuoles
Microsporogenesis									
1 Archesporium	−	−	−	−	1	+	−	−	−
2 Early pre-meiotic PMC	−	−	−	−	1	+	−	−	−
2 Late pre-meiotic PMC	+	(+)	−	(+)	1	+	−	−	−
4 Meiotic PMC	+	(+)	+	(+)	1	+	−	−	−
5 Early tetrad, cytokinesis	+	(+)	+	(+)	2	+	−	−	−
6 Middle tetrad stage	+	(+)	+	−	2	+	−	−	−
	en ek in								
7 Late tetrad stage	+ − −	(+)	+	−	2	−	+	−	−
8 Nonvacuolate microspores	+ − −	−	+	+	2	−	+	−	−
Pollen development									
9 Vacuolating Microspores	+ + −	−	+	+	2	−	(+)	++	+
10 Vacuolated pollen	+ + +	−	−	+	2	−	(+)	++	(+)
11 Engorging pollen	+ + +	−	(+)	(+)	Degenerate	−	−	−	−
12a Bicellular pollen with starch	+ + +	−	++	−	Degenerate	−	−	−	−
12b Bicellular pollen with starch and lipids	+ + +	+	++	−	0	−	−	−	−

[a] Data based on material collected both during the day and at night. Duration of development: one to several weeks, depending mainly on the temperature. en, Endexine; ek, ektexine; in, intine. ++, Abundant; +, present;(+), traces; −, absent.
[b] From Noher de Halac, et al. 1990.

From Archesporium to Meiosis

Developmental events of pollen ontogeny in *Oenothera* involve several peculiarities. In the staminal rudiment of the youngest flower bud, the archesporium is a mass of non-vacuolated cells located at the center of each anther lobule or future pollen sac: The other tissues remain meristematic and undifferentiated. Later, PMCs can be distinguished by their shape and volume from the prospective tapetal cells (Figure 13.1). PMCs undergo volumetric growth. Their cell walls thicken, stain dark with osmium and fluoresce with aniline blue, an indicator for callose deposition. Starch is present in plastids (Figures 13.2, 13.3), and small lipid drops lie in the cytoplasm.

During the meiotic prophase, the ribosome population of PMCs is reduced (Figure 13.2). The same occurs in *Lilium* during microsporogenesis (Dickinson and Heslop-Harrison 1977; Dickinson and Potter 1978) and in *Gasteria verrucosa* at the meiotic prophase (diplotene) during megasporogenesis (Willemse and Fransen-Verheisen 1978). Megaspore mother cells in *Impatiens, Allium,* and *Lilium* show a decrease in the number of ribosomes per cytoplasmic area during the meiotic prophase, a decrease that is assumed to be related to the small number of nuclear pores and the increase in the volume of nucleolus at this stage. The increase in the number of ribosomes per cytoplasmic area after metaphase I is related to the disintegration of the nuclear envelope and to the presence of nucleoluslike bodies (nucleoloids) in the cytoplasm after metaphase I (De Boer-De Jeu 1978). Whether ribosome renewal is a character of

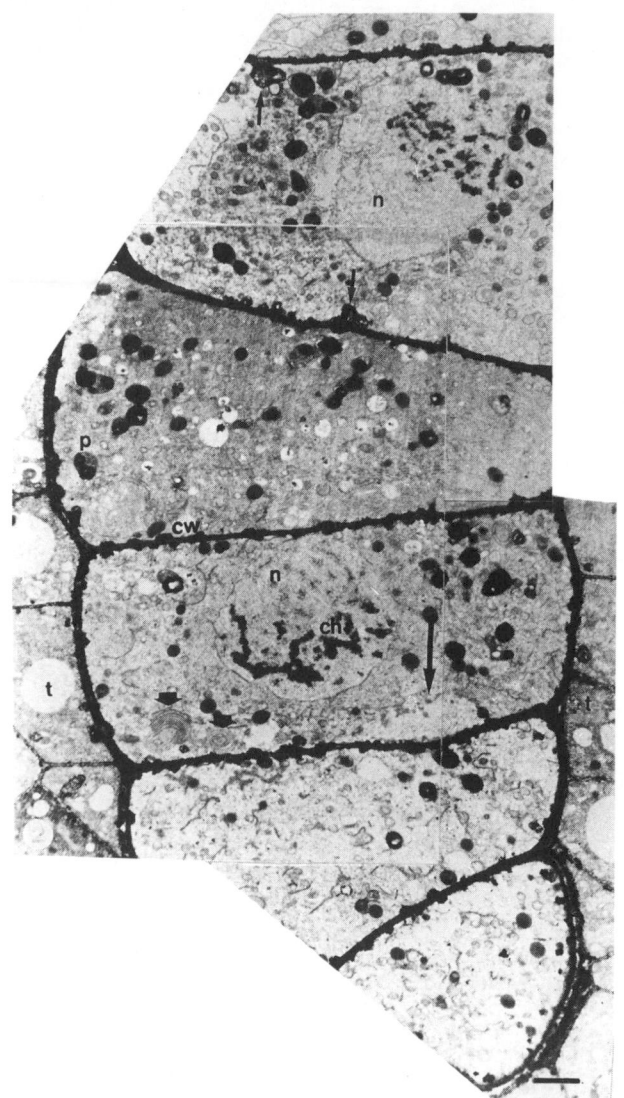

Figure 13.2. A set of PMCs of *Oenothera elata* × *glazioviana* at the meiotic prophase with pericytoplasmic bodies (*arrows* in the upper cell). The prospective apertural chamber is surrounded by endoplasmic reticulum membranes (*thick arrow*) and DMIs (*short arrows*) in the lower central cell; × 5950; ch, chromatin; cw, cell wall; n, nucleus; p, plastid; t, tapetal cell.

general occurrence during meiosis in plants remains, however, a matter of discussion (De Boer-De Jeu 1978).

Membrane inclusions (Dickinson 1981) or double-membrane inclusions (DMIs) (Knox 1984) appear in the PMC cytoplasm (Figures 13.3A,B). Double or multiple membrane-bound inclusions with more cytoplasmic ribosomes than surrounding cytoplasm are found during microsporogenesis and megasporogenesis (Dickinson and Heslop-Harrison 1977; Dickinson and Andrews 1977; Dickinson and Potter 1978). Significantly, this encapsulation is immediately followed by elimination from the cytoplasm of the major part of the ribosome population after cytokinesis. The ribosomes contained in these membranous inclusions remain unaffected by the lytic enzymes active elsewhere in the cytoplasm. DMIs disintegrate during the later stages

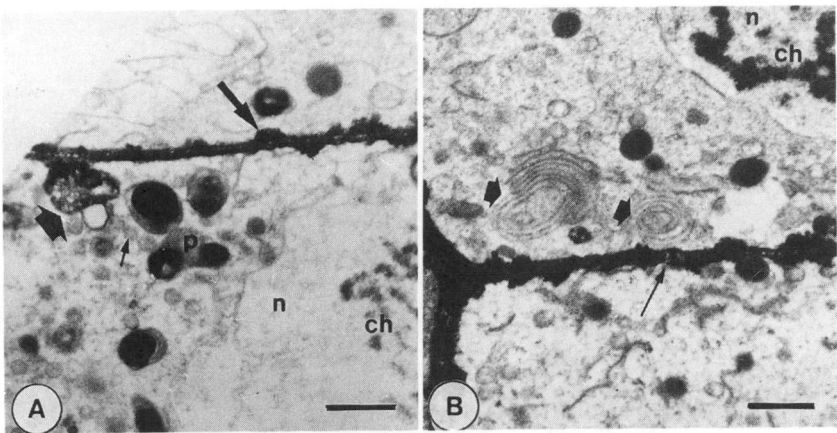

Figure 13.3. (A) Part of the upper PMC of Figure 13.2. Details of a pericytoplasmic body (*thick arrow*) and fused vesicles (*thin arrow*) are shown. Dark material accumulates inside the cell walls (*long arrow*). (B) Part of the lower central PMC of Figure 13.2. Details of the DMIs (*thick arrows*) and a connecting channel between cells (*thin arrow*) are shown; both × 14,050; ch, chromatin; n, nucleus; p, plastid.

and therefore are believed to be responsible for the increase in the ribosome population after cytokinesis. The above authors propose that the encapsulated cytoplasm fulfills two roles (a) it carries reserves necessary for post-meiotic development from the diplophase to the haplophase, and (b) it allows the continuity of protein synthesis through meiosis I and II, during which the major part of the protein-synthetizing apparatus is absent. DMIs might also have autolytic functions that contribute to ribosome population turnover, as do the similar membranous formations in other plant cells (Matile 1975). With Sudan black B stain for simultaneous detection of lipids and polysaccharides, cycles of lighter and darker cytoplasmic coloration were seen during meiosis. These color shades perhaps indicate an accumulation and a loss, respectively, of polar cell components such as ribosomal RNA. The Sudan black B test can be a suitable reaction to study the ribosomal cycle during microsporogenesis (Noher de Halac et al. 1992).

Several kinds of small vacuoles, vesicles, and paramural bodies are found in the cytoplasm of PMCs during active callose deposition (Figure 13.2). The vesicles having a light halo and a dark core may be involved in this process in other callose-bearing cells, such as pollen tubes of tomato (Pacini and Juniper 1984) and megaspores of *Oenothera* (Noher de Halac 1980b; cf. Figure 13.7A and Figure 13.14). The fusion of vesicles with plasmalemma without retraction of the membrane in PMCs leads to the formation of the paramural multivesicular bodies (Figures 13.2, 13.3A).

The apertural chambers begin to form at the meiotic prophase. Parallel endoplasmic reticulum membranes border the lighter cytoplasmic apertural chamber precursor zone (Figure 13.2).

Nuclear vacuoles become visible in PMCs at the end of the meiotic prophase (Figure 13.4). These vacuoles in *Oenothera* do not contain polysaccharides but contain dispersed nonpolar materials that do not react as neutral lipids (Noher de Halac et al. 1992). The nuclear vacuoles seem to be of general occurrence during meiosis in angiosperms, but their function is unclear. Nucleoloids appear in the cytoplasm of PMCs after the meiotic prophase and remain visible until the tetrad stage. The material of nucleoli and nucleoloids is poorly embedded by the Sudan black B stain and looks brownish-white, possibly due to the polar nature of their nucleic acids in combination with non-polar materials (Noher de Halac et al. 1992).

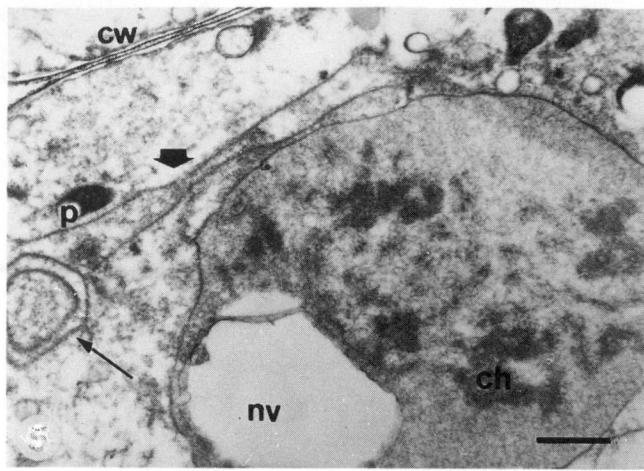

Figure 13.4. Part of the PMC of *Oenothera elata* × *glazioviana* at the end of prophase. A nucleus with a nuclear vacuole (nv) is shown. DMIs (*thin arrow*) are connected to parallel membranes of endoplasmic reticulum (*thick arrow*); × 11,730; ch, chromatin; cw, cell wall; p, plastid.

Tetrad of Microspores

Stages of tetrad development may be categorized as early, middle, and late. At the early tetrad stage, cytokinesis occurs (Figure 13.5), and each member of the tetrad becomes covered by a special callose wall. Callose appears dark blue with toluidine, electron dense with osmium tetroxide (Figures 13.5–13.7), brilliant white with Sudan black B, and fluorescent with aniline blue. The old fibrillar cellulosic cell wall of the PMC is seen at the surface of the tetrad (Figures 13.6, 13.7). Callose borders the connecting channels between microspores (Figure 13.7A), a general phenomenon in the microspore ontogeny (Knox 1987).

Osmiophylic granular material is visible outside the cellulosic PMC wall at the tetrad stage and in the loculus and on the tapetal walls (Figure 13.5). This material possibly originates from the eccrine and/or granulocrine secretion of the tapetal walls, and stains light with Sudan black B. Thus, it may comprise proteins, like the enzyme callase, as well as polysaccharides and/or the ektexine precursor materials (Noher de Halac et al. 1992). This material is loose and does not form a continuous layer; it can be assumed to be homologous to the tapetal membrane of other angiosperms (for a review, see Bhandari 1984).

Cytokinesis is simultaneous. Plastids with rounded starch grains are located near the site of the inner wall formation in the tetrad (Figure 13.5, *arrow*), as in the meiocytes of other angiosperms (Noher De Halac & Harte 1975,1977,1985; Bhandari and Sharma 1988; Rodkiewicz et al. 1988; Johri et al. 1992). The particular pattern of amyloplast aggregation in spore morphogenesis can be interpreted as the first manifestation of cell polarity during micro and megasporogenesis. Polarity, presumably a general feature in plant meiosis, has been found to be related to the activity of microtubules that direct the intracytoplasmic movements of organelles (Bednara et al. 1988; van Lammeren et al. 1988; Pearson 1989). Van Lammeren et al. (1989) found a remarkable arrangement of microfilaments in the cortical cytoplasm of microspores and pollen of *Gasteria*. They believe that this might point to an expression of polarity within the microspore and the pollen grain.

At the middle-tetrad stage, the first evidence of the exine precursor layer is observed in the accumulation of granular material in the pericytoplasmic compartment inside the callose layer (Figure 13.7A). Depots of osmiophylic material are seen in the pericytoplasmic compartment through electron microscopy (Figure 13.7B). It was assumed that the exine pattern is established in a pectocellulosic layer (the primexine) by the activity of the PMC genome and cytoplasm (Heslop-Harrison 1971b). In *Oenothera,* however, endexine forms before the release of microspores from the tetrad and stains brownish-white with Sudan black B. This result suggests the presence of polysaccharidic/proteinic and lipid components (Figure 13.5; Noher de Halac et al. 1992).

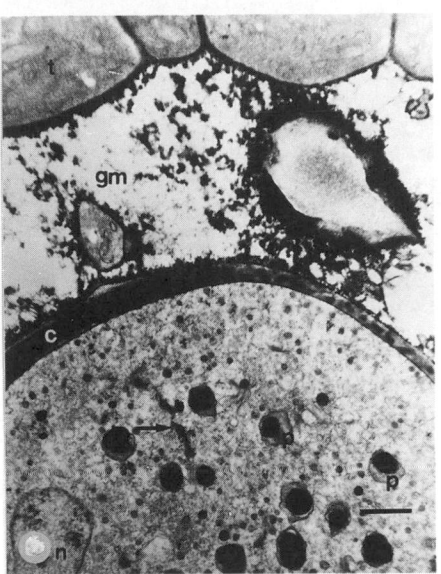

Figure 13.5. Part of an early tetrad of *Oenothera elata* × *glazioviana* covered by the callose wall (c) at cytokinesis (*long arrow*). Granular material sticks to the outer surface of the tetrad and to the tapetal cell walls; × 5950; gm, granular material; n, nucleus; p, plastid; t, tapetal cell.

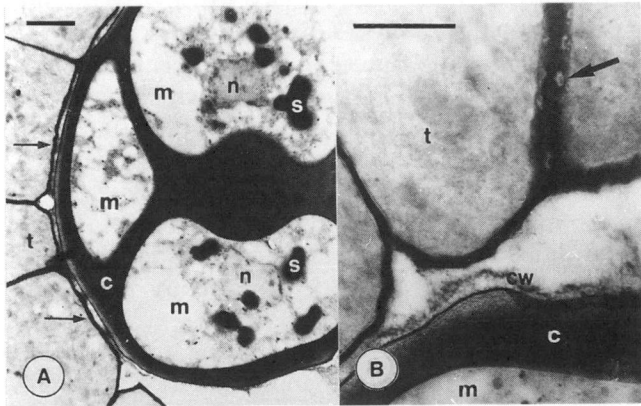

Figure 13.6. (A) Part of a middle tetrad of *Oenothera elata* × *glazioviana* showing the callose wall (c) and tapetum (t) with flattened cells still having a cellulosic wall (*arrow*); × 5000; (B) Part of the tapetum (t) at the middle tetrad stage with cells connected through groups of plasmodesmata (*arrow*). The tetrad is covered with callose wall (c) and the old cellulose wall (cw) of the PMC; × 12,470; m, microspore; n, nucleus; s, starch.

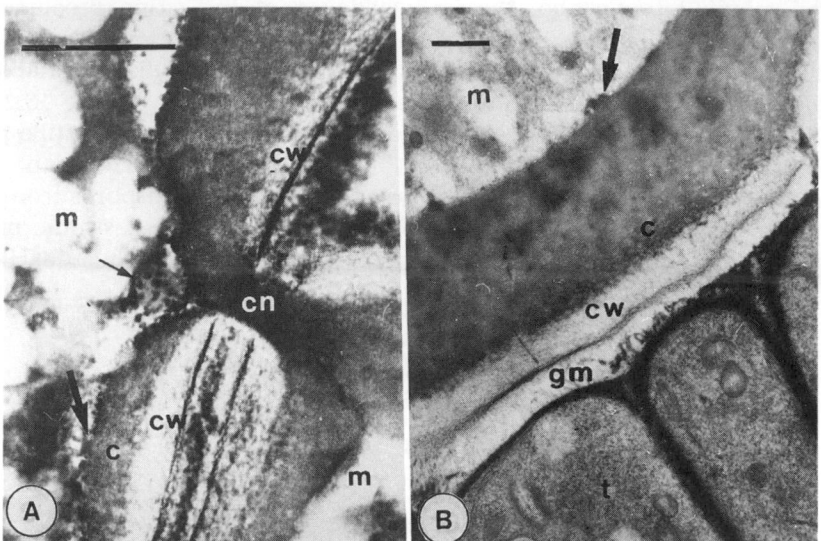

Figure 13.7. (A) Two adjacent tetrads in the anther of *Oenothera elata* × *glazioviana* showing the connecting channels (cn) and callose vesicles (c). The pericytoplasmic dark material is believed to be the precursor material for endexine (*thin arrow*); × 33,330; (B) Details of a middle tetrad. The wall is integrated with a peripheral zone of the granular material (gm) between the tapetal cell wall (t) and the tetrad; a fibrillar layer corresponding to the old cellulose wall (cw) of the PMC, the callose layer (c), and the inner dark formations represent the initial phase of endexine deposition (*thick arrow*) around the microspore (m) cytoplasm; × 12,960.

Microspore-release Stage

The late tetrad stage is characterized by a release of microspores from the tetrad induced by tapetum-produced callase activity (reviewed in Bhandari 1984). Microspores contain small vacuoles (Figure 13.8A,B) and amyloplasts with composed, round starch grains located around the nucleus. After the microspore release, "wheel-like" remnants of the inner tetrad walls (Figure 13.8A), which have polysaccharidic components are seen in the thecal fluid (Noher de Halac et al. 1992).

The entire sporoderm of the young microspore stains dark with toluidine blue (Figure 13.8A). The sporopolleninous endexine is produced by the metabolism of the haploid cell from the middle tetrad stage onwards and stains homogeneously dark with osmium tetroxide (Figure 13.8B, 13.9). The endexine layer reacts slightly to the lipid test with Sudan black B (Figure 13.10A). It gradually thickens by the apposition of materials produced by the microspore cytoplasm.

Fibrillar material is formed in the cytoplasm of PMCs that extrudes after the release of microspores from the tetrad and gives rise to three apertural chambers (oncus). Medium electron-dense vesicles are seen at the base of each apertural chamber after the release of microspores (Figure 13.8A) and later become flattened and osmiophilic (Figure 13.9). They possibly contain sporopollenin precursors, since the mature pollen grains have a ring of sporopollenin at the base of each oncus (Figure 13.11).

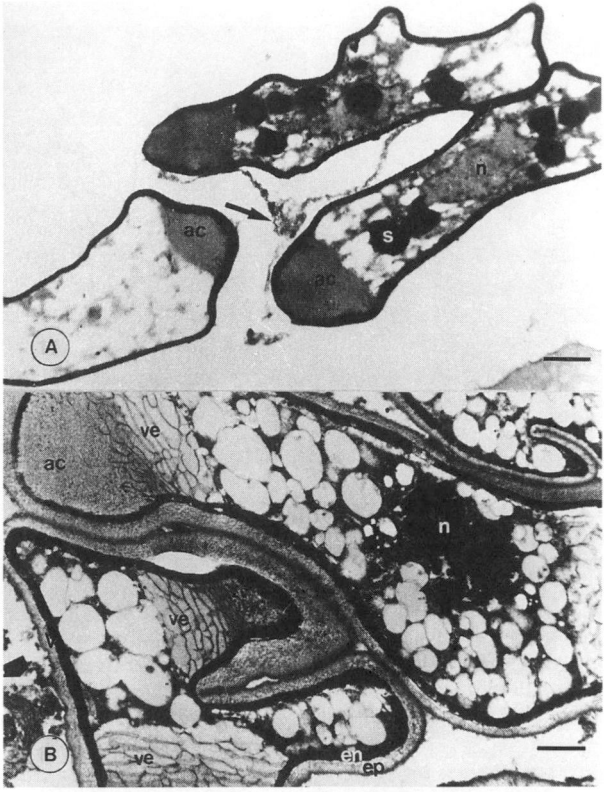

Figure 13.8. (A) Releasing microspores of *Oenothera elata* × *glazioviana*. The wheel-like formation (*arrow*) between the microspores is the wall material after callase activity. The sporoderm is homogeneously stained with toluidine blue. Endexine cannot be distinguished from the ektexine precursor layer; × 6190; (B) Details of the sporoderm and apertures. The endexine (en) is completed, and the ektexine precursor layer (ep) shows a fibrillar texture similar to the apertural chamber materials. Inside each apertural chamber (ac), apposition of light vesicles (ve) can be seen. Tapetal cell remnants stick to the sporoderm surface (*arrow*); × 7670; n, nucleus; s, starch.

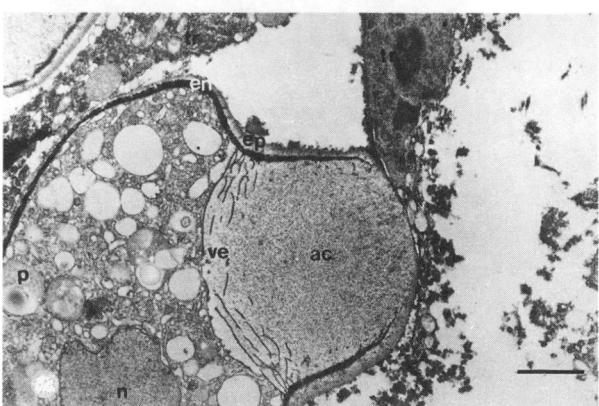

Figure 13.9. Part of a young microspore of *Oenothera elata* × *glazioviana* after its release from tetrad. The apertural chamber (ac) possesses dark, flattened vesicles (ve) at its inner side. The disintegrated tapetal-cell remnants (tr) floats in the thecal fluid and sticks partially to the ektexine precursor layer (ep). Endexine (en) is fully developed; × 9450; n, nucleus; p, plastid.

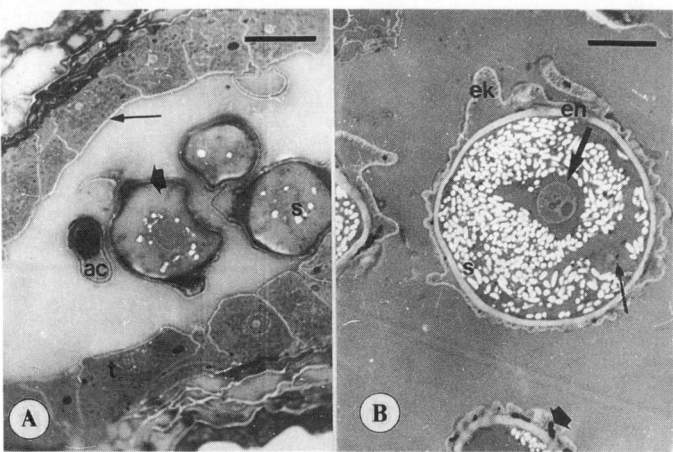

Figure 13.10. (A) The releasing nonvacuolated microspores (treated with Sudan black B for locating lipid and carbohydrate) of *Oenothera elata* × *glazioviana*. Round starch grains (s) are located near the nucleus. The endexine precursor layer and base of the apertural chambers (ac) show a positive reaction for lipids (*thick arrow*). Ektexine and the tapetal cell surface (*thin arrow*) stain alike with the test; × 925. (B) Mature pollen grains (Sudan black B tested) of *Oenothera elata*. Lens-shaped starch fills the cytoplasm of the vegetative cell. The vegetative nucleus is centrally located (*thick arrow*), and the generative cell without starch grains lies in its cytoplasm (*thin arrow*). Lipidic material (*short arrow*) is present in the pollen coat; × 867.

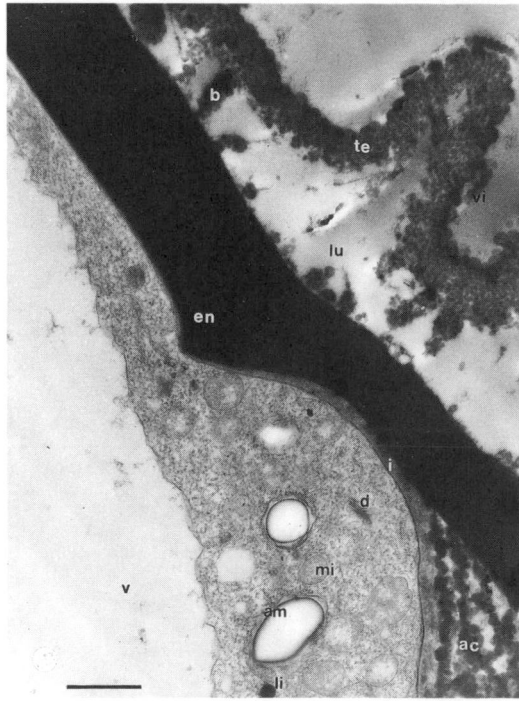

Figure 13.11. Bicellular pollen grain of *Oenothera elata* × *glazioviana*. Cytoplasm of the vegetative cell with mitochondria (mi), dictyosomes (d), scarce lipid drops (li), and amyloplasts (am) that contain elongate starch grains. The vacuole (v) is still visible. The sporoderm consists of intine (i), endexine (en), and ektexine with viscin threads (vi). The apertural chamber (ac) with sporopollenin granules lies at its base; × 23,260; b, baculum, lu, lumina; te, tectum.

Vacuolated Microspore Stage

Vacuolation and starch depletion are two remarkable features of cytoplasm at this stage. The sporoderm becomes a paracrystalline-beaded structure (Noher de Halac et al. 1990). Sporopollenin is seen as brownish-white with the Sudan black B test. At this time, microspores often have their apertural chambers inserted into invaginations of the tapetal cells, with ektexine in close contact with a Sudan black B positive layer of the wall of the tapetal cells (I. Noher de Halac, unpublished). Passage of materials to (or from) the microspores can be assumed on the basis of this observation (see the section on Tapetal Cells, below).

Pollen Stage

We distinguish four pollen stages: vacuolated pollen grains, engorging pollen grains, bicellular pollen grains with starch, and bicellular pollen grains with starch and lipids (Table 13.1). Each stage is characterized by the amount of vacuolation and the kind and location of reserve materials (Noher de Halac et al. 1992). The peculiarities of the normal sporoderms in pollen stages can be described with the concepts and terminology proposed by Skvarla et al. (1976) in their ultrastructural studies of Onagraceae. The exine consists of two fundamental units, the ektexine and the endexine. The former comprises an outer delicate network or reticulum of the branching sporopollenin rods that have a faintly paracrystalline-beaded appearance. This entire network is called the *tectum*. The rods perpendicular to the underlying juxtaposed endexine, termed either *columellae* or *bacula,* also show a paracrystalline-beaded form. A foot layer is poorly developed or entirely absent in the Onagraceae. The endexine lies immediately beneath the columella and the foot layer. It is generally of uniform thickness around the pollen grain and thicker within the apertures where denticulate lamellar layers are formed. The apertures comprise two parts, the basal endo-aperture and the external pore formed by the ektexine. They protrude through the external pores and show a coarsely lamellated endexine. Viscin threads (Skvarla et al. 1978) occur in the proximal pole (Noher de Halac and Harte 1985). Their surface texture is generally similar to that of their respective ektexines (Figure 13.11).

Lipids accumulate in the sporoderm at early pollen stages (Table 13.1). They occur on the ektexine and in the compartment between the ektexine and endexine (*lumina*) (Figure 13.10B). They are dissolved at the pollen-shedding stage. The adhesive lipid layer, usually known as the *pollenkit* (Hesse 1981), is absent in mature pollen grains.

The first mitosis of the vacuolated microspore is unequal (Figure 13.10B) and results in the vacuolated pollen grain (Table 13.1). The generative cell is laterally located, and the vegetative cell has a big central vacuole. A dramatic increase of volume occurs, perhaps because of hydration of the vacuole of the vegetative cell.

The engorging pollen stage (Figure 13.11; Table 13.1) is characterized by the gradual loading of the vegetative cell with spindlelike amyloplasts that contain single elongate starch grains. The vacuole becomes smaller and the generative cell migrates to the center of the pollen grain.

Reserves in the Vegetative and Generative Cells

Starch and lipids are alternatively or simultaneously present in different locations during pollen morphogenesis (Table 13.1). Starch grains appear either electron dense

(Figures 13.2, 13.3A, 13.5) or translucent (Figures 13.9, 13.13) under the electron micro-scope, a condition that can be explained by the affinity of osmium to the double cova-lent bonds at the starch grain surface. This finding confirms the assumption of starch complexity at the biochemical level (see Beck and Ziegler 1989).

At the early bicellular pollen stage, the vegetative cells are completely filled with spindlelike amyloplasts (Figure 13.10B). Later, cytoplasmic lipid bodies also become abundant. Based on the asynchronous starch and lipid accumulation in the vegetative cell, we consider two bicellular pollen stages: (a) with only starch, and (b) with starch and lipids (Table 13.1). Lipids are deposited in the vegetative cell when the lipid materials of the lumina are dissolved. Shed pollen in *Oenothera* contains both starch and lipids. In *Lilium* and several other taxa, pollen grains are shed starchless but with lipids and other soluble polysaccharides in the cytoplasms of their vegetative cells (Reznikova and Willemse 1982; Pacini and Franchi 1988). Variation among taxa in relation to pollen reserves is a character of evolutionary significance because of its relation to the pollination agent and the pollen grain volume (Baker and Baker 1979).

Amyloplasts are the most prominent organelles of the vegetative cells in *O. organensis* S_3 and S_4 pollen grains (Cresti et al. 1983). Amylogenesis/amylolysis waves have been recorded in the pollen ontogeny in many angiospermous species (Franchi and Pacini 1988; Pacini and Franchi 1988).

The generative cell has no starch (Figure 13.10B, despite having plastids (Diers 1962; Noher de Halac at al. 1992), because the first mitosis in the microspore is unequal; plastids of the smaller cytoplasm do not accumulate starch. Whereas those of the bigger cytoplasm become gradually loaded with single starch grains as vacuolation decreases. This remarkable difference between the generative and the vegetative cell lines in *Oenothera* provides evidence of a divergence in the metabolic path of the daughter cells of the first mitosis, consequent upon an asymmetric division. Whether this divergence is due to volume differences, preparation of the next division, isolation of the generative cell through a callose layer, or differential gene activity regulation needs further research.

Other observations concerning starch deposits in the pollen of *Oenothera* are (a) starch type may differ between the fertile and nonfertile pollen, as in *O. muricata* (Renner 1919), and (b) the amount of starch is smaller in pollen tubes growing on self-incompatible styles than in those growing on self-compatible ones, as in *O. organensis* (Dickinson & Lawson 1975); this difference in amount of starch could be related to increase in number of callose plugs in the former.

The major components of the native starch—amylose and amylopectin— are not uniform but represent populations of different molecular forms with regard to chain length and branching characteristics (see Beck and Ziegler 1989 for a review). Several differentiated forms of each relevant enzyme (isoenzymes or multiple form of an enzyme) are necessary to cope effectively with the variety of chain length and branching intensities exhibited by the native starch. The diploid and haploid cytoplasms in the *Oenothera* pollen ontogeny may differ in the type of enzymes that catalyze starch biosynthesis as well as starch degradation. Different isoenzymes (α-amylases) could be translated from different mRNAs emanated from different genes in the diploid and haploid cell, or the same active enzyme could be modified after the translation by different ways (Beck and Ziegler 1989) in different plant materials. Beck and Ziegler (1989) report examples of correlation of special isozyme patterns of α- and β-amylase with stages of development and tissue differentiation in *Araucaria* and rice seeds, respectively. They believe that a biochemical clue to the phenomenon of enzyme heterogeneity may be provided by the notion that the substrate(s) of the enzymic reac-tions may change during the course of development. Starch composition varies not only because of transmission between the particulate (granular) and soluble forms, but also as a result of alterations in the amylase:amylopectin ratio, e.g. during starch granule formation. In addition, changes in the length of the basic chain (C-chain) and the number of sidechains (A- and B-chains) attached to them may lead to amylopectin's exhibiting an either more trichitic or more racemose structure or even becoming a phytoglycogen. To elucidate the nature of the morphological and osmiophilic differences of starch in pollen ontogeny, detailed enzymatic and biochemical studies with amyloplast-isolation techniques are needed.

Tapetal Cells

The tapetum in *Oenothera* is secretory (parietal) and thus belongs to the basic subtype for angiosperms (Pacini et al. 1985). At the early and middle tetrad stages, the tapetal cells are binucleate. They do not lose their polysaccharidic cell walls after the tetrad stage (Figures 13.5–13.7, 13.10A). The cells are connected through plasmodesmata (Figure 13.6B), postulated to be related to the origin of viscin threads (Rowley et al. 1982). The form of the tapetal cells changes during pollen ontogeny. At first rounded, they gradually become flattened at the locular surface (Figure 13.6A). The cell walls are first osmiophilic (Figures 13.5–13.6) and stain dark with toluidine blue; later they become electron translucent. A membrane labyrinth develops at the locular surface. The material of the cell wall remains white with Sudan black B after the microspore-release stage (Figure 13.10A). Later, their plastids become filled with lipids and the cells undergo vacuolation and reabsorption (Noher de Halac 1986).

At least five identifiable functions can be assumed to be accomplished sequentially by the tapetal cells during pollen ontogeny, as deduced from morphological events:

1. Tapetal cells synthetize metabolic products like enzymes and sporopollenin precursors by involving their abundant ribosomes and well-developed rough endoplasmic reticulum (ER).

2. They secrete the produced materials by the eccrine and/or granulocrine way, as was assumed in a number of angiosperms (reviewed in Buchen and Sievers 1981). Tapetum cells assume a transfusional form during microspore release from the tetrad (Noher de Halac 1986). Some of them fall into the thecal-fluid, possibly a holocrine way of secretion (Figure 13.9), because the materials produced through cell disintegration mix with the locular sap.

3. The polysaccharidic/protein materials secreted by the tapetal cells stick to the immature sporoderm surface of the non-vacuolated microspores (Figures 13.8B, 13.9). Thus, special receptors in the glycocalyx (Rowley et al. 1982) on the exine-precursor layer could be responsible for the final physicochemical organization of the protosporopolleninous materials secreted by the tapetum in the form of the typical paracrystalline-beaded pattern of ektexine.

4. Tapetal cells are then involved in the formation of a transient lipidic pollen coat (Noher de Halac at al. 1992), or *pollenkit* (Dickinson and Lawson 1975, Hesse 1981; Cresti et al. 1983). In fact, the origin of these lipidic materials is believed to be the tapetal cells; the plastids of the tapetal cells become filled with lipid vesicles at the vacuolated pollen stage (Noher de Halac 1986). During the engorging stage of pollen, the tapetal cells become gradually

depleted of lipids, and the unpolar lipids are immediately recognized in the lumina and paracrystalline-beaded matrix of ektexine (Table 13.1). Catabolites of the tapetal cells, transformed in active acetate, could pass to the locular sap and be used as raw materials for lipid biosynthesis on the pollen grain surface (Noher de Halac at al. 1992).

5. The last activity of the tapetal cells is autolysis, which involves hydrolytic enzymes. The cells vacuolate and partially disintegrate. Their cytoplasmic remnants, including the hydrolytic enzymes, pass to the locular sap. These enzymes can be assumed to catalyze the dissolution of the materials of the transient pollen coat. The catabolites may be then incorporated into the vegetative cell during the engorgement stage and used as raw materials for starch and lipid biosynthesis in the vegetative cell.

The cytoplasmic remnants of the tapetal cells could become incorporated into the pollen walls at two moments. Once, before the completion of ektexine (Figure 13.9) and, then, at the dissolution of the transient pollen coat. This sequence can be assumed because at these moments the tapetal cells disintegrate in the thecal fluid. On the other hand, the tapetal cells can be assumed to synthesize different products (enzymes and/or recognition proteins) at each developmental stage, products that probably become located in the strategic sites of the exine. These products of tapetal origin may become functional at different moments of pollen differentiation and pollen-tube growth. The enzymatic pattern varies during anther development (Hedge and Andrade 1982; Raghavan 1984; Nave and Sawhney 1986; Sawhney and Nave 1986).

The nutritional role of the tapetum has an evolutionary significance. Engorgement of pollen can be seen as "heterophagic" activity that developed phylogenetically as an adaptive response to the need for energy incorporation in the dark environment of the anther loculum. This assumption is supported by the observation in *Oenothera* of an engorging stage, usually in the night collection of inflorescences (Noher de Halac et al. 1990), when photosynthetic activity in the anther is excluded. More investigation on the light-dependent/independent metabolic processes in pollen ontogeny is needed.

That the transient pollen coat fulfills mainly a nutritional role in *Oenothera* can be correlated to the presence of viscin threads in the pollen (Skvarla et al. 1978). The passive adherence of pollen to the bodies of pollinating agents is ensured by these structures; the *pollenkit* is thus unnecessary (Dickinson and Lawson 1975; Skvarla et al. 1978; Cresti et al. 1983).

Male Sterile Development

The breakdown of the time-sequence-programmed, gene-controlled functions leading to normal pollen development occurs from mutation of the controlling genes. Such an event causes abolition of male sex and leads to the evolution of new sex types, the male steriles in the angiosperms (reviewed in Kaul 1987). Male sterility was studied in the hybrid *O. elata* × *glazioviana* in homozygous plants with the genetic constitution *ster/ster* (Noher de Halac at al. 1990).

The first evidence of male sterile (mst) development visible in the tapetal cells by electron microscope includes abnormal vacuolation and/or osmiophilic deposits in vacuoles and the presence of loose dark bodies in the cytoplasm and pericytoplasmic spaces from the PMC stage onwards. These bodies are lipidic (I. Noher de Halac, unpublished). During microsporogenesis, the tapetal cells of mst anthers show poor development of the transfer structure and rough endoplasmic reticulum (RER) hypertrophy compared to the cells of normal anthers (Noher de Halac 1985b, 1986). These two observations can be interpreted as evidence of faults in protein synthesis and in the secretory process. The lipidic bodies become coalescent in mature anthers and, together with the lamellar, Sudan black B–positive materials, occupy most of the degenerating cytoplasm of the tapetal cells (Noher de Halac at al. 1990).

In sporogenic cells, the first evidence of mst development appears at the tetrad stage, where the callose layer stains lighter with toluidine blue than in normal anthers, and subsequently the shape of microspores in the tetrad is often abnormally irregular (Noher de Halac et al. 1990). The nonvacuolated free microspores are of irregular shape and the morphology of sporoderms is variable. The endexine is malformed, and the paracrystalline-beaded structure of the ektexine is never completed. The apertures have a visible oncus. At the vacuolated microspore stage, dark depots are adsorbed on the surface of the ektexine precursor layer (Figure 13.12A) and stick the degenerating microspores together. Later, the endexine dissolves, and microspores are covered by intine and remnants of the other layers (Figure 13.13). The dissolution of the malformed endexine materials and the death of cytoplasm have been thought to be caused by the hydrolytic activity of the tapetal cells (Noher de Halac et al. 1990). Under the electron microscope, dead mst microspores show sporoderms with lamellations and dark depots instead of the paracrystalline ektexine structure (Noher de Halac 1982). The lamellar and dark materials seen at the outside of the tapetal cells (Figure 13.12), on pollen surfaces, and on the apertural chambers were assumed to be lipid self-assemblies of unused sporopollenin precursors (Sitte 1981; Noher de Halac 1985b, 1986). This assumption is reinforced by the positive Sudan black B reactivity of these materials (I. Noher de Halac, unpublished) and by the findings of Guilford et al. (1988) that support the notion that sporopollenin is not a unique substance but rather a series of related biopolymers derived from largely saturated precursors, such as fatty acids.

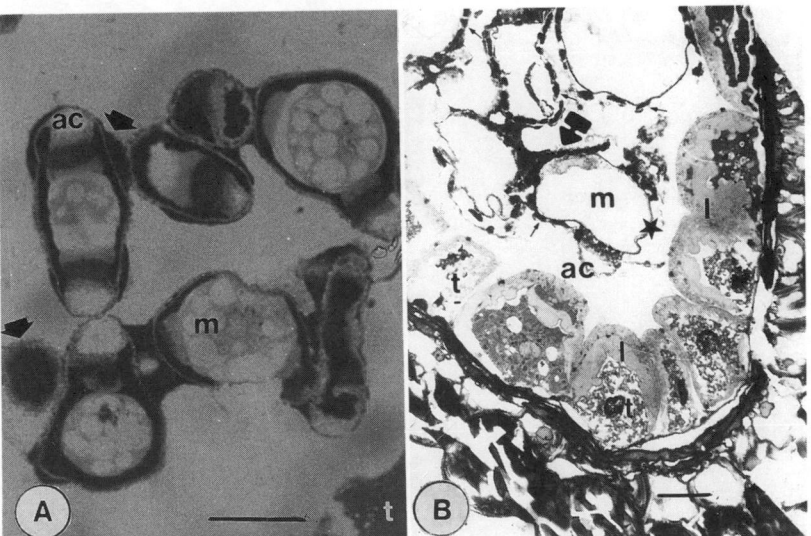

Figure 13.12. (A) Degenerated microspores in mst anthers of *Oenothera elata* × *glazioviana*. Dark material (*arrow*) holds the microspores together; × 900; (B) Degenerated microspores (m) in a more mature mst anther. Endexine is almost completely dissolved and the intine exposed (*star*). The dark material (*thick arrow*) keeps the microspores attached. The tapetal cells have degenerated cytoplasm and lamellar material (l) at the locular surface; × 600; ac, apertural chamber; m, microspore.

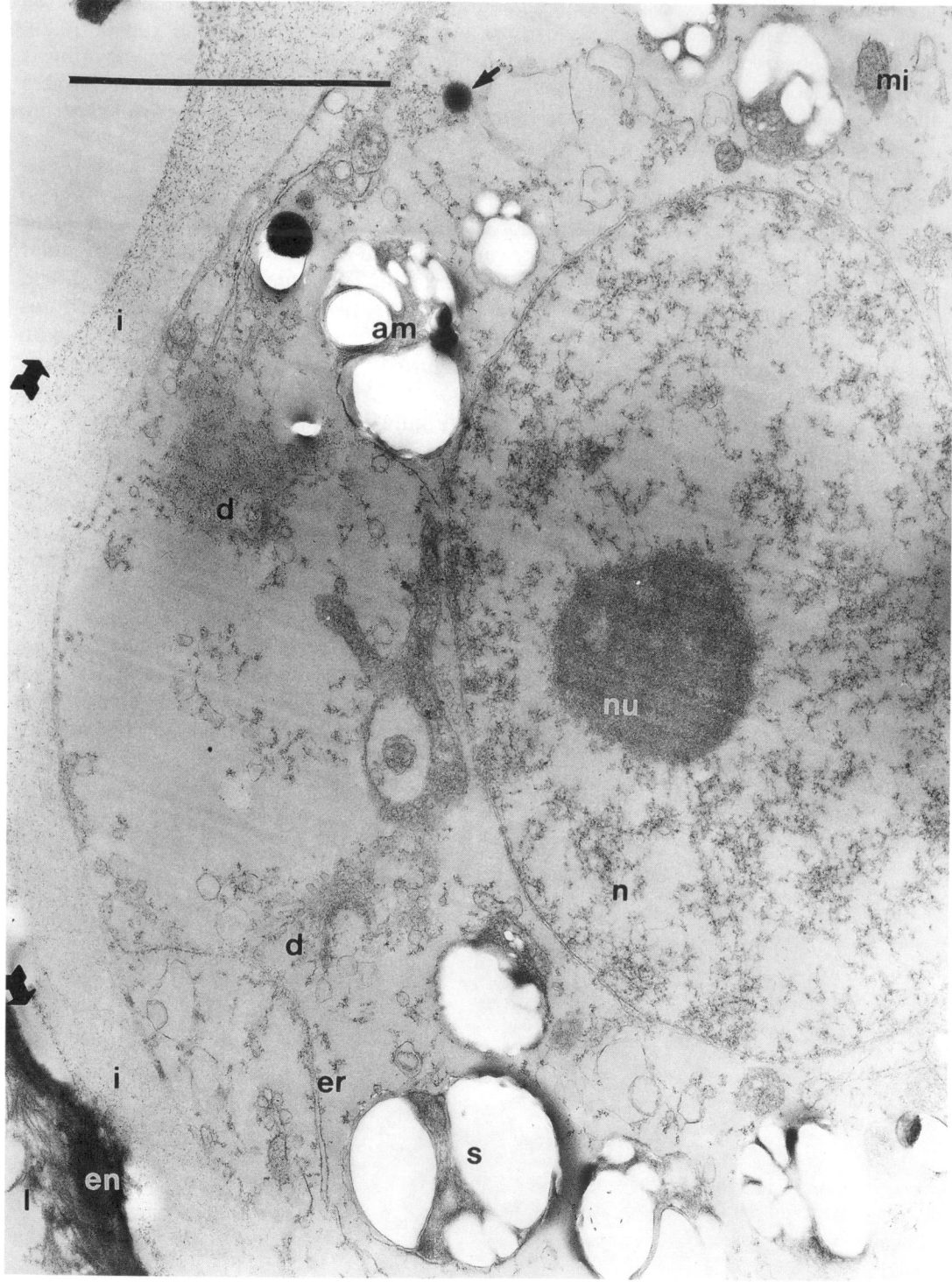

Figure 13.13. Degenerated microspore in a *mst* anther of *Oenothera elata* × *glazioviana*. Cytoplasm shows dictyosomes (d), endoplasmic reticulum (er), mitochondria (mi), lipids (*thin arrow*), and amyloplasts (am) with rounded starch grains (s). The intine (i) is fibrillar, and a light compartment (*thick arrow*) can be seen between the lamellar endexine (en) and the intine; × 55,800; l, lamellations; n, nucleus; nu, nucleolus.

POLLEN TUBE GROWTH AND INCOMPATIBILITY

The progamic phase begins when the pollen grains are transported to the stigmatic surface. There they germinate and produce pollen tubes that carry the generative cell and later the gametes to the ovule for fertilization (reviewed in van Went and Willemse 1984). Pollen tubes have callose walls and callose plugs that fluoresce with aniline blue, as in many other genera (Cresti and van Went 1976). The pollen tubes grow *in vitro* and on the stigmatic surface when pollinations are self-compatible. The ovule is reached by the pollen tube upon the maturation of the megagametophyte, and fertilization occurs.

Self-incompatibility systems are classified as heteromorphic or homomorphic. The heteromorphic self-incompatible species produce morphologically distinct types of flowers, whereas the homomorphic plants produce morphologically identical flowers (Clarke et al. 1989). *Oenothera* has both types; it belongs to one of the 24 families with heteromorphic self-incompatibility. It has a heterostyly in crosses like *O. elata* × *glazioviana* (Noher de Halac 1986), which ensures a mechanical barrier to illegitimate matings.

More than 70 families of angiosperms (including Onagraceae) have specific self-incompatibility genes (S-genes) that prevent inbreeding (reviewed in De Nettancourt 1984). There are two types of homomorphic self-incompatibility: gametophytic and sporophytic. In plants with a gametophytic system of self-incompatibility, the pollen expresses its own S-genotype. In contrast, the pollen phenotype of plants with a sporophytic system of control is determined by the S-genotype of the pollen-producing plant. S-allele-associated proteins, or glycoproteins, have been identified in style and stigma extracts (reviewed in Harris et al. 1989). *Oenothera organensis* demonstrates gemetophytic self-incompatibility (Emerson 1940) but differs from other species with this system in that the inhibition reaction, after a short germination, is located at the stigma level but not after it has penetrated the stigma and style (Knox 1979). The evidence of S-associated molecules in the pollen of this species is well recorded (reviewed in Gaude and Dumas 1987). Gaude and Dumas report that the S-specific antigen comprised about 20% of the pollen proteins; it diffused from the moistened pollen into isotonic media within 30 min. Individual pollen grains produced precipitates when sprinkled on the gel containing S-specific antisera. The antigenic substances could be located in the Sudan black B–rejecting cell-wall layer (intine) bordering the apertural chambers in the examined species (Figure 13.10B).

Compatible as well as incompatible pollinations were carried out in *O. organensis* pollen tubes (Dickinson and Lawson 1975). The self-incompatible pollen tubes were found to have a highly vacuolate cytoplasm and contain far less starch than the self-compatible tubes. The source of reserves for the growth of the tube was not apparent, but the presence of starch and dependence of the growth of tubes of some pollens upon the size of the grain suggest that important reserves are held within the grain. Whether the starch is used for the production of wall material, energy, or both is not clear. Dickinson and Lawson (1975) assumed that carbohydrate metabolism in pollen tubes was involved with the incompatibility reaction. They concluded that whatever the supply from stigma or style for the gametophytic incompatibility reaction in the stigmatic tissue may be, tube growth ultimately relies upon reserves in the pollen. Evidence on changes in carbohydrate metabolism (starch, callose, and PAS-positive material) in the incompatible pollen tubes in *O. organensis* points to a block in the breakdown of the storage reserves into short-chain precursors. Observations suggest that during the hydration phase, a stigmatic product accelerates starch catabolism in the initial growth zone of the incompatible pollen tubes. As a consequence, free carbo-hydrates (PAS-positive materials) increase in the cytoplasm and are remetabolized as callose plugs, thus interrupting the passage of starch to the tip of the pollen tube. The pollen-tube growth is arrested because of the lack of energy due to the scarce starch reserves in the pollen-tube tip. Nuclear activity can remain normal despite the lack of energy and the resultant arrest of growth.

Harte (1984) reinterpreted some genetic processes of gametophytes on the basis of her observations on *Oenothera*. She identified the incompatibility produced by the S-system in *O. organensis* as a gametophytic-sporophytic incompatibility system and dif-ferentiated it from the incompatibility system identified earlier as "selective fertiliza-tion." She concluded that a gene active in the pollen tube and the embryo sac is respon-sible for the chemotropic cooperation between gametophytes. The similarity of the pollen-tube and embryo-sac genes is a special case of incompatibility between two gametophytes, hence the term *gametophytic-gametophytic incompatibility system*. Harte (1984) proposed that *Oenothera* has developed still other possibilities to exhibit genetic influence on gametophytes. She speculated that the plastidial DNA (plastome) of *Oenothera* has a gene with at least two alleles that cooperates with one or more karyotic genes in influencing the germination of male gametophytes.

MEGAGAMETOPHYTE DEVELOPMENT
AND THE PHENOMENA OF POLARITY

A developmental process about which less is known than pollen ontogeny is megagametophyte ontogeny. Studies that compare both the morphogenetic paths in the Angiospermae are scarce. In members of the Ericaceae, comparisons of male and female developmental stages have shown a remarkable evolutionary significance (Palser et al. 1989).

Meiosis occurs in the megaspore mother cells (MMCs), which pass from the diploid to the haploid nuclear phase and produce four megaspores. Generally, only one of these cells in each ovule enters megagametogenesis. After undergoing three mitoses, it forms a megagametophyte. Variations on this normal pattern are of taxonomic sig-nificance and concern the number of megaspores involved in megagametophyte production, the number of mitotic divisions, and the final organization and number of the megagametophyte cells (Maheswari 1950; Rutishauser 1969). The megagameto-phyte contains at least one female gamete (for a review see van Went and Willemse 1984). Experimental work, including gamete isolation and *in vitro* fertilization, is being done on different taxa (Keijzer and Willemse 1988; Wanger et al. 1988). The peculiari-ties of ovule (Noher de Halac 1980a), megaspore, and megagametophyte differentia-tion were described in several species and hybrids of *Oenothera* (Noher de Halac and Harte 1975, 1977; Noher de Halac 1980b, c). The ovule is anatropous, bitegmic, and crassinucellate. The MMC is located near the chalaza and can be distinguished from the nucellar cells by shape and volume. One of the factors involved in morphogenesis during meiosis is the asynchrony of meiosis II (Noher de Halac and Harte 1975). Meiosis I leads to a diad and meiosis II to a tetrad. In Onagraceae, the chalazal cell of the diad usually has the second meiotic division delayed compared with the micropylar cell. In a number of observed cases, the second meiotic division was even absent in the chalazal cell, and the cell degenerated before the end of karyokinesis. Then, instead of a tetrad of megaspores, a triad is obtained. The delayed meiosis II is thought to be caused by nutritional gradients in the ovule (Noher de Halac and Harte 1975).

In most angiosperms, the chalazal cell of the diad is located near the hypostase, which limits the nutritional source of the ovular vascular strand. After meiosis II, the most chalazal cell becomes the functional megaspore. In *Oenothera,* however, the micropylar megaspore is usually the mother cell of the megagametophyte, and the polarity of the tetrad is inverted; the three chalazal megaspores degenerate. The callose layer also has an inverted polarity. In most angiosperms, the MMC is covered by a callose layer, which is discontinuous or thinner toward the chalazal tip of the MMC and later becomes thinner toward the chalazal member of the diad and tetrad (Rodkiewicz 1970; Kuran 1972). Because callose is thought to decrease the per-meability of cells to certain substances (Heslop-Harrison and Mackenzie 1968; Knox and Heslop-Harrison 1970), the discontinuity of the layer would be advantageous to the chalazal pole of the cells, which respond by growing faster and accelerating their karyokinesis. This scheme is inverted in *Oenothera* (Jalouzot-Romain 1970; Rodkiewicz and Kuran 1971; Noher de Halac and Harte 1975, 1977; Rodkiewicz and Sniezko 1978). The functional megaspore in some *Oenothera* species lies at the micropylar end of the tetrad (Figure 13.14). This location corresponds to the inverted position of the callose wall discontinuity from the MMC stage onward.

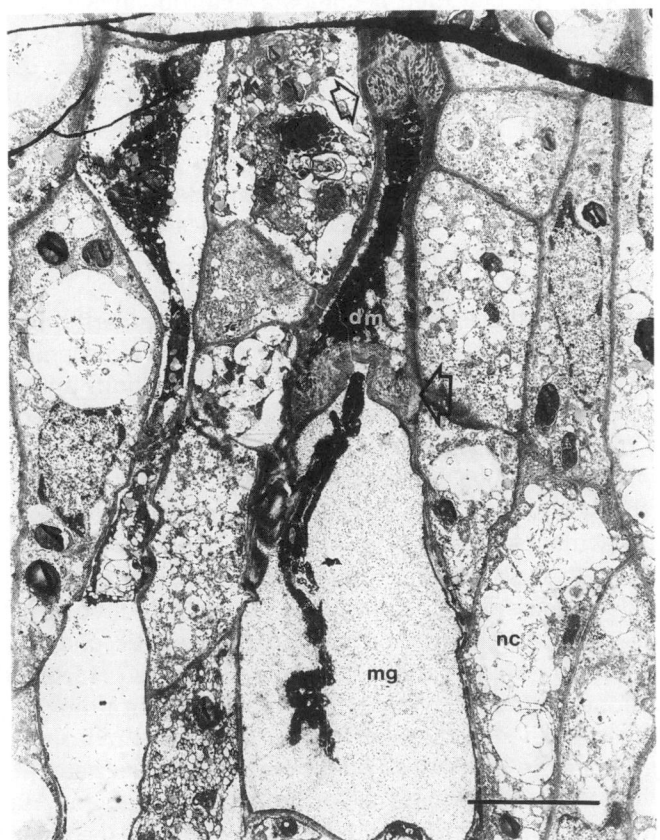

Figure 13.14. Megagametophyte of *Oenothera elata*. A degenerated megaspore (dm) is shown with callose (*arrows*) and surrounding nucellar cells (nc). The megaspore has pluglike callose masses at the chalazal and micropylar ends of the cell. The masses are formed by the depots of vesicles with a dark core and a lighter halo. The micropyle is oriented downward; × 2800; mg, megagametophyte.

In *Oenothera*, the crassinucellate ovule has a prominent nucellar tissue with abundant starch grains between micropyle and the differentiating megagametophyte. The future embryo sac can draw nutrition from this source. It is assumed that the nutrition from the micropylar side of the nucellus is a factor influencing the inversion of the polarity of the tetrad (Noher de Halac and Harte 1975, 1977).

Additional evidence of the relation of callose and nutritional supply to the polarity of structures is the development of twin megagametophytes in *Oenothera* species and hybrids with the chromosomic Renner complexes (Noher de Halac and Harte 1975, 1977; Sniezko and Harte 1984a, b; Harte and Sniezko, 1988). Twin megagametophytes originate by simultaneous growth of the micropylar and the chalazal members of the tetrad. In these examples the callose layer is absent around the MMC and the tetrad of megaspores and is present only in the internal walls of the latter. Asynchrony of meiosis II is generally absent in these examples. Both tip megaspores start growing to form megagametophytes, while the inner two megaspores degenerate. Later, the megagametophyte with the weaker genetic constitution degenerates, whereas the other emerges victorious in a competition for nutrients in the ovule (the Renner effect).

Studies with *Oenothera* support the notion that megagametophyte polarity is consequent to the polarity of the initial stages of development. The small archespore has no defined polarity axis; the cell then becomes a heteropolar MMC, first through the positioning of organelles and then through vacuolation (Noher de Halac and Harte 1975, 1977). When callose deposition becomes polar with a discontinuous tip, organelles also become polarly distributed (Rodkiewicz and Bednara 1974; Rodkiewicz 1978;; Noher de Halac and Harte 1985), possibly due to the nuclear repulsion and organelle movements in relation to the cytoskeleton of the cell, as was noted in *Gasteria verrucosa* and *Chamaenerion angustifolium* (Bednara et al. 1988; Willemse & van Lammeren 1988) and is assumed in microsporogenesis (van Lammeren et al. 1988). Organelle polarity was observed before in the tetrad of megaspores in *Epilobium* (Rodkiewicz and Bednara 1974).

The growth of one of the tetrad cells, i.e. the heteropolarity, is oriented towards the chalazal end of the ovule in most angiosperms; an inverted polarity characterizes the Onagraceae. Homopolarity is the identical growth of both ends of the tetrad, at least for a certain period. This peculiarity leads to the growth of two megaspores and the development of twin megagametophytes (Harte and Sniezko 1988). Another polarity occurs in tetrasporic megagametogenesis, which does not involve definition of a polarity axis in the MMCs. These cells can be interpreted to have a multipolar structure in conjunction with the absence of callose around the megaspore mother cell (Rodkiewicz 1970). All four of the nuclei obtained after meiosis participate in megagametophyte development. The polarity of the reproductive structures before and after meiosis in the angiospermous ovule is an ontogenetic character of the whole ovule and has evolutionary significance (Noher de Halac and Harte 1977).

Unequal divisions are another factor involved in determining megagametophyte morphology that is also related to cytoskeletal peculiarities. Environmental factors may influence polarity. Organelle movement might result from the perception of gravity or light by cells (Rodkiewicz and Bednara 1974; Noher de Halac and Harte 1985). When organelles accumulate at the micropylar side of the MMC, the micropylar cell after cytokinesis will have more organelles (especially plastids with starch) than the other cell (Noher de Halac 1980c). The increased number of organelles, in turn, determines the possibility of a higher metabolic activity, faster growth and differentiation, and competition advantages that lead to divergences in cell differentiation between the resultant daughter cells of a division.

Onagraceae have another peculiarity in their megagametogenesis, and this concerns the final number of cells. The *Oenothera*-type megagametophyte has only four cells instead of the seven of the *Polygonum*-type (Maheswari 1950). The fewer number may be a consequence of the direction of the nutrition-supply in relation to the position of the growing megagametophyte in the ovule since greater growth consumes more energy (Noher de Halac and Harte 1977). Active growth occurs in *Oenothera* megagametophytes exclusively in the pole located near the micropylar nucellar tissue, which is the source of food supply. The opposite end of the megagametophyte is far from the nutrition supply source and remains without nuclei. The lack of antipodes in the mature megagametophytes can be seen as a consequence of the initial position of the functional megaspore nucleus (Noher de Halac and Harte 1977).

In short, megasporogenesis and megagametogenesis demonstrate the following interacting factors that condition the polarity of cell structures:

1. Asynchronous and/or unequal cell divisions.

2. Organelle distribution due to intracytoplasmic movements in relation to nuclear repulsion and cytoskeletal activity.

3. Cell-to-cell interactions through plasmodesmata and localized absence of callose walls.

4. Perception of positional information (e.g. graviperception or light perception and ovular construction).

5. Biochemical gradient established through spatial and temporal nutritional and/or hormonal variations.

6. Genetic constitution or regulation of haploid determining the transcriptional differences.

7. Post-translational differences influenced by the environmental factors.

CONCLUDING REMARKS

The common characters of haploid cells in male and female gametophytes may be evidence for expression of haploid information. These characters provide the genetic information necessary for spore ontogeny, which may be transcribed and translated by means of protein-synthesis before or during the transitional stage between the diploid and the haploid nuclear phases. In both kinds of gametophyte, nuclear vacuoles are present at the end of prophase. The ribosome population of the cytoplasm shows a cycle of loss and gain in number and DMIs are formed, thus suggesting that a new protein-synthesis apparatus belonging to the haploid cell might set in. Callose walls develop in PMCs, MMCs, and later in tetrads by the activity of callose vesicles.

During pollen ontogeny, amylogenesis, amylolysis, and lipogenesis/lipolysis occur from meiosis to the mature pollen stage. Starch grains in amyloplasts of the diploid cytoplasm differ in morphology from those in the cytoplasm of the haploid vegetative cell, thus suggesting the possibility of biochemical differences in the enzyme/substrate specificity. Whether similar events can be described for the development of female gametophytes remains an open question. The time and location of reserves during microgametophyte ontogeny seem to be of evolutionary significance in relation to pollinating agents.

The three apertures of pollen grains in *Oenothera* are initiated at the PMC stage. A cytoplasmic zone is surrounded by parallel endoplasmic reticulum membranes during the meiotic prophase. After the microspore-releasing stage, the apertural chambers are extruded and then completed by apposition of the flattened cytoplasmic vesicles that could contain sporopollenin precursors.

Part of the pollen sporoderm forms inside the callose layer at the tetrad stage. At the moment of microspore release, the sporoderm comprises (a) an ektexine-precursor layer, which may correspond to the pectocellulosic/proteinic primexine and/or to the glycocalyx described by other authors; and (b) the endexine, which looks homogeneously dark with osmium tetraoxide. The mature exine is composed of endexine and a paracrystalline-beaded ektexine. Intine forms at the first mitosis. Shed pollen is without *pollen-kit,* and beaded viscin threads are present. The exine in *Oenothera* has a pattern common to the Onagraceae.

The tapetum is secretory, a character of great taxonomic interest. Its cells have polysaccharidic walls throughout the pollen ontogeny. At the tetrad stage, these cells are binucleate with abundant rough endoplasmic reticulum and loose ribosomes. Later they pass through a transfer phase and show a membrane labyrinth. At the microspore-release phase, some cells of the tapetal layer disintegrate. At the vacuolated pollen state, the plastids of the *in situ* tapetal cells become filled with lipid vesicles and are then reabsorbed after intensive vacuolation; the tapetal-cell remnants are then incorporated in the thecal fluid.

The tapetum probably first produces callase and precursors of sporopollenin for the ektexine accretion and later produces precursors for the transient lipidic materials embedding the exine by the activity of the plastids charged with lipid vesicles. These materials are secreted eccrinely, granulocrinely, and holocrinely at different moments of microspore and pollen ontogeny. The cytoplasm remnants of the diploid tapetal cells thus become incorporated into pollen walls at two stages.

Heterostyly and gametophytic self-incompatibility are present in *Oenothera.* The products of pollen grains and of the stigmatic and stylar tissues responsible for homomorphic gametophytic and heteromorphic incompatibility and the involvement of starch in these processes are partially known. Differences of polysaccharide metabolism among compatible/incompatible pollen tubes are of evolutionary value in *Oenothera.*

The megagametophyte is four-celled as in the rest of the Onagraceae. Peculiarities of megasporogenesis and megagametogenesis in *Oenothera* involve polarity phenomena believed to be related to the construction of the ovule, the nutritional supply to the sporogenous tissues and gametophytes, the callose wall discontinuities, and organelle distribution due to nuclear repulsion and the activity of the cytoskeletal structures.

Acknowledgments and Credit

The authors are grateful to Prof. Dr. Cornelia Harte for advice and for botanical materials, and to Graciela Fama and Lucia Artino for technical assistance. Grants by the CONICET and the CONICOR are thankfully acknowledged.

Table 13.1 is reprinted with permission from *Sexual Plant Reproduction,* Volume 3; copyright 1992 by Springer-Verlag, Heidelberg (Noher de Halac 1992).

LITERATURE CITED

Afzelius, B. M. 1956 Electron-Microscope investigations into exine stratification. *Grana Palynologica* 1:22–37.

Baker, H. G., and I. Baker. 1979. Starch in angiosperm pollen grains and its evolutionary significance. *Am. J. Bot.* 5:591–600.

Beck, E., and P. Ziegler. 1989. Biosynthesis and degradation of starch in higher plants. *Annu. Rev. Plant Physiol. Plant. Mol. Biol.* 40:95–117.

Bednara, J., A. A. M. van Lammeren, and M. T. M. Willemse. 1988. Microtubular configurations during meiosis and megasporogenesis in *Gasteria verrucosa* and *Charaemion angustifolium*. *Sexual Plant Reproduct.* 1:164–172.

Beer, R. A. 1905. On the development of the pollen grain and anther of some Onagraceae. *Beih. Bot. Zbl.* 19:286–313.

Bhandari, N. N. 1984. The microsporangium. In *Embryology of Angiosperms*. Ed. B. M. Johri. New York: Springer Verlag. 53–111.

Bhandari, N. N., and M. Sharma. 1988. Distribution of organelles in the meiocytes during microsporogenesis in *Solanum nigrum* Lin. *Tenth Int. Symp. on Sexual Reproduction in Higher Plants*. Siena University,. 12.

Brennicke, A., S. Moller, and P. A. Blanz. 1985. The 18S and 5S ribosomal RNA genes in Oenothera mitochondria. *Mol. Genet.* 198:404–410.

Brennicke, A., and B. Schwemmle. 1984. Inheritance of mitochondrial DNA in *Oenothera berteriana* and *O. odorata* hybrids. *Z. Naturforsch.* 39:191–192.

Buchen, B., and A. Sievers. 1981. Sporogenesis in plants. In *Cytomorphogenesis in Plants*. Ed. O. Kiermayer. Berlin: Springer Verlag. 401–421.

Clarke, A. E., M. A. Anderson, R. Bernatsky, E. C. Cornish, and S. -L. Mau. 1989. Molecular aspects of self-incompatibility. In *The Molecular Basis of Plant Development*. Ed. R. Goldberg. New York: Alan Liss. 87–98.

Cleland, R. E. 1972. *Oenothera:Cytogenetics and Evolution*. London: Academic Press.

Cresti, M., F. Ciampolini, and R. N. Kapil. 1983. Ultrastructure of S3 S4 genotype pollen grains of *Oenothera organensis*. *Acta Bot. Neerl.* 32:177–183.

Cresti, M., and J. L. van Went. 1976. Callose deposition and plug formation in *Petunia* pollen tubes in situ. *Planta* 133:35–40.

Cruden, R. E., and K. G. Jensen. 1979. Viscin threads pollination efficiency and low pollen-ovule ratios. *Am. J. Bot.* 66:875–879.

DeBoer-de Jeu, M. J. 1978. Megasporogenesis. A comparative study of the ultrastructural aspects of megagametogenesis in *Lilium, Allium* and *Impatiens*. *Meded. Landbouwhogesch. Wageningen.* 78:1–128.

De Nettancourt, D. 1984. Incompatibility. In *Encyclopedia of Plant Physiology*, N. S. Vol. 17, *Cellular Interactions*. Ed. H. F. Linskenes, J. Heslop-Harrison. Berlin: Springer Verlag. 624–639.

Dickinson, H. G. 1981. Cytoplasmic differentiation during microsporogenesis in higher plants. *Acta Soc. Bot. Pol.* 50:3–12.

Dickinson, H G. and L. Andrews. 1977. The role of membrane-bound cytoplasmic inclusions during gametogenesis in *Lilium longiflorum* Thunb. *Planta.* 134:229–240.

Dickinson, H. G., and J. Heslop-Harrison. 1977. Ribosomes, membranes and organelles during meiosis in angiosperms. *Philos. Trans. R. Soc. London Ser. B.* 277:327–342.

Dickinson, H. G., and J. Lawson. 1975. Pollen tube growth in stigma of *Oenothera organensis* following compatible and incompatible intraspecific pollination. *Proc. R. Soc. London Ser. B.* 188:327–344.

Dickinson, H. G., and U. Potter. 1978. Cytoplasmic changes accompanying the female meiosis in *Lilium longiflorum* THUNB. *J. Cell. Sci.* 29:147169.

Diers, L. 1962. Elektronen mikroskopische Beobachtungen an der generativen zelle von *Oenothera Hookeri* Torr et Gray. *Z. Naturforsch.* 18:562–566.

Echlin, P. 1971. The role of the tapetum during microsporogenesis of angiosperms. In

Pollen Development and Physiology. Ed. J. Heslop-Harrison. London: Butterworths. 41–61.

Emerson, S. 1940. Growth of incompatible pollen tubes in *Oenothera organensis. Bot. Gaz.* 101:890–911.

Eschrich, W., and H. B. Currier. 1964. Identification of callose by its diachrome and fluorochrome reactions. *Stain Technol.* 39:303–307.

Franchi, G. G., and E. Pacini. 1988. Pollen polysaccharide reserves in some plants of economic interest. In *Sexual Reproduction in Higher Plants.* Ed. M. Cresti, P. Gori, E. Pacini. Berlin/Heidelberg/New York: Springer Verlag. 473.

Gaude, T., and C. Dumas. 1987. Molecular and cellular events of self-incompatibility. *Int. Rev. Cytol.* 107:333–366.

Guilford, W. J., D. M. Schneider, J. Labovitz, and S. J. Opella. 1988. High resolution solid state ^{13}C NMR spectroscopy of sporopolenins from different plant taxa. *Plant Physiol.* 86:134–136.

Harris, P. J., J. A. Weinhandl, and A. E. Clarke. 1989. Effect on 'in vitro' pollen growth of an isolated style glycoprotein associated with self-incompatibility in *Nicotiana alata. Plant Physiol.* 89:360–367.

Harte, C. 1984. Genetic control of the development of the haploid generation in *Oenothera. Acta Soc. Bot. Pol.* 53:279–295.

Harte, C., and B. Bissinger. 1952. Entwicklungsgeschichtliche Untersuchung der durch die Faktoren fr und ster Bedingten Pollensterilität bei *Oenothera. Z. Induct. Abstamm. Vererbungsl.* 84:251–269.

Harte, C, and R. Sniezko. 1988. Polyembryony in *Oenothera.* In *Sexual Reproduction in Higher Plants.* Ed. M. Cresti, P. Gori, E. Pacini. Berlin/Heidelberg/New York: Springer Verlag. 413–418.

Hedge, B. B., L. Andrade. 1982. Anther development in *Datura:* Distribution of proteins, esterase, and adenosine triphosphatase. *Plant Sci. Lett.* 18:95–101.

Heslop-Harrison, J. 1971a. The cytoplasm and its organelles during meiosis. In *Pollen Development and Physiology.* Ed. J. Heslop-Harrison. London: Butterworths. 16–31.

———. 1971b. The pollen wall: Structure and development. In *Pollen Development and Physiology.* Ed. J. Heslop-Harrison. London: Butterworths. 75–98.

Heslop-Harrison, J. and A. Mackenzie. 1968. Autoradiography of soluble (2 ^{14}C) thymidine derivatives during meiosis and microsporogenesis in *Lilium* anthers. *J. Cell. Sci.* 2:387–400.

Hesse, M. 1981. The fine structure of the exine in relation to the stickiness of angiosperm pollen. *Rev. Palaeobot. Palynol.* 35:81–92.

Johri, B. M., K. B. Ambegaokar, and P. S. Srivastava. 1992. *Comparative Embryology of Angiosperms,* Vol. 1. Heidelberg: Springer-Verlag.

Johri, B. M., and P. S. Rao. 1984. Experimental embryology. In *Embryology of Angiosperms.* Ed. B. M. Johri. New York: Springer Verlag. 735–803.

Kaul, M. L. H. 1987 *Male Sterility.* Berlin/New York: Springer-Verlag.

Keijzer, C. J., M. T. M. Willemse. 1988. Tissue interactions in the developing locule of *Gasteria verrucosa* during microgametogenesis. *Acta Bot. Neerl.* 37:475–492.

Knox, R. B. 1979. *Flower.* McGraw Hill Yearbook (Science and Technology), London, New York: McGraw-Hill Book Co., Inc.

———. 1984. The pollen grain. In *Embryology of Angiosperms.* Ed. B. M. Johri. New York: Springer-Verlag. 197–271.

———. 1987. Pollen differentiation patterns and male function. In *Differentiation Patterns in Higher Plants.* New York: Academic Press. 33–51.

Knox, R. B., and J. Heslop-Harrison. 1970. Direct demonstration of the low permeability of the angiosperm meiotic tetrad using a fluorogenic ester. *Z. Pflanzenphysiol.* 62:451–459.

Kuran, H. 1972. Callose localization in the walls of megasporocytes and megaspores in the course of development of monospore embryosacs. *Acta Soc. Bot. Pol.* 41:509–539.

Lepouse, J., and M. F. Romain. 1967. Etude de l'utrastructure des enveloppes polliniques ches *Oenothera biennis. Pollen et Spores* 9:403–413.

Linskens, H. F. 1988. Present status and future prospects of sexual reproduction research in higher plants. In *Sexual Reproduction in Higher Plants*. Ed. M. Cresti, P. Gori, E. Pacini. Berlin/New York: Springer-Verlag. 451–459.

Maheshwari, P. 1950. *An Introduction to the Embryology of Angiosperms*. New York: McGraw Hill.

Matile, P. H. 1975. *The Lytic Compartment of Plant Cells*. New York: Springer-Verlag.

Nave, E. B., and V. K. Sawhney. 1986. Enzymatic changes in post-meiotic anther development in *Petunia hybrida*. I. Anther ontogeny and isozyme analysis. *J. Plant Physiol.* 125:451–465.

Noher de Halac, I. 1980a. Fine structure of nucellar cells during development of the embryo sac in *Oenothera biennis* L. *Ann. Bot.* 45:515–521.

_____. 1980b. Callose deposition during megagametogenesis in two species of *Oenothera*. *Ann. Bot.* 46:473–477.

_____. 1980c. Expresión génica en las megásporas y durante la megagametogénesis en especies de *Oenothera* (Onagraceae). In *Actas del IV Congress Latinoamer. y X Cong. Arg. Genética*. Buenos Aires: Soc. Arg. Genet. 2:161–169.

_____. 1982. Exine membranes of sterile pollen in *Oenothera hookeri* × *velans*. In 10^h *Int. Congr. Electron Microsc.* Frankfurt am Main: Deutsche Gesellschaft für elektronen Mikroskopie. 3:543–544.

_____. 1985a. Sterility of microspores in *Oenothera hookeri* × *velans*. In *Sexual Reproduction in Seed Plants, Ferns and Mosses*. Ed. M. T. M. Willemse, J. L. van Went. Wageningen: PUDOC. 47–49.

_____. 1985b. Stages of tapetal cell development in sterile anthers of *Oenothera hookeri* × *velans*. in *Sexual Reproduction in Seed Plants, Ferns and Mosses*. Ed. M. T. M. Willemse, J. L. van Went. Wageningen: Pudoc. 50–51.

_____. 1986. Pollen sterility in hybrids and species of *Oenothera*. In *Biotechnology and Ecology of Pollen*. Ed. D. L. Mulcahy, G. Bergamini Mulcahy, E. Ottaviano. New York: Springer-Verlag. 273–282.

Noher de Halac, I., G. Fama and A. Cismondi. 1992. Changes in lipids and polysaccharides during pollen ontogeny in *Oenothera* anthers. *Sex. Plant Rep.* 5:110–116.

Noher de Halac, I., A. Cismondi, and C. Harte. 1990. Pollen ontogenesis in *Oenothera* in genotypically normal anthers compared with the male sterile mutant *sterillis*. *Sex. Plant Rep.* 3:41–53.

Noher de Halac, I., and C. Harte. 1975. Female gametophyte competition in relation to polarization phenomena during megasporogenesis and development of the embryo sac in the genus *Oenothera*. In *Gamete Competition in Plants and Animals*. Ed. D. L. Mulcahy. Amsterdam: North Holland. 43–56.

_____. 1977. Different patterns of callose wall formation during megasporogenesis in two species of *Oenothera* (Onagraceae). *Plant Syst. Evol.* 127:23–28.

_____. 1985. Cell differentiation during megasporogenesis and megagametogenesis. Phytomorphology. 35:189–200.

Pacini, E. and G. G. Franchi. 1988. Amylogenesis and amylolysis during pollen grain development. In *Sexual Reproduction in Higher Plants*. Ed. M. Cresti, P. Gori, E. Pacini. Berlin/Heidelberg/New York: Springer Verlag. 181–186.

Pacini, E., G. G. Franchi, and M. Hesse. 1985. The tapetum: Its form, function and possible phylogeny in Embryophyta. *Plant Syst. Evol.* 149:155–185.

Pacini, E. and B. E. Juniper. 1984. The ultrastructure of pollen grain development in *Lycopersicum peruvianum*. *Caryologia*. 37:21–50.

Palser, B. F., J. L. Rouse, and E. G. Williams. 1989 Coordinated time table for megagametophyte development and pollen tube growth in *Rhododendron nuttalii* from anthesis to early post-fertilization. *Am. J. Bot.* 76:1167–1202.

Pearson, E. 1989. *Organization and Function of the Cytoskeleton in Pollen and Pollen Tubes*. Ph. D. Thesis, Catholic University of Nijmegen.

Raghavan, V. 1984. Protein synthetic activity during normal pollen development and during induced pollen embryogenesis in *Hyoscyamus niger*. *Can. J. Bot.* 62:2493–2513.

Renner, O. 1919. Über Sichtbarwerden der Mendelschen spaltung in Pollen von Oenothera-Bàstarden. Ber. Dtsch. Bot. Ges. 37:129–135.

Reznikova, S. A., and M. T. M. Willemse. 1981. Electron-microscopic and histochemical investigation of tissue of the developing lily anther in connection with metabolism of reserve nutrient substances. Fiziol. Rastenii. 28:1181–1189.

Rodkiewicz, B. 1970. Callose in cell walls during megasporogenesis in angiosperms. Planta 93:39–47.

———. 1976. Cytoplasm restructuring, isolation and polarization in meiocytes during megasporogenesis in angiosperms. Postepy Biol. Komorki 5:135–154.

Rodkiewicz, B., and J. Bednara. 1974. Distribution of organelles and starch grains during megasporogenesis in Epilobium. In Fertilization in Higher Plants. Ed. H. F. Linskens. Amsterdam: North Holland. 89–95.

Rodkiewicz, B., E. Duola, and K. Kudlicka. 1988. Organelle aggregations during microsporogenesis in Stangeria, Nymphaca, and Malva. In Sexual Reproduction in Higher Plants. Ed. M. Cresti et al. Berlin/Heidelberg/New York: Springer-Verlag 170–180. 1988. Visualization of microfilaments in cytoplasm and spindles of meiocytes, microspores and pollen of Gasteria verrucosa. In Sexual Reproduction in Higher Plants. Ed. M. Cresti, P. Gori, E. Pacini. Berlin/New York: Springer-Verlag. 476.

Rodkiewicz, B., and H. Kuran. 1971. The specificity of callose distribution in cell walls during megasporogenesis in Onagraceae, Caryophyllaceae and Scrophulariaceae. Ann. Univ. A. R. E. R. S. (Reims) 9:31–35.

Rodkiewicz, B., and R. Sniezko. 1978. Differentiation of functional megaspore in Onagraceae. Bull. Soc. Bot. Fr. Actualites Bot. 1–2:163–166.

Rowley, J R. 1971. Resolution of channels in the exine by translocation of colloidal iron. 29th Annu. Proc. Electron Microscopy. Soc. Amer., Ed. C. J. Arcenaux. Boston.

Rowley, J. R., A. O. Dahl, B. Walles and K. L. Huynti. 1983. Viscin threads considered as connective structures between pollen grains and tapetal cells. In Fertilization and Embryogenesis in Ovulated Plants. Ed. O. Erdelska. Bratislava, Czech.: Veda. 89–92.

Rowley, J. R., and J. J. Skvarla. 1974. Plasma membrane-glycocalyx origin of ubisch body wall. Pollen et Spores 16:442–448.

Rutishauser, A. 1969. Embriologie und Fortpflanzungsbiologie der Angiospermen. Berlin, Heidelberg: Springer-Verlag.

Sawhney, V. K. and E. B. Nave. 1986. Enzymatic change in post-meiotic anther development in Petunia hybrida II. Histochemical localization of esterase, peroxidase, malate and alcohol dehydrogenase. J. Plant Physiol. 125:467–473.

Schuster, W., and A. Brennicke. 1985. Termination codon in the apocytochrome b gene from Oenothera mitochondria. Curr. Genet. 9:157–163.

Sitte, P. 1981. Role of lipid self-assembly in subcellular morphogenesis. In Cell Biology Monographs, Vol. 8. Cytomorphogenesis in Plants. Ed. O. Kiermayer. New York: Springer-Verlag. 401–421.

Skvarla, J. J., P. H. Raven, W. F. Chissoe, and M. Sharp. 1978. An ultrastructural study of viscin threads in Onagracean pollen. Pollen et Spores 20:5–143.

Skvarla, J. J., P. H. Raven, and J. Praglowski. 1975. The evolution of pollen tetrads in Onagraceae. Am. J. Bot. 62:6–35.

Skvarla, J. J., P. H. Raven, and J. Praglowski. 1976. Ultrastructural survey of Onagraceae pollen. In The Evolutionary Significance of the Exine. Ed. I. K. Ferguson, J. Muller. London: Linnean Soc. 447–479.

Sniezko, R, and C. Harte. 1984a. Polarity and competition between megaspores in the ovule of Oenothera hybrids. Plant Syst. Evol. 144:83–97.

———. 1984b. Callose pattern and polarization phenomena in the ovules of hybrids between Oenothera hookeri and Oenothera suaveolens. Plant Syst. Evol. 147:79–90.

_____ . 1986. Development of polarity in the ovules of the F2-progeny of the Oenothera-hybrids *albicans-haplo-hookeri*. *Plant Syst. Evol.* 154:89–101.

Stanley, R. G., and H. F. Linskens. 1985. *Pollen Biologie Biochemie, Gewinnung und Verwendung. Amersee: Urs Freund Verlag.*

Van Lammeren, A. A. M., J. Bednara, and M. T. M. Willemse. 1988. Visualization of microfilaments in cytoplasm and spindles of meiocytes, microspores and pollen of *Gasteria verrucosa*. In *Sexual Reproduction in Higher Plants.* Ed. M. Cresti, P. Gori, E. Pacini. Berlin/New York: Springer-Verlag.

Van Lammeren, A. A. M., J. Bednara, and M. T. M. Willemse. 1989. Organization of the actin cytoskeleton during pollen development in *Gasteria verrucosa* (Mill.) H. Duval visualized with rhodamine-phalloidin. *Planta* 178:531–539.

Van Went, S. L., and M. T. M. Willemse. 1984. Fertilization. In *Embryology of Angiosperms.* Ed. B. M. Johri. New York: Springer-Verlag. 273–317.

Wanger, V. T., Y. Song, E. Matthys-Rochon, and C. Dumas. 1988. The isolated embryosac of *Zea mays:* Structural and ultrastructural observations. In *Sexual Reproduction in Higher Plants.* Ed. M. Cresti, P. Gori, E. Pacini. Berlin/New York: Springer-Verlag. 125–131.

Willemse, M. T. M., and M. A. W. Fransen-Verheisen. 1978. Cell organelles changes during megasporogenesis and megagametogenesis in *Gasteria verrucosa* (Mill.) H. Duval. *Bull. Soc. Bot. Fr.* 125:187–191.

Willemse, M. T. M., and A. A. M. van Lammeren. 1988. Structure and function of the microtubular cytoskeleton during megasporogenesis and embryo sac development in *Gasteria verrucosa* (Mill). H. Duval. *Sexual Plant Rep.* 1:74–82.

Chapter 14

The Angiosperm Embryo: Correlative Controls in Development, Differentiation, and Maturation

K. V. KRISHNAMURTHY

The embryo is the miniature sporophyte that is produced as the end-product of zygotic ontogeny in the seed. *In vivo* and *in vitro* experimental studies on the embryo of flowering plants have long been in progress, and with inputs from disciplines such as morphology, anatomy, genetics, biochemistry, cytology, histochemistry, ultrastructure, etc. the subject of the angiosperm embryo has now attained a fascinating facelift. The seemingly simple process of embryogenesis has turned out to be very complex and full of exciting problems (Evenari 1984). The zygote does not hold the exclusive patent to produce the future sporophyte, as the latter can be raised virtually from any living cell of the plant under suitable artificial culture conditions. Information drawn from studies on embryoids, the embryolike structures developed from such cultures and equated to "facsimiles" of embryos (Raghavan 1986), has also been used to interpret zygotic embryogeny whenever and wherever possible.

The zygote is the starting point for the development of the embryo; the process involved therein is termed *embryogenesis*. Embryogenesis involves an array of developmental episodes that occur in an ordered sequence and result finally in the mature embryo in which the structural and functional organization of the adult plant becomes imprinted. Development entails the interplay of a series of integrated and ontogenetically coordinated factors. Cell multiplication is progressively associated with the origin of new localized centers of growth, which, in turn, cause development of specific parts and organs of the embryo. Although a number of morphologically distinguishable contours such as the filamentous, globular, heart-shaped, torpedo, and mature embryos, form at different stages of embryo development, the entire gamut of events is to be looked upon as a continuous process in which any given stage is intimately related to the previous stage as well as to the stage that follows. This relationship is not to be conceived in terms of cell lineage and tier systems, but in terms of groups of cells that are specifically positioned in the multiplying mass of cells. During successive developmental stages, different chemical and structural components are fabricated and the cells organized into patterns distinctive of the different histogenic regions of the embryo.

During embryogenesis, physiological and biochemical factors intermingle with genetic controls. Their interaction is highly complicated and involves mechanisms not yet clearly delineated. The zygote and its products possess an internal environment of their own, which again interacts with the external environment present in the embryo sac/endosperm. The *modus operandi* of these factors is not yet clear (see also Johri et al. 1992; Srivastava and Johri 1992a).

In the following account on angiosperm embryogeny, routine information regarding the types of embryos and their developmental pathways has been deliberately omitted. Those interested may refer to Natesh & Rau (1984) and Raghavan (1968) and the literature cited therein.

TRANSFORMATION OF EGG INTO ZYGOTE

Cytological and Size Changes

The zygote is the fusion product of one of the male gametes carried by the pollen tube and the egg cell (Figure 14.1). The egg cell, comparatively poor in cytoplasmic organization and fairly quiescent metabolically prior to syngamy, undergoes sudden transformations, once fertilization has been effected. Many properties of the egg change during the first few hours. What mechanism triggers the egg cell to develop an embryo? It cannot be the fertilization alone, through which information is transmitted to the egg nucleus by the sperm nucleus, although in normal embryogeny fertilization seems to be the triggering mechanism. It must be something coupled to fertilization but also present independently; otherwise, there would be no case of apomictic embryos. Likewise, the trigger cannot be exclusively pollination (Evenari 1984). Much information is needed on this aspect.

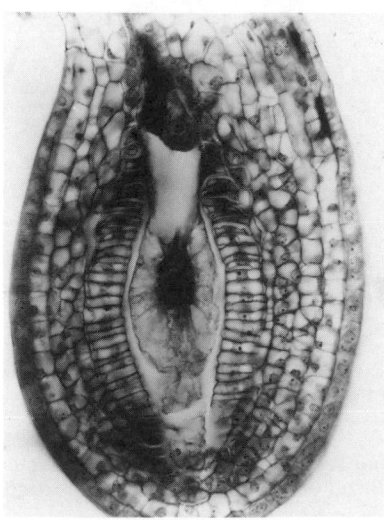

Figure 14.1. Lateral section of ovule of *Downingia bacigalupii* immediately after fertilization showing the zygote, darkly colored pollen tube, and the primary endosperm nucleus (after Kaplan 1969).

Dramatic changes occur in the number and postion of organelles of the egg when it becomes a zygote: these include regrouping and increase in the quantum of the endoplasmic reticulum; increase in starch grains in plastids; elaboration of additional cristae in mitochondria; generation of new populations of ribosomes and polysomes; and increase in dictyosome activity. All organelles clump around the nucleus, which itself shifts toward the chalazal pole, if it is not already there (Figure 14.2). The most notable change, however, is the formation of a wall around the egg (within 36–50 hr, depending on the species), which was devoid of a wall at its chalazal end prior to fertilization (details in Natesh and Rau 1984).

The size of the egg changes immediately after fertilization in some species. In cotton, within 8–10 hr after fertilization, the zygote decreases nearly to one half of its original size; shrinkage has also been noticed in some other taxa but is not as striking as in cotton (Pollock and Jensen 1964; Jensen 1968; Schulz and Jensen 1968a; Ashley 1972; Mogensen and Suthar 1979; Sehgal and Gifford 1979). Shrinkage is apparently characteristic of most zygotes that are to proceed with normal development. In a comparative ultrastructural study of normal and hybrid zygotes of *Hibiscus* species, Ashley (1972) reported that a pronounced shrinkage of the zygote coupled with cytological reorganization occurred only in the normal zygotes of selfed cases, whereas the hybrid zygotes, which do not give rise to embryos, hardly underwent shrinkage or cytological changes.

According to Jensen (1968), zygotic shrinkage is related to the osmotic gradient caused by the initial rapid growth of the endosperm (the central cell of the prefertilization embryo sac) that would cause water to move from the vacuole of the zygote to the endosperm. This growth results in the creation of a sudden disequilibrium between the zygote and the endosperm cavity around it. Ryczkowski (1960, 1971) indicated that the

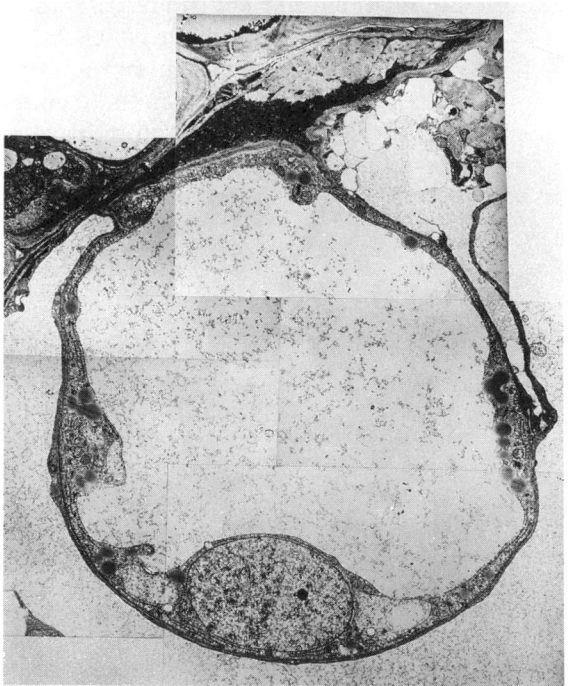

Figure 14.2. Electron micrograph of the longitudinal section of the zygote in *Quercus*. The zygote nucleus is positioned at the extreme chalazal end with most organelles associated with it (courtesy of Mogensen).

vacuole of the central cell/endosperm chamber constitutes an important reservoir of sugars, amino acids, and inorganic salts and that their concentrations in the chalazal and micropylar poles are totally different, thus establishing a physicochemical gradient with different pHs at different regions. This gradient appears to be different in the prefertilization stage, immediately after fertilization, and considerably after fertilization. Naturally, this difference in gradient will affect the osmoticum of the egg cell/zygote and embryo. In other words, the chalazal and micropylar regions of the central cell/endosperm have different "topophysic effects" (positional effects), in the sense of Evenari (1984). Its importance was stressed by Wardlaw (1955), who recognized different morphogenetic fields in the "embryo sac" (Figure 14.3).

Other possible factors that may be involved in zygotic shrinkage include: (a) the absence of a wall at the chalazal end of the egg, its development immediately after fertilization, and the consequent influence on the osmotic equilibrium between the zygote and its surroundings; (b) the sudden change from haploidy to diploidy and the possible impact of the incorporation of a male genome into the egg cell, thus changing its genome; and (c) the ultrastructural changes in the zygote such as those observed in the tubular endoplasmic reticulum in cotton.

Shrinkage is only a momentary phenomenon, however, and it is soon overcome by the zygote enlargement prior to the first division.

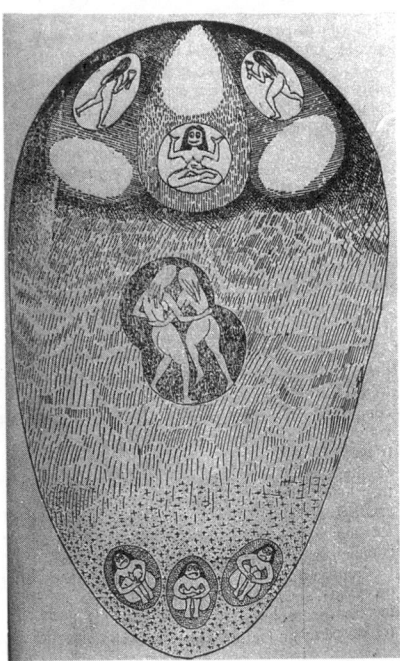

Figure 14.3. Mature angiospermous embryo sac. The difference in the morphogenetic fields in its different regions is shown (courtesy of Swamy).

Synthetic Abilities of the Zygote

Like the egg, the zygote (the young embryo as well) needs inputs from its immediate surroundings. Does the zygote have sufficient machinery of its own to synthesize its basic needs—proteins for example? Opinions differ. Many believe that the first proteins synthesized by the zygots are coded by the stores of mRNAs bequeathed from the egg cell. This scenario means that no RNA is synthesized by the zygote immediately after fertilization, and whatever mRNA is involved in the vigorous synthesis of proteins in the zygote is a leftover form the egg. This concept of involvement of residual mRNA of the egg in the protein synthesis of the zygote has been borrowed from animal embryology (Raghavan 1986). The proof for this viewpoint comes from instances in which egg cells parthenogenetically develop into embryos that obviously carry out the protein-synthesizing processes involved in zygote ontogeny.

The active synthetic ability of the zygote has also been reported, however. Studies on cotton indicate the formation of a new population of ribosomes in the cytoplasm of the egg immediately after fertilization (Jensen 1964, 1968). In tomato (Kadej and Kadej 1981), the ribosomal system of the egg is reported to undergo dissolution and a new population to rise at a distance from the zygote nucleus. During this period, the cytoplasm shows a sharp increase in the RNA-positive staining intensity. These features are interpreted as indications of active mRNA synthesis in the zygote. Similarly, the egg of *Nicotiana rustica* possesses two strongly RNA-positive bodies that increase in number after fertilization and that have been suggested to play an important role in the synthesis of key enzymes during early development of the proembryo (Sehgal & Gifford 1979).

Given these contradictions, it is likely that zygotes of some species synthesize proteins with newly formed mRNA and some with the help of the mRNA population bequeather from the egg cell. This area warrants further research.

Zygote Dormancy

Although in the majority of flowering plants the zygote is reported to embark on division immediately after syngamy, in some instances the zygote experiences a period of rest during the interval between fertilization and first division. This period may range from a few hours to several months. For example, in the *Nicotiana* species, dormancy may be prolonged for seven days whereas in species of *Pistacia* it may last from a few weeks to several months (Grundwag 1976).

Why some zygotes remain dormant for a variable duration and others divide more or less immediately after fertilization is unclear (Evenari 1984). The dormancy may be due to a delayed fusion of male and female nuclei after entry of the former into the egg cell cytoplasm. Because the male nucleus is considerably smaller than the female, it may not be evident in sections that pass through the center of the egg nucleus, thus leading to an erroneous assumption that what is being examined is a zygote nucleus. The occurrence of two nuclei, one larger and one smaller (male nucleus), in the "zygotes" of many ovules of *Pistacia* species (Grundwag 1976) supports this possibility. "Zygote" dormancy due to delayed fusion of male and female nuclei is evident also in some interspecific crosses of *Triticum* (Boyes & Thompson 1937).

Growth regulators apparently are not involved in zygote dormancy. Attempts to break zygote dormancy by growing ovules on media with various concentrations of growth regulators failed; likewise, the spraying or injecting of developing fruits with growth regulators was not successful (Grundwag 1976). The post-fertilization enclosure of the zygote with an intact wall all around is perhaps another factor that has a bearing on zygote dormancy. Since the zygote has a genetic makeup different from that of the surrounding cells, insulation and isolation form a prerequisite for its embarking on cell division, the failure of which is likely to result in zygote dormancy. In fact, in several species of *Rhododendron* and *Ledum groenlandicum* (Ericaceae), a callose wall is reported to be laid down around the zygote during the first two days after fertilization (Williams et al. 1984). The insulation of the newly formed zygote by the callose wall from the influence of neighboring cells of a different genotype probably carries significance in the subsequent induction of sporophytic development (i.e. formation of the embryo). Callose is known to be an excellent insulating agent in the meiocytes of plants in general and angiosperms in particular (Heslop-Harrison 1964; Krishnamurthy 1977). It is worth investigating within angiosperms whether the wall being laid down immediately after syngamy in the zygote also contains callose. An analogous situation exists in the development of embryoids from single cells under *in vitro* conditions. The embryoids are initiated from single cells that are physically isolated from other cells by a very thick wall (callose?) Although it has been doubted "whether physical isolation of the cell (by a very thick wall) is essential for embryogenesis" in culture conditions (Raghavan 1976), it is apparently important, since such an isolation also appears to occur in the true zygote. The failure of all changes hitherto described that take place in the egg cell immediately after fertilization may also singly and collectively affect zygote dormancy.

Polarity of Zygote and Embryo

One of the characteristic features of the sexually formed zygote and the subsequent embryo is polarity. Although the basic polarity of the zygote is inherited from the precursor egg cell, syngamy has further accentuated this basic polarity. Several cellular and subcellular features of the egg point to its polarized nature, and most of these have been discussed in detail (see Raghavan 1986).

The polarity of the egg and zygote is largely due to the polar electric gradients that already exist in the embryo sac, which were formed during meagasporogenesis and gametogenesis (details in Swamy 1974; Swamy and Krishnamurthy 1975a). Wardlaw (1955) postulated that differences exist in the physiological conditions of the micropylar and chalazal ends and the other regions of the embryo sac, and that these conditions influence the behavior of the constituent cells of the embryo sac positioned in different regions. In other words, the cells of the egg apparatus are subjected to a different morphogenetic field and influence when compared to the antipodals or polar nuclei (Figure 14.3). Such an effect was later designated by Evenari (1984) as the *topophysic effect*.

Only the zygote derived from the egg, and in occasional instances from the fertilized synergid, and that is subjected to the topophysic effect of the micropylar pole of the embryo sac, possesses polarized gradients; the embryos derived from this zygote retain their polarity throughout their develpment. Embryo initials such as the antipodals, nucellar cells, and integumentary cells that are subjected to a different topophysic effect (i.e. located in fields other than the micropylar pole) are not polarized from the beginning and the embryos derived from them are also not polarized structures. In these embryos, polarity is established at very late stages of development. The absence of polarity in these embryos in earlier stages of ontogeny is reflected not only in the planes and patterns of cell division but also in histogenic differentiation (Figure 14.4).

The evidence for the polarized nature of the sexually formed zygote is shown in its first division. The location of the first division spindle, its orientation with reference to the long axis of the zygote, and the ensuing wall coincide with the patternized distribution gradients of metabolites and organelles within the zygote. The first division products are unequal cells, because the zygotic division is asymmetric. As is well known, asymmetric divisions, wherever they occur, are the reflections of the strongly polarized nature of the dividing cells. The first division of the zygote is also significant, as in other asymmetrically dividing cells, in that the destinies of the two resultant daughter cells are different. Unequal partitioning of the zygotic cytoplasm probably elicits different modes of nuclear expression of the two resultant cells in the subsequent stages of development (see also Lyndon 1990).

Polar forces are maintained even during subsequent stages of embryogeny. This polarity becomes manifest in the globular embryo by the organization of the hypophysis at the root pole and the epiphysis at the shoot pole with the intervening part forming the embryo axis (Figure 14.4). The hypophysis and epiphysis become organized almost simultaneously and become distinctive from other cells of the globular embryo by their distinctive staining reactions and histochemical characteristics. Embryos developing from initials other than those located in the micropylar pole of the embryo sac [nucellar, integumentary, and antipodal(?) embryos], and embryoids that develop *in vitro,* do not show the differentiation of hypophysis and epiphysis and lack a polarized development (Swamy & Krishnamurthy 1981) (Figure 14.4).

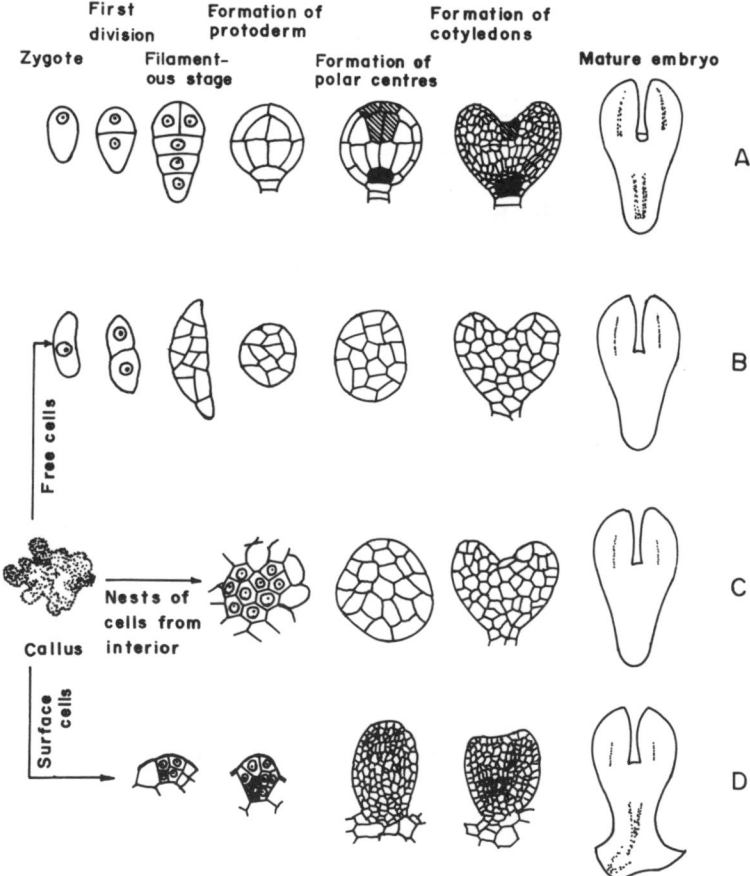

Figure 14.4.   The development of a typical, sexually produced dicotyledon embryo (A) and embryoids (B,C,D). (A) shows an organized, polarized development and the differentiation of hypophysis and epiphysis at opposite poles even at the globular stage. (B,C,D) shows an unorganized development until maturity of the embryo, no differentiation of hypophysis and epiphysis, and no early differentiation of protoderm (after Swamy and Krishnamurthy 1981).

CELL DIVISION, TECTONICS, AND CONTOUR CHANGES DURING EMBRYOGENY

Cell Division and Cell Enlargement

Wardlaw (1955) considered the zygote (and its products) as a complex, specific, diffusion reaction system that functions in conformity with the laws of physical chemistry and mathematics. It is also a gene-determined reaction system operating under the sustaining environmental conditions prevailing at the micropylar milieu of the embryo sac/endosperm. Therefore, the chains of reactions involved in it are collectively determined by its genome after interaction with the prevailing environmental milieu.

As mentioned above, the first division of the zygote is transverse and asymmetric in nearly all angiosperms so far studied. The position of the nucleus in the zygote foreshadows the disparity in volume of the two daughter cells formed. In all cases, the terminal cell is smaller than the basal one (see discussion in Sivaramakrishna 1978). The embryo is formed by subsequent divisions of these two cells. There is considerable variation in the extent of the respective contributions of the two cells to the embryo, however, on the basis of which five major types and many subtypes of embryogeny are recognized (see Johansen 1950; Crété 1963).

The outstanding feature of zygotic embryogeny is the orderly and almost predetermined sequence of cell divisions noticed. All such divisions strictly obey the physical laws that govern cell division in general. The most important of these are (a) Sachs' law that new walls intersect the old ones at right angles; (b) Sachs' law of equal masses in the daughter cells (barring asymmetric divisions); and (c) Errera'slaw that the new wall after karyokinesis is formed along the minimal area of the mother cell (D'Arcy Thompson 1942).

Cell divisions leading to embryoids in vitro as well as to embryos that develop in "fields" other than that of the micropylar milieu of the embryo sac do not obey the physical laws mentioned above and "discourage geometrical or mathematical analysis" (Steward 1958). This behavior is essentially due to the absence of forces that cause a polarizing gradient in the initiating cells, which are not kept in equilibrium with the neighboring cells and their immediate milieu (Swamy & Krishnamurthy 1981).

What is the relative contribution of cell division and cell enlargement to the organization of the mature embryo? At which stage of embryo development does one or the other relatively preponderate? It is generally assumed, but without much evidence, that cell division predominates during the early stages of embryogenesis and that cell enlargement prevails during the later period. In a few instances, cell multiplication has been assumed merely on the basis of the smaller size of the cells of older embryo without actually observing mitotic figures. Cell size has to be taken into account correlatively with the rate of increase in the size of the embryo during development. The embryo after the globular stage as a whole enlarges slowly, may not enlarge at all, or may even become smaller, especially between the late globular and mature stages.

In the embryo of cotton, Pollock and Jensen (1964) recorded progressively declining cell size in the embryo until about 100 cells were formed; at this stage the average cell size was about 1/20 of that of the zygote. Subsequently, the cell size was almost constant until about 1000 cells had been formed. Beyond that, cell size underwent further reduction by half. A similar condition exists in Capsella (Schulz and Jensen 1968b) and Quercus (Singh and Mogensen 1975).

In *Capsella* and cotton, the increase in cell number was found to be interrupted by a lag during cotyledon initiation, resulting in the formation of a sigmoid curve for cell number from zygote to globular embryo and another sigmoidal curve from heart-shaped to mature embryo (Pollock and Jensen 1964). Although cell number increased exponentially up to the formation of 40 cells in *Hordeum vulgare, Oryza sativa,* and wheat, rhythmic variations in cell numbers were observed subsequently (Nagato 1978). In *Glycine max,* cell increase was intense up to the initiation of the cotyledon, subsequent to which cell enlargement was predominant (Meinke et al. 1981).

These few studies point not only to the variations that are likely to be associated with the taxa studied but also to the need for further intensive studies with advanced techniques. Again the whole embryo has been taken into consideration without focusing attention on the different histogenic regions of the embryo that are blocked out as early as the globular stage. The degree of cell division and cell enlargement probably varies appreciably in different histogenic regions of the embryo. A similar statement can be made for cell doubling time: e.g. it is 20–22 hr in cotton (Pollock and Jensen 1964); 8–19.2 hr in wheat (Bennett et al. 1973); 9.2–12.9 hr in barley; 15.7–22.7 hr in *Secale cereale* (Forster and Dale 1983); and 42 hr in carrot (Gray et al. 1984). The mitotic cycle duration is already known to be different in the quiescent center of the root meristem (Clowes 1971), which is ontogenetically traceable and histologically similar to the hypophysis (Swamy & Krishnamurthy 1975b) of the globular embryo. The same holds true for the epiphysis and its product, the shoot apex, in the embryo (Swamy & Krishnamurthy 1977). Therefore, no generalizations can be made with reference to the cell doubling time of the embryo without specifying the histogenic region to which the data belong; an average value for the whole embryo would be misleading.

Is Cell Lineage Important in Embryogenesis?

The zygote divides by a transverse wall to form a basal cell and an apical cell. Of these, the apical cell engenders the embryo proper through a series of cell divisions. A number of embryologists believe that these cell divisions proceed in such an "orderly manner" that it is almost possible to predict, at each stage of embryogenesis of a given species, how and where the next divisions will take place. Such a belief, for example, enabled Souèges (1937) to establish his "Laws of Embryonomy," which were followed faithfully by many subsequent investigators. This classical approach, often called the "Cell Lineage Concept" or "Mosaic Theory" (Street 1976), has been spelled out by Johansen (1950), who states:

> In order to elucidate the laws of embryonomy with utmost precision and clarity and in as complete a manner as possible, the employment of formulae has become necessary. These formulae indicate precisely the relationships, which the individual cells present to one another during the course of their segmentations, with respect to their origin, to their number, to their disposition and to their eventual destination or their histogenic function. . . . Each and every cell has a reason for its existence, its origin can be demonstrated, its destination determined, and its position is invariably the same. A superfluous cell would seriously upset the harmonious balance.

Therefore, according to the cell lineage concept (a) great significance is to be attached to the order and planes of divisions in the young embryo; (b) during these divisions, the individual cells of the embryo inherit different cytoplasmic potentialities from different parts of the zygote; and (c) these differences determine the exact role they and their daughter cells play in organizing the embryo and its parts.

The cell lineage concept gained great support for many years and contributed much to the recognition of the major types of embryogenesis and the variations under each type (Johansen 1950). As a consequence, many embryologists tended to assess the type of embryo development from the first few divisions of the zygote and to allocate the ontogeny into one of the recognized types without looking beyond the globular stage (Philip 1972; see also Chapter 15).

The concept of cell lineage and its fixity has been questioned in recent years. It is questioned whether a reliable system of classifying angiosperm embryo ontogeny can be formulated on the basis of successive steps in the division of the zygote and a dogmatic emphasis on the destination of the cells formed. Even within the same taxon, distinct variations were observed in the early ontogeny of the embryo and cell lineages (Philip 1972; Periasamy 1977; Raghavan 1986). The "Regulative Theory of Embryo Organization" (in contrast to the Mosaic Theory), proposed by those who worked on somatic embryogenesis (see Street 1976), postulates that the segmentation patterns observed during early embryogeny are controlled solely by physical factors such as surface tensions (Berthhold 1886; D'Arcy Thompson 1942) and have no phylogenetic and taxonomic significance. It further emphasizes that during early development of the embryo, its constituent cells do not inherit distinct and specific cytoplasmic potentialities but remain undetermined and uncommitted. An embryogenetic "field" may exist in combination with a position effect, i.e. a given cell acts in the embryo in relation to the surrounding cells (Jensen 1974). In other words, it is not the cell or cell group itself that determines the future histogenetic region of the embryo it gives rise to, but the position that the cell or cell group occupies [the so-called "positional information" or "Wolpert model" (Wolpert 1970, 1971, 1981)] in the developing young embryo. Therefore, according to this school, allocation of parts of the mature embryo to initials at the 8–16 celled stage of the proembryo appears to be based on topographical correspondence of the initials with the parts of the mature embryo, rather than on the actual proof of derivation of parts from the initials. Angiosperm embryogeny should therefore not be looked upon as adhering to laws concerned with parsimony, origin, numbers, disposition, and destination of cells segmented by the zygote and the proembryo.

Studies made on embryoids that develop *in vitro* and on nonzygotic embryos that develop inside the ovules reveal that the same final product (mature embryo/embryoid) can be obtained by altogether different pathways and cell lineages. *In vivo* and *in vitro* sequences of the same taxon can create different cell lineages with developmental programs that result in identical structures (see also Raghavan and Srivastava 1982). This result reinforces the notion that the endproduct rather than the means of acheivement is of greater importance.

Symmetry Changes in the Embryo

The dicot embryo experiences three distinct morphological phases during its ontogeny—the filamentous, globular, and cordate phases. The filamentous phase results from the variable number of transverse divisions in the zygote. The globular phase is initiated by two successive, vertical divisions at right angles to one another in one, two, or (rarely) more of the outermost cells of the filamentous proembryo (Periasamy 1977). The globular embryo comprises a variable number of cells, depending upon the plant, but in all cases it culminates in the initiation of the epiphysis at the shoot pole and the hypophysis at the root pole. The differentiation of these two poles is a very important morphogenetic step because the further orderly development of the embryo depends on whether these two poles are formed (Swamy and Krishnamurthy 1975b, 1977). In the absence of the differentiation of epiphysis and hypophysis, no transition from globular to the cordate embryo takes place. If epiphysis does not differentiate, the cotyledons do not develop. For example, Caruso (1968) reported that the globular embryo does not prepare itself for the transition to the heart-shaped stage and does not have a normal shoot apex (i.e., epiphysis) in the reduced mutant tomato (Figure 14.5 A–D). The epiphysis becomes the quiescent part of the shoot apical meristem whereas the hypophysis forms the quiescent center of the root apical meristem. The globular embryo then switches over to the heart-shaped through the initiation of two lateral cotyledonary primordia from the embryonal axis nearer the epiphysis.

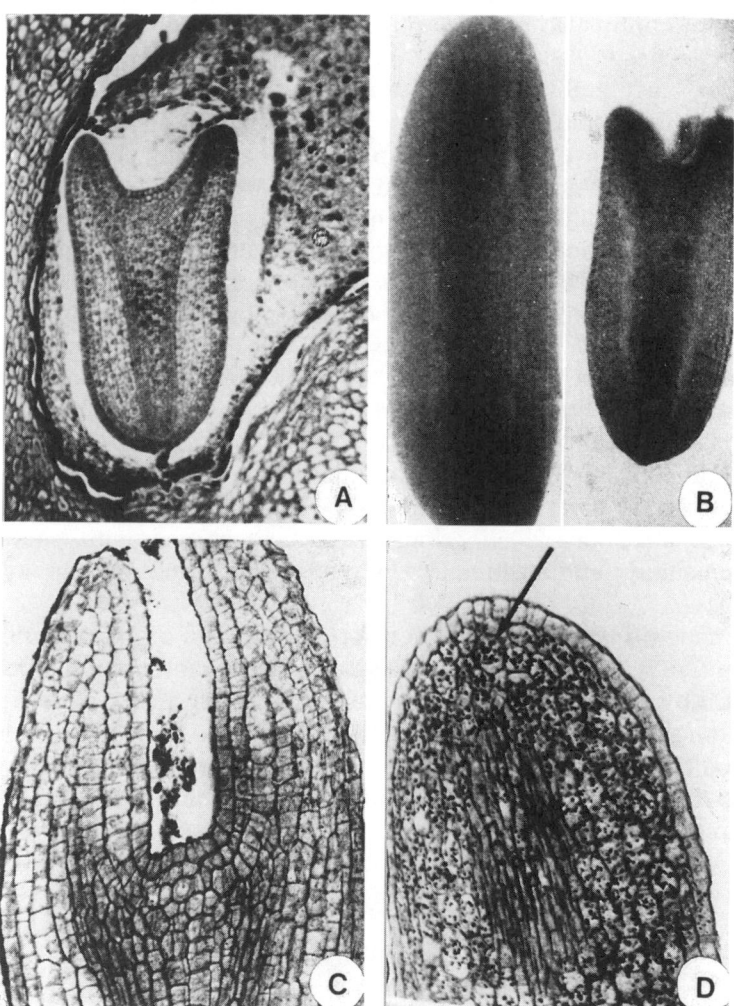

Figure 14.5. Normal and mutant embryos of tomato. (A) Median lateral section of normal torpedo stage embryo. (B) Whole mutant embryos of equal age, one without cotyledons and the other with cotyledons. (C) Longitudinal section of normal embryo with cotyledons and embryonic shoot apex. (D) Longitudinal section of mutant embryo without cotyledons and an organized shoot apex. *Arrow* shows starch grains in the apical cells of the shoot (after Caruso 1968).

Despite the ontogenetic similarity between the dicot and monocot embryos up to the octant stage, the form of the mature embryo is distinctly dissimilar in the two classes. Therefore, in monocotyledons, the filamentous and globular stages occur, but later the embryo assumes a different contour (not cordate) due to the formation of only one cotyledon.

All three morphological phases of embryogeny also involve conspicuous changes in symmetry. From the filamentous phase to the globular phase, the embryo becomes typically radially symmetrical, but this symmetry is lost in the next phase. In dicots, the radial symmetry of the globular embryo is changed into bilateral symmetry due to the initiation of two cotyledons, whereas in monocots symmetry is unilateral due to the initiation of only one cotyledon.

Only two explanations are possible for the orderly development of the embryo and the regular transitions in the symmetry of the embryo during its ontogeny. Either the embryo itself exerts self regulation or the control emanates from the surrounding milieu, especially the endosperm. Although we cannot totally disregard the first possibility, there appears to be more evidence for the second (Krishnamurthy 1988).

Endosperm failure invariably results in the arrest of embryo development (Srivastava and Johri 1992b). The literature demonstrates a close correlation between the stage of endosperm development and the stage of embryo development. At various crucial stages of embryogeny, specific physiological and morphological changes also seem to occur in the endosperm. The morphological changes are not clearly distinguishable in the cellular endosperm but in many nuclear and helobial endosperms at least three (slightly overlapping) morphological phases occur: the free nuclear phase; the cell wall formation phase; and the phase in which the storage products are deposited. The embryo shows distinct changes in symmetry corresponding to these phases. During the free nuclear endospermic phase, the development of the globular embryo phase is completed. At the time of initiation of wall formation in the nuclear endosperm, the hypophysis and epiphysis are differentiated and the cotyledonary primordia initiated in the embryo. When the storage products are deposited in the endosperm, a rapid development of cotyledon(s) occurs.

Endosperm and embryo development, in at least a few cases of seed failure, has brought to light the importance of the stage of cell wall formation in the nuclear endosperm in bringing about transition from the globular to heart-shaped phase of the embryo. If cell-wall formation is either absent or delayed in the nuclear endosperm of these abnormal cases, a corresponding absence or delay appears in the transition of the embryo from radial to bilateral (or unilateral) symmetry. As long as the endosperm does not become cellular, the globular embryo remains globular with or without an addition of cells. A good example of this was seen in *Argemone mexicana* treated with colchicine (Chopra and Rai 1958). The ontogeny of the embryo was normal until the globular stage, but instead of attaining the pre-heart shape, it increased in size without any differentiation until it was almost twice the size of the control embryos, after which the enlargement stoppped. The endosperm in this case never became cellular. In some *Citrus* crosses (Esen and Soost 1973), the triploid embryos never differentiate into a plumule-radicle axis with two cotyledons, but the globular embryos proliferate diversely due to continued mitotic activity. The endosperm, without becoming cellular, degernerates very early.

A careful perusal of the literature concerning the *in vitro* culture of zygotes, proembryos, and older embryos reveals that: (a) transitions from filamentous to globular and from globular to heart-shaped stages are possible only if the constituents of the culture medium are changed quantitatively, qualitatively, or both; (b) the younger the embryos, the more they lack biosynsthetic capacities; (c) the nutritional/regulatory requirements (including the proper osmoticum) of the zygote and proembryo are more exact than those of older embryos and, (d) the optimum conditions for in vitro growth of zygotes and proembryos imitate closely the composition of the environmental milieu of the embryo sac/endosperm at the corresponding stage of development.

An attempt has not yet been made to study the various embryological phenomena within the flower in a correlative manner. Endosperm development has been studied independently of embryo ontogeny, and a stagewise correlation of the events in the two structures has never been attempted. The histochemical and ultrastructural changes that take place at various stages of endosperm development need to be studied in collaboration with similar studies on the embryo. Such studies may reveal that changes in endosperm constitution bring about crucial changes in embryo symmetry.

Exegetic Embryo Dormancy

A phenomenon that appears to be related to the regulation of symmetry changes in the embryo is *exegetic dormancy*, which refers to the dormancy of embryos during embryogenesis (Evenari 1984). The embryo suddenly stops developing at a particular stage of ontogeny for a variable period, and then restarts. In some species, the dormancy may extend for as long as eight years before the seed reaches a "germinable" condition (Neal and Dye 1964). As early as 1946, Martin found this type of dormancy in about 46 angiospermous genera. The actual number of such taxa may be much greater. *Ilex* is one of the most familiar examples, of which 11 species have been reported to show exegetic dormancy (Hu 1975).

The reasons for exegetic dormancy are not clearly understood and may differ from species to species. The available data indicate that the controlling factor(s) lies in the tissue immediately around the embryo, e.g. nitrogen in the endosperm is in an insoluble form (Stokes 1952, 1953). In *Ilex aquifolium*, growth inhibitors in the endosperm and/or in the membrane-like testa interrupt embryogenesis (Hu et al. 1979).

How this inhibition is overcome is not clear. In *Heracleum spondylicum* , exegetic dormancy was overcome by low-temperature treatment (Stokes 1952, 1953). The growth of the embryo of this species was probably renewed when sufficiently low-temperature conditions prevailed. In *Ilex opaca*, when embryos were excised during the exegetic dormancy and grown in vitro, they resumed growth in dark conditions but failed to do so in light (Hu 1976). Hu (1976) concluded that the red-far red mechanism was involved. If this is true, however, why did the embryos become dormant inside the ovule where they were supposedly "in the dark" (Evenari 1984)? A number of speculations could be made, but the facts that would support such speculations are missing. Conclusive evidence, even for the involvement of a red–far red mechanism, is yet to be found.

It is interesting that the structure of exegetically dormant embryos is similar to dormant mature embryos of fully developed seeds of several taxa. This similarity becomes evident upon a comparison of the ultrastructure of cells of the two types of dormant embryos (Hu et al. 1979).

One logical conclusion of the studies on exegetically dormant embryos is that each step in embryogeny, especially the critical symmetry changes observed, is under sequential control that probably emanates from the endosperm. Thus, embryos are forced to remain dormant in the absence of factors that trigger their continued growth and lie in the endosperm.

Embryo Rotation and Nastic Movements

An interesting area of study is the rotational and nastic movements exhibited by growing embryos (Krishnamurthy and Senthil Kumar, 1992). In some species of *Polygala*, some of the growing embryos exhibit a rotation whereas others show a pendulous movement (simple harmonic movement) along their vertical axes. It could not be detected whether the embryo rotated during filamentous and globular stages because of its radial symmetry. It is feasible that the embryo rotated even during these earlier stages, as it did at later stages of development. Positive evidence for the presence of rotation was noticed from the heart-shaped stage onward. The ovule is anatropous, with a distinct raphe traversed by a prominent vascular trace. In transverse sections of the developing seed at successive stages of embryogenesis, special attention was paid to the orientation of the two developing cotyledons in relation to the position of the raphe bundle, which is fixed and was taken as the marker.

At the heart-shaped stage of the embryo, the line joining the raphe bundle, the center of the embryo, and the center of the cotyledons in transverse section was straight. During further development, the three points formed a triangle; the angles varied at different developmental stages, depending upon the disposition of the cotyledons of the embryo. At the end of seed development, the triangle formed by these three points was a right angle. In other words, in the initial stages, the two cotyledons were parallel to the raphe bundle, whereas in the mature seed the two cotyledons were at right angles to the raphe bundle, thus proving the incidence of rotation (Figure 14.6). It was found that the changed orientation in cotyledons was due to the rotation of the whole embryo. There was no way of verifying the speed of rotation or the number of rotations the embryo underwent before becoming fully mature. We assumed that there should have been at least two rotations (360°) between the heart-shaped stage and mature embryo.

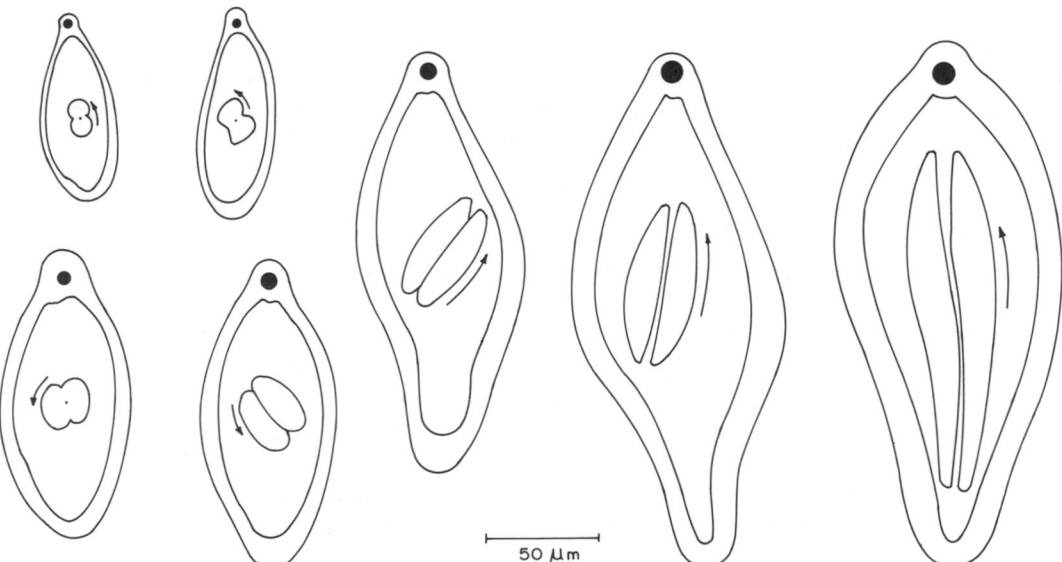

Figure 14.6. Transverse section of developing seeds of *Polygala* at successive stages; rotation of embryos is shown. The direction of rotation is indicated by *arrows*; the position of the raphe bundle, which is used as a marker, is shown by *solid black regions*.

Although the possibility of an embryo rotation was not considered by earlier investigators, the present study as well as some illustrations provided by Rao and Mary Roy (1981) for certain other species of *Polygala* indicate the occurrence of this phenomenon, at least in this genus. The exact significance of the rotation and nastic movements and their advantage to the embryo remain unclear.

HISTOLOGICAL DIFFERENTIATION

During embryogenesis, histological differentiation proceeds at specific regions of the developing embryo. Many early embryologists believed that histogenesis starts only during late embryogeny and becomes morphologically obvious only after the late globular stage (see Philip 1972) or heart-shaped embryo (Raghavan 1986). Consequently, a number of earlier researchers began their studies only from the globular stage of the embryo, under the impression that the histological ontogeny up to this stage is of no consequence. Again, by *histological differentiation,* they meant only the origin of the different meristems such as protoderm, ground meristem, procambium, and apical meristems. It should not be forgotten, however, that this morphological differentiation is preceded by distinct biochemical and histochemical changes, which can be demonstrated by special staining techniques, electron microscopy, and autoradiography, etc. Therefore, any attempt to deal with differentiation in the embryo should encompass not only the temporal and morphological aspects but also the physical, physiological, biochemical, and genetic bases of the differentiation phenomenon.

Importance of Cell Number in Differentiation

It has been postulated that a progressive increase in the number of cells may be an important factor determining histogenetic differentiation, because the various histogenic regions of the embryo do not appear simultaneously but differentiate during progressive growth of the embryo (see Raghavan 1986). Analysis of the literature, however, denies any such correlation between cell number and differentiation. In developing seeds of *Argemone mexicana* subjected to colchicine treatment, cell divisions continue in the globular embryo, resulting in large embryos with many cells at a stage when, in normal seeds, the globular embryos have passed on to the heart-shaped stage with a smaller number of constituent cells (Chopra and Rai 1958). In other words, the embryonic shoot apex does not differentiate and cotyledons do not form in the colchicine-treated embryos. In certain *Citrus* varieties, the triploid embryos obtained in a cross in which the endosperm degenerated early in development did not show differentiation into a plumule-radicle axis with two cotyledons, despite continued mitotic activity, i.e. increase in cell population (Esen & Soost 1973). In the "reduced" mutants of tomato (Caruso 1968), cell divisions and hence cell population kept increasing in the embryo but histogenetic differentiation was either poor or nonexistent. Embryos often developed without cotyledons and/or without organized shoot or root apices. These embryos were recognizable even at the very late globular stage. In the "modified" and "narrow" mutants of tomato, Caruso (1968) observed embryos that had one or two distinct cotyledonary structures but no active and differentiated shoot apex.

In crosses involving *Gossypium arboreum* and *G. hirsutum* (Weaver 1957), after ten days most embryos had not formed more than rudimentary cotyledons, although the number of cells apparently continued to increase. In ovules of *Eranthis* treated with phenylboric acid, some embryos did not exhibit a normal differentiation of cotyledon(s) (Haccius 1960). Lack of differentiation of root meristem and root cap was observed in *Avena* embryos subjected to maleic hydrazide (Mericle et al. 1955). These examples suggest that the process of differentiation in the developing embryo (irrespective of the type of tissue or organ that is differentiated) has no correlation with the number of constituent cells in the embryo at a given stage of development.

Genetic and Biochemical Bases of Differentiation

Histogenetic differentiation in the embryo appears to have a biochemical and genetic basis; the former is the effect of the latter. Cells in different locations of the developing embryo attain different genetic, cellular, and biochemical commitments, so the patterns of differentiation conform to the adult body plan characteristic of each species (Raghavan 1986). Biochemical reactions are triggered at appropriate times at appropriate loci of the developing embryo [due to sequential evocation of specific genes or *chreode, sensu* (Waddington 1957)] which can be analyzed by the specific proteins synthesized and the specific mRNA sequences employed.

A growing embryo synthesizes proteins (including enzymes) for normal development and histogenetic differentiation. A number of "house-keeping proteins" (Raghavan 1986) are synthesized along with a complement of enzymes for normal cellular metabolism; for cell specialization, histogenetic differentiation, and specific organ development, however, specific sets of proteins in excess of house-keeping proteins are synthesized. This process, according to Raghavan (1986), "implies that marked changes in gene-activity should be occurring at certain stages of embryogenesis to direct the transcription of structural genes." This gene-activity is different from that involved in the synthesis of storage proteins, which takes place during embryo maturation. Intensive studies are warranted to link the various differentaition phenomena observed during embryo development with specific types of protein synthesis.

Goldberg et al. (1981) made a detailed study of the mRNA patterns in the embryo of soybeans. They concluded that a change in form in the embryo (due to the process of histogenetic differentiation) was associated with an increase in mRNA complexity of the "rare" class of mRNA among the three ("superabundant," "moderate," and "rare") they found in the embryo. Investigation is needed to provide "evidence to link the synthesis of particular proteins among cell lineages with organogenesis in the embryo" (Raghavan 1986). Studies to date have investigated mainly the molecular biology, genome control, and synthesis of storage proteins in late embryogeny.

Differentiation of Different Tissue Regions

PROTODERM
The protoderm is perhaps the first to differentiate in the growing embryo. Its time of origin varies with taxa, but it is generally differentiated completely prior to the 16-celled stage of the embryo. In *Capsella* and a few other taxa, it differentiates in the octant stage. Once the protoderm is differentiated, its cells divide only anticlinally.

The differentiation of the protoderm is related to the cutting off of an internal cell in the embryo. Probably because of this relationship, Periasamy (1977) attached great importance to the cutting off of the internal cells in the proembryo and attempted to classify angiosperm embryogeny on this basis. According to Periasamy, the increasing exposure of newly formed cells of the zygote to the internal environment of the future embryo, rather than to the external environment of the endosperm, makes the segmentation of the first internal cell (which leads to the differentiation of the protoderm) an important morphogenetic event. The differentiation of the protoderm further increases exposure of the embryonal cells to its internal environment.

Although the cutting off of an internal cell and the subsequent initiation of the protoderm bring about a greater exposure of the newly formed cells to the internal environment of the embryo, the differentiation of the protoderm appears to be dependent on the regulatory effect of the extra-embryonal environment, especially one that prevails at the micropylar pole of the embryo sac. Embryos originating from nucellar and integumental cells do not form a protoderm at a stage corresponding to that of the zygotic embryo. The most peripheral layer of such embryos does not have regularly aligned cells; in addition, many of the cells undergo periclinal divisions even at very late stages of embryogeny, thereby disqualifying the layer as protoderm. A similar situation occurs in the embryoids produced *in vitro* from somatic cells and pollen grains (Swamy and Krishnamurthy 1981). In many embryoids, the differentiation of the protoderm not only is belated (see McWilliam et al. 1974; Haccius and Bhandari, 1975) but is often incomplete (Halperin and Wetherall 1964; Sussex, 1972). The reasons for such behavior can only be attributed to differences in the external environment to which the zygotic embryo, on the one hand, and the nonzygotic embryos and embryoids, on the other, are subjected. That a protoderm becomes differentiated, however, albeit belatedly, speaks of the basic control over its differentiation by the embryo proper, whether zygotic, nonzygotic, or somatic.

HYPOPHYSIS AND EPIPHYSIS

Almost concurrent with the differentiation of the protoderm, the hypophysis and epiphysis become initiated at the opposite poles of the globular embryo. As noted above, this differentiation implies that polarized gradients persist in the developing embryo. The *hypophysis* refers to a group of cells that become differentiated in the prospective root pole; the *epiphysis* is a similar zone in the prospective shoot pole (Souèges 1934). The hypophysis later forms an integral part of the root apical meristem and constitutes the base for the organization of the quiescent center (Swamy and Krishnamurthy 1975b). Similarly, the epiphysis becomes integrated into the shoot apical meristem as the prospective, relatively quiescent, central mother cell zone (Swamy and Krishnamurthy 1977, 1978).

The cells of hypophysis and epiphysis have identical histology, cytochemistry, and ultrastructure. They are larger than the adjacent cells of the embryo, less densely cytoplasmic, more vacuolated, and poorer in RNA and protein content (Rondet 1962; Pritchard 1964; Vallade 1972); they are large-nucleated (Figure 14.7A, B) and relatively quiescent or almost inactive mitotically (Sterling 1955). Experiments in which an exogenous supply of DNA analogues was used, such as H^3-thimidine, demonstrated the mitotic quiescence of these cells (Jones 1977; Clowes 1978). The epiphysis is comparable to the hypophysis in almost all the above characters.

The hypophysis and epiphysis remain more or less unaffected through embryogeny, both with respect to the number of constituent cells and their histology and ultrastructure (Sterling 1955; Swamy and Padmanabhan 1961; Vallade 1972). In a few plants there may be a slight increase in the number of constituent cells, and the newly formed cells possess characteristics identical to the earlier cells. There is no doubt that the quiescent center of the root is organized by the hypophysis. Claims regarding the disappearance of this zone during later stages of the embryogeny (Clowes 1958, 1961, 1978; Bryne 1973; McLeod and McLauchlin 1974) are likely to be based on faulty observations with nonmedian longitudinal sections (See Swamy and Krishnamurthy 1975; Gahan 1988).

The sexually produced zygotic embryo differs from similar structures derived from nucellar and integumental cells in the embryo sac and from the embryoids produced by somatic cells *in vitro* in that it possesses the hypophysis and epiphysis at opposite poles of the globular stage. The absence of the hypophysis and epiphysis is indicative of the existence of non-polarized gradients in structures other than zygotic embryos during most of their development. The differentiation of cells corresponding to hypophysis and epiphysis in the above structures takes place very late in ontogeny; only then do these structures become polarized and show evidence of organized development and differentiation.

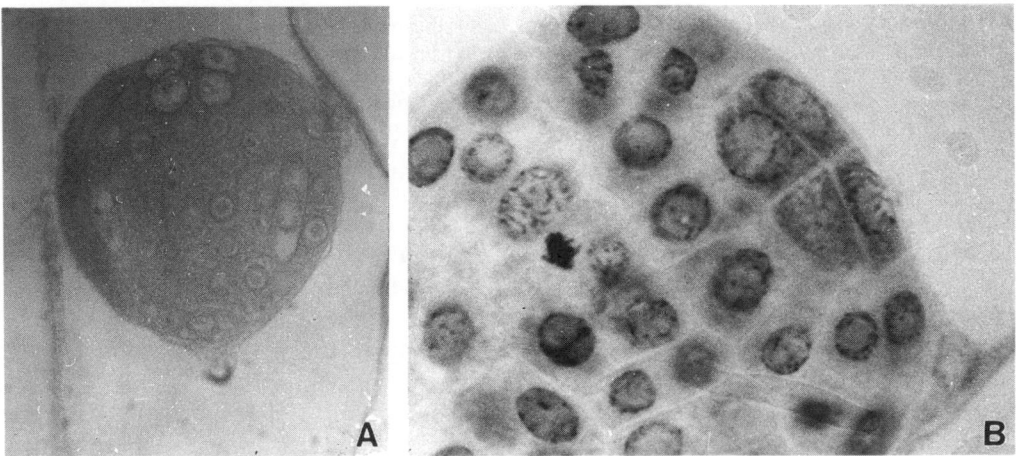

Figure 14.7. Embryos of *Stellaria media* with prominent epiphysis cells. The cells are large and contain big nuclei (after Pritchard 1964).

GROUND MERISTEM

The ground meristem and the provascular meristem are blocked out almost simultaneously during embryogeny (Figure 14.8). Both are derived from the cells of the central core of the late globular or early heart-shaped stage by way of cell enlargement, decreased stainability, and increased vacuolation. Depending upon the taxon, the ground meristem may produce only a cortex or both cortex and pith. The former situation occurs in *Phlox drummondii* (Miller and Wetmore 1945a, b). *Dianthus chinensis* (Buell 1952), *Sphenoclea zeylanica* (Swamy and Padmanabhan 1961), *Downingia bacigalupii* (Kaplan 1969), and *Stellaria media* (Ramji 1975). In these cases, the peripheral layer cells of the central meristematic core in the late globular embryo are the progenitors of the cortex of the mature embryo. During elongation of the embryo, these cells divide periclinally to form an embryonic cortex of 3–4 concentric layers. In *Juglans regia* (Nast 1941), *Pisum sativum* (Reeve 1948), *Nerium oleander* (Mahlberg 1960), and *Sesamum indicum* (Hanawa 1960), both pith and cortex develop from ground meristem. The first evidence of pith is the presence of enlarged light-staining cells in the central region of the globular embryo; by continued divisions, these cells differentiate as the pith of the hypocotyl part of the mature embryo.

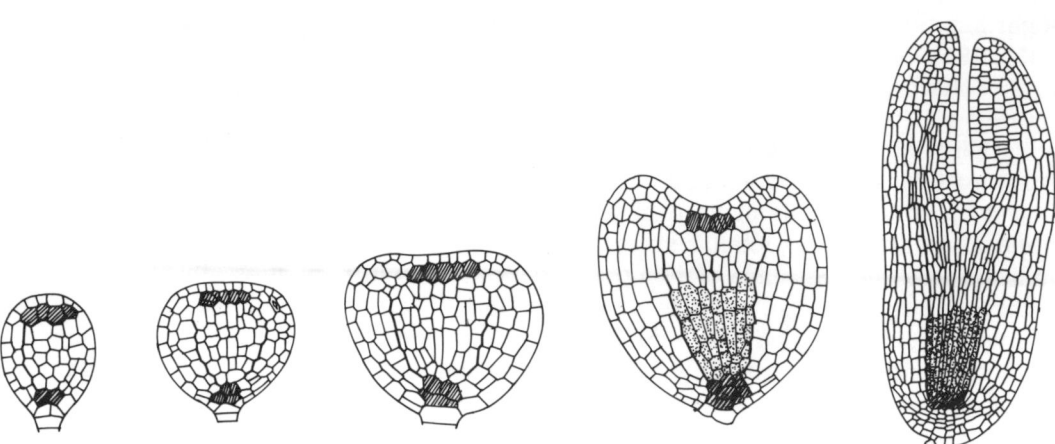

Figure 14.8. Stages in the development of the embryo of *Catharanthus roseus*. Differentiation of the hypophysis and epiphysis and of the protoderm, ground meristem, and central core. The hypophysis and epiphysis are *hatched*; the central core cells are *stippled*. There is slow increase in the number of cells of hypophysis and epiphysis as the embryo matures (after Philip 1972).

PROCAMBIALIZATION AND VASCULAR DIFFERENTIATION

Our knowledge regarding procambialization and vascular differentiation in embryos is meager (Esau 1965; Swamy and Krishnamurthy 1980b). This lack perhaps stems from a lack of understanding among past workers of the actual features of the procambium and also from a lack of biochemical markers for identifying the procambium and its activities in embryos (Shininger 1979).

Many past workers designated the whole central core of cells of the embryonic axis as procambium. This region was also called "pleurome" in accordance with the histogen concept of Hanstein (Reeve 1948), "stelar promeristem" (Gahan 1988), "provascular meristem" (Esau 1965), "residual meristem" (Meyer 1958), "prodesmogen" (Nast 1941), and "procambium in incipient stage" (Spurr 1949). Considering the entire zone as procambium implies that the procambium gives rise not only to vascular tissue but also to nonvascualr elements such as pith (wherever present), conjunctive parenchyma, pericycle, and endodermis (see also Swamy and Krishnamurthy 1980b).

This confusion caused problems in interpreting the wave of procambialization in the embryo and the temporal origin of the procambium. Esau (1965) admitted that the central core of cells of the embryonic axis at first retained the characteristics of the early embryonic cells and only gradually assumed the characteristics of the procambium. Not all cells of this central core become transformed into procambium, however. This will be evident after comparing the cytology and biochemistry of the cells of the central core with the characteristics of the procambium that differentiates from it (detailed discussion in Larson 1982; Iqbal and Ghouse 1990). Catesson (1984) compiled a list of characteristics of the procambium based on the data provided by Sterling (1946), Roland (1978), Larson (1982), and on her own observations. The characteristics are as follow: (a) presence of a single cell type; (b) small and isodiametric cells in sections; (c) cell division in any direction; (d) absence of intrusive growth; (e) cell wall of uniform thickness; (f) presence of proplastids and many small vacuoles; and (g) basophilic nature and intense staining with pyronin for RNA. Only a few of these traits are shared by all the cells of the central core of the embryonic axis.

It is true that in most embryos, the blocking out of the so-called provascular cells takes place in the central region of the late globular or early heart-shaped embryos (Esau 1965), but it is wrong to confuse it with procambial differentiation, as claimed by Nast (1941), Miller and Wetmore (1945a), Reeve (1948), Buell (1952), Balfour (1957), Mahlberg (1960), Hanawa (1960), and Kaplan (1969). The blocking out takes place as a continuous structure not only in the embryonic axis but also in the central core of the cotyledon(s), and this trait has given rise to confusion in interpreting the longitudinal wave of procambialization also. Consequently, we find such statements as the following: "The procambium of the cotyledons, hypocotyl, and the radicle is one continuous tissue system." It is, therefore, necessary to rethink and redescribe the course of events that take place during procambialization in embryos. Because of preconceived ideas and the false notion that the entire central core is procambium, we have been misled about the actual happenings in the embryos.

Procambilization of the embryo is noticed earliest in the first appendicular structure, the cotyledon. The linear derivatives of the subapical group of initials form the locus of differentiation of the median trace of the cotyledon. The blueprint for procambial development in the root is laid down much later, that is, after the preradicular meristematic center has become active. The medianly aligned linear derivatives of this meristem differentiate in part into the procambial system, in which the metaxylem locus becomes histologically distinctive (see Figure 14.9).

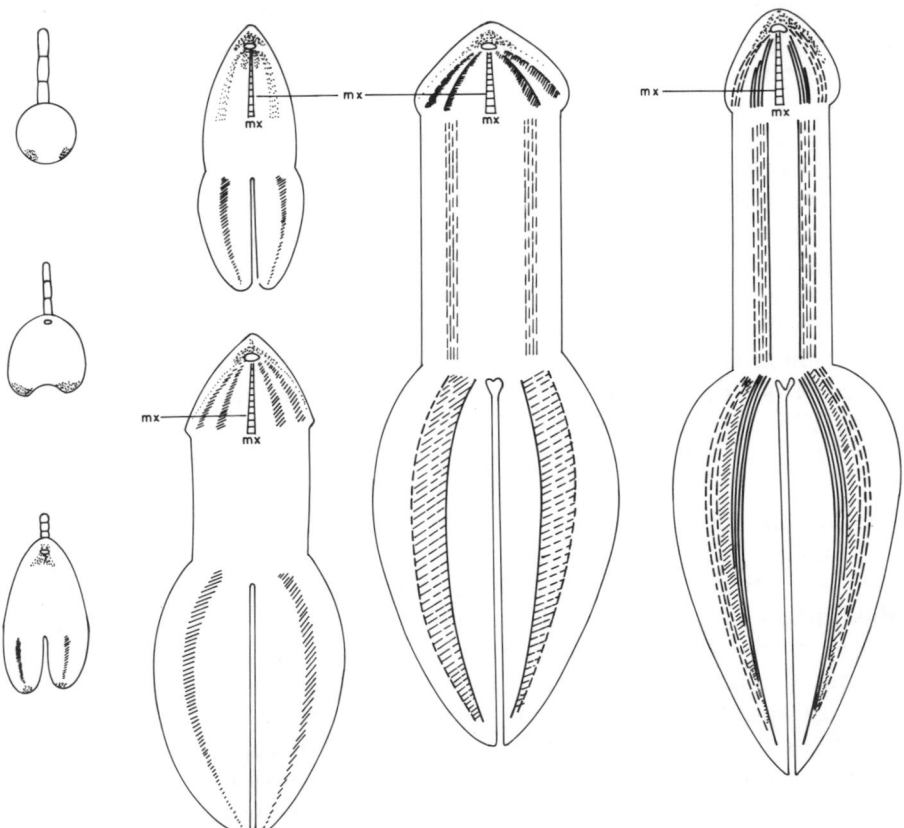

Figure 14.9. Stages of development of a dicot embryo. The location of meristematic regions (*stippled*), procambialization, and vascularization are shown. Procambial regions are *hatched* and xylem regions are represented by *broken lines*. The processes of procambialization and vascularization begin first in the cotyledons, then in the roots, and finally in the hypocotyl, thus showing a discontinuity; mx, metaxylem.

When procambial initiation has commenced in the cotyledon and the root regions, the hypocotyl part exhibits a conspicuous developmental lag (although possessing a central core of cells). This situation emphasizes that (a) the root and the hypocotyl are organs that are ontogenetically derived independently; (b) the procambial system of the cotyledon and of the root are directly related to the respective apical meristems; and (c) the cotyledonary procambium has no connection with that of the root or of the hypocotyl, as the latter exhibits a pronounced chronological lag in reference to procambialization (details in Swamy and Padmanabhan 1961; Philip 1972, 1974; Swamy and Krishnamurthy 1980a; Juncosa 1982, 1984a; Iqbal and Ghouse 1990).

The initiation of the pre-procambium is probably under the control of the parent plant. The control may come through hormones. Although cytological evidence does not permit an early detection of pre-procambial cells in the embryo (Miller and Wetmore 1945a; King and Heyes 1986), cytochemical markers have been devised for an early identification of these cells in vivo and in vitro (Caligo et al. 1986; Gahan 1988). The marker identified is carboxyl esterase, an enzyme associated with cell wall metabolism, which is active in cells destined to differentiate into vascular elements (Gahan 1981; Rana and Gahan 1982, 1983; Gahan and Bellani 1984). A careful perusal of the photographic illustrations provided in Gahan (1988) reveals that not all cells of the central core of the embryonic axis and cotyledons show the activity of the marker enzyme; the cells that show the reaction are likely to be the procambial cells.

The procambial cells that differentiate in the embryo are determined and committed to develop into vascular elements (see Meins and Binns 1979), i.e. this program persists irrespective of any subsequent programming events. On the contrary, the cells of the procortex are not rigid but plastic. We do not have adequate information on what causes the fixity of the procambial commitment, but the available information points to the involvement of specific genes. It has not yet been possible to identify the number of genes involved or the modality of their functioning, but it is likely that their expression is "embryo specific, let alone stelar promeristem-procambium specific (Dure 1985)" (Gahan 1988).

Information is deficient even on differentiation of vascular tissues from procambium in the embryo. This is particularly true of the phloem. Do the xylem and phloem elements follow a differentiation pattern and wave coincident with that of the procambium? If so, do all embryos? An answer to the first question can be attempted, but regarding the second, nothing can be said since the degree of morphological differentiation attained by the embryo in seeds varies widely even within the few taxa studied.

The differentiation of the first tracheary cells in the procambium strictly follows the corresponding temporal sequence described above for procambium. The earliest protoxylem and protophloem cells appear in the cotyledon and the root when only the procambial initiation is detected in the hypocotyl proper. Whereas the origin of the procambium in the cotyledon and root is traceable to the respective meristems (subapical group of initials and the root apical meristem), that of the hypocotyl is not related to any apical mersitematic units. On the contrary, the procambium differentiates from the constituent cells of the hypocotyl itself at appropriate loci. Vascularization of this procambium is also correspondingly delayed as compared with the cotyledon and root. Thus, by the time of the first appearance of protoxylem in the hypocotylar procabmium (generally soon after germination), the tracheary vascularization of the cotyledon and root exhibits almost complete differentiation (see Miller and Wetmore 1945a,b; Moens 1963; Philip 1972; Swamy & Krisnamurthy 1980a; Juncosa 1984a,b).

There are few studies on phloem differentiation. Phloem differentiation generally precedes that of xylem and this, too, is discontinuous (Philip 1972; see also Dauphiné and Rivière 1940; Nast 1941; Esau 1965).

ORIGIN AND DIFFERENTIATION OF APICAL MERISTEMS

Attention has been drawn to the differentiation of hypophysis and epiphysis in the globular embryo marking the two opposite poles. The cells constituting the two structures are relatively quiescent. The shoot apical meristem of the embryo is organized around the epiphysis, which serves as its nucleus. Similarly, the root apical meristem is organized with the hypophysis as its nucleus. The epiphysis forms the central mother cell zone of the shoot apex, whereas the hypophysis organizes the quiescent center of the root apex. In other words, the differentiation of the root and shoot apices begins with the organization of the hypophysis and epiphysis, respectively. Although the embryonic apices are very small, their origin and differentiation can be discerned, so it is wrong to assume that the shoot and root meristems have an undistinguishable origin (Raghavan 1986).

During the organization of the two meristems in the developing embryo, a change from the random distribution of cell divisions to a concentration of mitoses in the respective poles takes place around the quiescent epiphysis and hypophysis. Consequently, even within the very small embryonic root and shoot apices, a cytohistological zonation can be identified (Mahlberg 1960; Kaplan 1969). Since these changes become evident before the initiation of cotyledons, the latter can be considered as the first formative organs produced by the shoot apex. Once the cotyledon(s) is initiated, the shoot apex, in the majority of taxa, lapses into a state of quiescence or dormancy in the mature embryo. In some taxa, however, the embryonic shoot apex continues to produce primordia of at least a few leaves; in such instances, dormancy of the apex is not observed. This is especially true of certain water plants and a few legumes.

EMBRYO MATURATION

Definition of the Mature Embryo

Defining a mature embryo is made difficult by the varying connotations of the word "mature." *Mature* has been used to describe the final stage attained by a seminal embryo, i.e. an embryo with a root meristem at one end and a shoot meristem and one or two cotyledons at the other end connected by the hypocotyl–root axis. *Mature* has also been used to describe an embryo characterized by the cessation of cell division and, to some extent, cell expansion. Again, "maturity of an embryo is reckoned in terms of its ability to give rise to a normal seedling plant upon germination" (Raghavan 1986). The maturity of an embryo is difficult to define from its metabolic status, because subtle physiological changes continue to occur in the embryo even after the attainment of a morphologically mature structure. "Mature" seminal embryos are to a certain extent independent and autotrophic and are able to grow when supplied with a limited diet containing a few inorganic salts and sucrose. The critical stage at which the embryo attains this autonomy depends on the species in question, however (Batygina and Vasilyeva 1981). Some authors have even considered the weight of the embryo to identify its maturity. For example, in cotton, embryos weighing more than 100 mg (final weight 120 mg) were deemed to be mature (Dure et al. 1979). *Maturity* may be safely associated with a combination of most, if not all, of the attributes mentioned above.

Induction of dormancy is one of the final results of embryo maturation. It is regulated by the levels of GA and abscissic acid (ABA) but the precise mechanism remains unkown (Raghavan 1986). The many cytological changes that occur in the embryo include the culmination of synthesis of storage substances, extensive reduction in water content, increase in the size and complexity of the structure of the nucleolus, increase in the total cellular RNA, formation of smooth ER, and development of plastid-inclusion bodies (Villiers 1972a). The dormancy-breaking changes are triggered during germination and the embryo gives rise to a seedling.

Embryo maturity generally synchronizes with seed ripening, but in several species an apparently ripe seed may contain an immature embryo that continues to grow to maturity intraseminally after the seed is released. These intraseminal changes in the embryo, making it fit enough for germination, are collectively called *after-ripening*. A good example is the coconut palm. The fruits contain only undifferentiated embryos when they fall to the ground. In the soil, the embryos grow within the fruit and germinate. Other examples of after-ripening occur in *Crocus* and members of Ranunculaceae, Fumariaceae, Papaveraceae, and Umbelliferae. The after-ripening period varies from 8 days in *Fumaria* to nearly 12–18 months in some Ranunculaceae. Generally, the embryos of the after-ripening category do not have a dormant period. In all the above instances, the factors that promote after-ripening are intraseminal. In many orchids, the ripe seed contains an undifferentiated embryo (in globular stage), whose further growth depends on the "infection" of its cells with the specific mycorrhizal fungus with which the taxon is normally associated symbiotically (Withner 1959; Arditti 1979).

Several queries remain. Why in some taxa does embryo maturity coincide with seed ripening whereas in others there is no such correlation? Why is dormancy skipped in taxa showing after-ripening? Do these undifferentiated or partially differentiated embryos have a dormancy of the exegetic type? What is the physiolgical basis of after-ripening? Not many studies have addressed these questions, but some studies have found indications that GA and ABA are involved. That the addition of GA promotes germination of the *in vivo*-grown embryos taken out of non-after-ripened or partially after-ripened seeds (Beranger-Novat and Monin 1971; Côme and Durand 1971; Bianco and Bulard 1977; Jarvis and Wilson 1977) and that the GA content increases in embryos during the after-ripening (Isaia and Bulard 1978; Côme and Thèvenot 1982) indicate the role of GA in avoiding dormancy ("dormancy-breaking device") and promoting the continuance of embryogenesis. Experiments with apple indicate that ABA reverses the effect of GA (Barthe and Bulard 1978). The mechanism of action of GA and ABA on dormancy and after-ripening remains unknown, however.

Synthesis of Storage Substances

Mature embryos of several taxa are rich in proteins and other storage metabolites. Most, if not all, of these metabolites are synthesized when cell division almost stops and cell expansion commences in the developing embryo. The synthetic process, however, is built up progressively and culminates when the seminal embryo reaches maturity (Crouch 1979).

Compared with other storage products, embryo proteins have been the subject of intensive study mainly by those interested in gene action and expression during embryo development. Studies invoving cell-free translation systems, *in vivo* and *in vitro* pulse-labeling, and polypeptide and holoprotein accumulation patterns have been undertaken in addition to those using conventional techniques. The total protein fraction of an embryo broadly falls into two categories; heterogeneous metabolic proteins that include enzymes, ribosomal, chromosomal, and membrane proteins; and more homogeneous storage proteins (including lectins). The recognition by Osborne (1924) of the four types of proteins—albumins, globulins, prolamines, and glutelins—based on solubility classes is still valid. In legumes, the major storage proteins are the globulins, whereas prolamines and glutelins predominate in the cereals. Proteins appear to originate both in the vacuolar system and the plastids in cereals. In legumes, the vacuoles, rough endoplasmic reticulum, and dictyosomes are involved in the formation of the storage protein bodies.

An underlying question pertains to how the cells of the developing embryo synthesize the basic raw materials such as amino acids required to synthesize storage protein bodies and when this synthetic ability is attained during ontogeny. Although in most taxa studied the basic raw materials required for protein synthesis are shown to be obtained from the immediately surrounding maternal tissues and endosperm of the plant, in at least a few cases the embryo itself was found to synthesize the basic amino acids (Raghavan 1986). It may be expected that an embryo that is capable of synthesizing proteins should also be capable of synthesizing their precursors.

Active protein synthesis necessarily calls for active nucleic acid synthesis, because different types of proteins are to be coded during development. In general, RNA and DNA increase in parallel with protein accumulation in legumes. In cereals, the nucleic acid levels reach their maximum value at about the beginning of the storage protein accumuation. No direct evidence, however, implicates, the increase of nucleic acid in the increase of protein synthesis.

Precocious Germination and Vivipary

The ability of the embryo to germinate even before attaining "maturity" is called *precocious germination*. Although precocious germination is not found *in vivo*, many instances of young embryos directly germinating and producing seedlings *in vitro* have been recorded. The seedlings derived under these conditions are weak and invariably perish. In such cases, the embryos aviod the normal dormancy period characteristic of seminal embryos. In precocious germination, normal embryogenesis is replaced by alternate developmental programs that lead to germination in which certain steps, especially the later phases of embryogeny, are skipped. Research on this phenomenon has identified when during embryogenesis embryos are most vulnerable to precocious germination. Prior to this developmental phase, embryos fail to grow and germinate *in vitro*, whereas embryos beyond this phase germinate normally. This period, at least in a few cases, coincides with a period of active increase in fresh and dry weight and RNA content (Walbot 1971; Walbot et al. 1972).

Prolongation of embryogenic growth or induction of precocious germination depends essentially on the same biochemical marker(s) (Raghavan 1986); ABA is important in this regard (Ihle and Dure 1970, 1972). That the addition of ABA to culture medium inhibits precocious germination supports this statement (Dure et al. 1979). In normal ovules, ABA is believed to check precocious germination of embryos until they are mature. Once the controlling influence of ABA is lost, the embryo germinates normally. This control is effected through the influence of ABA on the synthesis of certain proteins (ABA-induced genic activity) (Dure et al. 1979). In cotton, for example, one set of proteins produced by young embryos is retained even at maturity whereas the synthesis of another set of proteins takes place only when the embryo approaches maturity. This second set is synthesized in immature cultured embryos only in the presence of ABA in the medium, whereas the first is produced even in its absence (Dure et al. 1981; see also Quatrano et al. 1983; Stinissen et al. 1984).

Whether the ABA-induced gene action noticed in embryogenesis/precocious germination is controlled by the embryo or by its surrounding tissue is unclear. Although evidence for the latter control comes from studies on cotton (Ihle and Dure 1970, 1972), data on the mutant embryos of *Arabidopsis thaliana* (Karssen et al. 1983) support autocontrol of the embryo.

A phenomenon related to precocious germination is vivipary. In this, the mature embryos skip the dormancy period characteristic of seminal embryos, and germinate while retained inside the fruit when the latter is still attached to the parent plant. It is reasonable to assume from the discussion of precocious germination that absence or very low amounts of ABA would promote vivipary (Ihle and Dure 1972). Sussex's (1975) studies on *Rhizophora mangle,* a viviparous plant, reveal that although the embryos are insensitive to ABA in culture, they have a high water content. Since ABA level is inversely correlated to high water content, we can assume that very low concentrations of ABA in the viviparous embryo might be sufficient to promote germination (see Walbot 1978).

Viability of Embryos

Embryo viability may be defined as the ability of the mature embryo to germinate and produce a seedling under favorable conditions. Embryos vary appreciably in their viability. In some taxa, the embryo loses viability immediatley after seed formation; in others, it can germinate even after several years (up to 250 yr in some cases). The normal viability period of most species, however, ranges from 5–30 yr. It can be prolonged in many cases under proper storage conditions.

The gradual loss of viability is often referred to as *aging.* A number of changes take place slowly in a mature embryo that lead finally to the total loss of viability (see Villiers 1967, 1971, 1972a,b; Berjak and Villiers 1970, 1972a–d; van Staden et al. 1975; Chatterjee et al. 1976; Vishnyakova et al. 1976). The following changes are more important: (a) damage to and disintegration of membrane-lined organelles such as plastids; (b) dispersion of ribosomes; (c) disapearance of dictyosomes; (d) rupture of lipid and protein bodies; (e) accumulation of toxic and/or mutagenic compounds resulting in chromosomal aberrations and inhibition of growth, as seen in many cereals; (f) accumulation of phenolics not noticed in viable embryos, as seen in cereals; (g) increase in acid phosphatase activity in the cytoplasm; (h) absence of further cell division; (i) extinguishment of mitochondrial functions leading to the loss of an ATP-generating system in the embryo, and; (j) reduction in or total lack of protein synthesis due to structurally and biochemically defective ribosomal and postribosomal fractions (see Raghavan 1986); loss of or defective enzyme machinery (in some cases at least one enzyme, Transferase I, involved in protein synthesis is found to be affected); and no new RNA synthesis. It may be concluded therefore that the loss of viability in embryos is caused by general damage to macromolecules, including nucleic acids (especially to their integrity), membrane compounds, and enzymes.

Aging embryos undergo autolysis in their cells, although at a slow speed. Autolysis is initiated by the appearance of cytolysomes (sensu; Villiers 1967), which arise by the fusion of segments of endoplasmic reticulum. This results in the fine compartmentalization of the cytoplasm and finally in the death of cells. A similar phenomenon is observed in aging embryo suspensors (Nagl 1977).

PROBLEMS AND PROSPECTS

Although during the last few decades many aspects of the angiosperm embryo have been studied, the following aspects require further attention:

1. One of the remarkable features of angiosperm zygotic embryogenesis is the ordered sequence of development that is completed with astounding precision. We know little about the factors that are responsible for this orderliness, nor do we understand how apparently similar final products are obtained by very diverse pathways in zygotic, somatic, pollen, and adventive embryogenies.

2. The starting point for zygotic embryogeny is the zygote, derived from the egg after fusion with one of the male gametes. This transition from haploidy (egg) to diploidy (zygote) brings about unprecedented transformations in the structure and behavior of the resultant cell. The triggering mechanism for such changes and its mode of action are yet to be identified. Another pertinent topic is the degree of autonomy of the zygote with reference to its synthetic abilities and possession of an appropriate machinery to carry out these activities. We need to learn about the proteins synthesized soon after transition from egg to zygote and the mRNA sequences involved therein.

3. The existence of polarized fields in the zygote and its division products is well recognized. Although circumstantial evidence indicates that this polarity is "inherited" from the embryo sac in which the zygote is located, we know little of the factors responsible for their sustenance through the developing embryo. Is a gradient in calcium ions involved in this process, as is known in some unipolar structures? Future studies alone can answer this.

4. The factors involved in the transition from filamentous to globular, globular to cordate, and cordate to the mature stage of the embryo deserve attention. Although the existence of an autocontrol by the embryo for these transitions is always probable, evidence for control emanating from the immediate milieu of the embryo must also be considered. Molecular and histochemical changes at different stages of embryogeny need to be studied in conjunction with similar investigations in the corresponding stages of the developing endosperm and other regions of the growing seed.

   Contour changes are preceded by histogenetic differentiation of specific regions of the developing embryo. Position is definitely a major controlling factor in the differentiation process, but the molecular and biochemical mechanisms involved have yet to be elucidated. There are indications that differentiation is a gene-controlled process and that these genes are likely to be evoked sequentially at appropriate loci in the developing embryo. In this context, gene expression studies in which protein syntheses are used as markers have shown the right direction for future research. There is room also for basic studies on the genetical basis of differentiation in the embryo, especially during younger stages of its development.

5. The phenomena of dormancy/vivipary/maturation/viability of embryos are so intimately interconnected that any light shed on one of these would also elucidate the other. Only a few taxa have thus far been studied from this perspective, however. The seminal embryo is a model system in which diverse studies regarding molecular control of development and differentiation could be attempted.

LITERATURE CITED

Arditti, J. 1979. Aspects of the physiology of orchids. *Adv. Bot. Res.* 7:421–655.

Ashley, T. 1972. Zygote shrinkage and subsequent development in some *Hibiscus* hybrids. *Planta* 108:303–317.

Balfour, E. 1957. The development of the vascular systems in *Macropiper excelsum* Forst. I. The embryo and seedling. *Phytomorphology* 7:354–364.

Barthe, P., and C. Bulard. 1978. Bound and free abscisic acid levels in dormant and after-ripened embryos of *Pyrus malus* L. CV. Golden Delicious. *Z. Pflanzenphysiol.* 90:201–208.

Batygina, T. B., and V. E. Vasilyeva. 1981. Experimental study of embryo differentiation in angiosperms. *Acta Soc. Bot. Pol.* 50:257–263.

Bennett, M. D., M. K. Rao, J. B. Smith, and M. W. Bayliss. 1973. Cell development in the anther, the ovule and the young seed of *Triticum aestivum* L. Var. *Chinese Spring*. *Philos. Trans. R. Soc. London Ser. B.* 266:39–81.

Beranger-Novat, N., and J. Monin. 1971. A propos de la levée de dormance des embryons d'*Euonymus europaeus* L. par l'acide gibbérellique. *Compt. Rend. Acad. Sci. Paris D* 272:1368–1371.

Berjak, P., and T. A. Villiers. 1970. Ageing in embryos. I. The establishment of the normal sequence of development in the root cap upon germination. *New Phytol.* 69:929–938.

——— . 1972a. Ageing in embryos II. Age-induced damage and its repair during early germination. *New Phytol.* 71:135–144.

——— . 1972b. Ageing in plant embryos. III. Acceleration of senescence following artifical ageing treatment. *New Phytol.* 71:513–518.

——— . 1972c. Ageing in plant embryos. IV. Loss of regulatory control in aged embryos. *New Phytol.* 71:1069–1074.

——— . 1972d. Ageing in plant embryos. V. Lysis of the cytoplassm in non-viable embryos. *New Phytol.* 71:1075–1079.

Berthold, G. D. W. 1886. *Studien über Protoplasma-mechanik*. Leipzig: Felix.

Bianco, J., and C. Bulard. 1977. Etude de la dormance embryonnaire chez *Sorbus aucuparia* L. Trav. *Scient. Parc. Natl. Vanoise* 8:147–155.

Boyes, J. W., and W. P. Thompson. 1937. The development of the endosperm and embryo in reciprocal interspecific crosses in cereals. *J. Genet.* 34:203–227.

Bryne, J. M. 1973. The root apex of *Malva sylvestris*. III. Lateral root development and the quiescent centre. *Am. J. Bot.* 60:657–662.

Buell, K. M. 1952. Developmental morphology in *Dianthus* I. Structure of the pistil and seed development. *Am. J. Bot.* 39:194–210.

Caligo, M. A., V. Nuti Ronchi, and M. Nozzolini. 1986. Proline and serine affect polarity and development of carrot somatic embryos. *Cell Differ.* 17:193–198.

Caruso, J. L. 1968. Morphogenetic aspects of leafless mutant in tomato. I. General patterns in development. *Am. J. Bot.* 55:1169–1176.

Catesson, A. M. 1984. La dynamique Cambiale. *Ann. Sci. Nat. Bot. Biol. Veg.* 6:23–43.

Chatterjee, A., P. K. Saha, P. Das Gupta, S. N. Ganguly, and S. M. Sircar. 1976. Chemical examination of viable and non-viable rice seeds. *Physiol. Plant.* 38:307–308.

Chopra, R. N., and K. S. Rai. 1958. Response of ovules of *Argemone mexicana* L. to colchicine treatment *in vivo*. *Phytomorphology* 8:107–113.

Clowes, F. A. L. 1958. Development of quiescent centres in root meristems. *New Phytol.* 57:85–88.

——— . 1961. *Apical Meristems*. Oxford: Blackwell.

——— . 1971. The proportion of cells that divide in root meristems of *Zea mays* L. *Ann. Bot.* 35:249–261.

——— . 1978. Origin of quiescence at the root pole of pea embryos. *Ann. Bot.* 42:1237–1239.

Cóme, D., and M. Durand. 1971. Influence de l'acide gibbérellique sur la levée de dormance des embryons de pommier (*Pyrus malus* L.) par le froid. *Compt. Rend. Acad. Sci. Paris* D 273:1937–1940.

Côme, D., and C. Thèvenot. 1982. Environmental control of embryo dormancy and germination. In *The Physiology and Biochemistry of Seed Development, Dormancy and Germination*. Ed. A. A. Khan. 2nd ed. Amsterdam: Elsevier Biomedical Press. 271–298.

Crété, P. 1963. Embryo. In *Recent Advances in the Embryology of Angiosperms*. Ed. P. Maheshwari. New Delhi: International Society of Plant Morphologists. 171–220.

Crouch, M. L. 1979. *Storage Proteins as Embryo-specific Developmental Markers in Zygotic, Microspore and Somatic Embryos of Brassica napus*. Ph.D. Thesis, Yale University, New Haven, CT.

D'Arcy Thompson, W. 1942. *On Growth and Form*. 2nd ed. Cambridge: Cambridge Univ. Press.

Dauphiné, A., and S. Rivière. 1940. Sur la présence de tubes criblés dans des embryons de graines non germées. *Compt. Rend. Acad. Sci. Paris* 211:359–361.

Dure, L. S. III, 1985. Embryogenesis and gene expression during seed formation. *Oxford Surv. Plant Mol. Cell Biol.* 2:179–197.

Dure, L. S. III., A. M. Capdevila, and S. C. Greenway. 1979. Messenger RNA domains in the embryogenesis and germination of cotton cotyledons. In *Genome Organization and Expression in Plants*. Ed. L. Leaver. New York: Plenum Press. 127–146.

Dure, L. S. III., S. C. Greenway, and G. A. Galau. 1981. Developmental biochemistry of cotton seed embryogenesis and germination: Changing messenger ribonucleic acid populations as shown by *in vitro* and *in vivo* protein synthesis. *Biochemistry* 20:4162–4168.

Esau, K. 1965. *Vascular Differentiation in Plants*. New York: Holt, Rinehart & Winston.

Esen A., and R. K. Soost. 1973. Seed development in *Citrus* with special reference to 2x × 4x crosses. *Am. J. Bot.* 60; 448–462.

Evenari, M. 1984. Seed physiology: From ovule to maturing seed. *Bot. Rev.* 50:143–170.

Forster, B. P., and J. E. Dale. 1983. A comparative study of early seed development in genotypes of barley and rye. *Ann. Bot.* 52:603–612.

Gahan, P. B. 1981. An early cytochemical marker of commitment to stelar differentiation in meristems for dicotyledonous plants. *Ann. Bot.* 48:769–775.

———. 1988. Xylem and phloem differentiation in perspective. In *Vascular Differentiation and Plant Growth Regulators*. Ed. L. W. Roberts, P. B. Gahan, R. Aloni. Berlin: Springer-verlag. 1–21.

Gahan, P. B., and L. M. Bellani. 1984. Identification of shoot apical meristem cells to form vascular elements in *Pisum sativum*. L. and *Vicia faba* L. *Ann. Bot.* 54:837–841.

Goldberg, R. B., G. Hoschek, S. H. Tam, G. S. Ditta, and R. W. Breidenbach. 1981. Abundance, diversity, and regulation of mRNA sequence sets in soybean embryogenesis. *Dev. Biol.* 83:201–217.

Gray, D., J. A. Ward, and J. R. A. Steckel. 1984. Endosperm and embryo development in *Daucus carota* L. *J. Exp. Bot.* 35:459–465.

Grundwag, M. 1976. Embryology and fruit development in four species of *Pistacia* L. (Anacardiaceae). *Bot. J. Linn. Soc.* 73:355–370.

Haccius, B. 1960. Experimentell induzierte Einkeimblattrigkeit bei *Eranthis hyemalis*. II. Monokotylie durch phenylborsaure. *Planta* 54:482–497.

Haccius, B., and N. N. Bhandari. 1975. Delayed histogen differentiation as a common primitive character in all types of non-zygotic embryos. *Phytomorphology* 25:91–94.

Halperin W., and D. F. Wetherell. 1964. Adventive embryony in tissue cultures of wild carrot, *Daucus carota*. *Am J. Bot.* 51:274–283.

Hanawa, J. 1960. Late embryogeny and histogenesis in *Sesamum indicum* L. *Bot. Mag.* 73:369–376.

Heslop-Harrison, J. 1964. Cell walls, cell membranes and protoplasmic connections during meiosis and pollen development. In *Pollen Physiology and Fertilization.* Ed. H. F. Linskens. Amsterdam: North-Holland. 39–47.

Hu, C. Y. 1975. *In vitro* culture of rudimentary embryos of eleven *Ilex* species. *J. Am. Soc. Hort. Sci.* 100:221–225.

––––––. 1976. Light-mediated inhibition of *in vitro* development of rudimentary embryos of *Ilex opaca. Am. J. Bot.* 63:651–656.

Hu, C. Y., F. Rogalski, and C. Ward. 1979. Factors maintaining *Ilex* rudimentary embryos in the quiescent state and the ultrastructural changes during *in vitro* activation. *Bot. Gaz.* 140:272–279.

Ihle, J. N., and L. S. Dure III. 1970. Hormonal regulation of translation inhibition requiring RNA synthesis. *Biochem. Biophys. Res. Commun.* 38:995–1001.

––––––. 1972. The developmental biochemistry of cotton seed embryogenesis and germination III. Regulation of the biosynthesis of enzymes utilized in germination. *J. Biochem.* 247:5048–5055.

Iqbal, M., and A. K. M. Ghouse. 1990. Cambial concept and organization. In *The Vascular Cambium.* Ed. M. Iqbal. Taunton, U.K.: Research Studies Press. 1–36.

Isaia, A., and C. Bulard. 1978. Relative levels of some bound and free gibberellins in dormant and after-ripened embryos of *Pyrus malus.* cv. *Golden Delicious. Z. Pflanzenphysiol.* 90:409–414.

Jarvis, B. C., and D. Wilson. 1977. Gibberellin effects within hazel (*Corylus avellana* L.) seeds during the breaking of dormancy. I. A direct effect of gibberellin on the embryonic axis. *New Phytol.* 78:397–401.

Jensen, W. A. 1964. Cell development during plant embryogenesis. In *Meristems and Differentiation, Brookhaven Symp. Biol.* 16:179–202.

––––––. 1968. Cotton embryogenesis: The Zygote. *Planta* 79:346–366.

––––––. 1974. Reproduction in flowering plants. In *Dynamic Aspects of Plant Ultrastructure.* Ed. A. W. Robards. London: McGraw-Hill. 481–503.

Johansen, D. A. 1950. *Plant Embryology. Embryogeny of the Spermatophyta.* Waltham, MA: Chronica Botanica Co.

Johri, B. M., K. B. Ambegaokar, and P. S. Srivastava. 1992. *Comparative Embryology of Angiosperms.* Heidelberg: Springer-Verlag.

Jones, P. A. 1977. Development of quiescent center in maturing embryonic radicles of pea (*Pisum sativum* L. V. Alaska). *Planta* 135:233–240.

Juncosa, A. M. 1982. Developmental morphology of the embryo and seedling of *Rhizophora mangle* L. (Rhizophoraceae). *Am. J. Bot.* 69:1599–1611.

––––––. 1984a. Embryogenesis and seedling development in *Cassipourea elliptica* (SW.) Poir. (Rhizophoraceae). *Am. J. Bot.* 71:170–179.

––––––. 1984b. Embryogenesis and developmental morphology of the seedling in *Bruguiera exaristata* Ding Hou (Rhizophoraceae). *Am. J. Bot.* 71:180–191.

Kadej, F., and A. Kadej. 1981. Ultrastructural organization of the tomato embryo sac at the time of fertilization. *Acta Soc. Bot. Pol.* 50:139–142.

Kaplan, D. R. 1969. Seed development in *Downingia. Phytomorphology* 19:253–278.

Karssen, C. M., D. L. C. Brinkhorst—van der Swan, A. E. Breekland, and M. Koorneef. 1983. Induction of dormancy during seed development by endogenous abscisic acid: Studies on abscisic acid deficient genotypes of *Arabidopsis thaliana* (L.) Heynh. *Planta* 157:158–165.

King, G. A., and J. K. Heyes. 1986. Morphology and cytology of pea embryo during histogenesis. *Ann. Bot.* 58:633–640.

Krishnamurthy, K. V. 1977. Meiotic induction in plants—A hypothesis. *Biology* (Kamaraj University) 1:15–17.

––––––. 1988. Endosperm controls symmetry changes in the developing embryos of angiosperms. *Proc. Indian Acad. Sci.* (Pl. Sci.) 98:257–259.

Krishnamurthy, K. V., and T. Senthil Kumar. 1992. Embryo rotation in *Polygala arvensis* Willd. *Beitr. Biol. Pflanzen* 67:55–58.

Larson, P. R. 1982. The concept of cambium. In *New Perspectives in Wood Anatomy*. Ed. P. Baas. The Hague: Nijhoff/Junk. 85–121.

Lyndon. R. F. 1990. *Plant Development—The Cellular Basis*. London: Unwin Hyman.

Mahlberg, P. G. 1960. Embryogeny and histogenesis in *Nerium oleander* L. I. Organization of primary meristematic tissues. *Phytomorphology* 10:118–131.

Martin, A. C. 1946. The comparative internal morphology of seeds. *Am. Midl. Nat.* 36:513–660.

McLeod, R. D., and S. M. McLauchlin. 1974. The development of a quiescent centre in lateral roots. *Ann. Bot.* 38:535–544.

McWilliam, A. A., S. M. Smith, and H. E. Street. 1974. The origin and development of embryoids in suspension cultures of carrot (*Daucus carota*). *Ann. Bot.* 38:243–250.

Meinke, D. W., J. Chen, and R. N. Beachy. 1981. Expression of storage-protein genes during soybean seed development. *Planta* 153:130–139.

Meins, F. J., and A. N. Binns. 1979. Cell determination in plant development. *BioScience* 29:221–225.

Mericle, L. W., A. E. Eunus, and R. P. Mericle. 1955. Effects of maleic hydrazide on embryonic development I. *Avena sativa. Bot. Gaz.* 117:142–147.

Meyer, C. F. 1958. Cell patterns in the early embryogeny of the McIntosh apple. *Am. J. Bot.* 45:341–349.

Miller, H. A., and R. H. Wetmore. 1945a. Studies in the developmental anatomy of *Phlox drummondii* Hook. I. The embryo. *Am. J. Bot.* 32:588–599.

_____. 1945b. Studies in the developmental anatomy of *Phlox drummondii* Hook II. The seedling. *Am. J. Bot.* 32:628–634.

Moens, P. 1963. La vascularization de l'embryon et la plantule de *Coffea canephora* Pierre. *Cellule* 64:71–126.

Mogensen, H. L., and H. K. Suthar. 1979. Ultrastructure of the egg apparatus of *Nicotiana tabacum* (Solanaceae) before and after fertilization. *Bot. Gaz.* 140:168–179.

Nagato, Y. 1978. Analysis on the growth of embryo in some Gramineae. *Jpn. J. Breed.* 28:97–105.

Nagl, W. 1977. "Plastolysomes"—Plastids involved in the autolysis of the embryo-suspensor in *Phaseolus. Z. Pflanzenphysiol.* 85:45–51.

Nast, C. 1941. The embryogeny and seedling morphology of *Juglans regia* L. *Lilloa* 6:163–205.

Natesh, S., and M. A. Rau. 1984. The embryo. In *Embryology of Angiosperms*. Ed. B. M. Johri. Berlin: Springer-Verlag. 377–443.

Neal, O. M., and A. P. Dye. 1964. A method of studying dormancy of holly seeds that required eight years to germinate. *Proc. West-Virginia, Acad. Sci.* 36:10.

Osborne, T. B. 1924. *The Vegetable Proteins*. 2nd ed. London: Longmans Green.

Periasamy, K. 1977. A new approach to the classification of angiosperm embryos. *Proc. Indian Acad. Sci.* 86B:1–13.

Philip, V. J. 1972. Embryogenesis and seedling anatomy of *Catharanthus roseus* (Linn.) G. Don. 1. Embryogeny and procambialization. *Cellule* 69:155–172.

_____. 1974. Embryogenesis and seedling anatomy of *Catharanthus roseus* (Linn.) G. Don. II. The seedling. *Cellule* 70:19–28.

Pollock, E. G., and W. A. Jensen. 1964. Cell development during early embryogenesis in *Capsella* and *Gossypium. Am. J. Bot.* 51:915–921.

Pritchard, H. N. 1964. A cytochemical study of embryo development in *Stellaria media. Am. J. Bot.* 51:472–479.

Quatrano, R. S., B. L. Ballo, J. D. Williamson, M. T. Hamblin, and M. Mansfield. 1983. ABA controlled expression of embryo-specific genes during wheat grain development. In *Plant Molecular Biology*. Ed. R. B. Goldberg. New York: Alan R. Liss. 343–353.

Raghavan, V. 1976. *Experimental Embryogenesis in Vascular Plants*. London: Academic Press.

_____. 1986. *Embryogenesis in Angiosperms.* Cambridge: Cambridge Univ. Press.

Raghavan, V., and P. S. Srivastava. 1982. Embryo culture. In *Experimental Embryology of Vascular Plants.* Ed. B. M. Johri. Berlin: Springer-Verlag. 195–230.

Ramji, M. V. 1975. Histology of growth with regard to embryos and apical meristems in some angiosperms I. Embryogeny of *Stellaria media. Phytomorphology* 25:131–145.

Rana, M. A., and P. B. Gahan. 1982. Initiation of determination of stelar elements in roots of *Pisum sativum. Ann. Bot.* 50:757–762.

_____. 1983. Determination of fascicular, interfascicular and cork cambia in dicotyledonous plants. *Saussurea* 14:51–60.

Rao, P. N., and M. J. A. Mary Roy. 1981. From embryo sac to seed in *Polygala* Linn. *Indian J. Bot.* 4:115–121.

Reeve, R. M. 1948. Late embryogeny and histogenesis in *Pisum. Am. J. Bot.* 35:591–602.

Roland, J. C. 1978. Early differences between radial walls and tangential walls of actively growing cambial zone. *IAWA Bull.* (N. S.) 1:7–10.

Rondet, P. 1962. L'Organogenèse an cours de l'embryogenèse chez l'*Alyssum maritimum* Lamk. *Comp. Rend. Acad. Sci. Paris* 255:2278–2280.

Ryczkowski, M. 1960. Changes of osmotic value during the development of the ovule. *Planta* 55:343–356.

_____. 1971. Physico-chemical (chalaza-micropyle) gradient in the developing endosperm and embryo. *Bull. Acad. Pol. Sci. Ser. Sci. Biol.* 19:801–806.

Schulz, R., and W. A. Jensen. 1968a. *Capsella* embryogenesis. The egg, zygote and young embryo. *Am. J. Bot.* 55:807–819.

_____. 1968b. *Capsella* embryogenesis: The early embryo. *J. Ultrastruct. Res.* 22:376–392.

Sehgal, C. B., and E. M. Gifford. 1979. Developmental and histochemical studies of the ovules of *Nicotiana rustica* L. *Bot. Gaz.* 140:180–188.

Shininger, T. L. 1979. The control of vascular development. *Annu. Rev. Plant Physiol.* 30:313–337.

Singh, A. P., and H. L. Mogensen. 1975. Fine structure of the zygote and early embryo in *Quercus gambelii. Am. J. Bot.* 62:105–115.

Sivaramakrishna, D. 1978. Size relationship of apical cell and basal cell in two celled embryos in angiosperms. *Can. J. Bot.* 56:1434–1438.

Souèges, R. 1934. L'hypophyse et l'epiphyse; les problèmes d'histogenise qui leur sont liés. *Bull. Soc. Bot. Fr.* 81:737–748; 749–778.

_____. 1937. *Les Lois du Développement.* Paris: Actualités Scientifiques et Industrielles, Hermann et Cie.

Spurr, A. R. 1949. Histogenesis and organization of the embryo in *Pinus strobus* L. *Am. J. Bot.* 26:629–641.

Srivastava, P. S., and B. M. Johri. 1992a. Angiosperm embryology in 2000 A.D. In *Seed Biology.* Ed. K. G. Mukerji, A. K. Bhatnagar, S. C. Tripathi, M. Bansal, M. Saxena. Calcutta, India: Naya Prokash. 1–19.

_____. 1992b. Endosperm culture. In *Plant Tissue Culture Manual: Fundamentals and Applications.* Ed. K. Lindsey. Dordrecht, Netherlands: Kluwer Academic Publ. 1–21.

Sterling, C. 1946. Growth and vascular development in shoot apex of *Sequoia sempervirens* (Lamb.) Endl. III. Cytological aspects of vascularization. *Am. J. Bot.* 33:35–45.

_____. 1955. Embryogeny in the lima bean. *Bull. Torrey Bot. Club* 82:325–338.

Steward, F. C. 1958. Growth and organized development of cultured cells III. Interrelations of growth from free cell to carrot plant. *Am. J. Bot.* 45:709–713.

Stinissen, H. M., W. J. Peumans, and E. de Langhe. 1984. Abscisic acid promotes lectin biosynthesis in developing and germinating rice embryos. *Plant Cell Rep.* 3:55–59.

Stokes, P. 1952. A physiological study of embryo development in *Heracleum sphondylium* L. I. *Ann. Bot.* 16:571–576.

———. 1953. A physiological study of embryo development in *Heracleum sphondylium* L. III. *Ann. Bot.* 17:157–175.

Street, H. E. 1976. Experimental embryogenesis—The totipotency of cultured plant cells. In *The Developmental Biology of Plants and Animals.* Ed. C. F. Graham & P. F. Wareing. Oxford: Blackwell Sci. Publ. 73–90.

Sussex, I. M. 1972. Somatic embryos in longterm carrot tissue cultures: Histology, cytology and development. *Phytomorphology* 22:50–59.

Sussex, I. M. 1975. Growth and metabolism of the embryo and attached seedling of the viviparous mangrove, *Rhizophora mangle. Am. J. Bot.* 62:948–953.

Swamy, B. G. L. 1974. On the presumed ancestry of the angiosperm embryo sac. *Phytomorphology* 24:102–106.

Swamy, B. G. L., and K. V. Krishnamurthy. 1975a. Embryo sac ontogenies in angiosperms—An elucidation. *Phytomorphology* 25:12–18.

———. 1975b. Certain conceptual aspects of meristems. I. On hypophysis and quiescent centre. *Phytomorphology* 25:60–65.

———. 1977. Certain conceptual aspects of meristems. II. Epiphysis and shoot apex. *Phytomorphology* 27:1–8.

———. 1978. Certain conceptual aspects of meristems. III. A model. *Phytomorphology* 28:1–7.

———. 1980a. *From Flower to Fruit.* New Delhi: Tata-McGraw Hill Book Company.

———. 1980b. On the origin of vascular cambium in dicotyledonous stems. *Proc. Indian Acad. Sci. (Plant Sci.)* 89:1–6.

———. 1981. On embryos and embryoids. *Proc. Indian Acad. Sci.* 90B:401–411.

Swamy, B. G. L., and D. Padmanabhan. 1961. Embryogenesis in *Sphenoclea zeylanica. Proc. Indian Acad. Sci.* 54B:169–187.

Vallade, J. 1972. Structure et fonctionnement du méristème lors de la formation de la jeune racine primaire chez un *Petunia hybrida* hort. *Compt. Rend. Acad. Sci. Paris* 274D:1027–1030.

van Staden, J., M. G. Gilliland, and N. A. C. Brown. 1975. Ultrastructure of dry viable and non-viable *Protea compacta* embryos. *Z. Pflanzenphysiol.* 76:28–35.

Villiers, T. A. 1967. Cytolysomes in long-dormant plant embryo cells. *Nature* 214:1356–1357.

———. 1971. Cytological studies in dormancy. I. Embryo maturation during dormancy in *Fraxinus excelsior. New Phytol.* 70:751–760.

———. 1972a. Cytological studies in dormancy. II. Pathological ageing changes during prolonged dormancy and recovery upon dormancy release. *New Phytol.* 71:145–152.

———. 1972b. Cytological studies in dormancy. III. Changes during low temperature dormancy release. *New Phytol.* 71:153–160.

Vishnyakova, I. A., N. P. Krasnook, R. I. Povarova, E.A Morgunova, and Z. T. Bukhtoyarova. 1976. Ultrastructure of cells of the embryos of viable and unviable rice seeds in the course of swelling. *Soviet Plant Physiol.* 23:307–311.

Waddington, C. H. 1957. *The Strategy of the Genes.* London: Allen & Unwin.

Walbot, V. 1971. RNA metabolism during embryo development and germination of *Phaseolus vulgaris. Dev. Biol.* 26:369–379.

———. 1978. Control mechanisms for plant embryogeny. In *Dormancy and Developmental Arrest. Experimental Analysis in Plants and Animals.* Ed. M. E. Clutter. New York: Acadamic Press. 113–166.

Walbot, V., M. Clutter, and I. M. Sussex. 1972. Reproductive development and embryogeny in *Phaseolus. Phytomorphology* 22:59–68.

Wardlaw, C. W. 1955. *Embryogenesis in Plants.* London: Methuen & Co.

Weaver, J. B., Jr. 1957. Embryological studies following interspecific crosses in *Gossypium.* 1. *G. hirsutum* × *G. arboreum. Am. J. Bot.* 44:209–214.

Williams, E. G., R. B. Knox, V. Kaul, and J. L. Rouse. 1984. Post-pollination callose development in ovules of *Rhododendron* and *Ledum* (Ericaceae): Zygote special wall. *J. Cell. Sci.* 69:127–135.

Withner, C. 1959. *Orchids.* New York: Ronald Press Co.

Wolpert, L. 1970. Positional information and pattern formation. In *Towards a Theoretical Biology,* Vol. 3. Ed. C. H. Waddington. Edinburgh: Edinburgh University Press. 198–230.

———. 1971. Positional information and pattern formation. *Curr. Top. Dev. Biol.* 6:183–224.

———. 1981. Positional information and pattern formation. *Philos. Trans. R. Soc. London Ser. B* 295:441–450.

Chapter 15

Morphogenesis of the Angiosperm Proembryo and a Classification Based on Phylogenetic Trend

K. PERIASAMY

Classification is an essential process in the advancement of scientific knowledge, as it brings order to a large, complex array of information. Although analytical in approach, its ultimate outcome is the synthesis of the available knowledge in a particular field. The value of a classification system depends on (a) the size of the field encompassed (the larger the field, the greater the value of the classification); and (b) the size of the ultimate unit it can identify or categorize (the smaller the unit, the greater the value). The basis for such a system stems from the parameters of similarities and differences that have clear-cut boundaries. The greater the number of parameters available, the more precise the classification will be. For example, if several units to be classified differ from one another in only one parameter, they can be classified into two groups only; if they differ in several parameters, the classification may reach the level of each individual unit.

Angiosperms exhibit a unique pattern of embryogeny in which the early sequence of segmentation and subsequent development do not provide many specific clues for classification. There are few features, other than the number of cotyledons in the mature embryo, that separate the monocots from the dicots and that serve as parameters for classification and phylogeny.

PREVIOUS CLASSIFICATIONS OF THE ANGIOSPERM EMBRYO

Formulation of definite laws or a classification for the angiosperm embryogeny was thought to be impossible by Coulter and Chamberlain (1912), but Schnarf (1929) proposed a classification based on the early segmentation pattern and on the relative contribution of the first two-celled stage to the mature embryo. This was later modified and elaborated by Johnasen (1950) and Maheshwari (1950). Another classification was put forward by Souèges (1939): this was more elaborate but hardly allowed a proper categorization of the embryo (for details, see Johri et al. 1992).

Johansen's classification identifies six embryo types, each with a number of variations; this classification was followed by most English workers. Souèges's system, on the other hand, includes several ranks such as Periods, Megarchetypes and Series. Both systems, however, emphasize the pattern of early segmentation of the proembryo, up to the third or fourth cell generation, and the relative contribution of the cells formed in the first three or four divisions to the different parts of the mature embryo. Although these criteria provide parameters for classification, no morphological, physiological, or phylogenetic significance can be attached to them. For example, the terminal cell of the two-celled proembryo may become a quadrant by dividing vertically and then transversely, or vice versa. Although these two sequences of division are important parameters in both classifications, the derivation of the quadrant in one way or the other seems to bear no significance on the subsequent development of the embryo; nor does it have any phylogenetic value.

The embryonic laws enunciated by Johansen and Souèges fail in many instances. In some cases (Maheshwari 1950), specific initials are lost even at the four-celled stage, and different individuals of the same species have different parts derived from the embryonic initials. Mestre (1967), in a simplified version of Souèges' classification, showed that the fate of the two primordial cells alone was stable enough to serve as a criterion in establishing an embryonic law. He considered for his classification the multiple shapes of irregularity seen during embryo development. Johansen also stated that it was not possible to follow cell lineage beyond the 16-celled stage. Therefore, the allocation of parts of the mature embryo to initials at the 8- or 16-celled stage is based more on the topographical correspondence of the intials with the embryo parts (because plant cells do not move from place to place like animal cells during embryogeny) than on evidence for actual derivation of the parts from the initials.

The uncertainty of determining the derivation of the embryo parts from embryonic initials is well exemplified by the following two views regarding the location of the initials of epicotyl and cotyledon in the monocot proembryo:

1. The initials of cotyledons are located in the terminal tier and those of the epicotyl are located in the subterminal tier formed in the second or third cell generation of the proembryo (Souèges 1954).

2. The initials of both epicotyl and cotyledon occur in the terminal tier, but the topography of the cells of the terminal quadrant that gives rise to the epicotyl and cotyledon differs in the monocot and dicot plant groups (Haccius 1952; Swamy 1962; Swamy and Lakshmanan 1962a,b).

These conflicting conclusions show that following the cell lineage of the first few cells of the proembryo is difficult and that the derivation of the mature embryo parts may be interpreted differently. Different interpretations are possible because the cell lineage can be determined exactly only as long as each tier of the proembryo comprises eight or fewer cells. Once the number of cells and the size of the proembryonal mass have increased, the tiers merge into one another, thus making an accurate observation of the cell lineage impossible.

Based on the differentiation of organs and tissues during embryogeny and the differentiation of the root cortex and stem apex, Yamazaki (1974) recognized four principal types—Polygonad, Soland, Onagrad, and Asterad—and an irregular type in which the exact pattern of differentiation of the root cortex is difficult to decipher. Subdivisions of these types have also been suggested. Gamopetalae, a group of dicotyledonous plants, has been assembled under four Super Orders—Ericanae, Gentianae, Lamianae, and Asteranae (Yamazaki 1974). This grouping appears to be more natural than those proposed for Gamopetalae by Melchior (1964), Cronquist (1968), and Takhtajan (1969).

An additional type of embryogeny, the Geraniad type, which encompassed all dicots, was later described (Yamazaki 1982). It emphasized that the pattern of differentiation of the initials of root cortex is constant not only in families but sometimes also at the level of Orders, and that this feature indicates the phylogenetic relationships of the dicots (see also Natesh and Rau 1984).

Given the shortcomings of the earlier classifications, Periasamy (1977) suggested a new approach to the subject. A detailed appraisal is made below.

THE PROEMBRYONAL ENVIRONMENT

Every living organism is the result of the interaction between its genome and the environment. Therefore, any change in the environment will affect the organism; this effect will be more significant during the formative stage of early ontogeny and can alter the pattern of development (Periasamy 1972).

The angiosperm zygote is initially surrounded by the central cell of the embryo sac; later the endosperm surrounds the proembryo, thus comprising the immediate environment for the proembryo. The zygotic genome is slightly altered from that of the mother plant through genetic recombinations that occur during meiosis and the syngamy that follows. The unique phenomenon of triple fusion makes the genome of the endosperm 3n whereas that of the zygote remains 2n.

The proembryo and endosperm seem to be in delicate biochemical balance for the proper sequence of their mutually dependent, respective development. An apomictic embryo, formed in the embryo-sac environment, differs from a zygotic embryo in its developmental sequences and fails to develop in the absence of endosperm formation, just as an adventive embryo differs from the zygote in its genome and consequently its biochemistry.

INTERNAL CELL FORMATION IN MORPHOGENESIS
OF THE PROEMBRYO

As early as 1849, Hofmeister regarded the uniseriate filament of cells produced by the first few transverse divisions as "Vorkeim" or proembryo. Later, the term was extended to cover the subsequent multiseriate globular stage to the point at which the radial symmetry is lost and a bilateral symmetry—the so-called "torpedo stage"—arises by the initiation of cotyledon(s). Nevertheless, from the viewpoint of surface relationships and morphogenesis, the proembryo growth may be divided into (a) a uniseriate filamentous phase (Figure 15.1A–F); (b) a multiseriate elongate phase wherein all the cells are exposed to the environment external to the proembryo (Figure 15.1G–L); and (c) a multiseriate globular stage wherein internal cells have no contact with the environment external to the proembryo (Figure 15.1M–R). The differentiation of the

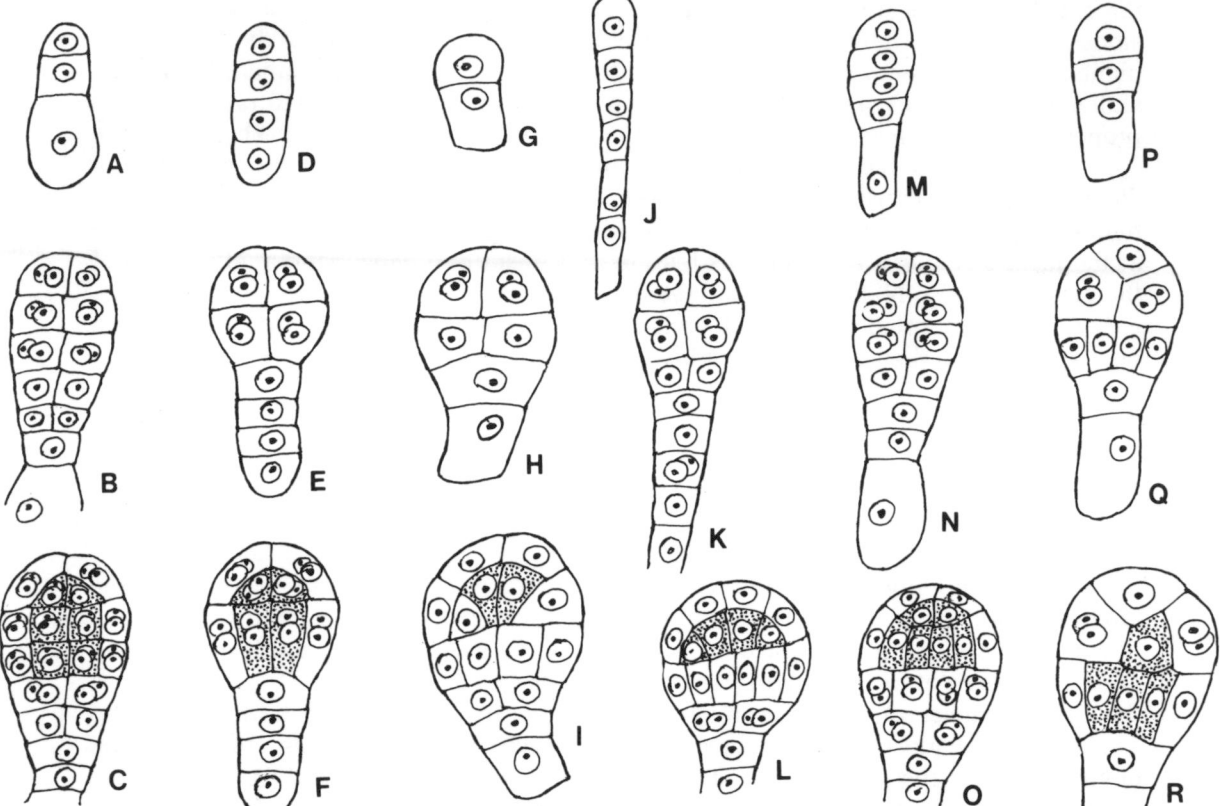

Figure 15.1. Proembryos at three stages of development: filamentous stage (*first horizontal row*), just before segmentation of the first internal cells (*second row*), and immediately after segmentation of the first internal cells (*third row*). Internal cells are *dotted*. The segmentation of internal cells does not alter the tier number. (A–C) *Sagittaria sagittaefolia* (EN 531; after Souèges 1931). (D–F) *Nicotiana tabacum* (EN 221; after Souèges 1937a). (G–I) *Melochia corchorifolia* (EN 241; after Venkata Rao 1951). (J–L) *Lobelia pyramidalis* (EN 351; after Subramanyam 1949). (M–O) *Sagina procumbens* (EN 432; after Souèges 1951). (P–R) *Geum urbanum* (EN 231; after Souèges 1948).

cotyledon(s), which changes radial symmetry into bilateral symmetry, does not provide any concrete parameter for classification even though it is a recognizable morphogenetic stage.

According to Wardlaw (1952), the proembryo may be regarded as a reaction system that produces changing patterns of organization. The segmentation of the first internal cell in the proembryo may be regarded as a significant morphogenetic event at the cellular level of organization, because the internal and external cells thereafter play different morphological and physiological roles. The external cells become protodermal cells directly, if they divide only anticlinally, or may produce protoderm initials after a few more periclinal divisions. The protoderm gives rise to an epidermal system that is in contact with the external environment and provides ventilation. The internal cells and their derivatives, on the other hand, do not become exposed to the external environment. They form various internal tissues by means of periclinal and anticlinal divisions, followed by divisions in diverse planes. Although the division and differentiation of internal cells are morphogenetically important, it is difficult to trace an exact sequence of division and derivation of tissues in terms of cell lineage or any other recognizable parameter that may be of use in classification and phylogeny.

PHYLOGENETIC SIGNIFICANCE OF THE PROTODERM

While tracing the process of apical growth in plants from the single apical cell of algae to the multicellular apex of angiosperms, Periasamy (1983) showed that there is a gradual shifting of protoderm isolation in the plant body, from the differentiated tissues to the embryonic, and that this represents a phylogenetic advance. Although non-tracheophytes lack a definite epidermal system, the embryos of tracheophytes, other than the angiosperms, do not have a clearly differentiated protoderm. Even in the adult plant, the shoot apex lacks a periclinally dividing protodermal layer or perigen (Periasamy 1983). The onset of a clear-cut organization into an anticlinally dividing surface layer and the internal layers is considered to be a major trend of phylogenetic specialization in the gymnospermous shoot apex (Pillai et al. 1972). Of the tissues derived from the shoot apex of petridophytes and gymnosperms, the outermost layer is clearly organized to perform the specific morphogenetic function of producing the epidermal system. Thus, the morphogenetic differentiation of a definite protoderm occurs in these taxa much later in ontogeny and stops short of the embryonic regions. In angiosperms, morphogenetic isolation of the protoderm reaches not only the adult shoot apex and the embryo but also the proembryo itself (Periasamy and Swamy 1964). This indicates that early morphogenetic isolation of the protoderm during ontogeny relates to phylogenetic advancement.

The stage at which the first internal cell is formed, as the first step for protoderm isolation, is easily detectable in the proembryo. This parameter is related to other well-defined parameters given below; hence, it is suitable for a meaningful classification based on morphogenesis and phylogeny.

FORMATION OF THE FIRST INTERNAL CELL: A BASIS FOR CLASSIFICATION

At the stage of segmentation of the first fully internal cell in the proembryo, proembryonic organization varies with regard to (a) total number of cell tiers present, (b) number of cells in each tier, and (c) location of the tier in which internal cells are formed. Based on delineation of cell lineages during early stages, Souèges had formulated more or less similar laws of embryonomy: (a) the law of origin, (b) the law of numbers, (c) the law of disposition, and (d) the law of destination.

Classification Based on Number of Tiers

The first division of the zygote is transverse in most angiosperms. Thus, the first morphogenetic activity leads to an increase in length. This division results in formation of unequal daughter cells. The terminal cell is generally smaller than the basal cell. The two cells are distinct from one another both cytologically and biochemically and exhibit an amplification of the reorganization and polarity that existed in the egg following fertilization. Nevertheless, Sivaramakrishna (1978) demonstrated that the two cells are essentially equal, and that if unequal, the terminal cell may even be larger. In addition, the basal cell is most often more vacuolated than the terminal cell. Subsequent divisions lead to an increase in the number of cells of the proembryo and to the formation of several cell tiers before the appearance of the first fully internal cell. Since the number of tiers thus formed is a primary parameter for classification, tier determination is an important element that needs to be clarified.

In angiosperm embryogeny, the term *tier* has been applied rather loosely to (a) single superposed cells and (b) a clearcut layer of more than one cell produced by longitudinal divisions (parallel to the long axis) of a single cell and arranged in the same transverse plane. The term should be restricted to the second category alone, however, because each cell is not considered a tier in uniseriate filamentous bodies.

The suspensor occupies the basal pole beyond root cap in the mature embryo and constitutes an *extra-embryonal part*. When the first internal cells are formed, the suspensor may be single-celled, uniseriate (Figure 15.1H–N), or multiseriate, i.e. where some cells may have divided longitudinally at the basal end and appear like tiers, while one or some longitudinally undivided cells intervene between them and the terminal part (Figures 15.1J, 15.2A–B).

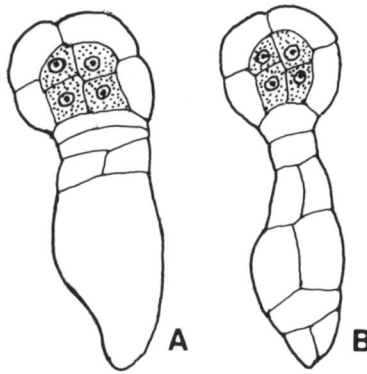

Figure 15.2.   Proembryos immediately after formation of the first internal cells (*dotted*): (A) *Sedum acre* (EN 221; after Souèges 1927). (B) *Saxifraga granulata* (EN 222; after Souèges 1937b).

The formation of morphogenetically significant tiers always starts at the terminal pole of the proembryo and proceeds toward the base. Hence, early longitudinal divisions at the basal end of the suspensor are of no morphogenetic value in the further development of the embryo. The tiers, significant for the present classification, thus end with the first vertically undivided cell that one sees when looking from the terminal to the basal end of the proembryo. Nevertheless, since the suspensor is a part of the proembryo and plays a considerable physiological role (Walbot et al. 1972; Nagl 1973; Alpi et al. 1975; Cionini et al. 1976), it cannot be ignored altogether. To consider the entire basal portion of the proembryo beyond the first vertically undivided cell as one tier (the *suspensor tier*), irrespective of the total number of cells or tiers that comprise it would be appropriate. For example, there would be only four tiers in the proembryo depicted in Figure 15.1K, and only three in those of Figures 15.1A and 15.2B.

Following the above, the first internal cell is not produced in angiosperms if the proembryo is less than two-tiered, and this may be delayed in a multitiered proembryo until six tiers are formed. The former represents the most advanced and the latter the least advanced type. Thus, the proembryos are categorized into five groups. In the first group, the first internal cells are formed when the proembryo is two-tiered, whereas in the second, third, fourth, and fifth groups, the cells are formed at the three-, four-, five-, and six-tier stage, respectively. If future studies reveal proembryos in which internal cell formation is delayed further, they will constitute more primitive sixth and seventh groups, and so on. The segmentation of internal cells in any tier does not alter the tier number but only the number of cells in the tier concerned. Hence, the total number of tiers present can be determined easily at the time of division or immediately afterward.

Classification Based on Number of Cells per Tier

Whereas tier formation is related to axial elongation of the proembryo, longitudinal cell division in the tiers is concerned with increase in its diameter. Before the formation of the first internal cells, all the tiers are distinct, and hence the number of cells per tier, which never exceeds eight, can be detected easily.

The foregoing discussion suggests that a decrease in the total number of cells present in all the tiers (counting the suspensor tier as one cell) relates to phylogenetic advancement. The number of cells in each tier and the variation of their distribution between the tiers at the time of the first internal-cell formation constitute the second rank, designated *Series,* under each Group. Whereas the cell number in the different tiers may vary from two to eight, the "internal cell" is not formed in a tier before the latter has become at least four-celled.

When internal cells are formed in a four-celled tier (this occurs always in the terminal tier), the four cells are equal in size, and the equal-sized internal cells are segmented by perclinal walls parallel to the outer surface (see Figures 15.1M–O, 15.3A,F,K,O). However, a four-celled terminal or subterminal tier may also, without cutting internal cells, become eight-celled by peculiarly curved walls such that none of the eight cells formed is wholly internal. Further, the orientation of the curved walls in the terminal tier differs from that in the subterminal tiers (see Figure 15.3H–J, P–R). Such eight-celled tiers, whether terminal or subterminal, comprise two groups of four cells each, with regard to shape and topography (Figure 15.3H–P). Internal cells may be segmented first either in four cells of any one group (Figure 15.3C,D,H,I, M,N, P,Q) or simultaneously in all eight cells (Figure 15.3E,J, N, R). Cell number in an eight-celled tier does not increase any further without segmentation of internal cells.

In some proembryos, the terminal tier may possess four to eight cells at the time of formation of internal cells. This is brought about by an oblique first division of the terminal cell, which results in a larger and a smaller cell. A wedge-shaped cell is then segmented by the larger cell. The two cells other than the wedge-shaped one, divide vertically to produce four cells, thus making the tier five-celled (Figure 15.3B). The wedge-shaped cell may also divide vertically to make the tier six-celled before the segmentation of internal cells. In such proembryos, as a rule, internal cells are produced first by the cells other than the wedge-shaped cell or by its derivatives (Figure 15.3B, G).

The two to eight cells of a tier are distributed variously in the proembryo, but follow a definite pattern because, as stated above, the morphogenetic wave of increase in the number of cells per tier always proceeds from terminal to basal tiers. Hence, until the time of segmentation of the first internal cells, the number of cells in any tier (excluding the suspensor tier) is equal to or less than the number of cells in a more terminally located adjacent tier. Besides, more than three tiers of four cells each or two tiers of eight cells each are not formed before the terminal cells are segmented.

The distribution of *series* under *groups* is as follows:

Group 1. Characterized by only two tiers, comprises three Series.
  Series 1. Terminal tier four-celled (Figure 15.4A–C).
  Series 2. Terminal tier more than four- but less than eight-celled (Figure 15.4D).
  Series 3. Terminal tier eight-celled (Figure 15.4E).
Group 2. Characterized by three tiers; includes five series.
  Series 1. Terminal tier four-celled; each of the other tiers less than four-celled (Figure 15.5A).
  Series 2. Two terminal tiers, each with four cells (Figure 15.5B, F).
  Series 3. Terminal tier more than four- but less than eight-celled; each of the other tiers four- or fewer celled (Figure 15.5C, G).
  Series 4. Terminal tier eight-celled; each other tier less than eight-celled (Figure 15.5D, H).
  Series 5. Two terminal tiers with eight cells each (Figure 15.5E, I).
Group 3. Marked with four tiers, contains six series.
  Series 1. Terminal tier four-celled; every other tier less than four-celled (Figure 15.6A).
  Series 2. Two terminal tiers, with four cells each; every other tier less than four-celled (Figure 15.6B, G).
  Series 3. Three or more terminal tiers with four cells each (Figure 15.6C, H).
  Series 4. Terminal tier more than four- but less than eight-celled; other tiers four- or less than four-celled (Figure 15.6D, 6I).
  Series 5. Terminal tier eight-celled; other tiers less than eight-celled (Figure 15.6E, J).
  Series 6. Two terminal tiers with eight cells each; other tiers less than eight-celled (Figure 15.6F, K).

Group 4 and group 5 would also have only six series similar to group 3, because, as stated above, the number of terminal tiers that become four-celled rarely exceeds three, and the maximum number of eight-celled terminal tiers is two before the segmentation of internal cells, irrespective of the number of tiers of the proembryo.

All series, except series 1, which is similar in all groups, are distinguished separately for each group, because the more significant, primary parameter of a group cannot be mingled with secondary parameter of a series. Series 4 and 5 of group 3 are similar to series 2 and 3 of group 1, and series 2, 4, 5, and 6 of group 3 are the same as series 2, 3, 4, and 5 of group 2.

Classification Based on Tier Location

Although in many proembryos, the first fully internal cells are formed in the terminal tier, they may be formed simultaneously in the terminal and adjacent subterminal tier or formed first in the subterminal tier. The first two conditions are considered to be more advanced than the last. This parameter, distinguishable in all groups except group 1, is called *variation*.

Variation 1: First internal cells formed in the terminal tier or simultaneously in the terminal and subterminal tiers (Figures 15.5A–E, 15.6A–D).
Variation 2: First internal cells formed in a subterminal tier (Figures 15.5F–I, 15.6G–K).

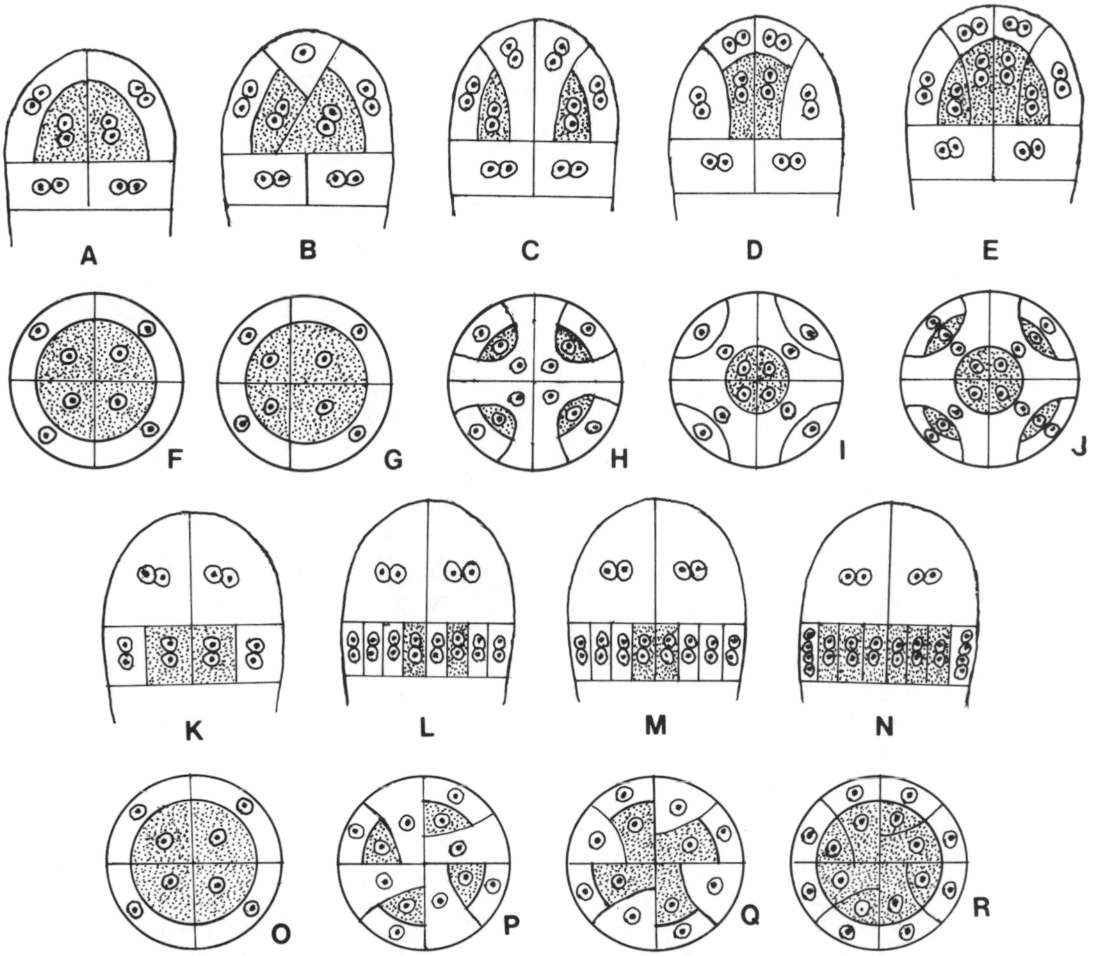

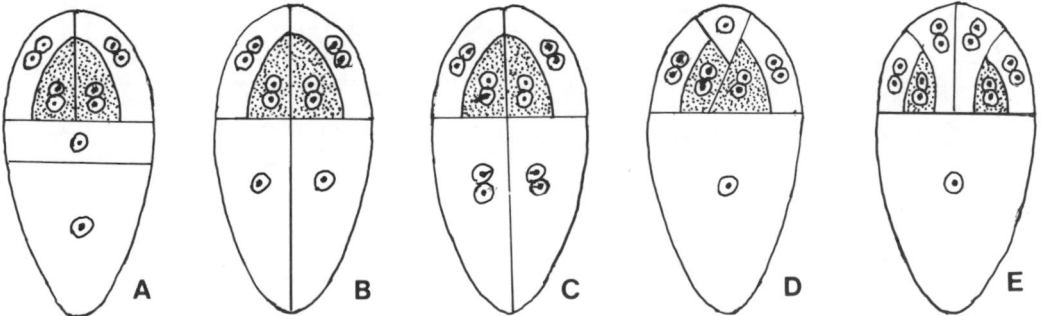

Figure 15.3. Segmentation of first internal cells (*dotted*), as seen in longitudinal and transverse section of the terminal and subterminal tiers of the proembryo. (A–J) Segmentation in terminal tier. (A–E) Longitudinal sections: (A) terminal tier four-celled; (B) terminal tier more than four but less than eight-celled; (C–E) terminal tier eight-celled. (F–J) Transverse sections corresponding to figures (A–E). (K–R) Segmentation in subterminal tier. (K–N) Longitudinal sections: (K) subterminal tier four-celled; (L–N) subterminal tier eight-celled. (O–R) Transverse sections corresponding to figures (K–N).

Figure 15.4. Longitudinal view of Group 1 embryos just after segmentation of the first internal cells: (A–C) Series 1; (D) Series 2; (E) Series 3.

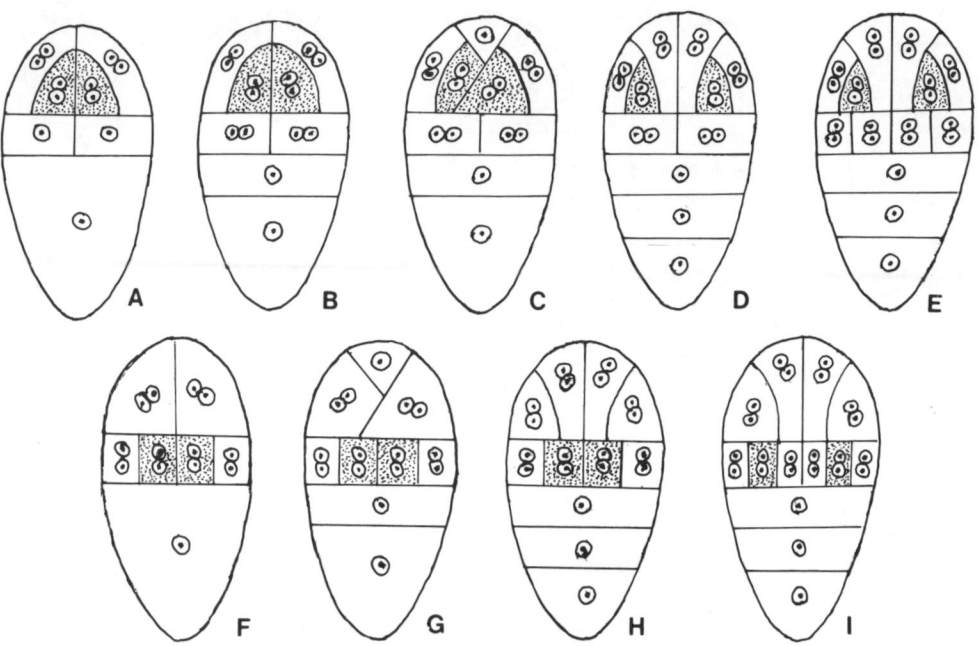

Figure 15.5. Longitudinal view of Group 2 embryos just after segmentation of the first internal cells: (A) Series 1; (B–E) Series 2 to 5, respectively, Variation 1; (F–I) Series 2 to 5, respectively, Variation 2.

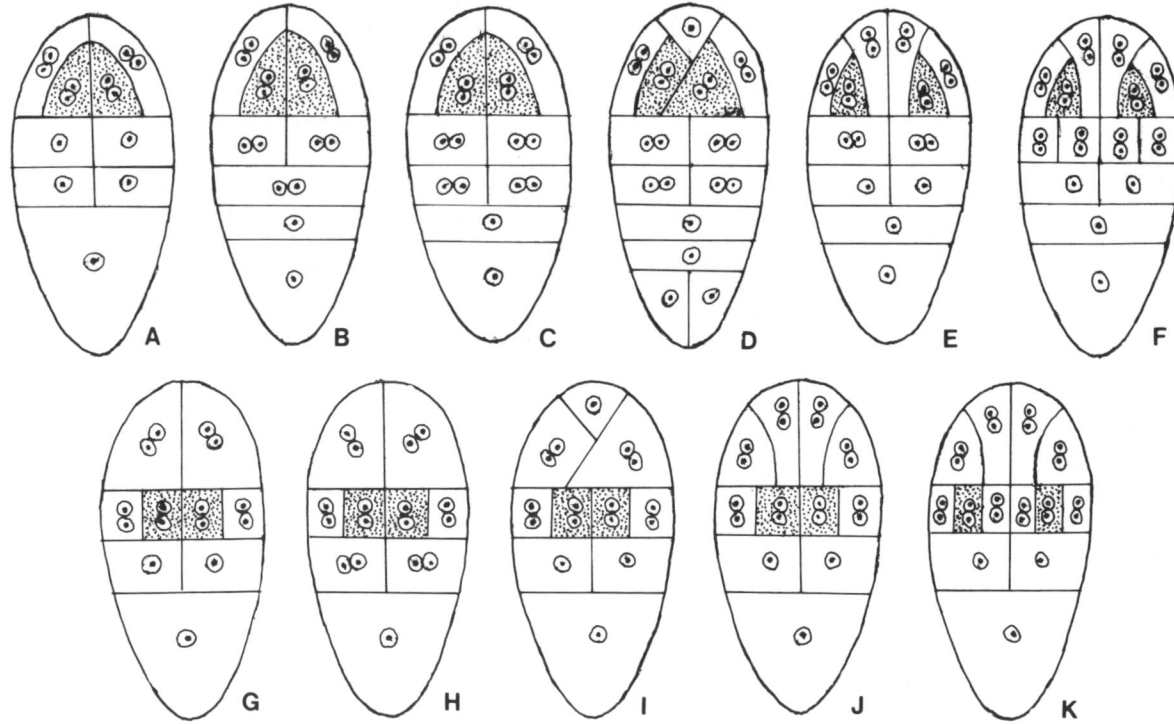

Figure 15.6. Longitudinal view of Group 3 embryos just after segmentation of the first internal cells: (A) Series 1; (B–F) Series 2 to 6, respectively, Variation 1; (G–K) Series 2 to 6, respectively, Variation 2.

GENERAL CONSIDERATIONS AND CONCLUSIONS

All the parameters on which this classification is based are serially numbered, hence an embryo can be characterized by a three-digit number, i.e. the *embryonic number* (EN), in which the first digit denotes the group number (1 to 5), the second digit indicates the series number (1 to 6), and the third digit shows the variation number (1 or 2).

This classification divides the angiosperm proembryos into a total of 45 kinds in 5 groups. If more groups are obtained, this number will correspondingly increase.

The classification is based upon a morphogenetic analysis of the angiosperm proembryo in accordance with an established phylogenetic trend. It does not consider the derivation of the different parts of the mature embryo or necessitate a study of the exact sequence of the first few divisions of the proembryo for determining the embryonic number. On the contrary, it concerns the composition of the different tiers during or immediately after segmentation of the first internal cells. This is easy because the proembryo does not have more than eight cells in any tier by that time. The use of numbers simplifies embryo characterization; however, this classification, like others, is applicable only to those embryos showing a regular, early ontogeny. Several angiosperms, marked with an irregular early embryogeny, lack definite and recognizable parameters (see Buvat 1989).

Periasamy (1977) determined the embryonic number of a random sample of 50 species, both dicotyledons and monocotyledons, and found a nearly normal distribution of groups, series, and variations (Table 15.1). For example, 222 is the embryonic number for *Papaver rhoeas*. As there are three tiers, the first digit refers to group 2 (vertical division in terminal and subterminal tiers), the second refers to series 2 under group 2 because the two terminal tiers have four cells each (after octant stage, the first wholly internal cells are formed), and the third digit refers to variation 2 because the first internal cells are formed in the subterminal tier.

Table 15.1. Distribution of 50 embryos by group, series, and variation.

Group	Number of embryos	Series	Number of embryos	Variation	Number of embryos
1	3	1	4	1	34
2	15	2	21	2	16
3	19	3	11		
4	10	4	5		
5	3	5	8		
		6	1		

Angiosperm taxonomy rests on external morphology, and the taxa so circumscribed often show many developmental, anatomical, physiological, and cytological similarities. In general, larger taxa are more prone to discrepancy. The taxonomic affinities, therefore, are confirmed by statistical correlations: taxa with a greater number of advanced features are thought to be more advanced than others. Whatever the validity of this approach, such statistics urge the establishment of the evolutionary status of every character. Although this is again based on taxonomic hierarchy, the taxa involved are large enough to be marked with a definite evolutionary status.

Most of our phylogenetic considerations rest on two general dicta: (a) ontogeny recapitulates phylogeny, and (b) phylogenetic advance comes about by successive modifications of ontogeny. The study of ontogeny is the only way to understand the operation of these dicta: however, the first has received more attention than the second, probably because the second is more concerned with morphogenesis than the first and is thus more difficult to assess and interpret. Despite spectacular advances in genetics and molecular biology, we have yet to reach even a hypothesis concerning how, starting from the gene, the morphogenesis of the specific morphology of a phenotypic expression (such as leaf shape, for example) is brought about.

LITERATURE CITED

Alpi, A., F. Tognoni, and F. D'Amato. 1975. Growth regulator levels in embryo and suspensor of *Phaseolus coccineus* at two stages of development. *Planta* 127:153–162.

Buvat, R. 1989. *Ontogeny, Cell Differentiation, and Structure of Vascular Plants.* Berlin: Springer-Verlag.

Cionini, P. G., A. Bennici, A. Alpi, and F. D'Amato. 1976. Suspensor gibberellin, and *in vitro* development of *Phaseolus coccineus* embryos. *Planta* 131:115–117.

Coulter, J. M., and C. J. Chamberlain. 1912. *Morphology of Angiosperms.* New York.

Cronquist, A. 1968. *The Evolution and Classification of Flowering Plants.* Boston: Houghton Mifflin.

Haccius, B. 1952. Die Embryoentwicklung bei *Ottelia alismoides* und des Problem des terminalen Monocotylenkeimblatts. *Planta* 40:443–460.

Hofmeister, F. 1849. *Die Entstehung des Embryo der Phanerogamen.* Leipzig.

Johansen, D. A. 1950. *Plant Embryology.* Waltham, MA: Chronica Botanica.

Johri, B. M., K. A. Ambegaokar, and P. S. Srivastava. 1992. *Comparative Embryology of Angiosperms.* Heidelberg: Springer-Verlag.

Maheshwari, P. 1950. *An Introduction to the Embryology of Angiosperms.* New York: McGraw Hill.

Melchior, H. 1964. *A. Engler's Syllabus der Pflanzenfamilien.* Bd 2. Berlin: Borntraeger.

Mestre, J. C. 1967. La signification phylogénétique de l'embryogénie. *Rev. Gen. Bot.* 74:273–324.

Nagl, W. 1973. The angiosperm suspensor and the mammalian trophoblast: Organs with similar cell structure and function. *Bull. Soc. Bot. Fr. Mem.* 298–302.

Natesh, S., and M. A. Rau. 1984. The embryo. In *Embryology of Angiosperms.* Ed. B. M. Johri. Heidelberg: Springer-Verlag. 377–443.

Periasamy, K. 1972. Contemporary thoughts in plant morphology. *Advances in Plant Morphology.* Ed. Y. S. Murty. Meerut, India: Sarita Prakashan. 33–45.

––––––. 1977. A new approach to the classification of angiosperm embryos. *Proc. Indian Acad. Sci.* 85:1–13.

––––––. 1983. Apical growth in plants. *Swamy Bot. Club News Lett.* 2:40–54.

Periasamy, K., and B. G. L. Swamy. 1964. Is the microsporangium of angiosperms wall-less? *Curr. Sci.* 33:835–838.

Pillai, S. K., B. Chacko, M. B. Bande, and R. Divakaran. 1972. The shoot apex in gymnosperms: Trends of specialization. In *Biology of the Land Plants.* Ed. V. Puri et al. Meerut, India: Sarita Prakashan 44–56.

Schnarf, K. 1929. *Vergleichende Embryologie der Angiospermen.* Berlin: Borntraeger.

Sivaramakrishna, D. 1978. Size relationship of apical cell and basal cell in two-celled embryos in angiosperms. *Can. J. Bot.* 56:1434–1438.

Souèges, R. 1927. Développement de l'embryon chez le *Sedum acre* L. *Bull. Soc. Bot. France* 74:234–251.

_____. 1931. L'embryon chez le *Sagittaria sagittaefolia* L. Le cône végétatif de la tige et L'extermite rediculaire chez le monocotyledones. *Ann. Sci. Nat. Bot.* 13:353–402.

_____. 1937a. *Les lois de Développement.* Paris: Hermen et Co.

_____. 1937b. *Triteres et Travaux Scientifiques.* Saint Dizier, France: Dexime Notice.

_____. 1939. *Embryogénie et Classification.* 2e fasc. *Essai d'un Systéme Embryogénique. Partie Générale,* Paris, France.

_____. 1948. *Embryogénie et Classification.* 3e. fasc. *Essai d'un Systéme Embryogénique. Partie Speciale:* Ire periode du systeme, Paris, France.

_____. 1951. *Embryogégenie et Classification.* 4e. fasc. *Essai d'un Systéme Embryogénique. Partie speciale.* 2e periode due systeme. Paris France.

_____. 1954. L'origin de cône végétatif de la tige et la question de la "Terminalite" du cotyledon des monocotyledones. *Ann. Sci. Nat. Bot. Paris* 15(Ser. 11):1–20.

Subramanyam, M. 1949. An embryological study of *Lobelia pyramidalis* Wall. with special reference to the mechanism of nutrition of the embryo in the family Lobeliaceae. *New Phytol.* 48:365–373.

Swamy, B. G. L. 1962. The origin of cotyledon and epicotyl in *Ottelia alismoides. Beitr. Biol. Pflanzen.* 39:1–16.

Swamy, B. G. L., and K. K. Lakshmanan. 1962a. The origin of epicotylary meristem and cotyledon in *Halophila ovata* Gaudich. *Ann. Bot.* (n.s.) 26:243–249.

_____. 1962b. Contributions to the embryology of Najadaceae. *J. Indian Bot. Soc.* 41:247–267.

Takhtajan, A. 1969. *Flowering Plants: Origin and Dispersal.* Edinburgh: Oliver and Boyd.

Venkata Rao, C. 1951. Contributions to the embryology of Sterculiaceae. III. *Melochia corchorifolia* L. *J. Indian Bot. Soc.* 30:122–131.

Walbot, V., T. Brandy, M. Clutter, and I. Sussex. 1972. Macromolecular synthesis during plant embryogeny: Rates of RNA synthesis in *Phaseolus coccineus. Dev. Biol.* 29:104–111.

Wardlaw, C. W. 1952. *Phylogeny and Morphogenesis.* London: Macmillan.

Yamazaki, T. 1974. A system of Gamopetalae based on embryology. *J. Fac. Sci. Univ. Tokyo, Sect.III, Bot.* 11:263–281.

Yamazaki, T. 1982. Recognized types in early development of the embryo and phylogeny in the dicotyledons. *Acta. Phytotax. Geobot.* 33:240–249.

Section IV
PHYLOGENETIC DEVELOPMENT

Chapter 16

Reconstruction of the Phylogeny of Seed Plants

A. D. J. MEEUSE

The role of anatomy in the phylogeny of seed plants is about as old as paleobotany (160 y), and seed plant taxonomy has long been based almost exclusively on external morphological features. Of necessity, the comparative analysis of structural features of recent plant groups has been used as a yardstick for the interpretation of fossils, but gradually so many data from Paleo- and Mesozoic vascular plants have accumulated that one may envisage the building up of a comparative morphology of stem (stelic) structures starting from the most primitive. Despite great strides made so far, however, a consensus as to whether all vascular plants are (or were originally) monostelic or primarily polystelic has not yet been possible. The early diversification of the tracheophytes suggests that there are several alternative organization plans of the Lycophyta, Sphenophyta, and (other) groups ancestral to true ferns, seed plants, and presumably some extinct groups. In view of the still unsorted data, discussion of the subject in greater detail is premature, but the continual increase in records will probably soon lead to an adequate understanding of the evolution of the vascular plants. The relevant publications are scattered and mostly so recent that they have not yet been properly summarized in manuals or literature surveys. The origin of the seed plants is fortunately already practically elucidated and can be retraced to the Lower Devonian.

My neological approach to seed plant evolution has been under attack from several angles. The simple truth is that we "new" morphologists base our deductions at least partly on the outcome of paleobotanical studies, so we are in a position to reconstruct an "upward" evolution of ancient morphomes (what became of them?) and can retrace the recent character states in a "downward" direction to their putative archetypes. This approach is more realistic, because "classical" morphology, which is based on nontangible and rigid tenets that can be challenged and replaced by alternative viewpoints when necessary, is merely typology in disguise.

The most glaring *testimonium paupertatis* of the "classical" approach is its failure to provide an acceptable answer to the awkward question of angiosperm origin and evolution. I have followed the scientific procedure of replacing a theory (and the framework of deductions and conclusions built around it) by other principles and basic assumptions largely based on discrete evidence from various sources (see Meeuse 1992).

HISTORICAL DATA

When Darwinian ideas began to pervade biological thinking, at first the evolution of the higher plants remained obscure for several reasons, the principal one being a leaning among botanists to accept certain current typological tenets as valid throughout and, therefore, applicable in a phylogenetic context (see Meeuse 1986, 1987, for details and also for references and the terminology used in the present chapter). It does not follow that all deductions emanating from "classical" morphology have to be rejected; the well-known Hofmeisterian generalization of the processes associated with the alternation of generations among the Cormophyta is the best but perhaps the only successful example.

At about the turn of the century, the outcome of paleobotanic studies—principally the discovery of Bennettitalian forms and the recognition of ancient seed plants since dubbed "seed ferns"—started to change the picture, but the conventional dicta concerning the morphological interpretation of the functional reproductive units (FRUs) of the angiosperms were not amended. To understand and explain the situation, one has to go back to the interpretation of the so-called magnoliophytic "flower" as a "metamorphosis" (in a Goethean sense) of the vegetative shoot (thus implying the equivalence of all floral appendages as modified trophophylls, the conventional "leaves"). A consequence of, or perhaps a prelude to this idea, was the postulation of only three separate and intransgressive categories of seed plant organs: leaf, stem, and root. The roots were considered to be (basically subterranean) modifications of stems and, hence, also caulomatic; in any event, they can be disregarded in the discussion of controversial issues concerning sporogenous organs.

The interpretation of fertile organs (gamomorphomes) as "leaves" of a sort, or at least as phyllomatic or "appendicular" entities, had one important consequence— understanding the nature of the sporangiate parts proper (anthers and ovules) of the highest seed plants. Until about the 1930s, phytomorphology was largely the morphology of the Magnoliophyta or at least strongly "angiosperm-centered" in the flowering plants that were used as yardsticks for the morphology of Lower Cormophyta and the Coniferophyta. The study of, among other things, developmental stages resulted in two opposite opinions—one accepting stem-borne ovules (Payer, etc.) and the other accepting leaf-borne ones (Celakovsky, etc.). There simply was no alternative! This controversy turned up time and again in a more or less modified form (phyllo- and stachyospermy of Sahni, phyllo- and stachyospermy of Lam; see Meeuse 1966a, 1972, 1986, and also for references to authors mentioned in this chapter but not included in the bibliography). The possibility of a different nature of the genitalia (i.e. their *sui generis* nature in respect to the vegetative organs or trophomorphomes) was pointed out by Grégoire and McLean Thompson, for example, but the ingrained dicta were tenacious and prevailed, largely owing to the authoritative publications of the typological Trollian school in Europe and the Eamsian morphologists in the United States.

Since in the meantime more and more fossilized remains of undoubtedly primitive vascular plants had been found in Devonian and even older strata (*Psilophyton* and other forms), one became confronted with plant forms without any differentiation in clearly phyllomic (and principally photosynthetizing) and manifestly caulomatic morphomes. Bower is quoted for the statement: "The sporangium is older than the leaf." He clearly envisaged a phylogenetically older situation in which the originally undifferentiated parts had somehow evolved into stelic caulomes and nonstelic phyllomes (or had acquired "leafy" organs originated from emergences). This in turn implies that the already present sporangia and their derivatives were not primarily a part of a leafy organ but led an independent existence, or at best became *secondarily* associated with a phyllomorphome. His perfectly logical deduction was almost completely disregarded in subsequent publications until about 1930, when W. Zimmermann, as a representative of the school of New Morphology, proposed his Telome Theory. He postulated a common organization plan of all early Tracheophyta inspired by the Devonian *Rhynia* and *Horneophyton* type of plant, based on an archetype with a dichotomously branched corm, of which some or all of the ultimate clado-morphomes or telomes bore terminal sporangia. This hypothesis implied that monophyletic evolution can be queried because: (a) *Rhynia* was of about Middle Devonian age, and (b) dissimilar fossils are known from older strata that reach back into the Silurian. This is of no consequence as far as the seed plants are concerned, however. It is quite clear what their Lower Devonian precursors were and how their vegetative parts developed into phyllomes and caulomes, the *ab initio* present sporangia evolving independently. The fundamental mistake Zimmermann made is that he postulated a divergent evolution of trophophylls from planated syntelomes without sporangia next to a semogenesis of "sporophylls" from so-called "mixed syntelomes" comprising telomes bearing terminal sporangia. Apart from the false homology (sterile telomes cannot possibly be the morphological equivalent of fertile ones: Meeuse 1966c, 1986), there is no evidence, as stated above, for such a development in the primitive Devonian plants accepted as ancestral to spermatophytes (*Protopteridium = Remillea, Svalbardia,* the early *Archaeopteris* type, etc.): their reproductive morphomes remain spatially separate from the trophophylls-to-be. Another unexplained difficulty is how derivatives of so-called "mixed syntelomes," which according to the theory incorporated single sporangia, could turn into gamomorphomes bearing the much more complex anthers, ovules, and cupules. Clearly, Zimmermann did the utmost to save the dictum of leaf-borne genitalia. The semogenetic origin from the cycadophytinous cupule is elucidated by the fossil record: sterile, telomelike cladomes originated (or modified from similar, sterile morphomes) near an ovule or a group of ovules started to envelop the sporangiate organs. To my mind the cupule is *sui generis* in respect of the phyllomes, but it is at any rate unacceptable within the framework of the classical dicta to find a leaf on a sporophyll, or a cladic organ for that matter. Ovuliferous cupules seemingly incorporated in a fertile frond, as in Carboniferous seed ferns, are not primarily leaf-borne but became secondarily associated with phyllomic elements.

The above-mentioned, compromising attempts by Sahni and Lam were partly intended to link gymnosperms and angiosperms by providing features that both kinds of seed plants were supposed to have in common. The gamomorphome of the female *Cycas* plant has so consistently been taken for the epitomization of the "sporophyll" concept that Sahni accepted the "phyllospermy" of all cycadalean FRUs against the "stachyospermy" of, for example, those of *Ginkgo*. Lam posed that in angiosperms both conditions occur, but why the angiospermous genitalia bear anthers or contain ovules instead of sporangia was left unexplained.

For various reasons, students of seed plant evolution have come to the conclusion that the Magnoliophyta are inevitably descendants of some kind of gymnosperm. However, the ingrained tenets regarding floral morphology prevented the crystallization of ideas because one met with some "unbridgeable gap" between gymnosperms and angiosperms in spite of the manifest resemblances. Three errors were committed: (a) the adherence to the above-mentioned, essentially Goethean concept of a "flower", (b) the failure to distinguish between cycadophytic and coniferophytinous seed plants (which groups evolved independently even since the Upper Devonian), and (c) the lack of understanding of the taxonomic affinities of the Gnetatae. The impact of the ante-dated floral concept on phylogenetic theories will be recapitulated presently. The origin of the flowering plants can be traced back to cycadophytinous forms; the evolution of the Coniferophytina is irrelevent in this connection. Because suitable candidates for a form progenitorial to the angiosperms were illusive for a long time, one "recon-structed"some retroactively, but these figments of the mind still have not materialized. The vexing absence of fossil angiospermoids led to far-fetched explanations as to why the anticipated, hypothetical ancestors had not been discovered, while the true reason—spurious premises—was not considered! The kinds of fossil FRUs that have so far come to light are not conformable to the hypothetical phaneranthous, polymerous, bisexual (and entomophilous) "flower" envisaged on account of false assumptions; if that kind of FRU existed at all at that time it must have been rare and it is not possibly archetypic in respect of all other early angiospermous ones.

Other items having an important bearing upon the phylogeny of the seed plants include the origin and evolution of the ovule and its accessory morphomes (Meeuse 1963a,b, 1974a, 1981; Meeuse and Bouman 1974; Boesewinkel and Bouman 1984; Bouman 1984) and of microsporangiate organs, and the semogenesis of the phyllomic trophomorphomes (leaves of various kinds). Although the phylogenetic history of the spermatophytes can be traced back to the Lower Devonian times, some space must be devoted to other groups of vascular plants. In his Telome Theory, Zimmermann postu-lated a monophyletic origin of the sporophytes of all tracheophytes from a common, Rhynia-like archetype, but this idea is rendered out of date. Their common precursor might have been a thallose gametophytic plant form bearing sessile sporangia, the vegetative sporophyte originating secondarily (Meeuse 1966b). The Lycophyta apparently evolved independently, probably since the Silurian; they have a singular type of trophophyll, namely the "enation leaf" or lycophyll, that almost certainly evolved from an enation (emergence) and not from a syntelomic archetype. The phylogenetic origin and taxonomic position of the true (= isosporous!) ferns is obscure, and the conventional "Filices" are presumably polyphyletic; the so-called water-ferns are incongruous and much more likely to be the depauperate survivors of the pteridosperms. Conceivably, some fern groups are descendants of Early Devonian forms from which also the seed plants originated, but they never developed a cambial growth in stem girth, nor did they become heterosporous like the latter (or hardly ever: Stauropteris?). Quite recently, Rothwell (1987) described Lower Carboniferous fossils combining features of indusiate fern groups, a finding that renders a Late Paleozoic radiation of at least these groups highly probable. It also confirms the independent evolution of seed plants (since the Devonian) and true ferns. The Sphenophyta may share an early origin with the seed plants (and some fern groups?), but they soon acquired and maintained a number of characteristic features (sporangia pendulous on apically recurved stalks; stems sharply jointed with a singular siphonostelic anatomy, etc.). There were also early land plants with laterally attached sporangia, but this type probably did not survive long.

It is, therefore, clear that the comparative morphology and anatomy of seed plants must start from Lower Devonian archetypes immediately preceding the so-called "progymnosperms" (Eo- or Protospermatophyta would be a more appropriate name), and subsequently one must take the principal and early diversification of the

latter into account. A direct comparison of, say, a coniferous strobilus ("cone") with
stroboloid polymorphomes of cycadophytinous forms (e.g. "flowers"), as has been done
in the past, is clearly not permissible, as their common precursory structures are far
more primitive than corresponding parts of protospermatophytic plants. The same
holds for the vegetative organs, so the evolutionary morphology of the
coniferophytinous and cycadophytinous plant groups must be treated separately. That
of archespermatophytic plants provides the only, ancient connection. I am inclined to
go even so far as to accept an appreciable number of parallelisms and convergencies of
seemingly homologous characters and character states in the two conventionally
gymnospermous groups (of which only one served as the ancestral group of the
angiosperms). The forms of siphongamy found in all recent Coniferophytina, barring
the very primitive Gingko, and the most advanced Cycadophytina (including all
flowering plants) are nowadays attributed to convergent evolution, and the progressive reduction of the vegetative gametophytes in both groups is a good example of
parallelism.

Character states manifestly derived from shared symplesiomorphies found in the
progymnosperms, such as the presence of tracheidal elements with bordered pits (and
their derivatives) in the secondary xylem and a primary vascularized integument, may
for the time being be accepted as homologous throughout the Spermatophyta. These
simple and straightforward starting-points expressed by several leading scientists are
continually threatened by peculiar viewpoints. To mention a single example: Some
representatives of the Gnetatae or Chlamydospermae have repeatedly been assigned to
a coniferophytinous taxon and others to a cycadophytinous one (see e.g. Meyen 1984).
This confuses the issue and denies the significance of whole sets of corresponding and
distinguishing features.

Recent attempts to save the theory of the uniaxial "flower" are chiefly centered on
the origin of the angiospermous carpel (see Meeuse 1987); the principal mistake is the
lack of understanding of the advent and the nature of the integuments and the
ovuliferous cupule. In many surveys and in quite a few manuals, one finds the remark
that the "classical" floral theory is "convenient through its simplicity and straight-
forwardness" and "has so often been shown to be valid and confirmed" or that alternative hypotheses are too conjectural to be acceptable—clearly mental inertia because
such alternatives have not been refuted by a critical point-for-point analysis. At one
time, nuclear and atomic physics was a relatively simple affair: An atomic nucleus
was surrounded by electrons. In due course, mainly theoretical considerations ushered
in the discovery of a whole range of elementary particles: protons, neutrons, positrons,
neutrinos, mesons, quarks, and gluons, to mention only the most important ones, but
no physicist would discard the theoretical background because the original conceptual
model was far less complicated and easier to understand—the hypotheses were taken
seriously and tested for their value.

In view of the steadily increasing number of angiospermoid fossils from the
critical Lower to Middle Cretaceous age, which provide tangible yardsticks that were
lacking before, the classical floral theory and its consequences appear to be untenable.
This immediately involves the question of the strictly mono- or pleiorheithric descent
of the flowering plants and the prevailing sex distribution in turn associated with the
reputedly early incidence of entomophily. Such considerations are largely based on
morphological evidence because that is all we can primarily glean from the lifeless
fossil remains. Still, a comparison of the fossils in question with similar or, even
better, clearly related, living taxa not only greatly enlightens the degree of advancement of these recent angiosperms and the apo- or plesiomorphy of their characters but
also their original floral ecology.

GENERALITIES

As stated above, phylogenetic approaches to the unraveling of semogenetic relationships ought to be based on tangible evidence, primarily on an adequate fossil record and secondarily on shared features of (groups of) recent taxa. The crux of the assessment is the question of homology (see Meeuse 1984, 1986). One only has to postulate a few things to arrive at morphome sequences found in a stratigraphical order, thus rendering the relation between successively appearing phenotypes a plausible one. Once a semogenetic sequence has been reconstructed, new finds provide links bridging gaps in fossil record and confirming the reliability of that sequence. Still, much depends on the inferences drawn from the evidence and the ensuing interpretations.

Such phene sequences (historical morphoclines) represent evolutionary phases of a morphome (or of other, associated or deducible features such as symmetry, nomomery and other spatial relations, anatomical characters, functional aspects such as pollination and diaspore dispersal, etc.), so that the complex of identifiable sequences found within the same group clearly reflects the evolutionary history of that taxon (i.e. of a lineage).

The most important character sequences are those involving what are by consensus singular and, hence, distinguishing and discriminating features of a given group of organisms up to the present time. The seed plants, for instance, are fully characterized by the combination of three consistent main features (of which the first is occasionally lost in herbaceous taxa): (a) secondary growth by means of one or sometimes several stem cambia, normally producing phloem centrifugally and xylem centripetally, the longitudinally oriented xylem elements being fiber tracheids with bordered pits or derivatives of this type; (b) heterospory, and (c) the possession of ovules, i.e. of megasporangium homologs surrounded by at least one integument (hardly ever redundant in a few angiospermous taxa). By means of these features, one can link the present seed plants with Upper Devonian fossils and the latter in turn to still older forms in which the characteristic spermatophytic features (such as heterospory, integument) were still lacking or not yet fully developed. The ancient spermatophytic characteristics, as already found in Devonian plants, are clearly symplesiomorphic in terms of cladistics, so that one can detect and recognize new developments and changes in a semogenetic sequence as apomorphies. Two very important apomorphies originated in the latest Devonian, namely, the two unique characteristics of the cycadophytinous spermatophytes: the cupule (the early precursor of the angiospermous carpel), and about simultaneously the lagenostome/salpinx (later to become the inner integument); these are symplesiomorphic among all cycadophytinous plant forms but apomorphic in the coniferophytina. Another difference between the conifero- and cycadophytinous groups is the different nature of their trophophylls (see below).

The above-sketched approach has to be preferred as a working hypothesis to the "classical" morphology. As intimated above, the neological deductions are self-correcting in that new discoveries continually augment and improve our insight without coming into conflict with the theory. Palynomorphs previously known only as *sporae diversae* have later been found *in situ* (within microsporangia), and this has thrown light on, or confirmed, their surmised taxonomic identity. As an example, the discovery of what is to all intents a chloranthaceous plant (see Friis et al. 1986) confirmed the identity of the already known palynomorph *Clavatipollenitis* previously suspected to represent the pollen grain of a taxon of chloranthaceous affinity.

A phytomorphology based on rigid and invariable dicta cannot be adjusted in such a way and is ambiguous by failing to indicate the polarity of a series of presumably homologous entities, whereas the fossil record is infallible in this respect as soon as adequate data have come to hand, thanks to the stratigraphical position of the stages of the morphocline that provides a (relative or absolute) time factor, and, hence, the direction of the progression, the polarity, of the semogenesis. It follows that I reject the Hennigian or cladistic approach precisely because the fossil evidence is *a priori* discarded categorically. This amounts to throwing away the baby with the bathwater.

METHODOLOGY

Our cognizance of the evolutionary history of a certain morphome is not only augmented by discoveries of previously unknown macrofossils but also by the application of new techniques to earlier recorded material. Scanning electron microscopy (SEM) is an example of an applicable methodological advance. Fossil material of leaves or other organs studied by SEM reveals details of the epidermal architecture and the stomatal apparatus that may provide clues to the affinity of the plant taxon concerned: Fossilized dissected leaves of Cretaceous age, originally referred to the Rutales on account of their dissected leaf type, proved to agree better with those of the Fagales (Rüffle 1980). Because at early times one did not expect that the present-day, almost always single-leaved oak and beech family was likely to have ancestors with dissected trophomorphomes, the connection long remained unrecognized. Certain additional arguments were obtained from the morphology of the first leaves of fagaceous seedlings (which may be lobed) and from the lobed leaves of certain *Quercus* cultivars (probably a throwback or atavism, possibly obtained from a coppice shoot) and the exceptional incidence of more or less lobed leaves in an occasional fagaceous taxon.

The microtechnical procedures to obtain sections of fossil material have also been improved, so that a greater range of variously impregnated (silicified, calcified, pyritized, or otherwise) plant fossils can be studied anatomically. Other evidence is provided by the development (ontogeny) of morphomes including seedling anatomy and morphology. As mentioned above, in some taxa seedlings produce first leaves of a kind reminiscent of the progenitorial type (e.g. dissected or compound and more or less clearly differing from the adult and undivided ones produced later). Likewise, coppice shoots of trees and large shrubs occasionally produce atypical leaves of an atavistic phenotype (horticulturists have developed new cultivars by taking cuttings from such shoots and propagating them vegetatively).

Ontogenetical analyses often provide useful pointers by demonstrating the secondary (= phylogenetically younger) coalescence, adnation, and fusion of primordial morphomes, thus suggesting a semogenesis starting from individual elements and characterized by a progressive unification of these elements; a corolla may originate as a whorl of 4 or 5 primordia on a floral apex but later develops into a continuous rim to form a sympetalous corolla (i.e. the developmental sequence "recapitulates" semogenesis). Another deduction based on the study of development is the origin of morphomes either as single primordia or as groups of associated primordia, in particular of "stamens" (merandra). Merandra originating as a cluster of primordia secondarily forming out of a single primary one were thought to be equivalent to a homotopic single one. This conventional interpretation required a secondary "splitting" or chorisis of a primordium leading to a secondary increase. Other interpretations, such as the posing of a primary polyandry, were not deemed acceptable because they clash with the concept of a uniaxial flower. My explanation starts from the assumption that the polyandry of clustered merandra is an original condition and reflects the origin of androecial members from originally "polyandrous" holandra (Meeuse 1974b).

Comparative ontogenetic studies may also lead to appreciations and evaluations with a semogenetic meaning. Examples are the initiation and development of ovular integuments, nucellus, and gametophyte. From what can be gleaned from the conditions in the Cycadales and some other living (gnetate) and fossil gymnosperms, in addition to those found in such primitive taxa as the Magnoliales and the Piperales, the angiospermous ovules originally contained a multicellular to massive nucellus (this is called crassinucellate) and they were bitegmic, with a more or less massive but always plurilayered and subdermally initiated outer, and a much thinner, dermally derived inner integument. The outer integument was vascularized, the inner one was not. The seed coat was exarillate, and when the seeds functioned as zoochorously dispersed diaspores they were sarcotestate. Starting from the original conditions still found in several Magnoliales, a number of semogenetic changes led to unitegmy; the ovules often but not always became tenuinucellate and sometimes acquired an aril, arillode, caruncle or elaiosome, or seed floss. Early angiosperms with indehiscent fruits also had exarillate seeds. By a judicious application of these criteria for plesiomorphy one can construe semogenetic sequences, but since the features under discussion are at least partly adaptive, one must avoid the pitfall of undue and unwarranted homologizations. Unitegmy, for instance, must have originated along three alternative pathways (or even more than three if parallel evolution occurred): (a) by the coalescence of two integuments, (b) through the reduction of the (redundant) inner one, and (c) by a process of "tegumentary shifting" (Bouman and Calis 1977). Tenuinucellate ovules are, similarly, the result of a special tendency—the telescoping of developmental stages and a precocity of development of the much reduced gametophyte, so that it required a smaller amount of nutrients.

Among the ultramicroscopical features, the painstaking and continuing studies of phloem microplastids (Behnke 1981) have contributed valuable evidence. Behnke's results indicate a close connection between the magnoliid and liliid clades, which supports other evidence to that effect. The magnolioid-nymphaeoid-ranunculoid nexus also has representatives with a type of microplastid found in other dicotyledonous clades, which, although confirming both the ancestry and a long-lasting diversification within the Magnoliidae s.l. and suggesting certain phylogenetic events, is not unequivocal as regards the time and the sequence of divergence of proliliates and of the hamameloid, rosoid, and dillenioid lineages, and of their phylogenetic relationships. Many phylogenetic relationships still remain more or less obscure or ambiguous if one applies only the available anatomical and morphological criteria. Evidence from other disciplines may be corroborative or at least provide some pointers aiding our provisional conclusions.

CHEMODIAGNOSTIC ANALYSES AND ECOLOGICAL ASPECTS

Bio-and phytochemical studies provide independent and frequently corroborative date, but also such features may have resulted from convergent evolution. The often taxonomically useful host–parasite relations are presumably associated with the distribution of special bioconstituents in the plant kingdom, but so far they have proved useful only at lower taxonomic levels (up to the order level).

The phytoconstituents referred to by the name of "secondary" plant substances are not involved in daily metabolic processes and are usually sequestered. One may interpret this as the deposition of metabolic slag, but this idea is simply refuted by the consideration that many of these products are synthesized by special biochemical pathways, which cost a good deal of energy and must have some purpose. Some of the pathways are phylogenetically "old" and for that reason may have evolutionary significance (Kubitzky and Gottlieb 1984a,b). It also follows that some or all secondary compounds must have some function, e.g. the deterrence of herbivores and parasites. The synthetic pathways, as intimated above, are firmly anchored in the genome, so that the presence or the absence of chemical substances by itself is strongly suggestive of relationships ("chemotaxonomy"). A good example of the usefulness of chemotaxonomic pointers is the positive Mäule reaction in the Gnetatae, an angiospermous feature not found in most of the coniferophytinous gymnosperms that refutes the alighment of any gnetate group within the Coniferophytina. A number of additional, shared chemical features emphasize a close relationship with angiosperms (especially with the Hamamelidae: Gottlieb and Kubitzky 1984a,b and personal communication). This is another confirmation of the hemi-angiospermous nature of the Gnetatae.

The use of amino acid sequences, DNA-hybridization, and serology is only fleetingly mentioned here because the results so far obtained do not contribute substantially to our insight in the evolution of the major spermatophyte clades; moreover, fossil material cannot be studied in this way.

PITFALLS

The essence of a morphophylogenetic approach to problems of relationship is the reconstruction of a genorheithrum (a stream of perpetuated but continually changing DNA codes) by the phenotypical expression of genes in semogenetic sequences, i.e. by character and character state evolution deducted from, preferably, paleobotanical data. This approach has its drawbacks, the principal one being the discontinuities in and the incompleteness of the fossil record. The ensuing uncertainties, aggravated by unwarranted interpretations and generalizations, create pitfalls resulting from false assessments of homology (i.e. of a morphological identity ensuing from a semogenetic continuity in time), of the opposite (ahomology, convergence of features appearing in separate and independent genorheithra), and of "polarity" (i.e. the assessment of directional changes in a semogenetic sequence; this is almost precluded when our paleobotanical records are adequate, but start to play a role when the fossil evidence is misinterpreted or altogether disregarded).

The advantage of the stratigraphically sequential fossil data is the absolute, serial appearance (or disappearance!) of features or character states in time. There can hardly be any doubt that sporangia are very ancient morphomes, because they occur in bryophytes and must have been present in the algal ancestors of the latter; their counterparts in all higher cormophytes (tracheophytes) are undoubtedly derived from them because they retained the original function of producing meiospores (a function that could not possibly be interrupted: the process of sexual reproduction was the only way of ultimate survival). Heterospory is an apomorphic condition with regard to homospory (because homospory is "older" and still consistently present in mosses and liverworts; heterospory appears later—significally as a parallelism—in most but not in all pteridophytic groups and in progymnosperms as a progression). In the same vein, a pollen sac and a nucellus are by consensus advanced derivatives of sporangia.

The fossil record may seem to be unequivocal, but there are pitfalls. An illustrative example is provided by the semogenesis of the cycadophytinous megaphyll (its independent evolution from the coniferophyll being unrecognized), but the issue became even more confused by the disregarding of the antiquity of the sporangium: sporangia existed before the originally undifferentiated sporophyte acquired procaulomatic and prophyllomic parts, and conceivably the whole vegetative sporophyte originated *de novo*. Leaf semogenesis, accordingly, began only after a fundamental anatomical, morphological, and functional distinction, and spatial separation of vegetative corm parts and sporangia had existed for quite a while. One should accept a *sui generis* status of the two morphome categories under discussion. Whatever changes they underwent later (such as a secondary close association between them), their ahomology was maintained. In terms of the Telome Theory, the corm parts of the progenitors of the seed plants consisted of telomes and mesomes, and the sporangia were borne terminally on some or all of the telomes. The supposed but clearly false homology of a telome bearing a terminal sporangium and a sterile telome without one led to unacceptable consequences, as discussed above. Once this spurious explanation of the evolutionary origin of more or less laminiform, sporangiate organs had become accepted, the issue was further confused by the application of the term "sporophyll" to every kind of sporangium-bearing organ. This suggests a homology of morphomes or polymorphomes bearing single sporangia (Lycophyta)), stalked synangial aggregates of sporangia (Shenophyta), sori of varied architecture and often indusiate (ferns), and synangia evolved into anthers and ovules (in angiosperms and some groups of gymnosperms). It is self-evident that each of these unequal structures must have had a special semogenetic history, so a comparative morphological analysis is condemnable if this point is not kept in sight.

Another cause of unacceptable deductions is the repeated mistake of selecting a certain feature as a major discriminating characteristic. The alleged "gap" between "gymnosperms" and "angiosperms" is an example. There are in fact enough transitions between the two groups, provided one throws out such notions as the phyllomic nature of the carpel and of the conventional "stamen" (Meeuse 1992).

How one may be led astray by following up the consequences of a very limited number of assumptions is exemplified by the classification of the gymnosperms proposed by Meyen (1984), said to be based on the fossil record (!). His principal argument is a seed (or ovule) character ("platyspermy" *versus* "radiospermy"), which is totally unsuitable because adaptive evolution inevitably moulded such organs into various shapes and led to a convergence of features without any cogent phylogenetic significance. Each of Meyen's three major groups (called Ginkgoopsida − sic! −, Pinopsida, and Cycadopsida, in a sense different from that of most workers) is a hodgepodge of unrelated taxa (with or without a cupule, coniferophyllous, or megaphyllous, with one ovular integument or with an at least incipient, additional inner one, etc.). Meyen has been criticized by several American paleobotanists (Beck 1985; Miller 1985; Rothwell 1985), to whose criticism it may be added that the distinction between Coniferophytina and Cycadophytina is not accounted for, and that the Gnetatae, so clearly angiospermoid, are dismembered and appear in more than one of Meyen's groups. Apparently much depends on the interpretation of the available data, and it is sad to note that so often factual evidence is forcibly twisted and moulded to fit a so-called "established" viewpoint; for instance, everything is being done to make all conventional gymnosperms unitegmic because otherwise one would have to accept the morphological identity of cupule and carpel. Fossil records of early angiosperms and advanced angiospermoids of Lower to Middle Cretaceous age have dispelled the notion that the floral morphology, sex distribution, and anthecology of the oldest angiosperms are still, and exclusively, retained in the recent holanthous, monoclinous, and entomophilous Magnoliales (and it may be added, of the notion of a strictly monophyletic evolution of the angiosperms).

It does not follow that data obtained from recent taxa would not provide important pointers. Chemical features, although hardly retained in fossil material, often yield good evidence. Anthecological studies of *Ephedra* (Bino et al. 1984a,b and unpublished data) have shown beyond reasonable doubt that an at least incipient ambisexuality and entomophily originated at a still "gymnospermous" level of evolutionary advancement and that a diversification already became manifest at that level (dicliny persisting in some forms, etc.). Such evidence is both corrective and confirmative.

Spurious notions and misinterpretations may play an even greater role in studies based on evidence from recent plant forms alone, because the deductions are not backed up by fossil data. One of the standing elementary mistakes is the repetition of the traditional bisection of the (recent) seed plants in gymno- and angiosperms as we have seen; one should also seriously consider an alternative subdivision of the flowering plants currently but erroneously divided into Di- and Monocotyledonae. One must avoid the pitfall of carrying through such "standing" classifications.

Another pitfall is hidden in the indiscriminate interpretation of abnormalities as if they were atavisms (see Meeuse 1986). If a leptoblastically "degenerated" and virescent FRU is adduced as an argument pleading in favor of interpretation of the normal condition of that FRU as a modified, leaf-bearing shoot, it has been assumed that this abnormally developed morphome aggregate (ideophenotype) is a throw-back—which it is not. If the teratological FRU recalls the original characteristics of a shoot, why has the presence of axillary buds in these terata never been recorded? Also, the incidence of more complex terata opposite a perianth member and almost always "replacing" a gamomorphome, usually a merandron, if interpreted as an atavism, would mean a kind of "stachyospory" of the substituted organ, which is at variance with the conventional floral concept. One must first make the atavistic nature of the phenomenon highly probable. The aberrant form may be a not previously existing mutant, or it may simply be the result of the ontogeny having been thrown out of gear.

Androgynous cones of representatives of the Pinales have occasionally been adduced as atavistic, but their aberrant nature is not supposed to have any phylogenetic meaning. Androgynous catkins of *Salix* and of Juglandaceae, however, have been interpreted as cogent pointers in favor of an original monocliny (and entomophily!) of the taxa concerned. There are indications that various causes may be responsible for an aberrant androgyny. The androgynous florets observed in normally dioecious species of willows usually do not contain normal genitalia but mostly structures intermediate between male and female ones; this suggests an abnormal but not atavistic development (which would require the presence of only strictly male and strictly female organs in the same FRU. That a single species of *Salix* is monoclinous does not mean that it is primitive—the species in question occurs in Brazil at the extreme range of the area of distribution of the genus, so that it is a "young" species.

The last group of pitfalls to be discussed here is the confusion of rudiments, oriments, and other seemingly reduced or degenerated elements. The anthoidal male FRUs of the Juglandaceae sometimes (*Juglans*) or consistently (e.g. in *Pterocarya fraxinifolia*) contain a finger-like protrusion in the center. The current idea that a unisexual "flower" is always a "reduced" ambisexual one almost automatically led to the interpretation of the central protrusion as a "pistillode" or vestigial pistil. This structure resembles a pistil neither morphologically nor anatomically. It is in fact the free tip of the cladic part of the precursory androclad that became transformed into an anthoid.

Similarly, as in the androgynous catkins of *Salix*, the supposedly "reduced" female morphomes found in the strobili of the functionally male *Welwitschia* plants and of male plants of several species of *Ephedra* and *Gnetum* have been adduced as an (unacceptable) argument in favor of a former monocliny of the Gnetatae. Ambisexual gymnosperms are conspicuous by their great rarity, and the morphomes in question are functionally very important by attracting insects (they exude a pollination droplet), so they represent an evolutionary advancement initiating both entomophily and monocliny rather than a vestigial morphome without a function. The reality is the other way round: the morphomes represent an incipient monocliny derived from dicliny.

RETROACTIVE AND CONTROVERSIAL INTERPRETATIONS

One of the glaring mistakes that phytomorphologists can make is the interpretation of the anatomy and morphology of more primitive, recent, and extinct tracheophytes, especially of nonangiospermous seed plants and their Devonian precursors, by using the architecture and structure of magnoliophytic morphomes as their yardstick and common denominator. Understandably, in the beginning, the ubiquity of the angiosperms suggested such an interpretation, also in the light of the adoption of such colloquial (but in fact unscientific) notions as "leaves," "stems," "flowers," "fruits," and "seeds." Up to about a century ago, structures such as a coniferous or cycadalean "cone" were called "flowers," and until recently especially French workers have applied the colloquial term "fleur" to such entities as the FRUs of *Ginkgo* and *Taxus*. Not infrequently, the FRUs of the Gnetatae have also been referred to as "flowers." The danger is two-fold: First, a homology is implied—things called by the same name are likely to belong to the same category—and, second, concomitant terms such as "perianth" have also been applied to parts of nonangiospermous FRUs.

The worst case is the tenet of the strongly magnolioid nature of the "flowers" (FRUs!) of the progenitors of the Magnoliophyta, an idea not based on tangible evidence from fossil material, but on the supposedly very primitive characteristics of the recent, large-flowered Magnoliales, chosen because they were taken to approach most closely the preconceived monaxial "flower" concept. The implications led to equally tenaceous dicta: The early angiosperms were said to be monoclinous, phaneranthous (polymerous and showy, i.e. provided with optical lures in the form of semaphylls), and insect-pollinated (or even specifically cantharophilous). The simple consideration that the Gymnosperms are and were predominantly or totally diclinous, hardly showy (not provided with semaphylls, possibly barring an odd Bennettitalean form), and usually anemophilous, renders the still current dictum of the primarity of the magnolioid "flower" type highly questionable. One also failed to explain how the prevalent dicliny changed into monocliny and where the semaphylls originated from.

An associated case is the persistence of the originally Goethean concept of the "flower" as a "metamorphosis" of a leafy twig, i.e. as a uniaxial structure in its "essence" comparable to a leaf-bearing stem (a vegetative shoot) whose foliar appendages somehow became fertile. Such views not only created an artificial barrier between gymnosperms and flowering plants, but also ruled out recognition of true homologies and semogeneses. In combination with other spurious ideas and the disregarding of possible divergencies and parallelisms, this stood in the way of a plausible answer to the question of the origin of the angiosperms (see e.g. Meeuse 1976a,b, 1977, 1982, 1992). Discoveries of a substantial number of Lower–Middle

Cretaceous angiospermoid fossils in the last two decades are decisive and will sooner or later render the total abandonment of the long-current, erroneous ideas and interpretations unavoidable.

Since by consensus the flowering plants are generally considered to be eustelic throughout, one tends to interpret the internal stem architecture of more primitive spermatophytes as though they were all eustelic. One should not preclude the possible occurrence of polystely in pre-angiosperms, however; this might be useful to bear in mind when trying to assess the plesio- or apomorphy of the stem anatomy of, for example, Aristolochiaceae, Nymphaeaceae, and Piperales (and of *Gnetum*).

Another angiosperm-centered way of thinking is the application of the term "leaf" to all kinds of assimilatory phyllomes. The magnoliophytic leaf is a megaphyll and as such is retraceable to the complex fronds of pre-angiospermous seed ferns, but other laminiform morphomes are not, or are only partly, homologous entities and should be denoted by lycophyllome, coniferophyll, etc. to emphasize the difference. In the same vein, the term "sporophyll" has been applied to all kinds of sporogenous cormophytic organs, thus somehow suggesting their homology, and also their homology with the angiospermous carpel, a usage that is totally confusing.

Conservative-minded phytomorphologists suggest that the neologists' phylogenetical approach is in fact inferred from recent forms retroactively. One could never have arrived at a comparative morphology and the semogenesis of the cormophytic phyllomes without relevant evidence from habit forms of early vascular plants, and could never have surmised the origin of the ovuliferous cupule of the seed ferns, or discovered how soon during seed plant evolution pollination droplets became evolved in the catching of pollen grains, to mention a few examples. There is certainly no retroactive interpretation here. The best example is provided by the utter failure of the classical morphology to arrive at an acceptable reconstruction of the evolutionary history of the flowering plants (Darwin's abominable mystery!). Reliable fossil records of angiospermoid and early magnoliophytic plants have at least put some considerable doubt upon the Euanthium or Ranalean Theory of the "flower" and upon the phylogenetic significance of the magnolialean type of angiosperm.

THE CLADISTIC APPROACH

In present-day Hennigian cladistics, the usefulness of evidence from fossils is denied on account of a Popperian axiom. The claim laid by its protagonists that it is the only way to "phylogenetic systematics" is, therefore, debatable.

Attempts to classify angiosperm clades (Hill and Crane 1982; Dahlgren and Bremer 1985) or even all seed plants (Crane 1986; Doyle and Donoghue 1986a,b) by a cladistic approach without precluding paleophytic evidence, still suffer from the major drawbacks (Meeuse 1986, 1987; Robinson 1986) that the result of any "cladistic" approach is primarily decided already by a number of partly tacit assumptions and by the wholesale adoption of previously published taxa, and, in addition, suffers from some procedural methods. In fact, the assessment of a primitive (plesiomorphic) versus an advanced (apomorphic) condition or character state is always decisive, especially in combination with features more segregational than others. The seed plants soon diverged (already in the Upper Devonian); the two principal clades evolved independently as Coniferophytina (with coniferophylls, without cupule and lagenostome/salpinx) and Cycadophytina (with megaphylls and with a cupule and a lagenostome/salpinx precursory to the inner integument). It is inane to merge progymno-sperms, all conventional gymnosperms, and all angiosperms, as though they represent a taxon to be subdivided and classified as Crane (1986) and Doyle and Donoghue (1986a) have done: The above-mentioned differences—that can be expressed as symplesio- and apomorphies—split up this artificial assembly and render it more surveyable, also because one can pin-point the more characteristic evolutionary trends and advancements within each major spermatophytic taxon without taking into account features and trends found in the other assembly. Another advantage is that each group can be compared separately with its putative progymnospermatophytic progenitors. There is, for instance, no reason to compare palynomorpyhs of cycadophytinous groups with those of coniferophytinous ones as though they belong to the same evolutionary clade, or megaphylls with coniferophylls as though they are homologues.

The story repeats itself in that the cycadophytinous clade must soon have segregated into two, one comprising the Laurasian seed-ferns of the lyginopterid and neuropterid types, and the other the glossopterid assembly with a primarily Gond-wanan distribution. By consensus, most or all of the Mesocycadophytes and the angiosperms are of glossopterid extraction; the Laurasian pteridosperms in my opinion only survive as the specialized aquatic Salviniales. Also in this case one should com-pare the advanced Mesozoic seed-ferns and angiosperms with glossopterid archetypes rather than with other groups of gymnospermous seed plants.

In my opinion, all above-mentioned cladistic efforts were doomed to fail (and, likewise, the comparable assessment of the taxonomic position of the Lactoridaceae in the magnolioid-ranunculoid assembly by Lammers et al. 1986). When Doyle and Donoghue (1986a) compare spermatophytic "leaves," they do not account for the funda-mental difference between conifero- and megaphylls. It follows that their relevant conclusions are misleading. Other tenets that they (and also Crane) adhere to obscure the picture even more; for example, the sporophyll concept and, in the case of the angiosperms, the false notion that the primary FRU type is retained in a more or less original state in the large-flowered, monoclinous, phaneranthous, and entomophilous Magnoliales. The comparison of various microsporangiate organs is incomplete if one disregards the divergent evolution of holandra and merandra and the advent of the androecial filaments (in Gnetatae and in angiosperms), and of course, the homology of cupule and carpel is a fundamental issue.

A semiquantification by evaluating character states as 0 (absent, or plesio-morphic, as the case may be) or 1 (present or apomorphic), or as 0, 1, and 2 (1 being intermediate) stands or falls with certain presuppositions. As an example, the primary oligandry of the *anthoids* (and general floral oligomery, for that matter) of *Lactoris* is scored as advanced (as secondary oligandry, i.e. in respect to a *Magnolia*-like *holanth*) by Lammers et al, but *Lactoris* is in fact much more primitive than they concluded!

It follows that the results of such cladistic data processing are unsatisfactory. The total output of cladistics dealing with seed plant evolution is, therefore, virtually nil and will remain unproductive as long as outdated dicta play such a major role. In view of (repeated) parallelisms and convergent evolution (hardly accounted for in cladistics), such efforts should be abandoned.

PHYLOGENY OF THE CONIFEROPHYTINA

The Coniferophytina are characterized by coniferophyllous trophophylls and the presence of only one integument. The xylem anatomy is conservative and essentially the same as that of the ancient Archaeopteridales (e.g. *Dadoxylon*). There are some advances, such as the occurrence of resin ducts in the wood of several genera of the Pinaceae. The formation of the secondary stem tissues is also plesiomorphic in that there is only a single cambium in each secondary caulomorphome that consistently produces phloem centrifugally and secondary xylem centripetally. The absolute dicliny is also a "primitive" condition, and so is the constantly arborescent and perennial habit form. The principal evolutionary advances took place in the gamomorphomes and the mode of reproduction. The phylogenetic progression is clear and supported by ample fossil evidence; it runs parallel with the subdivision in Ginkgoales, Taxales, and Pinales. I set forth the principal tendencies and ensuing sequences of character states nearly 30 years ago (Meeuse 1963a,b 1966a). These have been confirmed by the substantial increase of fossil records.

Advanced Archaeopteridales were heterosporous and apparently dioecious (although some were perhaps already monoecious); therefore, the dioecy of *Ginkgo* and the Taxales is clearly plesiomorphic. A characteristic feature of the reproductive regions of the Archaeopteridales in question is the "fertile frond" architecture. If we call the secondary axes pinnae, the ultimate bracteate pinnae consisted of a central cauloid morphome that bore a few sterile organs rather similar to its bract and to the trophomorphomes of the "sterile fronds" distally and proximally, and between them coaxial groups of sporangia that tended to form synangial aggregates. This situation is rather closely retained in the male *Ginkgo*, in which the gamomorphomes consist of a cladic portion bearing stalked synangia and *sometimes* also trophomorphomelike organs distally and/or proximally. From this condition, the other androgamomorphome types can easily be deduced. In *Taxus*, the stalked and androsynangia are still represented. In the extinct Cordaitales, a brachyblastic contraction coincided with a broadening of the synangial stalk, which came to bear a terminal tuft of sporangia. In Araucariaceae, the supporting stalk has become more scalelike, and the sporangia are pendulous to lie parallel with the broadened sublaminiform stalk; in the other pinalean groups, the sporangia became adnate to their supporting organ and the resulting coaxial fertile "scales" constitute the male cones, which are in turn borne coaxially on a cladomorphome and represent the original archaeopteridalean pinnae. The number of pollen sacs upon the whole became subject to oligomerization (to two units in *Pinus* and related genera).

The female gamomorphome evolved by at first developing ovules (clearly out of gynosynangia). Each ultimate megasporangiate cladic organ of the original fertile frond became a stalked ovule. A number of ovules and phyllomic parts had become brachyblastic in the mean time in Cordaitales. (Early ginkgoalean forms remained more primitive and bore coaxial stalked ovules in racemoid or fascicled arrangement—a dead-end alley of evolution; the only survivor, *Ginkgo biloba*, has oligomerized, binate, and sessile gamomorphomes that are sometimes atavistically developed and more or less racemoid.)

The condition in the Cordaitales is maintained in the Taxales: One to several ovules are borne on brachyblasts (which also bear phyllomorphomes), their aril-like outer cover is a novelty and an adaptation to endozoochory. As in the Cordaitales, the ovuliferous brachyblasts still exhibit a radial or helical build-up in contrast to the dorsolaterally flattened seed scales of the Coniferales. In Late Paleozoic and early

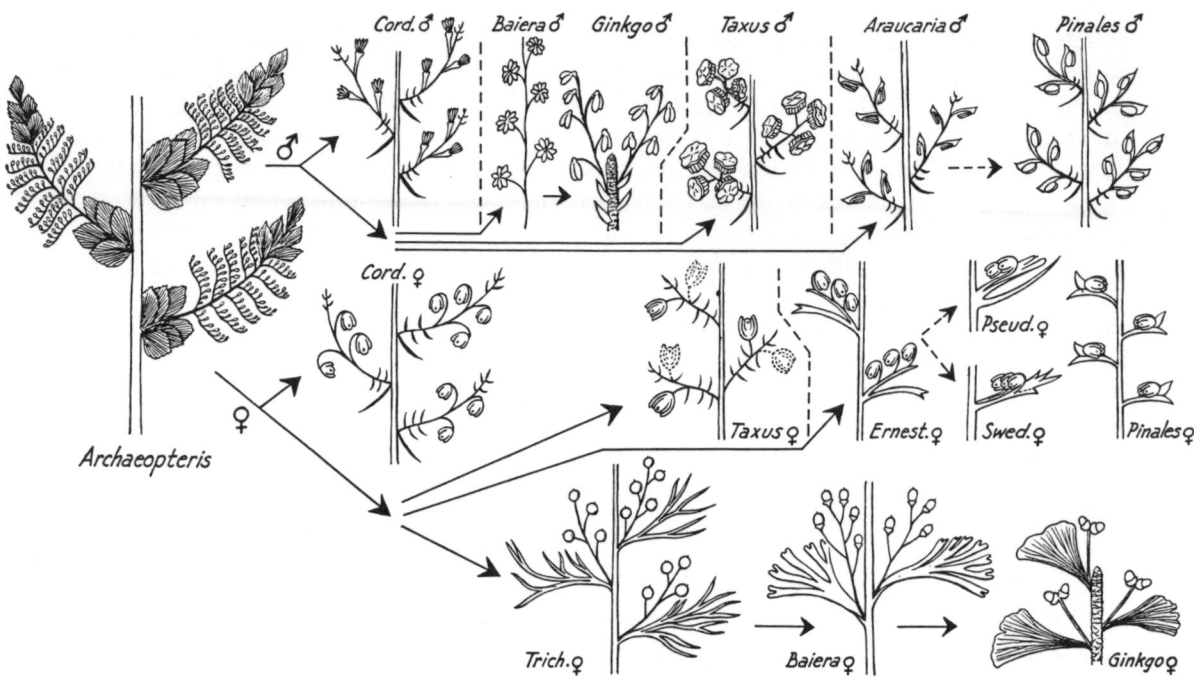

Figure 16.1. The evolution of the Coniferophytina. The starting point is a pinnate "mixed" frond of an Archeopteridalean form. The ultimate pinnules bore proximally and distally sterile phyllomes and between them coaxially inserted sporangia. Cord., *Cordianthus*; Ernest., *Ernestiodendron*; Pseud., *Pseudovoltzia*; Swed., *Swedenborgia*; Trich., *Trichopitys*. The principal tendencies were (1) a lateral coalescence of the coaxial groups of sporangia to form synangia, the female ones subsequently becoming transformed into an ovule (the condition represented in the Ginkgoales); and (2) a tendency toward a contraction (brachyblasty) of the original fertile pinnae, especially in the female strobili. The male reproductive organs still betray their origin in the Taxales: the stalked synangia remain arranged in capitate or fascicled groups that represent a fertile pinnule.

In the Cordaitales, the male organs became dorsolaterally flattened and bore sporangia; they occurred in groups representing a fertile pinna; their female organs were stalked ovules borne on a brachyblastic modification of the pinna inclusive of the distal and proximal sterile (and phyllomic) elements. In all groups, the morphomes derived from a pinna are bracteate. About the Cordaitales–conifers relation, it is clear that, provided one considers the transformation of a presumably helical phyllo- and stachyotaxis of the pinna into a bilateral symmetry, the homology is easily established. The fertile pinnules have become ovules borne on long stalks. The subsequent evolution can easily be visualized: the pinnule axis became broader and flatter: the sterile appendages became incorporated or disappeared, and the ovules became adnate, with the micropyles facing the axis (the ovules are adaxially attached at least in the precursors of the recent conifers). The Taxales resemble the cordaites in their female organs: brachyblasts bear organs and one pseudoterminal to several laterally attached ovules. In the most advanced Pinales, the original bract subtending the pinna became the bract-scale, which is usually fused with the seed-scale (after Meeuse 1963).

It is clear from the diagrams that the female coniferous cone represents a coaxial aggregate of bracteate pinnae (bract-scale/seed-scale units) and the male "cones" originated from pinnules (i.e. they contain axes of a higher order).

precursors of the recent conifers, there are transitions in that the flattening is not so manifest, apart from the independence of the seed scale. The flattening of the brachyblast that became a seed scale was concomitant with the incorporation and partial loss through oligomerization of the sterile elements and a shortening of the ovular stalks. In Cordaitales, the ovules were borne on stalks and apparently protruded beyond the vegetative parts, so that their preservation in fossils suggests either an adaxial or an abaxial position, but in recent form they are situated on the adaxial side of the seed scale. The ovules became partly incorporated and partly adnate to the seed scale, with the result that their micropyles are directed toward the cone axis. (Compare Figure 16.1). In all recent taxa, *Ginkgo* excepted, siphonogamy replaced zoidogamy. In conjunction with the tight packing of the cone in anthesis, siphonogamy is advantageous because the micropyles are better protected than if they were exposed.

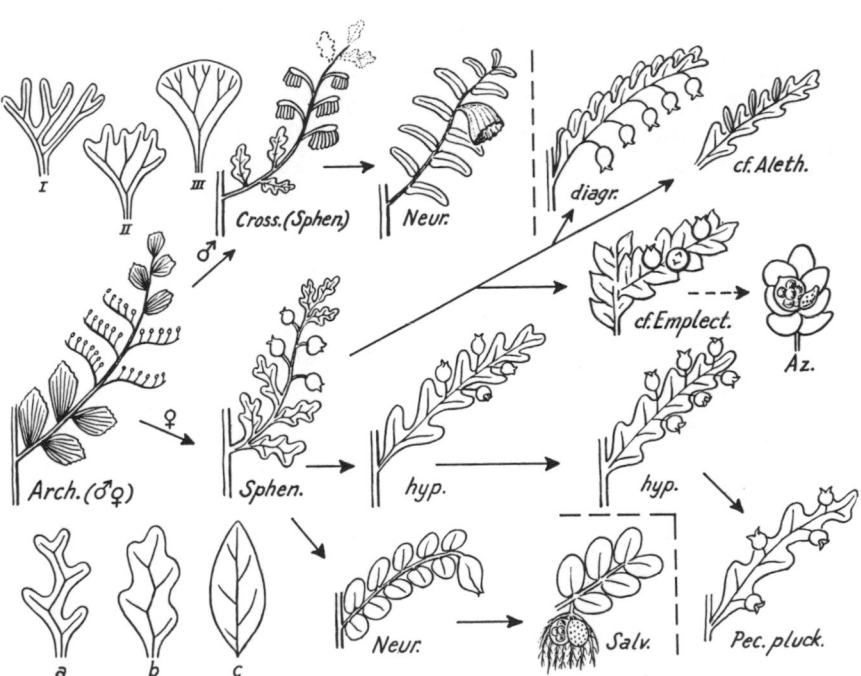

Figure 16.2. Suggested overall phylogeny of the Laurasian seed-ferns starting from an archeopteridalean archetype (which is probably not quite correct, but not too far off the mark): Principal trends in some groups are the simplification of the trophophylls, and secondary association of gamomorphomes with the latter. General trends are aggregation of sporangia, the gynosynangia becoming ovules (origin of vascular integument), and the advent of the salpinx/lagenostome.

No higher forms descended from this assembly. In contrast with current viewpoints, however, it may be suggested that they are not extinct and survive as the Salviniales (*Salvinia* being most reminiscent of the Neuropteridales and *Azolla* of the Lyginopteridales, cf. *Emplectopteris*). Arch., Archeopteridales; Cross., *Crossotheca*; Neur., Neuropteridales; Aleth., *Alethopteris* type; Emplect., *Emplectopteris*; Az., *Azolla*; Sphen., *Sphenophyllum*; Salv., *Salvinia*; Pec. Pluck., *Pecopteris pluckenetii*; diag., diagrammatic; hyp., hypothetical (after Meeuse 1963).

PHYLOGENY OF THE LAURASIAN PTERIDOSPERMS

The tentative phylogeny of this group is diagrammatically shown in Figure 16.2. It is suggested that these seed ferns became extinct in the Carboniferous (the period of their greatest diversification) and that their evolution would have ceased more or less abruptly. I believe that this is not true and that the seed-ferns of this group survived as the Salviniales (Meeuse 1961a): Their heterospory is absolutely incongruous in true ferns; the megasporangium is encased in an only secondarily closed, reduced, thin cupule (the conventional indusium) and has, in addition to what appears to be a thin integument, an apical differentiation agreeing with a salpinx/lagenostome. The latter is apparently not functional any longer, apparently because the original pollination syndrome involving a droplet exuded from the endostome ceased to exist and was replaced by a system operative in an aquatic environment.

If the salvinialean ovule and cupule had originated secondarily in an ancestral and supposedly isosporous fern group, their evolution would have taken place as a response to some obscure functional requirement. The same holds true for the Marsileales, incidentally—they also have a cupule, an integument, and a salpinx/lagenostome. Moreover, the motile androgametes of the latter, before they become uncoiled, are strongly reminiscent of the zoidiogametes of *Ginkgo* and the Cycadales whereas they are without a counterpart among the true ferns.

The survival of the "water ferns" is apparently attributable to the conserving capacity of their semi-aquatic habitat and to their strongly developed vegetative reproduction. Those of their features that are more or less incongruous in comparison with the extinct terrestrial seed ferns can be explained as new adaptive developments emanating from a life in a different habitat. As is apparent from the diagram, the Azollaceae are presumably of lyginopteridalean origin and the Salviniaceae are of neuropteridalean descent.

TENTATIVE PHYLOGENY OF THE GLOSSOPTERID CLADE AND THE ANGIOSPERMS

Several workers have come to the conclusion that the angiosperms are descendants of glossopterid seed ferns (see Figures 16.2, 16.3). I do not see any obstacles to this point of view, but stipulate that the magnoliophytes are not directly derived from a glossopterid archetype (Melville 1966) but from more advanced Mesozoic cycadophytes, which may collectively be called mesocycadophytes for convenience. This is a heterogeneous assembly comprising Bennettitales (Cycadeaoideales), Caytoniales, Czekanovskiales, Corystospermaceae, Peltaspermaceae, Pentoxylales, and a few other groups, including the Nilssoniales and their surviving descendants, the Cycadales.

Several authorities accept the origin of angiosperms from one or several of these taxa. By postulating a monophyletic evolution of the flowering plants, one has aprioristically narrowed down the possibilities. If the relationships between one of the Mesocycadophyta and angiosperms were indeed clear-cut, this connection would have been recognized long ago. By consensus, bennettitalean plants such as *Williamsonia* and similar forms are old enough—some are of Lower to Middle Cretaceous age—to have acted as progenitors of (some) angiosperms, but the more recent *Cycadeoidea*, although considered somehow ancestral to angiosperms (e.g. in the Euanthium

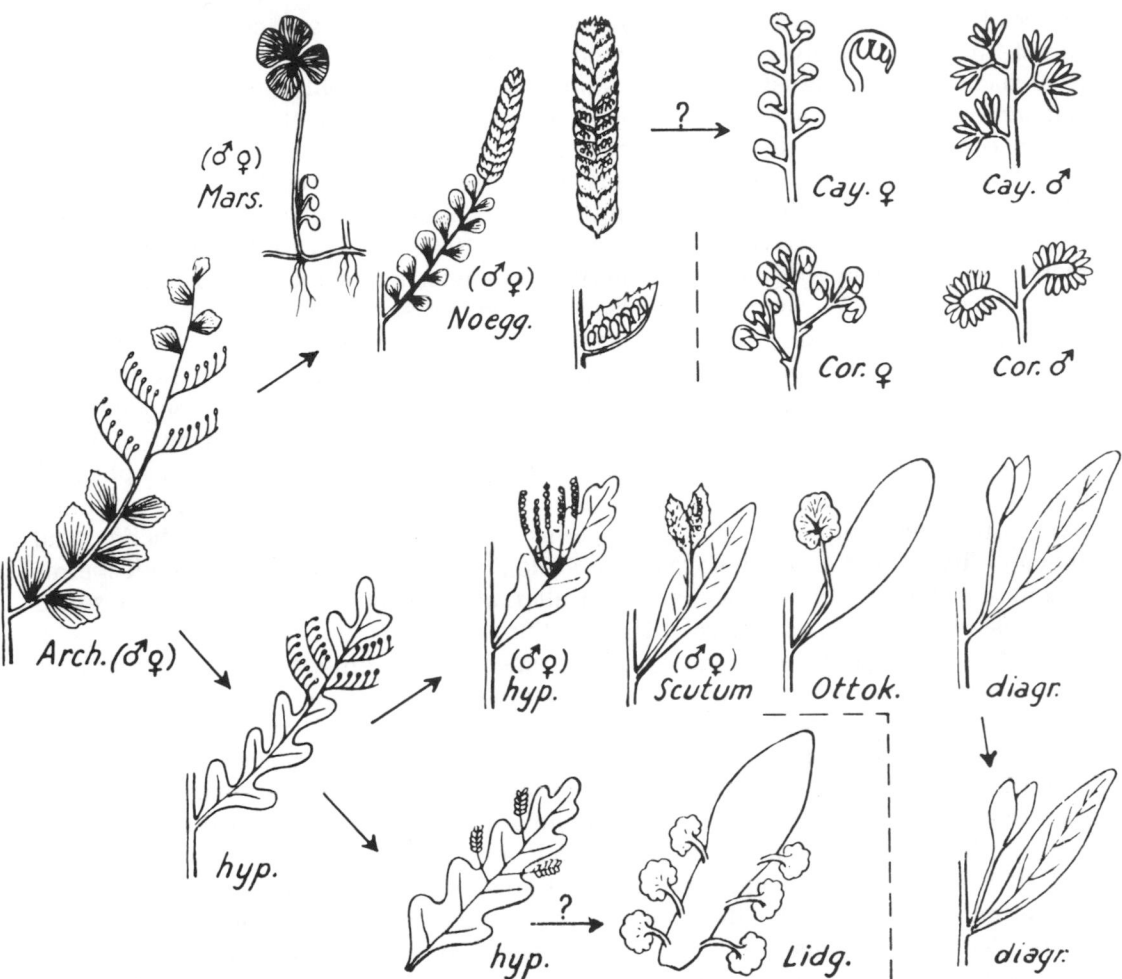

Figure 16.3. Suggested overall phylogeny of the Gondwanaland glossopterid assembly, including Noeggerathiales. Principal general trends are as in the Laurasian pteridosperms, but include a more pronounced tendency toward once-pinnate, palmate, or pedate to single leaves and toward a reticulate blade venation. Paleozoic to Early Mesozoic forms, said to be extinct, probably survive as the Marsileales. The Noeggerathiales must belong to the assembly, and the diversified Mesocyadophytic groups (of which only a selection is shown), including *Lidgettonia*, may have a greater morphological correspondence with them than with some more specialized taxa such as *Pluma, Scutum, Ottokaria*, etc. Arch., Archeopteridales; Mars., Marsileales; Noegg., Noeggerathiales; Cay., Caytoniales; Cor., Corystospermaceae; Ottok., *Ottokaria*; Lidg., *Lidgettonia*; diag., diagrammatic; hyp., hypothetical (after Meeuse 1963).

Hypothesis of Arber and Parkin 1907), is too recent to be eligible as ancestral to Lower Cretaceous angiosperms (or angiospermoids). One could not reconcile the female FRU of *Cycadeoidea* with the concept of the foliar carpel (hence Arber and Parkin borrowed the female strobilus of *Cycas*, dubbed "megasporophyll," as the archetype of such a carpel). The homology of cupule and carpel was not seriously considered (except by e.g. Krassilov 1984!), and the result was utter confusion and no real advance.

The Anthocorn Theory provides a common basis of comparison and enables us to compare fertile regions of all cycadophytes on the basis of gonoclads (which may be coaxially organized into an anthocorm). The caytonious gynoclad is prototypic in respect to an angiospermous gynoecium or a part thereof, each cupule becoming a carpel—the presumably already at anthesis closed cupule is to all intents a carpel! Gonoclads became transformed into anthoids by a brachyblastic contraction, and sometimes whole anthocorms developed into holanths, the gonoclads becoming adnate and incorporated in the floral receptacle.

The evolution of the angiosperms is associated with the advent of monocliny, and of a novel form of pollination once an originally "one-sided" plant-insect relation had become mutualistic (Meeuse 1977, 1978a,b, 1986, 1987). In contrast to current opinion, monocliny (and also zoophily) is apomorphic in angiosperms and one need not search for ambisexual FRUs among the mesocycadophytes so as to locate an angiosperm ancestor. The Gnetatae (Meeuse 1978a,b; Bino et al. 1984a,b) provide the clue: A partial transformation of unisexual FRUs into potentially ambisexual ones concomitant with an efficient pollen transfer by insects opened up a pathway to monocliny and zoophily. In other, strictly diclinous, representative Gnetatae, the advent of floral nectaries strongly suggests that an alternative road must have led to zoophily in diclinous angiosperms such as Cucurbitaceae and Euphorbiaceae (Bino et al. 1984a.,b). Since other progenitors of the angiosperms must have retained their dicliny and anemophily, the early morphological and ecological diversification of the angiosperms becomes plausible; the above-mentioned alternative FRU transformations increased the possibilities of morphological differentiation.

Since the general evolutionary advancements are manifest and the homologies cupule—carpel, holandron (monandron) — merandra plus perianth member (and potential semaphyll), gonoclad — anthoid and anthocorm — holanth form a convenient basis of comparison, the origin of the several major clades of angiosperms by a polyrheithric rather than a monophyletic form of evolution has become reduced to a comparison of a mesocycadophytic group with an angiospermous clade (or retroactively to a search for matching features of such a clade among a mesocycadophytic form).

The pin-pointing of corresponding features suggests a relation between (early) bennettitalean forms and the magnolioid-ranunculoid-caryophylloid and monocot clade. The Pentoxylales perhaps provide clues concerning the origin of monocots and the Gnetatae (whose "bennettitalean" character was recognized long ago: Arber and Parkin 1907) forming a link with hamamelidoid taxa. The various kinds of microsporangiate organs found among the Mesocycadophytes necessitate the supposition that the holandra and merandra of recent groups of angiosperm did not necessarily all originate in the same fashion. Laminiform holandra bearing androsynangia (protantherae) on the ventral (= adaxial) surface can easily be visualized as archetypic in respect to the androecial members of Magnoliaceae, Monimiaceae s.s., Juglandaceae, and a few other taxa with holandra, and also in respect to the merandra associated with a perianth member of ranunculoid groups and of all other taxa. The holandra with apparently abaxially borne synangia of fossils such as Caytonanthus (Caytoniales) and Pteruchus (Corystospermaceae) must have undergone a somewhat different transformation and could more easily result in "centrifugal" androecia [as found in Dilleniidae; this would not at all be illogical in the light of a polyphyletic descent of the flowering plants (Meeuse 1987)].

One must accept certain widespread advancements such as oligomerizations and brachyblasty often concomitant with adnations. Cupules (and carpels) may contain several ovules or only a single one, and this is reflected among the recent magnoliophytes: Compare, for example, the pluri-ovulate carpels of several Magnoliales with those of Piperales and, likewise, those of Liliales with the gynoecia of Poales and Cyperales. The number of monogyna (= cupules = carpels) borne on a gynoclad or androgynoclad also tends to become oligomerized; see, for example, the polymerous ones of *Magnolia* and the monomerous ones of Piperales. Gynoecial monomery and androecial oligomery are not necessarily a derived feature but may be an ancient apomorphy (see the monogynon of *Caytonia* against the oligomerous one of the Corystospermaceae).

Another advancement is the anatropous/campylotropous ovule, so widespread among the angiosperms, obviously apomorphic in respect to the orthotropous one of the mesocycadophytes, the Gnetatae, and a few angiospermous taxa. Anatropy is rare among primitively monomerous, angiospermous pistils and could only originate after the significance of an exposed exostome with pollination droplet ceased to exist and (other) morphogenetic causes, such as the advent of chalazogamy and spatial relationships (ovules becoming squeezed inside the ovary locule), started to play a role. The ab- or adaxial position of the micropyle in mesocycadophytic forms (adaxial in Corystospermaceae) is immaterial in this connection: As far as the evidence indicates, the chalazal and micropylar parts of their ovules lie opposite and not in each other's proximity as in truly anatropous ovules.

Once the morphological relations between various kinds of cycadophytinous gamomorphomes and their accessory organs has been properly understood and there are no longer any barriers preventing a direct linking of angiospermous FRUs and their mesocycadophytic precursors as a solid basis for the unraveling of evolution of the flowering plants, it follows that nonmorphological features, such as anatomical characters, gain in significance. If one assumes a connection between Pentoxylales and (some) monocotyledons (Meeuse 1961b) and finds agreements in, for example, their reproductive regions, the singular stem anatomy of *Pentoxylon* is not altogether without counterpart among the Liliatae. The secondary growth is unusual and the secondary xylem consists (apart from parenchymatous elements) of fiber tracheids with bordered pits, by consensus a very primitive tracheidal element. A peculiar kind of secondary growth resulting in a xylem with exclusively tracheidal cells of exactly the same type, as found in arborescent dracaenoids and species of *Aloe*, can hardly be a coincidence. The loss of an erect stem explains the possible origin of such forms as *Sansevieria* and the decline of the stem may well explain the loss of the secondary growth and the peculiar tracheids in both cauline and stemless monocots. I (Meeuse 1961a,b) accept a connection between Pentoxylales and Sparganiaceae, but not necessarily between all groups of monocots and the (Cretaceous!) Pentoxylales. For example, the monomery of the monogyna in *Carnoconites* is at variance with the (originally) pluri-ovulate condition of carpels of the Liliales (and Orchidales), Commelinales, Juncaceae, Zingiberales, and other monocot groups.

The corollary of this chapter is that the unraveling of the alleged "mystery" of angiosperm evolution has at least progressed to the status of a half-completed jigsaw puzzle: Some pieces still have to be fitted in to complete the picture. This achievement was accomplished through a neological approach, and one has to decide whether or not one wishes to embrace these deductions (which lead to a comprehensive and unambiguous system linking all seed plants) or to persist in playing blind man's buff (see, however, Meeuse 1992).

Still, one must remain critical. First, the glossopterid assembly was rather diversified but on the whole not arborescent. Certain angiospermous taxa with rhizomes or a caudex may well reflect their origin in their recent habit form. Second, the diversification of mesocycadophytes might have begun at an early time (say 200 million years ago or more), thus implying a still more ancient diversification of the angiosperms. Third, the classification of fossil mesocycadophytes is not at all clear. Forms referred to Bennettitales (= Cycadeoidales) date from Early Jurassic (or even earlier) times to the Upper Cretaceous, which does not render their homogeneity very likely. A subdivision is indicated also because the members do not share so many features (the leaves may be simple or pinnately compound; some forms were diclinous and others morphologically monoclinous; some were pachycaul to almost stemless with a caudex or an almost subterranean stem; some are supposed to have had a slender stem; etc.). The principal shared features are the pollen type and perhaps the stomatal apparatus, but what else? Did they all have seeds with a massive embryo, as in *Cycadeoidea*? Another question is whether all forms referred to the Bennettitales had the same anthecology: *Cycadeoidea* must have been practically angiospermous (because no pollen grains were found in the pollen chamber) and one wonders whether they had an *Ephedra* type of siphonogamy (with archegonia) or perhaps already the angiospermous type (without archegonia), and one can keep speculating. Was this taxon entomophilous? It seems that the answers have to wait until more relevant details have been discovered.

SUGGESTIONS FOR FURTHER STUDIES

Armed with cognizance and considerations set forth in the foregoing discussion, one ought to be able to search successfully for connections between pre-Cretaceous seed plants and angiosperms so as to elucidate gradually the origin of the various major clades of flowering plants. It will be clear that one has to rid oneself of the ingrained tenets concerning the reproductive organs of higher spermatophytes that have hampered progress.

One must also have an open mind as regards the mono- or pleiophyletic descent of the recent angiosperms: An accepted possible pleiorheithry permits a comparison of any somehow primitive taxon (e.g., Nymphaeales, Nelumbonales, Platanaceae, Juglandales, Piperales, monocot groups, and of course also a magnolioid-ranunculoid type) with prospective progenitors among the mesocycadophytes. This narrows down the possibilities, especially if one forgets about "flowers" and starts thinking in terms of anthocorms and gonoclads.

Farther down the geological time-scale, more information is required about the relation between glossopterid seed ferns and the mesocycadophytes. One must bear in mind that among the hemi-angiospermous forms, compound leaves were of more common occurrence than among the recent Magnoliophyta. One must probably concentrate on glossopterids with pinnately and palmately compound trophophylls and should not be led astray by the writings of Melville, who selected taxa with simple leaf blades to arrive at a gonophyll. There are hiatuses as regards the relation between the glossopterid seed ferns and pteridosperms of the Laurasian region (Lyginopteridales, Neuropteridales, Medullosae, etc.).

The study of the evolution of pollen grains has taken great strides but has contributed little toward the unraveling of angiosperm evolution, beyond the recognition of early angiospermlike palynomorphs. The principal differentiation is of course the scarcity of *in situ* records, as most types described are *sporae dispersae*. The comparative morphology of such sporomorphs is by itself usually inadequate to permit reliable semogenetic reconstructions—for instance, the advent of colporate pollen grains is still a major issue.

LITERATURE CITED

Arber, E. A. N., and J. Parkin. 1907. On the origin of angiosperms. *Bot. J. Linn. Soc.* 38:29–44.

Arber, E. A. N., and J. Parkin. 1907. Studies on the evolution of the angiosperms. The relationship of the Angiosperms to the Gnetales. *Ann. Bot.* 22:489–515.

Beck, C. B. 1985. A commentary of the views of S. V. Meyen. *Bot. Rev.* 51:273–294.

Behnke, H. D. 1981. Sieve-element characters. *Nordic J. Bot.* 1:381–400.

Bino, R. J., A. Dafni, and A. D. J. Meeuse. 1984a. Entomophily in the dioecious gymnosperm *Ephedra aphylla* Forsk. (= *E. alte* C. A. Mey), with some notes on *E. campylopoda* C. A. Mey. I. Aspects of the entomophilous syndrome. *Proc. Kon. Nederl. Akad. Wetensch. Amsterdam C* 87:1–13.

Bino, R. J., N. Devente, and A. D. J. Meeuse. 1984b. II. Pollination droplets, nectaries and nectarial secretion in *Ephedra*. *Proc. Kon. Nederl. Akad. Wetensch. Amsterdam C* 87:14–22.

Boesewinkel, F. D. and F. Bouman. 1984. The Seed: Structure. In *Embryology of the Angiosperms*. Ed. B. M. Johri. Berlin: Springer. 567–610.

Bouman, F. 1984. The ovule. In *Embryology of the Angiosperm*. Ed. B. M. Johri. Berlin: Springer. 123–157.

Bouman, F. and J. I. M. Calis. 1977. Integumentary shifting—A third way to unitegmy. *Ber. Deut. Bot. Ges.* 90:15–28.

Crane, P. R. 1985. Phylogenetic analysis of the seed plants and the origin of the Angiosperms. *Ann. Miss. Bot. Gard.* 72:716–793.

Dahlgren, R., and K. Bremer. 1985. Major clades of the Angiosperms. *Cladistics* 1:349–369.

Doyle, J. A., and M. J. Donoghue. 1986a. Seed plant phylogeny and the origin of angiosperms. An experimental cladistic approach. *Bot. Rev.* 52:321–431.

_____. 1986b. Relationships of angiosperms and Gnetales: A numerical cladistic analysis. In *Systemic and Taxonomic Approaches in Paleobotany*. (System. Assoc. Spec. Vol. 31) Eds. R. A. Spicer and B. A. Thomas. Oxford: Oxford Univ. Press. 177–198.

Friis, E. M., P. R. Crane, and K. R. Pedersen 1986. Floral evidence for Cretaceous chloranthoid angiosperms. *Nature* 320:163–164.

Hill, C. R., and P. R. Crane. 1982. Evolutionary cladistics and the origin of the Angiosperms. In *Problems of Phylogenetic Reconstruction*. Ed. K. A. Joysey and A. E. Friday. (System. Assoc. Spec. Vol. 21) London/New York: Academic Press. 269–361.

Krassilov, V. A. 1984. New paleobotanical data on origin and early evolution of angiospermy. *Ann. Miss. Bot. Garden.* 71:577–592.

Kubitzky, K., and O. R. Gottlieb. 1984a. Micromolecular patterns and the evolution and major classification of the angiosperms. *Taxon.* 33:375–391.

_____. 1948b. Phytochemical aspects of angiosperm origin and evolution. *Acta. Bot. Neerl.* 33:457–468.

Lammers, T. G., T. F. Stuesey, and O. M. Silva. 1986. Systematic relationships of the Lactoridaceae, an endemic family of the Juan Fernandez Islands, Chile. *Plant Syst. Evol.* 152:243–266.

Meeuse, A. D. J. 1961a. Marsileales and Salviniales—Living fossils? *Acta Bot. Neerl.* 10:257–260.

_____. 1961b. The Pentoxylales and the origin of the Monocotyledons. *Proc. Kon. Nederl. Akad. Wetensch. Amsterdam Ser. C.* 64:543–559.

_____. 1963a. From ovule to ovary: A contribution to the phylogeny of the megasporangium. *Acta Biotheor.* 16:127–182.

_____. 1963b. The so-called "megasporophyll" of *Cycas*—A morphological misconception. Its bearing on the phylogeny and the classification of the Cycadophyta. *Acta Bot. Neerl.* 12:119–128.

_____ . 1965. Angiosperms—Past and present. Phylogenetic botany and interpretative morphology of the flowering plants. *Adv. Front. Plant Sci.* (Spec. Vol.) 11:1–228.

_____ . 1966a. *Fundamentals of Phytomorphology*. New York: Ronald Press. 131.

_____ . 1966b. The early evolution of the Archegoniatae: A re-appraisal. *Acta Bot. Neerl.* 15:162–167.

_____ . 1966c. The homology concept in phytomorphology: Some moot points. *Acta Bot. Neerl.* 15:451–476.

_____ . 1967. Again: The growth habit of the early angiosperms. *Acta Bot. Neerl.* 15:33–41.

_____ . 1972. Sixty-five years of theories of the multiaxial flower. *Acta Biother.* 21:167–202.

_____ . 1974a. Megasporangium, nucellus and presemen: Their nomenclature and homology. *Acta Bot. Neerl.* 23:493–503.

_____ . 1974b. The different origins of petaloid semaphylls. *Phytomorphology* 23:88–99.

_____ . 1976a. Fundamental aspects of the evolution of the Magnoliophyta. In *Glimpses in Plant Research, Vol. 3*. Ed. P. K. K. Nair. Delhi: Vikas. 82–100.

_____ . 1976b. Origin of the angiosperms—Problem or inaptitude? *Phytomorphology* 25:373–379.

_____ . 1977. Coincidence of characters and angiosperm phylogeny. *Phytomorphology* 27:314–322.

_____ . 1978a. Nectarial secretion, floral evolution and the pollination syndrome in early angiosperms. *Proc. Kon. Nederl. Akad. Wetensch. Amsterdam Ser. C.* 300–326.

_____ . 1978b. The significance of the Gnetatae in connection with the early evolution of the Angiosperms. In *Glimpses in Plant Research, Vol 4*. Ed. P. K. K. Nair. Delhi: Vikas. 62–73.

_____ . 1981. Evolution of the Magnoliophyta: Current and dissident viewpoints. *Ann. Rev. Plant Sci.* New Delhi: Kalyani Publ. 2:393–442.

_____ . 1982. Floral theories in the light of some neological viewpoints concerning the morphology and anthecology of the oldest angiosperms. *Phytomorphology* 30:295–302.

_____ . 1984. Homology as an empirism. *J. Plant Anat. Morphol.* 1:9–24.

_____ . 1986. *Anatomy of Morphology*. Leiden: E. J. Brill Publ.

_____ . 1987. *All About Angiosperms*. Delft: Eburon.

_____ . 1992. *Angiosperm Evolution—Not an Abominable Mystery*. Delft: Eburon.

Meeuse, A. D. J., and F. Bouman. 1974. The inner integument—its probable origin and homology. *Acta Bot. Neerl.* 23:237–249.

Melville, R. 1960. A new theory of the angiosperm flower. *Nature* 188:14–18.

_____ . 1962. A new theory of the angiosperm flower. I. The gynoecium. *Kew Bull.* 16:1–50.

_____ . 1963. A new theory of the angiosperm flower. II. The androecium. *Kew Bull.* 17:1–63.

Meyen, S. V. 1984. Basic features of gymnosperm systematics and phylogeny as evidenced by the fossil record. *Bot. Rev.* 50:1–111.

Miller, C. N. Jr. 1985. A critical review of S. V. Meyen's "Basic features of gymnosperm systematics and phylogeny as evidenced by the fossil record." *Bot. Rev.* 51:295–318.

Robinson, H. 1986. A key to the common errors of cladistics. *Taxon* 35:309–311.

Rothwell, G. W. 1985. The role of comparative morphology and anatomy in interpreting the systematics of fossil gymnosperms. *Bot. Rev.* 319–327.

_____ . 1987. Complex Paleozoic Filicales in the evolutionary radiation of ferns. *Am. J. Bot.* 74:458–461.

Rüffle, L. 1980. Wachstum-Modus und Blatt-Morphologie bei altertümlichen Fagales und Hamamelidales der Kreide und der Gegenwart. In *100 Jahre Arboretum (1879–1979)* Berlin: Bot. Garden Issue. 329–341.

Author Index

Plant Index

Asterisks indicate fossil forms.

Subject Index

472

CONTRIBUTORS

R. K. BAMBER, 1 Trevalgan Place, St. Ives, 2075, Australia (formerly with Forestry Commission of New South Wales, Australia)

P. W. BARLOW, AFRC Institute of Arable Crops Research, Department of Agricultural Science, University of Bristol, Long Ashton Research Station, Long Ashton, Bristol, BS18 9AF, England

S. BHAMBIE, Department of Botany, Kurukshetra University, Kurukshetra 132 119 (Haryana), India

INES ADRIANA CISMONDI, Electron Microscopy Center, Catholic University at Cordoba, O. Trejo 323, 5000 Cordoba, Argentina

S. K. DATTA, Department of Botany, Visva-Bharati University, Santiniketan 731 235, India

DARLEEN A. DEMASON, Department of Botany and Plant Sciences, University of California, Riverside, California, 92521, U.S.A.

N. G. DENGLER, Department of Botany, University of Toronto, Toronto, Ontario M5S 1A1, Canada

B. A. FINERAN, Department of Plant and Microbial Sciences, University of Canterbury, Christchurch 1, New Zealand

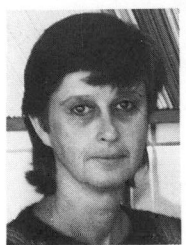

INES NOHER DE HALAC, Electron Microscopy Center, Catholic University at Cordoba, O. Trejo 323, 5000 Cordoba, Argentina

MUHAMMAD IQBAL, Department of Botany, Faculty of Science, Hamdard University, New Delhi 110 062, India

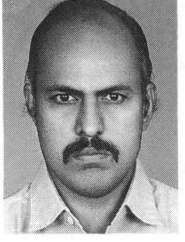

K. V. KRISHNAMURTHY, Department of Botany, Bharathidasan University, Tiruchirapalli 620 024 (Tamil Nadu), India

A. D. J. MEEUSE, Harrelaers 1, 1852 KT, Heiloo, the Netherlands (formerly with the Department of Botany, University of Amsterdam)

RANDY MOORE, Department of Biology, Wright State University, Dayton, Ohio 45435, U.S.A.

K. PERIASAMY, D-97, 9th Cross Thillainagar, Tiruchirapalli 620 018 (Tamil Nadu), India (formerly with the Department of Botany, Bharathidasan University, Tiruchirapalli)

AMBUJA PILLAI, C-139 Dayanand Narg, Tilaknagar, Jaipur 302 004, India (formerly with the Department of Botany, University of Rajasthan, Jaipur)

THOMAS L. ROST, Department of Botany, University of California, Davis, California 95616, U.S.A.

P. S. SRIVASTAVA, Department of Botany, Faculty of Science, Hamdard University, New Delhi 110 062, India

B. J. H. TER WELLE, Institute of Systemic Botany, University of Utrecht, 3584 CS Utrecht, the Netherlands